W9-AGB-480

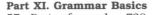

lessons thus far:

no adjectives
a writer can't teach a writer

THE
BEDFORD
HANDBOOK

last, first. "article name."
<u>Publisher/location</u>. date pub.
date looked up (address)

Fifth Edition

THE BEDFORD HANDBOOK

Diana Hacker

BEDFORD/ST. MARTIN'S
Boston ◆ New York

For Bedford/St. Martin's
President and Publisher: Charles H. Christensen
General Manager and Associate Publisher: Joan E. Feinberg
Managing Editor: Elizabeth M. Schaaf
Developmental Editor: Michelle McSweeney
Editorial Assistants: Joanne Diaz and Rebecca Jerman
Production Editor: Heidi L. Hood
Production Assistant: Stasia Zomkowski
Copyeditor: Barbara G. Flanagan
Text Design: Claire Seng-Niemoeller
Cover Design: Hannus Design Associates
Composition: CRWaldman Graphic Communications
Printing and Binding: RR Donnelley and Sons Company

Library of Congress Catalog Card Number: 97–72371

Manufactured in the United States of America.

2   1   0
l   k   j   i   h   g

For information, write: Bedford/St. Martin's, 75 Arlington Street, Boston, MA
02116   (617–426–7440)

ISBN: 0–312–16623–0 (Instructor's Annotated Edition)
      0–312–26063–6 (hardcover Student Edition)
      0–312–26062–8 (paperback Student Edition)

ACKNOWLEDGMENTS

Preface for Instructors

The first edition of *The Bedford Handbook*, then titled *Rules for Writers*, was written on a self-correcting IBM Selectric, a wonderful innovation, or so I thought at the time. You can easily imagine the technology that has helped me produce the fifth edition: a powerful computer, CD-ROM references, a color printer, e-mail, a fax machine, and an Internet browser. Although the philosophy of the book remains largely the same, the fifth edition is a major revision primarily because of the impact technology has had on all of us in the classroom.

This book's beginnings

When I began writing this book, I had been teaching long enough to know just what I wanted in a handbook. At Prince George's Community College, our teaching load is fifteen hours per semester, so there is all too little time for individualized grammar lessons. I wanted a handbook so clear and accessible that our students could learn from it on their own.

I had in mind a book that would give students what they seem to prefer—straightforward rules—but without suggesting that rules are absolutes or that writing well is simply a matter of following rules.

Further, because our students have such a range of abilities, I hoped for a book that would be useful for all of them, offering a little help or a lot of help depending on their needs. Finally, I envisioned a handbook that would support the philosophy of composition that we work so hard to convey in the classroom. Writing is a process, we tell our students, and revision is central to that process. Revision is not a punishment for failing to get things right the first time. Nor is it a perfunctory clean-up exercise. It occurs right on the pages of a rough draft, often messily, with cross-outs and insertions, and it requires an active mind, a mind willing to look at a draft from the point of view of the reader, to spot problems, and to choose solutions.

With these aims in mind, then, I began writing this book. And it was with them in mind that I rewrote it again and again, with each draft edging closer to my vision. Central to my vision—then and now—is the belief that a handbook, whether brief or full, should work primarily as a reference that students can use on their own.

The fifth edition

Three main challenges faced me as I prepared this fifth edition of *The Bedford Handbook*. First, because today's computer-age students want quick access to information, preferably through visuals, I hoped to simplify the book's reference system and enliven it with icons. Second, because technology has changed composing behaviors so dramatically over the past four years, I looked forward to bringing the book into the electronic age. And, finally, because many instructors assign writing based on one or two sources (rather than on personal experience or on many sources), I wanted to emphasize text-based writing early in the book, not just in later sections. The chart on page viii shows, very briefly, how I have tried to address these three challenges.

Following is a more detailed description of the book's features, both old and new.

Quick access through menus. Designed for student use, a new brief menu inside the front cover displays icons representing the book's eleven parts and lists only the numbered sections. By consulting this menu, students can quickly locate the icon and section number for the information they need. Then they can follow up the page reference or flip pages in search of the appropriate tabs. The tabs on the left-hand pages display the icons, and those on the right-hand pages give the section numbers.

The traditional, more detailed handbook menu, which is useful for instructors but too daunting for many students, now appears on the back endpapers.

Tutorials. Five tutorials in "How to Use This Book" show students how to use the brief and detailed menus, the index, the Glossary of Usage, and the directories to documentation models. I like to use two or three of the tutorials as a small-group classroom activity early in the semester; my students teach one another, and they get to know one another at the same time.

Hand-edited sentences. Most examples in *The Bedford Handbook* appear with handwritten revisions over faulty typeset sentences. Unlike paired incorrect and correct examples, hand-edited sentences highlight the revision, allowing students to grasp both the error and its correction at a glance. Further, hand-edited sentences model the process of revision that students should use when working on hard copies of their own drafts.

Clear, uncluttered page design, now with four colors. Because rules and hand-edited sentences are highlighted in a

New to the fifth edition

A REFERENCE DESIGNED FOR TODAY'S STUDENTS

—A brief menu, with icons, inside the front cover

—A detailed menu, with icons, inside the back cover

—New four-color page design to promote quick reference

—Fifty charts, fourteen of them new, address common student problems at a glance

A GUIDE FOR THE ELECTRONIC AGE

—Finding, evaluating, and documenting online sources

—Fifty grammar checker boxes

—Designing documents, including e-mail and Web pages

—*Research and Documentation in the Electronic Age,* available in print and online (http://www.bedford books.com/rd)

—An electronic version of the handbook, with exercises

A RESOURCE FOR STUDENTS WORKING WITH TEXTS

—A section on writing about texts, with a sample summary and a sample analysis

—A sample argument paper

—Two MLA research papers (one new), an APA paper, and new sample pages from a *Chicago*-style history paper

—More on integrating quotations, summaries, and paraphrases

—A thoroughly revised section on writing about literature, with more on integrating quotations, along with two sample papers (one new)

second color (red), *The Bedford Handbook* is easy to skim for quick answers to questions. The book's third and fourth colors (teal and beige) appear in charts and boxes; these charts and boxes are easy to find and, just as important, they are easy to skip.

Quick reference charts. Many of the handbook's full-page charts take students back to their own writing, helping them review their drafts for common problems such as fragments and subject-verb agreement. Other charts summarize important material: a checklist for global revision, strategies for avoiding sexist English, guidelines for evaluating Web sites, and so on.

"Looking at yourself as a writer" charts. When writers experience a problem repeatedly, often their difficulties can be traced to root causes: false or half-learned rules, fossilized habits, confused motivations, or needless fears. For example, a writer may be addicted to run-on sentences for cognitive or emotional reasons that cannot be addressed simply by learning rules and working on exercises. Other writers may have difficulty asserting a thesis because of cultural conflicts or a lack of confidence. In the "Looking at yourself as a writer" charts, I hope to encourage the kind of self-reflection that leads to those occasional moments of recognition and flashes of insight that help us all grow as writers.

Fifty grammar checker boxes. New to this edition are fifty boxes that show students just what current grammar checkers and spell checkers can do—and what they can't do. As you may have discovered in your own classes, some students produce strange errors because they have taken the advice of a grammar checker without first thinking. And many students believe that once they have run a grammar or spell checker, their problems are over.

To discover the capabilities and limits of current grammar checkers, I have run a large bank of exercise sentences (many containing errors), along with some student drafts, through two grammar checker programs that are commonly used on college campuses. The results, summarized in screened boxes with computer icons throughout the book, show that grammar checkers help with some but by no means all of the typical problems in a draft.

Emphasis on writing about texts. The fifth edition emphasizes writing about texts early in the book as well as later. A new Part II, Critical Thinking, shows students how to approach assignments based on one or two texts. Section 6, on entering into a conversation with authors, is illustrated with a sample summary and a sample analysis. Advice on constructing arguments now appears in section 7, along with a new sample paper.

Section 55, on writing about literature, now offers more advice on integrating quotations. There are two sample papers, one new.

Nine updated sections on researched writing. Part IX is now broken up into more sections to target important topics such as managing information, avoiding plagiarism, and integrating sources. Throughout Part IX, I assume that students are using electronic search tools in the library and perhaps at home. Advice on tracking down sources, managing information, and evaluating sources has therefore changed considerably.

Documentation models have also been updated, with much attention to electronic sources. Both MLA and ACW (Alliance for Computer Writing) models for electronic sources are given in section 53.

A new sample paper, which draws on both Internet and library sources, addresses a political debate concerning the mountain lion population in California. For instructors who prefer a topic based on a scholarly controversy, I have retained the paper on apes and language.

MLA, APA, and Chicago documentation. *Chicago*-style footnotes or endnotes are new to this edition. They, along with APA documentation, appear in section 56, far enough away from MLA style (section 53) to avoid confusion. All three sections include models for documenting online sources. The MLA section is marked with a vertical band of teal, the APA with red, and *Chicago* with gray. The APA paper has been retained, and *Chicago* style is illustrated with sample pages.

A section on document design. Both in the business world and in the academic world, writers are becoming increasingly interested in document design—the use of visual cues to help readers. In the fifth edition of *The Bedford Handbook*, the section on document design appears in Part I, The Writing Process. It includes the principles of document design, a model MLA paper without secondary sources, sample business formats, and advice on creating effective e-mail and Web pages. Manuscript guidelines for MLA research papers now appear in Part IX. Manuscript guidelines for APA and *Chicago*-style research papers are in Part X.

Help for culturally diverse students. Part VI focuses on ESL trouble spots, and ESL boxes throughout the book provide other tips for students who speak English as a second language. In addition, ESL material appears in these ancillaries: *Supplemental Exercises, Diagnostic Resources, Bedford Basics,* and *Background Readings.*

Section 27, on choosing standard English verb forms, helps students with such matters as omitted -s and -ed endings and omitted verbs, problems often caused by dialect differences.

Extensive exercises, some with answers. At least one exercise set accompanies nearly every section of the book. Most sets begin with five lettered sentences with answers in the back of the book so students can test their understanding independently. The sets then continue with ten numbered sentences whose answers appear only in the *Instructor's Annotated Edition,* so that instructors may use the exercises in class or assign them as homework.

To help students learn to use the handbook independently as a reference, I have included five tutorials in "How to Use This Book."

A *user-friendly index.* The index of *The Bedford Handbook* helps students find what they are looking for even if they don't know grammatical terminology. When facing a choice between *I* and *me,* for example, students may not know to look up "Case" or even "Pronoun, case of." They are more likely to look up "*I*" or "*me,*" so *The Bedford Handbook* includes index entries for "*I* versus *me*" and "*me* versus *I.*" Similar user-friendly entries appear throughout the index of the fifth edition.

A *wide array of ancillaries.* To make *The Bedford Handbook* more useful for both students and instructors, the publisher has improved the package of resources accompanying the handbook.

PRACTICAL RESOURCES FOR INSTRUCTORS
Instructor's Annotated Edition

Quizzes and Diagnostic Tests to Accompany The Bedford Handbook, with ESL versions (available on disk)

Transparencies to Accompany The Bedford Handbook

PROFESSIONAL RESOURCES FOR INSTRUCTORS
Background Readings for Instructors Using The Bedford Handbook

The Bedford Guide to Teaching Writing in the Disciplines

The Bedford Guide for Writing Tutors

The Bedford Bibliography for Teachers of Writing, Fourth Edition (available online: http://www.bedfordbooks.com/bb)

RESOURCES FOR STUDENTS
Bedford Basics: A Workbook for Writers, Third Edition (with Answer Key)

Answers to Exercises in The Bedford Handbook

Supplemental Exercises for The Bedford Handbook (with Answer Key)

Research and Documentation in the Electronic Age (available online: http://www.bedfordbooks.com/rd)

Preparing for the CLAST with The Bedford Handbook

Preparing for the TASP with The Bedford Handbook

SOFTWARE
The Electronic Bedford Handbook (Windows® and Macintosh)

MicroGrade: A Teacher's Gradebook (Windows® and Macintosh)

Acknowledgments

No author can possibly anticipate the many ways in which a variety of students might respond to a text: Where might students be confused? How much explanation is enough? What is too intimidating? Do the examples appeal to a range of students? Are they free of stereotypes? To help me answer such questions, nearly two hundred professors from more than one hundred colleges and universities contributed useful insights based on their varied experiences in the classroom.

For their many helpful suggestions, I would like to thank a perceptive group of reviewers:

John Ames, Santa Fe Community College
Andrea M. Atkin, Wake Forest University
Thomas Banks, Ohio Northern University
Sandra Blakeman, Hood College
Geoffrey L. Brackett, Pace University
Robert Bray, Middle Tennessee State University
Colleen Brice, Purdue University
Lois E. Bueler, California State University, Chico
Cheryl M. Clark, Miami-Dade Community College
Mark Coley, Tarrant County Junior College
Jeanne deMartinez, Harvard University
Stephen B. Dobranski, Georgia State University
Keith Dorwick, University of Illinois at Chicago
Nancy Downs, University of Illinois at Chicago
Donald E. Erskine, Clark College
Richard Fabrizio, Pace University
Irene R. Fairley, Northeastern University
Barbara Fister, Gustavus Adolphus College
Mark K. Fulk, John Brown University
Susan Galloway, St. Mary's University
Helen Gilbart, St. Petersburg Junior College
Stacy Hagen, Edmonds Community College
Kay Halasek, Ohio State University
Iris Rose Hart, Santa Fe Community College
Allen Hoey, Bucks County Community College
Ann Huse, Washington University in St. Louis
David J. Johnson, Bucks County Community College
Leela Kapai, University of the District of Columbia
Michael Kent, San Bernardino Valley College
Ken McAllister, University of Illinois at Chicago
Brian Michaels, St. John's River College
Mark S. Miller, Pikes Peak Community College
Susan J. Miller, Santa Fe Community College
Terry Miller, Indian River Community College
Joan T. Mims, West Chester University
Susanna Minton, Boston University
Ken Moon, Indian Hills Community College
Renate Muendel, West Chester University
Louis Nazario, Pueblo Community College
Matthew Parfitt, Boston University

Carolyn Sue Poor, Wharton County Junior College
Helon Raines, Armstrong State College
Barbara C. Rhodes, Central Missouri State University
Gerald Richman, Suffolk University
Jim Roth, Spokane Community College
Timothy John Schell, Clackamas Community College
Nancy Shankle, Abilene Christian University
Ellen Shull, Palo Alto College
Donald L. Skinner, Indian River Community College
J. Robert Thompson, Macomb Community College
Thomas A. Underwood, Boston University
Kurt Wagner, William Paterson College of New Jersey
Thomas P. Walsh, University of Nebraska at Omaha
Irwin Weiser, Purdue University
Elizabeth Westgard, Saint Mary-of-the-Woods College
Suellyn Winkle, Santa Fe Community College
Pat Zeller, Northwest State Community College

For helping me to see the strengths and deficiencies of the fourth edition, thanks go to the many instructors who took the time to answer a detailed questionnaire:

Andrea M. Atkin, Wake Forest University; Mark Bauer, Hawaii Pacific University; Ann Beebe, University of Kentucky; Judith Bentley, Cardinal Stritch College; Sandra Blakeman, Hood College; Curtis Bowman, University of Kentucky; Anne Boyle, Wake Forest University; Anna Brickhouse, Columbia University; Emerson Brown, Vanderbilt University; Lois E. Bueler, California State University, Chico; Mark Coley, Tarrant County Junior College; Catherine S. Cox, University of Pittsburgh at Johnstown; Sheryl Craig, Central Missouri State University; Julie Crosby, Columbia University; M. Francine Danis, Our Lady of the Lake University; Wendy Day, College of the Redwoods; Stephen B. Dobranski, Georgia State University; Michael Elliott, Columbia University; Richard Fabrizio, Pace University; Mark K. Fulk, John Brown University; Donald Gallo, Central Connecticut State University; Susan Galloway, St. Mary's University; Patricia B. Geehr, Fairleigh Dickinson University; Paul D. Green, West Chester University;

Phillip J. Hanse, Jamestown College; Patrick Harkins, Saint Mary-of-the-Woods College; Janet Ruth Heller, Grand Valley State University; Cathy Henrichs, Pikes Peak Community College; Barbara Henry, West Virginia State College; Roderick Hofer, Indian River Community College; Woodrow L. Holbein, The Citadel; Casey Huff, California State University, Chico; Ann Huse, Washington University in St. Louis; Greg Jewell, Madisonville Community College; Sally Joranko, John Carroll University; Michael O. Kent, San Bernardino Valley College; Sharon Killworth, University of Dayton; Pete N. Kinnar, Colorado Northwestern Community College; Dara Llewellyn, Florida Atlantic University; Laura Lomas, Columbia University; Dawn Mays, Los Angeles Pierce College; Margo Miller, University of Kentucky; Andrea R. Nagy, University of Virginia; Jill Orofino, Boston University; Judith G. Prats, University of Kentucky; Susan Rieke, Saint Mary College; Lecia Rosenthal, Columbia University; Ellen Shull, Palo Alto College; Rebecca Simoneaux, Pikes Peak Community College; Aviva Taubenfeld, Columbia University; Mary Kathryn Tri, University of Kentucky; Catherine Wadbrook, Texas A&M at Kingsville; Jie Wang, University of Illinois at Chicago; Elizabeth Westgard, Saint Mary-of-the-Woods College; Bernadette Wilkowski, Seton Hall University; Julie Witherow, Pikes Peak Community College; Pat Zeller, Northwest State Community College

Writing a handbook is truly a collaborative effort. Barbara Flanagan, Lloyd Shaw, and Barbara Fister helped me improve the research paper chapters; William Peirce assisted with the chapter on argument; Julia Sullivan and Beth Castrodale contributed to the chapter on writing about literature.

I am grateful as well to the authors of the book's ancillaries: to Leigh Ryan for her insightful *Guide for Writing Tutors*; to Glenn Blalock for his carefully edited *Background Readings*; to Wanda Van Goor, Mitch Evich, and Owen Shows for their work on *Quizzes and Diagnostic Tests*; to Wanda Van Goor for her lively exercises in *Bedford Basics*; to Barbara Fister for her expert contribution to *Research and Documentation in the Electronic Age*; and to Barbara Sloan and Carolyn Christensen

West and to Ellen Shull and Paula Tran for their useful guides *Preparing for the CLAST* and *Preparing for the TASP*.

I am indebted to the students whose essays appear in this edition—John Garcia, Andrew Knutson, Margaret Peel, Lauren Pent, Karen Shaw, and Tom Weitzel—not only for permission to use their work but for permission to adapt it for pedagogical purposes as well. My thanks also go to the many students who granted me permission to use their paragraphs or other short writings: Celeste Barrus, Stephen Chapman, Diana Crawford, Robert Diaz, Jim Drew, Connie Haley, William G. Hill, Matthew J. Holicek, Patricia Klein, Gary Laporte, Linda Lavelle, Kathleen Lewis, Chris Mileski, Danielle Portes, David Queen, Julie Reardon, Jeffrey Richardson, Margaret Stack, John Clyde Thatcher, Angela Ventresca, and David Warren.

Several talented editors have contributed to the book. Michelle McSweeney has been a first-rate developmental editor: tactful, savvy, and good-humored. Her knowledge of computers and the Internet proved invaluable as we worked to bring the fifth edition into the electronic age. Copyeditor Barbara Flanagan has once again brought grace and consistency to the final manuscript; her keen eye has saved me from many a blunder. Beth Castrodale helped out in many ways, especially with the literature and research sections; Rebecca Jerman checked facts and handled other matters too numerous to mention; and Joanne Diaz worked enthusiastically with the authors of many of the book's ancillaries.

Book editor Heidi Hood has expertly steered the book through production under impossible deadlines with the help of Stasia Zomkowski, Patricia Bergin, Jocelyn Humelsine, and Arthur Johnson; and managing editor Elizabeth Schaaf has once again orchestrated the production of the book and its ancillaries with her usual unflappable calm. Award-winning designer Claire Seng-Niemoeller has created a new four-color design that enlivens the book while preserving the clean, uncluttered pages featuring the hand-edited sentences.

Special thanks are due to publishers Chuck Christensen and Joan Feinberg. Fourteen years ago Chuck took a chance on an unknown community college professor with an inexplicable urge to write a handbook. I am deeply grateful to him for giving me this opportunity. In retrospect, I suppose Chuck knew that almost anyone could learn to write a handbook under the guidance of Joan Feinberg. Certainly a better teacher-editor could not have been found. Joan has consistently set a standard of excellence, and over the years she has nudged me toward it, always with intelligence, grace, and good humor. It would be impossible to overstate my gratitude.

Finally, a note of thanks goes to my mother, Georgiana Tarvin, and to Joseph and Marian Hacker, Robert Hacker, Greg Tarvin, Betty Renshaw, Bill Fry, Bill Mullinix, Joyce Neff Magnotto, Christine McMahon, Anne King, Wanda Van Goor, Melinda Kramer, Joan Naake, Bill Pierce, Lloyd Shaw, the Dougherty family, and Robbie and Austin Nichols for their support and encouragement; and to the many students over the years who have taught me that errors, a natural by-product of the writing process, are simply problems waiting to be solved.

Diana Hacker

Prince George's Community College

How to Use This Book

Though it is small enough to hold in your hand, *The Bedford Handbook* will answer most of the questions you are likely to ask as you plan, draft, and revise a piece of writing: How do I choose and narrow a topic? What can I do if I get stuck? How do I know when to begin a new paragraph? Should I write *none was* or *none were*? When does a comma belong before *and*? What is the difference between *accept* and *except*? How do I cite a source from the Internet?

How to find information with an instructor's help

When you are revising an essay that has been marked by your instructor, tracking down information is simple. If your instructor marks problems with a number such as *16* or a number and letter such as *12e*, you can turn directly to the appropriate section of the handbook. Just flip through the colored tabs on the upper corners of the right-hand pages until you find the number in question. The number *16*, for example, leads you to the rule "Tighten wordy sentences," and *12e* takes you to the subrule "Repair dangling modifiers." If your instructor uses an abbreviation such as *w* or *dm* instead of a number, consult the list of abbreviations and symbols on the next to the last page of the book (just before the endpapers), where you will find the name of the problems *(wordy; dangling modifier)* and the number of the section to consult.

How to find information on your own

With a little practice, you will be able to find information in this book without an instructor's help—usually by tracking the icons that appear in the brief menu inside the front cover. At times, you may want to consult the detailed menu inside the back cover, the index, the Glossary of Usage, or one of the directories to the documentation models.

THE FRONT ENDPAPERS   Usually the brief menu on the inside front cover is the fastest way into the book. Let's say you are having problems with run-on sentences. Your first step is to find the appropriate section—in this case "Grammatical Sentences," which is represented by a check mark icon. Next, find the appropriate numbered rule: "20 Revise run-on sentences." You can flip directly to the page number given (p. 296), or you can use the icon tabs on the left-hand pages and section number tabs on right-hand pages to help you find section 20.

THE BACK ENDPAPERS   When the numbered section you're looking for is broken up into quite a few lettered subsections, try consulting the detailed menu on the inside back cover.

THE INDEX   If you aren't sure which topic to choose from one of the menus, consult the index at the back of the book. For example, you may not realize that the issue of *is* versus *are* is a matter of subject-verb agreement (section 21). In that case, simply look up "*is* versus *are*" in the index and you will be directed to the exact pages you need.

THE GLOSSARY OF USAGE   When in doubt about the correct use of a particular word (such as *affect* and *effect, among* and *between,* or *hopefully*), consult the Glossary of Usage at the back of the book. This glossary explains the difference between commonly confused words; it also lists colloquialisms and jargon that are inappropriate in formal written English.

DIRECTORIES TO DOCUMENTATION MODELS When you are documenting a research paper with MLA, APA, or *Chicago* style, you can find documentation models by consulting the appropriate directories. The MLA directories to in-text citation models and to works cited models are easy to find: Just look for the pages marked with a vertical band of teal. The APA directories appear on pages marked with a vertical band of red. And the *Chicago* directories appear on pages marked with a vertical band of gray.

How to use this book for self-study

In a composition class, most of your time should be spent writing. Therefore it is unlikely that you will want to study all of the chapters in this book in detail. Instead you should focus on the problems that tend to crop up in your own writing. Your instructor (or your college's writing center) will be glad to help you design an individual program of self-study.

The Bedford Handbook has been designed so that you can learn from it on your own. By providing answers to some exercise sentences, it allows you to test your understanding of the material. Most exercise sets begin with five sentences lettered a–c and conclude with ten sentences numbered 1–10. Answers to the five lettered sentences appear near the end of the book.

Diana Hacker

Tutorials

The following tutorials will give you practice using the book's menus, index, Glossary of Usage, and MLA works cited directory. Answers to the tutorials begin on page 789.

TUTORIAL 1 Using the menus

Each of the following "rules" violates the principle it expresses. Using the brief menu inside the front cover or the detailed menu inside the back cover, find the section in *The Bedford Handbook* that explains the principle. Then fix the problem. Examples:

> *Tutors in*
> ~~In~~ the writing center/~~they~~ say that vague pronoun reference
> ^
> is unacceptable.   *23*

> *come*
> Be alert for irregular verbs that have ~~came~~ to you in the
> ^
> wrong form.   *27a*

1. A verb have to agree with its subject.
2. Each pronoun should agree with their antecedent.
3. About sentence fragments. You should avoid them.
4. Don't write a run-on sentence you must connect the clauses with a comma and a coordinating conjunction or with a semicolon.
5. Discriminate careful between adjectives and adverbs.
6. Proofread to see if you any words out.
7. Check for *-ed* verb endings that have been drop.
8. In most contexts, passive-voice verbs should be avoided.
9. In choosing proper pronoun case, follow the example of we teachers, whom are the experts.
10. Don't use no double negatives.
11. When dangling, watch your modifiers.
12. Its important to use apostrophe's correctly.
13. A writer must be careful not to shift your point of view.
14. If your sentence begins with a long introductory word group use a comma to separate the word group from the rest of the sentence.
15. Last but not least, avoid clichés like the plague.

TUTORIAL 2 Using the index

Assume that you have written the following sentences and want to know the answers to the questions in brackets. Use the index at the back of the book to locate the information you need, and edit the sentences if necessary.

1. Anybody taking the school bus to the volleyball game must bring in a permission slip signed by their parents. [Does the pronoun *Anybody* agree with *their*? If not, what is the best way to fix the problem?]
2. We had intended to go surfing but spent most of our vacation lying on the beach. [Should I use *lying* or *laying*?]
3. We only looked at two houses before buying the house of our dreams. [Is *only* in the right place?]
4. In Saudi Arabia it is considered ill-mannered for you to accept a gift. [Is it okay to use *you* to mean "anyone in general"?]
5. In Canada, Joanne picked up several bottles of maple syrup for her sister and me. [Should I write *for her sister and I*?]

TUTORIAL 3 Using the menus or the index

Imagine that you are in the following situations. Using either the menus or the index, find the information you need.

1. You are Ray Farley, a community college student who has been out of high school for ten years. You recall learning to punctuate items in a series by putting a comma between all items except the last two. In your college readings, however, you have noticed that most writers use a comma between all items. You're curious about the current rule. Which section of *The Bedford Handbook* will you consult?
2. You are Maria Sanchez, an honors student working in your university's writing center. Mike Lee, who speaks English as a second language, has come to you for help. He is working on a rough draft that contains a number of problems involving the use of articles (*a*, *an*, and *the*). You know how to use articles, but you aren't able to explain the rather complicated rules on their correct use. Which section of *The Bedford Handbook* will you and Mike Lee consult?

3. You are John Pell, engaged to marry Jane Dalton. In a note to Jane's parents, you have written *Thank you for giving Jane and myself such a generous contribution toward our honeymoon trip to Hawaii.* You wonder if you should write *Jane and I* or *Jane and me* instead. Upon consulting *The Bedford Handbook,* what do you learn?

4. You are Selena Young, a supervisor of interns at a housing agency. Two of your interns, Jake Gilliam and Susan Green, have writing problems involving *-s* endings on verbs. Gilliam tends to drop *-s* endings; Green tends to add them where they don't belong. You suspect that both problems stem from non-standard dialects spoken at home.

   Susan and Jake are in danger of losing their jobs because your boss thinks that anyone who writes *the tenant refuse* or *the landlords agrees* is beyond hope. You disagree. Susan and Jake are more intelligent than your boss supposes, and they have asked for your help. Where in *The Bedford Handbook* can they find the rules they need?

5. You are Joe Thompson, a first-year college student. Your friend Samantha, who has completed two years of college, seems to enjoy correcting your English. Just yesterday she corrected your sentence *I felt badly about her death* to *I felt bad about her death.* You're sure you've heard many educated persons, including professors, say *I felt badly.* Upon consulting *The Bedford Handbook,* what do you discover?

TUTORIAL 4   Using the Glossary of Usage

Consult the Glossary of Usage to see if the italicized words are used correctly. Then edit any sentences containing incorrect usage. Example:

                                            an
The pediatrician gave my daughter ~~a~~ injection for her allergy.

1. The *amount* of horses a Comanche warrior had in his possession indicated the wealth of his family.
2. This afternoon I plan to *lie* out in the sun and begin working on a tan.
3. That is the most *unique* floral arrangement I have ever seen.

4. Changing attitudes *toward* alcohol have *effected* the beer industry.
5. Jenny *should of* known better than to attempt that dive.
6. Everyone in our office is *enthused* about this project.
7. George and Pat are selling *there* house because now that *their* children are grown, *their* planning to move to Arizona.
8. Most sleds are pulled by no *fewer* than two dogs and no more than ten.
9. It is *man's* nature to think wisely and act foolishly.
10. Dr. Newman and *myself* have agreed to arrange the retirement party.

TUTORIAL 5 Using the directory to MLA works cited models

Assume that you have written a short research paper on the controversial growth of gambling operations on Indian reservations. You have cited the following sources in your paper, using MLA documentation, and you are ready to type your list of works cited. Turn to page 592 and use the MLA directory to locate the appropriate models. Then write a correct entry for each source and arrange the entries in a properly formatted list of works cited. *Note:* Do not number the entries in a list of works cited.

A book by Bruce E. Johansen entitled *Life and Death in Mohawk Country.* The book was published in Golden, Colorado, in 1993 by North American Press.

An e-mail about casinos on reservations in the Northeast, sent to you by Helen Codoga on April 10, 1997.

An article by Eric Schine entitled "First Gambling, Then a Bank: California Has Reservations," from the weekly magazine *Business Week.* The article appears on page 47 of the September 9, 1996, issue of the magazine.

An article by Sam Ridgebear entitled "Guilty Hands: Traditionalism and the Indian Gaming Industry" from the online journal *Many Voices: American Indian Students Journal.* The article appears in volume 1, issue 1, of this journal in 1995, and there is no pagination. You accessed the article through the Internet on April 2, 1997, at the following address: http://thecity.sfsu.edu/users/BANN/journal/guiltyhands.html.

A journal article by Mary H. Cooper entitled "Native Americans' Future: Do U.S. Policies Block Opportunities for Progress?" The article appears on pages 603 to 619 of *CQ Researcher,* which is paginated by volume. The volume number is 6 and the year is 1996.

An article by James Dao entitled "Gambling Proponents See Indian Casinos as Alternative," available through America Online in *The New York Times on America Online.* The article was published on January 30, 1997, and it appears on page B2 of the late edition of the print version of the *New York Times.* You accessed the online version on April 5, 1997.

Contents

PART II
Critical Thinking   137

PART III
Clear Sentences   181

PART V
Grammatical Sentences

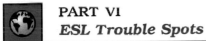

PART VI
ESL Trouble Spots 389

PART VII
Punctuation 425

PART VIII
Mechanics   487

PART IX
Researched Writing — 519

PART X
Literature and Other Disciplines 641

PART I

The Writing Process

Since it's not possible to think about everything all at once, most experienced writers handle a piece of writing in stages. Roughly speaking, those stages are planning, drafting, and revising. You should generally move from planning to drafting to revising, but be prepared to circle back to earlier stages whenever the need arises.

1

Generate ideas and sketch a plan.

Before attempting a first draft, spend some time generating ideas. Mull over your subject while listening to music or driving to work, jot down inspirations on scratch paper, and explore your insights with anyone willing to listen. At this stage you should be collecting information and experimenting with ways of focusing and organizing it to best reach your readers.

1a Assess the writing situation.

Begin by taking a look at the writing situation in which you find yourself. The key elements of the writing situation include your subject, the sources of information available to you, your purpose, your audience, and constraints such as length, document design, review sessions, and deadlines.

It is unlikely that you will make final decisions about all of these matters until later in the writing process—after a first draft, for example. Nevertheless, you can save yourself time by thinking about as many of them as possible in advance. For a quick checklist, see pages 14–15.

Subject

Frequently your subject will be given to you. In a psychology class, for example, you might be asked to explain Bruno Bettelheim's Freudian analysis of fairy tales. Or in a course on the history of filmmaking, you might be assigned an essay on the political impact of D. W. Griffith's silent film *The Birth of a Nation*. In the business world, your assignment might be to draft a quarterly sales report or craft a diplomatic letter to a customer who has complained about your firm's computer software.

Sometimes you will be free to choose your own subject. Then you will be wise to select a subject that you already know something about or one that you can reasonably investigate in the time you have. Students in composition classes have written successfully on all of the subjects listed here, most of which were later narrowed into topics suitable for essays of 500–750 words. By browsing through the lists, perhaps you can pick up some ideas of your own.

Education: computers in the classroom, an inspiring teacher, sex education in junior high school, magnet schools, a learning disability such as dyslexia, programmed instruction, parochial schools, teacher certification, a local program to combat adult illiteracy, creative means of funding a college education

Careers and the workplace: working in an emergency room, the image versus the reality of a job such as lifeguarding, a police officer's workday, advantages of flextime for workers and employers, company-sponsored day care, mandatory drug testing by employers, sex or racial discrimination on the job, the psychological effects of unemployment, the rewards of a part-time job such as camp counseling, e-mail privacy issues

Families: an experience with adoption, a portrait of a family member who has aged well, the challenges facing single parents, living with an alcoholic, a portrait of an ideal parent, growing up in a large family, the problems of split custody, an experience with child abuse, the depiction of parent-child relationships in a popular TV series, expectations versus the reality of marriage, overcoming sibling rivalry, the advantages or disadvantages of being a twin, overseeing a child's access to the World Wide Web

Health: a vegetarian diet, weight loss through hypnotism, a fitness program for the elderly, reasons not to smoke, the rights of smokers or nonsmokers, overcoming an addiction, Prozac as a treatment for depression, the side effects of a particular treatment for cancer, life as a diabetic, the benefits of an aerobic exercise such as swimming, caring for a person with AIDS

Sports and hobbies: an unusual sport such as free-fall parachuting or bungee jumping, surviving a wilderness program, bodybuilding, a sport from another culture, the philosophy of karate, the language of sports announcers, pros and cons of banning boxing, coaching a Little League team, cutting the costs of an expensive sport such as skiing, a portrait of a favorite sports figure, sports for the handicapped, the discipline required for a sport such as gymnastics, the rewards of a hobby such as woodworking, salary caps for professional athletes

The arts: working behind the scenes at a theater, censorship of rock and roll lyrics, photography as an art form, the Japanese tea ceremony, the influence of African art on Picasso, the appeal of a local art museum, a portrait of a favorite musician or artist, performing as a musician, a high school for the arts, the colorization of black-and-white films, science fiction as a serious form of literature, a humorous description of romance novels or hard-boiled detective thrillers

Social justice: an experience with racism or sexism, affirmative action, reverse discrimination, making public transportation accessible for the physically handicapped, an experience as a juror, a local program to aid the homeless, discrimination against homosexuals, pros and cons of a national drinking age of twenty-one

Death and dying: working on a suicide hotline, the death of a loved one, a brush with death, caring for terminally ill patients, assisted suicide, the Buddhist view of death, explaining death to a child, passive euthanasia, death with dignity, an out-of-body experience

Violence and crime: an experience with a gun, a wartime experience, violence on television news programs, visiting a friend in prison, alternative sentencing for first offenders, victims' rights, a successful program to eliminate violence in a public high school, Internet fraud, capital punishment, preventing terrorist attacks, domestic violence and the courts

Nature and ecology: safety of nuclear power plants, solar energy, wind energy, air pollution in the national parks, forest fires on the California coast, grizzly bears in Yellowstone, communication among dolphins, organic gardening, backpacking in the Rockies, marine ecology, cleaning up Boston Harbor, the preservation of beaches in Delaware

Science and technology: pros and cons of writing on a computer, genetic engineering, an experimental farming technique, a medical breakthrough, free speech and the Internet

Many of these subjects are too broad. Part of your challenge as a writer will be whittling broad subjects down to manageable topics. If you are limited to a few pages, for example, you could not possibly do justice to a subject as broad as "sports for the handicapped." You would be wise to restrict your paper to a topic more manageable in the space allowed—perhaps a description of the Saturday morning athletic program your college offers for handicapped children. The chart on page 7 suggests specific ways to narrow a subject to a topic.

Sources of information

Where will your facts, details, and examples come from? Can your topic be illustrated by personal experience, or will you need to search out relevant information through direct observation, interviews, questionnaires, reading, or the Internet?

PERSONAL EXPERIENCE You can develop many topics wholly through personal experience, depending of course on your own life experiences. The students who wrote about lifeguarding, learning disabilities, weight loss through hypnotism, and free-fall parachuting all spoke with the voice of experience, as did those who wrote about flextime, coaching a Little League team, and company-sponsored day care. When narrowing their subjects, those students chose to limit themselves to information they had at hand. For example, instead of writing about company-sponsored day care in general—a subject that would have required a great deal of research—one student limited her discussion to the successful day care center at the company for which she worked.

DIRECT OBSERVATION Direct observation is an excellent means of collecting information about a wide range of subjects, such as male-female relationships on the television program *Friends*, the clichéd language of sports announcers, or the appeal of a local art museum. For such subjects, do not rely on your memory alone; your information will be fresher and more detailed if you actively collect it, with a notebook or tape recorder in hand. As writer Stuart Chase advises young journalists assigned to report on their city's water system, "You will write a better article if you heave yourself out of a comfortable chair and go down in tunnel 3 and get soaked."

Ways to narrow a subject to a topic

SUBDIVIDING YOUR SUBJECT

Many subjects can be subdivided. Instead of writing about censorship of popular songs, for example, you might select a subdivision of this general subject: government labeling of CDs for content. Or instead of writing about homelessness in general, you might focus on the homeless in a particular city.

RESTRICTING YOUR PURPOSE

Often you can narrow your subject by restricting your purpose. For example, if your subject is drug testing in the workplace, you might at first hope to persuade readers that it should be banned in all situations. Upon further reflection, however, you might realize that this goal is more than you could hope to accomplish, given your word limit. By adopting a more limited purpose—to show that drug testing is unreliable, to argue that its use by private employers should be banned, or to demonstrate that it violates an innocent person's right to privacy—you would have a better chance of success.

RESTRICTING YOUR AUDIENCE

Another way to narrow your subject is to write for a particular audience. For example, instead of writing to a general audience on a subject such as teenage pregnancy, you might address persons with a special interest in the subject: young people, parents, or counselors working for Planned Parenthood.

CONSIDERING THE INFORMATION AVAILABLE TO YOU

One of the most natural ways to narrow a subject is to look at the information you have collected. If you have gathered a great deal of information on one aspect of your subject (for example, discrimination against persons with AIDS) and less information on other aspects (such as the causes of AIDS or promising treatments for AIDS), you may have found your topic.

INTERVIEWS AND QUESTIONNAIRES   Interviews and questionnaires can supply you with detailed and interesting information on a variety of subjects. A nursing student interested in the care of terminally ill patients might interview nurses at a hospice; a political science major might speak with a local judge to learn about alternative sentencing for first offenders; a future teacher might conduct a survey on the classroom use of computers in local elementary schools. It is a good idea to tape interviews to preserve any lively quotations that you might want to weave into your essay. (See pp. 544–45.) Keep questionnaires simple and specify a deadline to ensure that you get a reasonable number of responses.

READING   Reading will be your primary source of information for many college assignments, which will generally be of two kinds: analytical assignments that call for a close reading of one book, essay, or literary work and research assignments that send you to the library to consult a variety of sources on a particular topic. For analytical essays, you can usually assume that your reader is familiar with the work and has a copy of it at hand. You select details from the work not to inform readers but to support an interpretation. When you quote from the work, page references are often sufficient. For research papers, however, you cannot assume that your reader is familiar with your sources or has them close at hand. This means that you must formally document all quoted and summarized or paraphrased material (see 50). When in doubt about the need for formal documentation, consult your instructor.

THE INTERNET   If you have access to the Internet, take advantage of its many resources. To generate ideas, you might surf the Web, join chat groups and online discussion groups, or browse through online periodicals. Beware, however, that the wealth of information available through the Internet can be overwhelming, and Internet sources are not always reliable. For advice on using the Internet to explore your subject, see page 25. For advice on evaluating and documenting online sources, see pages 546–48 and 603–07.

Purpose

Your purpose will often be dictated by the specific writing situation that faces you. Perhaps you have been asked to take minutes for a club meeting, to draft a letter requesting payment from a client, or to describe the results of a biology experiment. Even though your overall purpose is fairly obvious in such situations, a close look at that purpose can help you make a variety of necessary decisions. How detailed should the minutes be? Is your purpose to summarize the meeting or to establish a careful record of discussion in case future controversies arise? How firmly should your letter request payment? Do you need the money at all costs, or do you hope to get it without risking loss of the client's business? How technical does your biology professor want your report to be?

In many writing situations, part of your challenge will be discovering a purpose. Consider, for example, the topic of magnet schools — schools that draw students from different neighborhoods because of features such as advanced science classes or late-afternoon day care. Your purpose could be to inform parents of the options available in your county. Or you might argue that the county's magnet schools are not promoting racial integration as had been planned. Or you might propose that the board of education create a magnet high school for the arts on your college campus.

Although no precise guidelines will lead you to a purpose, you can begin by asking yourself which one or more of the following aims you hope to accomplish.

PURPOSES FOR WRITING

to inform	to evaluate
to persuade	to recommend
to call readers to action	to request
to change attitudes	to propose
to analyze	to provoke thought
to argue	to express feelings
to theorize	to entertain
to summarize	to give aesthetic pleasure

It is surprising how often writers misjudge their own purposes: informing, for example, when they should be recommending; summarizing when they should be analyzing; or expressing feelings about problems instead of proposing solutions. Before beginning any writing task, therefore, pause to ask, "Why am I communicating with my readers?" And this question will lead you to another important question: "Just who are those readers?"

Audience

Audience analysis can often lead you to an effective strategy for reaching your readers. One writer, whose purpose was to persuade teenagers not to smoke, jotted down the following observations about her audience:

dislike lectures, especially from older people

have little sense of their own mortality

are concerned about physical appearance and image

want to be socially accepted

have limited budgets

This analysis led the writer to focus more on the social aspects of smoking (she pointed out, for instance, that kissing a smoker is like licking an ashtray) than on the health risks. Her audience analysis also warned her against adopting a preachy tone that her readers might find offensive. Instead of lecturing to her audience, she decided to draw examples from her own experience as a hooked smoker: burning holes in her best sweater, driving in zero-degree weather late at night in search of an open tavern to buy cigarettes, rummaging through ashtrays for stale butts, and so on. The result was an essay that reached its readers instead of alienating them.

The following checklist will help you decide how to approach your audience.

AUDIENCE CHECKLIST

How well informed are your readers about the subject?

What do you want them to learn about the subject?

How interested and attentive are they likely to be?

Will they resist any of your ideas?

What is your relationship to them: Employee to supervisor? Citizen to citizen? Expert to novice? Scholar to scholar?

How much time are they willing to spend reading?

How sophisticated are they as readers? Do they have large vocabularies? Can they follow long and complex sentences?

Of course, in some writing situations the audience will not be neatly defined for you. Nevertheless, many of the choices that you make as you write will tell readers who you think they are (novices or experts, for example), so it is best to be consistent—even if this means creating an audience that is in some sense a fiction.

BUSINESS AUDIENCES   Writers in the business world often find themselves writing for multiple audiences. A letter to a client, for instance, might be distributed to sales representatives as well. Readers of a report may include persons with and without technical expertise or readers who want details and those who prefer a quick overview. To satisfy the demands of multiple audiences, business writers have developed a variety of strategies: attaching cover letters to more detailed reports, adding boldface headings, placing summaries in the left margin, and so on.

ACADEMIC AUDIENCES In the academic world, considerations of audience can be more complex than they seem at first. Your professor will read your essay, of course, but most professors play multiple roles while reading. Their first and most obvious roles are as coach and judge; less obvious is their role as an intelligent and objective reader, the kind of person who might reasonably be informed, convinced, entertained, or called to action by what you have to say.

Some professors create writing assignments that specify an audience, such as a hypothetical supervisor, readers of a local newspaper, or fellow academics in a particular field of study. Other professors expect you to imagine an audience appropriate to your purpose and your subject. Still others prefer that you write for a general audience of educated readers— nonspecialists who can be expected to read with an intelligent, critical eye. When in doubt about an appropriate audience for a particular assignment, check with your professor.

Length and document design

Writers seldom have complete control over length and document design. Journalists usually write within strict word limits set by their editors, businesspeople routinely aim for conciseness, and most college assignments specify an approximate length.

Certain document designs may also be required by your writing situation. Specific formats are used in the business world for documents such as letters, memos, reports, budget analyses, and personnel records. In the academic world, you may need to learn precise conventions for lab reports, critiques, research papers, and so on. For most undergraduate essays, a standard format is acceptable (see 5b).

In some writing situations, you will be free to create your own document design, complete with headings, displayed lists, and perhaps even visuals, such as charts and graphs. Quite sophisticated results are now possible on computers, and both writers and readers are becoming increasingly interested in designs that improve readability. For a discussion of the principles of document design, see 5a.

Reviewers and deadlines

Professional and business writers rarely work alone. They work with reviewers, often called editors, who offer advice throughout the writing process. In the academic world, too, the use of reviewers is increasingly common. Some instructors will play the role of reviewer for you; others may ask you to visit your college's writing center. Still others schedule peer review sessions in class (sometimes conducted online, in a networked classroom). Such sessions give you a chance to hear what other students think about your draft in progress—and to play the role of reviewer yourself.

Deadlines are a key element of any writing situation. They tell you what is possible and help you plan your time. For complex writing projects, such as research papers, you'll need to plan your time quite carefully. By working backward from the final deadline, you can create a schedule of target dates for completing various parts of the process. (See p. 520 for an example.)

EXERCISE 1–1

Choose one of the subject areas mentioned on pages 3–5 and add at least five subjects to those already on the list. If other members of your class have also done this exercise, pool the results.

Checklist for assessing the writing situation

At the beginning of the writing process, you may not be able to answer all of the questions on this checklist. That's fine. Just be prepared to think about them later.

NOTE: It is not necessary to think about the elements of a writing situation in the exact order listed in this chart.

SUBJECT

— Has a subject (or a range of possible subjects) been given to you, or are you free to choose your own?

— Is your subject worth writing about? Can you think of any readers who might be interested in reading about it?

— How broadly can you cover the subject? Do you need to narrow it to a more specific topic (because of length restrictions, for instance)?

— How detailed should your coverage be?

SOURCES OF INFORMATION

— Where will your information come from: Personal experience? Direct observation? Interviews? Questionnaires? Reading? The Internet?

— If your information comes from reading or the Internet, what sort of documentation is required?

PURPOSE

— Why are you writing: To inform readers? To persuade them? To entertain them? To call them to action? Some combination of these?

Assessing the writing situation (*continued*)

AUDIENCE

— How well informed are your readers about the subject? What do you want them to learn about the subject?

— How interested and attentive are they likely to be? Will they resist any of your ideas?

— What is your relationship to them: Employee to supervisor? Citizen to citizen? Expert to novice? Scholar to scholar?

— How much time are they willing to spend reading?

— How sophisticated are they as readers? Do they have large vocabularies? Can they follow long and complex sentences?

LENGTH AND DOCUMENT DESIGN

— Are you working within any length specifications? If not, what length seems appropriate, given your subject, your purpose, and your audience?

— Must you use a particular design for your document? If so, do you have guidelines or examples that you can consult?

REVIEWERS AND DEADLINES

— Who will be reviewing your draft in progress—your instructor, a writing center tutor, your classmates, a friend, someone in your family?

— What are your deadlines? How much time will you need to allow for the various stages of writing, including typing and proofreading the final draft?

EXERCISE 1–2

Narrow five of the following subjects into topics that would be manageable for an essay of two to five pages.

COSTUME DESIGNER

 1. Working behind the scenes at a theater *STAGE*
 2. A sport from another culture *CRICKET*
 3. Domestic violence and the courts LAWYERS
 4. The advantages or disadvantages of being a twin MISTAKEN FOR YOUR TWIN
 5. An experience with adoption ABANDONMENT
 6. The side effects of a particular treatment for cancer KIMO
 7. Computers in the classroom DELL
 8. Parochial schools NEX PRESSMAN
 9. Performing as a musician HAVING CONFIDENCE
10. An experience with racism or sexism

FEMALE FOOTBALL ATHOLETE

EXERCISE 1–3

Which of the following subjects might be illustrated wholly by personal experience? For the others, suggest possible sources of information: direct observation, interviews, questionnaires, reading, or the Internet.

 1. The problems of split custody
 2. Working in an emergency room
 3. Backpacking in the Rockies
 4. The influence of African art on Picasso
 5. Violence on television news programs
 6. The discipline required for a sport such as gymnastics
 7. Photography as an art form
 8. Online marketing techniques
 9. A local program to aid the homeless
10. Visiting a friend in prison

EXERCISE 1–4

Suggest a purpose and an audience for five of the following subjects.

 1. A vegetarian diet
 2. Cutting the costs of an expensive sport such as skiing

3. The challenges facing single parents
4. Advantages of flextime for workers and employers
5. Growing up in a large family
6. Pros and cons of a national speed limit of sixty-five
7. Science fiction as a serious form of literature
8. An unusual sport such as bungee jumping
9. A police officer's workday
10. Working on a suicide hotline

EXERCISE 1–5

For each of the following paired items, choose the sentence or passage that is more effective, given the writer's purpose and audience. Be prepared to explain your choices.

1. Here are two notices sent out by dentists to remind patients to call for an appointment. Which notice is more effective?

   a. Things to do today:
      1. Floss.
      2. Call your dentist.
      It's time again for your regular dental checkup, so please call today for an appointment.

   b. It is the custom of this office to notify patients on record for periodical examination of the mouth. This service is rendered to safeguard previous work and to ensure future good health and appearance. May I suggest you call.

2. If you were writing an instruction booklet for machinists, which of the following sentences would you choose?

   a. Move the control lever to the reverse position after the machine stops.

   b. After the machine stops, move the control lever to the reverse position.

3. In an essay about a short story, which sentence announces a clearer interpretation?

   a. In "The Lottery," Shirley Jackson uses symbolism to reveal the emptiness of rituals and traditions and the dark side of human nature.

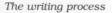
  b. Shirley Jackson's "The Lottery" uses subtle symbolism along with incongruities to exemplify the loss of significance of some rituals and traditions and flaws of human nature.

4. In a business letter promoting the writer's company to an audience aware of the company's former problems, which of the following sentences is more effective?

  a. At this point in time ours is a revitalized and emergent company no longer attached to outmoded marketing concepts, no longer subject to inbred managerial alliances, and never again dependent on reactionary governmental influences.

  b. We have revitalized our company with new marketing ideas, a forward-looking management, and a wider base of clients.

5. Which of the following sentences would be more effective in a campus newspaper article criticizing the food in the cafeteria's vending machines?

  a. First and foremost, the hamburgers that are sold in the cafeteria's machines are dry in texture and cold to the taste.

  b. When I turned to the machine, I decided to try a sizzling hamburger, lean and juicy. Instead, out came a small dry patty so cold that the fat was congealed in tiny globs on top of the meat.

1b Experiment with ways to explore your subject.

Instead of just plunging into a first draft, experiment with one or more techniques for exploring your subject, perhaps one of these:

listing	keeping a journal
clustering	talking and listening
asking questions	the Internet
freewriting	invention software
annotating texts and taking notes	

You can use most of these techniques whether you are working with pencil and paper or entering ideas into a computer.

Whatever technique you turn to, the goal is the same: to generate a wealth of ideas. At this early stage of the writing process, you should aim for quantity, not necessarily quality, of ideas. If an idea proves to be off the point, trivial, or too far-fetched, you can always throw it out later.

Listing

You might begin by simply listing ideas, putting them down in the order in which they occur to you—a technique sometimes known as "brainstorming." Here, for example, is a list one student writer jotted down:

The Phillips Collection

Washington, D.C.

1612 21st Street, close to Mass. Ave.

near Dupont Circle, in an interesting neighborhood

hard to find a parking space; better to take subway

elegant red brick townhouse, once home of Duncan and Marjorie Phillips (art collectors)

turned into a museum in 1918

facade reminds me of a bygone era—teas and debutante balls

free concerts on Sundays

mostly Impressionists, Postimpressionists, and modern masters

Renoir's *Luncheon of the Boating Party*—warm and joyful—you can almost smell the breeze off the Seine and hear the hum of conversation

you can wander through small rooms filled with paintings by Van Gogh, Degas, Cézanne, Bonnard, and Klee the Rothko room, with huge color paintings—pulsating, sensuous reds, yellows, blues, greens

the new wing—no more bygone era—clean and uncluttered lines appropriate for modern masters like Picasso, Pollock, Dalí, Braque

a walled garden

The ideas appear here in the order in which they first occurred to the writer. Later she felt free to rearrange them, to cluster them under general categories, to delete some, and to add others. In other words, she treated her initial list as a source of ideas and a springboard to new ideas, not as an outline.

Clustering

Unlike listing, the technique of clustering highlights relationships among ideas. To cluster ideas, write your topic in the center of a sheet of paper, draw a circle around it, and surround that with related ideas connected to it with lines. If

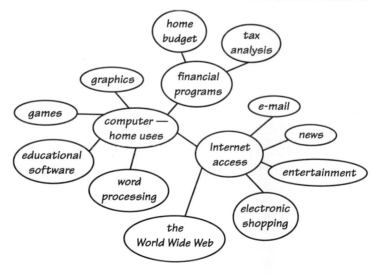

some of the satellite ideas lead to more specific clusters, write them down as well. The writer of the diagram on page 20 was exploring ideas for an essay on home uses for computers.

Asking questions

By asking relevant questions, you can generate many ideas — and you can make sure that you have adequately surveyed your subject. When gathering material for a story, journalists routinely ask themselves Who? What? When? Where? Why? and How? In addition to helping journalists get started, these questions ensure that they will not overlook an important fact: the date of a prospective summit meeting, for example, or the exact location of a neighborhood burglary.

Whenever you are writing about events, whether current or historical, the journalist's questions are one way to get started. One student, whose subject was the negative reaction in 1915 to D. W. Griffith's silent film *The Birth of a Nation,* began exploring her topic with this set of questions:

Who objected to the film?

What were the objections?

When were protests first voiced?

Where were protests most strongly expressed?

Why did protesters object to the film?

How did protesters make their views known?

In the academic world, scholars often generate ideas with questions related to a specific discipline: one set of questions for analyzing short stories, another for evaluating experiments in social psychology, still another for reporting field experiences in anthropology. If you are writing in a particular discipline, try to discover the questions that scholars typically explore. These are frequently presented in textbooks and software as checklists. See pages 646–47 for an example.

Freewriting

In its purest form, freewriting is simply nonstop writing. You set aside ten minutes or so and write whatever comes to you, without pausing to think about word choice, spelling, or even meaning. If you get stuck, you can write about being stuck, but you should keep your pencil moving. The point is to loosen up, relax, and see what happens. Even if nothing much happens, you have lost only ten minutes. It's more likely, though, that something interesting will emerge on paper—perhaps an eloquent sentence, an honest expression of feeling, or a line of thought worth exploring.

To explore ideas on a particular topic, consider using a technique known as *focused freewriting.* Again, you write quickly and freely—without regard for word choice, spelling, punctuation, or even paragraphing—but this time you focus on a subject and pay some attention to meaning. The following passage was freely written by a student who was recalling childhood visits to his grandparents' farm.

> Memories. Memories of Canton, Mississippi. We called it The Farm, like it was the only farm in the world. There was lots to keep us busy, 90 acres of untamed pastures. One of the first things that comes to mind is playing in the haybarn, climbing through the hay stacked high to the rafters. We would burrough a path between the bails tunnelling our way to the top. This was alot of fun until someone disturbed one of the many wasp nests making everyone scatter. Cruising the pastures, we enjoyed testing sound travel. We would spread out from each other and still talk at a normal tone audibly. I remember once getting over 100 yards away from my brother — although we would have to talk slowly and clearly, we could under-stand each other. Another game for the pasture was to lie on the ground, be very quiet, slow our breathing, and wait for the buzzards. We could never figure out how they knew we weren't dead.
>
> —David Queen, student

Despite the awkward beginning, the misspellings, and some problems with punctuation, this freewriting has potential. Its writer later polished some of the sentences and included them in an essay.

Annotating texts and taking notes

When you write about reading, one of the best ways to explore ideas is to mark up the text—on the pages themselves if you own the work, on photocopies if you don't. For examples of annotated texts, see pages 141, 143–44, and 643. In addition to annotating texts, you will often want to take notes on your reading (see 48).

Keeping a journal

A journal is a collection of personal, exploratory writings. An entry in a journal can be any length—from a single sentence to several pages—and it is likely to be informal and experimental.

In a journal, meant for your eyes only, you can take risks. In one entry, for example, you might do some freewriting or focused freewriting. In another, you might pose a series of interesting questions, whether or not you have the answers. In still another, you might play around with language for the sheer fun of it: writing "purple prose," for instance, or parodying the style of a favorite author or songwriter.

Keeping a journal can be an enriching experience in its own right, since it allows you to explore issues of concern to you without worrying about what someone else thinks. A journal can also serve as a sourcebook of ideas to draw on in future essays; on rare occasions, in fact, a journal entry may emerge as a polished essay of interest to readers other than yourself. Some writers find that they do their best work when writing for themselves, deliberately ignoring the constraints of a formal writing situation.

The writing process

Should you decide to keep a journal, here are some prompts to help you get started.

SOME IDEAS FOR JOURNAL WRITINGS

— Record some stories from your family's history.

— Describe some of your more interesting dreams.

— Write about a moral dilemma that you (or a friend or relative) once faced or that you now face.

— Describe a turning point in your life.

— Write a history of your involvement with a hobby or an art form; or write about current projects.

— Record your first impressions of a course you are taking this semester.

— Keep a running log of your involvement in a class that features interesting group discussions.

— Write an imaginary dialogue between two major historical figures you have read about, or a scientist and a philosopher, or characters in different novels.

— Comment on an interesting idea encountered in one of your college classes—a historical interpretation, a psychological theory, a new biological breakthrough.

— Parody the style of a favorite author or songwriter. Or mimic the style of a genre with which you are familiar (such as romances, hard-boiled detective novels, or sports writing).

Talking and listening

The early stages of the writing process need not be lonely. Many writers begin a writing project by brainstorming ideas in a group, debating a point with friends, or engaging in conversation with a professor. Others turn to themselves for company—by talking nonstop into a tape recorder.

If your computer is equipped with a modem, you can "virtually converse" by exchanging ideas through e-mail, by joining an Internet chat group, or by following a listserv discussion. If you are part of a networked classroom, you may be encouraged to exchange ideas with your classmates and instructor in an electronic workshop.

Talking can be a good way to get to know your audience. If you're planning to write a narrative, for instance, you can test its dramatic effect on a group of friends. Or if you hope to advance a certain argument, you can try it out on listeners who hold a different view.

As you have no doubt discovered, conversation can deepen and refine your ideas before you even begin to set them down on paper. Our first thoughts are not necessarily our wisest thoughts; by talking and listening to others we can all stretch our potential as thinkers and as writers.

The Internet

The Internet is a rich source of information that is fast and convenient to use, although its sheer magnitude can be overwhelming. A good way to begin exploring your subject on the Internet is through a search engine such as Yahoo! or Excite. A student looking for trends in teenage smoking, for example, might start by entering *teenage and smoking* in Excite's search box. Even a fairly focused subject such as this can unleash thousands of sites, however, so always be prepared to narrow your search to make it more manageable. In the smoking example, the student might modify the search to read *teenage and smoking and advertising*, which would cut the number of sites listed in half. For more detailed advice on using the Internet to research a subject, see 46d For advice on evaluating and documenting Internet sources, see 47c and 53.

Invention software

You may have access to invention software in a networked classroom, in your school's writing center, or even on your own computer. Invention software prompts you to think about your subject by raising a series of exploratory questions and sometimes by generating group discussion. To make the most of invention software, be sure to keep an open mind and allow yourself to explore the subject freely. For invention programs tailored to specific disciplines, check with your instructors.

EXERCISE 1-6

Generate a list of at least fifteen items for one of the subjects listed on pages 3–5.

EXERCISE 1-7

Using the technique of clustering or freewriting, explore one of the subjects listed on pages 3–5.

1c   Settle on a tentative focus.

As you explore your subject, you will begin to see possible ways to focus your material. At this point, try to settle on a tentative central idea. The more complex your subject, the more your initial central idea will change as your drafts evolve.

For many types of writing, your central idea can be asserted in one sentence, a generalization preparing readers for the supporting details that will follow. Such a sentence, which will ordinarily appear in the opening paragraph of your finished essay, is called a *thesis.* A successful thesis—like the following, all taken from articles in *Smithsonian*—points both the writer and the reader in a definite direction.

> Much maligned and the subject of unwarranted fears, most bats are harmless and highly beneficial.

Geometric forms known as fractals may have a profound effect on how we view the world, not only in art and film but in many branches of science and technology, from astronomy to economics to predicting the weather.

Aside from his more famous identities as colonel of the Rough Riders and president of the United States, Theodore Roosevelt was a lifelong professional man of letters.

The thesis sentence usually contains a key word or controlling idea that limits its focus. The preceding sentences, for example, prepare for essays that focus on the *beneficial* aspects of bats, the *effect* of fractals on how we view the world, and Roosevelt's identity as a writer, or *man of letters.*

It's a good idea to formulate a thesis early in the writing process, perhaps by jotting it on scratch paper, by putting it at the head of a rough outline, or by attempting to write an introductory paragraph that includes the thesis. Your tentative thesis will probably be less graceful than the thesis you include in the final version of your essay. Here, for example, is one student's early effort:

Although they both play percussion instruments, drummers and percussionists are very different.

The thesis that appeared in the final draft of the student's paper was more polished:

Two types of musicians play percussion instruments—drummers and percussionists— and they are as different as Quiet Riot and the New York Philharmonic.

Don't worry too soon about the exact wording of your thesis, however, because your main point may change as you refine your ideas.

For a more detailed discussion of the thesis, see 2a.

1d Sketch a tentative plan.

Once you have generated some ideas and formulated a tentative thesis, you may want to sketch an informal outline. Informal outlines can take many forms. Perhaps the most common is simply the thesis followed by a list of major supporting ideas.

> Hawaii is losing its cultural identity.
>
> — pure-blooded Hawaiians increasingly rare
>
> — native language diluted
>
> — natives forced off ancestral lands
>
> — little emphasis on native culture in schools
>
> — customs exaggerated and distorted by tourism

Clustering diagrams, often used to generate ideas, can also serve as rough outlines (see p. 20). And if you began by jotting down a list of ideas (see pp. 19–20), you may be able to turn the list into a rough outline by crossing out some ideas, adding others, and numbering the ideas to create a logical order.

Planning with headings

When writing a relatively long college paper or business document, consider using headings to guide readers. In addition to helping readers follow the organization of your final draft, headings can be a powerful planning tool, especially if you are working on a computer. You can type in your tentative thesis and then experiment with possible headings; once you have settled on the headings that work best, you can begin typing in chunks of text beneath each heading. Here, for example, is what one student typed into his laptop computer when planning a long history paper. The headings, written in the form of questions, are centered.

Although we will never know whether Nathan Bedford Forrest directly ordered the massacre of Union troops at Fort Pillow, evidence strongly suggests that he was responsible for it.

What happened at Fort Pillow?
Why do the killings qualify as a massacre?
Did Forrest order the massacre?
Did the men have reason to think Forrest wanted a massacre?

For more detailed advice about using headings, see page 111. For examples of papers that use headings, see pages 152–57, 616–26, and 691–700.

When to use a formal outline

Early in the writing process, rough outlines have certain advantages over their more formal counterparts: They can be produced more quickly, they are more obviously tentative, and they can be revised more easily should the need arise. However, a formal outline may be useful later in the writing process, after you have written a rough draft, especially if your subject matter is complex.

The following formal outline brought order to a complex subject, methods for limiting and disposing of nuclear waste. Notice that the student's thesis is an important part of the outline. Everything else in the outline supports it, either directly or indirectly.

Thesis: Although various methods for limiting or disposing of nuclear wastes have been proposed, each has serious drawbacks.

I. The process of limiting nuclear waste through partitioning and transmutation has serious drawbacks.
   A. The process is complex and costly.
   B. Nuclear workers' exposure to radiation would increase.

II. Antarctic ice sheet disposal is problematic for scientific and legal reasons.
   A. Our understanding of the behavior of ice sheets is too limited.
   B. An international treaty prohibits disposal in Antarctica.

III. Space disposal is unthinkable.
   A. The risk of an accident and resulting worldwide disaster is great.
   B. The cost is prohibitive.
   C. The method would be unpopular at home and abroad.

IV. Seabed disposal is unwise because we do not know enough about the procedure or its impact.
   A. Scientists have not yet solved technical difficulties.
   B. We do not fully understand the impact of such disposal on the ocean's ecology.

V. Deep underground disposal endangers public safety and creates political problems.
   A. Geologists disagree about the safest disposal sites, and no sites are completely safe.
   B. There is much political pressure against the plan from citizens who do not want their states to become nuclear dumps.

In constructing a formal outline, keep the following guidelines in mind.

1. Put the thesis at the top.
2. Make items at the same level of generality as parallel as possible (see 9).
3. Use sentences unless phrases are clear.
4. Use the conventional system of numbers and letters for the levels of generality.

   I.
      A.
      B.
         1.
         2.
            a.
            b.
               (1)
               (2)
                  (a)
                  (b)
   II.

5. Always use at least two subdivisions for a category, since nothing can be divided into fewer than two parts.
6. Limit the number of major sections in the outline; if the list of roman numerals begins to look like a laundry list, find some way of clustering the items into a few major categories with more subcategories.
7. Be flexible; in other words, be prepared to change your outline as your drafts evolve.

2

Rough out an initial draft.

As long as you treat an initial draft as a rough draft, you can focus your attention on ideas and organization, knowing that problems with sentence structure and word choice can always be dealt with later.

Overcoming writer's block

Before beginning a first draft, gather together your prewriting materials—lists, diagrams, outlines, freewriting, and so on. In addition to helping you get started, such notes and blueprints will encourage you to keep moving. With your earlier thoughts close by, you won't need to pause so frequently, staring at a blank page or screen in search of ideas. Writing tends to flow better when it is drafted relatively quickly, without many stops and starts. The trick, of course, is to relax—to overcome the fear that grips many of us as we face that blank page.

At one time or another, we all experience writer's block. But if writer's block is a chronic problem for you, consider whether you're being too hard on yourself. Do you demand that your sentences all be stylish and perfectly grammatical right from the start? Do you expect your ideas to emerge full-blown, like Athena from the head of Zeus?

Professional writers are not so tough on themselves. Jacques Barzun, for example, lets his rough-draft sentences be "as stupid" as they wish. Joan Didion acknowledges that she discovers ideas *as she writes;* for her, writing is a way of learning, not just a means of revealing already known truths. As Didion puts it, "I write entirely to find out what I'm thinking, what I'm looking at, what I see and what it means."

2a   For most types of writing, draft an introduction that includes a thesis.

The introduction announces the main point; the body develops it, usually in several paragraphs; the conclusion drives it home. You can begin drafting, however, at any point. If you find it difficult to introduce a paper that you have not yet written, you can write the body first and save the introduction for later.

For most writing tasks, your introduction will be a paragraph of 50 to 150 words. Perhaps the most common strategy is to open the paragraph with a few sentences that engage the reader and to conclude it with a statement of the essay's main point. The sentence stating the main point is called a *thesis.* (See 1c.) In the following examples, the thesis has been italicized.

> To the Australian aborigines, the Dreamtime was the time of creation. It was then that the creatures of the earth, including man, came into being. There are many legends about that mystical period, but unfortunately, the koala does not fare too well in any of them. *Slow-witted though it is in life, the koala is generally depicted in myth and folklore as a trickster and a thief.*   Roger Caras, "What's a Koala?"

> When I was sixteen, I married and moved to a small town to live. My new husband nervously showed me the house he had rented. It was after dark when we arrived there, and I remember wondering why he seemed so apprehensive about my reaction to the house. I thought the place seemed shabby but potentially cozy and quite livable inside. The morning sun revealed the reason for his anxiety by exposing the squalor outdoors. Up to that point, my contact with any reality but that of my own middle-class childhood had come from books. *The next four years in a small Iowa town taught me that reading about poverty is a lot different from living with it.*
> —Julie Reardon, student

Ideally, the sentences leading to the thesis should hook the reader, perhaps with one of the following:

a startling statistic or unusual fact

a vivid example

a description

a paradoxical statement

a quotation or bit of dialogue

a question

an analogy

a joke or an anecdote

Such hooks are particularly important when you cannot assume your reader's interest in the subject. Hooks are less necessary in scholarly essays and other writing aimed at readers with a professional interest in the subject.

Although the thesis frequently appears at the end of the introduction, it can just as easily appear at the beginning. Much work-related writing, in which a straightforward approach is most effective, commonly begins with the thesis.

> *Flextime scheduling, which has proved its effectiveness at the Library of Congress, should be introduced on a trial basis at the main branch of the Montgomery County Public Library.* By offering flexible work hours, the library can boost employee morale, cut down on absenteeism, and expand its hours of operation.   —David Warren, student

For some types of writing, it may be difficult or impossible to express the central idea in a thesis sentence; or it may be unwise or unnecessary to put a thesis sentence in the essay itself. A personal narrative, for example, may have a focus too subtle to be distilled in a single sentence, and such a sentence might ruin the story. Strictly informative writing, like that found in many business memos, may be difficult to summarize in a thesis. In such instances, do not try to force the central idea into a thesis sentence. Instead, think in terms of an overriding purpose, which may or may not be stated directly.

Characteristics of an effective thesis

An effective thesis should be a generalization, not a fact; it should be limited, not too broad; and it should be sharply focused, not too vague.

Because a thesis must prepare readers for facts and details, it cannot itself be a fact. It must always be a generalization demanding proof or further development.

> **TOO FACTUAL**   The first polygraph was developed by Dr. John A. Larson in 1921.
>
> **REVISED**   Because the polygraph has not been proved reliable, even under the most controlled conditions, its use by private employers should be banned.

Although a thesis must be a generalization, it must not be *too* general. You will need to narrow the focus of any thesis that you cannot adequately develop in the space allowed. Unless you were writing a book or a very long research paper, the following thesis would be too broad.

> **TOO BROAD**   Many drugs are now being used successfully to treat mental illnesses.

You would need to restrict the thesis, perhaps like this:

> **REVISED**   Despite its risks and side effects, Prozac is an effective treatment for depression.

Finally, a thesis should be sharply focused, not too vague. Beware of any thesis containing a fuzzy, hard-to-define word such as *interesting*, *good*, or *disgusting*.

TOO VAGUE	Many of the songs played on station WXQP are disgusting.

The word *disgusting* is needlessly vague. To sharpen the focus of this thesis, the writer should be more specific.

REVISED	Of the songs played on station WXQP, all too many depict sex crudely, sanction the beating or rape of women, or foster gang violence.

In the process of making a too-vague thesis more precise, you may find yourself outlining the major sections of your paper, as in the preceding example. This technique, known as *blueprinting*, helps readers know exactly what to expect as they read on. It also helps you, the writer, control the shape of your essay.

The thesis sentence is central to so many types of writing that it is discussed in several other sections of this book:

— in 6d, writing about texts

— in 7b and 7c, writing arguments

— in 49, research writing

— in 55, writing about literature

LOOKING AT YOURSELF AS A WRITER
The thesis sentence

In much college writing, you will need to state a thesis in your introduction and to support the thesis in the body of your essay. Although the thesis is usually only one sentence long, it can be surprisingly hard to write. When you have trouble formulating a good thesis, consider possible causes and cures for your difficulties.

CAUSE	You are trying to write the thesis sentence by itself.
CURE	Try drafting the whole introduction, placing the thesis sentence in context (usually at the end of the introduction).

The thesis sentence (continued)

CAUSE Once you have written a thesis, you tend to cling to it, even if the body of the essay doesn't exactly support it.

CURE View your initial thesis as tentative. As you draft an essay, you may discover a main idea that is more interesting than the one you began with. As writer E. M. Forster put it, "How do I know what I think until I see what I say?"

CAUSE You underestimate the importance of a clear thesis statement because you are unfamiliar with the academic world in which you are trying to write.

CURE Develop an appreciation for the goals of academic writing: to seek the truth, to argue a point, to propose solutions, to deepen insights, to clarify a theory, to challenge conventional wisdom. To reach any of these goals, you will need to articulate a thesis.

CAUSE You feel that a thesis sentence will not be significant unless it makes a grand, sweeping statement about life. But you lack the evidence to back up such a sweeping statement.

CURE Aim to do less, and you will accomplish more. As Darcy O'Brien advises writers, "Do not be grand. Try to get the ordinary into your writing. . . . Middletown today, not Mankind through the ages."

CAUSE You fear that a thesis sentence will sound too blunt. Perhaps this is because you come from a culture that values a more indirect approach. Or maybe you feel uncomfortable being assertive or lack the confidence to be assertive.

CURE Try to be flexible—to adapt to the needs of readers in your particular writing situation. You might also experiment with strategies for softening the tone of a thesis sentence without sacrificing clarity. With practice, writers can learn to assert a main idea simply and directly without sounding too blunt.

EXERCISE 2–1

In each of the following pairs, which sentence might work well as a thesis for a paper based on personal experience (not on reading)? What is the problem with the other one? Is it too factual? Too broad? Too vague?

1a. Of the many challenges facing single parents, the most difficult is learning to maintain a balance among work, school, a social life, and, most important, family.

 b. Single parents face many challenges, so they need to be well organized.

2a. From the time I was a young child, I have always had at least three cats.

 b. In addition to being the perfect size to be kept indoors, cats are clean, loving, graceful, and surprisingly intelligent animals.

3a. At the Special Olympics, disabled athletes are taught that with hard work and support from others they can accomplish anything: that they can indeed be winners.

 b. Working with the Special Olympics program is rewarding.

4a. Immigrants from many lands have made major contributions to American culture.

 b. When Uncle Jacob stepped onto Ellis Island with only a small suitcase and the clothes on his back, no one could have predicted that one day his stone carvings would grace many buildings and monuments in our nation's capital.

5a. History 201, taught by Professor Brown, is offered at 10 A.M. on Tuesdays and Thursdays.

 b. Whoever said that history is nothing but polishing tombstones must have missed History 201, because in Professor Brown's class history is very much alive.

EXERCISE 2–2

In each of the following pairs, which sentence might work well as a thesis for a paper based on reading? What is the problem with the other one? Is it too factual? Too broad? Too vague?

1a. So far, research suggests that zero-emissions vehicles are not a sensible solution to the problem of steadily increasing air pollution.

 b. Because air pollution is of serious concern to many people in the world today, several government agencies in the United States have implemented plans to begin solving the problem.

2a. Anorexia nervosa is a dangerous, sometimes deadly eating disorder found mainly in young, upper-middle-class teenagers.

 b. The eating disorder anorexia nervosa is rarely cured by one treatment alone; only by combining drug therapy with psychotherapy and family therapy can the patient begin the long, torturous journey to wellness.

3a. Although we cannot fully harness the powers that nature wields, we can manage most naturally occurring forest fires to benefit our national parks.

 b. The Yellowstone fires of 1988 taught many lessons to many people.

4a. Marijuana is classified by the Drug Enforcement Agency as a Schedule I drug.

 b. If marijuana was legalized for medical purposes, we could relieve some of the suffering associated with AIDS, cancer, and glaucoma.

5a. Was the man killed on July 22, 1934, in the alley next to the Biograph Theater in Chicago John Dillinger?

 b. Sweeping across the Midwest in the early 1930s, the Dillinger gang's crime wave epitomized the lawlessness of the era.

2b Fill out the body.

Before drafting the body of an essay, take a careful look at your introduction, focusing especially on your thesis sentence. What does the thesis promise readers? Try to keep this focus in mind.

It's a good idea to have a plan in mind as well. If your thesis sentence outlines a plan (see 2a) or if you have sketched a preliminary outline, try to block out your paragraphs accordingly. If you do not have a plan, you would be wise to pause for a moment and sketch one (see 1d). Of course it is also possible to begin without a plan—assuming you are prepared to treat your first attempt as a "discovery draft" that will almost certainly be tossed (or radically rewritten) once you discover what you really want to say.

For more detailed advice about paragraphs in the body of an essay, see section 4.

2c Attempt a conclusion.

The conclusion should echo the main idea, without dully repeating it. Often the concluding paragraph can be relatively short. By the end of the essay, readers should already understand your main point; your conclusion simply drives it home and perhaps suggests its significance.

In addition to echoing your main idea, a conclusion might summarize the essay's key points, pose a question for future study, offer advice, or propose a course of action. To end an essay detailing the social skills required of a bartender, one writer concludes with some advice:

> If someone were to approach me one day looking for the secret to running a good bar, I suppose I would offer the following advice: Get your customers to pour out their ideas at a greater rate than you pour out the liquor. You will both win in the end.   —Kathleen Lewis, student

To make the conclusion memorable, consider including a detail, example, or image from the introduction to bring readers full circle; a quotation or bit of dialogue; an anecdote; or a humorous, witty, or ironic comment. To end a narrative describing a cash register holdup, one student uses an anecdote that includes some dialogue:

> It took me a long time to get over that incident. Countless times I found myself gasping as someone "pointed" a dollar bill at me. On one such occasion, a jovial little man buying a toy gun for his son came up to me and said in a Humphrey Bogart impression, "Give me all your money, Sweetheart." I didn't laugh. Instead, my heart skipped a beat, for I had heard those words before. —Diana Crawford, student

Whatever concluding strategy you choose, avoid introducing wholly new ideas at the end of an essay. Also avoid apologies and other limp, indeterminate endings. The essay should end crisply, preferably on a positive note.

Do not become discouraged if the perfect conclusion eludes you at the rough-draft stage of the writing process. Because the conclusion is so closely tied to the rest of the essay in both content and tone, you may well decide to rework it (or even replace it) as your drafts evolve.

3

Make global revisions; then revise sentences.

For experienced writers, revising is rarely a one-step process. The larger elements of writing generally receive attention first—the focus, organization, content, and overall strategy. Improvements in sentence structure, word choice, grammar, punctuation, and mechanics come later.

GLOBAL REVISIONS

Revising is not just a matter of moving words around and correcting grammar. It involves much larger changes, global improvements that can be quite dramatic. Whole paragraphs might be dropped, others added. Material once stretched over two or three paragraphs might be condensed into one. Entire sections might be rearranged. Even the content may change, sometimes dramatically, for the process of writing stimulates thought.

Major revising can be difficult, sometimes even painful. You might discover, for example, that an essay's first three paragraphs are nothing but padding, that its central argument tilts the wrong way, and that you sound like a stuffed shirt throughout. But the sheer fact that you can see such problems in your writing is a sign of hope. Those opening paragraphs can be dropped, the argument's slant realigned, the voice made more human.

NOTE: When working on a computer, print out a hard copy so that you can read the draft as a whole rather than screen by screen. A computer screen focuses your attention on small chunks of text rather than the whole; a printout allows you to look at the entire paper when thinking about what global revisions to make.

Once you have decided what global revisions may be needed, the computer, of course, is an excellent tool. In fact, because the computer saves time, it encourages you to experiment with global revisions. Should you combine two paragraphs? Would your conclusion make a good introduction? Might several paragraphs be rearranged for greater impact? Will the addition of boldface headings improve readability? With little risk, you can explore the possibilities. When a revision misfires, it is easy to restore your original draft.

3a Get some distance, perhaps with the help of reviewers.

Many of us resist global revisions because we find it difficult to distance ourselves from a draft. We tend to review our work from our own, not from our audience's, perspective.

To distance yourself from a draft, begin by putting it aside for a while, preferably overnight or even longer. When you return to it, try to play the role of your audience as you read. Mark any places where your readers are likely to be confused, misled, or annoyed; look too for sentences and paragraphs that are not likely to persuade.

If at all possible, enlist the help of reviewers—persons willing to play the role of audience for you. Possible reviewers include peers, such as family members, friends, and other students; and professionals, such as professors, trained writing center tutors, and practicing writers. Ask your reviewers to focus on the larger issues of writing, not on the fine points. If they are at first preoccupied by fine points such as grammar and spelling, remind them that you are not ready to think about such matters. For the moment, you are interested in their response to the essay as a whole.

Many professors set aside class time for peer review sessions in which students respond to one another's drafts in written comments, discussions, or both. In some classrooms, students use e-mail or other forms of electronic communication to send and receive comments on one another's rough drafts.

A checklist for reviewers appears on page 51.

Guidelines for peer reviewers

If your instructor provides specific guidelines for peer reviewing, you should of course follow them. Some general guidelines follow on pages 46–48.

EXAMPLE OF GLOBAL REVISIONS

                Sports on TV--A Win or a Loss?

    Team sports are as much a part of Americain
life as Mom and apple pie, and they have a good
tendency to bring people together. They encourage
team members to cooperate with one another, they
also create shared enthusiasm among fans. Thanks
to television, this togetherness now seems available
to nearly all of us at the flick of a switch. We do
not have to buy tickets, and travel to a stadium,
to see the World Series or the Superbowl, these
games are on television. We can enjoy the game
in the comfort of our own living room. ~~After
Thanksgiving or Christmas dinner, the whole family
may gather around the TV set to watch football together.~~ It would appear that television has done
us a great service. But is this really the case?

*Although television does make sports more accessible, it also
creates a distance between the sport and the fans and between
athletes and the teams they play for.*

    *The advantage of television is that it provides sports fans
with greater convenience.*

                [insert]   ←
*We can see more games than if we had to attend each one in
person, and we can follow greater varieties of sports.*

EXAMPLE OF SENTENCE-LEVEL REVISIONS

> *Televised*
> Sports ~~on TV~~--A Win or a Loss?
>   ^

Team sports, ~~are~~ as much a part of America͜n

tend
life as Mom and apple pie, ~~and they have a good~~
              us
~~tendency~~ to bring ~~people~~ together. They encourage team
          ^   *and*
members to cooperate with one another, they ~~also~~ create
                              Because of
shared enthusiasm among fans. ~~Thanks to~~ television,
                              ^
this togetherness now seems available ~~to nearly all~~

~~of us~~ at the flick of a switch. ~~It would appear that~~

~~television has done us a great service.~~ But is this
                          makes
really the case? Although television ~~does make~~
                                     ^
sports more accessible, it also creates a distance

between the sport and the fans and between athletes
    their
and ~~the~~ teams. ~~they play for.~~
    ^   ^

The advantage of television is that it provides

sports fans with greater convenience. We do not

have to buy tickets/ and travel to a stadium/
                                        but
to see the World Series or the Super Bowl/ ~~these~~
                                     any ^
~~games are on television. We~~ can enjoy ~~the~~ game in
                              rooms. ^
the comfort of our own living ~~room.~~ We can see
                              ^
more games than if we had to attend each one in
                    a   *variety*
person, and we can follow greater ~~varieties~~ of
                          ^
sports.

READING THE DRAFT   As you read a classmate's draft, you may want to make a few marks in the margin: perhaps an asterisk (*) for sentences or passages that seem especially effective, a question mark (?) for spots that confuse you, a plus mark (+) for places where you'd like to hear more details. Don't get carried away, however. Remember that you are not "grading" a finished essay; you are helping a fellow writer get distance from a rough draft. Above all, do not mark errors in grammar, punctuation, and spelling. The writer can deal with such matters later.

WRITING COMMENTS   Although some professors may ask you to write comments on the draft of an essay, most prefer that you respond on a separate sheet of paper or in a separate computer file. In a networked classroom, you may be asked to respond online. Here are some ideas for framing written responses.

— In a sentence, describe the writer's apparent purpose and audience.

— In a sentence, explain what the introduction promises readers; in other words, explain what you as a reader expect to hear in the rest of the essay.

— List the two or three passages that best fulfill the promise of the introduction.

— List a few things that you would like to hear more about.

— Try to sketch a very simple outline of the draft— just the key ideas in support of the main point. (If this is difficult, the writer may need to work on organization.)

— Write down two or three sentences from the draft that you found particularly interesting or well written.

TALKING TO THE WRITER   If you have the opportunity to discuss your ideas with the writer—either in person or on-line—here are some guidelines to keep in mind.

— Try to open your conversation with descriptive, rather than evaluative, comments. For example, if the writer's subject is physical disabilities, you might begin by saying, "I think your point is that many adults are insensitive and patronizing when they encounter persons with physical disabilities."

— When you turn to evaluative comments, make the first ones positive. For example, you might mention that you found the writer's second paragraph a powerful example of insensitivity toward people with physical disabilities.

— An effective peer review session is a dialogue, not a monologue. Try to get the writer talking by asking questions—about the draft in progress and about the subject. As writers talk about their subject with an interested listener, they often recall useful details and vivid examples that might be included in the essay.

— If you have suggestions for improvement, try to tie them to the writer's goals. For instance, you might advise the writer to put the dramatic example of insensitivity toward physically disabled people last, where it will have the maximum impact on readers. Or you might suggest that a passage would gain power if abstractions were replaced with concrete details.

— Throughout the review session, look on yourself as a coach, not a judge, as a proposer of possibilities, not a dictator of revisions. It is the writer, after all, who will have to grapple with the task of improving the essay.

The writing process

—At the end of the review session, you might want to express interest in reading the writer's next revision or final draft. Such interest—if it is sincere—can be a powerful motivation for a writer.

3b Approach global revision in cycles.

The process of global revision can be overwhelming, so it is best to approach it in cycles, with each cycle encompassing a particular purpose for revising. Five common cycles of global revision are discussed in this section:

—Sharpening the focus
—Improving the organization
—Strengthening the content
—Clarifying the point of view
—Engaging the audience

You can handle these cycles in nearly any order, and you may be able to skip or combine some of them. A chart summarizing these cycles appears on page 50.

If you have asked someone to review your draft, you have already begun to see which of these cycles most need your attention. And by giving some thought to your overall purpose and audience, you'll discern even more clearly where your essay does—and does not—need major reworking.

Sharpening the focus

A draft is clearly focused when it fixes the reader's attention on one central idea and does not stray from that idea. You can sharpen the focus of a draft by clarifying the introduction (especially the thesis) and by deleting any text that is off the point.

CLARIFYING THE INTRODUCTION First you will want to make sure that your introduction looks and reads like an introduction. Can readers tell where the introduction stops and the body of the essay begins? Have you perhaps included material in the introduction that really belongs in the body of the essay? Is your introduction long-winded?

Next check to see whether the introduction focuses on the essay's main point. Does it let readers know what to expect as they read on? Does it make the significance of the subject clear so that readers will want to read on?

The most important sentence in the introduction is the thesis. (See 2a.) If your essay lacks a thesis, make sure that you have a good reason for not including one. If your thesis is poorly focused or if it doesn't accurately state the real point of the essay, you'll need to revise it.

DELETING TEXT THAT IS OFF THE POINT Compare the essay's introduction, particularly its thesis statement, with the body of the essay. Does the body of the essay fulfill the promise of the introduction? If not, one or the other must be adjusted. Either rebuild the introduction to fit the body of the paper or keep the introduction and delete any sentences or paragraphs that stray from its point.

Improving the organization

A draft is well organized when its major divisions are logical and easy for readers to follow. To improve the organization of your draft, consider taking one or more of the following actions: adding or sharpening topic sentences, moving blocks of text, reparagraphing, and inserting headings.

ADDING OR SHARPENING TOPIC SENTENCES Topic sentences, as you probably know, state the main ideas of the paragraphs in the body of an essay. (See 4a.) Topic sentences act as signposts for readers, announcing ideas to come.

Cycles of global revision (for writers)

SHARPENING THE FOCUS

Look for opportunities

— to clarify the introduction (especially the thesis)

— to delete text that is off the point

IMPROVING THE ORGANIZATION

Look for opportunities

— to add or sharpen topic sentences

— to move blocks of text

— to reparagraph and perhaps to add headings

STRENGTHENING THE CONTENT

Look for opportunities

— to add specific facts, details, and examples

— to emphasize major ideas

— to rethink your argument or central insight

CLARIFYING THE POINT OF VIEW

Look for opportunities

— to make the point of view more consistent

— to use a more appropriate point of view

ENGAGING THE AUDIENCE

Look for opportunities

— to let readers know why they are reading

— to motivate readers to read on

— to use a more appropriate tone

Checklist for global revision (for reviewers)

FOCUS

- Does the introduction focus on the main point?
- Is the thesis clear enough? (If there is no thesis, is there a good reason for omitting one?)
- Are any ideas off the point?

ORGANIZATION

- Does the writer give readers enough organizational cues (such as topic sentences or headings)?
- Should any text be moved?
- Are any paragraphs too long or short for easy reading?

CONTENT

- Are there enough facts, examples, and details to support major ideas?
- Are the parts proportioned sensibly? Do major ideas receive enough attention?
- How might the argument be strengthened?

POINT OF VIEW

- Is the draft free of distracting shifts in point of view?
- Is the point appropriate?

AUDIENCE APPEAL

- Does the draft accomplish its purpose—to inform us, to persuade us, to entertain us, to call us to action (or some combination of these)?
- Does the opening paragraph make us want to read on? Do we know why we are reading?
- Is the tone appropriate?

You can review the organization of a draft by reading only the topic sentences. Do they clearly support the essay's main idea? Do they make a reasonable sentence outline of the paper? If your draft lacks topic sentences, make sure you have a good reason for omitting these important signposts.

MOVING BLOCKS OF TEXT Improving the organization of a draft can be as simple as moving a few sentences from one paragraph to another or switching the order of paragraphs. Often, however, the process is more complex. As you move blocks of text, you may need to supply transitions to make them fit smoothly in the new positions; you may also need to rework topic sentences to make your new organization clear.

Before moving text, consider sketching a revised outline. Divisions in the outline might become topic sentences in the restructured essay. (See 1d.)

REPARAGRAPHING AND INSERTING HEADINGS Occasionally you can clarify the organization of a draft simply by combining choppy paragraphs or by dividing those that are too long for easy reading. (See 4f.)

In long documents, such as research papers or business reports, consider using headings to help readers follow your organization. Possible headings include phrases, declarative or imperative sentences, and questions. To draw attention to headings, consider centering them, putting them in boldface, underlining them, using all capital letters, or some combination of these. (See also pp. 111–14.)

Strengthening the content

In reviewing the content of a draft, consider whether any text (sentences, paragraphs, or longer passages) should be added or deleted, keeping in mind your readers' needs. Then, if your purpose is to argue a point, consider how persuasively you have proved your point to an intelligent, discerning audience. When necessary, rethink your argument.

ADDING TEXT   If any paragraphs or sections of the essay are developed too skimpily to be clear and convincing (a common flaw in rough drafts), you will need to add specific facts, details, and examples. This necessity will take you back to the beginning of the writing process: listing specifics, brainstorming ideas with friends or classmates, perhaps doing more research.

DELETING TEXT   Look for sentences and paragraphs that can be cut without serious loss of meaning. Perhaps you have repeated yourself or strayed from your point. Maybe you have given undue emphasis to minor ideas. Cuts may also be necessitated by word limits, such as those imposed by a college assignment or by the realities of the business world, where readers are often pressed for time.

RETHINKING YOUR ARGUMENT   A first draft presents you with an opportunity for rethinking your argument. You can often deepen your ideas about a subject by asking yourself some hard questions. Is your claim more sweeping than the evidence allows? Have you left out an important step in the argument? Have you dealt with the arguments of the opposition? Is your thinking flawed by logical fallacies? The more challenging your subject, the more likely you will find yourself adjusting your early thoughts. (For more about argumentative writing, see 7.)

Clarifying the point of view

If the point of view of a draft shifts confusingly or if it seems not quite appropriate for your purpose, audience, and subject, consider adjusting it.

The writing process

There are three basic points of view to choose from: the first person (*I* or *we*), the second person (*you*), and the third person (*he/she/it/one* or *they*). Each point of view is appropriate in at least some contexts, and you may need to experiment before discovering which one best suits your needs.

THE THIRD-PERSON POINT OF VIEW   Much academic and professional writing is best presented from the third-person point of view (*he/she/it/one* or *they*), which puts the subject in the foreground. The *I* point of view is usually inappropriate in such contexts because, by focusing attention on the writer, it pushes the subject into the background. Consider, for example, one student's first-draft description of the behavior of a species of frog that he had observed in the field.

> Each frog that *I* was able to locate in trees remained in its given tree during the entirety of *my* observation period. However, *I* noticed that there was considerable movement within the home tree.

Here the *I* point of view is distracting, as the student himself noticed when he began to revise his report. His revision focuses more on the frogs, less on himself.

> Each frog located in a tree remained in that tree throughout the observation period. The frogs moved about considerably, however, within their home trees.

Just as the first-person pronoun *I* can draw too much attention to the writer, the second-person pronoun *you* can focus unnecessarily on the reader. In the following sentence from a memo, for example, a supervisor writing to a sales manager needlessly draws attention to the reader:

> When *you* look at the numbers, *you* can clearly see that travel expenses must be cut back.

This sentence would be clearer and more direct if presented without the distraction of the *you* point of view:

> The numbers clearly show that travel expenses must be cut back.

Although the third-person point of view is often a better choice than the *I* or *you* point of view, it is by no means trouble-free. Writers who choose it can run into problems when they want to use singular pronouns in an indefinite sense. For example, when Miss Piggy says that a reason for jogging is "to improve *one's* emotional health and make *one* feel better about *oneself*," one wishes she wouldn't use quite so many *one*'s, doesn't one? The trouble is that American English, unlike British English, does not allow this pronoun to echo unself-consciously throughout a sentence. The repetitions sound stuffy.

Some years ago Americans would have said "to improve a person's emotional health and to make *him* feel better about *himself*," with the understanding that *him* really meant *him or her*. Today, however, this use of *him* is offensive to many readers and is best avoided. But, "to make *him or her* feel better about *himself or herself*" is distinctly awkward. So what is poor Miss Piggy to say?

Her only hope, it turns out, is a flexible and inventive mind. She might switch to the plural: *Joggers run to improve their emotional health and to make them feel better about themselves.* Or she could restructure the sentence altogether: *Jogging improves a person's emotional health and self-image.* (See 17f and 22a.)

THE SECOND-PERSON POINT OF VIEW   The *you* point of view, which puts the reader in the foreground, is appropriate if the writer is advising readers directly, as in giving tips on raising children or instructions on flower arranging. All imperative sentences, such as the advice for writers in this book, are written from the *you* point of view, although the word itself is frequently omitted and understood. "Sketch a plan" means "*You* should sketch a plan"; everyone knows this, so the *you* is not expressed.

In the course of giving advice or instructions, the actual word *you* may be appropriate and even desired. In advising gardeners about walkways, for example, newspaper columnist Henry Mitchell feels free to use the words *you* and *your* as the need arises:

> If *your* main walk is less than four feet wide, and if it is white concrete, then widen it, no matter what has to be sacrificed . . . and resurface it with brick, stone, or something less glaring and dull. Three flowers against a good-looking pavement will do more for *you* than thirty flowers against white concrete. [Italics added.]

Mitchell might have written this passage from the third-person point of view instead ("If *the gardener's* walk is less than four feet wide . . ."), but the effect would have seemed oddly indirect. Even at the risk of sounding a bit bossy, Mitchell has wisely selected the imperative (*you*) approach instead.

Notice that Mitchell's *you* means "you, the reader." It does not mean "you, anyone in general." Indefinite uses of *you,* such as the following example, are inappropriate in formal writing. (See 23d.)

> Young Japanese women wired together electronic products on a piece-rate system: The more *you* wired, the more *you* were paid.

Here the writer should have stayed with the third-person point of view instead.

> The more *they* wired, the more *they* were paid.

THE FIRST-PERSON POINT OF VIEW   If much of a writer's material comes from personal experience, the *I* point of view will prove most natural. It is difficult to imagine, for example, how James Thurber could have avoided the word *I* in describing his early university days:

> *I* passed all the other courses that *I* took at *my* university, but *I* could never pass botany. This was because all botany students had to spend several hours a week in a laboratory looking through a microscope at plant cells, and *I* could never see through a microscope. *I* never once saw a cell through a microscope. This used to enrage my instructor.
> [Italics added.]   —"University Days"

Thurber's *I* point of view puts the writer in the foreground, and since the writer is in fact the subject, this makes sense.

Writers who are aware that the first-person point of view is sometimes viewed as inappropriate in academic writing often overgeneralize the rule. Concluding that the word *I* is never appropriate, they go to extreme lengths to avoid it:

> Mama read with such color and detail that *one* could fancy *oneself* as the hero of the story.

Since the paper in which this sentence appeared was a personal reminiscence, the entire paper sounded more natural once the writer allowed himself to use the word *I:*

> Mama read with such color and detail that *I* could fancy *myself* as the hero of the story.

Engaging the audience

Considerations of audience often lead to global revision. Many rough drafts need a major overhaul because they are directed at no audience at all for no apparent purpose — written in a vacuum, so to speak. Readers are put off by such writing because when they don't know *why* they are reading, they suspect that a writer may be wasting their time. A good question to ask yourself about your own rough drafts, therefore, is the toughest question that a reader might ask: "So what?" If your draft can't pass the "So what?" test, you will need to rethink your entire approach; in fact, you may even decide to scrap the draft and start over.

Once you have made sure that your draft is directed at an audience — readers who stand to benefit in some way by reading it — you may still need to refine your tone. The tone of a piece of writing expresses the writer's feelings toward the audience, so it is important to get it right. If the tone seems too self-centered — or too flippant, stuffy, bossy, patronizing, opinionated, or hostile — obviously it should be modified.

Any piece of writing drafted in anger or frustration will almost certainly need to be toned down. The following rough draft, for example, was written by a secretary in response to criticisms of a newsletter sent out by the organization for which she worked.

Dear Mr. Martin:

I know our newsletter is crudely laid out, the reason being that I work under a tight deadline, and we can't afford any fancy desktop publishing equipment. Perhaps we'd do better if we had more funding.

I think you were wrong to dismiss the offending story as bragging about *Nuclear War: What's in It for You?* The book was nominated for the prize, a fact worthy of mention despite the fact that it did not win.

In any case, I am glad to hear that you liked the open letter to the president. Would that the *Philadelphia Inquirer* had liked it as well.

Sincerely,

Robbie Nichols

As she reached the last paragraph of the rough draft, the writer saw the need to be more diplomatic. Later, in a calmer and less defensive mood, she revised the letter like this:

Dear Mr. Martin:

We are glad to hear that you liked Roger Molander's "An Open Letter to the President." Would that the *Philadelphia Inquirer* had liked it as well.

I do think you were wrong to dismiss the sentence about *Nuclear War: What's in It for You?* as "bragging." It is a fairly direct sentence, and there may well be those among the faithful who wouldn't otherwise have known about its nomination for the prize.

Your comments about the physical layout of the story were, in fact, echoed by the staff here. The layout could not be changed, however, because of the limitations of our current computers.

Thank you for writing. Even though our newsletter has a limited circulation, we hope that Roger's open letter will elicit serious thought about the president's March 23 address on weapons in space.

Sincerely,

Robbie Nichols

SENTENCE-LEVEL REVISIONS

3c   Revise and edit sentences.

When you revise sentences, you focus on effectiveness; when you edit, you check for correctness. As with global revision, sentence revision may be approached in cycles, with each cycle focusing on a different purpose for making changes. The

The writing process

Cycles of sentence-level revision

The numbers in this chart refer to sections in this handbook.

STRENGTHENING SENTENCES

Look for opportunities

- —to use more active verbs (14a)
- —to prune excess words (16)

CLARIFYING SENTENCES

Look for opportunities

- —to balance parallel ideas (9)
- —to supply missing words (10)
- —to untangle mixed constructions (11)
- —to repair misplaced or dangling modifiers (12)
- —to eliminate distracting shifts (13)

INTRODUCING VARIETY

Look for opportunities

- —to combine choppy sentences (8a)
- —to break up long sentences (8d)
- —to vary sentence openings (15a)

REFINING THE STYLE

Look for opportunities

- —to choose language more appropriate for the subject and audience (17)
- —to choose more exact words (18)

An editing checklist

At first this checklist may seem overwhelming, but as your instructor responds to your writing and as you become familiar with the rules in this handbook, you'll begin to see which problems, if any, tend to cause you trouble. You can then devise a personal checklist of errors to look for as you edit. (The numbers in the chart refer to sections in this handbook.)

GRAMMAR

Sentence fragments (19)
Run-on sentences (20)
Subject-verb agreement (21)
Pronoun-antecedent agreement (22)
Pronoun reference (23)
Case of nouns and pronouns (24)
Case of *who* and *whom* (25)
Adjectives and adverbs (26)
Standard English verb forms (27)
Verb tense, mood, and voice (28)
ESL problems (29, 30, 31)

PUNCTUATION

The comma and unnecessary commas (32, 33)
The semicolon (34)
The colon (35)
The apostrophe (36)
Quotation marks (37)
End punctuation (38)
Other punctuation marks (39)

MECHANICS

Abbreviations and numbers (40, 41)
Italics (underlining) (42)
Spelling and the hyphen (43, 44)
Capital letters (45)

main purposes for revising sentences—to strengthen, clarify, vary, and refine them—are detailed in the chart on page 60. A checklist on editing for grammar, punctuation, and mechanics appears on page 61.

Some writers handle most sentence-level revisions directly at the computer, experimenting on screen with a variety of possible improvements. Other writers prefer to print out a hard copy of the draft, mark it up, and then return to the computer. Here, for example, is a rough-draft paragraph as one student edited it for a variety of sentence-level problems:

> Finally ~~we decided~~ *deciding* that perhaps our dream needed ~~some~~ prompting, ~~and~~ we visited a fertility doctor and began the expensive, time-consuming round of procedures that held out ~~the~~ *some* promise of ~~fulfilling our dream. All this was~~ *our dream's fulfillment. Our efforts, however, were* to no avail. ~~and~~ *As* ~~as~~ we approached the sixth year of our marriage, we ~~had reached the point where we couldn't~~ *could no longer* even discuss our childlessness without becoming very depressed. We questioned why this had happened to us. Why had we been singled out for ~~this~~ *such a* major disappointment?

The original paragraph was flawed by wordiness and an excessive reliance on structures connected with *and*. Such problems can be addressed through any number of acceptable revisions. The first sentence, for example, could have been changed like this:

```
    Finally we decided that perhaps our dream
                   After visiting
needed some prompting /. and we visited a fertility
        we                      ^
doctor, and began the expensive, time consuming
      ^                                    ^
                              promised hope
round of procedures that held out the promise of
                                          ^
fulfilling our dream.
```

Though some writers might argue about the effectiveness of these improvements compared with the previous revision, most would agree that both versions are better than the original.

Some of the paragraph's improvements involve less choice and are not so open to debate. The hyphen in *time-consuming* is necessary; a noun must be substituted for the pronoun *this* in the second sentence, which was being used more loosely than grammar allows; and the question mark in the next to last sentence must be changed to a period.

Software tools

Software can provide help with sentence-level revisions. Most word processors have spell checkers that will catch many but not all spelling errors, and some have thesauruses to help with word choice.

Some word processing programs are equipped with grammar checkers (sometimes called "style checkers" or "text analyzers"). When using a grammar checker, you need to be aware of what this tool can — and cannot — do. Grammar checkers are fairly good at flagging wordy sentences, jargon, slang, clichés, and passive verbs. But such problems represent only a small fraction of the sentence-level problems in a typical draft. Because so many problems — such as faulty parallelism, mixed constructions, and misplaced modifiers — lack mathematical precision, they slip right past the grammar checker. You should not assume, therefore, that once you have run your draft through a grammar checker, your grammar problems are over.

Throughout this book, you will find grammar checker advice linked to specific problems. For example, in section 14 you will learn that grammar checkers can flag most but not all passive verbs and that they flag passive constructions whether or not they are appropriate. In section 20 you will learn that grammar checkers flag some run-ons, miss others, and tell you that some sentences may be run-ons when in fact they are not.

The grammar checker advice is based on a large sample of correct and incorrect sentences that were run through two widely used grammar checker programs. For more details, see pages viii–x of the preface.

3d   Proofread the final manuscript.

After revising and editing, you are ready to prepare the final manuscript. (See 5b for guidelines.) At this point, make sure to allow yourself enough time for proofreading—the final and most important step in manuscript preparation.

Proofreading is a special kind of reading: a slow and methodical search for misspellings, typographical mistakes, and omitted words or word endings. Such errors can be difficult to spot in your own work because you may read what you intended to write, not what is actually on the page. To fight this tendency, try proofreading out loud, articulating each word as it is actually written. You might also try proofreading your sentences in reverse order, a strategy that takes your attention away from the meanings you intended and forces you to think about small surface features instead.

Although proofreading may be dull, it is crucial. Errors strewn throughout an essay are distracting and annoying. If the writer doesn't care about this piece of writing, thinks the reader, why should I? A carefully proofread essay, however, sends a positive message: It shows that you value your writing and respect your readers.

EXPOSITORY STUDENT ESSAY: EXPLAINING AN INSIGHT

Lauren Pent, who wrote "E-mail — Return to Sender?" (pp. 74–77), was responding to the following assignment.

> #### ASSIGNMENT: EXPLAINING AN INSIGHT
>
> When you explain an insight on a topic, you offer readers a fresh or interesting way of looking at it. In other words, you give them a way of understanding something that they may have understood differently before.
>
> You might challenge a conventional view that has not been validated by your own experience: the view, for example, that growing up in a small town is idyllic or that work as a flight attendant is glamorous. You might explain an insight about a group with which you are familiar: Harley-Davidson bikers, farmers, the physically challenged, or people from another culture. You might give readers a new way of looking at some aspect of the media: maybe by ridiculing the language of sports announcers, revealing stereotypes in a television series, explaining why *Star Trek* has had such lasting appeal, or showing that the history of rap music is more complex than most people think. Or you might give readers an insight into one of your special interests, such as photography, mountain climbing, or one of the martial arts.
>
> Your insight should appear in a thesis sentence early in the essay, most likely at the end of the introductory paragraph (see pp. 33–35 of *The Bedford Handbook*). For this assignment, your information should come from personal knowledge, interviews, or direct observation. Aim for an essay from 500 to 1,000 words long — from two to four typed pages, double-spaced.

Pent's planning materials

When she received her assignment, Lauren Pent considered several possibilities before settling on the topic of e-mail. Having just gone online herself, Pent understood the advantages of e-mail that her family and friends had been raving about. She wondered, though, whether e-mail wasn't perhaps being oversold.

To get started on her paper, Pent typed the following list of ideas into her computer:

```
e-mail--faster than "snail mail"

easy to use--no licking envelopes etc. (especially
when you're sending lots of copies of the same
message)

lots of people have free access at school or work
but most people in the world don't have computers
or modems, so e-mail is no use to them

I wonder why there isn't more junk e-mail. Will Ed
McMahon ever make it to cyberspace?

cost of e-mail? fees for online services, but you
can send multiple copies for the same price as one

e-mail is sort of impersonal. I'd rather get a
love letter or a birthday card through regular mail

what about privacy? especially in the workplace
```

Later Pent reread her list and concluded that her focus should be the advantages and disadvantages of e-mail, with an emphasis on the disadvantages that some people probably haven't thought about. With this focus in mind, she formulated a tentative thesis and sketched a rough outline.

E-mail has many advantages over regular mail, but there are several disadvantages that might not be so readily apparent.

    --Advantages

        --speed

        --low cost

        --easy to use

    --Disadvantages

        --no access for some people

        --lacks a personal touch

        --lack of privacy, especially in the workplace

NOTE: Pent later revised this rough outline after listening to what her peer reviewers had to say about her first draft.

Working from her list and rough outline, Pent wrote a first draft. She wrote it quickly, focusing more on ideas than on grammar, style, and mechanics. As you read her rough draft, consider what global changes you would recommend. Think about large issues such as focus, organization, content, and audience appeal.

PENT'S ROUGH DRAFT

E-mail--Return to Sender?

For many people, turning on the computer and checking for e-mail messages has become as much a part of their daily routine as a trip to the mailbox. The growing popularity of e-mail makes us wonder how could we have survived without it? E-mail has many advantages, including speed, never having to pay for postage and that we can send messages with ease. At the same time, however, there are several disadvantages that might not be so readily apparent.

There is no denying that e-mail has many advantages over regular mail through the U.S. Postal Service. The most obvious advantage is speed. We can send e-mail around the world in a matter of minutes with no more effort than it takes to press a few key on the computer. It is this terrific speed that has lead to our calling regular mail "snail mail." E-mail also has the advantage of being less expensive. Many people have access to e-mail for free through there work or school. And while some people may pay for e-mail through an online service, there is no increase in cost relative to the number of messages sent. It is the same price to send one message to one person as it is to send messages back and forth all day or to a hundred people.

In addition, e-mail allows us to send the same message to many people at the same time with little more effort than it takes to send a message to one person. There is never the trouble of photocopying the letter or printing out another copy or addressing and posting another envelope. Considering the ease, it is surprising there is not more junk e-mail then there is. Someday the direct marketing people will surely catch up with the electronic revolution, at least Ed McMahon hasn't made it to cyberspace yet.

Despite the convenience that e-mail provides, it has several disadvantages. For one thing, each person who uses e-mail must have their own e-mail address, so e-mail excludes anyone who doesn't

have access to a computer. Even having a computer
still does not mean that one has e-mail. One must
pay a monthly fee to an online service to have access to e-mail. It is only less expensive in the
sense that there is not a per-use charge as there
is with regular mail.

Assuming one does have access to e-mail without much effort or expense, there are still several advantages to regular mail. With e-mail all
messages look very much alike and this removes
some of the wonder of getting a message in the
first place. We have no handwriting to scrutinize,
no perfumed envelope to smell, no colors or designs to enjoy. E-mail is also limited by what one
can send. Attached files might let us send a copy
of a photo, but we wouldn't want to put it in a
frame. One will never get an e-mail care package
from home or an e-mail pop-up birthday card. For
these more personal things we must always resort
to regular mail.

In addition, there is the issue of privacy.
Especially in the business world. For example, its
probably not a great idea to complain about your
boss on the company e-mail, or write anything that
you would not truly mind sharing with others.

While e-mail gives us the ability to send
messages with convenience, speed, and little expense, it lacks the personality of regular mail.
There is no reason, however, to always choose one
over the other. Instead we should take advantage
of both, using each to its best advantage. E-mail

for quick notes, multiple mailings, and business
correspondence. Regular mail for messages that deserve a more personal touch. Regular mail will always take longer, but, as the old saying goes,
good things come to those who wait.

Peer review of Pent's draft

Before beginning to revise the draft, Pent brought it to class
for a peer review session. Three of her classmates read the
draft and responded to it, using the chart on page 51 as a
guideline for their discussion. Here are some of their most
useful comments and suggestions:

I'd like to hear more about why e-mail is convenient.

Your remark about junk mail and Ed McMahon was funny,
but wasn't it off the point?

I like your details about personal letters. You made me feel
nostalgic.

You talk about the cost of e-mail in two places. Shouldn't this
all be together? Also, is e-mail cheaper or not?

Dr. King is going to want you to sharpen your thesis (at the
end of the first paragraph).

In places, your use of the word *one* seemed sort of stiff. I like
it better when you use *we*, because it sounds friendlier.

I thought your point about privacy was a good one. Once my
little sister called up an e-mail sent by my boyfriend, and she
hasn't stopped teasing me since.

One of the things I like about e-mail is that people don't seem
to care as much if you make mistakes.

You made me see the advantages of e-mail, but maybe you
could beef up the part about disadvantages. Isn't the danger
of "flaming" a disadvantage? I know some people who have
gotten themselves in trouble in the business world.

Your second paragraph seems pretty long. Why not break it up so that you talk about the low cost of e-mail in one paragraph and its convenience in another?

I wasn't sure about your purpose and audience. The concluding paragraph gives advice to readers, but some parts of the paper make more of a social commentary.

Notice that Pent's classmates were focusing on global matters, not on sentence-level revisions. Because the draft needed a fair amount of work, it made little sense to tinker with its sentences, some of which would be thrown out anyway.

Pent's global revisions

With the help of her peer reviewers, Pent saw the need for a number of global revisions. Here, for example, is how she revised her opening paragraph to improve the focus of her paper:

For many people, turning on the computer and checking for e-mail messages has become as much a part of their daily routine as a trip to the mailbox. The growing popularity of e-mail makes us wonder how could we have survived without it? E-mail has many advantages, including speed, never having to pay for postage and that we can send messages with ease. ~~At the same time, however, there are several disadvantages that might not be so readily apparent.~~

In our enthusiasm for e-mail, however, it would be unwise of us to abandon the post office altogether. For some purposes, e-mail is a poor substitute for "snail mail," both in our personal lives and in the business world.

For Pent's sentence-level revisions of this same paragraph, see page 73.

In the following paragraph, Pent made three global revisions. She added a topic sentence at the beginning of the paragraph, she deleted text that was off the point, and she added new text describing another way in which e-mail is convenient.

> *There is no question that e-mail is convenient. It*
> ~~In addition,~~ e-mail allows us to send the same
> ^
> message to many people at the same time with
> little more effort than it takes to send a message
> to one person. There is never the trouble of
> photocopying the letter or printing out another
> copy or addressing and posting another envelope.
> ~~Considering this ease, it is surprising there is~~
> ~~not more junk e-mail then there is. Someday the~~
> ~~direct marketing people will surely catch up with~~
> ~~the electronic revolution, at least Ed McMahon~~
> ~~hasn't made it to cyberspace yet.~~
> *E-mail is also convenient because it lends itself to an informal*
> *style that makes composing a message relatively easy; in*
> *addition, readers of e-mail tolerate more mistakes than*
> *readers of conventional mail, and their tolerance saves*
> *us time.*

If you compare Pent's final draft (pp. 74–77) with her earlier draft (pp. 67–70), you will notice other global revisions: breaking a long paragraph into two paragraphs, deleting and adding more chunks of text, sharpening topic sentences, making the point of view more consistent by using *we* instead of *people* or *one*, and so on.

Pent's sentence-level revisions

Once Pent had written a second draft, she felt ready to devote her full attention to matters of style and correctness. Here, for example, are the first two paragraphs as Pent edited them. Notice that even though Pent had run all of her drafts through a spell checker, the second paragraph still contained both a typographical error and a misspelling. The spell checker didn't flag *key* and *lead* because they are real words.

For many ~~people~~ *of us,* turning on the computer and checking for e-mail messages has become as much a part of ~~their~~ *our* daily routine as a trip to the mailbox. The growing popularity of e-mail makes us wonder how ~~could we have~~ *we ever* survived without it. E-mail has many advantages/ *over regular mail,* including speed, ~~never~~ *low cost, and convenience.* ~~having to pay for postage and that we can send messages with ease.~~ In our enthusiasm for e-mail, however, ~~it~~ *we* would be unwise ~~of us~~ to abandon the post office altogether. For some purposes, e-mail is a poor substitute for "snail mail," both in our personal lives and in the business world.

There is no denying that e-mail has many advantages over regular mail. ~~through the U.S. Postal Service.~~ The most obvious advantage is speed. We can send e-mail around the world in a

matter of minutes with no more effort than it
takes to press a few key*s* on the computer. It is
this ~~terrific~~ speed that has ~~lead~~ *led* to our calling
regular mail "snail mail."

When Pent finished making all of her revisions, she carefully proofread and corrected her paper before turning in the final draft shown here.

PENT'S FINAL DRAFT

                    E-mail--Return to Sender?

        For many of us, turning on the computer and
checking for e-mail messages has become as much a
part of our daily routine as a trip to the mailbox. The growing popularity of e-mail makes us
wonder how we ever survived without it. E-mail
has many advantages over regular mail, including
speed, low cost, and convenience. In our enthusiasm
for e-mail, however, we would be unwise to abandon
the post office altogether. For some purposes,
e-mail is a poor substitute for "snail mail,"
both in our personal lives and in the business
world.

        There is no denying that e-mail has many
advantages over regular mail. The most obvious advantage is speed. We can send e-mail around the
world in a matter of minutes with no more effort
than it takes to press a few keys on the computer.
It is this speed that has led to our calling regular mail "snail mail."

E-mail also has the advantage of being less expensive, for most people, than regular mail. Many people have access to e-mail for free through their work or school. And while some people may pay for e-mail through an online service, there is no increase in cost relative to the number of messages sent. It is the same price to send one message to one person as it is to send messages back and forth all day or to a hundred people. Finally, if we consider the costs saved in long-distance phone bills in addition to the costs saved in postage, most e-mail users surely come out ahead.

There is no question that e-mail is convenient. It allows us to send the same message to many people at the same time with little more effort than it takes to send a message to one person. When sending multiple copies of a message, we avoid the trouble of photocopying the letter, printing out additional copies, addressing envelopes, and posting the mail. E-mail is also convenient because it lends itself to an informal style that makes composing a message relatively easy; in addition, readers of e-mail tolerate more mistakes than readers of conventional mail, and their tolerance saves us time.

Despite the many benefits that e-mail provides, it is not always appropriate. Before dashing off another piece of e-mail--in our private lives or in the business world--we need to pause and consider whether the post office or a carrier such as Federal Express or UPS might be more fitting.

It would be sad to think that letters from friends might become obsolete. With e-mail, unfortunately, all messages look very much alike, and this sameness removes some of the wonder of getting a message in the first place. We have no handwriting to scrutinize, no perfumed envelope to smell, no colors or textures to enjoy. E-mail is also limited by what we can send. Attached files might let us send a copy of a photo, but we wouldn't want to put it in a frame. We will never receive an e-mail care package from home or an e-mail pop-up birthday card. For these more personal things we must still rely on regular mail. Besides, opening old computer files is never as much fun as pulling a musty shoebox out of the closet to browse through old letters and photos.

In the business world, as in our personal lives, e-mail is not always an appropriate medium. First, there is the issue of privacy. Because of its electronic transmission in networked systems, e-mail may be accessible to co-workers and supervisors. It's probably not a good idea to complain about the boss on the company e-mail or to write anything that shouldn't be shared with strangers or potential enemies. A second problem with e-mail is its informality. For much company business, a

certain level of courtesy and formality is desirable; e-mail can seem inappropriate because of its
relatively slapdash quality. And finally, because
of its speed, e-mail encourages "flaming," sending
off rapid-fire emotional messages that can get a
businessperson in serious trouble.

While e-mail gives us the ability to send
messages with convenience, speed, and little expense, it lacks the personality and authority of
regular mail. Luckily, however, we needn't always
choose one over the other. Instead we should take
advantage of both, using each to its best advantage: e-mail for quick notes, multiple mailings,
and routine business correspondence; regular mail
for personal messages and for formal or private
business correspondence. Regular mail will always
take a bit longer, but at times good things are
worth waiting for.

4

Build effective paragraphs.

Except for special-purpose paragraphs, such as introductions and conclusions (see 2a and 2c), paragraphs are clusters of information supporting an essay's main point (or
advancing a story's action). Aim for paragraphs that are
clearly focused, well developed, organized, coherent, and neither too long nor too short for easy reading.

4a Focus on a main point.

A paragraph should be unified around a main point. The point should be clear to readers, and all sentences in the paragraph must relate to it.

Stating the main point in a topic sentence

As readers move into a paragraph, they need to know where they are—in relation to the whole essay—and what to expect in the sentences to come. A good topic sentence, a one-sentence summary of the paragraph's main point, acts as a signpost pointing in two directions: backward toward the thesis of the essay and forward toward the body of the paragraph.

Like a thesis statement (see 1c and 2a), a topic sentence is more general than the material supporting it. Usually the topic sentence comes first.

> *Nearly all living creatures manage some form of communication.* The dance patterns of bees in their hive help to point the way to distant flower fields or announce successful foraging. Male stickleback fish regularly swim upside-down to indicate outrage in a courtship contest. Male deer and lemurs mark territorial ownership by rubbing their own body secretions on boundary stones or trees. Everyone has seen a frightened dog put his tail between his legs and run in panic. We, too, use gestures, expressions, postures, and movement to give our words point. [Italics added.]
>
> —Olivia Vlahos, *Human Beginnings*

Sometimes the topic sentence is introduced by a transitional sentence linking it to earlier material. In the following paragraph, the topic sentence (italicized) has been delayed to allow for a transition.

But flowers are not the only source of spectacle in the wilderness. *An opportunity for late color is provided by the berries of wildflowers, shrubs, and trees.* Baneberry presents its tiny white flowers in spring but in late summer bursts forth with clusters of red berries. Bunchberry, a ground-cover plant, puts out red berries in the fall, and the red berries of wintergreen last from autumn well into winter. In California, the bright red, fist-sized clusters of Christmas berries can be seen growing beside highways for up to six months of the year. [Italics added.]

— James Crockett et al., *Wildflower Gardening*

Occasionally the topic sentence may be withheld until the end of the paragraph—but only if the earlier sentences hang together so well that the reader perceives their direction, if not their exact point. The opening sentences of the following paragraph state facts, so they are supporting material rather than topic sentences, but they strongly suggest a central idea. The topic sentence at the end is hardly a surprise.

Tobacco chewing starts as soon as people begin stirring. Those who have fresh supplies soak the new leaves in water and add ashes from the hearth to the wad. Men, women, and children chew tobacco and all are addicted to it. Once there was a shortage of tobacco in Kaobawa's village and I was plagued for a week by early morning visitors who requested permission to collect my cigarette butts in order to make a wad of chewing tobacco. Normally, if anyone is short of tobacco, he can request a share of someone else's already chewed wad, or simply borrow the entire wad when its owner puts it down somewhere. *Tobacco is so important to them that their word for "poverty" translates as "being without tobacco."* [Italics added.]

—Napoleon A. Chagnon, *Yanomamo: The Fierce People*

Although it is generally wise to use topic sentences, at times they are unnecessary. A topic sentence may not be needed if a paragraph continues developing an idea clearly introduced in a previous paragraph, if the details of the paragraph unmistakably suggest its main point, or if the paragraph appears in a narrative of events where generalizations might interrupt the flow of the story.

Sticking to the point

Sentences that do not support the topic sentence destroy the unity of a paragraph. If the paragraph is otherwise well focused, such offending sentences can simply be deleted or perhaps moved elsewhere. In the following paragraph describing the inadequate facilities in a high school, the information about the word processing instructor (in italics) is clearly off the point.

> As the result of tax cuts, the educational facilities of Lincoln High School have reached an all-time low. Some of the books date back to 1985 and have long since shed their covers. The lack of lab equipment makes it necessary for four to five students to work at one table, with most watching rather than performing experiments. The few computers in working order must share one dot matrix printer. *Also, the word processing instructor left to have a baby at the beginning of the semester, and most of the students don't like the substitute.* As for the furniture, many of the upright chairs have become recliners, and the desk legs are so unbalanced that they play seesaw on the floor.

Sometimes the cure for a disunified paragraph is not as simple as deleting or moving material. Writers often wander into uncharted territory because they cannot think of enough evidence to support a topic sentence. Feeling that it is too soon to break into a new paragraph, they move on to new ideas for which they have not prepared the reader. When this happens, the writer is faced with a choice: Either find more evidence to support the topic sentence or adjust the topic sentence to mesh with the evidence that is available.

LOOKING AT YOURSELF AS A WRITER
Topic sentences

Professors and business supervisors often complain about the writing that is submitted to them, and one of their loudest complaints concerns topic sentences. Why, they wonder, do so many students and employees have trouble stating the point of a paragraph in its first sentence?

If you have experienced this difficulty, ask yourself why. Here are some common causes and cures.

CAUSE You haven't decided how to organize your draft, so you don't know what key idea to express in the topic sentence for each paragraph.

CURE Jot down an informal outline and build a topic sentence for each key point in the outline. It's best to do this before drafting, but you can do it later as well.

CAUSE You are focusing on details and forget the reader's need to see how the details fit into the overall structure of the essay. The forward flow of writing tempts nearly all of us to blur the structure while we are drafting.

CURE As you revise a draft, pay special attention to organization, inserting (or sharpening) topic sentences as needed.

CAUSE You are trying to link the opening sentence of a new paragraph to the last sentence of the previous paragraph.

CURE When you move into a new paragraph, don't worry about subtle links between sentences. Pay attention instead to links between larger chunks of text—the move from one topic to another.

CAUSE You are aware that some professional writers, especially journalists and informal essayists, do not always use clear topic sentences.

Topic sentences (continued)

CURE   Develop a flexible approach to writing. In some contexts, topic sentences may not be so important. In
the academic world, however, topic sentences are
often necessary for clarifying the lines of an argument or reporting the research in a field. In the business world, topic sentences (along with headings)
are essential, since readers often scan for information.

EXERCISE 4–1

Underline the topic sentence in the following paragraph and eliminate any material that does not clarify or develop the central idea.

Historically, quilt making has served as an important
means of social, political, and artistic expression for women.
In the nineteenth century, especially, quilting circles provided
one of the few opportunities for the women of a community to
forge social bonds outside of their families. Once a week or
more, they came together to sew as well as trade small talk,
advice, and news. They used dyed cotton fabrics much like
the fabrics quilters use today; surprisingly, quilters' basic materials haven't changed that much over the years. Sometimes
the women joined their efforts in the support of a political
cause, making quilts that would be raffled to raise money for
temperance societies, hospitals for sick and wounded soldiers,
and the fight against slavery. The abolitionist movement, in
particular, led one activist, Sarah Grimke, to memorably
express her hopes for herself and fellow quilters: "May the
points of our needles prick the slave owner's conscience."
Quilt making also afforded women a means of artistic expression at a time when they had few other creative outlets.
Within their socially acceptable roles as homemakers, many
quilters subtly—and perhaps subconsciously—pushed back
at the restrictions placed on them by experimenting with
color, design, and technique.

4b   Develop the main point.

Though an occasional short paragraph is fine, particularly if it functions as a transition or emphasizes a point, a series of brief paragraphs suggests inadequate development. How much development is enough? That varies, depending on the writer's purpose and audience.

For example, when she wrote a paragraph attempting to convince readers that it is impossible to lose fat quickly, health columnist Jane Brody knew that she would have to present a great deal of evidence because many dieters want to believe the opposite. She did *not* write:

> When you think about it, it's impossible to lose—as many diets suggest—10 pounds of *fat* in ten days, even on a total fast. Even a moderately active person cannot lose so much weight so fast. A less active person hasn't a prayer.

This three-sentence paragraph is too skimpy to be convincing. But the paragraph that Brody wrote contains enough evidence to convince even skeptical readers.

> When you think about it, it's impossible to lose —as many diets suggest— 10 pounds of *fat* in ten days, even on a total fast. A pound of body fat represents 3,500 calories. To lose 1 pound of fat, you must expend 3,500 more calories than you consume. Let's say you weigh 170 pounds and, as a moderately active person, you burn 2,500 calories a day. If your diet contains only 1,500 calories, you'd have an energy deficit of 1,000 calories a day. In a week's time that would add up to a 7,000-calorie deficit, or 2 pounds of real fat. In ten days, the accumulated deficit would represent nearly 3 pounds of lost body fat. Even if you ate nothing at all for ten days and maintained your usual level of activity, your caloric deficit would add up to 25,000 calories. . . . At 3,500 calories per pound of fat, that's still only 7 pounds of lost fat.
> — Jane Brody, *Jane Brody's Nutrition Book*

4c Choose a suitable pattern of organization.

Although paragraphs (and indeed whole essays) may be patterned in any number of ways, certain patterns of organization occur frequently, either alone or in combination:
examples and illustrations, narration, description, process,
comparison and contrast, analogy, cause and effect, classification and division, and definition. There is nothing particularly magical about these patterns (sometimes called
methods of development). They simply reflect some of the
ways in which we think.

Examples and illustrations

Examples, perhaps the most common pattern of development, are appropriate whenever the reader might be tempted
to ask, "For example?" Though examples are just selected instances, not a complete catalog, they are enough to suggest
the truth of many topic sentences, as in the following paragraph.

> Normally my parents abided scrupulously by "The
> Budget," but several times a year Dad would dip into his bat-
> tered, black strongbox and splurge on some irrational, totally
> satisfying luxury. Once he bought over a hundred comic
> books at a flea market, doled out to us thereafter at the tan-
> talizing rate of two a week. He always got a whole flat of pan-
> sies, Mom's favorite flower, for us to give her on Mother's Day.
> One day a boy stopped at our house selling fifty-cent raffle
> tickets on a sailboat and Dad bought every ticket the boy had
> left—three books' worth.   —Connie Hailey, student

Illustrations are extended examples, frequently presented in story form. Because they require several sentences
apiece, they are used more sparingly than examples. When
well selected, however, they can be a vivid and effective
means of developing a point. The writer of the following para-

graph uses illustrations to demonstrate that Harriet Tubman, famous conductor on the underground railway for escaping slaves, was a genius at knowing how and when to retreat.

> Part of Harriet Tubman's strategy of conducting was, as in all battle-field operations, the knowledge of how and when to retreat. Numerous allusions have been made to her moves when she suspected that she was in danger. When she feared the party was closely pursued, she would take it for a time on a train southward bound. No one seeing Negroes going in this direction would for an instant suppose them to be fugitives. Once on her return she was at a railway station. She saw some men reading a poster and she heard one of them reading it aloud. It was a description of her, offering a reward for her capture. She took a southbound train to avert suspicion. At another time when Harriet heard men talking about her, she pretended to read a book which she carried. One man remarked, "This cannot be the woman. The one we want can't read or write." Harriet devoutly hoped the book was right side up.
> —Earl Conrad, *Harriet Tubman*

Narration

A paragraph of narration tells a story or part of a story. Narrative paragraphs are usually arranged in chronological order, but they may also contain flashbacks, interruptions that take the story back to an earlier time. The following paragraph, from Jane Goodall's *In the Shadow of Man*, recounts one of the author's experiences in the African wild.

> One evening when I was wading in the shallows of the lake to pass a rocky outcrop, I suddenly stopped dead as I saw the sinuous black body of a snake in the water. It was all of six feet long, and from the slight hood and the dark stripes at the back of the neck I knew it to be a Storm's water cobra—a deadly reptile for the bite of which there was, at that time, no serum. As I stared at it an incoming wave gently deposited part of its body on one of my feet. I remained motionless, not

even breathing, until the wave rolled back into the lake, drawing the snake with it. Then I leaped out of the water as fast as I could, my heart hammering.

—Jane Goodall, *In the Shadow of Man*

Description

A descriptive paragraph sketches a portrait of a person, place, or thing by using concrete and specific details that appeal to one or more of our senses—sight, sound, smell, taste, and touch. Consider, for example, the following description of the grasshopper invasions that devastated the midwestern landscape in the late 1860s.

> They came like dive bombers out of the west. They came by the millions with the rustle of their wings roaring overhead. They came in waves, like the rolls of the sea, descending with a terrifying speed, breaking now and again like a mighty surf. They came with the force of a williwaw and they formed a huge, ominous, dark brown cloud that eclipsed the sun. They dipped and touched earth, hitting objects and people like hailstones. But they were not hail. These were live demons. They popped, snapped, crackled, and roared. They were dark brown, an inch or longer in length, plump in the middle and tapered at the ends. They had transparent wings, slender legs, and two black eyes that flashed with a fierce intelligence.   —Eugene Boe, "Pioneers to Eternity"

Process

A process paragraph is patterned in time order, usually chronologically. A writer may choose this pattern either to describe a process or to show readers how to perform a process. The following paragraph describes what happens when water freezes.

> In school we learned that with few exceptions the solid phase of matter is more dense than the liquid phase. Water, alone among common substances, violates this rule. As water

begins to cool, it contracts and becomes more dense, in a perfectly typical way. But about four degrees above the freezing point, something remarkable happens. It ceases to contract and begins expanding, becoming less dense. At the freezing point the expansion is abrupt and drastic. As water turns to ice, it adds about one-eleventh to its liquid volume.

—Chet Raymo, "Curious Stuff, Water and Ice"

Here is a paragraph explaining how to perform a "roll cast," a popular fly fishing technique:

Begin by taking up a suitable stance, with one foot slightly in front of the other and the rod pointing down the line. Then begin a smooth, steady draw, raising your rod hand to just above shoulder height and lifting the rod to the 10:30 or 11:00 position. This steady draw allows a loop of line to form between the rod top and the water. While the line is still moving, raise the rod slightly, then punch it rapidly forward and down. The rod is now flexed and under maximum compression, and the line follows its path, bellying out slightly behind you and coming off the water close to your feet. As you power the rod down through the 3:00 position, the belly of the line will roll forward. Follow through smoothly so that the line unfolds and straightens above the water.

—*The Dorling Kindersley Encyclopedia of Fishing*

Comparison and contrast

To compare two subjects is to draw attention to their similarities, although the word *compare* also has a broader meaning that includes a consideration of differences. To contrast is to focus only on differences.

Whether a comparison-and-contrast paragraph stresses similarities or differences, it may be patterned in one of two ways. The two subjects may be presented one at a time, block style, as in the following paragraph of contrast.

So Grant and Lee were in complete contrast, representing two diametrically opposed elements in American life. Grant was the modern man emerging; beyond him, ready to come on the stage, was the great age of steel and machinery, of crowded cities and a restless burgeoning vitality. Lee might have ridden down from the old age of chivalry, lance in hand, silken banner fluttering over his head. Each man was the perfect champion of his cause, drawing both his strengths and weaknesses from the people he led.

—Bruce Catton, "Grant and Lee: A Study in Contrasts"

Or a paragraph may proceed point by point, treating the two subjects together, one aspect at a time. The following paragraph uses the point-by-point method to contrast the writer's academic experiences in an American high school with those in an Irish convent.

Strangely enough, instead of being academically inferior to my American high school, the Irish convent was superior. In my class at home, *Love Story* was considered pretty heavy reading, so imagine my surprise at finding Irish students who could recite passages from *War and Peace.* In high school we complained about having to study *Romeo and Juliet* in one semester, whereas in Ireland we simultaneously studied *Macbeth* and Dickens's *Hard Times,* in addition to writing a composition a day in English class. In high school, I didn't even begin algebra until the ninth grade, while at the convent seventh graders (or their Irish equivalent) were doing calculus and trigonometry.   —Margaret Stack, student

Analogy

Analogies draw comparisons between items that appear to have little in common. Writers turn to analogies for a variety of reasons: to make the unfamiliar seem familiar, to provide a concrete understanding of an abstract topic, to argue a point, or to provoke fresh thoughts or changed feelings about a subject. In the following paragraph, physician Lewis

Thomas draws an analogy between the behavior of ants and that of humans. Thomas's analogy helps us to understand the social behavior of ants and forces us to question the superiority of our own human societies.

> Ants are so much like human beings as to be an embarrassment. They farm fungi, raise aphids as livestock, launch armies into wars, use chemical sprays to alarm and confuse enemies, capture slaves. The families of weaver ants engage in child labor, holding their larvae like shuttles to spin out the thread that sews the leaves together for their fungus gardens. They exchange information ceaselessly. They do everything but watch television.
> —Lewis Thomas, "On Societies as Organisms"

Although analogies can be a powerful tool for illuminating a subject, they should be used with caution in arguments. Just because two things may be alike in one respect, we cannot conclude that they are alike in all respects. (See *false analogy*, p. 172.)

Cause and effect

When causes and effects are a matter of argument, they are too complex to be reduced to a simple pattern (see p. 173). However, if a writer wishes merely to describe a cause-and-effect relationship that is generally accepted, then the effect may be stated in the topic sentence, with the causes listed in the body of the paragraph.

> The fantastic water clarity of the Mount Gambier sinkholes results from several factors. The holes are fed from aquifers holding rainwater that fell decades—even centuries—ago, and that has been filtered through miles of limestone. The high level of calcium that limestone adds causes the silty detritus from dead plants and animals to cling together and settle quickly to the bottom. Abundant bottom vegetation in the shal-

low sinkholes also helps bind the silt. And the rapid turnover of water prohibits stagnation.

—Hillary Hauser,
"Exploring a Sunken Realm in Australia"

Or the paragraph may move from cause to effects, as in this paragraph from a student paper on the effects of the industrial revolution on American farms.

The rise of rail transport in the nineteenth century forever changed American farming—for better and for worse. Farmers who once raised crops and livestock to sustain just their own families could now make a profit by selling their goods in towns and cities miles away. These new markets improved the living standard of struggling farm families and encouraged them to seek out innovations that would increase their profits. On the downside, the competition fostered by the new markets sometimes created hostility among neighboring farm families where there had once been a spirit of cooperation. Those farmers who couldn't compete with their neighbors left farming forever, facing poverty worse than they had ever known.   —Chris Mileski, student

Classification and division

Classification is the grouping of items into categories according to some consistent principle. Philosopher Francis Bacon was using classification when he wrote that "some books are to be tasted, others to be swallowed, and some few to be chewed and digested." Bacon's principle for classifying books is the degree to which they are worthy of our attention, but books of course can be classified according to other principles. For example, an elementary school teacher might classify children's books according to their level of difficulty, or a librarian might group them by subject matter. The principle of classification that a writer chooses ultimately depends on the purpose of the classification.

The following paragraph classifies species of electric fish.

> Scientists sort electric fishes into three categories. The first comprises the strongly electric species like the marine electric rays or the freshwater African electric catfish and South American electric eel. Known since the dawn of history, these deliver a punch strong enough to stun a human. In recent years, biologists have focused on a second category: weakly electric fish in the South American and African rivers that use tiny voltages for communication and navigation. The third group contains sharks, nonelectric rays, and catfish, which do not emit a field but possess sensors that enable them to detect the minute amounts of electricity that leak out of other organisms.
>
> —Anne Rudloe and Jack Rudloe, "Electric Warfare: The Fish That Kill with Thunderbolts"

Division takes one item and divides it into parts. As with classification, division should be made according to some consistent principle. Dividing a tree into roots, trunk, branches, and leaves makes sense; listing its components as branches, wood, water, and sap does not, for the categories overlap.

The following passage describes the components that make up a baseball:

> Like the game itself, a baseball is composed of many layers. One of the delicious joys of childhood is to take apart a baseball and examine the wonders within. You begin by removing the red cotton thread and peeling off the leather cover—which comes from the hide of a Holstein cow and has been tanned, cut, printed, and punched with holes. Beneath the cover is a thin layer of cotton string, followed by several hundred yards of woolen yarn, which make up the bulk of the ball. Slice into the rubber and you'll find the ball's heart—a cork core. The cork is from Portugal, the rubber from southeast Asia, the covers are American, and the balls are assembled in Costa Rica.
>
> —Dan Gutman, *The Way Baseball Works*

Definition

A definition puts a word or concept into a general class and then provides enough details to distinguish it from others in the same class. For example, in one of its senses the term *grit* names the class of things that birds eat, but it is restricted to those items — such as small pebbles, eggshell, and ashes — that help the bird grind food.

Many definitions may be presented in a sentence or two, but abstract or difficult concepts may require a paragraph or even a full essay of definition. In the following paragraph, the writer defines envy as a special kind of desire.

> Envy is so integral and so painful a part of what animates human behavior in market societies that many people have forgotten the full meaning of the word, simplifying it into one of the synonyms of desire. It is that, which may be why it flourishes in market societies: democracies of desire, they might be called, with money for ballots, stuffing permitted. But envy is more or less than desire. It begins with the almost frantic sense of emptiness inside oneself, as if the pump of one's heart were sucking on air. One has to be blind to perceive the emptiness, of course, but that's just what envy is, a selective blindness. *Invidia,* Latin for envy, translates as "nonsight," and Dante had the envious plodding along under cloaks of lead, their eyes sewn shut with leaden wire. What they are blind to is what they have, God-given and humanly nurtured, in themselves.   —Nelson W. Aldrich, Jr., *Old Money*

Extended definitions frequently make use of other patterns of development, such as examples, illustrations, or comparison and contrast. Here, for example, is a paragraph that uses a number of illustrations to define the typical teenage victim in a "slasher" film.

> Since teenagers are the target audience for slasher films, the victims in the films are almost always independent, fun-loving, just-out-of-high-school partygoers. The girls all love to

take late-night strolls alone through the woods or to skinny-
dip at midnight in a murky lake. The boys, eager to impress
the girls, prove their manhood by descending alone into
musty cellars to restart broken generators or by chasing psy-
chotic killers into haylofts and attics. Entering dark and
gloomy houses, young men and women alike decide suddenly
that now's a good time to save a few bucks on the family's
electric bill—so they leave the lights off. After hearing a noise
within the house, they always foolishly decide to investigate,
thinking it's one of their many missing friends or pets. Disre-
garding the "safety in numbers" theory, they branch off in
separate directions, never to see each other again. Or the
teenagers fall into the common slasher-movie habit of walking
backward, which naturally leads them right into you-know-
who. Confronted by the ax-wielding maniac, the senseless
youths lose their will to survive, close their eyes, and scream.
—Matthew J. Holicek, student

EXERCISE 4-2

Write a paragraph modeled on one of the patterns discussed in this
section. Some possible topics—most of which you'll need to restrict—
are listed here.

Examples or illustrations: sexism in a comic strip, ways to include protein in a vegetarian diet, the benefits of a particular
summer job, community services provided by your college, violence on the six o'clock news, educational software for children

Narration: the active lifestyle of a grandparent, life with an alcoholic, working in an emergency room, the benefits (or problems) of intercultural dating, growing up in a large family, the
rewards of working in a nursing home, an experience that
taught you a lesson, a turning point in your life

Description: your childhood home, an ethnic neighborhood,
a rock concert, a favorite painting in an art gallery, a garden,
a classic car, a hideous building or monument, a style of
dress, a family heirloom (such as a crazy quilt or a collection
of Christmas tree ornaments), a favorite park or retreat

Process: how to repair something, how to develop a successful job interview style, how to ask someone out on a date, how to practice safe scuba diving, how to build a set for a play, how to survive in the wilderness, how to train a dog, how to quit smoking, how to make bread

Comparison and contrast: two neighborhoods, teachers, political candidates, colleges, products; country living versus city living; the stereotype of a job versus the reality; a change in attitude toward your family's religion or ethnic background

Analogy: between a family reunion and a circus, between training for a rigorous sport and boot camp, between settling an argument and being a courtroom judge, between a dogfight and a boxing match, between raising a child and tending a garden

Cause and effect: the effects of water pollution on a particular area, the effects of divorce on a child, the effects of an illegal drug, why a particular film or television show is popular, why an area of the country has high unemployment, why early training is essential for success as a ballet dancer, violinist, or athlete

Classification: types of clothing worn on your college campus, types of people who join online chat groups, types of dieters, types of television weather reports, types of rock bands, types of teachers

Definition: an Internet addict, an ideal parent or teacher, an authoritarian personality, an intellectual, a sexist, anorexia nervosa, a typical heroine in a Harlequin romance, a typical blind date

4d Consider possible ways of arranging information.

In addition to choosing a pattern of development (or a combination of patterns), you may need to make decisions about arrangement. If you are developing a paragraph with examples, for instance, you'll need to decide how to order the examples. Or if you are contrasting two items point by point, you'll need to decide which points to discuss first, second, and so on. Often considerations of purpose and audience will help you make these choices.

Three of the most common ways of arranging information are treated in this section: time order, spatial order, and order of climax. Other possible arrangements include order of complexity (from simple to complex), order of familiarity (from most familiar to least familiar), and order of audience appeal (from "safe" ideas to those that may challenge the audience's views).

Order of time

Time order, usually chronological, is appropriate for a variety of purposes such as narrating a personal experience, telling an anecdote, describing an experiment, or explaining a process. The following paragraph, arranged in chronological order, is from an account of the author's travels on the back roads of America.

> Orion Saddle Road, after I was committed to it, narrowed to a single rutted lane affording no place to turn around; if I met somebody, one of us would have to back down. The higher I went, the more that idea unnerved me—the road was bad enough driving forward. The compass swung from point to point, and within five minutes it had touched each of the three hundred sixty degrees. The clutch started pushing back, and ruts and craters and rocks threw the steering wheel into nasty jerks that wrenched to the spine. I understood why, the day before, I'd thought there could be no road over the Chiricahuas; there wasn't. No wonder desperadoes hid in this inaccessibility.
> —William Least Heat Moon, *Blue Highways*

Time order need not be chronological. For example, you might decide to arrange events in the order in which they were revealed to you, not in the order in which they happened. Or you might choose to begin with a dramatic moment and then flash back to the events that led up to it.

Order of space

For descriptions of a location or a scene, a spatial arrangement will seem natural. Imagine yourself holding a video camera and you'll begin to see the possibilities. Might you pan the scene from afar and then zoom to a close-up? Would you rather sweep the camera from side to side—or from top to bottom? Or should you try for a more impressionistic effect, focusing the camera on first one and then another significant feature of the scene?

The writer of the following paragraph describes the contents of a long, narrow pool hall by taking us from the front to the back.

> The pool tables were in a line side by side from the front to the back of the long, narrow building. The first one was the biggest, and the best snooker players used it. Beyond it were the other tables used by lesser players, except for the last one. This was the bank's pool table, used only by the best players in the county.   —William G. Hill, student

Order of climax

When ideas are presented in the order of climax, they build toward a conclusion. Consider the following paragraph describing the effects on workers of long-term blue-collar employment. All of the examples have an emotional impact, but the final one—even though it might at first seem trivial—is the most powerful. It shows us just how degrading blue-collar work can become.

> I met people who taught me about human behavior. I saw people take amphetamines to keep up with ever-rising production rates. I saw good friends, and even relatives, physically attack each other over job assignments that would mean a few cents' difference. I observed women cheating on their husbands and men cheating on their wives. I watched women hand over their entire paycheck to a bookie. I saw

pregnant women, their feet too swollen for shoes, come to work in slippers. I saw women with colds stuff pieces of tissue up their nostrils so they wouldn't have to keep stopping to blow their nose.   —Linda Lavelle, student

Because the order of climax saves the most dramatic examples for the end, it is appropriate only when readers are likely to persist until the end. In much business writing, for example, you cannot assume that readers will read more than the first couple of sentences of a paragraph. In such cases, you will be wise to open with your most powerful examples, even at the risk of allowing the paragraph to fizzle at the end.

4e Make paragraphs coherent.

When sentences and paragraphs flow from one to another without discernible bumps, gaps, or shifts, they are said to be coherent. Coherence can be improved by strengthening the various ties between old information and new. A number of techniques for strengthening those ties are detailed in this section.

Linking ideas clearly

In the first draft of a paragraph or an essay, writers do not always link their ideas as clearly as possible. To check a draft for clear connections among ideas, try to look at it from the point of view of a reader. Think in terms of the reader's expectations.

WHAT READERS LOOK FOR IN A PARAGRAPH   As you know, readers usually expect to learn a paragraph's main point in a topic sentence early in the paragraph. Then, as they move into the body of the paragraph, they expect to encounter specific details, facts, or examples that support the topic sentence—either directly or indirectly. Consider the following example, in which all of the sentences following the topic sentence directly support it.

> A passenger list of the early years of the Orient Express would read like a *Who's Who of the World*, from art to politics. Sarah Bernhardt and her Italian counterpart Eleonora Duse used the train to thrill the stages of Europe. For musicians there were Toscanini and Mahler. Dancers Nijinsky and Pavlova were there, while lesser performers like Harry Houdini and the girls of the Ziegfeld Follies also rode the rails. Violinists were allowed to practice on the train, and occasionally one might see trapeze artists hanging like bats from the baggage racks.
>
> —Barnaby Conrad III, "Train of Kings"

If a sentence does not directly support the topic sentence, readers expect it to support another sentence in the paragraph and therefore to support the topic sentence indirectly. Composition scholar Francis Christensen has invented a useful system for numbering the sentences in a paragraph to depict the hierarchic connections among sentences that readers look for. The topic sentence, being most general, receives the number 1, and any sentences that directly support it receive the number 2. Sentences that support level 2 sentences receive the number 3, and so on. Here, for example, is Christensen's numbering system as applied to a paragraph by columnist Ellen Goodman.

1. In the years since Kitty Genovese's murder, social scientists have learned a great deal about bystander behavior.
    2. They've learned that the willingness to intervene depends on a number of subtle factors beyond fear.
        3. It turns out that people are less likely to help if they are in a crowd of bystanders than if they are the only one.
            4. Their sense of responsibility is diffused.

    4. If the others aren't helping, they begin to reinterpret what they are seeing.

  3. People are also more passive in urban neighborhoods or crowded city spots where they suffer from "excessive overload" or simply turn off.

  3. They rarely get involved if they believe that the victim knows the assailant.

    4. This is especially true if the crime being witnessed is . . . a rape or attempted rape.

Because the sentences in this paragraph are arranged in a clear hierarchy, readers can easily follow the writer's train of thought.

To check one of your own paragraphs for clear connections among ideas, look to see if the hierarchic chain has been broken at any point. The topic sentence should announce the main idea, and the rest of the sentences should support it either directly or indirectly. When a sentence supports the topic sentence indirectly, it must support an earlier sentence that is clearly linked (directly or indirectly) to the topic sentence. If you can't find such a sentence, you'll need to add one or rethink the entire chain of ideas.

    WHAT READERS LOOK FOR IN AN ESSAY Like the sentences within paragraphs, the paragraphs within an essay should be arranged in a clear hierarchy. Readers expect to learn the essay's main point in the first paragraph, often in a thesis statement (see 2a). And by scanning the topic sentence of each paragraph in the body of the essay, readers hope to understand how each paragraph connects with what has come before. As a rule, a topic sentence should tell readers whether the information they are about to read supports the thesis statement directly or supports a key idea in the essay, which in turn supports the thesis.

Consider the following thesis statement and topic sentences, taken from an essay by student Thu Hong Nguyen. Each of Nguyen's topic sentences supports the thesis statement directly.

THESIS STATEMENT IN OPENING PARAGRAPH
From the moment she is mature enough to understand commands, to the day she is married off, to the time when she bears her own children, a Vietnamese woman tries to establish a good name as a diligent daughter, a submissive wife, and an altruistic mother.

TOPIC SENTENCE IN FIRST BODY PARAGRAPH
In order to be approved of by everyone, a Vietnamese daughter must work diligently to help her parents.

TOPIC SENTENCE IN SECOND BODY PARAGRAPH
Once she enters an arranged marriage, a good Vietnamese woman must submit to her husband.

TOPIC SENTENCE IN THIRD BODY PARAGRAPH
Finally, to be recognized favorably, a Vietnamese woman must sacrifice herself for the benefit of the children it is her duty to bear.

Topic sentences do not always have to interlock with the thesis quite so tightly as in Nguyen's essay. Nevertheless, by scanning the opening sentence or two of each paragraph, readers should have at least a rough sense of the connections among ideas within the whole essay.

Repeating key words

Repetition of key words is an important technique for gaining coherence. To prevent repetitions from becoming dull, you can use variations of a key word (*hike, hiker, hiking*), pronouns referring to the word (*gamblers . . . they*), and synonyms (*run, spring, race, dash*). In the following paragraph describing plots among indentured servants in the seventeenth century, historian Richard Hofstadter binds sentences together by repeating the key word *plots* and echoing it with a variety of synonyms (which are italicized).

Plots hatched by several servants to run away together occurred mostly in the plantation colonies, and the few recorded servant *uprisings* were entirely limited to those colonies. Virginia had been forced from its very earliest years to take stringent steps against *mutinous plots,* and severe punishments for *such behavior* were recorded. Most servant *plots* occurred in the seventeenth century: a contemplated *uprising* was nipped in the bud in York County in 1661; apparently led by some left-wing offshoots of the *Great Rebellion,* servants *plotted* an *insurrection* in Gloucester County in 1663, and four leaders were condemned and executed; some discontented servants apparently joined *Bacon's Rebellion* in the 1670's. In the 1680's the planters became newly apprehensive of discontent among the servants "owing to their great necessities and want of clothes," and it was feared that they would *rise up* and *plunder* the storehouses and ships; in 1682 there were plant-cutting *riots* in which servants and laborers, as well as some planters, took part. [Italics added.]

—Richard Hofstadter, *America at 1750*

Using parallel structures

Parallel structures are frequently used within sentences to underscore the similarity of ideas (see 9). They may also be used to bind together a series of sentences expressing similar information. In the following passage describing folk beliefs, anthropologist Margaret Mead presents similar information in parallel grammatical form.

Actually, almost every day, even in the most sophisticated home, something is likely to happen that evokes the memory of some old folk belief. The salt spills. A knife falls to the floor. Your nose tickles. Then perhaps, with a slightly embarrassed smile, the person who spilled the salt tosses a pinch over his left shoulder. Or someone recites the old rhyme, "Knife falls, gentleman calls." Or as you rub your nose you think, That means a letter. I wonder who's writing?

—Margaret Mead, "New Superstitions for Old"

A less skilled writer might have varied the structure, perhaps like this: *The salt gets spilled. Mother drops a knife on the floor. Your nose begins to tickle.* But these sentences are less effective; Mead's parallel structures help tie the passage together.

Maintaining consistency

Coherence suffers whenever a draft shifts confusingly from one point of view to another or from one verb tense to another. (See 13.) In addition, coherence can suffer when new information is introduced with the subject of each sentence. As a rule, a sentence's subject should echo a subject or object in the previous sentence.

The following rough-draft paragraph is needlessly hard to read because so few of the sentences' subjects are tied to earlier subjects or objects. The subjects appear in italics.

> *One* goes about trapping in this manner. At the very outset *one* acquires a "trapping" state of mind. A *library* of books must be read, and preferably *someone* with experience should educate the novice. *Preparing* for the first expedition takes several steps. The *purchase* of traps is first. A *pair* of rubber gloves, waterproof *boots*, and the grubbiest *clothes* capable of withstanding human use come next to outfit the trapper for his adventure. Finally, the *decision* has to be made on just what kind of animals to seek, what sort of bait to use, and where to place the traps.

Although the writer repeats a number of key words, such as *trapping*, the paragraph seems disconnected because new information is introduced with the subject of each sentence.

To improve the paragraph, the writer used the first-person pronoun as the subject of every sentence. The revision is much easier to read.

> *I* went about trapping in this manner. To acquire a "trapping" state of mind, *I* read a library of books and talked at

length with an experienced trapper, my father. Then *I* purchased the traps and outfitted myself by collecting a pair of rubber gloves, waterproof boots, and the grubbiest clothes capable of withstanding human use. Finally, *I* decided just what kinds of animals to seek, what sort of bait to use, and where to place my traps. — John Clyde Thatcher, student

Notice that Thatcher combined some of his original sentences. By doing so, he was able to avoid excessive repetitions of the pronoun *I*. Notice, too, that he varied his sentence openings (most sentences do not begin with *I*) so that readers are not likely to find the repetitions tiresome.

Providing transitions

Transitions are bridges between what has been read and what is about to be read. Transitions help readers move from sentence to sentence; they also alert readers to more global connections of ideas—those between paragraphs or even larger blocks of text.

SENTENCE-LEVEL TRANSITIONS Certain words and phrases signal connections between (or within) sentences. Frequently used transitions are included in the following list.

TO SHOW ADDITION
and, also, besides, further, furthermore, in addition, moreover, next, too, first, second

TO GIVE EXAMPLES
for example, for instance, to illustrate, in fact, specifically

TO COMPARE
also, in the same manner, similarly, likewise

TO CONTRAST
but, however, on the other hand, in contrast, nevertheless, still, even though, on the contrary, yet, although

TO SUMMARIZE OR CONCLUDE
in other words, in short, in summary, in conclusion, to sum up, that is, therefore

TO SHOW TIME
after, as, before, next, during, later, finally, meanwhile, then, when, while, immediately

TO SHOW PLACE OR DIRECTION
above, below, beyond, farther on, nearby, opposite, close, to the left

TO INDICATE LOGICAL RELATIONSHIP
if, so, therefore, consequently, thus, as a result, for this reason, since

Skilled writers use transitional expressions with care, making sure, for example, not to use *consequently* when an *also* would be more precise. They are also careful to select transitions with an appropriate tone, perhaps preferring *so* to *thus* in an informal piece, *in summary* to *in short* for a scholarly essay.

In the following paragraph, taken from an argument that dinosaurs had the " 'right-sized' brains for reptiles of their body size," biologist Stephen Jay Gould uses transitions (italicized) with skill.

I don't wish to deny that the flattened, minuscule head of the large bodied "Stegosaurus" houses little brain from our subjective, top-heavy perspective, *but* I do wish to assert that we should not expect more of the beast. *First of all*, large animals have relatively smaller brains than related, small animals. The correlation of brain size with body size among kindred animals (all reptiles, all mammals, *for example*) is remarkably regular. *As* we move from small to large animals, from mice to elephants *or* small lizards to Komodo dragons, brain size increases, *but* not so fast as body size. *In other words*, bodies grow faster than brains, *and* large animals have low ratios of brain weight to body weight. *In fact*, brains grow only about two-thirds as fast as bodies. *Since* we have no reason to believe that large animals are consistently stupider than their smaller relatives, we must conclude that large animals require relatively less brain to do as well as smaller animals. *If* we do not recognize this relationship, we are likely to underestimate the mental power of very large animals, dinosaurs in particular. [Italics added.]

—Stephen Jay Gould, "Were Dinosaurs Dumb?"

CAUTION: Do not be too self-conscious about plugging in transition words while you are drafting sentences; overuse of these signals can seem heavy-handed. Usually, you will use transitions quite naturally, just where readers need them. If you (or your reviewers) discover places where readers cannot easily move from sentence to sentence in your rough draft, you can always add transition words as you revise.

PARAGRAPH-LEVEL TRANSITIONS Paragraph-level transitions usually link the *first* sentence of a new paragraph with the *first* sentence of the previous paragraph. In other words, the topic sentences signal global connections.

Look for opportunities to allude to the subject of a previous paragraph (as summed up in its topic sentence) in the topic sentence of the next one. In his essay "Little Green Lies," Jonathan H. Alder uses this strategy in the following topic sentences, which appear in a passage describing the benefits of plastic packaging.

Consider septic packaging, the synthetic packaging for the "juice boxes" so many children bring to school with their lunch. [*Rest of paragraph omitted.*]

What is true for juice boxes is also true for other forms of synthetic packaging. [*Rest of paragraph omitted.*]

TRANSITIONS BETWEEN BLOCKS OF TEXT In long essays, you will need to alert readers to connections between blocks of text more than one paragraph long. You can do this by inserting transitional sentences or short paragraphs at key points in the essay. Here, for example, is a transitional paragraph from a student research paper by Karen Shaw. It announces that the first part of her paper has come to a close and the second part is about to begin.

> Although the great apes have demonstrated significant language skills, one central question remains: Can they be taught to use that uniquely human language tool we call grammar, to learn the difference, for instance, between "ape bite human" and "human bite ape"? In other words, can an ape create a sentence?

Another strategy to help readers move from one block of text to another is to insert headings in your essay. Headings, which usually sit above blocks of text, allow you to announce a new topic boldly, without the need for subtle transitions.

4f If necessary, adjust paragraph length.

Most readers feel comfortable reading paragraphs that range between 100 and 200 words. Shorter paragraphs force too much starting and stopping, and longer ones strain the reader's attention span. There are exceptions to this guideline, however. Paragraphs longer than 200 words frequently appear in scholarly writing, where they suggest seriousness and depth. Paragraphs shorter than 100 words occur in newspapers because of narrow columns; in informal essays to quicken the pace; and in business letters, where readers routinely skim for main ideas.

In an essay, the first and last paragraphs will ordinarily be the introduction and conclusion. These special-purpose paragraphs are likely to be shorter than the paragraphs in the body of the essay. Typically, the body paragraphs will follow the essay's outline: one paragraph per point in short essays, a group of paragraphs per point in longer ones. Some ideas require more development than others, however, so it is best to be flexible. If an idea stretches to a length unreasonable for a paragraph, you should divide the paragraph, even if you have presented comparable points in the essay in single paragraphs.

Paragraph breaks are not always made for strictly logical reasons. Writers use them for the following reasons as well.

REASONS FOR BEGINNING A NEW PARAGRAPH

— to mark off the introduction and conclusion

— to signal a shift to a new idea

— to indicate an important shift in time or place

— to emphasize a point (by placing it at the beginning or the end, not in the middle, of a paragraph)

— to highlight a contrast

— to signal a change of speakers (in dialogue)

— to provide readers with a needed pause

— to break up text that looks too dense

Beware of using too many short, choppy paragraphs, however. Readers want to see how your ideas connect, and they become irritated when you break their momentum by forcing them to pause every few sentences. Here are some reasons you might have for combining some of the paragraphs in a rough draft.

REASONS FOR COMBINING PARAGRAPHS

— to clarify the essay's organization

— to connect closely related ideas

— to bind together text that looks too choppy

EXERCISE 4–3

Use Francis Christensen's numerical system (see 4e) to indicate the relations among sentences in the following paragraph.

Once children have learned to read, they go far beyond their textbooks and explore the popular books written just for them. In order to see how these books portray men and women, I decided to visit the St. Peter Public Library. One book I found, *The Very Worst Thing*, tells of the adventures of a little boy on his first day in a new school. He arrives at school wearing the new sweater his mother has knit for him and is greeted by his teacher, Miss Pruce, and his male principal. At recess, the girls jump rope and toss a ball back and forth while the boys choose football teams and establish a tree house club. For show-and-tell that day, Henry, his new friend, brings a snake and some mice; Alice shows her foreign dolls; and Elizabeth demonstrates how to make fudge with Rice Krispies. In another book, *Come Back, Amelia Bedelia*, Amelia is fired from her job of baking for Mrs. Rogers, so she tries to find work as a beautician, a seamstress, a file clerk, and a secretary for a doctor. After trying all of these jobs unsuccessfully, she goes back to Mrs. Rogers and gets back her old job by making cream puffs. The rest of the books I looked at contained similar sex-role stereotypes—boys wear jeans and T-shirts, set up lemonade stands, and play broomball, while girls wear dresses, play dress-up, and jump rope. Men are businessmen, soldiers, veterinarians, and truck drivers. Women are housewives, teachers, and witches who make love potions for girls wanting husbands.

—Patricia Klein, student

EXERCISE 4–4

If you were to divide the paragraph in Exercise 4–3 into two paragraphs, at what point would you make the break? Why?

EXERCISE 4–5

Looking again at the paragraph in Exercise 4–3, find examples of the following techniques for gaining coherence: repetition of key words, parallel structures, and transitions.

5

Choose an appropriate document design.

The term *document* is broad enough to describe anything you might write in an English class, in other classes across the curriculum, in the business world, and in everyday life. How you design a document (format it on the page) can affect how it is received.

Instructors have certain expectations about how a college paper should look (see 5b). Employers too expect documents such as business letters and memos to be formatted in standard ways (see 5c). Even peers who read your e-mail and World Wide Web pages will appreciate an effective document design (see 5d and 5e).

5a Become familiar with the principles of document design.

Well-designed documents — such as memos, résumés, manuals, and reports — have always been important in the business world, where writers must compete for the attention of readers. By using lists, headings, and a variety of visual cues, business and technical writers make documents accessible to all segments of an audience: readers who want a quick overview, those who are scanning for specific information, those who need in-depth coverage of a topic, and so on.

Document design is becoming increasingly important in

the academic world as well. The information explosion has placed unprecedented demands on instructors' and students' time, so professional articles and student essays must be as accessible as possible. Fortunately, today's computers and printers provide academic writers with design tools that were once prohibitively expensive. With access to software, a student can enhance an essay with boldface headings, formally displayed lists, and even graphs, charts, and other visuals.

Good document design promotes readability, but what this means depends on your purpose and audience and perhaps on other elements of your writing situation, such as your subject and any length restrictions. (See the checklist on pp. 14–15.) All of your design choices—word processing options and use of headings, displayed lists, and other visuals—should be made in light of your specific writing situation.

Format options

Most typewriters and word processing programs present you with several format options. Before you begin typing, you should make sure that your margins, line spacing, and justification are set appropriately. If a number of fonts (typeface styles and sizes) are available, you should also determine which is most appropriate for your purposes.

MARGINS, LINE SPACING, AND JUSTIFICATION   For documents written on 8½" × 11" paper, you should leave a margin of between one and one and a half inches on all sides of the page. These margins prevent the text from looking too crowded, and they allow room for annotations, such as an instructor's comments or an editor's suggestions.

Most manuscripts-in-progress are double-spaced to allow room for editing. Final copy is often double-spaced as well, since single-spacing is less inviting to read. But at times the advantages of double-spacing are offset by other considerations. In a business memo, for example, you may single-space to fit the memo on one easily scanned page. And in a technical report, you might single-space to save paper, for both ecological and financial reasons.

Word processing programs usually give you a choice between a justified and an unjustified (ragged) right margin. When the text is justified, all of the words line up against the right margin, as they do on a typeset page like the one you are now reading. Unfortunately, text that has been justified on a computer can be hard to read. The problem is that extra space is added between words in some lines, creating "rivers" of white that can be quite distracting. In addition, right-justified margins may create a need for excessive hyphenation at the ends of lines. Unless you have the technology to create the real look of a typeset page, you should turn off the justification feature.

FONTS If you have a choice of fonts, you should select a normal size (10 to 12 points) and a style that is not too off-beat. Although unusual styles of type, such as those that look handwritten, may seem attractive, they slow readers down. We all read more efficiently when a text meets our usual expectations.

CAUTION: Never write or type a college essay or any other document in all capital letters. Research shows that readers experience much frustration when they are forced to read more than a few words in a row printed in all capital letters.

Headings

There is little need for headings in short essays, especially if the writer uses paragraphing and clear topic sentences to guide readers. In more complex documents, however, such as research papers, grant proposals, business reports, and even Web-based documents, headings can be a useful visual cue for readers.

Headings help readers see at a glance the organization of a document. If more than one level of heading is used, the headings also indicate the hierarchy of ideas — as they do throughout this book.

Headings serve a number of functions, depending on the needs of different readers. When readers are simply looking up information, headings will help them find it quickly. When readers are scanning, hoping to pick up the gist of things, headings will guide them. Even when readers are committed enough to read every word, headings can help. Efficient readers preview a document before they begin reading; when previewing and while reading, they are guided by any visual cues the writer provides.

CAUTION: Avoid using more headings (or more levels of headings) than you really need. Excessive use of headings can make a text choppy.

PHRASING HEADINGS Headings should be as brief and as informative as possible. Certain styles of headings — the most common being *-ing* phrases, noun phrases, questions, and imperative sentences — work better for some purposes, audiences, and subjects than others.

Whatever style you choose, use it consistently for headings on the same level. In other words, headings on the same level of organization should be written in parallel structure (see 9), as in the following examples. The first set of headings appeared in a report written for an environmental think tank, the second in a history textbook, the third in a mutual fund brochure, and the fourth in a garden designer's newsletter.

-ING HEADINGS
Safeguarding the earth's atmosphere

Charting the path to sustainable energy

Conserving global forests

Triggering the technological revolution

Strengthening international institutions

NOUN PHRASE HEADINGS
The economics of slavery

The sociology of slavery

Psychological effects of slavery

QUESTIONS AS HEADINGS
How do I buy shares?

How do I redeem shares?

What is the history of the fund's performance?

What are the tax consequences of investing in the fund?

IMPERATIVE SENTENCES AS HEADINGS
Fertilize roses in the fall.

Feed them again in the spring.

Prune roses when dormant and after flowering.

Spray roses during their growing season.

PLACING AND HIGHLIGHTING HEADINGS Headings on the same level of organization should be positioned and highlighted in a consistent way. For example, you might center your first-level headings and print them in boldface; then you might place the second-level headings flush left (against the left margin) and underline them, like this:

First-level heading

Second-level heading

Headings are usually centered or placed flush left, but at times you might decide to indent them a half inch or five spaces from the left margin, like a paragraph indent. Or in a business document, you might place headings in a column to the left of the text.

To highlight headings, consider using boldface, italics or underlining, all capital letters, color, larger or smaller typeface than the text, a different font, or some combination of these:

 *The writing process*

boldface	color
italics	larger typeface
<u>underlining</u>	smaller typeface
ALL CAPITAL LETTERS	different font

On the whole, it is best to use restraint. Excessive highlighting results in a page that looks too busy, and it defeats its own purpose, since readers have trouble sorting out which headings are more important than others.

Important headings can be highlighted by using a fair amount of white space around them. Less important headings can be downplayed by using less white space or even by running them into the text (as with the small all-capitals heading on p. 115).

Displayed lists

Lists are easy to read or scan when they are displayed rather than run into your text. You might reasonably choose to display the following kinds of lists:

— steps in a process
— materials needed for a project
— parts of an object
— advice or recommendations
— items to be discussed
— criteria for evaluation (as in checklists)

Displayed lists should usually be introduced with an independent clause followed by a colon (see 35a and the preceding list). Periods are not used after items in a list unless the items are sentences.

Lists are most readable when they are presented in parallel grammatical form (see 9). In the sample list, for instance, the items are all noun phrases. As with headings, some kinds of lists might be more appropriately presented as *-ing* phrases, as imperative sentences, or as questions.

To draw the reader's eye to a list, consider using bullets (circles or squares) or dashes if there is no need to number the items. If there is some reason to number the items, use an arabic number followed by a period for each item.

Although displayed lists can be a useful visual cue, they should not be overdone. Too many of them will give a document a choppy, cluttered look. And lists that are very long (sometimes called "laundry lists") should be avoided as well. Readers can hold only so many ideas in their short-term memory, so if a list grows too long, you should find some way of making it more concise or clustering similar items.

Visuals

Visuals such as charts, graphs, tables, diagrams, maps, and photographs convey information concisely and vividly. In a student essay not intended for publication, you can use another person's visuals as long as you credit the borrowing (see 50). And with access to computer graphics, you can create your own visuals to enhance an essay, a report, or an electronic document.

This section suggests when charts, graphs, tables, and diagrams might be appropriate for your purposes. It also discusses where you might place such visuals.

USING CHARTS, GRAPHS, TABLES, AND DIAGRAMS In documents that help readers follow a process or make a decision, flow charts can be useful; for an example, see page 295 of this book. Pie charts are appropriate for indicating ratios or apportionment, as in the following example.

The writing process

PIE CHART

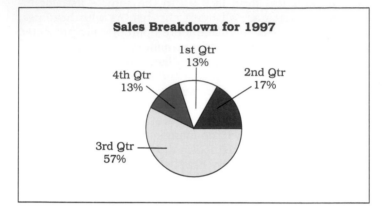

LINE GRAPH

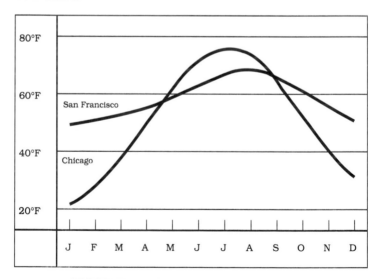

**MONTHLY MEAN TEMPERATURE IN
SAN FRANCISCO AND CHICAGO**

BAR GRAPH

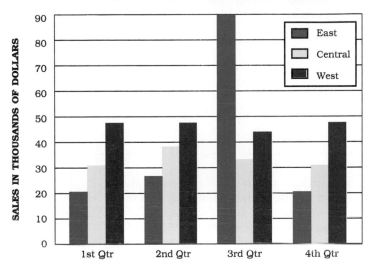

SALES BREAKDOWN BY REGION, **1997**

Line graphs and bar graphs illustrate disparities in numerical data. Line graphs are appropriate when you want to illuminate trends over a period of time, such as trends in sales, in unemployment, or in population growth. Bar graphs can be used for the same purpose. In addition, bar graphs are useful for highlighting comparisons, such as vote totals for rival political candidates or the number of refugees entering the United States during different time periods.

Tables are not as visually interesting as line graphs or charts, but they allow for inclusion of specific numerical data, such as exact percentages. The following table presents the responses of students and faculty to one question on a campus-wide questionnaire.

The writing process

TABLE

Is American education based too much on European history and values?

	PERCENT		
	NO	UNDECIDED	YES
Nonwhite students	21	25	54
White students	55	29	16
Nonwhite faculty	15	20	65
White faculty	57	27	16

Diagrams are useful—and sometimes indispensable—in scientific and technical writing. It is more concise, for example, to use the following diagram than to explain the chemical formula in words.

PLACING VISUALS A visual may be placed in the text of a document, near a discussion to which it relates, or it can be put in an appendix, labeled, and referred to in the text.

Placing visuals in the text of a document can be tricky. Usually you will want the visual to appear close to the sen-

DIAGRAM

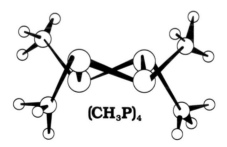

$(CH_3P)_4$

tences that relate to it, but page breaks won't always allow this placement. At times you may need to insert the visual at a later point and tell readers where it can be found or, with the help of software, you may be able to make the text flow around the visual.

In newsletters and in business and technical documents, page layout is both an art and a science. The best way to learn how to lay out pages is to work with colleagues who have had experience solving the many problems that can arise.

5b For academic essays, use standard manuscript formats.

If your instructor provides formal guidelines for formatting an essay — or a more specialized document such as a lab report, a case study, or a research paper — you should of course follow them. Otherwise, use the manuscript format that is standard for the discipline in which you are writing.

In most English and humanities classes, you will be asked to use the MLA (Modern Language Association) format. The sample papers on pages 616–26 and 627–40 illustrate this format. For more detailed advice about MLA manuscript guidelines, see 54a. If you have been asked to use APA (American Psychological Association) or *Chicago*-style manuscript guidelines, see 56a–56f.

MLA ESSAY FORMAT

Double-
spacing
throughout

⬆ 1"

⬇ ½"

Weitzel 1

Tom Weitzel

Dr. Fry

English 101

16 April 1997

Title,
centered

Who Goes to the Races?

½"
indent ⟷ A favorite pastime of mine is observing people, and

my favorite place to observe is at the horse races. After

many encounters with the racing crowd, I have discovered

that there are four distinct groups at the track: the

once-a-year bunch, the professionals, the clubhouse set,

and the unemployed.

The largest group at the track consists of those who

show up once a year. They know little about horses or betting

and rely strictly on racetrack gimmick sheets and newspaper

1" ⟷ predictions for selecting possible winners. If that strategy ⟷ 1"

doesn't work, they use intuition, lucky numbers, favorite

colors, or appealing names. They bet larger amounts as the

day goes along, gambling on every race, including long-shot

bets on exactas and daily doubles. The vast majority go home

broke and frustrated.

More subtle and quiet are the professionals. They fol-

low the horses from track to track and live in campers and

motor homes. Many are married couples, some are retired, and

all are easily spotted with their lunch sacks, water jugs,

and binoculars. Since most know one another, they section

themselves off in a particular area of the stadium. All rely

⬆ 1"

MLA ESSAY FORMAT *(continued)*

½"

1"

Weitzel 2

on the racing form and on personal knowledge of each horse, jockey, and track in making the proper bet. They bet only on the smart races, rarely on the favorites. Never do they bet on exactas or daily doubles. More often than not they either break even or go home winners.

Isolated from the others is the clubhouse set. Found either at the cocktail lounge or in the restaurant, usually involved in business transactions, these racing fans rarely see a race in person and do their betting via the waiter. It's difficult to tell whether they go home sad, happy, or in between. They keep their emotions to themselves.

The most interesting members of the racetrack population are the unemployed. They will be found not in the clubhouse, but right down at the rail next to the finish line. Here one can discover the real emotion of the race-track--the screaming, the cursing, and the pushing. The unemployed are not in it for the sport. Betting is not a game for them, but a battle for survival. If they lose, they must borrow enough money to carry them until the next check comes in, and then, of course, they head right back to the track. This particular group arrives at the track beaten and leaves beaten.

I have probably lost more money than I have won at the track, but observing these four interesting groups of people makes it all worthwhile.

1"   1"

5c For business documents, use standard business formats.

This section provides guidelines for preparing business letters, résumés, and memos. For a more detailed discussion of these and other business documents—proposals, reports, executive summaries, and so on—consult a business writing textbook or take a look at examples currently being written at the organization for which you are writing.

Business letters

In writing a business letter, be direct, clear, and courteous, but do not hesitate to be firm if necessary. State your purpose or request at the beginning of the letter and include only pertinent information in the body. By being as direct and concise as possible, you show that you value your reader's time.

A sample business letter appears on page 123. This letter is typed in what is known as "block" style. The return address at the top and the close and signature at the bottom are lined up just to the right of the center of the width of the page. The inside address, the salutation, and the body of the letter are flush left (against the left margin). The paragraphs are not indented.

If you choose to indent your paragraphs, you are using "semiblock" style, which is considered less formal. If you choose to move all elements of the letter flush left, you are using the most formal style, "full block." This style is usually preferred when the letter is typed on letterhead stationery that gives the return address of the writer or the writer's company.

When writing to a woman, use the abbreviation *Ms.* in the salutation unless you know that the woman prefers another form of address. If you are not writing to a particular

BUSINESS LETTER IN BLOCK FORM

Return address —— 121 Knox Road, #6
College Park, MD 20740
March 4, 1997

Linda Hennessee, Managing Editor
World Discovery
1650 K Street, NW
Washington, DC 20036

—— Inside address

Dear Ms. Hennessee: ——— Salutation

Please accept my application for the summer editorial internship listed with
the Career Development Center at the University of Maryland. Currently I
am a junior at the University of Maryland, with a double major in English
and Latin American studies.

Over the past three years I have gained considerable experience in newspaper and magazine journalism, as you will see on my enclosed résumé. I am
familiar with the basic procedures of editing and photographic development, but my primary interests lie in feature writing and landscape photography. My professional goal is to work as a photojournalist with an international focus, preferably for a major magazine. I cannot imagine a better introduction to that career than a summer at *World Discovery*.

—— Body

I am available for an interview almost any time and can be reached at
301-555-2651. My e-mail address is jrichard@umdcp.edu.

I look forward to hearing from you.

Close ——— Sincerely,

Signature —— *Jeffrey Richardson*

Jeffrey Richardson

Enc.

person, you can use the salutation *Dear Sir or Madam* or you can address the company itself—*Dear Solar Technology.*

Below the signature, flush left, you may include the abbreviation *Enc.* to indicate that something is enclosed with the letter or the abbreviation *cc* followed by a colon and the name of someone who is receiving a copy of the letter.

Résumés

An effective résumé gives relevant information in a clear and concise form. The trick is to present yourself in the best possible light without going on at length and wasting your reader's time.

A sample résumé appears on page 125. Notice that the writer has used bullets to make his résumé easy to scan. Notice too that he presents his work experience in reverse chronological order—to highlight his most recent accomplishments.

When you send out your résumé, you should include a letter that tells what position you seek and where you learned about it (see p. 123). The letter should also summarize your education and past experience, relating them to the job you are applying for. End the letter with a suggestion for a meeting, and tell your prospective employer when you will be available.

Memos

Business memos (short for *memorandums*) are a form of communication used within a company or organization. Usually brief and to the point, a memo reports information, makes a request, or recommends an action. The format of a memo, which varies from company to company, is designed for easy distribution, quick reading, and efficient filing.

Most memos display the date, the name of the recipient, the name of the sender, and the subject on separate lines at the top of the page. Many companies have preprinted forms for memos, and some word processing programs allow you

RÉSUMÉ

Jeffrey Richardson

121 Knox Road, #6
College Park, MD 20740
301–555–2651

OBJECTIVE   To obtain an editorial internship with a magazine

EDUCATION

Fall 1994–   University of Maryland
present   • B.A. expected in June 1998
                      • Double major: English and Latin American studies
                      • GPA: 3.7 (on a 4-point scale)

EXPERIENCE

Fall 1995–   Photo editor, *The Diamondback*, college paper
present   • Shoot and print photographs
                      • Select and lay out photographs and other visuals

Summer   Intern, *The Globe,* Fairfax, Virginia
1996   • Wrote stories about local issues and personalities
                      • Interviewed political candidates
                      • Edited and proofread copy
                      • Contributed photographs
                      • Coedited "The Landscapes of Northern Virginia:
                        A Photoessay"

Summers   Tutor, Fairfax County ESL Program
1994   • Tutored Latino students in English as a Second Language
1995   • Trained new tutors

ACTIVITIES   Photographers' Workshop, Spanish Club

REFERENCES   Available upon request

BUSINESS MEMO

Commonwealth Press

MEMORANDUM

February 28, 1997

To: Production, promotion, and editorial assistants

cc: Stephen Chapman

From: Helen Brown

Subject: New computers for staff

We will receive the new personal computers next week for the assistants in production, promotion, and editorial. In preparation, I would like you to take part in a training program and to rearrange your work areas to accommodate the new equipment.

Training Program

A computer consultant will teach in-house workshops on how to use our spreadsheet program. If you have already tried the program, be prepared to discuss any problems you have encountered.

Workshops for our three departments will be held in the training room at the following times:

- Production: Monday, March 10, 10:00 a.m. to 2:00 p.m.
- Promotion: Wednesday, March 12, 10:00 a.m. to 2:00 p.m.
- Editorial: Friday, March 14, 10:00 a.m. to 2:00 p.m.

Lunch will be provided in the cafeteria. If you cannot attend, please let me know by March 3.

Allocation and Setup

To give everyone access to a computer, we will set up the new computers as follows: two in the assistants' workspace in production; two in the area outside the conference room for the promotion assistants; and two in the library for the editorial assistants.

Assistants in all three departments should see me before the end of the week to discuss preparation of the spaces for the new equipment.

to call up a memo template that prints standard memo lines — "To," "cc" (for others receiving a copy of the memo), "From," and "Subject" — at the top of the page.

Because readers of the memos are busy people, you cannot assume that they will read your memo word for word. Therefore the subject line should describe the subject as clearly and concisely as possible, and the introductory paragraph should get right to the point. In addition, the body of the memo should be well organized and easy to scan. To promote scanning, use headings where possible and display any items that deserve special attention by setting them off from the text. A sample memo with headings and a displayed list appears on page 126.

5d Follow the conventions of e-mail.

Communicating by electronic mail (or e-mail) has many benefits. Unlike conventional "snail" mail messages, e-mail messages are sent and received immediately after they are written — to and from anywhere in the world at any time. And although e-mail can be as quick as a telephone call, it provides a bit more time than conversation allows for framing ideas and thoughtful responses. As with all writing, you should keep your audience and purpose clearly in mind as you draft e-mail. But you should also be aware of the special conventions of this fast-paced form of communication.

Keeping messages brief and direct

Because the purpose of e-mail is to relay and receive information quickly, it is a courtesy to keep each message as brief as possible and to state your point early. Your message may be just one of many that your reader has to wade through. Always fill in the subject line with a clear, concise description of what your message is about (*Dec. 4 meeting agenda* is clearer than *Miscellaneous notes*). If you are making a request or a recommendation, state it right away, if possible in the first few sentences (*Can you get your report to me by Monday?* or *I think we need two committees to study the impact of the proposed building*). For long, detailed messages that may fill more than two computer screens, consider providing a summary at the beginning, such as the following:

> The study on improving the work environment at DeVincent Company includes three key recommendations: (1) acquire additional space for the growing customer service division, (2) improve lighting and reduce background noise in cubicle areas, and (3) add another break room for the third and fourth floors.

Maintaining an appropriate tone

It is appropriate for e-mail to be more informal than other types of writing; you may even alienate your reader if you are too formal. In general, maintain a tone that is friendly and conversational, yet respectful. The first-person (*I*) and second-person (*you*) points of view are standard in e-mail, and contractions are usually acceptable.

Though you should always try to keep messages as brief as possible, you can avoid a blunt tone by including an appropriate greeting and closing. You may also want to open with a brief personal note or include a bit of humor when communicating with friends and colleagues.

TOO FORMAL AND BLUNT

Now that the regional conference has concluded, it is my responsibility to assemble the agenda for the 1997 planning meeting. In order to do so in a timely fashion, I need your ideas about issues to cover in the meeting by October 25.

Expressions like *it is my responsibility* and *in order to do so in a timely fashion* make this message sound formal and stilted, and the lack of a greeting and closing give it a cold, blunt tone.

REVISED

Dear Carolyn,

I enjoyed seeing you and the other members of the steering committee at the regional conference. Now that I'm back in the office, I need to start putting together the agenda for our 1997 planning meeting. If you have any preliminary thoughts about issues to cover, could you please e-mail them to me by October 25? Thanks, Carolyn. I look forward to hearing from you.

Best,
Ada

As with all forms of writing, your tone in e-mail should suit your subject and audience. In business and academic contexts or in writing to someone you don't know well, you will probably want to use a more formal tone than you would when, say, making social plans with friends. Regardless of your subject and audience, you should always avoid harsh or flippant language in e-mail.

NOTE: Some e-mailers use emoticons (combinations of symbols that look like faces turned sideways) and acronyms (such as *TIA* for "thanks in advance"). Though you may be tempted to use these shortcuts, it is usually better to convey your tone and meaning through words, especially in business and academic contexts. Readers who are unfamiliar with emoticons and e-mail abbreviations may be confused by them, and even readers who understand these shortcuts may be annoyed by them.

Designing e-mail

Consider using the following elements to design e-mail messages that are easy to scan and easy to digest. See the sample e-mail message on page 132 for an example of good design.

SHORT PARAGRAPHS In academic writing, short paragraphs often indicate inadequate development. In e-mail messages, however, short paragraphs make it easier for readers to see divisions among key ideas within the limits of a computer screen. As in other forms of writing, each paragraph in an e-mail message should be built around a main point. Indicate a new paragraph with a hard return and a tab indent or with a line of space.

HEADINGS In brief e-mail messages of a paragraph or two, headings probably aren't necessary. But in longer messages containing categories of information, headings can break up blocks of text and help readers scan for items of special interest.

Because many e-mail programs cannot produce boldface, underlining, or italics, set off each heading on a line by itself with a line of space above it. Word all the headings in parallel form (see "Phrasing Headings," p. 112).

DISPLAYED LISTS For an e-mail message that includes a list or steps in a procedure, consider displaying the information with asterisks, dashes, or numbers. (See the sample e-mail message on p. 132.)

SIMPLE FORMATTING Word processing software allows writers to use an endless variety of fonts and type styles in documents. The type options in e-mail programs, however, are usually more limited. You can't be sure that your recipient's e-mail system will be able to reproduce special formatting even if you can include it. It is best, therefore, to keep formatting simple, relying on white space, indentations, and simple lists to design your messages.

CAUTION: Avoid the temptation to use all capital letters to highlight whole sentences or paragraphs. All-capital text is so difficult to read, especially in long stretches, that among e-mailers it is known as "shouting."

Following e-mail etiquette

E-mail, like other forms of communication, has its own etiquette, which varies slightly depending on your purpose and audience. Essentially, when writing and responding to others, you should take care to be prompt, clear, and courteous. Here are some principles to keep in mind:

— Check your e-mail frequently and respond to messages promptly.

— Fill in subject lines to help readers sort through their messages and set priorities.

— Include a brief greeting (such as *Hi, Gloria* or *Dear Professor Hartley*) and a brief closing (such as *Bye for now* or *Sincerely*).

— Avoid writing in all capital letters or all lowercase letters.

— Resist "flaming"— spouting off angry or insulting messages.

— Forward messages from others only when you are certain the original sender would approve.

— Restrict your use of copyrighted materials to short passages, and always name the author, title, and publication source.

Revising e-mail

Although standards for revision are not as high for fast-paced e-mail as for other forms of written communication, resist the temptation to send off a message without reading it first. Check to make sure that your tone is tactful, that your main point is clear and concise, and that your message is free of errors in grammar, punctuation, spelling, and mechanics.

E-MAIL MESSAGE

```
Return-Path:  <dportes@umass-boston.edu>
Date:         Fri, 22 Nov 1996 22:31:45-0500
To:           rdayson@newhoriz.org
From:         Danielle Portes <dportes@umass-boston.edu>
Subject:      Telephone interview on Dec. 4
cc:           Helen Tran <htran@umass-boston.edu>
```

Dear Ms. Dayson:

Thank you for taking the time to speak with me last week about my research project. As we agreed, I am sending some questions for you to consider before our phone interview on December 4 at 2 p.m.

QUESTIONS ABOUT GUESTS

--What symptoms of stress do guests--both women and their children--show when they first arrive at the shelter?

--What problems, in addition to the abuse itself, must guests deal with (for example, lack of support from family or friends, financial concerns, problems in dealing with police and courts)?

--Can you think of any past or current guests who might agree to an interview?

QUESTIONS ABOUT STAFFERS

--What are the main stresses that staffers face? How do they cope with these stresses?

--What do staffers see as the rewards as well as the drawbacks of the job?

--On average, how many guests does each staffer work with every day? every week?

--Can you think of any past or current staffers who might agree to an interview?

I appreciate your considering these questions and look forward to our interview.

Sincerely,
Danielle Portes
Phone: 617-555-7777

5e Creating effective Web sites.

At some point you may be asked to create a World Wide Web site as part of a school or work assignment, or you may decide to build one for your personal use. Although this book can't begin to explain all the technical aspects of creating a Web site, included here are design and organizational hints to help you make the most of this new medium. For more detailed information on creating a Web site, see *Style Guide for Online Hypertext* (http://www.w3.org/pub/WWW/Provider /Style), written by Web founder Tim Berners-Lee.

Organizing information

If you have browsed the World Wide Web, you may have noticed that the most effective sites are the simplest ones — those that give you quick and easy access to what you're looking for. The overall organization of a Web site can be found on its home page, which welcomes visitors, introduces them to the site, and gives them an overview of its contents (see the sample on p. 135).

From the home page, visitors navigate via "links," words or visual images that, at the click of the mouse, send them to other pages within the site or to other locations on the Web. In a typical Web site, the home page contains the most general information, and internal pages are more specific.

Before creating a Web site, make an outline of the hierarchy of the information you will present: a home page linked to internal pages, which can in turn be linked to other pages in your site or on the Web. As is true in print documents, important items, such as a company name, should receive more prominence than items of lesser importance, such as a copyright date. To help you weigh the relative importance of material, think about what your readers will most likely be looking for. Why are they visiting your site in the first place? What are they expecting to find?

Breaking up text

Because the Internet is so vast, online surfers move quickly from page to page. Visitors to your page won't have the patience to scroll through long passages of text. To keep your readers' attention, present your material as concisely as possible, and break up text with headings and displayed lists (see pp. 111–15). And, where appropriate, highlight information with visuals such as clip art, photos, or even animation.

Linking to other sites

One of the most useful features of World Wide Web documents is the ability to create links to other Internet locations. You will probably decide to add some links to other sites from your Web page, but use care when doing so. Especially when creating academic or professional Web sites, keep in mind that any links you include should be relevant to your subject.

A link to another site is an implicit endorsement of that site, so you should evaluate potential sites before linking to them. As a courtesy to readers, periodically visit the sites you have links to; remove any links to sites that are outdated or nonfunctioning, and reroute links to sites that have moved.

Testing your site

When you create a Web site, you are publishing a document that represents you or your organization. Therefore, before you upload your new site to the Web, you should be certain that all your links are working and that all your text has been properly coded.

As you would in a print document, you should use a clear and grammatical writing style, carefully proofread your text, and give proper credit to any material you may have borrowed from other sources.

SAMPLE WEB PAGE

PART II

Critical Thinking

Critical thinking

Most college assignments, especially those based on reading, call for critical thinking: an open-minded, reasoned analysis of a political, scholarly, or literary issue. At times you will be asked to write a documented, researched essay in which you draw conclusions about a variety of sources arguing different points of view (see 46–54). Or you may be asked to analyze a literary work, such as a short story or a poem (see 55).

Many assignments, however, ask you to respond critically to just one or two essays (see 6) or to construct your own argument, which may or may not be based on written sources (see 7).

6

Writing about texts: Enter into a conversation with authors.

Like critical thinking, critical reading is active, not passive. To develop the habit of critical reading, imagine yourself entering into a conversation with the authors who are making a claim on your attention.

6a Acquaint yourself with an author.

For a book, the dust jacket and preface can serve as your introduction to the author. For an article in a magazine or newspaper, look for a brief description of the author, which often appears at the end of the article. If you are reading a selection in an anthology, look for a headnote describing the author's credentials and reputation.

You can further your acquaintance with an author by trying to understand his or her writing situation. Look for any clues about the social and historical context in which the piece was written. Most readings will provide you with answers to at least some of the following questions:

—Is the writer contributing to a larger conversation? In other words, is there a body of literature on the subject that he or she is responding to? If so, who are the key players?

—Does the author have a stake in the matter, some personal or political agenda? What values does the author hold dear?

—What are the conventions of the type of book, magazine, newspaper, or scholarly journal for which the author is writing?

—Was the author working within length restrictions that have affected his or her coverage of the issue?

—What audience does the author appear to be addressing?

—What purpose does the author hope to accomplish?

Of course, the best way to get to know an author is by reading. Authors reveal themselves on the page in many ways: through their tone, their assumptions (whether stated or hidden), their handling of evidence, and their tactics. They even reveal themselves by what they choose not to say.

CAUTION: As you get to know an author, keep an open mind. Do not let your personal beliefs prevent you from listening to new ideas or opposing viewpoints. And do not allow yourself to be prejudiced either for or against an author just because he or she belongs to an organization, such as the National Rifle Association or Planned Parenthood, that suggests possible bias. The author's arguments may or may not be reasonable. Listen first, assess the arguments, and then decide what you think.

6b Read actively, with a pencil in hand.

Although you may be fond of highlighters, a pencil promotes active reading in ways that a highlighter cannot. With a highlighter, you just identify key sentences, usually on a first reading; on a second reading, you are often tempted to read only what's highlighted. More important, you can't write down your thoughts, questions, and reactions with a highlighter.

A pencil offers greater flexiblity. You can underline key sentences or you can draw an asterisk or other symbol in the margin to mark them. And you can scribble your insights all over the pages—not just on a first reading, but on rereadings as well. Finally, if you change your mind while rereading, you can erase your early comments and replace them with new insights.

Beginning the conversation: Understanding the text

Let's assume that you have been asked to read two articles on the issue of legalizing drugs: "Drug Policy and the Intellectuals" by William J. Bennett and "Our Current Drug Legislation: Grounds for Reconsideration" by Michael Tooley. Your assignment is to write a summary of one article and then to write a critical analysis (not necessarily negative criticism) of the other.

The articles appear in an anthology with brief headnotes that help you place the readings in context. The headnote for the Bennett article mentions that Bennett was born in 1943, has a law degree from Harvard, and served both as secretary of education and as "drug czar" (director of the Office of National Drug Control Policy). The headnote also tells you that the article was originally a speech; it was delivered at Harvard in 1989 while Bennett was serving as drug czar. Michael Tooley, you learn from the other headnote, is a philosophy professor at the University of Colorado. His essay originally appeared in a 1994 newsletter put out by the University of Colorado's Center for Values and Social Policy.

Tooley's title, "Our Current Drug Legislation: Grounds for Reconsideration," makes you suspect that Tooley is in favor of legalizing drugs. Bennett's title, "Drug Policy and the Intellectuals," is less informative, but you have no doubt that Bennett opposes legalizing drugs. Also, you suspect that he has contempt for the intellectuals mentioned in his title. His contemptuous use of the term *intellectuals* is bold, you might think, considering Bennett's audience at Harvard. Most speakers don't begin by insulting their audience, so you are curious to see what Bennett is up to.

Here is the first paragraph of Bennett's "Drug Policy and the Intellectuals," with a few comments penciled in the margins:

> The issue I want to address is our national drug policy and the intellectuals. Unfortunately, the issue is a little one-sided. There is a very great deal to say about our national drug policy, but much less to say about the intellectuals — except that by and large, they're against it. Why they should be against it is an interesting question, perhaps more a social-psychological question than a properly intellectual one. But whatever the reasons, I'm sorry to say that on properly intellectual grounds the arguments mustered against our current drug policy by America's intellectuals make for very thin gruel indeed.

ho does he ean exactly?

's tone ems sort arrogant.

Thesis?

Why this metaphor?

Bennett's speech is quite long, seven dense book pages when printed, and because it is a speech there are no headings to help you follow the structure. After reading the opening paragraph, though, you know what you'll be looking for: Bennett's attacks on the arguments that intellectuals are making against the government's current drug policy.

As you begin reading, you notice that the speech is somewhat rambling, with many twists and turns and asides. You realize that uncovering the real structure of Bennett's speech is going to take some work. At this point, you might pull out your laptop computer and attempt to bring order to what you have read. Your first notes could be quite simple, something like this:

— long introduction: focuses mainly on the intellectuals, both liberal and conservative, who advocate legalizing drugs; contrasts them with intellectuals in the medical and scientific communities, who are trying to solve the drug problem

— body of speech: provides counterarguments to each of the claims made by proponents of legalizing drugs

— conclusion: calls upon intellectuals to help solve the drug problem

With this overview in mind, you might attempt to outline the body of the speech. Usually, you would begin by listing the speaker's key points, but Bennett organizes the body of his speech around the claims made by his opponents. A good way to start, then, is by listing the claims Bennett *disagrees* with. Turning again to your laptop, you might decide to put these claims as simply as possible, in your own words, like this:

— Legalization would eliminate the dealers' profit motive.

— The drug problem can be easily solved by legalizing drugs.

— Drug use would not go up if drugs were legalized.

— It costs too much to enforce drug laws.

— Legalization would reduce the crime rate.

— Drug users hurt only themselves.

— Drug laws restrict our liberty.

— Drug enforcement doesn't work.

With a list of these claims in front of you, you would begin looking for Bennett's counterarguments. You might insert these beneath each of the claims listed on your computer screen, again using your own words. Here, for example, is what you could type under one of them:

—It costs too much to enforce drug laws.

> The cost of legalizing drugs would be much higher: Think of drug-related accidents, lost productivity, hospital emergency admissions, school dropouts, premature babies, and the high costs of treatment.

With a list of Bennett's key counterarguments, you are well on your way to understanding them. And as you begin assessing those counterarguments, your understanding will deepen.

Talking back: Questioning the text

Let's assume that you have read both Bennett's and Tooley's articles and you understand each author's central claim and key arguments. Even as you were reading to understand, you were beginning to question the text. But now, as you reread, you are ready to react more strongly: questioning each author's assumptions, evidence, and tactics. You begin by jotting comments in the margins of the text (or a photocopy of the text). Here, for example, are comments you might make in the margins of two paragraphs from Tooley's article. These are the first and the last paragraphs of a four-paragraph introduction.

t the
bject
s been
scussed.

Why is the American policy debate not focused more intensely on the relative merits or demerits of our current approach to drugs and of possible alternatives to it? The lack of discussion of this issue is rather striking, given that America has the most serious drug problem in the world, that alternatives to a prohibitionist approach are under serious consideration in other countries, and that the grounds for reconsidering our current approach are, I shall argue, so weighty. . . .

I guess he's for legalizing drugs. Why doesn't he say so?

True? How is he defining "drug problem"?

I want to turn in detail to perhaps the two most important reasons for reconsidering our current drug policy: first, the difficulty of providing any adequate justification for the restrictions that prohibitive laws place on people's liberty; and second, the enormous social and personal costs associated with a <u>prohibitionist</u> approach.

Biased language?

This first reason seem off the point Is it really worth half o our attentio

Aren't there important aspects of the subject that he's ignoring?

Once you have marked up the text with your questions and comments, you might turn to your laptop again to type in Tooley's claims (as you understand them) together with your rough notes that question his assumptions, evidence, and tactics:

—Prohibition doesn't work.

One short paragraph backs up this claim—says that we ban heroin yet have the worst problem in the world (is this true?) and that prohibition of alcohol didn't work (is this a fair analogy?).

—There is no reason for making a distinction between drugs that are currently illegal (like marijuana, heroin, and LSD) and those that are legal (alcohol and nicotine).

Only one paragraph—no real evidence here, just a rhetorical tactic. Asks us to imagine we were on a desert island with an unlimited supply of tobacco and opium. Then asks us which one we'd want our kids addicted to. (But we aren't on a desert island—we live in a complex world in which people need to work, among other things. Can opium, i.e., heroin, addicts hold down jobs?)

— A law is justified only if it prevents someone from harming others.

> A long philosophical discussion based on the unproved assumption that people using drugs legally wouldn't be harming anyone else (but what about PCP, which makes people violent, or crack cocaine, which makes mothers irresponsible?). Am I right that if using drugs does harm others this long philosophical defense of libertarianism is irrelevant? Am I missing something here?

—The cost of prohibiting drugs is too high.

> Costs to society—crime and violence, cost of prosecuting and jailing offenders, crowded jails that result in violent criminals being released too soon. Yes, these are high costs, but Tooley doesn't even discuss the costs we'd bear if drugs were legal. It's not fair of him to ignore these.

> Costs to drug users—loss of freedom when sent to jail, "forced into a life of crime," drugs not regulated and so aren't safe, AIDS from shared needles. Why is he so sympathetic to drug users? Why does he say they are "forced" into committing crimes?

Widening the conversation

If the author of a work were available for a chat—in person, on the phone, or online—that would be an ideal way to widen your conversation. But authors are rarely available to chat with their readers. Nevertheless, you can widen your conversation with an author in two ways: by talking with other readers and by reading works by other authors on the same subject (or other works by the same author).

In many classes where readings are assigned, you will have the opportunity to discuss them, in large or small groups or perhaps online. Take advantage of this opportunity, for it's an excellent way to test your initial responses to a reading. For example, a classmate might challenge you to think further about a long section of the Tooley article that you had initially thought off the point: the philosophical defense of libertarianism. After talking to classmates, you might come to think that Tooley is more interested in a defense of libertarianism than in the drug issue, even though the surface structure of the article suggests the opposite. With a revised view of Tooley's purpose, your assessment of the article could certainly change.

A second way to widen your conversation with an author is to read other works on the same subject, especially those written by authors with opposing views. If you were writing about Bennett's and Tooley's views on the legalization of drugs, for example, you could turn to your anthology and read two other essays on the same subject: one by political scientist James Q. Wilson, who opposes legalization, the other by Kurt Schmoke, former mayor of Baltimore, who favors it. And if you had the time, you could of course head to the library for recent articles on the subject — or sit down at your computer and surf the Net.

Drawing conclusions

The more you learn about a subject, the more you realize how much you don't know about it. It is tempting, therefore, to throw up your hands in despair and declare that the ultimate truth about a subject is beyond your grasp. It is even tempting to suspect that the truth is beyond anyone's grasp. But remember that some writers and readers are much closer to the elusive truth than others. Not all opinions are created equal. Some opinions are more informed and better reasoned than others.

Even though you may not have studied a subject exhaustively, at some point you need to draw conclusions about it. This is especially true in the political arena, where you must make up your mind and vote. It is also true in the academic and business worlds, where you will be faced with writing assignments and deadlines.

6c Summarize to demonstrate your understanding.

Your first written responses to a text should be tentative—maybe just your annotations on the text itself and a set of rough notes. By not committing yourself to a more finished piece of writing too soon, you keep your mind open to new ideas.

When you feel ready to respond to a text more formally, try writing a summary first. A summary is neutral in tone and demonstrates that you have understood the author's key ideas. Once you have demonstrated your understanding, you will be ready to meet the real challenge of critical thinking: analyzing the text. An analysis evaluates the text, showing how well it succeeds in enlightening readers about the issue in question.

Your goal in writing a summary is to articulate an author's main idea and key points as simply and as briefly as possible, without sacrificing accuracy. If the article you have read is complex, summarizing it will be an intellectual challenge. Since most summaries must be fairly short, part of your challenge will be in deciding what *not* to include. That means making judgments about what is most important.

When you sit down to write a summary, don't get tangled up in details: Think big. Find the author's central idea for the whole piece—the thesis—and then try to divide the whole into a few major ideas, each of which may be developed in several paragraphs. Some authors highlight their major ideas by providing headings introducing chunks of text, but many do not.

Here are some general guidelines for writing a summary:

—Keep your planning materials simple: just the author's main point and a list of key ideas.

—In the first sentence or two, mention the title of the reading, the name of the author, and the author's thesis or central purpose.

—Use a neutral tone; be objective.

—Write from the third-person point of view, and use the present tense: *Tooley argues* . . . [not *I thought that* or *you will see that*].

—Put all or most of the summary in your own words; if you borrow a phrase or a sentence from the author, put it in quotation marks.

—Limit yourself to presenting the author's key points.

—Be brief; work within any word limits assigned.

Following is a summary of Michael Tooley's article. Although the article is controversial and may contain some flawed reasoning, notice that the summary maintains an objective tone.

SAMPLE SUMMARY

In "Our Current Drug Legislation: Grounds for Reconsideration," Michael Tooley argues that we should reconsider our prohibitionist approach to drugs. The introduction of the article sets forth two brief arguments: that prohibiting drugs does not work and that there is no good reason for the law to distinguish between drugs such as heroin and drugs such as alcohol and nicotine. The body of the article focuses on what Tooley calls "the two most important reasons for reconsidering our current drug policy." The first of these is philosophical and political: Tooley argues that a law is justified only if it prevents someone from harming others, and he states that a person's drug use does not harm others. He rejects other justifications for a law: to enforce morality and to protect people from themselves. Tooley's second main point is that the cost of prohibiting drugs is too high. He mentions the crime and violence associated with illegal drugs, the cost of prosecuting and jailing drug users, and the cost to society when violent criminals are released from prisons to make room for drug offenders. He also lists the costs to drug users: loss of freedom, a life of crime, unsafe drugs, and the health risk of AIDS from shared needles. In short, Tooley's position is grounded in his libertarian philosophy and his view that a prohibitionist approach costs too much.

6d Analyze to demonstrate your critical thinking.

When an assignment calls for an analysis, read the whole assignment carefully, along with any models provided, to see just what is required. The formal definition of *analysis*—the separation of the whole for the purpose of studying the parts—doesn't tell you much. Here are some questions that instructors usually want you to address when they ask you to analyze a nonfiction reading:

—What is the author's thesis or central purpose?

—How does the author structure the text? In other words, what are the key parts and how do they relate to one another and to the thesis?

—How convincing is the evidence given in support of the thesis?

—How effectively has the author addressed the concerns and assumptions of his or her audience?

—What is the significance of the author's contribution to the larger conversation about the subject?

—How effectively does the author anticipate objections and refute opposing viewpoints? (See 7e.)

—Does the author fall prey to any logical fallacies? (See 7g.)

Depending on your assignment, it may not be necessary to address all of these questions. Also, there is no need to address the questions one at a time—or in just this order.

NOTE: An analysis of a work of literature is quite different, calling for an interpretation. (See 55.)

When it comes time to write your analysis, you will need to decide on your own thesis and an organizational plan.

Your thesis

In an analysis, your thesis may be more complex than the thesis sentences you have written for other papers (see 2a). In fact, at times you may need to express your thesis in more than one sentence. For an analysis of the Tooley article, for example, here is a possible thesis statement you might come up with:

Philosopher Michael Tooley's essay "Our Current Drug Legislation: Grounds for Reconsideration" sets forth a libertarian argument in favor of reconsidering the legalization of drugs.

> This argument is strong when applied to illegal drugs, such
> as marijuana, that do little harm to nonusers; but it is weak
> when applied to many harder drugs.

A sample paper analyzing Bennett's speech appears on
pages 152–57. The thesis of that paper is placed at the end
of the opening paragraph.

Your organizational plan

Your analysis needs an introduction and a conclusion, usually each a paragraph long. You can organize the body of your
analysis in a number of ways; your thesis will often lead you
to a sensible plan. For example, consider the plan you
would probably use for a paper based on the thesis just
mentioned:

—Tooley's libertarian argument
—Tooley's argument applied to drugs such as marijuana
—Tooley's argument applied to harder drugs

CAUTION: Do not organize your analysis by tracing the author's ideas paragraph by paragraph. Such a structure
nearly always leads you to focus too much on repeating
or parroting the text and too little on your own analysis
of the text.

In the paper analyzing Bennett's speech, notice that the
thesis dictates the organization (p. 152). Because the analysis is fairly long, the writer has decided to use three headings to help readers follow the organization. Notice also that
when quoting Bennett, the writer provides a page number in
parentheses. Handled according to MLA style (see 53), these
page numbers refer to pages in the anthology where the

Bennett speech is printed. An MLA "Works Cited" page may or may not be required for a paper based on one source in an assigned anthology or a reader. If a "Works Cited" page is required, it follows the text of the paper and appears on a separate page (see p. 157).

SAMPLE ANALYSIS

William Bennett and the Intellectuals

In his speech "Drug Policy and the Intellectuals," Willam Bennett challenges his audience at Harvard daringly, by attacking intellectuals. It is easy to imagine the tension in the room. Bennett wins over his audience of intellectuals, however, in two ways: (1) by calling upon their talents in his opening and closing remarks and (2) by delivering an impassioned, yet largely fair, attack on the arguments of intellectuals who favor legalizing drugs.

Bennett's opening and closing remarks

In his opening remarks, Bennett comes close to insulting his audience of intellectuals, stopping short of an insult by referring to those he is attacking as "they" (not "you"). Early in the speech, he diplomatically praises some intellectuals, especially in medicine and science, who are using their talents to combat the drug problem. In a further diplomatic move, Bennett makes clear that his speech will not be politically partisan. Bennett will be criticizing intellectuals, whether

on the left or the right, who hold either or both
of these views: that the drug problem can be
solved by legalization and that the problem is so
hopeless we should give up trying to fix it.

In his closing remarks, Bennett calls upon
the talents of the intellectuals sitting in his
audience. People living in drug-plagued neighborhoods are the "real drug experts," he says, and
they haven't given up the fight: in city after
city they are "reclaiming their neighborhoods,
working with police, setting up community activities, getting addicts into treatment, saving their
children" (362). Why, he wonders, would the intellectuals want to do less? He asks, "Isn't it time
we had more drug control scholars?" (364).

In a final diplomatic move, Bennett ends his
speech not with condemnation but with an invitation: "We are grappling with complicated, stub-
born policy issues, and I encourage you to join
us. . . . I invite America's deep thinkers to get
with the program, or at the very least, to get in
the game" (364).

Bennett's arguments

The opening and closing sections of Bennett's
speech, which focus on the intellectuals, act as
a frame for the longer central section. In this
central section Bennett attacks the arguments in
favor of legalizing drugs, calling them "a recipe
for a public policy disaster" (360). Although some
of Bennett's counterarguments are stronger than

others, on the whole they are a fair assessment of the views Bennett opposes.

Bennett's least convincing arguments attempt to counter the claims that legalization would eliminate the drug dealers' profit motive, that legalization would reduce the crime rate, and that drug laws restrict our liberty. Bennett barely discusses the liberty issue. As for the drug dealers' profit motive, he suggests--oddly, I think--that most drug dealers aren't making much of a profit right now. He means that over a long time, they don't profit; but we all know that in the short run many of them make very large profits.

Bennett's argument concerning the crime rate is only partly convincing. He refers vaguely to "research" showing that most drug criminals were doing crime before they "got into drugs" and says that most addicts would continue to commit crimes if drugs were legal (362). While this could be true, surely the extent and seriousness of the crimes would be reduced. Bennett makes one argu- ment about crime, however, that is hard to refute: If drugs were legal for adults, many dealers would shift their market to teenagers, who would be restricted from buying drugs.

One of Bennett's strongest arguments chal- lenges those who claim that legalization is a simple way to eliminate the drug problem. He rightly criticizes them for failing to describe the kind of world they are proposing, for failing to answer questions like these:

> Would crack be legal? How about PCP?
> Or smokable heroin? Or ice? Would they
> all be stocked at the local convenience
> store, perhaps just a few blocks from
> an elementary school? And how much would
> they cost? (360-61)

Bennett also argues convincingly that, contrary to the claims of legalization advocates, drug use would go up if drugs were legal. When cocaine was available only in expensive powder form, he says, it was not widely used; but when it became available in inexpensive vials of crack, cocaine use skyrocketed. If drugs were legal, they would be easy to get, and they would be cheaper as well. Common sense tells us that more people would use drugs.

Legalization advocates focus on the high cost of enforcing drug laws. Bennett correctly chides them for not asking an important question: What would be the costs of legalization? Bennett tells us:

> We would have more drug-related acci-
> dents at work, on the highways, and in
> the airways. We would have even bigger
> losses in worker productivity. Our hos-
> pitals would be filled with drug emer-
> gencies. We would have more school kids
> on dope, and that means dropouts. More
> pregnant women would buy legal cocaine,

and then deliver tiny, premature infants. (361)

And to these costs, says Bennett, we can add the
costs of "treatment, social welfare, and
insurance" (361).

Legalization advocates assume that drug use
hurts only the user. Bennett questions this as-
sumption. In addition to the high costs to society
just mentioned, Bennett points out that drugs "destroy families" and "ruin friendships" and "are a
threat to the life of the mind" (362).

Finally, Bennett addresses the issue of drug
enforcement, which his opponents say doesn't--and
can't--work. His evidence here is anecdotal and
therefore only partly convincing. But at this
point in the speech, Bennett has given us reason
for thinking that we must make it work.

Conclusion

Bennett's speech began with some tension--a
conservative thinker facing a largely liberal
audience of intellectuals. Bennett overcomes this
tension first through diplomacy, then through a
series of largely solid arguments, and finally
with a positive appeal: a call for using the
intellectuals' collective intelligence to solve a
problem that is not beyond hope.

[NEW PAGE]

Work Cited

Bennett, William J. "Drug Policy and the Intellec-
     tuals." Current Issues and Enduring Questions:
     A Guide to Critical Thinking and Argument,
     with Readings. Ed. Sylvan Barnet and Hugo
     Bedau. Boston: Bedford, 1996. 358-64.

7

Construct reasonable arguments.

In argumentative writing, you take a stand on a debatable issue. The issue being debated might be a matter of public policy: Should religious groups be allowed to meet on school property? What is the least dangerous way to dispose of nuclear waste? Should a state enact laws rationing medical care? On such questions, reasonable persons can disagree.

Reasonable men and women also disagree about many scholarly issues. Psychologists debate the validity of behaviorism; historians interpret the causes of the Civil War quite differently; biologists conduct genetic experiments to challenge the conclusions of other researchers.

Your goal, in argumentative writing, is to change the way your readers think about a subject or to convince them to take an action that they might not otherwise be inclined to take. Do not assume that your audience already agrees with you; instead, envision skeptical readers who will make up their minds after listening to both sides of the debate. To convince such readers, you will need to build arguments strong enough to stand up to the arguments put forward by your opponents (sometimes called *the opposition*).

7a　Plan a strategy.

Planning a strategy for an argumentative essay is much like planning a debate for a speech class. A good way to begin is to list your arguments and the arguments of the opposition and then consider the likely impact of these arguments on your audience. If the arguments of the opposition look very powerful, you may want to rethink your position. By modifying your initial position—perhaps by claiming less or by proposing a less radical solution to a problem—you may have a greater chance of persuading readers to change their views.

Listing your arguments

Let's say that your tentative purpose (which may change as you think about your audience and the opposition) is to argue in favor of lowering the legal drinking age from twenty-one to eighteen. Here is a list of possible arguments in favor of this point of view.

—Society treats eighteen-year-olds as mature for most purposes.

　　They can vote.

　　They can go away to college.

　　At eighteen, men must register with Selective Service and be available for a possible draft.

—Age is not necessarily an indication of maturity.

—The current drinking age is unfair, since many older Americans were allowed to drink at eighteen.

—An unrealistic drinking age is almost impossible to enforce, and it breeds disrespect for the law.

—In European countries that allow eighteen-year-olds to drink, there is less irresponsible teenage drinking than in our country.

Listing the arguments of the opposition

The next step is to list the key arguments of the opposition. Here are some possible arguments *against* lowering the drinking age to eighteen.

— Teenage drinking frequently leads to drunk driving, which in turn leads to many deaths.

— Teenage drinking sometimes leads to date rape and gang violence.

— Alcoholism is a serious problem in our society, and a delayed drinking age can help prevent it.

— If the legal age were eighteen, many fifteen- and sixteen-year-olds would find a way to purchase alcohol illegally.

If possible, you should talk to someone who disagrees with your view or read some articles that are critical of your position. By familiarizing yourself with the views of the opposition, you can be reasonably sure you have not overlooked an important argument that might be used against you.

Considering your audience

Once you have listed the major arguments on both sides, think realistically about the impact they are likely to have on your intended audience. If your audience is the voting age population in the United States, for example, consider how you might assess some of the arguments of each side of the drinking age question.

Looking at your list, you would see that your audience, which includes many older Americans, might not be impressed by the suggestion that age is no sign of maturity or by the argument that because eighteen-year-olds are old enough to attend college they should be allowed to drink. You would decide to emphasize your other arguments instead. Americans who remember a time when young men were drafted, for example, might be persuaded that it is unfair to ask a man to die for his country but not allow him to drink. And anyone who has heard of Prohibition might be moved by the argument that an unrealistic drinking regulation can breed disrespect for the law.

As for the arguments of the opposition, clearly the first one on the list is the most powerful. Statistics show that drunk driving by teenagers causes much carnage on our highways and that teenagers themselves are frequently the victims. To have any hope of convincing your audience, you would need to take this argument very seriously; it would be almost impossible to argue successfully that reducing highway deaths is not important.

Rethinking your position

After exploring both sides of an argument, you may decide to modify your initial position. Maybe your first thoughts about the issue were oversimplified, too extreme, or mistaken in some other respect. Or maybe, after thinking more about your readers, you see little hope of persuading them of the truth or wisdom of your position.

If you were writing about the drinking age, for example, you might decide to modify your position in light of your audience. To have a better chance of convincing the audience, you could argue that eighteen-year-olds *in the military* should be allowed to drink. Or you could argue that eighteen-year-olds should be allowed to drink beer and wine, not hard alcohol. Or you could link your proposal to new tough laws against drunk driving.

7b Frame a thesis and state your major arguments.

A thesis is a sentence that expresses the main point of an essay. (See 2a.) In argumentative writing, your thesis should clearly state your position on the issue you have chosen to write about. Let's say your issue is the high insurance rates that most companies set for young male drivers. After thinking carefully about your own views, the arguments of the opposition, and your audience (the general public), you might state your position like this:

> Although young male drivers have a high accident rate, insurance companies should not be allowed to discriminate against anyone who has driven for the past two years without a traffic violation.

Notice that this is a debatable point, one about which reasonable persons can disagree. It is not merely a fact (for example, that companies do set higher rates for young males). Nor is it a statement of belief (for example, that differing rates are always unfair). Neither facts nor beliefs can be substantiated by reasons, so they cannot serve as a thesis for an argument.

Once you have framed a thesis, try to state your major arguments, preferably in sentence form. Together, your thesis and your arguments will give you a rough outline of your essay. Consider the following rough outline of an essay written by Julian L. Simon, a business professor at the University of Maryland. Simon argues for an easing of restrictions on immigration into the United States. His thesis frames the issue in economic terms, and his major arguments are economic reasons that support his thesis.

Thesis: Despite claims that increased immigration would hurt the economy, the evidence strongly suggests that new immigrants strengthen the economy in a variety of ways.

—Immigrants do not cause native unemployment, even among low-paid and minority groups.

—Immigrants do not overuse welfare services.

—Immigrants bring high-tech skills that the economy needs badly.

—Immigration is lower than it was in the peak years at the turn of the century.
—Natural resources and the environment are not at risk from immigration.
—Immigration reduces the social costs of the elderly, which can't be cut.

Some of the sentences in your rough outline might become topic sentences of paragraphs in your final essay. (See 4a.)

7c Draft an introduction that states your position without alienating readers.

In argumentative writing, your introduction should state your position on an issue in a clear thesis sentence (see 2a and 7b), and it should do this without needlessly alienating the audience whom you hope to convince. Where possible, try to establish common ground with readers who may not be in initial agreement with your views.

One student, who argued against allowing prayer in public schools, established common ground with readers who disagreed with her by explaining that she once shared their views. Her introduction ends with a clear thesis that states her current position on the issue.

> During most of my school years, the Lord's Prayer was a part of our opening exercises. I never gave it a second thought, and I never heard anyone complain about it. So when prayer in the schools became an issue in the courts, I was surprised to hear that anyone viewed it as a threat to individual rights or as a violation of the division between church and state. But now that I've thought about it, I would not like to see the practice of prayer in the schools reinstituted.

In her first draft, the student began the introduction like this: *I do not think prayer should be allowed in schools.*

This sentence clearly stated her position, but its blunt tone was likely to alienate readers who favor school prayer. The student wisely decided to establish common ground with her readers before stating her position. Notice that her new thesis statement, at the end of the introduction, is as clear as her original thesis but has a much more reasonable tone.

One way to establish common ground with readers who disagree with your position is to show that you share common values. If your subject is school prayer, for instance, you might show that even though you oppose allowing prayer in schools, you believe in the value of prayer. The writer of the following introduction successfully used this strategy.

> Although the Supreme Court has ruled against prayer in public schools on First Amendment grounds, many people still feel that prayers should be allowed. These people, most of whom hold strong religious beliefs, are well intentioned. What they fail to realize is that the Supreme Court decision, although it was made on legal grounds, makes good sense on religious grounds as well. Prayer is too important to be trusted to our public schools.

Like the writer of the other introduction about school prayer, this writer sounds reasonable. He states his position clearly and firmly in a thesis at the end of the paragraph, but because he takes into consideration the values of those who disagree with him, readers are likely to approach his essay with an open mind.

7d Support each argument with specific evidence.

When presenting the arguments for your position, you will of course need to back them up with evidence: facts, statistics, examples and illustrations, expert opinion, and so on. Depending on the issue you have chosen to write about, you may or may not need to do some reading to gather evidence.

Some argumentative topics, such as whether class attendance should be required at your college or university, can be developed through personal experience and maybe questionnaires or interviews. Most debatable topics, however, require some research.

If any of your evidence is based on reading, you will need to document your sources. Documentation gives credit to your sources and shows readers how to track down a source in case they want to assess its credibility or explore the issue further. (See 50a and 53.)

Using facts and statistics

A fact is something that is known with certainty because it has been objectively verified: The capital of Wyoming is Cheyenne. Carbon has an atomic weight of 12. John F. Kennedy was assassinated on November 22, 1963. Statistics are collections of numerical facts: More than three-quarters of U.S. households currently own a VCR. North America holds only 4 percent of the world's proven oil reserves; together, Iraq, Kuwait, and Saudi Arabia own 44 percent.

Most arguments are supported at least to some extent by facts and statistics. For example, if you were arguing against mandatory class attendance, you might include facts about the attendance policies of professors in several disciplines; you could also report statistics on the views of students.

Andrew Knutson, the student who wrote the argument paper on pages 177–80, gathered a few facts and statistics from two printed sources and one Internet source. When he used a statistic from one of these sources, he documented it with an MLA (Modern Language Association) citation in parentheses, like this:

> Currently the responsibility of educating about 75% of undocumented children is borne by just a few states—California, New York, Texas, and Florida (Edmondson 1).

Knutson got this statistic from an article by Brad Edmondson. The parenthetical citation at the end of the sentence names the author of the source and gives the page number. Complete information about the source appears in a "Works Cited" list at the end of the paper (see p. 180). (See 50 and 53 for more detailed information about citing sources.)

Writers and politicians often use statistics in selective ways to bolster their partisan views. If you suspect that a writer's handling of statistics is not quite fair, read authors with opposing views, who may give you a fuller understanding of the numbers. For example, one writer might argue that a capital gains tax cut would benefit the middle class because more than half the people earning capital gains have incomes less than $50,000 per year. By reading more about the subject, however, you might discover that although the statistic is true, the real beneficiaries of a capital gains tax cut would be millionaires, whose average capital gains earnings are more than one hundred times greater than those of the average person making under $100,000 per year.

Some objective sources for statistics are *Statistical Abstract of the United States, American Statistics Index,* and *Statistical Yearbook.*

Using examples and anecdotes

Examples and anecdotes (illustrative stories) alone rarely prove a point, but when used in combination with other forms of evidence, they flesh out an argument and bring it to life. In an essay arguing against mandatory class attendance, you might give examples of class sessions that were obviously a waste of time, maybe because the professor simply read from the textbook or because you were asked to play games that had nothing to do with the subject.

In a research essay, Karen Shaw used several examples from a variety of sources to show that apes are capable of using language creatively (see p. 633).

Citing expert opinion

Although they are no substitute for careful reasoning of your own, the views of an expert can contribute to the force of your argument. You might interview an educational psychologist on learning styles, for example, to help support your argument that class attendance is not the only way to learn. Or, if you were arguing in favor of mandatory class attendance, you might interview a dean to learn about academic goals (such as increased tolerance for persons from other cultures) that can be accomplished only through class attendance.

When you rely on expert opinion, you should be certain that your source is, in fact, an expert in the field you are covering. In some cases you may need to provide an explanation of what makes your source an expert. Use particular caution when gathering research from online sources (see 47).

If you include expert testimony in your paper, you must document your sources. You can summarize or paraphrase the expert's opinion or you can quote the expert's exact words. For important advice on appropriate use of written sources, see the chart on page 583.

7e   Anticipate objections; refute opposing arguments.

Readers who already agree with you need no convincing, although a well-argued case for their own point of view is always welcome. But indifferent and skeptical readers may resist your arguments because they have minds of their own. To give up a position that seems reasonable, a reader has to see that there is an even more reasonable one. In addition to presenting your own case, therefore, you should review the chief arguments of the opposition and explain what you think is wrong with them.

There is no best place in an essay to deal with the opposition. Often it is useful to summarize the opposing position early in your essay. After stating your thesis but before developing your own arguments, you might have a paragraph beginning *Critics of this view argue that. . . .* But sometimes a better plan is to anticipate objections as you develop your case paragraph by paragraph. Wherever you decide to deal with opposing arguments, do your best to refute them. Show that those who oppose you are not as persuasive as they claim because their arguments are flawed or because your arguments to the contrary have greater weight.

7f Establish common ground.

As you refute opposing arguments, try to establish common ground with readers who are not in initial agreement with your views. If you can show that you share your readers' values, they may be able to switch to your position without giving up what they feel is important. For example, to persuade people opposed to shooting deer, a state wildlife commission would have to show that it too cares about preserving deer and does not want them to die needlessly. Having established these values in common, the commission might be able to persuade critics that a carefully controlled hunting season is good for the deer population because it prevents starvation caused by overpopulation. Likewise, if those opposed to hunting want to persuade the commission to ban the hunting season, they would need to show that the commission could achieve its goals by some other feasible means, such as expanding the deer preserve or increasing the food supply to support an increased herd.

People believe that intelligence and decency support their side of an argument. To change sides, they must continue to feel intelligent and decent. Otherwise they will persist in their opposition.

7g Avoid common mistakes in reasoning.

Certain errors in reasoning occur frequently enough to deserve special attention. In both your reading and your writing, you will want to be alert to common mistakes in inductive and deductive reasoning and to certain mistakes known as logical fallacies.

Using inductive reasoning with care

When you reason inductively, you draw a conclusion from an array of facts. For example, you might conclude that a professor is friendly because he or she smiles frequently and talks to students after class or that fifty-five miles per hour is a safer speed limit than sixty-five miles per hour because there are fewer deaths per accident at that speed.

Inductive reasoning deals in probability, not certainty. For a conclusion based on inductive reasoning to be highly probable, the evidence must be sufficient, representative, and relevant. Consider, for example, how you would evaluate the following conclusion, drawn from evidence gathered in a survey.

> **CONCLUSION** The majority of households in our city would subscribe to cable television if it were available.
>
> **EVIDENCE** In a recent survey, 356 of the 500 households questioned say they would subscribe to cable television.

Is the evidence sufficient? That depends. In a city of 10,000, the 500 households are a 5 percent sample, sufficient for the purposes of marketing research. But in a city of 2 million, the households would amount to one-fortieth of 1 percent of the population, an inadequate sample on which to base an important decision.

Is the evidence representative? Again, that depends. The

cable company would trust the survey if it knew that the sample had been carefully constructed to reflect the age, sex, geographic distribution, and income of the city's population as a whole. If, however, the 500 households were concentrated in one wealthy neighborhood, the company would be wise to question the survey's conclusion.

Is the evidence relevant? The answer is a cautious yes. The survey question is directly linked to the conclusion. A question about the number of hours spent watching television, by contrast, would not be relevant, because it would not be about *subscribing* to *cable* television. In addition, a cautious interpreter of the evidence would want to know whether people who *say* they would subscribe tend to subscribe *in fact.* By looking at marketing research done in other cities, the cable television company could determine— through a new round of inductive reasoning—how many of the 356 households who say they would subscribe are likely in fact to subscribe.

Using deductive reasoning with care

When you reason deductively, you draw a conclusion from two or more assertions (called premises).

> The police do not give speeding tickets to people driving less than five miles per hour over the limit. Sam is driving fifty-nine miles per hour in a fifty-five-mile-per-hour zone. Therefore, the police will not give Sam a speeding ticket.

The conclusion is true only if the premises are true. If the police sometimes give tickets for less than five-mile-per-hour violations or if the speedometer is inaccurate, Sam cannot safely conclude that he will avoid a ticket.

Deductive reasoning can often be structured in a three-step argument called a *syllogism.* The three steps are the major premise, the minor premise, and the conclusion:

1. Anything that increases radiation in the environment is dangerous to public health. (Major premise)
2. Nuclear reactors increase radiation in the environment. (Minor premise)
3. Therefore, nuclear reactors are dangerous to public health. (Conclusion)

The major premise is a generalization. The minor premise is a specific case. The conclusion follows from applying the generalization to the specific case.

Many deductive arguments do not state one of the premises but rather leave the reader to infer it, as in the following example:

Violent crime is increasing.

Therefore, we should reinstate the death penalty.

The minor premise, that violent crime is increasing, may be true, but the major premise, that the death penalty deters violent criminals, is a debatable issue. A careful reader will uncover this hidden major premise and question the whole argument.

Deductive arguments break down if one of the premises is not true or if the conclusion does not logically follow from them. For example, consider this argument:

The deer population in our state should be preserved. During hunting season hundreds of deer are killed. Therefore, the hunting season should be discontinued.

To challenge this argument, the state's wildlife commission might agree with both the major and minor premises but question whether the conclusion follows logically from them. True, the deer population should be preserved; true, deer are killed during hunting season. However, in an area where deer have no natural enemies, herds become too large for the forest vegetation to support them. The overpopulated herds strip the leaves and bark from the young trees, killing the trees before dying of starvation themselves. The commission might conclude, therefore, that a limited hunting season helps preserve a healthier and more stable population of deer.

Avoiding logical fallacies

Some errors in reasoning are so common that writers and readers call them by name: hasty generalization, non sequitur, false analogy, and so on. Such errors are known as *logical fallacies*.

HASTY GENERALIZATION   A hasty generalization is a conclusion based on insufficient or unrepresentative evidence.

> Deaths from drug overdoses in Metropolis have doubled in the past three years. Therefore, more Americans than ever are dying from drug abuse.

Data from one city do not justify a conclusion about the whole United States.

Many hasty generalizations contain words like *all, every, always,* and *never,* when qualifiers such as *most, many, usually,* and *seldom* would be more accurate. Go over your writing carefully for such general statements and make sure that you have enough data to verify your position or that you qualify the statements.

A *stereotype* is a hasty generalization (usually derogatory) about a group. Examples: Women are bad bosses; politicians are corrupt; people without children are self-centered; computer programmers are nerds. Stereotyping is common because of our human tendency to perceive selectively. We tend to see what we want to see; that is, we notice evidence confirming our already formed opinions and fail to notice evidence to the contrary. For example, if you have concluded that politicians are corrupt, your stereotype will be confirmed by occasional news reports of legislators being indicted — even though every day the newspapers describe conscientious officials serving the public honestly and well. Generalizations about people must be based on numerous typical cases and not contradicted by many exceptions. And even conclusions that are generally valid — that Americans tend to place a high value on individual rights, for example — will have significant exceptions because what is generally true about groups of people will not be true of all individuals within those groups.

NON SEQUITUR A non sequitur (Latin for "does not follow") is a conclusion that does not follow logically from preceding statements or that is based on irrelevant data.

Mary loves good food; therefore, she will be an excellent chef.

Mary's love of good food does not guarantee that she will be able to cook it well.

FALSE ANALOGY An analogy points out a similarity between two things that are otherwise dissimilar. Analogies can be an effective means of illustrating a point (see 4c), but they are not proof. In a false analogy, a writer falsely assumes that because two things are alike in one respect, they must be alike in others.

If we can put humans on the moon, we should be able to find a cure for the common cold.

Putting humans on the moon and finding a cure for the common cold are both scientific challenges, but the technical problems confronting medical researchers are quite different from those solved by space scientists.

EITHER . . . OR FALLACY The *either . . . or* fallacy is the suggestion that only two alternatives exist when in fact there are more.

> Either learn how to program a computer or you won't be able to get a decent job after college.

In fact, many occupations do not require the ability to program a computer.

FAULTY CAUSE-AND-EFFECT REASONING Careless thinkers often assume that because one event follows another, the first is the cause of the second. This common fallacy is known as *post hoc,* from the Latin *post hoc, ergo propter hoc,* meaning "after this, therefore because of this." Like a non sequitur, it is a leap to an unjustified conclusion.

> Since Governor Smith took office, unemployment of minorities in the state has decreased by 7 percent. Governor Smith should be applauded for reducing unemployment among minorities.

The writer must show that Governor Smith's policies are responsible for the decrease in unemployment; it is not enough to show merely that the decrease followed the governor's taking office.

Demonstrating the connection between causes and effects is rarely a simple matter. For example, to explain why an introductory chemistry course has a very high failure rate, you would begin by listing possible causes: inadequate preparation of students, poor teaching, large class size, unavailability of qualified tutors, and so on. Next you would need to investigate each possible cause by gathering statistical data. For example, to see whether inadequate preparation of students contributes to the high failure rate, you might do a statistical comparison of the math and science backgrounds of successful and failing students. Or to see whether large class size is a contributing cause, you might run a pilot program of small classes and then compare grades in the small classes with those in the larger ones. Only after thoroughly investigating all of the possible causes would you be able to weigh the relative impact of each cause and then suggest appropriate remedies.

CIRCULAR REASONING AND BEGGING THE QUESTION Suppose you go to see a doctor about a rash you suddenly developed. "I have a rash," you say to the doctor. "What is your diagnosis?" The doctor answers, "You have allergitis." When you ask, "What's that?" the doctor replies, "It's a rash." This is an example of circular reasoning: No real information has been introduced; by a trick of semantics you have wound up back where you started.

Like circular reasoning, begging the question is a way of ducking the issue. Instead of supporting the conclusion with evidence and logic, the writer simply restates the conclusion in different language.

> Faculty and administrators should not be permitted to come to student council meetings because student council meetings should be for students only.

The writer has given no reason for this position but has merely repeated the point.

APPEALS TO EMOTION Many of the arguments we see in the media strive to win our sympathy rather than our intelligent agreement. A TV commercial suggesting that you will be thin and sexy if you drink a certain diet beverage is making a pitch to emotions. So is a political speech that recommends electing John D'Eau because he is a devoted husband and father who fought for his country in Vietnam.

The following passage illustrates several types of emotional appeals.

This progressive proposal to build a large ski resort in the state park has been carefully researched by Fidelity, the largest bank in the state; furthermore, it is favored by a majority of the local merchants. The only opposition comes from narrow-minded, do-gooder environmentalists who care more about trees than they do about people; one of their leaders was actually arrested for disturbing the peace several years ago.

Words with strong positive or negative connotations, such as *progressive* and *do-gooders,* are examples of *biased language.* Attacking the persons who hold a belief (environmentalists) rather than refuting their argument is called *ad hominem,* a Latin term meaning "to the man." Associating a prestigious name (Fidelity) with the writer's side is called *transfer.* Claiming that an idea should be accepted because a large number of people are in favor (the majority of merchants) is called the *bandwagon appeal.* Bringing in irrelevant issues (the arrest) is a *red herring,* named after a trick used in fox hunts to mislead the dogs by dragging a smelly fish across the trail.

In examining your own and other people's writing for errors of logic, you will find that logical fallacies are frequently not so clear-cut that a casual reader can spot them immediately. Often they show up in combination. To recognize such fallacies in your own writing takes discipline, but you can do it if you train yourself to become a skeptical and demanding reader — the kind of person who measures all claims against the evidence.

EXERCISE 7–1

Explain what is illogical in the following brief arguments. It may be helpful to identify the logical fallacy or fallacies by name. Answers to lettered sentences appear in the back of the book.

a. All of my blind dates have been embarrassing disasters, so I know this one will be too.
b. If you're old enough to vote, you're old enough to drink. Therefore, the drinking age should be lowered to eighteen.
c. This country has been run too long by old, out-of-date, out-of-touch, entrenched politicians protecting the special interests that got them elected.
d. It was possible to feed a family of four on $100 a week before Governor Leroy took office and drove up food prices.
e. If you're not part of the solution, you're part of the problem.

1. Whenever I wash my car, it rains. I have discovered a way to end all droughts—get all the people to wash their cars.
2. Our current war on drugs has not worked. Either we should legalize drugs or we should turn the drug war over to our armed forces and let them fight it.
3. College professors tend to be sarcastic. Three of my five professors this semester make sarcastic remarks.
4. Although Ms. Bell's book on Joe DiMaggio was well researched, I doubt that an Australian historian can contribute much to our knowledge of an American baseball player.
5. Self-righteous nonsmoking fanatics have eroded our basic individual freedoms by railroading the passage of oppressive antismoking laws that interfere with our natural right to make our own decisions.
6. If professional sports teams didn't pay athletes such high salaries, we wouldn't have so many kids breaking their legs at hockey and basketball camps.
7. Ninety percent of the students oppose a tuition increase; therefore, the board of trustees should not pass the proposed increase.
8. If the president had learned the lesson of Vietnam, he would realize that sending U.S. troops into a foreign country can only end in disaster.
9. A mandatory ten-cent deposit on bottles and cans will eliminate litter because everyone I know will return the containers for the money rather than throw them away.
10. Soliciting money to save whales and baby seals is irresponsible when thousands of human beings can't afford food and shelter.

SAMPLE ARGUMENT PAPER

In the following paper, student Andrew Knutson argues that Americans should continue to educate the children of illegal immigrants. Notice that Knutson is careful to establish common ground with readers who may hold a different view. Notice too that he attempts to refute the arguments of the opposition before laying out his own arguments.

In writing the paper, Knutson consulted two written sources and one Internet source. When he quotes from or uses statistics from a source, he cites the source with an MLA (Modern Language Association) in-text citation. Citations in the paper refer readers to the list of works cited at the end of the paper. (See 50 and 53 for detailed advice on citing sources.)

SAMPLE ARGUMENT PAPER

Why Educate the Children of Illegal Immigrants?

Immigration laws have been a subject of debate throughout American history, especially in states such as California and Texas, where immigrant populations are high. Recently, some citizens have been questioning whether we should continue to educate the children of illegal immigrants. While this issue is steeped in emotional controversy, we must not allow divisive "us against them" rhetoric to cloud our thinking. Yes, educating undocumented immigrants costs us, but not educating them would cost us much more.

Those who propose barring the children of illegal immigrants from our schools have understandable worries. They worry that their state taxes will rise as undocumented children crowd their

school systems. They worry about the crowding
itself, given the loss of quality education that
comes with large class sizes. They worry that
school resources will be deflected from their children because of the linguistic and social problems
that many of the newcomers face. And finally, they
worry that even more illegal immigrants will cross
our borders because of the lure of free education.

This last worry is probably unfounded. It
is unlikely that many parents are crossing the
borders solely to educate their children. More
likely, they are in desperate need of work, economic opportunity, and possibly political asylum.
As Charles Wheeler of the National Immigration Law
Center asserts, "There is no evidence that access
to federal programs acts as a magnet to foreigners
or that further restrictions would discourage illegal immigrants" (qtd. in Public Agenda).

The other concerns are more legitimate, but
they can be addressed by less drastic measures
than barring children from schools. Currently the
responsibility of educating about 75% of undocumented children is borne by just a few states--
California, New York, Texas, and Florida (Edmondson 1). One way to help these and other states is
to have the federal government pick up the cost of
educating undocumented children, with enough funds
to alleviate the overcrowded classrooms that cause
parents such concern. Such cost shifting could
have a significant benefit, for if the federal gov-

ernment had to pay, it might work harder to stem
the tide of illegal immigrants.

So far, attempts to bar undocumented children
from public schools have failed. In the 1982 case
of Plyler v. Doe, the Supreme Court ruled on the
issue. In a 5-4 decision, it overturned a Texas
law that allowed schools to deny education to
illegal immigrants as a means of "preserving financial resources, protecting the state from an
influx of illegal immigrants, and maintaining high
quality education for resident children" (McCarthy
128). The Court considered these issues but concluded that in the long run the costs of educating
immigrant children would pale in comparison to the
costs--both to the children and to society--of not
educating them.

It isn't hard to figure out what the costs of
not educating these children would be. The costs
to innocent children are obvious: loss of the
opportunity to learn English, to understand American culture and history, to socialize with other
children in a structured environment, and to grow
up to be successful, responsible adults.

The costs to society as a whole are fairly
obvious as well. That is why we work so hard to
promote literacy and prevent students from dropping out of school. An uneducated populace is dangerous to the fabric of society, contributing to
social problems such as vandalism and crime, an
underground economy, gang warfare, teenage preg-

nancy, substance abuse, and infectious and transmissible diseases. The health issue alone makes it worth our while to educate the children of undocumented immigrants, for when children are in school, we can make sure they are inoculated properly, and we can teach them the facts about health and disease.

Do we really want thousands of uneducated children growing up on the streets, where we have little control over them? Surely not. The lure of the streets is powerful enough already. Only by inviting all children into safe and nurturing and intellectually engaging schools can we combat that power. Our efforts will be well worth the cost.

[NEW PAGE]

Works Cited

Edmondson, Brad. "Life without Illegal Immigrants." American Demographics May 1996:1.

McCarthy, Martha M. "Immigrants in Public Schools: Legal Issues." Educational Horizons 71 (1993): 128-30.

Public Agenda. "Exploiting Fears." Admissions Decisions: Should Immigration Be Restricted? Online. World Wide Web. 7 Oct. 1996. Available http://www.vote-smart.org/issues /Immigration/chap2/imm2itx.html.

PART III

Clear Sentences

8

Coordinate equal ideas; subordinate minor ideas.

When combining two or more ideas in one sentence, you have two choices: coordination or subordination. Choose coordination to indicate that the ideas are equal or nearly equal in importance. Choose subordination to indicate that one idea is less important than another.

> **GRAMMAR CHECKERS** do not catch the problems with coordination and subordination discussed in this section. Not surprisingly, computer programs have no way of sensing the relative importance of ideas.

Coordination

Coordination draws attention equally to two or more ideas. To coordinate single words or phrases, join them with a coordinating conjunction or with a pair of correlative conjunctions (see 57g). To coordinate independent clauses — word groups that could stand alone as a sentence — join them with a comma and a coordinating conjunction or with a semicolon:

, and	, but	, or	, nor
, for	, so	, yet	;

The semicolon is often accompanied by a conjunctive adverb such as *moreover, furthermore, therefore,* or *however* or by a transitional phrase such as *for example, in other words,* or *as a matter of fact.* (See the chart on p. 184 for a more complete list.)

Assume, for example, that your intention is to draw equal attention to the following two ideas.

Grandmother lost her sight. Her hearing sharpened.

To coordinate these ideas, you can join them with a comma and the coordinating conjunction *but* or with a semicolon and the conjunctive adverb *however.*

Grandmother lost her sight, but her hearing sharpened.

Grandmother lost her sight; however, her hearing sharpened.

It is important to choose a coordinating conjunction or conjunctive adverb appropriate to your meaning. In the preceding example, the two ideas contrast with one another, calling for *but* or *however.*

Subordination

To give unequal emphasis to two or more ideas, express the major idea in an independent clause and place any minor ideas in subordinate clauses or phrases. (For specific subordination strategies, see the chart on p. 185.)

Deciding which idea to emphasize is not a matter of right and wrong but is determined by the meaning you intend. Consider the two ideas about Grandmother's sight and hearing.

Grandmother lost her sight. Her hearing sharpened.

If your purpose is to stress your grandmother's acute hearing rather than her blindness, subordinate the idea about her blindness.

As she lost her sight, Grandmother's hearing sharpened.

To focus on your grandmother's growing blindness, subordinate the idea about her hearing.

Though her hearing sharpened, Grandmother gradually lost her sight.

Using coordination to combine sentences of equal importance

1. Consider using a comma and a coordinating conjunction. (See 32a.)

   , and   , but   , or   , nor
   , for   , so   , yet

   ▶ In Orthodox Jewish funeral ceremonies, the shroud is
                      and the
   a simple linen vestment ~~. The~~ coffin is plain wood with

   no adornment.

2. Consider using a semicolon and a conjunctive adverb or transitional phrase. (See 34b.)

also	in addition	now
as a result	in fact	of course
besides	in other words	on the other hand
consequently	in the first place	otherwise
finally	meanwhile	still
for example	moreover	then
for instance	nevertheless	therefore
furthermore	next	thus
however		

                               therefore,
   ▶ Tom Baxter has been irritating me lately ~~,~~ ; I avoid him

   whenever possible.

3. Consider using a semicolon alone. (See 34a.)

                           he
   ▶ Nicklaus is like fine wine ~~.~~ ; ~~He~~ gets better with time.

Using subordination to combine sentences of unequal importance

1. Consider putting the less important idea in a subordinate clause beginning with one of the following words. (See 59b.)

after	before	that	which
although	even though	unless	while
as	if	until	who
as if	since	when	whom
because	so that	where	whose

▶ *When my*
  ~~My~~ son asked his great-grandmother if she had been a
   ^   *she*
  slave~~.~~, ~~She~~ became very angry.
     ^

▶ My sister owes much of her recovery to a bodybuilding
          that she
  program~~.~~/~~She~~ began ~~the program~~ three years ago.
      ^

2. Consider putting the less important idea in a phrase. (See 59a, 59c, 59d, and 59e.)

▶ Karate~~,~~ ~~is~~ a discipline based on the philosophy of
      ^
  nonviolence~~.~~/ ~~It~~ teaches the art of self-defense.
             ^
    E
▶ ~~Alvin was~~ ~~e~~ncouraged by his professor to apply for the
       Alvin
  job~~.~~/ ~~He~~ filed an application on Monday morning.
  ^
                        my eyes scanning
▶ I reached for the knife out of habit~~.~~/ ~~My eyes scanned~~
                          ^
  the long shiny blade for a price sticker. In a low,

  steady voice, my customer said, "This is a holdup."

Clear sentences

8a Combine choppy sentences.

Short sentences demand attention, so you should use them primarily for emphasis. Too many short sentences, one after the other, make for a choppy style.

If an idea is not important enough to deserve its own sentence, try combining it with a sentence close by. Put any minor ideas in subordinate structures such as phrases or subordinate clauses.

▶ We keep our use of insecticides, herbicides, and fungicides
  because we
  to a minimum/ ~~We~~ are concerned about the environment.
              ^

A minor idea is now expressed in a subordinate clause beginning with *because*.

▶ The Chesapeake and Ohio Canal, ~~is~~ a 184-mile waterway
                                ^
  constructed in the 1800s/, ~~It~~ was a major source of
                          ^
  transportation for goods during the Civil War.

A minor idea is now expressed in an appositive phrase (*a 184-mile waterway constructed in the 1800s*).

                    E
▶ ~~Sister Consilio was~~ ⁄nveloped in a black robe with only her
                              Sister Consilio
  face and hands visible/, ~~She~~ was an imposing figure.
                        ^

A minor idea is now expressed in a participial phrase beginning with *Enveloped*.

Although subordination is ordinarily the most effective technique for combining short, choppy sentences, coordination is appropriate when the ideas are equal in importance.

▶ The hospital decides when patients will sleep and wake/, It
                                                      and
dictates what and when they will eat/, It tells them when

they may be with family and friends.

Equivalent ideas are expressed in a coordinate series.

ESL

When combining sentences, do not repeat the subject of
the sentence; also do not repeat an object or adverb in an
adjective clause. See 31b and 31c.

▶ The apartment that we moved into it needed many

repairs.

▶ Tanya climbed into the tree house that the boys were

playing in. it.
         ^

LOOKING AT YOURSELF AS A WRITER
Choppy sentences

Combining choppy sentences is a natural part of revision for
most writers, but if your writing style is unusually choppy,
ask yourself why. Here are three common causes and cures.

CAUSE You are afraid of writing run-on sentences, so you
play it safe by keeping your sentences short.

CURE You are right to be concerned about run-on sentences, but try not to worry about them while drafting. Often you can fix a run-on sentence by subordinating minor ideas — the same strategy that usually
works for combining choppy sentences. (See 20d.)

Choppy sentences (continued)

CAUSE You aren't sure how to punctuate sentences that contain subordinate clauses and phrases, so you keep your sentences simple.

CURE Take a few risks when drafting. You can get help with punctuation later—from your instructor or your school's writing center or by consulting Part VII of *The Bedford Handbook*.

CAUSE You are not yet comfortable with the subordination strategies that are necessary for a smooth writing style.

CURE When combining choppy sentences in your drafts, consult the chart on page 185, which gives examples of subordination strategies.

EXERCISE 8–1

In the following paragraphs, combine choppy sentences by subordinating minor ideas or by coordinating ideas of equal importance. More than one effective revision is possible.

Imposing a salary cap on professional athletes is an unfair practice. We may object to a system in which a football player can earn a hundred times more than a schoolteacher. We should not single out professional athletes. No other profession is subjected to a limitation on its earnings. The public never complains about this. Why should Bill Gates or Tom Cruise be allowed to earn million upon million, but not Ken Griffey, Jr.? Athletes earn their money just as honestly as everyone else. They should be given the same earning opportunities.

Sports franchises are much like other corporations in this country. They are profit-seeking businesses. Superstars such as Michael Jordan and Wayne Gretzky increase profits by attracting more fans. Their salaries should reflect that increase.

Some team owners claim that teams in larger cities can afford to pay high player salaries. They say that teams in smaller cities are forced out of the market. The owners believe that salaries should be regulated. This would equally distribute the best players around the country. The owners have a valid point. They are forgetting an important issue: The teams' profits and owners' salaries don't have caps, so why should the players' salaries be limited?

It is sad for fans to see a favorite player move to another team for a better contract. Athletes are the heroes of our youth. We would like to believe that they would loyally play for one team for their entire career, regardless of money. But would we be willing to work for the same company our entire lives, no matter the pay? Would we accept that at a certain point in our earnings we could expect no more raises, even though we would be forced into retirement by age forty? We live in a capitalist society. It is unfair to expect athletes to play by different rules than the rest of us.

8b Avoid ineffective or excessive coordination.

Coordinate structures are appropriate only when you intend to draw the reader's attention equally to two or more ideas: *Professor Naake praises loudly, and she criticizes softly.* If one idea is more important than another—or if a coordinating conjunction does not clearly signal the relation between the ideas—you should subordinate the less important idea.

> **INEFFECTIVE** Closets were taxed as rooms, and most colonists stored their clothes in chests or clothes presses.
>
> **IMPROVED** Because closets were taxed as rooms, most colonists stored their clothes in chests or clothes presses.

The revision subordinates the less important idea by putting it in a subordinate clause. Notice that the subordinating conjunction *Because* signals the relation between the ideas more clearly than the coordinating conjunction *and.*

Clear sentences

Because it is so easy to string ideas together with *and*, writers often rely too heavily on coordination in their rough drafts. The cure for excessive coordination is simple: Look for opportunities to tuck minor ideas into subordinate clauses or phrases.

> *When*
> ▶ Jason walked over to his new Miata, ~~and~~ he saw that its
>   ^
>
> windshield had been smashed.

The minor idea has become a subordinate clause beginning with *When*.

> *noticing*
> ▶ My uncle, ~~noticed~~ my frightened look, ~~and~~ told me that
>   ^   ^
>
> Grandma had to feel my face because she was blind.

The less important idea has become a participial phrase modifying the noun *uncle*.

> *After four hours,*
> ▶ ~~Four hours went by, and~~ a rescue truck finally arrived, but
>   ^
>
> by that time we had been evacuated in a helicopter.

Three independent clauses were excessive. The least important idea has become a prepositional phrase.

EXERCISE 8–2

Combine or restructure the following sentences by subordinating minor ideas or by coordinating ideas of equal importance. You must decide which ideas are minor because the sentences are given out of context. Revisions of lettered sentences appear in the back of the book. Example:

> *where they*
> The crew team finally returned to shore, ~~and~~ had a party on
>   *to celebrate*   ^
> the beach ~~and celebrated~~ the start of the season.
>   ^

a. An instruction manual is enclosed with your computer, and it is user-friendly.
b. Part of my earnings went toward the purchase of a ten-speed bicycle. I hoped the bicycle would serve as my primary form of transportation.
c. There are five fishing piers on the island. Each pier has a bait and tackle shop.
d. Student volunteers from Baltimore City Community College help the younger children with reading and math. These are the children's weakest subjects.
e. The home study course seemed to have everything I was looking for, and I thought my troubles were over, but in reality they were just beginning.

1. Mary will graduate from high school in June. She has not yet decided on a college.
2. I noticed that the sky was glowing orange and red. I bent down to crawl into the bunker.
3. The Market Inn is located at 2nd and E Streets. It doesn't look very impressive from the outside. The food, however, is excellent.
4. Cocaine is an addictive drug and it can seriously harm you both physically and mentally, if death doesn't get you first.
5. These particles are known as "stealth liposomes," and they can hide in the body for a long time without detection.
6. Our waitress was costumed in a kimono. She had painted her face white. She had arranged her hair in an upswept lacquered beehive.
7. He walked up to the pitcher's mound. He dug his toe into the ground. He swung his arm around backward and forward. Then he threw the ball and struck the batter out.
8. Agnes was another girl I worked with. She was a hyperactive child.
9. The lift chairs were going around very fast. They were bumping the skiers into their seats.
10. The first football card set was released by the Goudey Gum Company in 1933. The set featured only three football players. They were Red Grange, Bronko Nagurski, and Knute Rockne.

8c   Do not subordinate major ideas.

If a sentence buries its major idea in a subordinate construction, readers may not give the idea enough attention. Express the major idea in an independent clause and subordinate any minor ideas.

▶   Lanie, who now walks with the help of braces*/.* *had polio as*
         had polio as a child,
    a child.

The writer wanted to focus on Lanie's ability to walk, but the original sentence buried this information in an adjective clause. The revision puts the major idea in an independent clause and tucks the less important idea into an adjective clause (*who had polio as a child*).

▶   *As*
    I was driving home from my new job, heading down Ranchitos

    Road, *when* my car suddenly overheated.

The writer wanted to emphasize that the car was overheating, not the fact of driving home. The revision expresses the major idea in an independent clause, the less important idea in an adverb clause (*As I was driving home from my new job*).

8d   Do not subordinate excessively.

In attempting to avoid short, choppy sentences, writers sometimes go to the opposite extreme, putting more subordinate ideas into a sentence than its structure can bear. If a sentence collapses of its own weight, occasionally it can be restructured. More often, however, such sentences must be divided.

▶ Our job is to stay between the stacker and the tie machine

If they do,

watching to see if the newspapers jam/. ~~in which case~~ we
^

pull the bundles off and stack them on a skid, because

otherwise they would back up in the stacker.

EXERCISE 8–3

In each of the following sentences, the idea that the writer wished
to emphasize is buried in a subordinate construction. Restructure
each sentence so that the independent clause expresses the major
idea and lesser ideas are subordinated. Revisions of lettered sentences appear in the back of the book. Example:

Although

Catherine has weathered many hardships, ~~although~~ she has
^

rarely become discouraged. [*Emphasize that Catherine has*

rarely become discouraged.]

a. We experienced a routine morning at the clinic until an infant
   in cardiac arrest arrived by ambulance. [*Emphasize the arrival
   of the infant.*]
b. My 1969 Camaro, which is no longer street legal, is an original
   SS396. [*Emphasize the fact that the car is no longer street legal.*]
c. This highly specialized medical training, which usually takes
   four years to complete, is called a "residency." [*Emphasize the
   length of time.*]
d. Although native Hawaiians try to preserve their ancestors'
   sacred customs, outsiders have forced changes on them.
   [*Emphasize the Hawaiians' attempt to preserve their customs.*]
e. Ash Lawn, the restored home of our fifth president, James
   Monroe, is located only two miles from Monticello. [*Emphasize
   that Ash Lawn is the restored home of our fifth president.*]

1. The ivy-covered dormitories, located about a mile from most
   of the classrooms, date from the early nineteenth century.
   [*Emphasize where the dormitories are located.*]

2. I was losing consciousness when my will to live kicked in. [*Emphasize the will to live.*]

3. Louis's team worked with the foreign mission by building new churches and restoring those damaged by hurricanes. [*Emphasize the building and restoring.*]

4. The rotor hit, gouging a hole about an eighth of an inch deep in my helmet. [*Emphasize that the rotor gouged a hole in the helmet.*]

5. Although Sarah felt that we lacked decent transportation, our family owned a Jeep, a pickup truck, and a sports car. [*Emphasize Sarah's feeling that the family lacked decent transportation.*]

9

Balance parallel ideas.

If two or more ideas are parallel, they are easier to grasp when expressed in parallel grammatical form. Single words should be balanced with single words, phrases with phrases, clauses with clauses.

A kiss can be a comma, a question mark, or an exclamation point.   —Mistinguett

This novel is not to be tossed lightly aside, but to be hurled with great force.   —Dorothy Parker

In matters of principle, stand like a rock; in matters of taste, swim with the current.   —Thomas Jefferson

Writers often use parallelism to create emphasis. (See 14c.)

GRAMMAR CHECKERS do not flag faulty parallelism. Because computer programs have no way of assessing whether two or more ideas are parallel in meaning, they fail to catch the faulty parallelism in sentences such as this: *In my high school, boys were either jocks, preppies, or studied constantly.*

9a Balance parallel ideas in a series.

Readers expect items in a series to appear in parallel grammatical form. When one or more of the items violate readers' expectations, a sentence will be needlessly awkward.

▶ Abused children commonly exhibit one or more of the

following symptoms: withdrawal, rebelliousness,
depression.
restlessness, and ~~they are depressed.~~
^

The revision presents all of the items as nouns.

▶ Hooked on romance novels, I learned that there is nothing
having
more important than being rich, looking good, and ~~to have~~ a
^
good time.

The revision uses *-ing* forms for all items in the series.

▶ After assuring us that he was sober, Sam drove down the
went through
middle of the road, ran one red light, and two stop signs.
^

The revision adds a verb to make the three items parallel:
drove . . . , ran . . . , went through . . . .

Clear sentences

NOTE: In headings and lists, aim for as much parallelism as the content allows. (See 5a.)

9b Balance parallel ideas presented as pairs.

When pairing ideas, underscore their connection by expressing them in similar grammatical form. Paired ideas are usually connected in one of these ways:

— with a coordinating conjunction such as *and, but,* or *or*

— with a pair of correlative conjunctions such as *either . . . or* or *not only . . . but also*

— with a word introducing a comparison, usually *than* or *as*

Parallel ideas linked with coordinating conjunctions

Coordinating conjunctions (*and, but, or, nor, for, so,* and *yet*) link ideas of equal importance. When those ideas are closely parallel in content, they should be expressed in parallel grammatical form.

▶ At Lincoln High School, vandalism can result in suspen-
expulsion
sion or even ~~being expelled~~ from school.
^

The revision balances the nouns *suspension* and *expulsion*.

▶ Many states are reducing property taxes for home-
extending
owners and ~~extend~~ financial aid in the form of tax credits to
^
renters.

The revision balances the verb *reducing* with the verb *extending*.

Parallel ideas linked with correlative conjunctions

Correlative conjunctions come in pairs: *either . . . or, neither . . . nor, not only . . . but also, both . . . and, whether . . . or.* Make sure that the grammatical structure following the second half of the pair is the same as that following the first half.

▶ The shutters were not only too long but also ~~were~~ too wide.

> The words *too long* follow *not only*, so *too wide* should follow *but also.* Repeating *were* creates an unbalanced effect.

to
▶ I was advised either to change my flight or ⌃ take the train.

> *To change my flight,* which follows *either,* should be balanced with *to take the train,* which follows *or.*

Comparisons linked with than *or* as

In comparisons linked with *than* or *as,* the elements being compared should be expressed in parallel grammatical structure.

to ground
▶ It is easier to speak in abstractions than ~~grounding~~ ⌃ one's

thoughts in reality.

▶ Mother could not persuade me that giving is as much a joy
receiving.
as ~~to receive.~~
⌃

> *To speak in abstractions* is balanced with *to ground one's thoughts in reality. Giving* is balanced with *receiving.*

NOTE: Comparisons should also be logical and complete. (See 10c.)

9c Repeat function words to clarify parallels.

Function words such as prepositions (*by*, *to*) and subordinating conjunctions (*that*, *because*) signal the grammatical nature of the word groups to follow. Although they can sometimes be omitted, include them whenever they signal parallel structures that might otherwise be missed by readers.

▶ Many smokers try switching to a brand they find distasteful
  to
  or a low tar and nicotine cigarette.
   ^

In the original sentence the prepositional phrase was too complex for easy reading. The repetition of the preposition *to* prevents readers from losing their way.

▶ The ophthalmologist told me that Julie was extremely
  that
  farsighted but corrective lenses would help considerably.
        ^

A second subordinating conjunction helps readers sort out the two parallel ideas: *that* Julie was extremely farsighted and *that* corrective lenses would help.

NOTE: If it is possible to streamline the sentence, repetition of the function word may not be necessary.

▶ The board reported that its investments had done well

  in the first quarter but ~~that they~~ had since dropped in

  value.

Instead of linking two subordinate clauses beginning with *that*, the revision balances the two parts of a compound predicate— *had done well in the first quarter* and *had since dropped in value.*

EXERCISE 9–1

Edit the following sentences to correct faulty parallelism. Revisions of lettered sentences appear in the back of the book. Example:

> **We began the search by calling the Department of Social**
>   *requesting*
> **Services and ~~requested~~ a list of licensed day care centers in**
>   ^
> **our area.**

a. The system has capabilities such as communicating with other computers, processing records, and mathematical functions.
b. The personnel officer told me that I would answer the phone, welcome visitors, distribute mail, and some typing.
c. The African elephants are endangered primarily because poachers kill them and having less and less space to live in.
d. How ideal it seems to raise a family here in Winnebago instead of the air-polluted suburbs.
e. In combat the soldiers were brave but sometimes foolish— because of poor training, lack of confidence, and having little experience.

1. The summer of our engagement, we saw a few plays, attended family outings, and a few parties.
2. Roger explained to the immigration officer that his visa had expired and of his applying to have it renewed.
3. The examiners observed us to see if we could stomach the grotesque accidents and how to cope with them.
4. During basic training, I was not only told what to do but also what to think.
5. Activities on Wednesday afternoons include fishing trips, dance lessons, and computers.
6. Tony found that it was faster to ride his bike than driving into the city.
7. More plants fail from improper watering than any other cause.
8. Your adviser familiarizes you with the school and how to select classes appropriate for your curriculum.

9. The winner of the gluttony contest swallowed six large pancakes, slurped down a cream pie, gobbled six waffles, and four pastries in front of the dumbfounded judges.

10. Esperanza is responsible for stocking merchandise, writing orders for delivery, and sales of computers.

LOOKING AT YOURSELF AS A WRITER
Parallelism

Nearly all writers encounter occasional problems with parallelism. Here are some common causes and cures.

CAUSE   You don't realize how awkward faulty parallelism can sound to readers.

CURE   Read aloud some sentences containing faulty parallelism (sentences in 9 or in Exercise 9–1, for example) to hear how awkward they sound. You can use the same read-aloud strategy for your own drafts.

CAUSE   You worry so much about sentence variety that you introduce it in inappropriate contexts.

CURE   Learn to appreciate the power of parallelism. In your reading, notice how skilled writers use parallelism to emphasize connections among ideas. Shakespeare has Hamlet say "to die, to sleep, perchance to dream" (not "to die, to sleep, perchance some dreaming").

CAUSE   You can't think of the right word or you're not sure how to spell the word that's needed to complete your parallel ideas.

CURE   Check a thesaurus or a dictionary.

EXERCISE 9–2

Describe the parallel structure in the following passages and discuss how the use of parallelism contributes to the effectiveness of each. (Also see 14c, which discusses parallel structure.)

1. All respect we may have had for politicians, preachers, lawyers, governors, Presidents, senators, congressmen was utterly destroyed as we watched them temporizing and compromising over right and wrong, over legality and illegality, over constitutionality and unconstitutionality.　　—Eldridge Cleaver
2. One of the devastating weaknesses of university learning, of the store of knowledge and opinion that has been handed down through academic training, has been its almost total erasure of women's experience and thought from the curriculum, and its exclusion of women as members of the academic community.
　　　　　　　　　　　　　　　　　　　—Adrienne Rich
3. Knowing others is wisdom; knowing the self is enlightenment. Mastering others requires force; mastering the self needs strength.　　　　　　　　　　　　　　　—Lao-tzu
4. How can I love the man who raped my mother, killed my father, enslaved my ancestors, dropped atomic bombs on Japan, killed off the Indians, and keeps me cooped up in the slums?
　　　　　　　　　　　　　　　　　　　—Malcolm X
5. I don't want to achieve immortality through my work. I want to achieve it through not dying.　　　　　　　—Woody Allen

10

Add needed words.

Do not omit words necessary for grammatical or logical completeness. Readers need to see at a glance how the parts of a sentence are connected.

ESL

Languages sometimes differ in the need for certain words. In particular, be alert for missing verbs, articles, subjects, or expletives. See 29e, 30, and 31a.

> **GRAMMAR CHECKERS** do not flag the vast majority of missing words. They can, however, catch some missing verbs (see 27e). Although they can flag some missing articles (*a*, *an*, and *the*), they often suggest that an article is missing when in fact it is not. (See also 30.)

10a Add words needed to complete compound structures.

In compound structures, words are often omitted for economy: *Tom is a man who means what he says and* [*who*] *says what he means.* Such omissions are perfectly acceptable as long as the omitted words are common to both parts of the compound structure.

If the shorter version defies grammar or idiom because an omitted word is not common to both parts of the compound structure, the word must be put back in.

▶ Some of the regulars are acquaintances whom we see at
 who
work or live in our community.
 ^

The word *who* must be included because *whom . . . live in our community* is not grammatically correct.

 accepted
▶ I never have and never will accept a bribe.
 ^

Have . . . accept is not grammatically correct.

 in
▶ Many of these tribes still believe and live by ancient laws.
 ^

Believe . . . by is not idiomatic in English.

NOTE: Even when the omitted word is common to both parts of the compound structure, occasionally it must be inserted to avoid ambiguity. The sentence *My favorite English professor and mentor influenced my choice of a career* suggests that the professor and mentor are the same person. If they are not, *my* must be repeated: *My favorite English professor and my mentor influenced my choice of a career.*

10b Add the word *that* if there is any danger of misreading without it.

If there is no danger of misreading, the word *that* may be omitted when it introduces a subordinate clause. *The value of a principle is the number of things [that] it will explain.* Occasionally, however, a sentence might be misread without *that.*

▶ Looking out the family room window, Sarah saw her favorite
                    that
                          ^

    tree, which she had climbed so often as a child, was gone.

    Sarah didn't see the tree; she saw that the tree was gone.

               that
▶ Many civilians believe the air force has a vigorous exercise
               ^

    program.

    The word *that* tells readers to expect a clause, not just *the air force,* as the direct object of *believe.*

10c Add words needed to make comparisons logical and complete.

Comparisons should be made between items that are alike. To compare unlike items is illogical and distracting.

▶ Henry preferred the hotels in Pittsburgh to ^*those in* Philadelphia.

Hotels must be compared with hotels.

▶ Some say that Ella Fitzgerald's renditions of Cole Porter's songs are better than any other ~~singer.~~ ^*singer's.*

Ella Fitzgerald's renditions cannot be logically compared to a singer. The revision uses the possessive form *singer's,* with the word *renditions* being implied.

Sometimes the word *other* must be inserted to make a comparison logical.

▶ Chicago is larger than any ^*other* city in Illinois.

Since Chicago is not larger than itself, the original comparison was not logical.

Sometimes the word *as* must be inserted to make a comparison grammatically complete.

▶ Ben is as talented ^*as,* if not more talented than, the other

actors.

The construction *as talented* is not complete without a second *as*: *as talented as . . . the other actors.*

Finally, comparisons should be complete enough to ensure clarity. The reader should understand what is being compared.

INCOMPLETE Brand X is less salty.

COMPLETE Brand X is less salty than Brand Y.

Also, there should be no ambiguity. In the following sentence, two interpretations are possible.

AMBIGUOUS   Ken helped me more than my roommate.

CLEAR   Ken helped me more than *he helped* my roommate.

CLEAR   Ken helped me more than my roommate *did.*

10d Add the articles *a, an,* and *the* where necessary for grammatical completeness.

Articles are sometimes omitted in recipes and other instructions that are meant to be followed while they are being read. Such omissions are inappropriate, however, in nearly all other forms of writing, whether formal or informal.

> Blood can be drawn only by *a* doctor or by *an* authorized person who has been trained in *the* procedure.

It is not always necessary to repeat articles with paired items: *We bought a computer and printer.* However, if one of the items requires *a* and the other requires *an,* both articles must be included.

> We bought a computer and *an* ink-jet printer.

Articles can cause special problems for speakers of English as a second language. See 30.

ESL

EXERCISE 10–1

Add any words needed for grammatical or logical completeness in the following sentences. Revisions of lettered sentences appear in the back of the book. Example:

that
The officer at the desk feared the prisoner in the interroga-
^

tion room would escape.

a. Dip paintbrush into paint remover and spread thick coat on small section of door.
b. Christopher had an attention span longer than the other students.
c. SETI (the Search for Extraterrestrial Intelligence) has and will continue to excite interest among space buffs.
d. Samantha got along better with the chimpanzees than Albert.
e. We were glad to see Yellowstone National Park was recovering from the devastating forest fire.

1. The forests of North America are much more extensive than Europe.
2. Producers of violent video games are not capable or interested in regulating themselves.
3. In my opinion, Jane's dependence on tranquilizers is no healthier than the alcoholic or the addict.
4. Our nursing graduates are as skilled, if not more skilled than, those of any other state college.
5. American English has borrowed more words from Spanish than from any language.
6. A good source of vitamin C is a grapefruit or orange.
7. Very few black doctors were allowed to serve in the Civil War, and their qualifications had to be higher than white doctors.
8. Darryl was both gratified and apprehensive about his scholarship to UCLA.
9. Hector understood the problem with the engine would not go away.
10. It was obvious that the students liked the new teacher more than the principal.

11

Untangle mixed constructions.

A mixed construction contains parts that do not sensibly fit together. The mismatch may be a matter of grammar or of logic.

> **GRAMMAR CHECKERS** can flag *is when, is where,* and *reason . . . is because* constructions (11c), but they fail to identify nearly all other mixed constructions, including sentences as tangled as this one: *Depending on the number and strength of drinks, the amount of time that has passed, and one's body weight determines the concentration of alcohol in the blood.*

11a Untangle the grammatical structure.

Once you head into a sentence, your choices are limited by the range of grammatical patterns in English. (See 58 and 59.) You cannot begin with one grammatical plan and switch without warning to another.

MIXED	For most drivers who have a blood alcohol content of .05 percent double their risk of causing an accident.
REVISED	For most drivers who have a blood alcohol content of .05 percent, the risk of causing an accident is doubled.
REVISED	Most drivers who have a blood alcohol content of .05 percent double their risk of causing an accident.

The writer began with a long prepositional phrase that was destined to be a modifier but then tried to press it into service as the subject of the sentence. This cannot be done. If the sentence is to begin with the prepositional phrase, the writer must finish the sentence with a subject and verb (*risk . . . is doubled*). The writer who wishes to stay with the original verb (*double*) must head into the sentence another way: *Most drivers. . . .*

▶ *Being*
~~When an employee is~~ promoted without warning can be
    ^
alarming.

The adverb clause *When an employee is promoted without warning* cannot serve as the subject of the sentence. The revision replaces the adverb clause with a gerund phrase, a word group that can function as the subject. (See 59b and 59c.)

▶ Although many pre-Columbian peoples achieved a high level

of civilization, ~~but~~ they were unfamiliar with the wheel.

The *Although* clause is subordinate, so it cannot be linked to an independent clause with the coordinating conjunction *but*.

Occasionally a mixed construction is so tangled that it defies grammatical analysis. When this happens, back away from the sentence, rethink what you want to say, and then say it again as clearly as you can.

MIXED   In the whole-word method children learn to recognize entire words rather than by the phonics method in which they learn to sound out letters and groups of letters.

REVISED   The whole-word method teaches children to recognize entire words; the phonics method teaches them to sound out letters and groups of letters.

ESL

English does not allow double subjects; nor does it allow an object or an adverb to be repeated in an adjective clause. See 31b and 31c.

▶ The squirrel that came down our chimney ~~it~~ did much damage.

▶ Hearing screams, Serena ran over to the pool that her daughter was swimming in. ~~it.~~
                                                    ^

11b Straighten out the logical connections.

The subject and the predicate should make sense together; when they don't, the error is known as *faulty predication.*

▶ We decided that ~~Tiffany's welfare~~ would not be safe living
       Tiffany
       ^
with her mother.

Tiffany, not her welfare, may not be safe.

▶ Under the revised plan, the elderly/~~who now receive a double~~
           double personal exemption for the
           ^
~~personal exemption,~~ will be abolished.

The exemption, not the elderly, will be abolished.

An appositive and the noun to which it refers should be logically equivalent. When they are not, the error is known as *faulty apposition.*

> *Tax accounting,*
> ▶ ~~The tax accountant,~~ a very lucrative field, requires
>   ^
>
>   intelligence, patience, and attention to mathematical
>
>   detail.

The tax accountant is a person, not a field.

11c   Avoid *is when, is where,* and *reason . . . is because* constructions.

In formal English many readers object to *is when, is where,* and *reason . . . is because* constructions on either grammatical or logical grounds. Grammatically, the verb *is* (as well as *are, was,* and *were*) should be followed by a noun that renames the subject or by an adjective that describes it, not by an adverb clause beginning with *when, where,* or *because.* (See 58b and 59b.) Logically, the words *when, where,* and *because* suggest relations of time, place, and cause— relations that do not always make sense with *is, was,* or *were.*

>   *a disorder suffered by people who,*
> ▶ Anorexia nervosa is ~~where people,~~ believing they are too fat,
>   ^
>
>   diet to the point of starvation.

Anorexia nervosa is a disorder, not a place.

> ▶ ~~The reason~~ I missed the exam ~~is~~ because my motorcycle
>
>   broke down.

The writer might have changed *because* to *that* (*The reason I missed the exam is that my motorcycle broke down*), but the revision above is more concise.

LOOKING AT YOURSELF AS A WRITER
Mixed constructions

An occasional mixed construction is nothing to worry about; just revise oddly structured sentences when you encounter them. But if many of your sentences are spinning out of control, try to discover why. Here are some common causes of mixed constructions, each of which suggests its own cure.

CAUSE You don't know what you want to say about your subject, so you wind up in a tangle of words.

CURE Spend more time on prewriting activities (see 1b). Begin drafting only when you have some promising ideas to work with.

CAUSE You are attempting to write in a style more sophisticated than you can handle.

CURE Write in a simpler, more direct style. Readers appreciate plain English more than you may think. (See 17a and 17b.)

CAUSE While drafting, you are overly conscious of style—of how you "sound" on paper.

CURE Focus on your meaning and often the style will take care of itself. Besides, you can always improve the sound of your sentences later.

CAUSE You cling to a particular sentence opening, even though you can't find the right words to finish the sentence.

CURE Experiment with alternatives; maybe you should open the sentence another way. When handwriting, make cross-outs and insertions; when working on a computer, delete and insert text until you get the sentence you want.

Clear sentences

EXERCISE 11–1

Edit the following sentences to untangle mixed constructions. Revisions of lettered sentences appear in the back of the book. Example:

> L
> ~~By~~ loosening the soil around your jade plant will help the air
>
> and nutrients penetrate to the roots.

a. The name of the song is called "Words Unspoken."
b. In a trial conducted in England, which included both pre- and post-menopausal women, showed slightly different results.
c. It is through the misery of others that has made old Harvey rich.
d. A cloverleaf is when traffic on limited-access freeways can change direction.
e. Bowman established the format in which future football card companies would emulate for years to come.

1. Early diagnosis of prostate cancer is often curable.
2. Depending on the number and strength of drinks, the amount of time that has passed since the last drink, and one's body weight determines the concentration of alcohol in the blood.
3. Dyslexia is where people have a learning disorder that impairs reading ability.
4. Although I feel that Mr. Dawe is an excellent calculus instructor, but a few minor changes in his method would benefit both him and his class.
5. The reason the Inuit were forced to eat their dogs was because the caribou, on which they depended for food, migrated out of reach.
6. After Cooke refused to take a Breathalyzer test, she was given a motor skills test and then placed her under arrest.
7. Thailand has been transformed into one of the fastest-growing stock exchanges in the world.
8. In this box contains the key to your future.
9. Who would have thought that a department store salesperson could be a life-threatening job?
10. Using surgical gloves is a precaution now worn by dentists to prevent contact with the patients' blood and saliva.

12

Repair misplaced and dangling modifiers.

Modifiers, whether they are single words, phrases, or clauses, should point clearly to the words they modify. As a rule, related words should be kept together.

> **GRAMMAR CHECKERS** can flag split infinitives, such as *to carefully and thoroughly sift* (12d). However, they don't alert you to other misplaced modifiers or dangling modifiers, including howlers like this one: *When a young man, my mother enrolled me in tap dance classes, hoping I would become the next Gregory Hines.*

12a Put limiting modifiers in front of the words they modify.

Limiting modifiers such as *only, even, almost, nearly,* and *just* should appear in front of a verb only if they modify the verb: *At first, I couldn't even touch my toes, much less grasp them.* If they limit the meaning of some other word in the sentence, they should be placed in front of that word.

> *only*
> ▶ Lasers ~~only~~ destroy ‸ the target, leaving the surrounding
>
> healthy tissue intact.

> *even*
> ▶ Our team didn't ~~even~~ score ‸ once.
>
> *Only* limits the meaning of *the target,* not *destroy. Even* modifies *once,* not *score.*

The limiting modifier *not* is frequently misplaced, suggesting a meaning the writer did not intend.

> *Not all*
> ▶ ~~All~~ wicker is ~~not~~ antique.
>   ^

The original version means that no wicker is antique. The revision makes the writer's real meaning clear.

12b Place phrases and clauses so that readers can see at a glance what they modify.

Although phrases and clauses can appear at some distance from the words they modify, make sure your meaning is clear. When phrases or clauses are oddly placed, absurd misreadings can result.

> **MISPLACED** The king returned to the clinic where he had undergone heart surgery in 1992 in a limousine sent by the White House.
>
> **REVISED** Traveling in a limousine sent by the White House, the king returned to the clinic where he had undergone heart surgery in 1992.

The revision corrects the false impression that the king underwent heart surgery in a limousine.

> *On the walls*
> ▶ ~~There~~ are many pictures of comedians who have performed
>   ^
> at Gavin's. ~~on the walls.~~
>   ^

The comedians weren't performing on the walls; the pictures were on the walls.

>   *150-pound,*
> ▶ The robber was described as a six-foot-tall man with a heavy
>   ^
> mustache. ~~weighing 150 pounds.~~
>   ^

The robber, not the mustache, weighed 150 pounds. The revision makes this clear.

Occasionally the placement of a modifier leads to an ambiguity, in which case two revisions will be possible, depending on the writer's intended meaning.

AMBIGUOUS   The exchange students we met for coffee occasionally questioned us about our latest slang.

CLEAR   The exchange students we occasionally met for coffee questioned us about our latest slang.

CLEAR   The exchange students we met for coffee questioned us occasionally about our latest slang.

In the original version, it was not clear whether the meeting or the questioning happened occasionally. The revisions eliminate the ambiguity.

12c Move awkwardly placed modifiers.

As a rule, a sentence should flow from subject to verb to object, without lengthy detours along the way. When a long adverbial clement separates a subject from its verb, a verb from its object, or a helping verb from its main verb, the result is usually awkward.

> ▶ ~~Our son,~~ ^A^ after doctors told him that he would never walk
> ^*our son*^ without a cane, began an intensive program of
> rehabilitation.^^

There is no reason to separate the subject *Our son* from the verb *began* with a long adverb clause.

► ~~Oscar Lewis spent,~~ *I*n researching *The Children of Sanchez,*
Oscar Lewis spent
hundreds of hours living with the Sanchez family in a slum
⌃
of Mexico City.

The *in* phrase needlessly separated the verb *spent* from its object, *hundreds of hours.*

► ~~Many students have,~~ *B*y the time they reach their senior
many students have
year, completed all the graduation requirements for
⌃
their major.

The helping verb *have* should be closer to its main verb, *completed.*

EXCEPTION: Occasionally a writer may choose to delay a verb or an object to create suspense. In the following passage, for example, Robert Mueller inserts the *after* phrase between the subject *women* and the verb *walk* to heighten the dramatic effect.

> I asked a Burmese why women, after centuries of following
> their men, now walk ahead. He said there were many
> unexploded land mines since the war.
>
> — Robert Mueller

ESL

English does not allow an adverb to appear between a verb and its object. See 31d.

easily.
► Yolanda lifted ~~easily~~ the fifty-pound weight⁄

12d Do not split infinitives needlessly.

An infinitive consists of *to* plus a verb: *to think, to breathe, to dance.* When a modifier appears between *to* and the verb, an infinitive is said to be "split": *to carefully balance.* If a split infinitive is obviously awkward, it should be revised.

▶ *If possible, the*
~~The~~ patient should try to~~, if possible,~~ avoid going up and
^
down stairs.

Usage varies when a split infinitive is less awkward than the preceding one. To be on the safe side, however, you should not split such infinitives, especially in formal writing.

formally.
▶ The candidate decided to ~~formally~~ launch her campaign.
^

When a split infinitive is more natural and less awkward than alternative phrasing, most readers find it acceptable: *We decided to actually enforce the law* is a perfectly natural construction in English. *We decided actually to enforce the law* is not.

EXERCISE 12–1

Edit the following sentences to correct misplaced or awkwardly placed modifiers. Revisions of lettered sentences appear in the back of the book. Example:

in a telephone survey
Answering questions can be annoying. ~~in a telephone survey.~~
^ ^

a. At our warehouse sale, cash, MasterCard, or Visa will only be accepted.
b. All thin people are not anorexic or bulimic.
c. Celia received a flier about a workshop on making a kimono from a Japanese nun.

d. Jurors are encouraged to carefully and thoroughly sift through the evidence.
e. Each state would set a program into motion of recycling all reusable products.

1. Bob almost ate the whole chicken.
2. The orderly confessed that he had given a lethal injection to the patient after ten hours of grilling by the police.
3. Several recent studies have encouraged heart patients to more carefully watch their cholesterol levels.
4. All passengers were, as the train reached the border, asked to have their passports ready.
5. He promised never to remarry at her deathbed.
6. The recordings were all done at the studio of the late Jimi Hendrix named Electric Ladyland.
7. The old Marlboro ads depicted a man on a horse smoking a cigarette.
8. All fresh vegetables are not salt free.
9. The Secret Service was falsely accused of mishandling the attempted assassination by the media.
10. The smog was so bad that we could only see a hundred yards ahead.

12e Repair dangling modifiers.

A dangling modifier fails to refer logically to any word in the sentence. Dangling modifiers are usually introductory word groups (such as verbal phrases) that suggest but do not name an actor. When a sentence opens with such a modifier, readers expect the subject of the following clause to name the actor. If it doesn't, the modifier dangles.

DANGLING Deciding to join the navy, the recruiter enthusiastically pumped Joe's hand. [*Participial phrase*]

DANGLING Upon seeing the barricade, our car screeched to a halt. [*Preposition followed by a gerund phrase*]

DANGLING To please the children, some fireworks were set off a day early. [*Infinitive phrase*]

DANGLING Though only sixteen, UCLA accepted Martha's application. [*Elliptical clause with an understood subject and verb*]

These dangling modifiers falsely suggest that the recruiter decided to join the navy, that the car saw the barricade, that the fireworks intended to please the children, and that UCLA is only sixteen years old.

To repair a dangling modifier, you can revise the sentence in one of two ways:

1. Name the actor immediately following the introductory modifier, or
2. turn the modifier into a word group that names the actor.

▶ Upon entering the doctor's office, a skeleton. <del>caught my attention.</del>
   I noticed

▶ <del>Upon entering</del> the doctor's office, a skeleton caught my attention.
   As I entered

A dangling modifier cannot be repaired simply by moving it: *A skeleton caught my attention upon entering the doctor's office.* The sentence still suggests—absurdly—that the skeleton entered the doctor's office.

▶ <del>Opening</del> the window to let out a huge bumblebee, the car accidentally swerved into the lane of oncoming cars.
   When the driver opened

The car didn't open the window; the driver did. The writer has revised the sentence by putting the driver in the opening modifier.

▶ After completing seminary training, ~~women's~~ access to the
women have often been denied
^

pulpit, ~~has often been denied.~~
^

The women (not their access to the pulpit) complete the training. The writer has revised the sentence by making *women* (not *women's access*) the subject.

LOOKING AT YOURSELF AS A WRITER
Dangling modifiers

Most writers encounter occasional problems with dangling modifiers. Here are a few of the most common causes and cures.

CAUSE   You are trying to avoid using the word *I*, so you write a sentence like this: *At the age of twenty, my father let me drive his restored Mustang.*

CURE   Don't be afraid to use the word *I* in a personal narrative or in other writing that is clearly about you: *When I turned twenty, my father let me drive his restored Mustang.*

CAUSE   You are writing in the passive voice, with the subject of your sentence receiving the action instead of doing it, like this: *To finance the rescue effort, thousands of dollars were donated.*

CURE   Write in the active voice unless you have a good reason for choosing the passive: *To finance the rescue effort, citizens donated thousands of dollars.* (See 14a and 28c.)

CAUSE   To achieve sentence variety, you are putting certain modifiers up front in a sentence —without noticing that they dangle.

Dangling modifiers (*continued*)

CURE Keep the modifier up front, for variety, but add an actor to it. Or change the subject of the sentence so that it names the actor.

CAUSE You think your sentence is clear even though the modifier dangles.

CURE In fact, you may be right. Be aware, though, that some readers—especially English professors—find dangling modifiers distracting.

EXERCISE 12–2

Edit the following sentences to correct dangling modifiers. Most sentences can be revised in more than one way. Revisions of lettered sentences appear in the back of the book. Example:

> *a student must complete*
> To acquire a degree in almost any field, ~~two science courses.~~
> ^   ^
> ~~must be completed.~~

a. Reaching the heart, a bypass was performed on the severely blocked arteries.
b. To enter college early, more than good grades are required.
c. While dining at night, the lights along the Baja coastline created a romantic atmosphere perfect for our first anniversary.
d. While still a beginner at tennis, the coaches recruited my sister to train for the Olympics.
e. After returning to Jamaica, Marcus Garvey's Back to Africa movement slowly died.

1. When flashing, do not speed through a yellow light.
2. At the age of twelve, my grandparents took me on my first balloon ride.

Checking for dangling modifiers

First look for the most common trouble spots:

SENTENCES OPENING WITH A VERBAL

There are three kinds of verbals (see also 59c):

-ing verb forms such as *walking* (present participles)

-ed, -d, -en, -n, or *-t* verb forms such as *planted, eaten, taught* (past participles)

to verb forms such as *to become* (infinitives)

▶ Excited about winning the championship, a raucous *we held*

celebration was held in the locker room.

SENTENCES OPENING WITH A WORD GROUP CONTAINING A VERBAL

▶ After swimming across the lake, the lifeguard scolded *I swam*

me for risking my life.

SENTENCES OPENING WITH AN ELLIPTICAL CLAUSE (A CLAUSE WITH OMITTED WORDS)

▶ Although only four years old, my father insisted that I *I was*

learn to read.

3. By following this new procedure, our mailing costs will decrease significantly.
4. As president of the missionary circle, one of Grandmother's duties is to raise money for the church.
5. When investigating burglaries and thefts, it was easy for me to sympathize with the victims because I had been a victim myself.

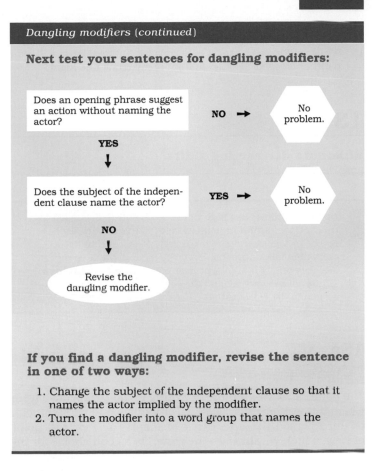

Dangling modifiers (continued)

Next test your sentences for dangling modifiers:

Does an opening phrase suggest an action without naming the actor? → **NO** → No problem.

YES ↓

Does the subject of the independent clause name the actor? → **YES** → No problem.

NO ↓

Revise the dangling modifier.

If you find a dangling modifier, revise the sentence in one of two ways:

1. Change the subject of the independent clause so that it names the actor implied by the modifier.
2. Turn the modifier into a word group that names the actor.

6. Spending four hours on the operating table, a tumor as large as a golf ball was removed from the patient's stomach.
7. As a child growing up in Nigeria, my mother taught me to treat all elders with respect.
8. After becoming eligible to win these bonuses, a sales quota must be maintained for six consecutive months.

9. Thinking that justice had finally prevailed, Lydia's troubles were just beginning.
10. While working as a ranger in Everglades National Park, a Florida panther crossed the road in front of my truck one night.

13

Eliminate distracting shifts.

> GRAMMAR CHECKERS do not flag the shifts discussed in this section: shifts in point of view; shifts in verb tense, mood, or voice; and shifts between direct and indirect questions or quotations. Even the most obvious errors like this one will slip right past most grammar checkers:
> *My three-year-old fell into the pool and to my surprise she swims to the shallow end.*

13a Make the point of view consistent in person and number.

The point of view of a piece of writing is the perspective from which it is written: first person (*I* or *we*), second person (*you*), or third person (*he/she/it/one* or *they*). The *I* (or *we*) point of view, which emphasizes the writer, is a good choice for informal letters and writing based primarily on personal experience. The *you* point of view, which emphasizes the reader, works well for giving advice or explaining how to do something. The third-person point of view, which emphasizes the subject, is appropriate in formal academic and professional writing.

Writers who are having difficulty settling on an appropriate point of view sometimes shift confusingly from one to another. The solution is to choose a suitable perspective and then stay with it.

▶ One week our class met in a junkyard to practice rescuing a

victim trapped in a wrecked car. We learned to dismantle the

                         We   *our*
car with the essential tools. ~~You~~ were graded on ~~your~~ speed

  our
and ~~your~~ skill in extricating the victim.

The writer should have stayed with the *we* point of view. *You* is inappropriate because the writer is not addressing readers directly. *You* should not be used in a vague sense meaning "anyone." (See 23d.)

  You
▶ ~~Everyone~~ should purchase a lift ticket unless you plan to

spend most of your time walking or crawling up a steep hill.

Here *you* is an appropriate choice because the writer is giving advice directly to readers.

  Police officers are
▶ ~~A police officer is~~ often criticized for always being there when

they aren't needed and never being there when they are.

Although the writer might have changed *they* to *he* or *she* (to match the singular *officer*), the revision in the plural is more concise. (See also 17f and 22a.)

13b Maintain consistent verb tenses.

Consistent verb tenses clearly establish the time of the actions being described. When a passage begins in one tense and then shifts without warning and for no reason to another, readers are distracted and confused.

▶ There was no way I could fight the current and win. Just as I
was losing hope, a stranger ~~jumps~~ *jumped* off a passing boat and ~~swims~~ *swam*
toward me.

Writers often encounter difficulty with verb tenses when writing about literature. Because fictional events occur outside the time frames of real life, the past and the present tenses may seem equally appropriate. The literary convention, however, is to describe fictional events consistently in the present tense.

▶ The scarlet letter is a punishment sternly placed upon
Hester's breast by the community, and yet it ~~was~~ *is* an
extremely fanciful and imaginative product of Hester's own
needlework.

13c Make verbs consistent in mood and voice.

Unnecessary shifts in the mood of a verb can be as distracting as needless shifts in tense. There are three moods in English: the *indicative,* used for facts, opinions, and questions; the *imperative,* used for orders or advice; and the *subjunctive,* used in certain contexts to express wishes or conditions contrary to fact (see 28b).

The following passage shifts confusingly from the indicative to the imperative mood.

▶ The officers advised us against allowing anyone into our
homes without proper identification. ~~Also,~~ *They also suggested that we* alert neighbors to
vacation schedules.

Since the writer's purpose was to report the officers' advice, the revision puts both sentences in the indicative.

A verb may be in either the active voice (with the subject doing the action) or the passive voice (with the subject receiving the action). (See 28c.) If a writer shifts without warning from one to the other, readers may be left wondering why.

▶ When the tickets are ready, the travel agent notifies the
    lists each ticket
client*,/* ~~Each ticket is then listed~~ on a daily register form*,* and
files
a copy of the itinerary*.* ~~is filed.~~

The passage began in the active voice (*agent notifies*) and then switched to the passive (*ticket is listed, copy is filed*). Because the active voice is clearer and more direct, the writer changed all the verbs to the active voice.

13d Avoid sudden shifts from indirect to direct questions or quotations.

An indirect question reports a question without asking it: *We asked whether we could take a swim.* A direct question asks directly: *Can we take a swim?* Sudden shifts from indirect to direct questions are awkward. In addition, sentences containing such shifts are impossible to punctuate because indirect questions must end with a period and direct questions must end with a question mark. (See 38b.)

▶ I wonder whether the sister knew of the theft and, if so, ~~did~~
    whether she reported
~~she report~~ it to the police.

The revision poses both questions indirectly. The writer could also ask both questions directly: *Did the sister know of the theft and, if so, did she report it to the police?*

An indirect quotation reports someone's words without quoting word for word: *Annabelle said that she is a Virgo.* A direct quotation presents the exact words of a speaker or writer, set off with quotation marks: *Annabelle said, "I am a Virgo."* Unannounced shifts from indirect to direct quotations are distracting and confusing, especially when the writer fails to insert the necessary quotation marks, as in the following example.

▶ Mother said that she would be late for dinner and ~~please do~~ *asked me not to*

~~not~~ leave for choir practice until Dad ~~comes~~ home. *came*

The revision reports all of the mother's words. The writer could also quote directly: *Mother said, "I will be late for dinner. Please do not leave for choir practice until Dad comes home."*

LOOKING AT YOURSELF AS A WRITER
Shifts

Shifts in a rough draft alert you to choices you must make as a writer. Once you have made those choices—by deciding on an appropriate point of view or tense, for example—eliminating shifts in the final draft will be a simple matter.

Shifts in point of view

CAUSE You are trying to avoid the word *I* or the word *you* in a context where these pronouns may be appropriate.

CURE Consider drafting your essay from the *I* or the *you* point of view. For appropriate uses of these points of view, see pages 55–57.

CAUSE You are trying to avoid sexist language without resorting to the wordy *he or she* construction.

CURE Consider writing in the plural. (See 22a.)

CAUSE You have selected the pronoun *one* in an attempt to include both men and women, but repeating *one* seems awkward, so you shift to another pronoun such as *their* or *you*.

Shifts (continued)

CURE You are right that repetitions of *one* sound awkward, at least to American ears: *One must watch one's pronouns.* Try another point of view instead: *Writers must watch their pronouns. You must watch your pronouns.*

Shifts in tense

CAUSE To make the action of a narrative more immediate, you are casting it in the present tense, but at times you shift to the past.

CURE Read your narrative to yourself twice—once using all present-tense verbs and once using all past-tense verbs. Then choose the tense that you feel sounds better. If you are still in doubt, ask another writer for advice.

CAUSE You are writing about events in a literary work, and you're not sure whether to use the present or the past tense.

CURE Choose the present tense, since that is the literary convention.

Shifts from indirect to direct questions or quotations

CAUSE By inserting direct questions or quotations, you hope to make your style more vivid, but you end up mixing direct and indirect questions or quotations.

CURE You are right that adding direct questions or quotations can make your writing more lively. Consider revising your sentence to use the direct approach consistently.

CAUSE In spoken English you hear such shifts all the time, and they don't seem to bother anyone.

CURE Be aware that the standards for written English are stricter than those for spoken English.

EXERCISE 13–1

Edit the following sentences to eliminate distracting shifts. Revisions of lettered sentences appear in the back of the book. Example:

> *they*
> For most people, quitting smoking is not easy once ~~you~~ are
>   ^
> hooked.

a. My hopes rise and fall as Joseph's heart started and stopped. The doctors insert a large tube into his chest, and the blood flowed from the incision onto the floor.
b. After the count of three, Mikah and I placed the injured woman on the scoop stretcher. Then her vital signs were taken by me.
c. A minister often has a hard time because they have to please so many different people.
d. We drove for eight hours until we reached the South Dakota Badlands. You could hardly believe the eeriness of the landscape at dusk.
e. The question is whether ferrets bred in captivity have the instinct to prey on prairie dogs or is this a learned skill.

1. Everyone should protect yourself from the sun, especially on the first day of extensive exposure.
2. The police told us that the island was being evacuated because of the coming storm. Also, take the northern route to the mainland.
3. A courtroom lawyer has more than a touch of theater in their blood.
4. Struggling with the boxes, I knew I was failing the performance test. You looked to the testing officer for a sign of mercy, but it never came.
5. The artist has often been seen as a threat to society, especially when they refuse to conform to conventional standards of taste.
6. Phil said that he would be happy to set up the new computer and when could he come over and get started.
7. As I was pulling in the decoys, you could see and hear the geese heading back to the bay.

8. Rescue workers put water on her face and lifted her head gently onto a pillow. Finally, she opens her eyes.
9. With a little self-discipline and a desire to improve oneself, you too can enjoy the benefits of running.
10. A politician is often criticized for breaking promises that they made during their election campaigns.

14

Emphasize your point.

Within each sentence, emphasize your point by expressing it in the subject and verb, the words that receive the most attention from readers. As a rule, choose an active verb and pair it with a subject that names the person or thing doing the action.

Within longer stretches of prose, you can draw attention to ideas deserving special emphasis by using a variety of techniques, often involving an unusual twist or some element of surprise.

14a Prefer active verbs.

Active verbs express meaning more emphatically and vigorously than their weaker counterparts—forms of the verb *be* or verbs in the passive voice. Forms of the verb *be* (*be, am, is, are, was, were, being, been*) lack vigor because they convey no action. Verbs in the passive voice lack strength because their subjects receive the action instead of doing it (see 28c and 58c).

LOOKING AT YOURSELF AS A WRITER
The passive voice

If you are frequently tempted to use the passive voice in contexts where the active voice would be more effective, consider some common causes and cures.

CAUSE In an attempt to avoid using the word *I* or *you*, you resort to the passive voice, like this: *In my excitement, my glass of iced tea was knocked over. Before a hard workout, warmup exercises are advised.*

CURE Feel free to use the words *I* and *you* when they are appropriate: *In my excitement, I knocked over my glass of iced tea. Before a hard workout, you should do some warmup exercises.* (See pp. 55–57 for a discussion of appropriate uses of *I* and *you*.)

CAUSE At work, you are surrounded by writers who use the passive voice, and you are picking up the habit from them.

CURE Look at your co-workers' writing with a critical eye, noting when their use of the passive is effective— and when it is not. Then look at your own writing with an equally critical eye.

CAUSE Your major is science or technology, disciplines in which use of the passive is often appropriate.

CURE Shift gears when you are taking classes outside of your major. In most disciplines, the active voice usually emphasizes your point more clearly than the passive.

CAUSE To make your writing flow, you often pick up a word from the tail end of one sentence and use it in the opening of the next sentence, like this: *The polygraph is an instrument that measures physiological responses to questions as a way of detecting possible deception. Possible deception is detected by examiners for a variety of purposes.*

> *The passive voice (continued)*
>
> **CURE**   Rethink your concept of "flow." Ideas flow best when they are clear, and the active voice is usually clearer: *The polygraph is an instrument that measures physiological responses to questions as a way of detecting possible deception. Examiners use the polygraph for a variety of purposes.*

Although the forms of *be* and passive verbs have legitimate uses, if an active verb can carry your meaning, use it.

BE VERB   A surge of power *was* responsible for the destruction of the pumps.

PASSIVE   The pumps *were destroyed* by a surge of power.

ACTIVE   A surge of power *destroyed* the pumps.

Even among active verbs, some are more active—and therefore more vigorous and colorful—than others. Carefully selected verbs can energize a piece of writing.

> ▶ The goalie crouched low, ~~reached~~ *swept* out his stick, and ~~sent~~ *hooked* the rebound away from the mouth of the net.

When to replace *be* verbs

Not every *be* verb needs replacing. The forms of *be* (*be, am, is, are, was, were, being, been*) work well when you want to link a subject to a noun that clearly renames it or to an adjective that describes it: *History is a bucket of ashes. Scoundrels are always sociable.* And when used as helping verbs before present participles (*is flying, are disappearing*) to express ongoing action, *be* verbs are fine: *Derrick was plowing the field when his wife went into labor.* (See 29a.)

If using a *be* verb makes a sentence needlessly wordy, however, consider replacing it. Often a phrase following the verb will contain a word (such as *destruction*) that suggests a more vigorous, active alternative (*destroyed*).

▶ Burying nuclear waste in Antarctica would ~~be in violation of~~ *violate*
an international treaty.

Violate is less wordy and more vigorous than *be in violation of*.

▶ Escaping into the world of drugs, I ~~was rebellious about~~ *rebelled against* every
rule set down by my parents.

Rebelled against is more active than *was rebellious about*.

When to replace passive verbs

In the active voice, the subject of the sentence does the action; in the passive, the subject receives the action.

ACTIVE   Hernando *caught* the fly ball.

PASSIVE   The fly ball *was caught* by Hernando.

In passive sentences, the actor (in this case *Hernando*) frequently disappears from the sentence: *The fly ball was caught.*

In most cases, you will want to emphasize the actor, so you should use the active voice. To replace a passive verb with an active alternative, make the actor the subject of the sentence.

▶ ~~The transformer was struck by a bolt of lightning,~~ *A bolt of lightning struck the transformer,* plunging
us into darkness.

The active verb (*struck*) makes the point more forcefully than the passive verb (*was struck*).

The passive voice is appropriate when you wish to emphasize the receiver of the action or to minimize the importance of the actor. For example, in the sentence about the fly ball, you would choose the active voice if you wanted to emphasize the actor, Hernando: *Hernando caught the fly ball.* But you would choose the passive voice if you wanted to emphasize the ball and the catch: *The fly ball was caught by Hernando.* (See 28c.)

ESL Some speakers of English as a second language avoid the passive voice even when it is appropriate. For advice on appropriate uses of the passive, see 28c.

GRAMMAR CHECKERS are fairly good at flagging passive verbs, such as *were given* (14a), but some passive verbs slip past these programs. Two words of caution are in order, however. First, because passive verbs are sometimes appropriate, you—not the computer program—must decide whether to make a passive verb active. (See 14a and 28c for guidelines on choosing active or passive verbs.)

Second, grammar checkers sometimes incorrectly flag verbs as passive. It's not surprising that a computer program can't distinguish between a true passive, such as *is managed*, and a *be* verb followed by a past participle functioning as an adjective, such as *are indebted.*

14b As a rule, choose a subject that names the person or thing doing the action.

In weak, unemphatic prose, both the actor and the action may be buried in sentence elements other than the subject and the verb. In the following sentence, for example, the actor

Clear sentences

and the action both appear in prepositional phrases, word groups that do not receive much attention from readers.

> **WEAK** Exposure to Dr. Martinez's excellent teaching had the effect of inspiring me to major in education.

> **EMPHATIC** Dr. Martinez's excellent teaching inspired me to major in education.

Consider the subjects and verbs of the two versions — *exposure had* versus *teaching inspired.* Clearly the latter expresses the writer's point more emphatically.

     Cocaine used   *cause*
▶ ~~The use of cocaine~~ by pregnant women can ~~be a major~~
    ^

~~contributor to~~ severe brain damage in infants.

In the original version, the subject and verb — *use can be* — express the point blandly. *Cocaine can cause* alerts readers to the dangers of cocaine more emphatically than *use can be.*

EXERCISE 14–1

Revise any weak, unemphatic sentences by replacing *be* verbs or passive verbs with active alternatives and, if necessary, by naming in the subject the person or thing doing the action. Some sentences are emphatic; do not change them. Revisions of lettered sentences appear in the back of the book. Example:

    The ranger doused the campfire before giving us
    ~~The campfire was doused by the ranger before we were given~~
    ^

    a ticket for unauthorized use of a campsite.

a. The Prussians were victorious over the Saxons in 1745.
b. The entire operation is managed by Ahmed, the producer.
c. Finally the chute caught air and popped open with a jolt at about 2,000 feet.
d. There were fighting players on both sides of the rink.
e. At recess, Ms. Robinson joined us in our games. She jumped rope, played dodgeball, and even climbed on the jungle gym.

1. Just as the police closed in, two shots were fired by the terrorists from the roof of the hotel.
2. Julia was successful in her first attempt to pass the bar exam.
3. The bomb bay doors rumbled open and freezing air whipped through the plane.
4. Listening to the music of Charlie Parker and John Coltrane had the effect of inspiring me to take up the saxophone.
5. The only responsibility I was given by my parents was putting gas in the brand-new Mitsubishi they bought me my senior year.

14c Experiment with techniques for gaining special emphasis.

By experimenting with certain techniques, usually involving some element of surprise, you can draw attention to ideas that deserve special emphasis. Use such techniques sparingly, however, or they will lose their punch. The writer who tries to emphasize everything ends up emphasizing nothing.

Using sentence endings for emphasis

You can highlight an idea simply by withholding it until the end of a sentence. The technique works something like a punch line. In the following example, the sentence's meaning is not revealed until its very last word.

> The only completely consistent people are the dead.
> — Aldous Huxley

Two types of sentence that withhold information until the end deserve special mention: the inversion and the periodic sentence. The *inversion* reverses the normal subject-verb order, placing the subject at the end, where it receives unusual emphasis. (Also see 15c.)

> In golden pots are hidden the most deadly poisons.
> —Thomas Draxe

The *periodic* sentence opens with a pile-up of modifiers and withholds the subject and verb until the end. It draws attention to itself because it contrasts with the cumulative sentence, which is used more frequently. A *cumulative* sentence begins with the subject and verb and adds modifying elements at the end.

PERIODIC
Twenty-five years ago, at the age of thirteen, while hiking in the mountains near my hometown of Vancouver, Washington, I came face to face with the legendary Goat Woman of Livingston Mountain.   —Tom Weitzel, student

CUMULATIVE
A metaphysician is one who goes into a dark cellar at midnight without a light, looking for a black cat that is not there.   —Baron Bowan of Colwood

Using parallel structure for emphasis

Parallel grammatical structure draws special attention to paired ideas or to items in a series. (See 9.) When parallel ideas are paired, the emphasis falls on words that underscore comparisons or contrasts, especially when they occur at the end of a phrase or clause.

> We must *stop talking* about the *American dream* and *start listening* to the *dreams of Americans*.
>
> —Reubin Askew

In a parallel series, the emphasis falls at the end, so it is generally best to end with the most dramatic or climactic item in the series.

> Sister Charity enjoyed passing out writing punishments: translate the Ten Commandments into Latin, type a thousand-word essay on good manners, copy the New Testament with a quill pen.   —Marie Visosky, student

Using punctuation for emphasis

Obviously the exclamation point can add emphasis, but you should not overuse it. As a rule, the exclamation point is more appropriate in dialogue than in ordinary prose.

> I oozed a glob of white paint onto my palette, whipped some medium into it, loaded my brush, and announced to the class, "Move over, Michelangelo. Here I come!"
>   —Carolyn Goff, student

A dash or a colon may be used to draw attention to word groups worthy of special attention. (See 35a, 35b, and 39a.)

> The middle of the road is where the white line is—and that's the worst place to drive.   —Robert Frost

> I turned to see what the anemometer read: The needle had pegged out at 106 knots.   —Jonathan Shilk, student

Occasionally, a pair of dashes may be used to highlight a word or an idea.

> [My friend] was a gay and impudent and satirical and delightful young black man—a slave—who daily preached sermons from the top of his master's woodpile, with me for sole audience.   —Mark Twain

Using an occasional short sentence for emphasis

Too many short sentences in a row will fast become monotonous (see 8a), but an occasional short sentence, when played off against longer sentences in the same passage, will draw attention to an idea.

> The great secret, known to internists and learned early in marriage by internists' wives [or husbands], but still hidden from the general public, is that most things get better by themselves. Most things, in fact, are better by morning.
>   —Lewis Thomas

Clear sentences

EXERCISE 14–2

Discuss the methods used to achieve emphasis in the following paragraphs.

> Unseen in the jungle, but present, are tapirs, jaguars, many species of snake and lizard, ocelots, armadillos, marmosets, howler monkeys, toucans and macaws and a hundred other birds, deer, bats, peccaries, capybaras, agoutis, and sloths. Also present in this jungle, but variously distant, are Texaco derricks and pipelines, and some of the wildest Indians in the world, blowgun-using Indians, who killed missionaries in 1956 and ate them.   —Annie Dillard

> My Uncle Tom worked as a blacksmith in the B & O yards near Harpers Ferry. That was a good job too. Though he walked the four-mile round trip to and from the shop daily in sooty railroader's clothes, Uncle Tom was well off. His house contained a marvel I had never seen before: an indoor bathroom. This was enough to mark Uncle Tom a rich man, but in addition he had a car. And such a car. It was an Essex, with windows that rolled up and down with interior hand cranks, not like my father's Model T with the isinglass windows in side curtains that had to be buttoned onto the frame in bad weather. Uncle Tom's Essex even had cut-glass flower vases in sconces in the backseat. He was a man of substance. When he rolled up in his Essex for Ida Rebecca's command appearances on Sunday afternoons in Morrisonville, wearing a white shirt and black suit, smoking his pipe, his pretty red-haired wife Goldie on the seat beside him, I felt pride in kinship to so much grandeur.   —Russell Baker

15

Provide some variety.

When a rough draft is filled with too many same-sounding sentences, try injecting some variety—as long as you can do so without sacrificing clarity or ease of reading.

GRAMMAR CHECKERS are of little help with sentence variety. It takes a human ear to know when and why sentence variety is needed.

Some programs tell you when you have used the same word to open several sentences, but sometimes it is a good idea to do so — if you are trying to highlight parallel ideas, for example (see p. 101).

15a Vary your sentence openings.

Most sentences in English begin with the subject, move to the verb, and continue along to the object, with modifiers tucked in along the way or put at the end. For the most part, such sentences are fine. Put too many of them in a row, however, and they become monotonous.

Adverbial modifiers, being easily movable, can often be inserted ahead of the subject. Such modifiers might be single words, phrases, or clauses.

> *Eventually a*
> ▶ A̶ few drops of sap ~~eventually~~ began to trickle into the
>   ^
> bucket.

Like most adverbs, *eventually* does not need to appear close to the verb it modifies (*began*).

> *Just as the sun was coming up, a*
> ▶ A̶ pair of black ducks flew over the blind . ~~just as the sun was~~
>   ^   ^
> ~~coming up.~~

The adverb clause, which modifies the verb *flew*, is as clear at the beginning of the sentence as it is at the end.

Adjectives and participial phrases can frequently be moved to the beginning of a sentence without loss of clarity.

A

Clear sentences

Dejected and withdrawn,
▶ Edward, ~~dejected and withdrawn,~~ nearly gave up his search
   ^
   for a job.

                A   *John and I*
▶ ~~John and I,~~ Anticipating a peaceful evening, sat down at the
                                                              ^
   campfire to brew a cup of coffee.

CAUTION: When beginning a sentence with an adjective or a participial phrase, make sure that the subject of the sentence names the person or thing described in the introductory phrase. If it doesn't, the phrase will dangle. (See 12e.)

15b Use a variety of sentence structures.

A writer should not rely too heavily on simple sentences and compound sentences, for the effect tends to be both monotonous and choppy. (See 8a and 8b.) Too many complex or compound-complex sentences, however, can be equally monotonous. If your style tends to one or the other extreme, try to achieve a better mix of sentence types.

The major sentence types are illustrated in the following sentences, all taken from Flannery O'Connor's "The King of the Birds," an essay describing the author's pet peafowl.

SIMPLE	Frequently the cock combines the lifting of his tail with the raising of his voice.
COMPOUND	Any chicken's dusting hole is out of place in a flower bed, but the peafowl's hole, being the size of a small crater, is more so.
COMPLEX	The peacock does most of his serious strutting in the spring and summer when he has a full tail to do it with.

COMPOUND **COMPLEX**	The cock's plumage requires two years to attain its pattern, and for the rest of his life, this chicken will act as though he designed it himself.

For a fuller discussion of sentence types, see 60a.

15c Try inverting sentences occasionally.

A sentence is inverted if it does not follow the normal subject-verb-object pattern. (See 58c.) Many inversions sound artificial and should be avoided except in the most formal contexts. But if an inversion sounds natural, it can provide a welcome touch of variety.

▶ *Opposite the produce section is a*
  ~~A~~ refrigerated case of mouth-watering cheeses; ~~is opposite~~
     ^   ^
  ~~the produce section;~~ a friendly attendant will cut off just the

  amount you want.

The revision inverts the normal subject-verb order by moving the verb, *is*, ahead of its subject, *case*.

▶ *Set at the top two corners of the stage wore huge*
  ~~Huge~~ lavender hearts outlined in bright white lights. ~~were set~~
     ^   ^
  ~~at the top two corners of the stage.~~

In the revision the subject, *hearts*, appears after the verb, *were set*. Notice that the two parts of the verb are also inverted—and separated from one another—without any awkwardness or loss of meaning.

Inverted sentences are used for emphasis as well as for variety. (See 14c.)

15d   Consider adding an occasional question or quotation.

An occasional question can provide a welcome change of pace, especially at the beginning of a paragraph, where it engages the reader's interest.

> Virginia Woolf, in her book *A Room of One's Own,* wrote that in order for a woman to write fiction she must have two things, certainly: a room of her own (with key and lock) and enough money to support herself.
> *What then are we to make of Phillis Wheatley, a slave, who owned not even herself?* This sickly, frail black girl who required a servant of her own at times—her health was so precarious—and who, had she been white, would have been easily considered the intellectual superior of all the women and most of the men in the society of her day. [Italics added.]
> —Alice Walker

Quotations can also provide variety, for they add other people's voices to your own. These other voices might be bits of dialogue.

> When we got back upstairs, Dr. Haney and Captain Shiller, the head nurse, were waiting for us by the elevator. As the nurse hurried off, pushing Todd, the doctor explained to us what would happen next.
> "Mrs. Barrus," he began, "this last test is one we do only when absolutely necessary. It is very painful and hard on the patient but we have no other choice." Apologetically, he went on. "I cannot give him an anesthetic." He waited for the statement to sink in.   —Celeste L. Barrus, student

Or they might be quotations from written sources:

> Even when she enters the hospital on the brink of death, the anorexic will refuse help from anyone and will continue to deny needing help, especially from a doctor. At this point, re-

ports Dr. Steven Levenkron, the anorexic is most likely "a frightened, cold, lonely, starved, and physically tortured, exhausted person—not unlike an actual concentration camp inmate" (29). In this condition she is ultimately force-fed through a tube inserted in the chest.

— Jim Drew, student

Notice that the quotation from a written source is documented with a citation in parentheses. (See 50.)

EXERCISE 15–1

Edit the following paragraph to increase variety in sentence structure.

I have spent thirty years of my life on a tobacco farm, and I cannot understand why people smoke. The whole process of raising tobacco involves deadly chemicals. The ground is treated for mold and chemically fertilized before the tobacco seed is ever planted. The seed is planted and begins to grow, and then the bed is treated with weed killer. The plant is then transferred to the field. It is sprayed with poison to kill worms about two months later. Then the time for harvest approaches, and the plant is sprayed once more with a chemical to retard the growth of suckers. The tobacco is harvested and hung in a barn to dry. These barns are havens for birds. The birds defecate all over the leaves. After drying, these leaves are divided by color, and no feces are removed. They are then sold to the tobacco companies. I do not know what the tobacco companies do after they receive the tobacco. I do not need to know. They cannot remove what I know is in the leaf and on the leaf. I don't want any of it to pass through my mouth.

EXERCISE 15–2

Discuss how the writers of the following paragraphs provide variety.

I was then a listening child, careful to hear the very different sounds of Spanish and English. Wide-eyed with hearing, I'd listen to sounds more than to words. First, there were English (*gringo*) sounds. So many words were still unknown to me that when the butcher or the lady at the drugstore said something, exotic polysyllabic sounds would bloom in the midst of their sentences. Often the speech of people in public seemed to me very loud, booming with confidence. The man behind the counter would literally ask, "What can I do for you?" But by being so firm and clear, the sound of his voice said that he was a *gringo*; he belonged in public society.

—Richard Rodriguez

Our own house was an appalling sight from the outside. The siding, originally white, sprouted leprous gray patches where the paint was peeling away. Bark hung down from the huge dead elm in the front yard like long, limp scabs. The tree and a doorless garage leaned ominously toward our house. To the north, weeds grew up around a lonely, abandoned shack. To the south, a run-down house covered with rotting, gray asbestos shingles crouched, a weathered outhouse several steps from the back door. Farther south along the frozen, muddy road huddled a tiny one-room dwelling isolated in a swampy hollow. Barely glimpsed through a sea of stiffly dried weeds, the roofs of two ramshackle chicken coops rounded out the view from our yard. Our forgotten lane lacked street lamps and house numbers and was denied even the dignity of a street sign at the corner.

— Julie Reardon, student

Word Choice

16

Tighten wordy sentences.

In a rough draft we are rarely economical: We repeat our-selves, we belabor the obvious, we cushion our thoughts in verbiage. As a general rule, advises writer Sidney Smith, "run a pen through every other word you have written; you have no idea what vigor it will give your style."

Long sentences are not necessarily wordy, nor are short sentences always concise. A sentence is wordy if it can be tightened without loss of meaning.

> **GRAMMAR CHECKERS** can flag some, but not all, wordy constructions. Most programs alert you to common redundancies, such as *true fact*, and empty or inflated phrases, such as *in my opinion* or *in order that*. In addition, they alert you to wordiness caused by passive verbs, such as *is determined* (see also 14a). They are less helpful in identifying sentences with needlessly complex structures.

16a   Eliminate redundancies.

Writers often repeat themselves unnecessarily. Afraid, per-haps, that they won't be heard the first time, they insist that a teacup is small *in size* or yellow *in color,* that married people should cooperate *together,* that a fact is not just a fact but a *true* fact. Such redundancies may seem at first to add emphasis. In reality they do just the opposite, for they divide the reader's attention.

▶ Black slaves were ~~thought of or~~ stereotyped as lazy even

though they were the main labor force of the South.

▶ Daniel ~~is now employed~~ at a private rehabilitation center
  ^works^

~~working~~ as a registered physical therapist.

Though modifiers ordinarily add meaning to the words they modify, occasionally they are redundant.

▶ Sylvia ~~very hurriedly~~ scribbled her name, address, and phone number on the back of a greasy napkin.

▶ Joel was determined ~~in his mind~~ to lose weight.

The words *scribbled* and *determined* already contain the notions suggested by the modifiers *very hurriedly* and *in his mind.*

16b Avoid unnecessary repetition of words.

Though words may be repeated deliberately, for effect, repetitions will seem awkward if they are clearly unnecessary. When a more concise version is possible, choose it.

▶ Our fifth patient, in room six, is *a* mentally ill. ~~patient.~~

▶ The best teachers help each student to ~~become a better~~
  ^grow^

~~student~~ both academically and emotionally.

16c Cut empty or inflated phrases.

An empty phrase can be cut with little or no loss of meaning. Common examples are introductory word groups that apologize or hedge: *in my opinion, I think that, it seems that, one must admit that,* and so on.

Word choice

O
► ~~In my opinion,~~ ¢ur current immigration policy is misguided

on several counts.

► ~~It seems that~~ *Lonesome Dove* is one of Larry McMurtry's

most ambitious novels.

Readers understand without being told that they are hearing
the writer's opinion or educated guess.

Inflated phrases can be reduced to a word or two without loss of meaning.

INFLATED	CONCISE
along the lines of	like
as a matter of fact	in fact
at all times	always
at the present time	now, currently
at this point in time	now, currently
because of the fact that	because
by means of	by
by virtue of the fact that	because
due to the fact that	because
for the purpose of	for
for the reason that	because
have the ability to	be able to, can
in light of the fact that	because
in the nature of	like
in order to	to
in spite of the fact that	although, though
in the event that	if
in the final analysis	finally
in the neighborhood of	about
until such time as	until

if
► We will file the appropriate papers ~~in the event that~~ we are
                                        ^
unable to meet the deadline.

16d Simplify the structure.

If the structure of a sentence is needlessly indirect, try simplifying it. Look for opportunities to strengthen the verb.

▶ The financial analyst claimed that because of volatile market

conditions she could not ~~make an~~ estimate ~~of~~ the company's

future profits.

The verb *estimate* is more vigorous and more concise than *make an estimate of*.

The colorless verbs *is*, *are*, *was*, and *were* frequently generate excess words.

          monitors and balances
▶ The secretary ~~is responsible for monitoring and balancing~~
         ^

the budgets for travel, contract services, and personnel.

The revision is more direct and concise. Actions originally appearing in subordinate structures have become verbs replacing *is*.

The expletive constructions *there is* and *there are* (or *there was* and *there were*) can also generate excess words. The same is true of expletive constructions beginning with *it*. (See 58c.)

   A
▶ ~~There is~~ ~~A~~nother module ~~that~~ tells the story of Charles

Darwin and introduces the theory of evolution.

         H   *must*
▶ ~~It is important that~~ ~~H~~ikers remain inside the park
          ^

boundaries.

Checking for wordy sentences

Look especially for these common trouble spots:

REDUNDANCIES (16a)

▶ Passive euthanasia is the ~~act or~~ practice of allowing terminally ill patients to die.

▶ The colors of the reproductions were ~~precisely~~ exact.

UNNECESSARY REPETITION OF WORDS (16b)

▶ ~~The quilt that was~~ *T*/he highlight of Grandmother's collection was a crazy quilt dating from 1889.

EMPTY OR INFLATED PHRASES (16c)

▶ Although ~~it seemed that~~ it was unlikely that the call was for me, I was so excited that I ran to the phone.

▶ The ring costs *about* ~~in the neighborhood of~~ sixty dollars.

NEEDLESSLY INDIRECT STRUCTURES (16d)

▶ The institute was established to *train* ~~provide training for~~ highway agency employees.

Wordy sentences *(continued)*

> ~~There was~~ _A a deranged vagrant ^{was} pestering the persons in line, spouting biblical quotations one minute and shouting obscenities the next.

> ~~It is imperative that~~ _A ~~a~~ll police officers ^{must} follow strict procedures when apprehending a suspect.

> Last summer, a horse. ^{my parents gave me} ~~was given to me by my parents.~~

NEEDLESSLY COMPLEX STRUCTURES (16e)

> We visited Charlottesville, ~~which is~~ the home of the historic University of Virginia.

> Our landlord was an elderly bachelor,/~~and it was~~ ^{who taught us} ~~through his guid~~ance that ~~we were able~~ to appreciate country life.

> When I approached the window, the guard took the form/, ~~He~~ asked me a few questions, and then ~~he~~ told me to see another guard, who would do a physical search.

Expletive constructions do have legitimate uses, however. For example, they are appropriate when a writer has a good reason for delaying the subject. (See 58c.)

Finally, verbs in the passive voice may be needlessly indirect. When the active voice expresses your meaning as well, use it. (See 14a and 28c.)

▶ All too often, athletes with marginal academic skills. ~~have~~
    our coaches have recruited
    ^
    ~~been recruited by our coaches.~~

16e Reduce clauses to phrases, phrases to single words.

Word groups functioning as modifiers can often be made more compact. Look for any opportunities to reduce clauses to phrases or phrases to single words.

▶ We took a side trip to Monticello, ~~which was~~ the home of Thomas Jefferson.

▶ For her birthday we gave Jess a stylish vest. ~~made of silk.~~
                                                  silk
                                                  ^   ^

EXERCISE 16–1

Edit the following sentences for wordiness. Revisions of lettered sentences appear in the back of the book. Example:

The Wilsons moved into the house ~~in spite of the fact that~~
                                   even though
                                   ^
the back door was only ten yards from the train tracks.

a. The drawing room in the west wing is the room that is said to be haunted.

b. Even the placement of ten terry cloth towels stuffed under the door did nothing to stop the flow.

c. In my opinion, Bloom's race for the governorship is a futile exercise.

d. Mr. Barker still hasn't paid last month's rent yet.

e. In the heart of Beijing lies the Forbidden City, which is an imperial palace built in very ancient times during the Ming dynasty.

1. Seeing the barrels, the driver immediately slammed on his brakes.

2. The thing data sets are used for is communicating with other computers.

3. The cat escaped during the time that I was asleep.

4. The opening words of the Declaration of Independence, which sum up in total America's entire rationale for its very existence, were the subject of considerable debate in 1776.

5. You will be the departmental travel coordinator for all members of the department.

6. Martin Luther King, Jr., was a man who set a high standard for future leaders to meet.

7. The professor knew from past experience that few students would refer back to their notes.

8. A typical autocross course consists of at least two straight aways, and the rest of the course is made up of numerous slaloms and several sharp turns.

9. We are asking for your help and cooperation in reducing the cost of our mailings.

10. The price of driving while drunk or while intoxicated can be extremely high.

LOOKING AT YOURSELF AS A WRITER
Wordy sentences

Editing for wordiness is a natural part of the writing process, especially in the business world, where conciseness (without loss of meaning) is highly valued. In the academic world, you may be tempted to adopt a wordy style for the following reasons.

Wordy sentences (continued)

CAUSE   You are padding your essay to reach the word limit established in the assignment.

CURE   Find an approach to the assignment that interests you; then do prewriting activities such as listing or clustering before you begin drafting. (See pp. 19–20.)

CAUSE   You are mimicking the indirect, wordy style that is unfortunately common in academic textbooks and journal articles.

CURE   Try not to be impressed by intelligent people who write badly. In your reading, notice that the best writers waste no words; they make each word count.

CAUSE   You fear that a simple, direct style will not sound intelligent — that more words will suggest a greater depth of ideas.

CURE   Look at yourself as a reader. Don't you resent having to wade through wordy sentences? Do you view them as a sign of the writer's intelligence?

17

Choose appropriate language.

Language is appropriate when it suits your subject, engages your audience, and blends naturally with your own voice.

To some extent, your choice of language will be governed by the conventions of the genre in which you are writing. When in doubt about the conventions of a particular genre — lab reports, informal essays, business memos, and so on — take a look at models written by experts in the field.

17a Stay away from jargon.

Jargon is specialized language used among members of a trade, profession, or group. Use jargon only when readers will be familiar with it; even then, use it only when plain English will not do as well.

Sentences filled with jargon are likely to be long and lumpy. To revise such sentences, you must rewrite them, usually in fewer words.

> **JARGON**   For years the indigenous body politic of South Africa attempted to negotiate legal enfranchisement without result.

> **REVISED**   For years the indigenous people of South Africa negotiated in vain for the right to vote.

Though a political scientist might feel comfortable with the original version, jargon such as *body politic* and *legal enfranchisement* is needlessly complicated for ordinary readers.

Broadly defined, jargon includes puffed-up language designed more to impress readers than to inform them. The following are common examples from business, government, higher education, and the military, with plain English translations in parentheses

ameliorate (improve)	indicator (sign)
commence (begin)	optimal (best, most favorable)
components (parts)	parameters (boundaries, limits)
endeavor (try)	peruse (read, look over)
exit (leave)	prior to (before)
facilitate (help)	utilize (use)
factor (consideration, cause)	viable (workable)
impact (v.) (affect)	

Sentences filled with jargon are hard to read, and they are often wordy as well.

▶ All ~~employees functioning in the capacity of~~ work-study
        must prove that they are currently enrolled.
students ~~are required to give evidence of current enrollment.~~
    ^

            begin
▶ Mayor Summers will ~~commence~~ his term of office by
improving   ^   *poor neighborhoods.*
~~ameliorating~~ living conditions in ~~economically deprived zones.~~
^   ^

17b Avoid pretentious language, most euphemisms, and "doublespeak."

Hoping to sound profound or poetic, some writers embroider their thoughts with large words and flowery phrases, language that in fact sounds pretentious. Pretentious language is so ornate and often so wordy that it obscures the thought that lies beneath.

        parents become old,
▶ When our ~~progenitors reach their silver-haired and golden~~
        ^   *entomb*   *old-age homes*
~~years,~~ we frequently ~~ensepulcher~~ them in ~~homes for~~
                        ^   ^
                                                    dead.
~~senescent beings~~ as if they were already among the ~~deceased.~~
                                                        ^

The writer of the original sentence had turned to a thesaurus (a dictionary of synonyms and antonyms) in an attempt to sound educated. When such a writer gains enough confidence to speak in his or her own voice, pretentious language disappears.

Related to pretentious language are euphemisms, nice-sounding words or phrases substituted for words thought to sound harsh or ugly. Like pretentious language, euphemisms are wordy and indirect. Unlike pretentious language, they are sometimes appropriate. It is our social custom, for example, to use euphemisms when speaking or writing about death (*Her sister passed on*), excretion (*I have to go to the bathroom*), sexual intercourse (*They did not sleep together until they were married*), and the like. We may also use euphemisms out of concern for someone's feelings. Telling parents, for example, that their daughter is "unmotivated" is more sensitive than saying she's lazy. Tact or politeness, then, can justify an occasional euphemism.

Most euphemisms, however, are needlessly evasive or even deceitful. Like pretentious language, they obscure the intended meaning.

EUPHEMISM	PLAIN ENGLISH
adult entertainment	pornography
preowned automobile	used car
economically deprived	poor
selected out	fired
negative savings	debts
strategic withdrawal	retreat or defeat
revenue enhancers	taxes
chemical dependency	drug addiction
downsize	lay off
correctional facility	prison

The term *doublespeak*, coined by George Orwell in his novel *1984*, applies to any deliberately evasive or deceptive language, including euphemisms. Doublespeak is especially common in politics, where missiles are named "Peacekeepers," airplane crashes are termed "uncontrolled contact with the ground," and a military retreat is described as "tactical redeployment." Business also gives us its share of doublespeak. When the manufacturer of a pacemaker writes that its product "may result in adverse health consequences in pacemaker-dependent patients as a result of sudden 'no output' failure," it takes an alert reader to grasp the message: The pacemakers might suddenly stop functioning and cause a heart attack or even death.

Word choice

> **GRAMMAR CHECKERS** can be helpful in identifying jargon and pretentious language. For example, they commonly advise against using words such as *utilize, finalize, facilitate,* and *effectuate.* You may find, however, that a program advises you to "simplify" language that is not jargon or pretentious language and may in fact be appropriate in academic writing. Sometimes you can direct the program to change the style level from standard to formal.

EXERCISE 17–1

Edit the following sentences to eliminate jargon, pretentious or flowery language, euphemisms, and doublespeak. You may need to make substantial changes in some sentences. Revisions of lettered sentences appear in the back of the book. Example:

> *mastered*
> After two weeks in the legal department, Sue has ~~worked~~
> *office*   *performance has*
> into the routine, ~~of the office,~~ and her ~~functional and self-~~
> ^   ^   ^
> ~~management skills have~~ exceeded all expectations.

a. Pay no heed to those who attempt to dissuade you from attaining what you desire.
b. In order that I may increase my expertise in the area of delivery of services to clients, I feel that participation in this conference will be beneficial.
c. Have you ever been accused of flagellating a deceased equine?
d. When Sal was selected out from his high-paying factory job, he learned what it was like to be economically depressed.
e. Passengers should endeavor to finalize the customs declaration form prior to exiting the aircraft.

1. We learned that the mayor had been engaging in a creative transfer of city employees' pension funds.
2. As I approached the edifice of confinement where my brother was incarcerated, several inmates loudly vocalized a number of lewd remarks.

3. The nurse announced that there had been a negative patient-care outcome due to a therapeutic misadventure on the part of the surgeon.
4. When we returned from our evening perambulation, we shrank back in horror as we surmised that our domestic dwelling was being swallowed up in hellish flames.
5. The bottom line is that the company is experiencing a negative cash flow.

LOOKING AT YOURSELF AS A WRITER
Jargon and pretentious language

In the academic and business worlds, you may be tempted to use jargon and pretentious language for several reasons.

CAUSE You're surrounded by jargon and pretentious language—at work or in your academic field—so you are picking it up, by osmosis.

CURE Develop an appreciation for good writing. Notice that the best writers can manage an elevated style without losing their human voices.

CAUSE You're afraid that if you present your ideas clearly, they will seem too simple.

CURE Give clear writing a try—and see if it sells. You can usually tell which professors or supervisors value a straightforward style and which are impressed by pompous language.

CAUSE Having discovered a thesaurus, you are using it for the wrong reason.

CURE Use a thesaurus or a dictionary to choose the best word, not necessarily the fanciest one. (See pp. 270–71.)

CAUSE You are experimenting with style, and your attempts at creativity and sophistication sometimes backfire.

CURE Continue to experiment, but be prepared—in the words of one writer—to "murder your darlings."

17c Avoid obsolete, archaic, and invented words.

Obsolete words are words found in the writing of the past that have dropped out of use entirely. Archaic words are old words that are still used, but only in special contexts such as literature or advertising. Although dictionaries list obsolete words such as *recomfort* and *reechy* and archaic words such as *anon* and *betwixt*, these words are not appropriate for current use.

Invented words (also called *neologisms*) are words too recently created to be part of standard English. Many invented words fade out of use without becoming standard. *Palimony, technobabble,* and *infomercial* are neologisms that may not last. *Printout, flextime,* and *Internet* are no longer neologisms; they have become standard English. Avoid using invented words in your writing unless they are given in the dictionary as standard or unless no other word expresses your meaning.

17d In most contexts, avoid slang, regional expressions, and nonstandard English.

Slang is an informal and sometimes private vocabulary that expresses the solidarity of a group such as teenagers, rock musicians, or football fans; it is subject to more rapid change than standard English. For example, the slang teenagers use to express approval changes every few years; *cool, groovy, neat, wicked, awesome,* and *stylin'* have replaced one another within the last three decades. Sometimes slang becomes so widespread that it is accepted as standard vocabulary. *Jazz,* for example, started out as slang but is now generally accepted to describe a style of music.

Although slang has a certain vitality, it is a code that not everyone understands, and it is very informal. Therefore, it is inappropriate in most written work.

▶ If we don't begin studying for the final, a whole semester's
   will be wasted.
   work ~~is going down the tubes.~~
       ^

                                              disgust you.
▶ The government's "filth" guidelines for food will ~~gross you~~
                                                         ^
~~out.~~

Regional expressions are common to a group in a geographical area. *Let's talk with the bark off* (for *Let's speak
frankly*) is an expression in the southern United States, for
example. Regional expressions have the same limitations as
slang and are therefore inappropriate in most writing.

▶ John was four blocks from the house before he remembered
   turn on
   to ~~cut~~ the headlights. ~~on.~~
      ^   ^

▶ I'm not ~~for~~ sure, but I think the dance has been postponed.

As you probably know, many people speak two varieties
of English — standard English, used in academic and business situations, and a nonstandard dialect, spoken with
close acquaintances who share a regional or social heritage.
In written English, a dialect may be used in dialogue, to reflect actual speech, but in most other contexts it is out of
place. Like slang and regionalisms, nonstandard English is
a language shared by a select group. Standard English, by
contrast, is accessible to all.

If you speak a nonstandard dialect, try to identify the
ways in which your dialect differs from standard English.
Look especially for the following features of nonstandard
English, which commonly cause problems in writing.

Misuse of verb forms such as *began* and *begun* (See 27a.)

Omission of -*s* endings on verbs (See 27c.)

Omission of *-ed* endings on verbs (See 27d.)
Omission of necessary verbs (See 27e.)
Double negatives (See 26d.)

17e Choose an appropriate level of formality.

In deciding on a level of formality, consider both your subject and your audience. Does the subject demand a dignified
treatment, or is a relaxed tone more suitable? Will readers
be put off if you assume too close a relationship with them,
or might you alienate them by seeming too distant?

For most college and professional writing, some degree
of formality is appropriate. In a letter applying for a job, for
example, it is a mistake to sound too breezy and informal.

TOO INFORMAL	I'd like to get that receptionist's job you've got in the paper.
MORE FORMAL	I would like to apply for the receptionist's position listed in the *Peoria Journal Star.*

Informal writing is appropriate for private letters, e-mail,
articles in popular magazines, and business correspondence
between close associates. Like spoken conversation, it allows
contractions (*don't, I'll*) and colloquial words (*kids, buddy*).
Vocabulary and sentence structure are rarely complex.

In choosing a level of formality, above all be consistent.
When a writer's voice shifts from one level of formality to another, readers receive mixed messages.

▶ Once a pitcher for the Cincinnati Reds, Bob shared with me
    began
the secrets of his trade. His lesson ~~commenced~~ with his
    thrown   ^
famous curveball, ~~implemented~~ by tucking the little finger
    ^

behind the ball instead of holding it straight out. Next he
revealed
~~elucidated~~ the mysteries of the sucker pitch, a slow ball
^
coming behind a fast windup.

Words such as *commenced* and *elucidated* are inappropriate for
the subject matter, and they clash with informal terms such as
sucker pitch and *fast windup.*

GRAMMAR CHECKERS can flag slang and some informal
language. Be aware, though, that they tend to be conservative on the matter of using contractions. If your ear tells
you that a contraction such as *isn't* or *doesn't* strikes the
right tone, stay with it.

EXERCISE 17-2

Edit the following paragraph to eliminate slang and maintain a consistent level of formality.

> The graduation speaker really blew it. He should have
> discussed the options and challenges facing the graduating
> class. Instead, he shot his mouth off at us and trashed us
> for being lazy and pampered. He did make some good points,
> however. Our profs have certainly babied us by not holding
> fast to deadlines, by dismissing assignments that the class
> ragged them about, by ignoring our tardiness, and by handing
> out easy C's like hotcakes. Still, we resented this speech as
> the final word from the college establishment. It should have
> been the orientation speech when we started college.

17f Avoid sexist language.

Sexist language is language that stereotypes or demeans
men or women, usually women. Some sexist language reflects genuine contempt for women: referring to a woman as

a "broad," for example, or calling a lawyer a "lady lawyer," or saying in an advertisement, "If our new sports car were a lady, it would get its bottom pinched."

Other forms of sexist language, while they may not suggest conscious sexism, reflect stereotypical thinking: referring to nurses as women and doctors as men, using different conventions when naming or identifying women and men, or assuming that all of one's readers are men. (See the chart on p. 268.)

Still other forms of sexist language result from outmoded traditions. The pronouns *he, him,* and *his,* for instance, were traditionally used to refer indefinitely to persons of either sex.

    TRADITIONAL   A journalist is stimulated by *his* deadline.

Today, however, such usage is widely viewed as sexist because it excludes women and encourages sex-role stereotyping—the view that men are somehow more suited than women to be journalists, doctors, and so on.

One option, of course, is to substitute *his or her* for *his: A journalist is stimulated by his or her deadline.* This strategy is fine in small doses, but it becomes awkward when repeated throughout an essay. A better strategy, many writers have discovered, is simply to write in the plural.

    REVISED   *Journalists* are stimulated by *their* deadlines.

Yet another strategy is to recast the sentence so that the problem does not arise.

    REVISED   A journalist is stimulated by *a* deadline.

When sexist language occurs throughout an essay, it is sometimes possible to adjust the essay's point of view. If the essay might be appropriately rewritten from the *I,* the *we,* or the *you* point of view, the problem of sexist English will not arise. (See pp. 53–57.)

Like the pronouns *he, him,* and *his,* the nouns *man* and *men* were once used indefinitely to refer to persons of either sex. Current usage demands gender-neutral terms for references to both men and women.

INAPPROPRIATE	APPROPRIATE
chairman	chairperson, moderator, chair, head
clergyman	member of the clergy, minister, pastor
congressman	member of Congress, representative, legislator
fireman	firefighter
foreman	supervisor
mailman	mail carrier, postal worker, letter carrier
mankind	people, humans
manpower	personnel
policeman	police officer
salesman	salesperson, sales associate, salesclerk, sales representative
to man	to operate, to staff
weatherman	weather forecaster, meteorologist
workman	worker, laborer

GRAMMAR CHECKERS are good at flagging sexist words, such as *mankind,* but they may also flag words, such as *girl* and *woman,* when they aren't being used in a sexist manner. It's sexist to call a woman a girl or a doctor a woman doctor, but you don't need to avoid the words *girl* and *woman* entirely and replace them with needlessly abstract terms like *female* and *individual.* All in all, just use your common sense. It's usually easy to tell when a word is offensive—and when it is not.

Although grammar checkers can flag sexist words, they cannot flag other kinds of sexist language, such as inconsistent treatment of men and women.

Avoiding sexist language

Avoid occupational stereotypes.

▶ After the nursing student graduates, ~~she~~ must face a

he or she

difficult state board examination.

When naming and identifying men and women, be consistent.

▶ Running for city council are Jake Stein, an attorney,

and ~~Mrs.~~ Cynthia Jones, a professor of English. ~~and~~

~~mother of three.~~

Do not write to an audience of men alone.

▶ If you are a senior government official, your ~~wife~~ is

spouse

required to report any gifts ~~she~~ receives that are

he or she

valued at more than $100.

Avoid using *he* to mean "he or she" or *him* to mean "him or her."

(For a variety of revision strategies, see the chart on pp. 328–29.)

▶ ~~Every applicant wants~~ to know how much ~~he~~ will make.

All applicants want   *they*

Avoid using *-man* words to refer to persons of either sex.

▶ A ~~fireman~~ must always be on call, even when ~~he is~~ off

firefighter

duty.

EXERCISE 17–3

Edit the following sentences to eliminate sexist language or sexist assumptions. Revisions of lettered sentences appear in the back of the book. Example:

> *Scholarship athletes*   *their*
> A scholarship athlete must be as concerned about his
>   ^   *they are*   *their*   ^
> academic performance as he is about his athletic
>   ^   ^
>
> performance.

a. Mrs. Geralyn Farmer, who is a mayor's wife, is the chief surgeon at University Hospital. Dr. Paul Green is her assistant.
b. If a young graduate is careful about investments, he can accumulate a significant sum in a relatively short period.
c. An elementary school teacher should understand the concept of nurturing if she intends to be a success.
d. The vice president for community affairs asked Elizabeth and Joseph to serve as cochairmen of the Red Cross blood drive.
e. If man does not stop polluting his environment, mankind will perish.

1. I have been trained to doubt an automobile mechanic, even if he has an excellent reputation.
2. If a high school graduate makes a career in the armed forces, he can retire with a comfortable pension before the age of fifty.
3. In the gubernatorial race, Lena Weiss, a defense lawyer and mother of two, easily defeated Harvey Tower, an architect.
4. My brother hired a lady lawyer who is a partner in the firm of Harris and Porter.
5. Peter Atlas and Dorea Smith own a large and successful bookstore. Peter handles the financial affairs, and Dorea, who is charming and attractive, directs all marketing efforts and manages the employees.

18

Find the exact words.

Whatever you want to say, claimed French writer Gustave Flaubert, "there is but one word to express it, one verb to give it movement, one adjective to qualify it; you must seek until you find this noun, this verb, this adjective." Even if you are not reaching for such perfection in your writing, you will sometimes find yourself wishing for better words. The dictionary is the obvious first place to turn, a thesaurus the second.

A good desk dictionary — such as *The American Heritage Dictionary, The Random House College Dictionary,* or *Merriam-Webster's Collegiate* or *New World Dictionary of the American Language* — lists synonyms and antonyms for many words, with helpful comments on shades of meaning. Under *fertile,* for example, *Webster's New World Dictionary* carefully distinguishes the meanings of *fertile, fecund, fruitful,* and *prolific:*

> SYN. — *fertile* implies a producing, or power of producing, fruit or offspring, and may be used figuratively of the mind; *fecund* implies the abundant production of offspring or fruit, or, figuratively, of creations of the mind; *fruitful* specifically suggests the bearing of much fruit, but it is also used to imply fertility (of soil), favorable results, profitableness, etc.; *prolific,* a close synonym for *fecund,* more often carries derogatory connotations of overly rapid production or reproduction — ANT. *sterile, barren*

If the dictionary doesn't yield the word you need, try a book of synonyms and antonyms such as *Roget's International Thesaurus* (or its online equivalent). In the back of *Roget's* is an index to the groups of synonyms that make up the bulk of the book. Look up the adjective *still,* for example, and you will find references to lists containing the words *dead, motionless, silent,* and *tranquil.* If *tranquil* is close to the word you have in mind, turn to its section in the front of the book. There you will find a long list of synonyms, including such words as *quiet, quiescent, reposeful, calm, pacific, halcyon, placid,* and *unruffled.* Unless your vocabulary is better than average, the list will contain words you've never heard or with which you are only vaguely familiar. Whenever you are tempted to use one of these words, look it up in the dictionary first to avoid misusing it.

On discovering the thesaurus, many writers use it for the wrong reasons, so a word of caution is in order. Do not turn to a thesaurus in search of exotic, fancy words — such as *halcyon* — with which to embellish your essays. Look instead for words that exactly express your meaning. Most of the time these words will be familiar to both you and your readers. *Tranquil* was probably the word you were looking for all along.

GRAMMAR CHECKERS can flag some nonstandard idioms, such as *comply to,* and many clichés, such as *leave no stone unturned.* In addition, they can flag commonly confused words such as *principal* and *principle* or *affect* and *effect,* although you must decide which word is correct in your context. Grammar checkers are less helpful with the other problems discussed in section 18: choosing words with appropriate connotations, using concrete language, and using figures of speech appropriately.

18a Select words with appropriate connotations.

In addition to their strict dictionary meanings (or *denotations*), words have *connotations,* emotional colorings that affect how readers respond to them. The word *steel* denotes "made of or resembling commercial iron that contains carbon," but it also calls up a cluster of images associated with steel, such as the sensation of touching it. These associations give the word its connotations—cold, smooth, unbending.

If the connotation of a word does not seem appropriate for your purpose, your audience, or your subject matter, you should change the word. When a more appropriate synonym does not come quickly to mind, consult a dictionary or a thesaurus.

▶ The model was ~~skinny~~ ^{slender} and fashionable.

The connotation of the word *skinny* is too negative.

▶ As I covered the boats with marsh grass, the ~~perspiration~~ ^{sweat} I

had worked up evaporated in the wind, and the cold morning

air seemed even colder.

The term *perspiration* is too dainty for the context, which suggests vigorous exercise.

EXERCISE 18–1

Use a dictionary or thesaurus to find at least four synonyms for each of the following words. Be prepared to explain any slight differences in meaning.

1. decay (verb)	3. hurry (verb)	5. secret (adjective)
2. difficult (adjective)	4. pleasure (noun)	6. talent (noun)

EXERCISE 18–2

For each of the words italicized in the following passages, consider alternatives that the writer might have chosen instead. (A dictionary and a thesaurus will lead you to other possibilities.) Then discuss why the author probably selected the word he or she did.

1. The forest, *choked* by growth and *shadow*, was like a jungle; the air hung thick with heat, *muting* the sound of their progress. Breathing in a *pungent steam* of sweet grasses and tangy needles, rotting wood and sunbaked fungi, she followed as best she could, *plunging* through the thicket to keep up with the young man ahead.

—Diana West

2. A change of just a few degrees in atmospheric temperature over the next century would be *catastrophic*. A *parade* of scientists appearing before a Senate committee in June *painted* a *graphic* picture of what that could mean: melting icecaps and rising sea levels that would *inundate* seaboard cities and drown thousands in *fierce* storms; rainfall shifts that would make the deserts *bloom* and turn *breadbaskets* into *dustbowls*; and, of course, heat everywhere.

—Matthew L. Wald

18b Prefer specific, concrete nouns.

Unlike general nouns, which refer to broad classes of things, specific nouns point to definite and particular items. *Film*, for example, names a general class, *science fiction film* names a narrower class, and *Jurassic Park* is more specific still. Other examples: *team, football team, Denver Broncos; music, symphony, Beethoven's Ninth; work, carpentry, cabinetmaking.*

Unlike abstract nouns, which refer to qualities and ideas (*justice, beauty, realism, dignity*), concrete nouns point to immediate, often sensory experience and to physical objects (*steeple, asphalt, lilac, stone, garlic*).

Specific, concrete nouns express meaning more vividly than general or abstract ones. Although general and abstract language is sometimes necessary to convey your meaning, ordinarily prefer specific, concrete alternatives.

▶ The senator spoke about the challenges of the future:
  of famine, pollution, dwindling resources, and terrorism.
  problems ~~concerning the environment and world peace.~~
    ^

Nouns such as *thing, area, aspect, factor,* and *individual* are especially dull and imprecise.

▶ A career in transportation management offers many ~~things.~~ *rewards.*

▶ Try pairing a trainee with an ~~individual with technical experience.~~ *experienced technician.*

18c Do not misuse words.

If a word is not in your active vocabulary, you may find yourself misusing it, sometimes with embarrassing consequences. Imagine the chagrin of the young woman who wrote that the "aroma of pumpkin pie and sage stuffing acted as an *aphrodisiac*" when she learned that aphrodisiacs are drugs or foods stimulating sexual desire. Such blunders are easily prevented: When in doubt, check the dictionary.

▶ The fans were ~~migrating~~ *climbing* up the bleachers in search of seats.

▶ Mrs. Johnson tried to fight but to no ~~prevail.~~ *avail.*

▶ Drugs have so ~~diffused~~ *permeated* our culture that they touch all segments of society.

Be especially alert for misused word forms — using a noun such as *absence, significance,* or *persistence,* for example, when your meaning requires the adjective *absent, significant,* or *persistent.*

▶ Most dieters are not ~~persistence~~ *persistent* enough to make a permanent change in their eating habits.

EXERCISE 18–3

Edit the following sentences to correct misused words. Revisions of lettered sentences appear in the back of the book. Example:

all-absorbing.
The training required for a ballet dancer is ~~all-absorbent~~.
                                              ^

a. We regret this delay; thank you for your patients.
b. Those who believe that books written for children are all sweetness and light are suffering from an allusion.
c. Liu Kwan began his career as a lawyer, but now he is a real estate mongrel.
d. When Robert Frost died at age eighty-eight, he left a legacy of poems that will make him immoral.
e. In general, the Internet has had a positive affect on our society.

1. Waste, misuse of government money, security and health violations, and even pilfering have become major dilemmas at the FBI.
2. Did you understand the significant of the list?
3. Grand Isle State Park is surrounded on three sides by water.
4. The Old World nuance of the restaurant intrigued us.
5. Tom Jones is an illegal child who grows up under the care of Squire Allworthy.

LOOKING AT YOURSELF AS A WRITER
Misused words

Most writers choose the wrong word now and then, but if you find yourself misusing a great many words, consider why. Here are some common causes and cures.

CAUSE You have a fondness for fancy words, such as *penultimate,* that are not in your active vocabulary.

CURE Write in a simpler style. Readers appreciate plain English more than you may think. (See 17a and 17b.) *Penultimate* probably isn't in their active vocabulary either.

Word choice

Misused words *(continued)*

CAUSE You tend to mix up easily confused words such as *accept* and *except*.

CURE Turn to the Glossary of Usage at the back of this book whenever you are in doubt about such words. Or consult a dictionary.

CAUSE Your vocabulary is not as strong as you'd like it to be.

CURE This cure will take time. The best way to improve your vocabulary is to read, and the best way to develop the habit of reading is to choose magazines and books that you enjoy. Seeing new words used properly, in context, will help you learn to use them in your own writing.

18d Use standard idioms.

Idioms are speech forms that follow no easily specified rules. The English say "Maria went *to hospital*," an idiom strange to American ears, which are accustomed to hearing *the* in front of *hospital*. Native speakers of a language seldom have problems with idioms, but prepositions sometimes cause trouble, especially when they follow certain verbs and adjectives. When in doubt, consult a good desk dictionary.

UNIDIOMATIC	IDIOMATIC
abide with (a decision)	abide by (a decision)
according with	according to
agree to (an idea)	agree with (an idea)
angry at (a person)	angry with (a person)
capable to	capable of
comply to	comply with
desirous to	desirous of
different than (a person or thing)	different from (a person or thing)

UNIDIOMATIC	IDIOMATIC
intend on doing	intend to do
off of	off
plan on doing	plan to do
preferable than	preferable to
prior than	prior to
superior than	superior to
sure and	sure to
try and	try to
type of a	type of

ESL

Because idioms follow no particular rules, you must learn them individually. You may find it helpful to keep a list of idioms that you frequently encounter in conversation and in reading.

EXERCISE 18–4

Edit the following sentences to eliminate errors in the use of idiomatic expressions. If a sentence is correct, write "correct" after it. Answers to lettered sentences appear in the back of the book. Example:

> We agreed to abide ~~with~~ *by* the decision of the judge.

a. Queen Anne was so angry at Sarah Churchill that she dismissed her once faithful servant.

b. Prior to the Russians' launching of *Sputnik*, *-nik* was not an English suffix.

c. Dad told us to be sure and visit the ghost towns of Nevada.

d. For the frightened refugees, the dangerous trek across the mountains was preferable than life in a war zone.

e. The baby fell off of the couch and landed on the soft cushion of the dog's bed.

1. Be sure and report on the danger of releasing genetically engineered bacteria into the atmosphere.

2. Why do you assume that embezzling bank assets is so different than robbing the bank?

3. Most of the class agreed to Sylvia's view that domestic terrorism is a very dangerous problem.
4. It was hard to predict what type of a prank Luis would play next.
5. Andrea intends on joining the Peace Corps after graduation.

18e Avoid worn-out expressions (clichés).

The frontiersman who first announced that he had "slept like a log" no doubt amused his companions with a fresh and unlikely comparison. Today, however, that comparison is a cliché, a saying that has lost its dazzle from overuse. No longer can it surprise.

To see just how dully predictable clichés are, put your hand over the right-hand column below and then finish the phrases on the left.

cool as a	cucumber
beat around	the bush
blind as a	bat
busy as a	bee, beaver
crystal	clear
dead as a	doornail
out of the frying pan and	into the fire
light as a	feather
like a bull	in a china shop
playing with	fire
nutty as a	fruitcake
selling like	hotcakes
starting out at the bottom	of the ladder
water under the	bridge
white as a	sheet, ghost
avoid clichés like the	plague

The cure for clichés is frequently simple: Just delete them. When this won't work, try adding some element of surprise. One student, for example, who had written that she had butterflies in her stomach, revised her cliché like this:

> If all of the action in my stomach is caused by butterflies, there must be a horde of them, with horseshoes on.

The image of butterflies wearing horseshoes is fresh and unlikely, not dully predictable like the original cliché.

18f Use figures of speech with care.

A figure of speech is an expression that uses words imaginatively (rather than literally) to invigorate an idea or make abstract ideas concrete. Most often, figures of speech compare two seemingly unlike things to reveal surprising similarities. For example, Richard Selzer compares an aging surgeon who has lost his touch to an old lion whose claws have become blunted. Readers enjoy such fresh comparisons, and you will find that creating them is one of the greatest pleasures in writing.

In a *simile,* the writer makes a comparison explicitly, usually by introducing it with *like* or *as.* One student, for instance, writes of his grandfather, "By the time cotton had to be picked, his neck was as red as the clay he plowed." In one of his short stories, William Faulkner describes the eyes of a plump old woman who had locked herself in her house for years as "like two small pieces of coal pressed into a lump of dough." J. D. Salinger's troubled adolescent Holden Caulfield in *The Catcher in the Rye* finds one of his fellow students "as sensitive as a goddam toilet seat," and actress Mae West tells us that men are "like streetcars. There's always another one around the corner."

In a *metaphor,* the *like* or *as* is omitted, and the comparison is implied. For example, Mark Twain's Huck Finn describes his drunken father's face as "fish-belly white." In the

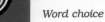

Old Testament's Song of Solomon, a young woman compares the man she loves to a fruit tree: "With great delight I sat in his shadow, and his fruit was sweet to my taste." And a student poet describes a fierce summer storm like this: "It growls and barks at me, / jumping at its leash, / as if it guards the gates of heaven."

Although figures of speech are useful devices, writers sometimes use them without thinking through the images they evoke. This can result in a *mixed metaphor,* the combination of two or more images that don't make sense together.

▶ Crossing Utah's salt flats in his new Corvette, my father flew
   at jet speed.
   ~~under a full head of steam.~~
   ^

Flew suggests an airplane, while *under a full head of steam* suggests a steamboat or a train. To clarify the image, the writer should stick with one comparison or the other.

▶ Our office had decided to put all controversial issues on a

   back burner. ~~in a holding pattern.~~
              ^

Here the writer is mixing stoves and airplanes. Simply deleting one of the images corrects the problem.

EXERCISE 18–5

Edit the following sentences to replace worn-out expressions and clarify mixed figures of speech. Revisions of lettered sentences appear in the back of the book. Example:

                        the color drained from his face.
When he heard about the accident, ~~he turned white as a~~
                                              ^
~~sheet.~~

a. John stormed into the room like a bull in a china shop.
b. The president thought that the scientists were using science as a sledgehammer to grind their political axes.

c. The Cubs easily beat the Mets, who were in the soup early in the game today at Wrigley Field.

d. We ironed out the sticky spots in our relationship.

e. Sasha told us that he wasn't willing to put his neck out on a limb.

1. I could read him like a book; he had egg all over his face.

2. Tears were strolling down the child's face.

3. The dean of students acted like a big fish in a little pond.

4. There are too many cooks in the broth here at corporate headquarters.

5. We told Al that he was playing with fire when we learned that he intended to spy on the trustees' meeting.

EXERCISE 18–6

Identify the figurative language in the following sentences. Be prepared to discuss why you think these passages are effective.

1. The kitchen was a great machine that set our lives running; it whirred down a little only on Saturdays and holy days.

    —Alfred Kazin

2. If growing up is painful for the Southern Black girl, being aware of her displacement is the rust on the razor that threatens the throat —Maya Angelou

3. She sat looking about her with eyes as impersonal, almost as stony, as those with which the granite Rameses in a museum watches the froth and fret that ebbs and flows about his pedestal. —Willa Cather

4. As the sweeping scythe of plague turned bustling towns into sepulchers and emptied the countryside, it reshaped European history. —Nicole Duplaix

5. In a word, we [Afro-Americans] are bringing down the curtain on this role you have cast us in and we will no longer be a party to our own degradation. —John Oliver Killens

PART V

Grammatical Sentences

19

Repair sentence fragments.

A sentence fragment is a word group that pretends to be a sentence. Sentence fragments are easy to recognize when they appear out of context, like these:

> On the old wooden stool in the corner of my grandmother's kitchen.

> And immediately popped their flares and life vests.

When fragments appear next to related sentences, however, they are harder to spot.

> On that morning I sat in my usual spot. On the old wooden stool in the corner of my grandmother's kitchen.

> The pilots ejected from the burning plane, landing in the water not far from the ship. And immediately popped their flares and life vests.

Recognizing sentence fragments

To be a sentence, a word group must consist of at least one full independent clause. An independent clause has a subject and a verb, and it either stands alone or could stand alone.

To test a word group for sentence completeness, use the flow chart on page 295. For example, by using the flow chart, you can see exactly why *On the old wooden stool in the corner of my grandmother's kitchen* is a fragment: It lacks both a subject and a verb. *And immediately popped their flares and life vests* is a fragment because it lacks a subject.

ESL

Unlike some languages, English does not allow omission of subjects (except in imperative sentences); nor does it allow omission of verbs. See 31a and 29e.

GRAMMAR CHECKERS can flag as many as half of the sentence fragments in a sample; but that means, of course, that they miss half or more of them. If fragments are a serious problem for you, you will still need to proofread for them.

Sometimes you will get "false positives," sentences that have been flagged but are not fragments. For example, one program flagged this complete sentence as a possible fragment: *I bent down to crawl into the bunker.* When a program spots a possible fragment, you should check to see if it is really a fragment. You can do this by using the flow chart on page 295.

Repairing sentence fragments

You can repair most fragments in one of two ways: Either pull the fragment into a nearby sentence or turn the fragment into a sentence.

▶ On that morning I sat in my usual spot~~.~~/ ~~On~~ the old wooden _{on}

  stool in the corner of my grandmother's kitchen.

▶ The pilots ejected from the burning plane, landing in the

  water not far from the ship. ~~And~~ immediately popped their _{They}

  flares and life vests.

19a Attach fragmented subordinate clauses or turn them into sentences.

A subordinate clause is patterned like a sentence, with both a subject and a verb, but it begins with a word that marks it as subordinate. The following words commonly introduce subordinate clauses:

after	even though	so that	when	whom
although	how	than	where	whose
as	if	that	whether	why
as if	in order that	though	which	
because	rather than	unless	while	
before	since	until	who	

Subordinate clauses function within sentences as adjectives, as adverbs, or as nouns. They cannot stand alone. (See 59b.)

Most fragmented clauses beg to be pulled into a sentence nearby.

▶ Jane will address the problem of limited on-campus parking/
if
~~If~~ she is elected special student adviser.

If introduces a subordinate clause that modifies the verb *will address*. (For punctuation of subordinate clauses appearing at the end of a sentence, see 33f.)

at
▶ Although we seldom get to see wildlife in the city/, ~~At~~ the zoo
   ^

we can still find some of our favorites.

Although introduces a subordinate clause that modifies the verb *can find.* (For punctuation of subordinate clauses appearing at the beginning of a sentence, see 32b.)

If a fragmented clause cannot be attached to a nearby sentence or if you feel that attaching it would be awkward, try rewriting it. The simplest way to turn a subordinate clause into a sentence is to delete the opening word or words that mark it as subordinate.

▶ Population increases and uncontrolled development

    are taking a deadly toll on the environment. ~~So that~~ ~~i~~n

    I

    many parts of the world, fragile ecosystems are

    collapsing.

19b Attach fragmented phrases or turn them into sentences.

Like subordinate clauses, phrases function within sentences as adjectives, as adverbs, or as nouns. They cannot stand alone. Fragmented phrases are often prepositional or verbal phrases; sometimes they are appositives, words or word groups that rename nouns or pronouns. (See 59a, 59c, and 59d.)

Often a fragmented phrase may simply be pulled into a nearby sentence.

▶ The panther lay quite motionless behind the rock/. ~~Waiting~~

    waiting

    silently for its prey.

Waiting silently for its prey is a verbal phrase. (For punctuation of verbal phrases, see 32e.)

▶ Mary is suffering from agoraphobia/. ~~A~~ fear of the outside

    a

    world.

A fear of the outside world is an appositive renaming the noun *agoraphobia.* (For punctuation of appositives, see 32e.)

If a fragmented phrase cannot be pulled into a nearby sentence effectively, turn the phrase into a sentence. You may need to add a subject, a verb, or both.

▶ In the computer training session, Eugene explained how to
install our new software. ~~Also~~ *He also taught us* how to organize our files,
connect to the Internet, and back up our hard drives.

The word group beginning *Also how to organize* is a fragmented verbal phrase. The revision turns the fragment into a sentence by adding a subject and a verb.

19c Attach other fragmented word groups or turn them into sentences.

Other word groups that are commonly fragmented include parts of compound predicates, lists, and examples introduced by *such as, for example,* or similar expressions.

Parts of compound predicates

A predicate consists of a verb and its objects, complements, and modifiers (see 58b). A compound predicate includes two or more predicates joined by a coordinating conjunction such as *and, but,* or *or.* Because the parts of a compound predicate share the same subject, they should appear in the same sentence.

▶ The woodpecker finch of the Galápagos Islands carefully
selects a twig of a certain size and shape./ ~~And~~ *and* then uses
this tool to pry out grubs from trees.

Notice that no comma appears between the parts of a compound predicate. (See 33a.)

Lists

When a list is mistakenly fragmented, it can often be attached to a nearby sentence with a colon or a dash. (See 35a and 39a.)

▶ It has been said that there are only three indigenous
American art forms/: M̶u̶s̶i̶c̶a̶l̶ comedy, jazz, and soap
   musical

opera.

Examples introduced by such as, for example, *or similar expressions*

Expressions that introduce examples (or explanations) can lead to unintentional fragments. Although you may begin a sentence with some of the following words or phrases, make sure that what you have written is a sentence, not a fragment.

also	for instance	or
and	in addition	such as
but	like	that is
especially	mainly	
for example	namely	

Sometimes fragmented examples can be attached to the preceding sentence.

▶ The South has produced some of our greatest twentieth-
century writers/, S̶u̶c̶h̶ as Flannery O'Connor, William
   such

Faulkner, Alice Walker, Tennessee Williams, and Thomas

Wolfe.

At times, however, it may be necessary to turn the fragment into a sentence.

▶ If Eric doesn't get his way, he goes into a fit of rage. For
example, ~~lying~~ *he lies* on the floor screaming or ~~opening~~ *opens* the cabinet
doors and then ~~slamming~~ *slams* them shut.

The writer corrected this fragment by adding a subject — *he* —
and substituting verbs for the verbals *lying, opening,* and
slamming.

LOOKING AT YOURSELF AS A WRITER
Sentence fragments

An occasional sentence fragment, used deliberately, can be
effective, but unintentional sentence fragments are serious
errors. If you tend to write unintentional fragments, try to
discover why.

CAUSE   You worry that you will write a run-on sentence (a
comma splice or a fused sentence).

CURE   You are right to be concerned about run-on sentences, but you may be worrying too much about
them while drafting. When you reach the editing
stage of the writing process, try proofreading for
both fragments and run-ons by using the flow charts
on pages 295 and 307.

CAUSE   Feeling that a sentence should be a certain length,
you insert a period at some convenient point when it
has reached that length.

CURE   Make punctuation decisions based on sentence
structure, not length. The following comma rules tell
you when to use a comma (or no punctuation) instead of a period: 32b, 32e, 33e, and 33f.

CAUSE   You are trying to emphasize the idea in the fragment
by putting it in its own sentence.

CURE   Consider using other strategies for emphasis, such
as the dash or the colon. (See 19c.)

19d Exception: Occasionally a fragment may be used deliberately, for effect.

Skilled writers occasionally use sentence fragments for the following special purposes.

FOR EMPHASIS	Following the dramatic Americanization of their children, even my parents grew more publicly confident. *Especially my mother.* — Richard Rodriguez
TO ANSWER A QUESTION	Are these new drug tests 100 percent reliable? *Not in the opinion of most experts.*
AS A TRANSITION	*And now the opposing arguments.*
EXCLAMATIONS	*Not again!*
IN ADVERTISING	*Fewer calories. Improved taste.*

Although fragments are sometimes appropriate, writers and readers do not always agree on when they are appropriate. Therefore you will find it safer to write in complete sentences.

EXERCISE 19–1

Repair any fragment by attaching it to a nearby sentence or by rewriting it as a complete sentence. If a word group is correct, write "correct" after it. Revisions of lettered sentences appear in the back of the book. Example:

One Greek island that should not be missed is Mykonos̸ A

vacation spot for Europeans and a playpen for the rich.

a. As I stood in front of the microwave, I recalled my grandmother bending over her old black stove. And remembered what she taught me: that any food can have soul if you love the people you are cooking for.

b. The resort was full of attractions. Three swimming pools, four restaurants, five bars, and every game imaginable, including a life-sized chess set.

c. I stepped on some frozen moss and started sliding down the face of a flat rock toward the falls. Suddenly I landed on another rock.

d. We need to stop believing myths about drinking. That strong black coffee will sober you up, for example, or that a cold shower will straighten you out.

e. On Sundays, James scrupulously read the newspaper's employment listings. Scrutinizing every position that held even the remotest possibility.

1. Sitting at a sidewalk café near the Sorbonne, I could pass as a French student. As long as I kept my mouth shut.

2. Mother loved to play all our favorite games. Canasta, Monopoly, hide-and-seek, and even kick-the-can.

3. The horses were dressed up with hats and flowers. Some even wore sunglasses.

4. The archaeologists worked very slowly. Examining and labeling every pottery shard they uncovered.

5. The geologists were interested in visiting the Seychelles. The only midocean islands in the world that are formed of granite.

6. If a woman from the desert tribe showed anger toward her husband, she was whipped in front of the whole village. And shunned by the rest of the women.

7. A tornado is a violent whirling wind. One that produces a funnel-shaped cloud and moves over land in a slim path of destruction.

8. Keiko arrived in the village of Futagami. Where she was to spend the summer with her grandparents.

9. In my three years of driving, I have never had an accident. Not one wreck, not one fender bender, not even a little dent.

10. Aspiring bodybuilders must first ascertain their strengths and weaknesses. And then decide what they want to achieve.

EXERCISE 19-2

Repair each fragment in the following paragraphs by attaching it to a sentence nearby or by rewriting it as a complete sentence.

Surfing the Internet now competes with watching television as our national pastime. People, it seems, have a natural ability to sit for hour upon hour. Passively watching images flit before their eyes. Whether these appear on a TV screen or a computer screen doesn't seem to make much difference. What counts are the images themselves. Not where they come from.

Web surfing is the cyber-age equivalent of channel surfing. Both of which appeal to us because of their constant promise of something better around the corner. When 1950s TV viewers got bored with Howdy Doody, they turned off the set. Or switched to a channel with no programming and stared at the test pattern. Today, with eighty or more channels to choose from, the demanding spectator is no longer forced to watch anything uninteresting. The Internet is the next logical step in this constant broadening of choice. Taking us from eighty channels to an almost infinite number of screens.

But there is at least one major risk of a culture based on images. That the written word may become an endangered species. As our brains eventually adapt to greater and greater levels of stimulation. Will we continue to be able to focus on a page of print? Already, members of the TV generation have a much harder time reading than their parents did. What, many people are wondering, will become of the Internet generation?

Before we send out too many alarms, however, we should remember that the Internet is still in its infancy. Already, Web browsers are helping us limit the dizzying number of choices that face us on the World Wide Web. By giving us powerful search tools that zero in on whatever aspect of a topic we are most interested in. And there is some evidence that those who spend time surfing the Net are doing more, not less, reading. Unlike TV viewers. Some Net surfers prefer to run their eyes over the words on the screen. An activity that is, after all, reading. Others download information and read the printouts. While it is true that television has reduced our nation's level of literacy, the Internet could well advance it. Only the future will tell.

Checking for sentence fragments

First look for the most common trouble spots:

WORDS INTRODUCING SUBORDINATE CLAUSES (19a)

although	even though	that	where	who
as if	how	though	whether	whom
because	if	unless	which	whose
before	so that	when	while	why

▶ Pat could not come skiing with us/ ~~Because~~ *because* she had

broken her leg.

PHRASES (19b)

▶ The air force sent me to Chanute, Illinois/, ~~Home~~ *home* of

the USAF Fire Academy.

PARTS OF COMPOUND PREDICATES (19c)

▶ Pressing the gun to my shoulder, I laid my cheek to

the stock/ ~~And~~ *and* sighted the target.

WORDS INTRODUCING LISTS OR EXAMPLES (19c)

for example	like	namely
for instance	mainly	such as

▶ You already know some gestures in sign language/,

~~Such~~ *such* as a wave for "hello" and a shake of the head for

"no."

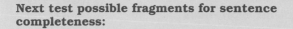

Sentence fragments (*continued*)

Next test possible fragments for sentence completeness:

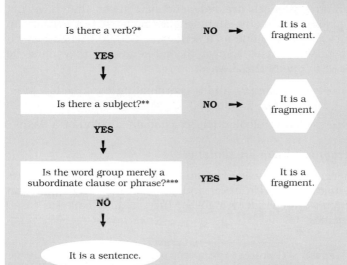

Is there a verb?*   **NO** ➡ It is a fragment.

YES ⬇

Is there a subject?**   **NO** ➡ It is a fragment.

YES ⬇

Is the word group merely a subordinate clause or phrase?***   **YES** ➡ It is a fragment.

NO ⬇

It is a sentence.

* Do not mistake verbals for verbs. (See 59c.)
** The subject of a sentence may be *you*, understood. (See 58a.)
*** A sentence may open with a subordinate clause, but the sentence must also include an independent clause. (See 59b.)

If you find any fragments, try one of these methods of revision:

1. Attach the fragment to a nearby sentence.
2. Turn the fragment into a sentence.

Grammatical sentences

20

Revise run-on sentences.

Run-on sentences are independent clauses that have not been joined correctly. An independent clause is a word group that can stand alone as a sentence. (See 60.) When two independent clauses appear in one sentence, they must be joined in one of these ways:

—with a comma and a coordinating conjunction (*and, but, or, nor, for, so, yet*)

—with a semicolon (or occasionally a colon or a dash)

Recognizing run-on sentences

There are two types of run-on sentences. When a writer puts no mark of punctuation and no coordinating conjunction between independent clauses, the result is called a *fused sentence*.

FUSED ┌─────── INDEPENDENT CLAUSE ───────┐
Gestures are a means of communication for everyone

┌─────── INDEPENDENT CLAUSE ───────┐
they are essential for the hearing impaired.

A far more common type of run-on sentence is the *comma splice*—two or more independent clauses joined by a comma without a coordinating conjunction. In some comma splices, the comma appears alone.

COMMA   Gestures are a means of communication for everyone,
SPLICE   they are essential for the hearing impaired.

In other comma splices, the comma is accompanied by a joining word that is *not* a coordinating conjunction. There are only seven coordinating conjunctions in English: *and, but, or, nor, for, so,* and *yet.* Notice that all of these words are short — only two or three letters long.

> **COMMA** Gestures are a means of communication for everyone,
> **SPLICE** however, they are essential for the hearing-impaired.

However is a transitional expression, not a coordinating conjunction (see 20b).

To review your writing for possible run-on sentences, use the charts on pages 306–07.

GRAMMAR CHECKERS can flag only about 20 to 50 percent of the run-on sentences in a sample. The programs tend to be cautious, telling you that you "may have" a run-on sentence; you will almost certainly get a number of "false positives," sentences that have been flagged but are not run-ons. For example, a grammar checker flagged the following acceptable sentence as a possible run-on: *They believe that requiring gun owners to purchase a license is sufficient.*

If you have a problem with run-ons, you will need to proofread for them even after using a grammar checker. Also, if your program spots a "possible" run-on, you will need to check to see if it is in fact a run-on, perhaps by using the flow chart on page 307.

Revising run-on sentences

To revise a run-on sentence, you have four choices:

1. Use a comma and a coordinating conjunction (*and, but, or, nor, for, so, yet*).

▶ Gestures are a means of communication for everyone, ~~but~~ they
are essential for the hearing-impaired.

2. Use a semicolon (or, if appropriate, a colon or a dash). A semicolon may be used alone; it can also be accompanied by a transitional expression.

▶ Gestures are a means of communication for everyone↓; they are essential for the hearing-impaired.

                                                  ; however,
▶ Gestures are a means of communication for everyone↓ they are essential for the hearing-impaired.

3. Make the clauses into separate sentences.

                                              They
▶ Gestures are a means of communication for everyone↓. ~~they~~ are essential for the hearing-impaired.

4. Restructure the sentence, perhaps by subordinating one of the clauses.

    Although gestures
▶ ~~Gestures~~ are a means of communication for everyone, they are essential for the hearing-impaired.

One of these revision techniques usually works better than the others for a particular sentence. The fourth technique, the one requiring the most extensive revision, is often the most effective.

20a Consider separating the clauses with a comma and a coordinating conjunction.

There are seven coordinating conjunctions in English: *and, but, or, nor, for, so,* and *yet.* When a coordinating conjunction joins independent clauses, it is usually preceded by a comma. (See 32a.)

> *and*
> ▶ The paramedic asked where I was hurt, as soon as I told
>   ^
>
> him, he cut up the leg of my favorite pair of jeans.

> ▶ Many government officials privately admit that the polygraph
>   *yet*
> is unreliable, ~~however,~~ they continue to use it as a security
>   ^
>
> measure.

However is a transitional expression, not a coordinating conjunction, so it cannot be used with only a comma to join independent clauses. (See 20b.)

20b Consider separating the clauses with a semicolon (or, if appropriate, with a colon or a dash).

When the independent clauses are closely related and their relation is clear without a coordinating conjunction, a semicolon is an acceptable method of revision. (See 34a.)

> ▶ Tragedy depicts the individual confronted with the fact of
>
> death; comedy depicts the adaptability and ongoing survival
>   ^
>
> of human society.

A semicolon is required between independent clauses that have been linked with a transitional expression (such as *however, therefore, moreover, in fact,* or *for example*). For a longer list, see the chart on page 306. (See also 34b.)

> ▶ The timber wolf looks much like a large German shepherd;
>   ^
>
> however, the wolf has longer legs, larger feet, a wider head,
>
> and a long, bushy tail.

▶ Everyone in my outfit had a specific job/; as a matter of fact,
        ^

most of the officers had three or four duties.

If the first independent clause introduces the second or if the second clause summarizes or explains the first, a colon or a dash may be an appropriate method of revision. (See 35b and 39a.) In formal writing, the colon is usually preferred to the dash.

                              : This
▶ Nuclear waste is hazardous ~~this~~ is an indisputable fact.
                                    ^

20c Consider making the clauses into separate sentences.

▶ Why should we spend money on expensive space
              We
exploration/? ~~we~~ have enough underfunded programs here
          ^

on earth.

Since one independent clause is a question and the other is a statement, they should be separate sentences.

                                              Then
▶ I gave the necessary papers to the police officer. ~~then~~ he said
                                                  ^

I would have to accompany him to the police station, where

a counselor would talk with me and call my parents.

Because the second independent clause is quite long, a sensible revision is to use separate sentences.

20d Consider restructuring the sentence, perhaps by subordinating one of the clauses.

If one of the independent clauses is less important than the other, turn it into a subordinate clause or phrase. (For more about subordination, see 8, especially the chart on p. 185.)

▶ Of the many geysers in Yellowstone National Park, the most
  famous is Old Faithful, ~~it~~ sometimes reaches 150 feet in
  ^*which*^
  ^
  height.

▶ ~~The~~ new health plan was explained to the employees in my
  When the
  ^
  division, everyone agreed to give it a try.

▶ Saturday afternoon Julie came running into the house/~~she~~

  ~~wanted~~ to get permission to go to the park.

  Minor ideas in these sentences are now expressed in subordinate clauses or phrases.

LOOKING AT YOURSELF AS A WRITER
Run-on sentences

Run-on sentences are considered serious errors because they
suggest that the writer doesn't understand basic sentence
structure. Unfortunately, the errors are fairly common, even
among writers who are otherwise reasonably proficient. If you
frequently write run-on sentences, consider the following possible causes and cures.

CAUSE Because you want your writing to flow smoothly
         from one idea to the next, you tend to string ideas
         together with commas. Run-on sentences sound bet-
         ter to you than a series of short, choppy sentences
         or a chain of ideas strung together with *and*'s.

CURE You are right to want your writing to flow, but you'll
         need to turn to other strategies for making this hap-
         pen. One of the best strategies for achieving sen-
         tence flow is subordination. (See 20d, 8a, and 8b.)

CAUSE Feeling that a sentence should be a certain length,
         you tend to keep it going until it has reached that
         length.

> ## Run-on sentences (*continued*)
>
> **CURE** Make punctuation decisions based on sentence structure, not length. The following punctuation rules show you ways of joining independent clauses correctly: 32a, 34a, 34b, 35b, 39a.
>
> **CAUSE** You enjoy using formal-sounding transitional expressions like *therefore, however,* and *moreover,* and you confuse these words with coordinating conjunctions meaning the same thing (*so, but,* and).
>
> **CURE** In most contexts, prefer the simpler coordinating conjunctions (*and, but, or, nor, for, so, yet*), which do not create run-on sentences.
>
> **CAUSE** You are confused by the term "comma splice," which focuses your attention on the comma and prevents you from seeing several possibilities for revision.
>
> **CURE** You are right that the term "comma splice" is confusing, especially since some revision strategies do not use a comma. Consider all four strategies.

EXERCISE 20–1

Revise any run-on sentences using the method of revision suggested in brackets. Revisions of lettered sentences appear in the back of the book. Example:

> *Because*
> **Orville was obsessed with his weight, he rarely ate anything**
> ^
> **sweet and delicious.** [*Restructure the sentence.*]

a. The city had one public swimming pool, it stayed packed with children all summer long. [*Restructure the sentence.*]

b. The building is being renovated, therefore at times we have no heat, water, or electricity. [*Use a comma and a coordinating conjunction.*]

c. Why shouldn't a divorced wife receive half of her husband's pen-sion and retirement benefits, she was her husband's partner for many years. [*Make two sentences.*]

d. Suddenly there was a loud silence, the shelling had stopped. [*Use a semicolon.*]

e. The experience taught Juanita a lesson, she could not always rely on her parents to bail her out of trouble. [*Use a colon.*]

1. For the first time in her adult life, Lucia had time to waste, she could spend a whole day curled up with a good book. [*Use a semicolon.*]

2. The city government had good reason to fear a major earth-quake, most of the business district was built on a landfill. [*Re-structure the sentence.*]

3. The next time an event is canceled because of bad weather, don't blame the meteorologist, blame nature. [*Make two sen-tences.*]

4. Mr. Romero is an excellent linguist he has been studying Chi-nese dialects for twenty years. [*Restructure the sentence.*]

5. The president of Algeria was standing next to the podium he was waiting to be introduced. [*Restructure the sentence.*]

6. On most days I had only enough money for bus fare, lunch was a luxury I could not afford. [*Use a semicolon.*]

7. There was one major reason for John's wealth, his grandfather had been a multimillionaire. [*Use a colon.*]

8. The neighborhood was ruled by gangs, what kind of environ-ment was this for my ten-year-old son? [*Make two sentences.*]

9. Lindsey is a top competitor she has been riding since the age of seven. [*Restructure the sentence.*]

10. Wind power for the home is a supplementary source of energy, it can be combined with electricity, gas, or solar energy. [*Re-structure the sentence.*]

EXERCISE 20-2

Revise any run-on sentences using a technique that you find ef-fective. If a sentence is correct, write "correct" after it. Revisions of lettered sentences appear in the back of the book. Example:

I ran the three blocks as fast as I could, ~~however,~~ *but* I missed

the bus.

a. Ted never drove the vintage cars that he had inherited, however, he could not bring himself to sell them.
b. The duck hunter set out his decoys in the shallow bay and then settled in to wait for the first real bird to alight.
c. In the Middle Ages, the streets of London were dangerous places, it was safer to travel by boat along the Thames.
d. Researchers were studying the fertility of Texas land tortoises they X-rayed all the female tortoises to see how many eggs they had.
e. We had planned to spend the last few days of our vacation at the beach, the hurricane, however, brought us home in a hurry.

1. Are you able to endure boredom, isolation, and potential violence, then the army may well be the adventure for you.
2. Jet funny cars are powered by jet engines, these engines are the same type that are used on fighter aircraft and helicopters.
3. If one of the dogs should happen to fall through the ice, it would be cut loose from the team and left to its fate, the sled drivers could not endanger the rest of the team for just one dog.
4. The volunteers worked hard to clean up and restore calm after the tornado, as a matter of fact, many of them did not sleep for the first three days of the emergency.
5. Nuclear power plants produce energy by fission, a process that generates radioactive waste.
6. The floor around the refreshment stand was sticky, I was lucky to make it away with both shoes on my feet.
7. The center of the French Quarter of New Orleans is Jackson Square, this square is one of the most beautiful urban spaces in the United States.
8. We didn't trust her, she had lied before.
9. I pushed open the first door with my back, turning to open the second door, I encountered a young woman in a wheelchair holding it open for me.
10. If you want to lose weight and keep it off, consider this advice, don't try to take it off faster than you put it on.

EXERCISE 20–3

In the following rough draft, revise any run-on sentences.

Some parents and educators argue that requiring uniforms in public schools would improve student behavior and performance. They think that uniforms give students a more professional attitude toward school, moreover they believe that uniforms help create a sense of community among students from diverse backgrounds. Parents and educators holding these views are well meaning, however they should take a second look at the arguments against requiring school uniforms in public schools.

Uniforms do create a sense of community, they do this, however, by stamping out individuality. People spend most of their working lives having to conform to one dress code or another. Youth is a time to express originality, it is a time to develop a sense of self. One important way young people express their identities is through the clothes they wear. Of course, it could be argued that the self-patrolled dress code of high school students is ultimately stricter than that of any company, nevertheless, trying to control dress habits from above will only lead to resentment or to mindless conformity.

If children are going to act like adults, they need to be treated like adults, they need to be made responsible for their own choices. Telling young people what to wear to school merely prolongs their childhoods. Education is not just a matter of learning facts and figures, it also involves growing up and understanding how to function in the real world.

Most public schools must take everyone who applies, this includes students and parents who are opposed to school uniforms. Uniforms may be a good idea for private schools, they may even be a good idea for a few public "alternative" schools that parents and their children can choose. In most public schools, however, school uniforms should not be required.

Checking for run-on sentences

First look for the most common trouble spots:

TRANSITIONAL EXPRESSIONS

also	in addition	now
as a result	in fact	of course
besides	in other words	on the other hand
consequently	in the first place	otherwise
finally	meanwhile	still
for example	moreover	then
for instance	nevertheless	therefore
furthermore	next	thus
however		

▶ We usually think of children as innocent and guileless/;
^
however, they are often cruel and unjust.

EXAMPLE OR EXPLANATION IN SECOND CLAUSE

He
▶ Martin looked out the window in astonishment: ~~he~~ had
^
never seen snow before.

CLAUSES EXPRESSING CONTRAST

but
▶ Most of his contemporaries had made plans for their
retirement, Tom had not.
^

PRONOUN AS SUBJECT OF SECOND CLAUSE

who
▶ Claudia, was full of energy and enthusiasm, ~~she~~ tackled
^
the job at once.

Run-on sentences (*continued*)

Next test your sentences for correctness:

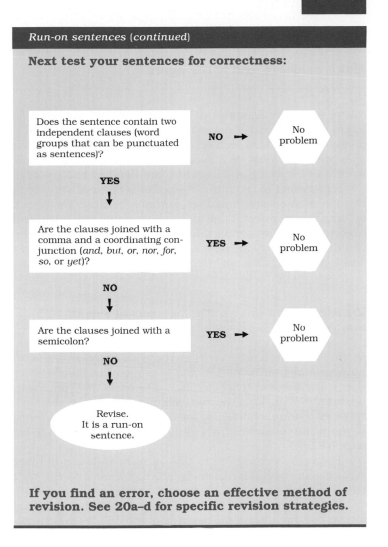

Does the sentence contain two independent clauses (word groups that can be punctuated as sentences)? → **NO** → No problem

YES

Are the clauses joined with a comma and a coordinating conjunction (*and, but, or, nor, for, so,* or *yet*)? → **YES** → No problem

NO

Are the clauses joined with a semicolon? → **YES** → No problem

NO

Revise. It is a run-on sentence.

If you find an error, choose an effective method of revision. See 20a–d for specific revision strategies.

21

Make subjects and verbs agree.

Native speakers of standard English know by ear that *he talks, she has,* and *it doesn't* (not *he talk, she have,* and *it don't*) are standard subject-verb combinations. For such speakers, problems with subject-verb agreement arise only in certain tricky situations, which are detailed in 21b–21k.

If you don't trust your ear—perhaps because you speak English as a second language, perhaps because you speak or hear nonstandard English in your community—you will need to learn the standard forms explained in 21a. Even if you do trust your ear, take a quick look at 21a to see what "subject-verb agreement" means.

21a Consult this section for standard subject-verb combinations.

In the present tense, verbs agree with their subjects in number (singular or plural) and in person (first, second, or third). The present-tense ending *-s* (or *-es*) is used on a verb if its subject is third-person singular; otherwise the verb takes no ending. Consider, for example, the present-tense forms of the verb *love,* given at the beginning of the chart on page 310.

The verb *be* varies from this pattern; unlike any other verb, it has special forms in *both* the present and the past tense. These forms appear at the end of the chart on page 310.

If you aren't confident that you know the standard forms, use the charts on pages 310 and 311 as you proof-read for subject-verb agreement. You may also want to take a look at 27c, which discusses the matter of -s endings in some detail.

GRAMMAR CHECKERS attempt to flag faulty subject-verb agreement, but they have mixed success. They fail to flag many problems; in addition, they flag a number of correct sentences, usually because they have misidentified the subject, the verb—or both.

If you are good at identifying subjects and verbs and seeing whether they agree, the grammar checker can be of some use to you, since you will be able to tell when a flagged sentence really has a problem and when it doesn't. Even so, bear in mind that the program won't catch all problems.

If you are not confident of your ability to identify subjects and verbs and see whether they agree, the grammar checker can do you serious harm. Writing center tutors report that some bizarre errors result when students don't have the confidence to reject the computer program's incorrect advice—or don't stop to think before accepting it. For example, without thinking first, one student changed *is* to *am* in this sentence because the computer said that the subject *I* agreed with the verb *am*, not with *is*: *Eating raw limpets, I found out, am like trying to eat art gum erasers.* You can imagine this student's embarrassment upon reading this sentence later. Slow down before taking the computer's advice. And when in doubt, rely on your handbook and your own good sense, not on the grammar checker.

Subject-verb agreement at a glance

PRESENT-TENSE FORMS OF *LOVE*
(A TYPICAL VERB)

	SINGULAR		PLURAL	
FIRST PERSON	I	love	we	love
SECOND PERSON	you	love	you	love
THIRD PERSON	he/she/it	loves	they	love

PRESENT-TENSE FORMS OF *HAVE*

	SINGULAR		PLURAL	
FIRST PERSON	I	have	we	have
SECOND PERSON	you	have	you	have
THIRD PERSON	he/she/it	has	they	have

PRESENT-TENSE FORMS OF *DO*

	SINGULAR		PLURAL	
FIRST PERSON	I	do/don't	we	do/don't
SECOND PERSON	you	do/don't	you	do/don't
THIRD PERSON	he/she/it	does/doesn't	they	do/don't

PRESENT-TENSE AND PAST-TENSE
FORMS OF *BE*

	SINGULAR		PLURAL	
FIRST PERSON	I	am/was	we	are/were
SECOND PERSON	you	are/were	you	are/were
THIRD PERSON	he/she/it	is/was	they	are/were

When to use the -s (or -es) form of a present-tense verb

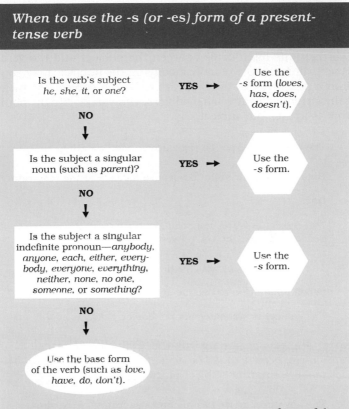

Is the verb's subject *he, she, it,* or *one*?

YES → Use the -s form (*loves, has, does, doesn't*).

NO ↓

Is the subject a singular noun (such as *parent*)?

YES → Use the -s form.

NO ↓

Is the subject a singular indefinite pronoun—*anybody, anyone, each, either, everybody, everyone, everything, neither, none, no one, someone,* or *something*?

YES → Use the -s form.

NO ↓

Use the base form of the verb (such as *love, have, do, don't*).

EXCEPTION: Choosing the correct present-tense form of *be (am, is,* or *are)* is not quite so simple. See the chart on the previous page for both present- and past-tense forms of *be*.

ESL CAUTION: Do not use the -s form of a verb that follows a helping verb such as *can, must,* or *should.* (See 29a.)

21b   Make the verb agree with its subject, not with a word that comes between.

Word groups often come between the subject and the verb. Such word groups, usually modifying the subject, may contain a noun that at first appears to be the subject. By mentally stripping away such modifiers, you can isolate the noun that is in fact the subject.

The *tulips* in the pot on the balcony *need* watering.

▶ High levels of air pollution cause~~s~~ damage to the respiratory tract.

> The subject is *levels,* not *pollution.* Strip away the phrase *of air pollution* to hear the correct verb: *levels cause.*

▶ The slaughter of pandas for their pelts ~~have~~ *has* caused the panda population to decline drastically.

> The subject is *slaughter,* not *pandas* or *pelts.*

NOTE: Phrases beginning with the prepositions *as well as, in addition to, accompanied by, together with,* and *along with* do not make a singular subject plural.

▶ The governor, as well as his press secretary, ~~were~~ *was* shot.

> To emphasize that two people were shot, the writer could use *and* instead: *The governor and his press secretary were shot.*

21c   Treat most subjects joined with *and* as plural.

A subject with two or more parts is said to be compound. If the parts are connected by *and,* the subject is nearly always plural.

Leon and Jan often *jog* together.

have
▶ **Jill's natural ability and her desire to help others ~~has~~ led to**
^
a career in the ministry.

Ability and desire is a plural subject, so its verb should be *have*.

EXCEPTIONS: When the parts of the subject form a single unit
or when they refer to the same person or thing, treat the subject as singular.

Strawberries and cream was a last-minute addition to the menu.

Sue's friend and adviser was surprised by her decision.

When a compound subject is preceded by *each* or *every*, treat
it as singular.

Each tree, shrub, and vine needs to be sprayed.

Every car, truck, and van is required to pass inspection.

This exception does not apply when a compound subject is
followed by *each: Alan and Marcia each have different ideas.*

21d With subjects joined with *or* or *nor* (or by
either . . . or or *neither . . . nor*), make the verb agree
with the part of the subject nearer to the verb.

A driver's *license* or credit *card is* required.

A driver's *license* or two credit *cards are* required.

is
▶ **If a relative or neighbor ~~are~~ abusing a child, notify the police**
^
immediately.

> ▶ Neither the lab assistant nor the students ~~was~~ ^{were} able to download the information.

The verb must be matched with the part of the subject closer to it: *neighbor is* in the first sentence, *students were* in the second.

NOTE: If one part of the subject is singular and the other is plural, put the plural one last to avoid awkwardness.

21e Treat most indefinite pronouns as singular.

Indefinite pronouns are pronouns that do not refer to specific persons or things. The following commonly used indefinite pronouns are singular:

anybody	each	everyone	nobody	somebody
anyone	either	everything	none	someone
anything	everybody	neither	no one	something

Many of these words appear to have plural meanings, and they are often treated as such in casual speech. In formal written English, however, they are nearly always treated as singular.

Everyone on the team *supports* the coach.

> ▶ Each of the furrows ~~have~~ ^{has} been seeded.

> ▶ Everybody who signed up for the ski trip ~~were~~ ^{was} taking lessons.

The subjects of these sentences are *Each* and *Everybody*. These indefinite pronouns are third-person singular, so the verbs must be *has* and *was*.

The indefinite pronouns *none* and *neither* are considered singular when used alone.

None is immune to this disease.

Neither is able to attend.

When these pronouns are followed by prepositional phrases with a plural meaning, however, usage varies. Some experts insist on treating the pronouns as singular, but many writers disagree. It is safer to treat them as singular.

None of these trades *requires* a college education.

Neither of those pejoratives *fits* Professor Brady.

A few indefinite pronouns (*all, any, some*) are singular or plural depending on the noun or pronoun they refer to.

Some of the *lemonade has* disappeared.

Some of the *rocks were* slippery.

21f   Treat collective nouns as singular unless the meaning is clearly plural.

Collective nouns such as *jury, committee, audience, crowd, class, troop, family*, and *couple* name a class or a group. In American English, collective nouns are nearly always treated as singular: They emphasize the group as a unit. Occasionally, when there is some reason to draw attention to the individual members of the group, a collective noun may be treated as plural. (Also see 22b.)

SINGULAR   The *class respects* the teacher.

PLURAL   The *class are* debating among themselves.

To underscore the notion of individuality in the second sentence, many writers would add a clearly plural noun such as *members:*

PLURAL   The class *members are* debating among themselves.

▶ The scout troop ~~meet~~ ^meets^ in our basement on Tuesdays.

The troop as a whole meets in the basement; there is no reason to draw attention to its individual members.

▶ A young couple ~~was~~ ^were^ arguing about politics while holding hands.

The meaning is clearly plural. Only individuals can argue and hold hands.

NOTE: The phrase *the number* is treated as singular, *a number* as plural.

SINGULAR   *The number* of school-age children *is* declining.

PLURAL   *A number* of children *are* attending the wedding.

NOTE: When units of measurement are used collectively, treat them as singular; when they refer to individual persons or things, treat them as plural.

SINGULAR   *Three-fourths* of the pie *has* been eaten.

PLURAL   *One-fourth* of the drivers *were* drunk.

21g Make the verb agree with its subject even when the subject follows the verb.

Verbs ordinarily follow subjects. When this normal order is reversed, it is easy to become confused. Sentences beginning with *there is* or *there are* (or *there was* or *there were*) are inverted; the subject follows the verb.

There *are* surprisingly few *children* in our neighborhood.

▶ There ~~was~~ a social worker and a crew of twenty volunteers at
    were
    ^
the scene of the accident.

The subject *worker and crew* is plural, so the verb must be *were*.

Occasionally you may decide to invert a sentence for variety or effect. When you do so, check to make sure that your subject and verb agree.

▶ At the back of the room ~~is~~ a small aquarium and an enormous
    are
    ^
terrarium.

The subject *aquarium and terrarium* is plural, so the verb must be *are*. If the correct sentence seems awkward, begin with the subject: *A small aquarium and an enormous terrarium are at the back of the room.*

21h Make the verb agree with its subject, not with a subject complement.

One basic sentence pattern in English consists of a subject, a linking verb, and a subject complement: *Jack is a securities lawyer.* Because the subject complement names or describes the subject (*Jack*), it is sometimes mistaken for the subject. (See 58b on subject complements.)

These *problems are* a way to test your skill.

▶ A tent and a sleeping bag ~~is~~ the required equipment for all
_{are} (correction above "is")

campers.

Tent and bag is the subject, not *equipment*.

▶ A major force in today's economy ~~are~~ women — as earners,
_{is} (correction above "are")

consumers, and investors.

Force is the subject, not *women*. If the corrected version seems awkward, make *women* the subject: *Women are a major force in today's economy — as earners, consumers, and investors.*

21i *Who, which,* and *that* take verbs that agree with their antecedents.

Like most pronouns, the relative pronouns *who, which,* and *that* have antecedents, nouns or pronouns to which they refer. Relative pronouns used as subjects of subordinate clauses take verbs that agree with their antecedents.

Take a *suit that travels* well.

Problems can arise with the constructions *one of the* and *only one of the.* As a rule, treat *one of the* constructions as plural, *only one of the* constructions as singular.

▶ Our ability to use language is one of the things that set*s̸* us

apart from animals.

The antecedent of *that* is *things,* not *one.* Several things set us apart from animals.

▶ **Dr. Barker knew that Frank was the only one of his sons who**
was
~~were~~ **responsible enough to handle the estate.**
^

The antecedent of *who* is *one,* not *sons.* Only one son was responsible enough.

LOOKING AT YOURSELF AS A WRITER
Subject-verb agreement

Subject-verb agreement causes trouble for most of us, largely because of the many tricky contexts that tempt us to choose the wrong verb. But if you find subject-verb agreement unusually troublesome, consider possible sources of your difficulties.

CAUSE You are confused about the rules on when to use the -*s* form of a verb. For example, you may think that a "plural" verb takes an -*s* ending, just like most plural nouns. Or you may think that *all* singular subjects demand a verb with an -*s* ending, not just third-person singular subjects.

CURE Trust the chart on page 310. Don't let yourself get confused by half-learned rules.

CAUSE You can't find the simple subject of the sentence (or clause).

CURE You are at a serious disadvantage as a writer if you cannot find the subject of a sentence. Turn to 58a for help. If you need more practice, check with your instructor or a writing center tutor.

CAUSE You aren't sure whether the subject is singular or plural.

CURE Look up the appropriate rule in 21. There is no need to memorize all of these rules; just know where to find them.

See also "Looking at Yourself as a Writer: Problems with -*s* endings on verbs" (p. 370).

21j   Words such as *athletics*, *economics*, *mathematics*, *physics*, *statistics*, *measles*, *mumps*, and *news* are usually singular, despite their plural form.

▶   Statistics ~~are~~ among the most difficult courses in our program.
                ^ *is*

EXCEPTION: When they describe separate items rather than a collective body of knowledge, words such as *athletics*, *mathematics*, *physics*, and *statistics* are plural: *The statistics on school retention rates are impressive.*

21k   Titles of works, company names, words mentioned as words, and gerund phrases are singular.

▶   *Lost Cities* ~~describe~~ the discoveries of many ancient
                  ^ *describes*

civilizations.

▶   Delmonico Brothers ~~specialize~~ in organic produce and
                        ^ *specializes*

additive-free meats.

▶   *Controlled substances* ~~are~~ a euphemism for illegal drugs.
                            ^ *is*

A gerund phrase consists of an *-ing* verb form followed by any objects, complements, or modifiers (see 59c). Treat gerund phrases as singular.

▶   Encountering busy signals ~~are~~ troublesome to our clients,
                              ^ *is*

so we have hired two new switchboard operators.

EXERCISE 21–1

Underline the subject (or compound subject) and then select the verb that agrees with it. (If you have difficulty identifying the subject, consult 58a.) Answers to lettered sentences appear in the back of the book. Example:

Someone in the audience ((has)/have) volunteered to partici-

pate in the experiment.

a. The city's rich history and its exciting cultural life (has/have) made Paris a popular tourist destination.
b. Shelters for teenage runaways (offers/offer) a wide variety of services.
c. Each of the twenty-five actors (was/were) given a five-minute tryout, and only three of us were called back for a more intensive audition.
d. The chances of your being promoted (is/are) excellent.
e. When Governor John White returned to Roanoke, he found that there (was/were) no signs of life or traces of the settlers he had left behind.

1. Neither the professor nor his assistants (was/were) able to solve the mystery of the eerie glow in the laboratory.
2. Four years of research (has/have) gone into making our software suitable for the Japanese market.
3. Located at the south end of the complex (was/were) an Olympic size pool, two basketball courts, and four tennis courts.
4. The most significant lifesaving device in automobiles (is/are) air bags.
5. The old iron gate and the brick wall (makes/make) our courthouse appear older than its fifty years.
6. The dangers of smoking (is/are) well documented.
7. Every year, during the midsummer festival, the smoke of village bonfires (fills/fill) the sky.
8. When food supplies (was/were) scarce, the slaves had to make do with the less desirable parts of the animals.
9. There (is/are) several pots of herbs on the balcony.
10. Hidden under the floorboards (was/were) a bag of coins and a rusty sword.

EXERCISE 21–2

Edit the following sentences to eliminate problems with subject-verb agreement. If a sentence is correct, write "correct" after it.

Answers to lettered sentences appear in the back of the book. Example:

were
Jack's first days in the infantry ~~was~~ grueling.
　　　　　　　　　　　　　　　　　　　^

a. High concentrations of carbon monoxide results in headaches, dizziness, unconsciousness, and even death.
b. Not until my interview with Dr. Hwang were other possibilities opened to me.
c. After hearing the evidence and the closing arguments, the jury was sequestered.
d. Crystal chandeliers, polished floors, and a new oil painting has transformed Sandra's apartment.
e. The board of directors, ignoring the wishes of the neighborhood, has voted to allow further development.

1. Fully 30 percent of the channel's programming consist of commercials.
2. Of particular concern are penicillin and tetracycline, antibiotics used to make animals more resistant to disease.
3. The presence of certain bacteria in our bodies is one of the factors that determine our overall health.
4. No one who has ever seen the northern lights has forgotten the experience.
5. Every year a number of kokanee salmon, not native to the region, is introduced into Flathead Lake.
6. Mathematics has always been one of my strongest subjects.
7. Neither the explorer nor his companions was ever seen again.
8. At MGM Studios at Disney World, the wonders of moviemaking comes alive.
9. SEACON is the only one of our war games that emphasize scientific and technical issues.
10. The key program of Alcoholics Anonymous are the twelve steps to recovery.

22

Make pronouns and antecedents agree.

A pronoun is a word that substitutes for a noun. (See 57b.) Many pronouns have antecedents, nouns or pronouns to which they refer. A pronoun and its antecedent agree when they are both singular or both plural.

SINGULAR   *Dr. Sarah Simms* finished *her* rounds.

PLURAL   The *doctors* finished *their* rounds.

The pronouns *he, his, she, her, it,* and *its* must agree in gender (masculine, feminine, or neuter) with their antecedents, not with the words they modify.

Jane visited *her* [not *his*] brother in Denver.

GRAMMAR CHECKERS do not flag problems with pronoun-antecedent agreement. It takes a human eye to see that a singular noun, such as *logger,* does not agree with a plural pronoun, such as *their,* in a sentence like this: *The logger in the Northwest relies on the old forest growth for their living.*

22a   Do not use plural pronouns to refer to singular antecedents.

Writers are frequently tempted to use plural pronouns to refer to two kinds of singular antecedents: indefinite pronouns and generic nouns.

Grammatical sentences

Indefinite pronouns

Indefinite pronouns refer to nonspecific persons or things. Even though some of the following indefinite pronouns may seem to have plural meanings, treat them as singular in formal English.

anybody	either	neither	somebody
anyone	everybody	nobody	someone
anything	everyone	none	something
each	everything	no one	

In class *everyone* performs at *his or her* [not *their*] own fitness level.

When a plural pronoun refers mistakenly to a singular indefinite pronoun, you can usually choose one of three options for revision.

1. Replace the plural pronoun with *he or she* (or *his or her*).
2. Make the antecedent plural.
3. Rewrite the sentence so that no problem of agreement exists.

▶ When someone has been drinking, ~~they are~~ *he or she is* likely to speed.

▶ When ~~someone has~~ *drivers have* been drinking, they are likely to speed.

▶ *A driver who* ~~When someone~~ has been drinking/~~they are~~ *is* likely to speed.

Because the *he or she* construction is wordy, often the second or third revision strategy is more effective. Be aware that the traditional use of *he* (or *his*) to refer to persons of either sex is now widely considered sexist. (See 17f.)

Generic nouns

A generic noun represents a typical member of a group, such as a typical student, or any member of a group, such as any lawyer. Although generic nouns may seem to have plural meanings, they are singular.

> Every *runner* must train rigorously if *he or she wants* [not *they want*] to excel.

When a plural pronoun refers mistakenly to a generic noun, you will usually have the same three revision options as just mentioned for indefinite pronouns.

▶ A medical student must study hard if ~~they want~~ *he or she wants* to succeed.

▶ ~~A medical student~~ *Medical students* must study hard if they want to succeed.

▶ A medical student must study hard ~~if they want~~ to succeed.

22b Treat collective nouns as singular unless the meaning is clearly plural.

Collective nouns such as *jury, committee, audience, crowd, class, troop, family, team,* and *couple* name a class or a group. Ordinarily the group functions as a unit, so the noun should be treated as singular; if the members of the group function as individuals, however, the noun should be treated as plural. (See also 21f.)

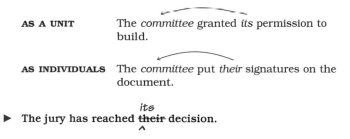

AS A UNIT The *committee* granted *its* permission to build.

AS INDIVIDUALS The *committee* put *their* signatures on the document.

▶ The jury has reached ~~their~~ *its* decision.

There is no reason to draw attention to the individual members of the jury, so *jury* should be treated as singular. Notice also that the writer treated the noun as singular when choosing the verb *has,* so for consistency the pronoun must be *its.*

their
▶ The audience shouted "Bravo" and stamped ~~its~~ feet.
                                              ^

It is difficult to see how the audience as a unit can stamp *its* feet. The meaning here is clearly plural, requiring *their.*

22c   Treat most compound antecedents connected by *and* as plural.

Joanne and John moved to the mountains, where *they* built a log cabin.

22d   With compound antecedents connected by *or* or *nor* (or by *either . . . or* or *neither . . . nor*), make the pronoun agree with the nearer antecedent.

Either *Bruce* or *James* should receive first prize for *his* sculpture.

Neither the *mouse* nor the *rats* could find *their* way through the maze.

NOTE: If one of the antecedents is singular and the other plural, as in the second example, put the plural one last to avoid awkwardness.

EXCEPTION: If one antecedent is male and the other female, do not follow the traditional rule. The sentence *Either Bruce or Ann should receive the blue ribbon for her sculpture* makes no sense. The best solution is to recast the sentence: *The blue ribbon for best sculpture should go to Bruce or Ann.*

EXERCISE 22–1

Edit the following sentences to eliminate problems with pronoun-antecedent agreement. Most of the sentences can be revised in more than one way, so experiment before choosing a solution. If a sentence is correct, write "correct" after it. Revisions of lettered sentences appear in the back of the book. Example:

> *Recruiters*
> ~~The recruiter~~ may tell the truth, but there is much that they
> ∧
> choose not to tell.

a. I can be standing in front of a Xerox machine, with parts scattered around my feet, and someone will ask me to let them make a copy.
b. The sophomore class elects its president tomorrow.
c. The instructor has asked everyone to bring their own tools to carpentry class.
d. An eighteenth-century architect was also a classical scholar; they were often at the forefront of archaeological research.
e. If anyone is caught smoking on the premises, they will be severely reprimanded.

1. If a driver refuses to take a blood or breath test, he or she will have their licenses suspended for six months.
2. Why should we care about the timber wolf? One answer is that they have proven beneficial to humans by killing off weakened prey.
3. When a client is going to be late or cannot make an appointment, half the time they fail to inform us.
4. Seven qualified Hispanic agents applied, each hoping for a career move that would let them use their language and cultural training on more than just translations and drug deals; the job went to a non-Hispanic who was taking a crash course in Spanish.
5. If anyone notices any suspicious activity, they should report it to the police.
6. The troop was expected to operate as a unit and carry out their orders without discussion.
7. David lent his motorcycle to someone who allowed their friend to use it.

Checking for problems with pronoun-antecedent agreement

First look for the most common trouble spots:

INDEFINITE PRONOUNS (SINGULAR) (22a)

anybody	each	everyone	nobody	somebody
anyone	either	everything	none	someone
anything	everybody	neither	no one	something

> *No one* will see a salary increase until *he or she has* [not *they have*] been employed for two years.

GENERIC NOUNS (SINGULAR) (22a)

A generic noun names a typical person or thing (such as a typical teacher) or any person or thing (such as any employee of a company).

> *An adult panda* must consume ninety pounds of bamboo if *it is* [not *they are*] to remain healthy.

COLLECTIVE NOUNS (SINGULAR UNLESS THE MEANING IS CLEARLY PLURAL) (22b)

audience	committee	crowd	majority	team
class	couple	family	minority	troop

> The *committee* selected *its* [not *their*] new chairperson last night.

Choose an effective revision strategy that avoids sexist language.

Because many readers object to sexist language, avoid the use of *he, him,* and *his* as shorthand for *he or she, him or her,* and *his* or *hers*. Also try to be sparing in your use of *he or she* and *his or her*, since these expressions can become awkward, especially when repeated several times in a short passage. Where possible, seek out more graceful alternatives.

USE AN OCCASIONAL *HE OR SHE* (OR *HIS OR HER*).

► In our office, everyone works at ~~their~~ own pace.
  (*his or her*)

MAKE THE ANTECEDENT PLURAL.

► ~~An employee~~ on extended leave may continue their life
  (*Employees*)

insurance.

RECAST THE SENTENCE.

► The amount of annual leave a federal worker may

accrue depends on ~~their~~ length of service.

► ~~If a~~ child ~~is~~ born to parents who are both
  (*A*)

schizophrenic/ ~~they have~~ a high chance of being
  (*has*)

schizophrenic.

► A year later someone finally admitted ~~that they were~~
  (*to being*)

involved in the kidnapping.

► I was taught that no one could escape the fires of
  (*who wanted to reach heaven*)

purgatory. ~~if they wanted to reach heaven.~~

8. The crowd danced through the streets of Rio, wearing elaborate hats, crowns, and garlands on its head.
9. The applicant should be bilingual if they want to qualify for this position.
10. A graduate student needs to be willing to take on a sizable debt unless they have wealthy families.

LOOKING AT YOURSELF AS A WRITER
Pronoun-antecedent agreement

Like all writers, at times you will find yourself wrestling with the problem of pronoun-antecedent agreement. Here is why the problem is so pervasive.

CAUSE You hear faulty pronoun agreement in speech all the time, and you probably don't see much wrong with it, since it rarely interferes with clarity.

CURE Be aware that standards in writing tend to be stricter than those in speech.

CAUSE You don't want to use sexist English, and you find *he or she* awkward — so you resort to using plural pronouns such as *their* with singular antecedents such as *swimmer*.

CURE Choose plural antecedents or find a clever way around the problem. The chart on page 329 shows several possibilities.

23

Make pronoun references clear.

Pronouns substitute for nouns; they are a kind of shorthand. In a sentence like *After Andrew intercepted the ball, he kicked it as hard as he could,* the pronouns *he* and *it* substitute for the nouns *Andrew* and *ball.* The word a pronoun refers to is called its *antecedent.*

> **GRAMMAR CHECKERS** do not flag problems with faulty pronoun reference. Although a computer program can identify pronouns, it has no way of knowing which words, if any, they refer to. For example, grammar checkers miss the fact that the pronoun *it* has an ambiguous reference in the following sentence: *The thief stole the woman's purse and her car and then destroyed it.* Did the thief destroy the purse or the car? It takes human judgment to realize that readers might be confused.

23a Avoid ambiguous or remote pronoun reference.

Ambiguous pronoun reference occurs when the pronoun could refer to two possible antecedents.

▶ When Gloria set the pitcher on the glass-topped table/. it broke.
The pitcher broke when Gloria set it

▶ Tom told James, that he had won the lottery."
"You have
"

What broke—the table or the pitcher? Who won the lottery—Tom or James? The revisions eliminate the ambiguity.

Remote pronoun reference occurs when a pronoun is too far away from its antecedent for easy reading.

▶ After the court ordered my ex-husband to pay child support,

he refused. Approximately eight months later, we were back

in court. This time the judge ordered him to make payments

directly to the Support and Collections Unit, which would in

turn pay me. For the first six months I received regular

my ex-husband
payments, but then they stopped. Again ~~he~~ was summoned
                                         ^

to appear in court; he did not respond.

The pronoun *he* was too distant from its antecedent, *ex-husband*, which appeared several sentences earlier.

23b   Generally, avoid broad reference of *this, that, which,* and *it.*

For clarity, the pronouns *this, that, which,* and *it* should ordinarily refer to specific antecedents rather than to whole ideas or sentences. When a pronoun's reference is needlessly broad, either replace the pronoun with a noun or supply an antecedent to which the pronoun clearly refers.

▶ More and more often, especially in large cities, we are finding

our fate
ourselves victims of serious crimes. We learn to accept ~~this~~
                                                         ^

with minor gripes and groans.

For clarity the writer substituted a noun (*fate*) for the pronoun *this,* which referred broadly to the idea expressed in the preceding sentence.

▶ **Romeo and Juliet were both too young to have acquired much**
      a fact
wisdom, which accounts for their rash actions.
         ^

The writer added an antecedent (*fact*) that the pronoun *which* clearly refers to.

EXCEPTION: Many writers view broad reference as acceptable when the pronoun refers clearly to the sense of an entire clause.

> If you pick up a starving dog and make him prosperous, he
> will not bite you. This is the principal difference between a
> dog and a man.   —Mark Twain

23c Do not use a pronoun to refer to an implied antecedent.

A pronoun should refer to a specific antecedent, not to a word that is implied but not present in the sentence.

                                          the braids
▶ **After braiding Ann's hair, Sue decorated** ~~them~~ **with ribbons.**
                                             ^

The pronoun *them* referred to Ann's braids (implied by the term *braiding*), but the word *braids* did not appear in the sentence.

Modifiers, such as possessives, cannot serve as antecedents. A modifier may strongly imply the noun that the pronoun might logically refer to, but it is not itself that noun.

               Euripides
▶ **In** ~~Euripides'~~ *Medea,* **he describes the plight of a woman**
                       ^
rejected by her husband.

The pronoun *he* cannot refer logically to the possessive modifier *Euripides'*. The revision substitutes the noun *Euripides* for the pronoun *he,* thereby eliminating the problem.

23d Avoid the indefinite use of *they, it,* and *you.*

Do not use the pronoun *they* to refer indefinitely to persons who have not been specifically mentioned. *They* should always refer to a specific antecedent.

▶ Sometimes a list of ways to save energy is included with the
  gas bill. For example, ~~they suggest~~ *the gas company suggests* setting a moderate
  ∧

  temperature for the hot water heater.

The word *it* should not be used indefinitely in constructions such as "It is said on television . . ." or "In the article it says that. . . ."

▶ ~~In~~ *T*he report ~~it~~ points out that lifting the ban on Compound

  1080 would prove detrimental, possibly even fatal, to the

  bald eagle.

The pronoun *you* is appropriate when the writer is addressing the reader directly: *Once you have kneaded the dough, let it rise in a warm place for at least twenty-five minutes.* (See p. 55.) Except in informal contexts, however, the indefinite *you* (meaning "anyone in general") is inappropriate.

▶ In Ethiopia ~~you don't~~ *one doesn't* need much property to be considered
  ∧

  well-off.

If the pronoun *one* seems too stilted, the writer might recast the sentence: *In Ethiopia a person doesn't need much property to be considered well-off.*

23e To refer to persons, use *who, whom,* or *whose,* not *that* or *which.*

In most contexts, use *who, whom,* or *whose* to refer to persons, *that* or *which* to refer to animals or things. Although *that* is occasionally used to refer to persons, it is more polite to use a form of *who*. *Which* is reserved only for animals or things, so it is impolite to use it to refer to persons.

▶ When he heard about my seven children, four of ~~which~~ *whom*

continue to live at home, Vincent smiled and said,

"I love children."

▶ Fans wondered how an out-of-shape old man ~~that~~ *who* walked

with a limp could play football.

NOTE: Occasionally *whose* may be used to refer to animals and things to avoid the awkward *of which* construction.

▶ A major corporation, ~~the~~ name ~~of which~~ *whose* will be in tomorrow's

paper, has been illegally dumping toxic waste in the harbor

for years.

EXERCISE 23–1

Edit the following sentences to correct errors in pronoun reference. In some cases you will need to decide on an antecedent that the pronoun might logically refer to. Revisions of lettered sentences appear in the back of the book. Example:

Following the breakup of AT&T, many other companies

began to offer long-distance phone service. ~~This~~ has led to

The competition

^

lower long-distance rates.

a. The detective removed the bloodstained shawl from the body and then photographed it.
b. In Professor Jamal's class, you are lucky to earn a C.
c. We have a staff of experienced technicians that will service your copier within two hours of a service call.
d. The Comanche braves' lifestyle was particularly violent; they gained respect for their skill as warriors.
e. All students can secure parking permits from the campus police office; they are open from 8 A.M. until 8 P.M.

1. Our German conversation group is made up of six people, three of which I had never met before.
2. Many people believe that the polygraph test is highly reliable if you employ a licensed examiner.
3. The sky was still leaden and foggy, but we thought it would burn off.
4. Because of Paul Robeson's outspoken attitude toward fascism, he was labeled a Communist.
5. In the encyclopedia it states that male moths can smell female moths from several miles away.
6. When Aunt Harriet put the cake on the table, it collapsed.
7. France satisfies nearly 80 percent of its electrical needs through nuclear power. They have not had a serious mishap to date, but will their luck continue?
8. Be sure to visit Istanbul's bazaar, where they sell everything from Persian rugs to electronic calculators.
9. If you have a sweet tooth, visit the confectioner's shop, where it is still made as it was a hundred years ago.
10. Time and time again, I fell for materialistic guys that gave me nothing but pain.

24

Distinguish between pronouns such as *I* and *me*.

The personal pronouns in the following chart change what is known as case form according to their grammatical function in a sentence. Pronouns functioning as subjects (or subject complements) appear in the *subjective* case; those functioning as objects appear in the *objective* case; and those showing ownership appear in the *possessive* case.

	SUBJECTIVE CASE	OBJECTIVE CASE	POSSESSIVE CASE
SINGULAR	I	me	my
	you	you	your
	he/she/it	him/her/it	his/her/its
PLURAL	we	us	our
	you	you	your
	they	them	their

Pronouns in the subjective and objective cases are frequently confused. Most of the rules in this section specify when to use one or the other of these cases (*I* or *me, he* or *him,* and so on). Rule 24g details a special use of pronouns and nouns in the possessive case.

> GRAMMAR CHECKERS can flag some incorrect pronouns and explain the rules for using *I* or *me, he* or *him, she* or *her, we* or *us,* and *they* or *them.* For example, grammar checkers correctly flagged *we* in the following sentence, suggesting that *us* should be used as the object of the preposition *for: I say it is time for we parents to revolt.*
>
> You should not assume, however, that a computer program will catch all incorrect pronouns. For example, grammar checkers did not flag *more than I* in this sentence, where the writer's meaning requires *me: I get a little jealous that our dog likes my neighbor more than I.*

24a   Use the subjective case (*I, you, he, she, it, we, they*) for subjects and subject complements.

When personal pronouns are used as subjects, ordinarily your ear will tell you the correct pronoun. Problems sometimes arise, however, with compound word groups containing a pronoun, so it is not always safe to trust your ear.

▶ Joel ran away from home because his stepfather and ~~him~~ *he*
had quarreled.

> *His stepfather and he* is the subject of the verb *had quarreled.* If we strip away the words *his stepfather and,* the correct pronoun becomes clear: *he had quarreled* (not *him had quarreled*).

When a pronoun is used as a subject complement (a word following a linking verb), your ear may mislead you, since the incorrect form is frequently heard in casual speech. (See subject complement, 58b.)

▶ Sandra confessed that the artist was ~~her.~~ *she.*

> The pronoun *she* functions as a subject complement with the linking verb *was.* In formal, written English, subject complements must be in the subjective case. If your ear rejects *artist was she* as too stilted, try rewriting the sentence: *Sandra confessed that she was the artist.*

24b   Use the objective case (*me, you, him, her, it, us, them*) for all objects.

When a personal pronoun is used as a direct object, an indirect object, or the object of a preposition, ordinarily your ear will lead you to the correct pronoun. When an object is compound, however, you may occasionally become confused.

▶ Janice was indignant when she realized that the salesclerk

her.
was insulting her mother and ~~she.~~
^

Her mother and her is the direct object of the verb *was insulting.* Strip away the words *her mother and* to hear the correct pronoun: *was insulting her* (not *was insulting she*).

me
▶ Geoffrey went with my family and ~~I~~ to King's Dominion.
^

Me is the object of the preposition *with.* We would not say *Geoffrey went with I.*

When in doubt about the correct pronoun, some writers try to avoid making the choice by using a reflexive pronoun such as *myself.* Such evasions are nonstandard, even though they are used by some educated persons.

me
▶ The Egyptian cab driver gave my husband and ~~myself~~ some
^

good tips on traveling in North Africa.

My husband and me is the indirect object of the verb *gave.* For correct uses of *myself,* see the Glossary of Usage.

24c Put an appositive and the word to which it refers in the same case.

Appositives are noun phrases that rename nouns or pronouns. A pronoun used as an appositive has the same function (usually subject or object) as the word(s) the appositive renames.

I,
▶ At the drama festival, two actors, Christina and ~~me,~~ were
^

selected to do the last scene of *King Lear.*

The appositive *Christina and I* renames the subject, *actors.*

▶ The college interviewed only two applicants for the job,

me.
Professor Stevens and ~~I.~~
                        ^

The appositive *Professor Stevens and me* renames the direct object *applicants*.

24d Following *than* or *as*, choose the pronoun that expresses your meaning.

When a comparison begins with *than* or *as*, your choice of a pronoun will depend on your intended meaning. Consider, for example, the difference in meaning between these sentences:

My husband likes football better than I.

My husband likes football better than me.

Finish each sentence mentally and its meaning becomes clear: *My husband likes football better than I [do]. My husband likes football better than [he likes] me.*

▶ Even though he is sometimes ridiculed by the other boys,

they.
Norman is much better off than ~~them.~~
                              ^

They is the subject of the verb *are*, which is understood: *Norman is much better off than they [are].* If the correct English seems too formal, you can always add the verb.

her.
▶ We respected no other candidate as much as ~~she.~~
                                            ^

This sentence means that we respected no other candidate as much as *we respected her. Her* is the direct object of an understood verb.

24e When deciding whether *we* or *us* should precede a noun, choose the pronoun that would be appropriate if the noun were omitted.

▶ ~~Us~~ *We* tenants would rather fight than move.

▶ Management is short-changing ~~we~~ *us* tenants.

No one would say *Us would rather fight than move* or *Management is short-changing we*.

24f Use the objective case for subjects and objects of infinitives.

An infinitive is the word *to* followed by the base form of a verb. (See 59c.) Subjects of infinitives are an exception to the rule that subjects must be in the subjective case. Whenever an infinitive has a subject, it must be in the objective case. Objects of infinitives also are in the objective case.

▶ The crowd expected Chris and ~~I~~ *me* to defeat Tracy and ~~he~~ *him* in the doubles championship.

Chris and me is the subject of the infinitive *to defeat; Tracy and him* is the direct object of the infinitive.

24g Use the possessive case to modify a gerund.

A pronoun that modifies a gerund or a gerund phrase should appear in the possessive case (*my, our, your, his/her/its, their*). A gerund is a verb form ending in *-ing* that functions as a noun. Gerunds frequently appear in phrases, in which case the whole gerund phrase functions as a noun. (See 59c.)

> My father always tolerated ~~us~~ talking after the lights were
> ^{our}
> out.

The possessive pronoun *our* modifies the gerund *talking.*

Nouns as well as pronouns may modify gerunds. To form the possessive case of a noun, use an apostrophe and an *-s* (*a victim's rights*) or just an apostrophe (*victims' rights*). (See 36a.)

> We had to pay a fifty-dollar fine for ~~Brenda~~ driving without a
> ^{Brenda's}
> permit.

The possessive noun *Brenda's* modifies the gerund phrase *driving without a permit.*

Gerund phrases should not be confused with participial phrases, which function as adjectives, not as nouns: *We saw Brenda driving a yellow convertible.* Here *driving a yellow convertible* is a participial phrase modifying the noun *Brenda.* (See 59c.)

Sometimes the choice between the objective or the possessive case conveys a subtle difference in meaning:

We watched *them* dancing.

We watched *their* dancing.

In the first sentence the emphasis is on the people; *dancing* is a participle modifying the pronoun *them.* In the second sentence the emphasis is on the dancing; *dancing* is a gerund, and *their* is a possessive pronoun modifying the gerund.

NOTE: Do not use the possessive if it creates an awkward effect. Try to reword the sentence instead.

> **AWKWARD** The president agreed to the applications' being reviewed by a faculty committee.
>
> **REVISED** The president agreed that the applications could be reviewed by a faculty committee.
>
> **REVISED** The president agreed that a faculty committee could review the applications.

EXERCISE 24–1

Edit the following sentences to eliminate errors in case. If a sentence is correct, write "correct" after it. Answers to lettered sentences appear in the back of the book. Example:

Grandfather cuts down trees for neighbors much younger

than ~~him~~.
‸ *he.*

a. My Ethiopian neighbor was puzzled by the dedication of we joggers.
b. The jury was astonished when the witness suddenly confessed that the murderer was none other than he.
c. Sue's husband is ten years older than her.
d. Everyone laughed whenever Sandra described how her brother and her had seen the Loch Ness monster and fed it sandwiches.
e. We appreciate you bringing this problem to our attention.

1. The chain stores are threatening the survival of us shopkeepers.
2. The mysterious old woman handed Natasha and him a gold coin each.

Checking for problems with pronoun case

Look for the most common trouble spots; where possible, apply a test for the correct pronoun.

COMPOUND WORD GROUPS (24a, 24b)

Test: Mentally strip away the rest of the compound word group.

> While diving for pearls, [Ikiko and] *she* found a treasure chest full of gold bars.

> The most traumatic experience for [her father and] *me* occurred long after her operation.

PRONOUN AFTER *IS, ARE, WAS,* OR *WERE* (24a)

In formal English, remember to use the subjective-case pronouns *I, he, she, we,* and *they* after the linking verbs *is, are, was,* and *were.*

> The panel was shocked to learn that the undercover agent was *she.*

APPOSITIVES (24c)

Test: Mentally strip away the word group that the appositive renames.

> [The chief strategists], Dr. Bell and *I*, could not agree on a plan.

> The company could afford to send only [one of two researchers], Dr. Davis or *me*, to Paris.

Pronoun case (continued)

PRONOUN AFTER *THAN* OR *AS* (24d)

Test: Mentally complete the sentence.

> The supervisor claimed that she was much more experienced than *I* [was].

> Gloria admitted that she liked Greg's twin better than [she liked] *him*.

WE OR *US* BEFORE A NOUN (24e)

Test: Mentally delete the noun.

> *We* [women] really have come a long way.

> Sadly, discrimination against *us* [women] occurs in most cultures.

PRONOUN BEFORE OR AFTER AN INFINITIVE (24f)

Remember that both subjects and objects of infinitives take the objective case.

> Ms. Wilson asked John and *me* to drive the senator and *her* to the airport.

PRONOUN OR NOUN BEFORE A GERUND (24g)

Remember to use the possessive case when a pronoun modifies a gerund.

> There is only a small chance of *his* bleeding excessively because of this procedure.

3. The patient began suffering from the delusion that him and his family were constantly being followed and observed.
4. A professional counselor advised the division chief that Marco, Fidelia, and myself should be allowed to apply for the opening.
5. My adjustment to a new career was compounded by me becoming a single parent.
6. For a moment, I thought the farmer's dogs were going to attack Danny and I.
7. The swirling cyclone caused he and his horse to race for shelter.
8. The winners of the art competition, Justine and I, will spend a month studying painting in Florence.
9. During the testimony the witness pointed directly at the defendant and announced that the thief was him.
10. Despite our different backgrounds, a close friendship developed between Esperanza and I.

25

Distinguish between *who* and *whom*.

The choice between *who* and *whom* (or *whoever* and *whomever*) occurs primarily in subordinate clauses and in questions. *Who* and *whoever*, subjective-case pronouns, are used for subjects and subject complements. *Whom* and *whomever*, objective-case pronouns, are used for objects. (For more about pronoun case, see 24.)

 GRAMMAR CHECKERS can flag some sentences with a misused *who* or *whom* and explain the nature of the error. For example, grammar checkers flagged the subject pronoun *who* in the following sentence, suggesting correctly that the context calls for the object pronoun *whom*: *One of the women who Martinez hired became the most successful lawyer in the agency.*

However, at times the programs skip past a misused *who* or *whom*, as they did with this sentence: *Now that you have studied with both musicians, whom in your opinion is the better teacher?* The programs could not tell that the object pronoun *whom* functions as the subject of the verb *is*.

25a In subordinate clauses, use *who* and *whoever* for subjects or subject complements, *whom* and *whomever* for all objects.

When *who* and *whom* (or *whoever* and *whomever*) introduce subordinate clauses, their case is determined by their function *within the clause they introduce*. To choose the correct pronoun, you must isolate the subordinate clause and then decide how the pronoun functions within it. (See subordinate clauses, 59b.)

In the following two examples, the pronouns *who* and *whoever* function as the subjects of the clauses they introduce.

> who
> ▶ The prize goes to the runner ~~whom~~ collects the most points.
>   ^

The subordinate clause is *who collects the most points.* The verb of the clause is *collects,* and its subject is *who.*

> whoever
> ▶ He tells that story to ~~whomever~~ will listen.
>   ^

The writer selected the pronoun *whomever,* thinking that it was the object of the preposition *to.* However, the object of the preposition is the entire subordinate clause *whoever will listen.* The verb of the clause is *will listen,* and its subject is *whoever.*

Who occasionally functions as a subject complement in a subordinate clause. Subject complements occur with linking verbs (usually *be, am, is, are, was, were, being,* and *been*). (See 58b.)

> ►
> The receptionist knows ~~whom~~ you are.
> *who*
> ^

The subordinate clause is *who you are.* Its subject is *you,* and its subject complement is *who.*

When functioning as an object in a subordinate clause, *whom* (or *whomever*) appears out of order, before both the subject and the verb. To choose the correct pronoun, you must mentally restructure the clause.

> ►
> You will work with our senior industrial engineers, ~~who~~ you
> *whom*
> ^
>
> will meet later.

The subordinate clause is *whom you will meet later.* The subject of the clause is *you,* the verb is *will meet,* and *whom* is the direct object of the verb. This becomes clear if you mentally restructure the clause: *you will meet whom.*

When functioning as the object of a preposition in a subordinate clause, *whom* is often separated from its preposition.

> ►
> The tutor ~~who~~ I was assigned to was very supportive and
> *whom*
> ^
>
> helpful.

Whom is the object of the preposition *to.* In this sentence, the writer might choose to drop *whom: The tutor I was assigned to was very supportive and helpful.*

NOTE: Inserted expressions such as *they know, I think,* and *she says* should be ignored in determining whether to use *who* or *whom.*

▶ All of the show-offs, bullies, and tough guys in school want
to take on a big guy ~~whom~~ they know will not hurt them.
　　　　　　　　　　　　who

Who is the subject of *will hurt,* not the object of *know.*

25b In questions, use *who* and *whoever* for subjects, *whom* and *whomever* for all objects.

When *who* and *whom* (or *whoever* and *whomever*) are used to open questions, their case is determined by their function within the question. In the following example, *who* functions as the subject of the question.

▶ ~~Whom~~ was responsible for creating that computer virus?
　　Who

When *whom* functions as the object of a verb or the object of a preposition in a question, it appears out of normal order. To choose the correct pronoun, you must mentally restructure the question.

▶ ~~Who~~ did the committee select?
　　Whom

Whom is the direct object of the verb *did select.* To choose the correct pronoun, restructure the question: *The committee did select whom?*

▶ ~~Who~~ did you enter into the contract with?
　　Whom

Whom is the object of the preposition *with,* as is clear if you recast the question: *You did enter into the contract with whom?*

USAGE NOTE: In spoken English, *who* is frequently used to open a question even when it functions as an object: *Who did Joe replace?* Although some readers will accept such constructions in informal written English, it is safer to use *whom: Whom did Joe replace?*

EXERCISE 25-1

Edit the following sentences to eliminate errors in the use of *who* and *whom* (or *whoever* and *whomever*). If a sentence is correct, write "correct" after it. Answers to lettered sentences appear in the back of the book. Example:

> *whom*
> What is the name of the person ~~who~~ you are sponsoring for
>   ^
> membership in the club?

a. In his first production of *Hamlet*, who did Laurence Olivier replace?

b. Who was Martin Luther King's mentor?

c. Datacall allows you to talk to whoever needs you no matter where you are in the building.

d. The bank doors were locked, and whomever was inside remained there until the police officers arrived.

e. One of the women who Martinez hired became the most successful lawyer in the agency.

1. When medicine is scarce and expensive, physicians must give it to whomever has the best chance to survive.

2. Who was accused of receiving Mafia funds?

3. According to the Greek myth, the Sphinx devoured those who could not answer her riddles.

4. The only interstate travelers who get pulled over for speeding are the ones whom cannot afford a radar detector.

5. I was introduced to Jake's brother, who I had never met before.

Checking for problems with who and whom

Look for common trouble spots; where possible, apply a test for correct usage.

IN A SUBORDINATE CLAUSE

Isolate the subordinate clause. Then read its subject, verb, and any objects, restructuring the clause if necessary. Some writers find it helpful to substitute *he* for *who* and *him* for *whom.*

> Samuels hoped to become the business partner of (whoever/whomever) found the treasure.

> Test: . . . *whoever* found the treasure. [. . . *he* found the treasure.]

> Ada always seemed to be bestowing a favor on (whoever/whomever) she worked for.

> Test: . . . she worked for *whomever.* [. . . she worked for *him.*]

IN A QUESTION

Read the subject, verb, and any objects, rearranging the sentence structure if necessary.

> (Who/Whom) conferred with Roosevelt and Stalin at Yalta in 1945?

> Test: *Who* conferred . . . ?

> (Who/Whom) did the committee nominate?

> Test: The committee did nominate *whom*?

26

Choose adjectives and adverbs with care.

Adjectives ordinarily modify nouns or pronouns; occasionally they function as subject complements following linking verbs. Adverbs modify verbs, adjectives, or other adverbs. (See 57d and 57e.)

Many adverbs are formed by adding *-ly* to adjectives (*normal, normally; smooth, smoothly*). But don't assume that all words ending in *-ly* are adverbs or that all adverbs end in *-ly*. Some adjectives end in *-ly* (*lovely, friendly*) and some adverbs don't (*always, here, there*). When in doubt, consult a dictionary.

ESL

In English, adjectives are not pluralized to agree with the words they modify: *The red* [not *reds*] *roses were a wonderful surprise.*

GRAMMAR CHECKERS can flag a number of problems with adjectives and adverbs: some misuses of *bad* or *badly* and *good* or *well*; some double comparisons, such as *more meaner;* some absolute comparisons, such as *most unique;* and some double negatives, such as *can't hardly.* However, the programs slip past more problems than they find. Programs ignored errors like these: *could have been handled more professional* and *hadn't been bathed regular.*

26a Use adverbs, not adjectives, to modify verbs, adjectives, and adverbs.

When adverbs modify verbs (or verbals), they nearly always answer the question When? Where? How? Why? Under what conditions? How often? or To what degree? When adverbs modify adjectives or other adverbs, they usually qualify or intensify the meaning of the word they modify. (See 57e.)

The incorrect use of adjectives in place of adverbs to modify verbs occurs primarily in casual or nonstandard speech.

▶ The arrangement worked out ~~perfect~~ *perfectly* for everyone.

▶ The manager must see that the office runs ~~smooth~~ *smoothly* and ~~efficient.~~ *efficiently.*

The adverb *perfectly* modifies the verb *worked out;* the adverbs *smoothly* and *efficiently* modify the verb *runs.*

The incorrect use of the adjective *good* in place of the adverb *well* is especially common in casual and nonstandard speech.

▶ We were surprised to hear that Louise had done so ~~good~~ *well* on the CPA exam.

The adverb *well* (not the adjective *good*) should be used to modify the verb *had done.*

NOTE: The word *well* is an adjective when it means "healthy," "satisfactory," or "fortunate": *I am very well, thank you. All is well. It is just as well.*

Adjectives are sometimes used incorrectly to modify adjectives or adverbs.

▶ For a man eighty years old, Joe plays golf ~~real~~ well.
    really
    ^

▶ We were ~~awful~~ sorry to hear about your uncle's death.
    awfully
    ^

Only adverbs can be used to modify adjectives or other adverbs. *Really* intensifies the meaning of the adverb *well*, and *awfully* intensifies the meaning of the adjective *sorry*. The writers could substitute other intensifiers: *very well, terribly sorry.*

ESL

Placement of adjectives and adverbs can be a tricky matter for second language speakers. See 31c.

26b   Use adjectives, not adverbs, as complements.

Adjectives ordinarily precede nouns, but they can also function as subject complements or as object complements.

Subject complements

A subject complement follows a linking verb and completes the meaning of the subject. (See 58b.) When an adjective functions as a subject complement, it describes the subject.

Justice is *blind.*

Problems can arise with verbs such as *smell, taste, look,* and *feel,* which sometimes, but not always, function as linking verbs. If the word following one of these verbs describes the subject, use an adjective; if it modifies the verb, use an adverb.

ADJECTIVE The detective looked *cautious.*

ADVERB The detective looked *cautiously* for fingerprints.

The adjective *cautious* describes the detective; the adverb *cautiously* modifies the verb *looked.*

Linking verbs suggest states of being, not actions. Notice, for example, the different meanings of *looked* in the preceding examples. To look cautious suggests the state of being cautious; to look cautiously is to perform an action in a cautious way.

▶ The lilacs in our backyard smell especially ~~sweetly~~ this year.

sweet

▶ Lori looked ~~well~~ in her new raincoat.

good

The verbs *smell* and *looked* suggest states of being, not actions. Therefore, they should be followed by adjectives, not adverbs. (Contrast with action verbs: *We smelled the flowers. Lori looked for her raincoat.*)

Object complements

An object complement follows a direct object and completes its meaning. (See 58b.) When an adjective functions as an object complement, it describes the direct object.

Sorrow makes us *wise.*

Object complements occur with verbs such as *call, consider, create, find, keep,* and *make.* When a modifier follows the direct object of one of these verbs, check to see whether it functions as an adjective describing the direct object or as an adverb modifying the verb.

ADJECTIVE The referee called the plays *perfect.*

ADVERB The referee called the plays *perfectly.*

The first sentence means that the referee considered the plays to be perfect; the second means that the referee did an excellent job of calling the plays.

▶ God created all men and women ~~equally.~~ *equal.*
^

> The adjective *equal* is an object complement describing the direct object *men and women.*

26c Use comparatives and superlatives with care.

Most adjectives and adverbs have three forms: the positive, the comparative, and the superlative.

POSITIVE	COMPARATIVE	SUPERLATIVE
soft	softer	softest
fast	faster	fastest
careful	more careful	most careful
bad	worse	worst
good	better	best

Comparative versus superlative

Use the comparative to compare two things, the superlative to compare three or more.

▶ Which of these two brands of toothpaste is ~~best?~~ *better?*
^

▶ Though Shaw and Jackson are impressive, Hobbs is the ~~more~~ *most*
^
  qualified of the three candidates running for mayor.

Form of comparatives and superlatives

To form comparatives and superlatives of most one- and two-syllable adjectives, use the endings *-er* and *-est: smooth, smoother, smoothest; easy, easier, easiest.* With longer adjec-

ad

tives, use *more* and *most* (or *less* and *least* for downward comparisons): *exciting, more exciting, most exciting; helpful, less helpful, least helpful.*

Some one-syllable adverbs take the endings *-er* and *-est* (*fast, faster, fastest*), but longer adverbs and all of those ending in *-ly* form the comparative and superlative with *more* and *most* (or *less* and *least*).

The comparative and superlative forms of the following adjectives and adverbs are irregular: *good, better, best; well, better, best; bad, worse, worst; badly, worse, worst.*

▶ The Kirov is the ~~talentedest~~ ballet company we have seen.
  most talented

▶ Lloyd's luck couldn't have been ~~worser~~ than David's.
  worse

Double comparatives or superlatives

Do not use double comparatives or superlatives. When you have added *-er* or *-est* to an adjective or adverb, do not also use *more* or *most* (or *less* or *least*).

▶ Of all her family, Julia is the ~~most~~ happiest about the move.

▶ That is the most ~~inanest~~ joke I have ever heard.
  inane

Absolute concepts

Avoid expressions such as *more straight, less perfect, very round*, and *most unique*. Either something is unique or it isn't. It is illogical to suggest that absolute concepts come in degrees.

▶ That is the most ~~unique~~ wedding gown I have ever seen.
  unusual

▶ The painting would have been even more ~~priceless~~ had it
  valuable

been signed.

26d   Avoid double negatives.

Standard English allows two negatives only if a positive meaning is intended: *The orchestra was not unhappy with its performance.* Double negatives used to emphasize negation are nonstandard.

Negative modifiers such as *never, no,* and *not* should not be paired with other negative modifiers or with negative words such as *neither, none, no one, nobody,* and *nothing.*

▶ Management is not doing ~~nothing~~ to see that the trash is
  anything

  picked up.

▶ George won't ~~never~~ forget that day.
  ever

▶ I enjoy living alone because I don't have to answer to ~~nobody.~~
  anybody.

The double negatives *not . . . nothing, won't never,* and *don't . . . nobody* are nonstandard.

The modifiers *hardly, barely,* and *scarcely* are considered negatives in standard English, so they should not be used with negatives such as *not, no one,* or *never.*

▶ Maxine is so weak she ~~can't~~ hardly climb stairs.
  can

EXERCISE 26–1

Edit the following sentences to eliminate errors in the use of adjectives and adverbs. If a sentence is correct, write "correct" after it. Answers to lettered sentences appear in the back of the book. Example:

> When I watched Carl run the 440 on Saturday, I was amazed
> at how ~~good~~ he paced himself.
> *well*

a. When Tina began breathing normal, we could relax.
b. All of us on the team felt badly about our performance.
c. This incident could have been handled more professional if lines of communication had been kept open.
d. The vaulting box, more commonly known as the horse, is the easiest of the four pieces of equipment to master.
e. Fiona has developed the most unique Web site I've ever seen.

1. When answering the phone, you should speak clearly and courteous.
2. Who was more upset about the loss? Was it the coach or the quarterback or the owner of the team?
3. We wanted a hunting dog. We didn't care if he smelled badly, but we really did not want him to smell bad.
4. The green bagels looked and tasted real peculiar.
5. After checking to see how bad I had been hurt, my sister dialed 911.
6. If the college's Web page had been updated more regular, students would have learned about the new course offerings.
7. Professor Brown's public praise of my performance on the exam made me feel a little strangely.
8. Of all of my relatives, Uncle Roberto is the most cleverest.
9. With the budget deadline approaching, our office hasn't hardly had time to handle routine correspondence.
10. Marcia performed very well at her Drama Club audition.

27

Choose standard English verb forms.

In nonstandard English, spoken by those who share a regional or cultural heritage, verb forms sometimes differ from those of standard English. In writing, use standard English verb forms unless you are quoting nonstandard speech or using nonstandard forms for literary effect. (See 17d.)

Except for the verb *be,* all verbs in English have five forms. The following chart lists the five forms and provides a sample sentence in which each might appear.

BASE FORM	Usually I (*walk, ride*).
PAST TENSE	Yesterday I (*walked, rode*).
PAST PARTICIPLE	I have (*walked, ridden*) many times before.
PRESENT PARTICIPLE	I am (*walking, riding*) right now.
-S FORM	He/she/it (*walks, rides*) regularly.

Both the past-tense and past-participle forms of regular verbs end in *-ed* (*walked, walked*). Irregular verbs form the past tense and past participle in other ways (*rode, ridden*).

The verb *be* has eight forms instead of the usual five: *be, am, is, are, was, were, being, been.*

GRAMMAR CHECKERS can flag some misused irregular verbs, such as *had drove* or *Lucia swum,* but they miss about twice as many errors as they find.

27a   Use the correct forms of irregular verbs.

For all regular verbs, the past-tense and past-participle forms are the same (ending in *-ed* or *-d*), so there is no danger of confusion. This is not true, however, for irregular verbs, such as the following.

BASE FORM	PAST TENSE	PAST PARTICIPLE
go	went	gone
fight	fought	fought
fly	flew	flown

The past-tense form, which never has a helping verb, expresses action that occurred entirely in the past. The past participle is used with a helping verb — either with *has, have,* or *had* to form one of the perfect tenses or with *be, am, is, are, was, were, being,* or *been* to form the passive voice.

PAST TENSE   Last July, we *went* to Paris.

PAST PARTICIPLE   We have *gone* to Paris twice.

When you aren't sure which verb form to choose (*went* or *gone, began* or *begun,* and so on), consult the list of common irregular verbs that starts on the next page. Choose the past-tense form if the verb in your sentence doesn't have a helping verb; choose the past-participle form if it does.

In nonstandard English speech, the past-tense and past-participle forms may differ from those of standard English, as in the following sentences.

▶ Yesterday we ~~seen~~ *saw* an unidentified flying object.

▶ The reality of the situation finally ~~sunk~~ *sank* in.

The past-tense forms *saw* and *sank* are required because there are no helping verbs.

▶ The truck was apparently ~~stole~~ *stolen* while the driver ate lunch.

▶ The teacher asked Dwain if he had ~~did~~ *done* his homework.

Because of the helping verbs, the past-participle forms are required: *was stolen, had done.*

When in doubt about the standard English forms of irregular verbs, consult the following list or look up the base form of the verb in the dictionary, which also lists any irregular forms. (If no additional forms are listed in the dictionary, the verb is regular, not irregular.)

Common irregular verbs

BASE FORM	PAST TENSE	PAST PARTICIPLE
arise	arose	arisen
awake	awoke, awaked	awaked, awoke
be	was, were	been
beat	beat	beaten, beat
become	became	become
begin	began	begun
bend	bent	bent
bite	bit	bitten, bit
blow	blew	blown
break	broke	broken
bring	brought	brought
build	built	built
burst	burst	burst
buy	bought	bought
catch	caught	caught
choose	chose	chosen
cling	clung	clung
come	came	come
cost	cost	cost
deal	dealt	dealt
dig	dug	dug
dive	dived, dove	dived
do	did	done
drag	dragged	dragged
draw	drew	drawn
dream	dreamed, dreamt	dreamed, dreamt
drink	drank	drunk
drive	drove	driven
eat	ate	eaten
fall	fell	fallen
fight	fought	fought
find	found	found
fly	flew	flown
forget	forgot	forgotten, forgot

BASE FORM	PAST TENSE	PAST PARTICIPLE
freeze	froze	frozen
get	got	gotten, got
give	gave	given
go	went	gone
grow	grew	grown
hang (suspend)	hung	hung
hang (execute)	hanged	hanged
have	had	had
hear	heard	heard
hide	hid	hidden
hurt	hurt	hurt
keep	kept	kept
know	knew	known
lay (put)	laid	laid
lead	led	led
lend	lent	lent
let (allow)	let	let
lie (recline)	lay	lain
lose	lost	lost
make	made	made
prove	proved	proved, proven
read	read	read
ride	rode	ridden
ring	rang	rung
rise (get up)	rose	risen
run	ran	run
say	said	said
see	saw	seen
send	sent	sent
set (place)	set	set
shake	shook	shaken
shoot	shot	shot
shrink	shrank	shrunk
sing	sang	sung
sink	sank	sunk
sit (be seated)	sat	sat
slay	slew	slain
sleep	slept	slept
speak	spoke	spoken

BASE FORM	PAST TENSE	PAST PARTICIPLE
spin	spun	spun
spring	sprang	sprung
stand	stood	stood
steal	stole	stolen
sting	stung	stung
strike	struck	struck, stricken
swear	swore	sworn
swim	swam	swum
swing	swung	swung
take	took	taken
teach	taught	taught
throw	threw	thrown
wake	woke, waked	waked, woken
wear	wore	worn
wring	wrung	wrung
write	wrote	written

27b Distinguish among the forms of *lie* and *lay*.

Writers and speakers frequently confuse the various forms of *lie* (meaning "to recline or rest on a surface") and *lay* (meaning "to put or place something"). *Lie* is an intransitive verb; it does not take a direct object: *The tax forms lie on the table.* The verb *lay* is transitive; it takes a direct object: *Please lay the tax forms on the coffee table.* (See 58b.)

In addition to confusing the meaning of *lie* and *lay*, writers and speakers are often unfamiliar with the standard English forms of these verbs.

BASE FORM	PAST TENSE	PAST PARTICIPLE	PRESENT PARTICIPLE
lie	lay	lain	lying
lay	laid	laid	laying

► Sue was so exhausted that she ~~laid~~ *lay* down for a nap.

The past-tense form of *lie* ("to recline") is *lay.*

▶ The patient had ~~laid~~ *lain* in an uncomfortable position all night.

The past-participle form of *lie* ("to recline") is *lain*. If the correct English seems too stilted, recast the sentence: *The patient had been lying in an uncomfortable position all night.*

▶ Mary ~~lay~~ *laid* the baby on my lap.

The past-tense form of *lay* ("to place") is *laid*.

▶ My mother's letters were ~~laying~~ *lying* in the corner of the chest.

The present participle of *lie* ("to rest on a surface") is *lying*.

EXERCISE 27–1

Edit the following sentences to eliminate problems with irregular verbs. If a sentence is correct, write "correct" after it. Answers to lettered sentences appear in the back of the book. Example:

Was it you I ~~seen~~ *saw* last night at the concert?

a. Noticing that my roommate was shivering and looking pale, I rung for the nurse.
b. When I get the urge to exercise, I lay down until it passes.
c. Grandmother had drove our new jeep to the sunrise church service on Savage Mountain, so we were left with the station wagon.
d. Last June my cousin Lucia swum the length of the lake in forty minutes.
e. In her basement, Sandra discovered letters dating from the Civil War that had lain untouched for years.

1. How did the detective know that the suspect had went to the officer on the night of the murder?
2. Laying on the operating table, I could hear only the beating of my heart.

3. The burglar must have gone immediately upstairs, grabbed what looked good, and took off.

4. In just a week the ground had froze, and the first winter storm had left over a foot of snow.

5. Jet lag must have caught up with me; I lay down for a nap yesterday afternoon—and woke up this morning.

6. Lincoln took good care of his legal clients; the contracts he drew for the Illinois Central Railroad could never be broke.

7. Have you ever dreamed that you were falling from a cliff or flying through the air?

8. I locked my brakes, leaned the motorcycle to the left, and laid it down to keep from slamming into the fence.

9. In her junior year, Cindy run the 440-yard dash in 51.1 seconds.

10. Larry claimed that he had drank a bad soda, but Esther suspected the truth.

27c   Use -s (or -es) endings on present-tense verbs that have third-person singular subjects.

All singular nouns (*child, tree*) and the pronouns *he, she,* and *it* are third-person singular; indefinite pronouns such as *everyone* and *neither* are also third-person singular. When the subject of a sentence is third-person singular, its verb takes an -s or -es ending in the present tense. (See also 21.)

	SINGULAR		**PLURAL**	
FIRST PERSON	I	know	we	know
SECOND PERSON	you	know	you	know
THIRD PERSON	he/she/it	knows	they	know
	child	knows	parents	know
	everyone	knows		

In nonstandard speech, the -s ending required by standard English is sometimes omitted.

▶ Ellen taught him what he ~~know~~ *knows* about the software.

► Sulfur dioxide ~~turn~~ leaves yellow, ~~dissolve~~ marble, and ~~eat~~
  ^{turns}   ^{dissolves}   ^{eats}

away iron and steel.

> The subjects *he* and *sulfur dioxide* are third-person singular, so
> the verbs must end in *-s*.

CAUTION: Do not add the *-s* ending to the verb if the subject
is not third-person singular.

The writers of the following sentences, knowing they
sometimes dropped *-s* endings from verbs, overcorrected by
adding the endings where they don't belong.

► I prepare~~s~~ program specifications and logic diagrams.

> The writer mistakenly concluded that the *-s* ending belongs on
> present-tense verbs used with *all* singular subjects, not just
> *third-person* singular subjects. The pronoun *I* is first-person
> singular, so its verb does not require the *-s*.

► The dirt floors require~~s~~ continual sweeping.

> The writer mistakenly thought that the *-s* ending on the verb
> indicated plurality. The *-s* goes on present-tense verbs used
> with third-person *singular* subjects.

Has *versus* have

In the present tense, use *has* with third-person singular subjects; all other subjects require *have.*

	SINGULAR		**PLURAL**	
FIRST PERSON	I	have	we	have
SECOND PERSON	you	have	you	have
THIRD PERSON	he/she/it	has	they	have

In some dialects, *have* is used with all subjects. But standard English requires *has* for third-person singular subjects.

Grammatical sentences

▶ This respected musician almost always ~~have~~ ^{has} a message to convey in his work.
^

▶ As for the retirement income program, it ~~have~~ ^{has} finally been established.
^

The subjects *musician* and *it* are third-person singular, so the verb should be *has* in each case.

CAUTION: Do not use *has* if the subject is not third-person singular. The writers of the following sentences were aware that they often wrote *have* when standard English requires *has*. Here they are using what appears to them to be the "more correct" form, but in an inappropriate context.

▶ My business law classes ~~has~~ ^{have} helped me to understand more about contracts.
^

▶ I ~~has~~ ^{have} much to be thankful for.
^

The subjects of these sentences—*classes* and *I*—are third-person plural and first-person singular, so standard English requires *have*. *Has* is used with third-person singular subjects only.

Does *versus* do *and* doesn't *versus* don't

In the present tense, use *does* and *doesn't* with third-person singular subjects; all other subjects require *do* and *don't*.

	SINGULAR		**PLURAL**	
FIRST PERSON	I	do/don't	we	do/don't
SECOND PERSON	you	do/don't	you	do/don't
THIRD PERSON	he/she/it	does/doesn't	they	do/don't

The use of *don't* instead of the standard English *doesn't* is a feature of many dialects in the United States. Use of *do* for *does* is rarer.

▶ Grandfather really ~~don't~~ have a place to call home.
   ^doesn't^

▶ ~~Do~~ she know the correct procedure for setting up the
   ^Does^

experiment?

Grandfather and *she* are third-person singular, so the verbs should be *doesn't* and *does*.

Am, is, and are; was and were

The verb *be* has three forms in the present tense (*am, is, are*) and two in the past tense (*was, were*). Use *am* and *was* with first-person singular subjects; use *is* and *was* with third-person singular subjects. With all other subjects, use *are* and *were*.

	SINGULAR		**PLURAL**	
FIRST PERSON	I	am/was	we	are/were
SECOND PERSON	you	are/were	you	are/were
THIRD PERSON	he/she/it	is/was	they	are/were

▶ Judy wanted to borrow Tim's notes, but she ~~were~~ too shy to
   ^was^

ask for them.

The subject *she* is third-person singular, so the verb should be *was*.

▶ Did you think you ~~was~~ going to drown?
   ^were^

The subject *you* is second-person singular, so the verb should be *were*.

If -s verb forms are a serious problem for you, ask yourself why. Here are the most common causes and cures.

CAUSE Your informal spoken English may differ from standard English in its use of -s forms.

CURE Listen carefully to your own casual speech (or the casual speech of family and friends) and compare it with the chart on page 310. Make a list of any differences that you need to be alert to.

CAUSE You may be confused about the rules on when to use the -s form of a verb. For example, you may mistakenly think that a "plural" verb takes an -s ending, just like most plural nouns.

CURE When proofreading, consult the chart on page 311, which shows when to use -s verb forms. Don't let yourself get confused by half-learned rules.

CAUSE When you proofread your final draft, you read for meaning, so you don't notice small surface features such as missing word endings.

CURE Proofread your draft out loud—slowly—articulating the words just as they are written on the page. If you still have trouble, ask your instructor or a writing center tutor for help.

CAUSE When it is difficult to pronounce an -s ending, you may have trouble hearing that the -s is needed—even when you proofread out loud. For example, many speakers do not articulate the -s in verbs like *costs* and *asks* and nouns like *tests* and *desks*.

CURE Be alert for words that give you difficulty. Probably they end in what grammarians call "consonant clusters." Here are some commonly used verbs and nouns that end in consonant clusters: *acts*, *asks*, *clasps*, *costs*, *crafts*, *desks*, *expects*, *grasps*, *lists*, *masks*, *risks*, *tests*, and *wasps*.

GRAMMAR CHECKERS can catch some missing -s endings on verbs and some misused -s forms of the verb. Unfortunately, they flag quite a few correct sentences, so you need to know how to interpret what the programs tell you. (See the grammar check advice on p. 309 for more detailed information.)

27d Do not omit *-ed* endings on verbs.

Speakers who do not fully pronounce *-ed* endings sometimes omit them unintentionally in writing. Failure to pronounce *-ed* endings is common in many dialects and in informal speech even in standard English. In the following frequently used words and phrases, for example, the *-ed* ending is not always fully pronounced.

advised	developed	prejudiced	supposed to
asked	fixed	pronounced	used to
concerned	frightened	stereotyped	

When a verb is regular, both the past tense and the past participle are formed by adding *-ed* to the base form of the verb.

Past tense

Use an *-ed* or *-d* ending to express the past tense of regular verbs. The past tense is used when the action occurred entirely in the past.

> ▶ Over the weekend, Ed ~~fix~~ _fixed_ his brother's skateboard and tuned
>
> up his mother's 1955 Thunderbird.

▶ Last summer my counselor ~~advise~~ me to ask my chemistry
                           advised
                            ^

   instructor for help.

Past participles

Past participles are used in three ways: (1) following *have,
has,* or *had* to form one of the perfect tenses; (2) following
be, am, is, are, was, were, being, or *been* to form the passive
voice; and (3) as adjectives modifying nouns or pronouns.
The perfect tenses are listed on pages 377–78, and the passive voice is discussed in 28c. For a discussion of participles
functioning as adjectives, see 59c.

▶ Robin has ~~ask~~ me to go to California with her.
          asked
          ^

   Has asked is present perfect tense (*have* or *has* followed by a
   past participle).

▶ Though it is not a new phenomenon, domestic violence is
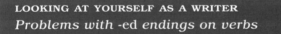
   ~~publicize~~ more frequently than before.
   publicized
   ^

   Is publicized is a verb in the passive voice (a form of *be* followed
   by a past participle).

LOOKING AT YOURSELF AS A WRITER
Problems with -ed endings on verbs

If you have difficulty spotting missing *-ed* endings, consider
possible sources of the problem.

CAUSE   Like most people, you don't always pronounce *-ed*
            endings, so you tend not to hear them as you proof-
            read.

CURE   Try proofreading out loud in a formal-sounding voice.
            When speaking formally, most people enunciate word
            endings more clearly.

Problems with *-ed* **endings on verbs** *(continued)*

CAUSE When you proofread a final draft, you read for meaning, so you don't notice small surface features such
as missing word endings.

CURE Again, reading out loud usually works. Read slowly,
articulating the words just as they are written on the
page. If you still have trouble, ask your instructor or
a writing center tutor for help. Proofreading is a skill
that can be learned.

CAUSE You don't proofread your final draft carefully enough
or you try to proofread for too many problems at once.

CURE Take time to proofread. Until you become a skilled
proofreader, you may need to go over your work several times.

▶ All aerobics classes end in a cool-down period to stretch
tightened
~~tighten~~ muscles.
   ^

The past participle *tightened* functions as an adjective modifying the noun *muscles*.

GRAMMAR CHECKERS can catch some missing *-ed* endings,
but they tend to slip past as many as they catch. For example, although programs flagged *was accustom*, they ignored *has change* and *was pass*.

27e Do not omit needed verbs.

Although standard English allows some linking verbs and
helping verbs to be contracted, at least in informal contexts,
it does not allow them to be omitted.

Linking verbs, used to link subjects to subject complements, are frequently a form of *be: be, am, is, are, was, were, being, been.* (See 58b.) Some of these forms may be contracted (*I'm, she's, we're, you're, they're*), but they should not be omitted altogether.

>   *are*
> ► When we out there in the evening, we often hear the
>   ^
>
> helicopters circling above.

>   *is*
> ► Alvin a man who can defend himself.
>   ^

Helping verbs, used with main verbs, include forms of *be, do,* and *have* or the words *can, will, shall, could, would, should, may, might,* and *must.* (See 57c.) Some helping verbs may be contracted (*he's leaving, we'll celebrate, they've been told*), but they should not be omitted altogether.

>   *have*
> ► We been in Chicago since last Thursday.
>   ^

>   *would*
> ► Do you know someone who be good for the job?
>   ^

Speakers of English as a second language sometimes have problems with omitted verbs and correct use of helping verbs. See 29e and 29a.

GRAMMAR CHECKERS are fairly good at flagging omitted verbs, but they do not catch all of them. For example, programs caught the missing verb in this sentence: *He always talking.* But in the following, more complicated sentence, they did not catch the missing verb: *We often don't know whether he angry or just talking.*

EXERCISE 27–2

Edit the following sentences to eliminate problems with *-s* and *-ed* verb forms and with omitted verbs. If a sentence is correct, write "correct" after it. Answers to lettered sentences appear in the back of the book. Example:

> *has*
> The psychologist ~~have~~ so many problems in her own life that
> *doesn't* ^
> she ~~don't~~ know how to advise anyone else.
> ^

a. The cops was after my hot rod Lincoln. We was passing cars like they was standing still.
b. The museum visitors were not suppose to touch the exhibits.
c. Our church has all the latest technology, even a close-circuit television.
d. We often don't know whether he angry or just joking.
e. Our express mail costs this past year have risen 25 percent.

1. Most psychologists agree that no one performs well under stress.
2. Have there ever been a time in your life when you were too depressed to get out of bed?
3. We were ask to sign a contract committing ourselves to not smoking for forty-eight hours.
4. Today a modern school building covers most of the old grounds.
5. Although he has been in two accidents this year, David is not a bad driver. He just unlucky.
6. The training for security checkpoint screeners, which takes place in an empty airplane hangar, consist of watching out-of-date videos.
7. Bettelheim claims that fairy tales stimulates the child's unconscious thoughts.
8. The ball was pass from one player to the other so fast that even the TV crew miss some of the exchanges.
9. Do he have enough energy to hold down two jobs while going to night school?
10. How would you feel if a love one had been a victim of a crime like this?

Grammatical sentences

28

Use verbs in the appropriate tense, mood, and voice.

28a Choose the appropriate verb tense.

Tenses indicate the time of an action in relation to the time of the speaking or writing about that action.

The most common problem with tenses—shifting confusingly from one tense to another—is discussed in 13. Other problems with tenses are detailed in this section, after the following survey of tenses.

GRAMMAR CHECKERS do not flag the problems with tense discussed in this section. Although some programs may tell you that *had had* is incorrect, in fact it is often correct. See p. 380.

Survey of tenses

English has three simple tenses (past, present, and future) and three perfect tenses (present perfect, past perfect, and future perfect). In addition, there is a progressive form of each of these six tenses.

SIMPLE TENSES The simple present tense is used primarily to describe habitual actions (*Jane walks to work*) or to refer to actions occurring at the time of speaking (*I see a cardinal in our maple tree*). It is also used to state facts or general truths and to describe fictional events in a literary work (see p. 379). The present tense may even be used to express future actions that are to occur at some specified time (*The semester begins tomorrow*).

The simple past tense is used for actions completed entirely in the past (*Yesterday Jane walked to work*).

The simple future tense is used for actions that will occur in the future (*Tomorrow Jane will walk to work*) or for actions that are predictable, given certain causes (*Meat will spoil if not properly refrigerated*).

In the following chart, the simple tenses are given for the regular verb *walk,* the irregular verb *ride,* and the highly irregular verb *be.*

SIMPLE PRESENT

SINGULAR		PLURAL	
I	walk, ride, am	we	walk, ride, are
you	walk, ride, are	you	walk, ride, are
he/she/it	walks, rides, is	they	walk, ride, are

SIMPLE PAST

SINGULAR		PLURAL	
I	walked, rode, was	we	walked, rode, were
you	walked, rode, were	you	walked, rode, were
he/she/it	walked, rode, was	they	walked, rode, were

SIMPLE FUTURE

I, you, he/she/it, we, they   will walk, ride, be

PERFECT TENSES More complex time relations are indicated by the perfect tenses (which consist of a form of *have* plus the past participle). The present perfect tense is used for an action that began in the past and is still going on in the present (*Jane has walked to work for years*) or an action that began in the past and is finished by the time of speaking or writing (*Jane has discovered a new restaurant on Elm Street*).

The past perfect tense is used for an action already completed by the time of another past action (*Jane hailed a cab after she had walked several blocks in the rain*) or for an action already completed at some specific past time (*By 8:30, Jane had walked two miles*). (See also pp. 380–81.)

The future perfect tense is used for an action that will be completed before or by a certain future time (*Jane will have left Troy by the time Jo arrives*).

PRESENT PERFECT
I, you, we, they   have walked, ridden, been
he/she/it   has walked, ridden, been

PAST PERFECT
I, you, he/she/it, we, they   had walked, ridden, been

FUTURE PERFECT
I, you, he/she/it, we, they   will have walked, ridden, been

PROGRESSIVE FORMS   The simple and perfect tenses already discussed have progressive forms that describe actions in progress. The present progressive form is used for actions currently in progress (*Jane is writing a letter*) or for future actions that are to occur at some specified time (*Jane is leaving for Chicago on Monday*).

The past progressive is used for past actions in progress (*Jane was writing a letter last night*).

The future progressive is used for future actions in progress (*Jane will be traveling next week*).

PRESENT PROGRESSIVE
I   am walking, riding, being
he/she/it   is walking, riding, being
you, we, they   are walking, riding, being

PAST PROGRESSIVE
I, he/she/it   was walking, riding, being
you, we, they   were walking, riding, being

FUTURE PROGRESSIVE
I, you, he/she/it, we, they   will be walking, riding, being

Like the simple tenses, the perfect tenses have progressive forms. The perfect progressive forms express the length of time an action is, was, or will be in progress. *Jane has been walking to work for five years* (present perfect progressive). *Jane had been walking to work until she was mugged* (past perfect progressive). *Jane will have been walking to work for five years by the end of this month* (future perfect progressive).

PRESENT PERFECT PROGRESSIVE

I, you, we, they	have been walking, riding, being
he/she/it	has been walking, riding, being

PAST PERFECT PROGRESSIVE

I, you, he/she/it, we, they had been walking, riding, being

FUTURE PERFECT PROGRESSIVE

I, you, he/she/it, we, they will have been walking, riding, being

ESL

The progressive forms are not normally used with mental activity verbs such as *believe*. See page 393.

Special uses of the present tense

Use the present tense when writing about events in a literary work, when expressing general truths, and when quoting, summarizing, or paraphrasing an author's views.

When writing about a work of literature, you may be tempted to use the past tense. The convention, however, is to describe fictional events in the present tense. (See also 13b.)

▶ In Masuji Ibuse's *Black Rain,* a child ~~reached~~ for a pome-
                                            reaches
granate in his mother's garden, and a moment later he
                                is
~~was~~ dead, killed by the blast of the atomic bomb.

Scientific principles or general truths should appear in the present tense, unless such principles have been disproved.

revolves
▶ Galileo taught that the earth ~~revolved~~ around the sun.
          ^

Since Galileo's teaching has not been discredited, the verb should be in the present tense. The following sentence, however, is acceptable: *Ptolemy taught that the sun revolved around the earth.*

When you are quoting, summarizing, or paraphrasing the author of a nonliterary work, use present-tense verbs such as *writes, reports, asserts,* and so on. (See p. 575 for a more complete list.) This convention is usually followed even when the author is dead (unless a date specifies the time of writing).

writes
▶ Baron Bowan of Colwood ~~wrote~~ that a metaphysician is "one
          ^
who goes into a dark cellar at midnight without a light,

looking for a black cat that is not there."

EXCEPTION: When you are documenting a paper with the APA (American Psychological Association) style of in-text citations, which include a date after the author's name, use past-tense verbs such as *reported* or *demonstrated* or present perfect verbs such as *has reported* or *has demonstrated.*

E. Wilson (1996) reported that positive reinforcement alone was a less effective teaching technique than a mixture of positive reinforcement and constructive criticism.

The past perfect tense

The past perfect tense consists of a past participle preceded by *had* (*had worked, had gone, had had*). (See pp. 377–78.)

This tense is used for an action already completed by the time of another past action or for an action already completed at some specific past time.

> Everyone *had spoken* by the time I arrived.

> Everyone *had spoken* by 10:00 A.M.

Writers sometimes use the simple past tense when they should use the past perfect.

▶ We built our cabin high on a pine knoll, forty feet above an
                                                   had been
   abandoned quarry that ~~was~~ flooded in 1920 to create a lake.
                              ^

The building of the cabin and the flooding of the quarry both occurred in the past, but the flooding was completed before the time of building.

                                                    had
▶ By the time we arrived at the party, the guest of honor left.
                                                          ^

The past perfect tense is needed because the action of leaving was completed at a specific past time (*by the time we arrived*).

Some writers tend to overuse the past perfect tense. Do not use the past perfect if two past actions occurred at the same time.

▶ When we arrived in Paris, Pauline ~~had~~ met us at the train

   station.

Sequence of tenses with infinitives and participles

An infinitive is the base form of a verb preceded by *to*. (See 59c.) Use the present infinitive to show action at the same time as or later than the action of the verb in the sentence.

raise
▶ The club had hoped to ~~have raised~~ a thousand dollars by
                        ^

April 1.

> The action expressed in the infinitive (*to raise*) occurred later than the action of the sentence's verb (*had hoped*).

Use the perfect form of an infinitive (*to have* followed by the past participle) for an action occurring earlier than that of the verb in the sentence.

have joined
▶ Dan would like to ~~join~~ the navy, but he did not pass the
                    ^

physical.

> The liking occurs in the present; the joining would have occurred in the past.

Like the tense of an infinitive, the tense of a participle is also governed by the tense of the sentence's verb. Use the present participle (ending in *-ing*) for an action occurring at the same time as that of the sentence's verb.

> Hiking the Appalachian Trail in early spring, we spotted many wildflowers.

Use the past participle (such as *given* or *helped*) or the present perfect participle (*having* plus the past participle) for an action occurring before that of the verb.

> *Discovered* off the coast of Florida, the *Atocha* yielded many treasures.

> *Having worked* her way through college, Melanie graduated debt-free.

28b Use the subjunctive mood in the few contexts that require it.

There are three moods in English: the *indicative,* used for facts, opinions, and questions; the *imperative,* used for orders or advice; and the *subjunctive,* used in certain contexts to express wishes, requests, or conditions contrary to fact. Of these moods, only the subjunctive causes problems for writers.

Forms of the subjunctive

In the subjunctive mood, present-tense verbs do not change form to indicate the number and person of the subject (see 21). Instead, the subjunctive uses the base form of the verb (*be, drive, employ*) with all subjects.

> It is important that you *be* [not *are*] prepared for the interview.
>
> We asked that she *drive* [not *drives*] more slowly.

Also, in the subjunctive mood, there is only one past-tense form of *be: were* (never *was*).

> If I *were* [not *was*] you, I'd proceed more cautiously.

Uses of the subjunctive

The subjunctive mood appears only in a few contexts: in contrary-to-fact clauses beginning with *if* or expressing a wish; in *that* clauses following verbs such as *ask, insist, recommend, request,* and *suggest;* and in certain set expressions.

IN CONTRARY-TO-FACT CLAUSES BEGINNING WITH *IF* When a subordinate clause beginning with *if* expresses a condition contrary to fact, use the subjunctive mood.

▶ If I ~~was~~ *were* a member of Congress, I would vote for that bill.

▶ We could be less cautious if Jake ~~was~~ *were* more trustworthy.

The verbs in these sentences express conditions that do not exist: The writer is not a member of Congress, and Jake is not trustworthy.

Do not use the subjunctive mood in *if* clauses expressing conditions that exist or may exist.

If Dana *wins* the contest, she will leave for Barcelona in June.

IN CONTRARY-TO-FACT CLAUSES EXPRESSING A WISH In formal English, the subjunctive is used in clauses expressing a wish or desire; in informal speech, however, the indicative is more common.

FORMAL I wish that Dr. Kurtinitis *were* my professor.

INFORMAL I wish that Dr. Kurtinitis *was* my professor.

IN *THAT* CLAUSES FOLLOWING VERBS SUCH AS *ASK, INSIST, RECOMMEND, REQUEST,* AND *SUGGEST* Because requests have not yet become reality, they are expressed in the subjunctive mood.

▶ Professor Moore insists that her students ~~are~~ *be* on time.

▶ We recommend that Lambert ~~files~~ *file* form 1050 soon.

IN CERTAIN SET EXPRESSIONS The subjunctive mood, once more widely used in English, remains in certain set expressions: *Be* that as it may, as it *were, come* rain or shine, far *be* it from me, and so on.

GRAMMAR CHECKERS rarely flag problems with the subjunctive mood. They may at times question your correct use of the subjunctive, since your correct use will seem to violate the rules of subject-verb agreement (see 21). For example, one program suggested using *was* instead of *were* in the following correct sentence: *This isn't my dog; if it were, I would feed it.* Because the sentence describes a condition contrary to fact, the subjunctive form *were* is correct.

EXERCISE 28–1

Edit the following sentences to eliminate errors in verb tense or mood. If a sentence is correct, write "correct" after it. Answers to lettered sentences appear in the back of the book. Example:

> *had been*
> After the path ~~was~~ plowed, we were able to walk through the
>   ∧
> park.

a. The palace of Knossos in Crete is believed to have been destroyed by fire around 1375 B.C.E.
b. Watson and Crick discovered the mechanism that controlled inheritance in all life: the workings of the DNA molecule.
c. In 1941 Hitler decided to kill the Jews. But Himmler and his SS were there three years ahead of him; they had mass murder in mind since 1938.
d. This isn't the Waldorf; if it were, we wouldn't be here.
e. In the feminist rewriting of "Sleeping Beauty," the girl was not awakened by a prince.

1. By the time we arrived, the cake had been eaten.
2. They had planned to have adopted a girl, but they got twin boys.
3. My sister Deanna was outside playing with the new puppies that were born only a few weeks earlier.
4. As soon as my aunt applied for the position of pastor, the post was filled by an inexperienced seminary graduate who had been so hastily snatched that his mortarboard was still in midair.

5. They had planned to have gone to Canada last summer, but they were unable to coordinate their vacations.
6. Don Quixote, in Cervantes's novel, was an idealist ill suited for life in the real world.
7. The hurricane tore up the palm trees, lifted them over the hotel roof, and had dropped them into the swimming pool.
8. I would like to have been on the *Mayflower* but not to have lived through the first winter.
9. When the doctor said "It's a girl," I was stunned. For nine months I dreamed about playing baseball with my son.
10. If men and women were angels, no government would be necessary.

28c Use the active voice unless you have a good reason for choosing the passive.

Transitive verbs (verbs that take a direct object) appear in either the active or the passive voice. (See 58c.) In the active voice, the subject of the sentence does the action; in the passive, the subject receives the action. Although both voices are grammatically correct, the active voice is usually more effective because it is simpler, more direct, and less wordy.

ACTIVE   The committee *reached* a decision.

PASSIVE   A decision *was reached* by the committee.

To transform a sentence from the passive to the active voice, make the actor the subject of the sentence.

▶ For the opening flag ceremony, ~~a dance was choreographed~~
    choreographed a dance
    ~~by~~ Mr. Martins to the song "Two Hundred Years and Still
                    ^
    a Baby."

The revision emphasizes Mr. Martins by making him the subject.

> *We did not take down the*
> ~~The~~ Christmas decorations ~~were not taken down~~ until
> ^
> **Valentine's Day.**

Very often the actor does not even appear in a passive-voice sentence. To turn such a sentence into the active voice, the writer must decide on an appropriate subject, in this case *We*.

The passive voice is appropriate if you wish to emphasize the receiver of the action or to minimize the importance of the doer.

APPROPRIATE
PASSIVE   Many native Hawaiians *are forced* to leave their beautiful beaches to make room for hotels and condominiums.

APPROPRIATE
PASSIVE   As the time for harvest approaches, the tobacco plants *are sprayed* with a chemical to retard the growth of suckers.

The writer of the first sentence wished to emphasize the receivers of the action, Hawaiians. The writer of the second sentence wished to focus on the tobacco plants, not on the people spraying them.

Some speakers of English as a second language tend to avoid the passive voice even when it is appropriate. For advice on transforming an active-voice sentence to the passive, see 58c.

GRAMMAR CHECKERS can flag many, but not all, passive verbs, and in some cases they flag verbs that aren't passive. Be aware, however, that passive verbs are sometimes appropriate, so you must decide whether to use an active verb instead. (For more detailed information, see the grammar checker advice on p. 235.)

EXERCISE 28–2

Change the following sentences from the passive to the active voice. You may need to invent an actor to be the subject in the active voice. Revisions of lettered sentences appear in the back of the book. Example:

> *We*
> ~~It was~~ learned from the test that our son was reading on the
>   ^
> second-grade level.

a. Each cell in the monastery was painted by Fra Angelico.
b. Carbon dating is used by scientists to determine the approximate age of an object.
c. As the patient undressed, scars were seen on his back, stomach, and thighs. We suspected child abuse.
d. It was noted right away that the taxi driver had been exposed to Americans because he knew all the latest slang.
e. Diseases have been discovered by researchers more often than cures.

1. For as long as I can remember, grace has been said before every meal at our house.
2. No loyalty at all was shown by the dog to his owner, who had mistreated him.
3. It can be concluded that a college education provides a significant economic advantage.
4. The land was ruthlessly stripped of timber before the settlers realized the consequences of their actions.
5. Home equity loans were explained to me by the assistant manager.

PART VI

ESL Trouble Spots

Part VI has a special audience: speakers of English as a second language (ESL) who have learned English but continue to have problems in a few trouble spots.

29

Be alert to special problems with verbs.

Both native and nonnative speakers of English encounter the following problems with verbs, which are treated elsewhere in this handbook:

> problems with subject-verb agreement (21)
>
> misuse of verb forms (27)
>
> problems with tense, mood, and voice (28)

This section focuses on features of the English verb system that cause special problems for second language speakers.

29a Match helping verbs and main verbs appropriately.

Only certain combinations of helping verbs and main verbs are allowed in English. The correct combinations are discussed in this section, after the following review of helping verbs and main verbs.

Review of helping verbs and main verbs

Helping verbs always appear before main verbs. (See 57c.)

> **HV** **MV** **HV** **MV**
> We *will leave* for the picnic at noon. *Do* you *want* a ride?

Some helping verbs — *have, do,* and *be* — change form to indicate tense; others, known as modals, do not.

FORMS OF *HAVE, DO,* AND *BE*
have, has, had
do, does, did
be, am, is, are, was, were, being, been

MODALS
can, could, may, might, must, shall, should, will, would (*also* ought to)

Every main verb has five forms (except *be*, which has eight forms). The following list shows these forms for the regular verb *help* and the irregular verb *give*. (See 27a for a list of common irregular verbs.)

BASE FORM	help, give
PAST TENSE	helped, gave
PAST PARTICIPLE	helped, given
PRESENT PARTICIPLE	helping, giving
-S FORM	helps, gives

Modal + base form

After the modals *can, could, may, might, must, shall, should, will,* and *would,* use the base form of the verb.

▶ My cousin will send~~s~~ us photographs from her wedding.

▶ We could ~~spoke~~ Spanish when we were young.
  ^speak^

CAUTION: Do not use *to* in front of a main verb that follows a modal. (*Ought to* is an exception.)

▶ Gina can ~~to~~ drive us home if we miss the bus.

Do, does, *or* **did** + *base form*

After helping verbs that are a form of *do,* use the base form of the verb.

The helping verbs *do, does,* and *did* are used in three ways: (1) to express a negative meaning with the adverb *not* or *never,* (2) to ask a question, and (3) to emphasize a main verb used in a positive sense.

▶   Mariko does not want~~s~~ any more dessert.

▶   Did Janice ^{*buy*} ~~bought~~ the gift for Katherine?

▶   We do ^{*hope*} ~~hoping~~ that you will come to the party.

Have, has, *or* **had** + *past participle (perfect tenses)*

After the helping verb *have, has,* or *had,* use the past participle to form one of the perfect tenses. (See 28a.) Past participles usually end in *-ed, -d, -en, -n,* or *-t.* (See 27a.)

▶   On cold nights many churches in the city have ^{*offered*} ~~offer~~ shelter

     to the homeless.

▶   An-Mei has not ^{*spoken*} ~~speaking~~ Chinese since she was a child.

The helping verb *have* is sometimes preceded by a modal helping verb such as *will: By nightfall, we will have driven five hundred miles.* (See also perfect tenses, 28a.)

Form of **be** + *present participle (progressive forms)*

After the helping verb *be, am, is, are, was, were,* or *been,* use the present participle to express a continuing action. (See progressive forms, 28a.)

building
► Carlos is ~~build~~ his house on a cliff overlooking the Pacific
            ^

Ocean.

driving
► Uncle Roy was ~~driven~~ a brand-new red Corvette.
                ^

The helping verb *be* must be preceded by a modal (*can, could, may, might, must, shall, should, will,* or *would*): *Edith will be going to Germany soon.* The helping verb *been* must be preceded by *have, has,* or *had*: *Andy has been studying English for five years.* (See also progressive forms, 28a.)

CAUTION: Certain verbs are not normally used in the progressive sense in English. In general, these verbs express a state of being or mental activity, not a dynamic action. Common examples are *appear, believe, belong, contain, have, hear, know, like, need, see, seem, taste, think, understand,* and *want.*

want
► I ~~am wanting~~ to see August Wilson's *Fences* at Arena Stage.
     ^

Some of these verbs, however, have special uses in which progressive forms are normal. (*We are thinking about going to the Bahamas.*) You will need to make a note of exceptions as you encounter them.

Form of be + *past participle (passive voice)*

When a sentence is written in the passive voice, the subject receives the action instead of doing it: *Melissa was given a special award.* (See 28c.)

To form the passive voice, use *be, am, is, are, was, were, being,* or *been* followed by a past participle (usually ending in *-ed, -d, -en, -n,* or *-t*).

written
► *Bleak House* was ~~write~~ by Charles Dickens.
                   ^

> honored
> ▶ The scientists were ~~honor~~ for their work with dolphins.
>   ^

When the helping verb is *be, being,* or *been,* it must be preceded by another helping verb. *Be* must be preceded by a
modal such as *will: Senator Dixon will be defeated. Being*
must be preceded by *am, is, are, was,* or *were: The child was
being teased. Been* must be preceded by *have, has,* or *had:
I have been invited to a party.*

CAUTION: Although they may seem to have passive meanings, verbs such as *occur, happen, sleep, die,* and *fall* may
not be used to form the passive voice because they are intransitive. Only transitive verbs, those that take direct objects, may be used to form the passive voice. (See transitive
and intransitive verbs, 58b.)

▶ The earthquake ~~was~~ occurred last Wednesday.

GRAMMAR CHECKERS can catch some mismatches of helping and main verbs. They can tell you, for example, that the
base form of the verb should be used after certain helping
verbs, such as *did* and *could,* in incorrect sentences like
these: *Did you understood my question? Could Alan comes
with us?*

Programs can also catch some, but not all, problems
with main verbs following forms of *have* or *be.* For example, grammar checkers flagged *have spend,* explaining that
the past participle *spent* is required, and they flagged *are
expose,* suggesting that either *exposed* or *exposing* is required. However, programs failed to flag problems in many
sentences, such as these: *Sasha has change her major
three times. The provisions of the contract were broke by
both parties.*

EXERCISE 29–1

Revise any sentences in which helping and main verbs do not match. You may need to look at the list of irregular verbs in 27a to determine the correct form of some irregular verbs. Answers to lettered sentences appear in the back of the book. Example:

Maureen should finds̸ an apartment closer to campus.

a. We will making this a better country.
b. There is nothing in the world that TV has not touch on.
c. Did the landlord told you that he's going to raise the rent?
d. A hard wind was blown while we were climbing the mountain.
e. The child's innocent world has been taking away from him.

1. We haven't spoke to our cousins in several weeks, but we expect to hear from them during the holidays.
2. A serious accident was happened at the corner of Main Street and First Avenue last night.
3. Have you find your wallet yet?
4. I have ate Thai food only once before.
5. How often does Sandy takes her daughter to the doctor?

29b In conditional sentences, choose verbs with care.

Conditional sentences state that one set of circumstances depends on whether another set of circumstances exists. Choosing verbs in such sentences can be tricky, partly because two clauses are involved: usually an *if* or a *when* or an *unless* clause and an independent clause.

Three kinds of conditional sentences are discussed in this section: factual, predictive, and speculative.

Factual

Factual conditional sentences express factual relationships. These relationships might be scientific truths, in which case the present tense is used in both clauses.

If water *cools* to 32°, it *freezes*.

Or they might be present or past relationships that are habitually true, in which case the same tense is used in both clauses.

When Sue *bicycles* along the canal, her dog *runs* ahead of her.

Whenever the coach *asked* for help, I *volunteered*.

Predictive

Predictive conditional sentences are used to predict the future or to express future plans or possibilities. In such a sentence, an *if* or *unless* clause contains a present-tense verb; the verb in the independent clause usually consists of the modal *will, can, may, should,* or *might* followed by the base form of the verb.

If you *practice* regularly, your tennis game *will improve*.

We *will lose* our remaining wetlands unless we *act* now.

Speculative

Speculative conditional sentences are used for three purposes: (1) to speculate about unlikely possibilities in the present or future, (2) to speculate about events that did not happen in the past, and (3) to speculate about conditions that are contrary to fact. Each of these purposes requires its own combination of verbs.

UNLIKELY POSSIBILITIES Somewhat confusingly, English uses the past tense in an *if* clause to speculate about a possible but unlikely condition in the present or future. The verb in the independent clause consists of *would, could,* or *might* plus the base form of the verb.

If I *had* the time, I *would travel* to Senegal.

If Stan *studied* harder, he *could master* calculus.

In the *if* clause, the past-tense form *were* is used with subjects that would normally take *was: Even if I were* [not *was*] *invited, I wouldn't go to the picnic.* (See also 28b.)

EVENTS THAT DID NOT HAPPEN English uses the past perfect tense in an *if* clause to speculate about an event that did not happen in the past or to speculate about a state of being that was unreal in the past. (See past perfect tense, 28a.) The verb in the independent clause consists of *would have, could have,* or *might have* plus the past participle.

> If I *had saved* enough money, I *would have traveled* to Senegal last year.

> If Aunt Grace *had been* alive for your graduation, she *would have been* very proud.

CONDITIONS CONTRARY TO FACT To speculate about conditions that are currently unreal or contrary to fact, English usually uses the past-tense verb *were* (never *was*) in an *if* clause. (See 28b.) The verb in the independent clause consists of *would, could,* or *might* plus the base form of the verb.

> If Grandmother *were* alive today, she *would be* very proud of you.

> I *would make* children's issues a priority if I *were* president

 GRAMMAR CHECKERS do not flag problems with conditional sentences. The programs miss even obvious errors, such as this one: *Whenever I washed my car, it rains.*

EXERCISE 29–2

Edit the following conditional sentences for problems with verbs. In some cases, more than one revision is possible. Suggested revisions of lettered sentences appear in the back of the book. Example:

had
If I ~~have~~ the money, I would meet my friends in Barcelona
^
next summer.

a. He would have won the election if he went to the inner city to campaign.
b. If Martin Luther King, Jr., was alive today, he would be appalled by the violence in our inner cities.
c. Whenever there is a fire in our neighborhood, everybody came out to watch.
d. We will lose our largest client unless we would update our computer system.
e. If I live in southern California, I wouldn't need to buy a winter coat.

1. If it would not be raining, we could go fishing.
2. If everyone has voted in the last election, the results would have been very different.
3. You would have met my cousin if you came to the party last night.
4. When dark gray clouds appeared on a hot summer afternoon, a thunderstorm often follows.
5. Our daughter would have drowned if Officer Blake didn't risk his life to save her.

29c Become familiar with verbs that may be followed by gerunds or infinitives.

A gerund is a verb form that ends in *-ing* and is used as a noun: *sleeping, dreaming.* (See 59c.) An infinitive is the base form of the verb preceded by the word *to: to sleep, to dream.* The word *to* is not a preposition in this use but an infinitive marker. (See 59c.)

A few verbs may be followed by either a gerund or an infinitive; others may be followed by a gerund but not by an infinitive; still others may be followed by an infinitive (either directly or with a noun or pronoun intervening) but not by a gerund.

Verb + gerund or infinitive

These commonly used verbs may be followed by a gerund or an infinitive, with little or no difference in meaning:

begin	continue	like	start
can't stand	hate	love	

I love *skiing.*   I love *to ski.*

With a few verbs, however, the choice of a gerund or infinitive changes the meaning dramatically:

forget	remember	stop	try

She stopped *speaking* to Lucia. [She no longer spoke to Lucia.]

She stopped *to speak* to Lucia. [She paused so that she could speak to Lucia.]

Verb + gerund

These verbs may be followed by a gerund but not by an infinitive:

admit	discuss	imagine	put off	risk
appreciate	enjoy	miss	quit	suggest
avoid	escape	postpone	recall	tolerate
deny	finish	practice	resist	

Have you finished *decorating* [not *to decorate*] the tree?

Bill enjoys *playing* [not *to play*] the piano.

Verb + infinitive

These verbs may be followed by an infinitive but not by a gerund:

agree	decide	manage	pretend	want
ask	expect	mean	promise	wish
beg	have	offer	refuse	
claim	hope	plan	wait	

We plan *to visit* [not *visiting*] the Yucatán next week.

Jill has offered *to water* [not *watering*] the plants while we are away.

Verb + noun or pronoun + infinitive

With certain verbs in the active voice, a noun or pronoun must come between the verb and the infinitive that follows it. The noun or pronoun usually names a person who is affected by the action.

advise	command	have	persuade	tell
allow	convince	instruct	remind	urge
cause	encourage	order	require	warn

The dean encourages *you to apply* for the scholarship.

The class asked *Luis to tell* the story of his escape.

A few verbs may be followed either by an infinitive directly or by an infinitive preceded by a noun or pronoun.

| ask | expect | need | want | would like |

We asked *to speak* to the congregation.

We asked *Rabbi Abrams to speak* to our congregation.

Verb + noun or pronoun + unmarked infinitive

An unmarked infinitive is an infinitive without *to*. A few verbs (known as "causative verbs") may be followed by a noun or pronoun and an unmarked (but not a marked) infinitive.

have ("cause")   let ("allow")   make ("force")

Absence makes *the heart grow* [not *to grow*] fonder.

Please let *me pay* [not *to pay*] for the tickets.

GRAMMAR CHECKERS can flag some, but not all, problems with gerunds and infinitives following verbs. For example, programs flagged many sentences with misused infinitives, such as these: *Have you finished to weed the garden? Chris enjoys to play tennis.* Programs were less successful at flagging sentences with misused present participles, skipping past incorrect sentences like this one: *We want traveling to Hawaii next spring.*

EXERCISE 29–3

Form sentences by adding gerund or infinitive constructions to the following sentence openings. In some cases, more than one kind of construction may be possible. Possible sentences for lettered items appear in the back of the book. Example:

Please remind *your sister to call me.*
                ^

a. I enjoy
b. Will you help Samantha
c. The team hopes
d. Ricardo and his brothers miss
e. The babysitter let

1. Pollen makes
2. The club president asked
3. Next summer we plan
4. Waverly intends
5. Please stop

29d Become familiar with commonly used two-word verbs.

Many verbs in English consist of a verb followed by a preposition or adverb known as a *particle*. (See 57c.) A two-word verb (also known as a *phrasal verb*) often expresses an idiomatic meaning that cannot be understood literally. Consider the verbs in the following sentences, for example:

> We *ran across* Professor Magnotto on the way to the bookstore.
>
> Calvin *dropped in* on his adviser this morning.
>
> Regina told me to *look* her *up* when I got to Seattle.

As you probably know, *ran across* means "encountered," *dropped in* means "paid an unexpected visit," and *look up* means "get in touch with." When you were first learning English, however, these two-word verbs must have suggested strange meanings.

Some two-word verbs are intransitive; they do not take direct objects. (See 58b.)

> This morning I *got up* at dawn.

Transitive two-word verbs (those that take direct objects) have particles that are either separable or inseparable. Separable particles may be separated from the verb by the direct object.

> Lucy *called* the wedding *off*.

When the direct object is a noun, a separable particle may also follow the verb immediately.

> At the last minute, Lucy *called off* the wedding.

When the direct object is a pronoun, however, the particle must be separated from the verb.

> Why was there no wedding? Lucy *called* it *off* [not *called off* it].

Inseparable particles must follow the verb immediately. A direct object cannot come between the verb and the particle.

> The police will *look into* the matter [not *look* the matter *into*].

The following list includes common two-word verbs. If a particle can be separated from the verb by a direct object, a pronoun is shown between the verb and the particle: *ask (someone) out*. When in doubt about the meaning of a two-word verb, consult the dictionary.

COMMON TWO-WORD VERBS

ask (someone) out
break down
bring (something or
  someone) up
burn (something) down
burn down
burn (something) up
burn up
call (something) off
call (someone) up
clean (something) up
clean up
come across
cut (something) up
do (something) over
drop in (on someone)
drop (someone or
  something) off
drop out (of something)
fill (something) out

fill (something) up
get along (with someone)
get away (with something)
get up
give (something) away
give (something) back
give in
give up
go out (with someone)
go over (something)
grow up
hand (something) in
hand (something) out
hang (something) up
help out
help (someone) out
keep on (doing something)
keep up (with someone
  or something)
leave (something) out

COMMON TWO-WORD VERBS

look into (something)

look (something) over

look (something) up

make (something) up

pick (something) out

pick (someone) up

pick (something) up

play around

point (something) out

put (something) away

put (something) back

put (something) off

put (something) on

put (something) out

put (something) together

put up (with someone or something)

quiet down

run across (someone or something)

run into (someone or something)

run out (of something)

see (someone) off

shut (something) off

speak to (someone)

speak up

stay away (from someone or something)

stay up

take care of (someone or something)

take off

take (something) off

take (someone) out

take (something) over

think (something) over

throw (something) away

throw (something) out

try (something) on

try (something) out

turn (something) down

turn (something) on

turn up

wake up

wake (someone) up

wear out

wrap (something) up

EXERCISE 29–4

From the list of two-word verbs, choose ten verbs, preferably ones whose meaning you are not sure of. First look up the verbs in the dictionary; then use each verb in a sentence of your own.

29e Do not omit needed verbs.

Some languages allow the omission of the verb when the meaning is clear without it; English does not.

is
▶ Jim ^ exceptionally intelligent.

are
▶ Many streets in San Francisco ^ very steep.

30

Use the articles *a*, *an*, and *the* appropriately.

Except for occasional difficulty in choosing between *a* and *an*, native speakers of English encounter few problems with articles. To speakers whose native language is not English, however, articles can prove troublesome, for the rules governing their use are surprisingly complex. This section summarizes those rules.

The definite article *the* and the indefinite articles *a* and *an* signal that a noun is about to appear. The noun may follow the article immediately or modifiers may intervene (see 57a and 57d).

the candidate, the exceptionally well qualified *candidate*

a sunset, a spectacular *sunset*

an apple, an appetizing *apple*

Articles are not the only words used to mark nouns. Other noun markers (sometimes called *determiners*) include possessive nouns (*Helen's*), numbers, and the following pronouns: *my, your, his, her, its, our, their, whose, this, that, these, those, all, any, each, either, every, few, many, more, most, much, neither, several, some.*

Usually an article is not used with another noun marker. Common exceptions include expressions such as *a few, the most,* and *all the.*

> **GRAMMAR CHECKERS** can flag some missing or misused articles, pointing out, for example, that an article usually precedes a word such as *paintbrush* or *vehicle* or that the articles *a* and *an* are not usually used before a noncount noun such as *sugar* or *advice*.
>
> However, the programs fail to flag many missing or misused articles. For example, in two paragraphs with eleven missing or misused articles, grammar checkers caught only two of the problems. In addition, the programs frequently suggest that an article is missing when it is not. For example, one program suggested that an article might be needed before *teacher* in this correct sentence: *My social studies teacher entered me in a public-speaking contest.*

30a Use *a* (or *an*) with singular count nouns whose specific identity is not known to the reader.

Count nouns refer to persons, places, or things that can be counted: *one girl, two girls; one city, three cities; one apple, four apples.* Noncount nouns refer to entities or abstractions that cannot be counted: *water, steel, air, furniture, patience, knowledge.* It is important to remember that noncount nouns vary from language to language. To see what nouns English categorizes as noncount nouns, refer to the list on page 408.

If a singular count noun names something not known to the reader—perhaps because it is being mentioned for the first time, perhaps because its specific identity is unknown even to the writer—the noun should be preceded by *a* or *an* unless it has been preceded by another noun marker. *A* (or *an*) usually means "one among many" but can also mean "any one."

                              a
▶ Mary Beth arrived in limousine.
                            ^

                                   an
▶ We are looking for apartment close to the lake.
                           ^

NOTE: *A* is used before a consonant sound: *a banana, a tree, a picture, a hand, a happy child. An* is used before a vowel sound: *an eggplant, an occasion, an uncle, an hour, an honorable person.* Notice that words beginning with *h* can have either a consonant sound (*hand, happy*) or a vowel sound (*hour, honorable*). (See also the Glossary of Usage: *a, an.*)

30b Do not use *a* (or *an*) with noncount nouns.

A (or *an*) is not used to mark noncount nouns, such as *sugar, gold, honesty,* or *jewelry.* A list of commonly used noncount nouns is given in the chart on page 408.

▶ Claudia asked her mother for ~~an~~ advice.

If you want to express an approximate amount, you can often use one of the following quantifiers with a noncount noun.

QUANTIFIER	NONCOUNT NOUN
a great deal of	candy, courage
a little	salt, rain
any	sugar, homework
enough	bread, wood, money
less	meat, violence
little (*or* a little)	knowledge, time
more	coffee, information
much (*or* a lot of)	snow, pollution
plenty of	paper, lumber
some	tea, news, work

Commonly used noncount nouns

FOOD AND DRINK

bacon, beef, bread, broccoli, butter, cabbage, candy, cauliflower, celery, cereal, cheese, chicken, chocolate, coffee, corn, cream, fish, flour, fruit, ice cream, lettuce, meat, milk, oil, pasta, rice, salt, spinach, sugar, tea, water, wine, yogurt

NONFOOD SUBSTANCES

air, cement, coal, dirt, gasoline, gold, paper, petroleum, plastic, rain, silver, snow, soap, steel, wood, wool

ABSTRACT NOUNS

advice, anger, beauty, confidence, courage, employment, fun, happiness, health, honesty, information, intelligence, knowledge, love, poverty, satisfaction, truth, wealth

OTHER

biology (and other areas of study), clothing, equipment, furniture, homework, jewelry, luggage, lumber, machinery, mail, money, news, poetry, pollution, research, scenery, traffic, transportation, violence, weather, work

NOTE: A few noncount nouns may also be used as count nouns, especially in informal English: *Bill loves chocolate; Bill offered me a chocolate. I'll have coffee; I'll have a coffee.*

To express a more specific amount, you can often precede a noncount noun with a unit word that is typically associated with it. Here are some common combinations.

A OR AN + UNIT + OF	NONCOUNT NOUNS
a bottle of	water, vinegar
a carton of	ice cream, milk, yogurt
an ear of	corn
a head of	cabbage, lettuce
a loaf of	bread
a piece of	meat, furniture, advice
a pound of	butter, sugar
a quart of	milk, ice cream
a slice of	bread, bacon

CAUTION: Noncount nouns do not have plural forms, and they should not be used with numbers or words suggesting plurality (such as *several, many, a few, a couple of, a number of*).

▶ We need some information̶s̶ about rain forests.

        much
▶ Do you have ~~many~~ money with you?
        ^

30c Use *the* with most nouns whose specific identity is known to the reader.

The definite article *the* is used with most nouns whose identity is known to the reader. (For exceptions, see 30d.) Usually the identity will be clear to the reader for one of the following reasons:

—The noun has been previously mentioned.

—A phrase or a clause following the noun restricts its identity.

- —A superlative such as *best* or *most intelligent* makes the noun's identity specific.

- —The noun describes a unique person, place, or thing.

- —The context or situation makes the noun's identity clear.

▶ A truck loaded with dynamite cut in front of our van.

When <u>*the*</u> truck skidded a few seconds later, we almost plowed into it.
^

The noun *truck* is preceded by *A* when it is first mentioned. When the noun is mentioned again, it is preceded by *the* since readers now know the specific truck being discussed.

▶ Bob warned me that <u>*the*</u> gun on the top shelf of the cupboard
^

was loaded.

The phrase *on the top shelf of the cupboard* identifies the specific gun.

▶ Our petite daughter dated <u>*the*</u> tallest boy in her class.
^

The superlative *tallest* restricts the identity of the noun *boy*.

▶ During an eclipse, one should not look directly at <u>*the*</u> sun.
^

There is only one sun in our solar system, so its identity is clear.

▶ Please don't slam <u>*the*</u> door when you leave.
^

Both the speaker and the listener know which door is meant.

30d Do not use *the* with plural or noncount nouns meaning "all" or "in general"; do not use *the* with most singular proper nouns.

When a plural or a noncount noun means "all" or "in general," it is not marked with *the*.

▶ ~~The~~ ^F^ fountains are an expensive element of landscape design.

▶ In some parts of the world, ~~the~~ rice is preferred to all other

grains.

As you probably know, proper nouns—which name specific people, places, or things—are capitalized. Although there are many exceptions, *the* is not used with most singular proper nouns, such as *Judge Ito, Spring Street,* or *Lake Huron.* However, *the* is used with plural proper nouns, such as *the United Nations, the Bahamas,* and *the Finger Lakes.*

Geographical names create problems because there are so many exceptions to the rules. When in doubt, consult the chart on page 412 or ask a native speaker.

EXERCISE 30-1

Articles have been omitted from the following story, adapted from *Zen Flesh, Zen Bones,* compiled by Paul Reps. Insert the articles *a, an,* and *the* where English requires them and be prepared to explain the reasons for your choices.

Moon Cannot Be Stolen

Ryokan, who was Zen master, lived simple life in little hut at foot of mountain. One evening thief visited hut only to discover there was nothing in it to steal.

Ryokan returned and caught him. "You may have come

Geographical names

WHEN TO OMIT *THE*

streets, squares, parks	Ivy Street, Union Square, Denali National Park
cities, states, counties	Miami, Idaho, Bee County
most countries	Italy, Nigeria, China
continents	South America, Africa
bays, single lakes	Tampa Bay, Lake Geneva
single mountains, islands	Mount Everest, Crete

WHEN TO USE *THE*

united countries	the United States, the Republic of China
large regions, deserts	the East Coast, the Sahara
peninsulas	the Iberian Peninsula
oceans, seas, gulfs	the Pacific, the Dead Sea, the Persian Gulf
canals and rivers	the Panama Canal, the Amazon
mountain ranges	the Rocky Mountains, the Alps
groups of islands	the Solomon Islands

long way to visit me," he told prowler, "and you should not return empty-handed. Please take my clothes as gift." Thief was bewildered. He took Ryokan's clothes and slunk away. Ryokan sat naked, watching moon. "Poor fellow," he mused, "I wish I could give him this beautiful moon."

31

Be aware of other potential trouble spots.

31a Do not omit subjects or the expletive *there* or *it*.

English requires a subject for all sentences except impera-
tives, in which the subject *you* is understood (*Give to the
poor*). (See 58a.) If your native language allows the omission
of an explicit subject in other sentences or clauses, be especially alert to this requirement in English.

▶ ~~Have~~ a large collection of baseball cards.
       I have

▶ Your aunt is very energetic; seems young for her age.
                                 she

When the subject has been moved from its normal position before the verb, English sometimes requires an expletive (*there* or *it*) at the beginning of the sentence or clause.
(See 58c.) *There* is used at the beginning of a sentence or
clause to draw the reader's (or listener's) attention to the location or existence of something.

▶ ~~Is~~ an apple in the refrigerator.
   There is

▶ As you know, are many religious sects in India.
             there

Notice that the verb agrees with the subject that follows it:
apple is, sects are. (See 21g.)

     In one of its uses, the word *it* functions as an expletive,
to call attention to a subject following the verb.

> *It is*
> ► ~~Is~~ healthy to eat fruit and grains.
>   ^

> *It is*
> ► ~~Is~~ clear that we must change our approach.
>   ^

The subjects of these sentences are *to eat fruit and grains* (an infinitive phrase) and *that we must change our approach* (a noun clause). (See 59c and 59b.)

As you probably know, the word *it* is also used as the subject of sentences describing the weather or temperature, stating the time, indicating distance, or suggesting an environmental fact.

> It is raining in the valley, and it is snowing in the mountains.

> In July, it is very hot in Arizona.

> It is 9:15 A.M.

> It is three hundred miles to Chicago.

> It gets noisy in our dorm on weekends.

 GRAMMAR CHECKERS can flag some sentences with a missing expletive (*there* or *it*), but they often misdiagnose the problem, suggesting that if a sentence opens with a word such as *Is* or *Are,* it may need a question mark at the end. Consider this sentence, which grammar checkers flagged: *Are two grocery stores on Elm Street.* Clearly, the sentence doesn't need a question mark. What it needs is an expletive: *There are two grocery stores on Elm Street.*

31b Do not repeat the subject of a sentence.

English does not allow a subject to be repeated in its own clause.

▶ **The doctor ~~she~~ advised me to cut down on salt.**

The pronoun *she* repeats the subject *doctor*.

The subject of a sentence should not be repeated even if a word group intervenes between the subject and the verb.

▶ **The car that had been stolen ~~it~~ was found.**

The pronoun *it* repeats the subject *car*.

31c Do not repeat an object or an adverb in an adjective clause.

In some languages an object or an adverb is repeated later in the adjective clause in which it appears; in English such repetitions are not allowed. Adjective clauses begin with relative pronouns (*who, whom, whose, which, that*) or relative adverbs (*when, where*), and these words always serve a grammatical function within the clauses they introduce. (See 59b.) Another word in the clause cannot also serve that same grammatical function.

When a relative pronoun functions as the object of a verb or the object of a preposition, do not add another word with the same function later in the clause.

▶ **The puppy ran after the car that we were riding in. ~~it~~.**
                                                         ^

The relative pronoun *that* is the object of the preposition *in*, so the object *it* is not allowed.

Even when the relative pronoun has been omitted, do not add another word with its same function.

▶ The puppy ran after the car we were riding in. ~~it.~~
^

The relative pronoun *that* is understood even though it is not present in the sentence.

Like a relative pronoun, a relative adverb should not be echoed later in its clause.

▶ The place where I work ~~there~~ is one hour from my apartment in the city.

The adverb *there* should not echo the relative adverb *where*.

GRAMMAR CHECKERS can flag certain sentences with repeated subjects or objects, but they misdiagnose the problem as two independent clauses incorrectly joined. For example, programs flagged this sentence: *The roses that they brought home they cost three dollars each.* The sentence does not have two independent clauses incorrectly joined. The problem with the sentence is that *they* repeats the subject *roses.*

EXERCISE 31-1

In the following sentences, add needed subjects or expletives and delete any repeated subjects, objects, or adverbs. Answers to lettered sentences appear in the back of the book. Example:

Nancy is the woman whom I talked to ~~her~~ last week.

a. Are some cartons of ice cream in the freezer.
b. Are several emergency telephone numbers listed next to the phones at the hotel.
c. The prime minister she is the most popular leader in my country.

d. Juana wants to travel to many countries that she has read about them.
e. The king, who had served since the age of sixteen, he was an old man when he died.

1. My cousin she is coming to visit this summer.
2. In this city is difficult to find a high-paying job.
3. The water is beautiful at the beach where we swim there.
4. Is a banyan tree in our backyard.
5. The neighbor we trusted he was a thief.

31d Place adjectives and adverbs with care.

Adjectives modify nouns or pronouns; adverbs modify verbs, adjectives, or other adverbs (see 57d and 57e). Both native and nonnative speakers encounter problems in the use of adjectives and adverbs (see 26). For nonnative speakers, the placement of adjectives and adverbs can also be troublesome.

Placement of adjectives

No doubt you have already learned that in English adjectives usually precede the nouns they modify and that they may also appear following linking verbs. (See 26h and 58b.)

Janine wore a *new* necklace. Janine's necklace was *new*.

When adjectives pile up in front of a noun, however, you may sometimes have difficulty arranging them. English is quite particular about the order of cumulative adjectives, those not separated by commas. (See 32d.)

Janine was wearing a *beautiful antique silver* necklace [not *silver antique beautiful* necklace].

Usual order of cumulative adjectives

ARTICLE OR OTHER NOUN MARKER

a, an, the, her, Joe's, two, many, some

EVALUATIVE WORD

attractive, dedicated, delicious, ugly, disgusting

SIZE

large, enormous, small, little

LENGTH OR SHAPE

long, short, round, square

AGE

new, old, young, antique

COLOR

yellow, blue, crimson

NATIONALITY

French, Scandinavian, Vietnamese

RELIGION

Catholic, Protestant, Jewish, Muslim

MATERIAL

silver, walnut, wool, marble

NOUN/ADJECTIVE

tree (as in *tree house*), kitchen (as in *kitchen table*)

THE NOUN MODIFIED

house, sweater, bicycle, bread, woman, priest

The chart on page 418 shows the order in which cumulative adjectives ordinarily appear in front of the noun they modify. This list is just a general guide; don't be surprised when you encounter exceptions.

NOTE: Long strings of cumulative adjectives tend to be awkward. As a rule, use no more than two or three of them between the article (or other noun marker) and the noun modified. Here are several examples:

a beautiful old pine table	Susan's large round painting
two enormous French urns	some small blue medicine
an exotic purple jungle flower	bottles

Placement of adverbs

Adverbs modifying verbs appear in various positions: at the beginning or end of the sentence, before or after the verb, or between a helping verb and its main verb.

Slowly, we drove along the rain-slick road.

Mia handled the teapot *very carefully.*

Martin *always* wins our tennis matches.

Christina is *rarely* late for our lunch dates.

My daughter has *often* spoken of you.

An adverb may not, however, be placed between a verb and its direct object.

carefully.
▶ Mother wrapped ~~carefully~~ the gift./
                                      ^

The adverb *carefully* may be placed at the beginning or at the end of this sentence or before the verb. It cannot appear after the verb because the verb is followed by the direct object *the gift.*

> **GRAMMAR CHECKERS** do not flag problems with the place-
> ment of adjectives and adverbs. They can, however, flag a
> few other problems with adjectives and adverbs. See the
> grammar checker advice on page 352.

EXERCISE 31-2

Using the chart on page 418, arrange the following modifiers and
nouns in their proper order. Answers to lettered items appear in the
back of the book. Example:

> *two new French racing bicycles*
> **new, French, two, bicycles, racing**

a. woman, young, an, Vietnamese, attractive
b. dedicated, a, priest, Catholic
c. old, her, sweater, blue, wool
d. delicious, Joe's, Scandinavian, bread
e. many, cages, bird, antique, beautiful

1. round, two, marble, tables, large
2. several, yellow, tulips, tiny
3. a, sports, classic, car
4. courtyard, a, square, small, brick
5. charming, restaurants, Italian, several

31e   Distinguish between present participles and past participles used as adjectives.

Both present and past participles may be used as adjectives.
The present participle always ends in *-ing*. Past participles
usually end in *-ed*, *-d*, *-en*, *-n*, or *-t*. (See 27a.)

PRESENT PARTICIPLES	confusing, speaking
PAST PARTICIPLES	confused, spoken

Participles used as adjectives can precede the nouns they modify; they can also follow linking verbs, in which case they describe the subject of the sentence. (See 58b.)

It was a *depressing* movie. Jim was a *depressed* young man.

The essay was *confusing.* The student was *confused.*

A present participle should describe a person or thing causing or stimulating an experience; a past participle should describe a person or thing undergoing an experience.

The lecturer was *boring* [not *bored*].

The audience was *bored* [not *boring*].

In the first example, the lecturer is causing boredom, not experiencing it. In the second example, the audience is experiencing boredom, not causing it.

The participles that cause the most trouble for nonnative speakers are those describing mental states:

annoying / annoyed	exhausting / exhausted
boring / bored	fascinating / fascinated
confusing / confused	frightening / frightened
depressing / depressed	satisfying / satisfied
exciting / excited	surprising / surprised

GRAMMAR CHECKERS do not flag problems with present and past participles used as adjectives. Not surprisingly, the programs have no way of knowing the meaning a writer intends. For example, both of the following sentences could be correct, depending on the writer's meaning: *My roommate was annoying. My roommate was annoyed.*

EXERCISE 31-3

Edit the following sentences for proper use of present and past participles. If a sentence is correct, write "correct" after it. Answers to lettered sentences appear in the back of the book. Example:

> *excited*
> Danielle and Monica were very ~~exciting~~ to be going to a
>   ^
>
> Broadway show for the first time.

a. Listening to everyone's complaints all day was irritated.
b. During the long lecture, many students appeared tiring.
c. He was not pleased with his grades last semester.
d. The violence in recent movies is often disgusted.
e. He has been amazed by the skill of his opponent in chess.

1. After doing a great deal of research, the scientist made a fascinated discovery.
2. That blackout was the most frightened experience I've ever had.
3. I couldn't concentrate on my homework because I was distracted.
4. The directions for the new board game seem extremely complicating.
5. Do you think acting is a fulfilled career?

31f Become familiar with common prepositions that show time and place.

The most frequently used prepositions in English are *at, by, for, from, in, of, on, to,* and *with.* Each of these prepositions has a variety of uses that must be learned gradually, in context.

Prepositions that indicate time and place can be difficult to master because the differences among them are subtle and idiomatic. The chart in this section limits itself to four troublesome prepositions that show time and place: *at, on, in,* and *by.*

Not every possible use is listed in the chart, so don't be surprised when you encounter exceptions and idiomatic

At, on, in, *and* by *to show time and place*

Showing time

AT   *at* a specific time: *at* 7:20, *at* dawn, *at* dinner

ON   *on* a specific day or date: *on* Tuesday, *on* June 4

IN   *in* a part of a 24-hour period: *in* the afternoon, *in* the daytime [but *at* night]

     in a year or month: *in* 1999, *in* July

     in a period of time: finished *in* three hours

BY   *by* a specific time or date: *by* 4:15, *by* Christmas

Showing place

AT   *at* a meeting place or location: *at* home, *at* the club

     at the edge of something: sitting *at* the desk

     at the corner of something: turning *at* the intersection

     at a target: throwing the snowball *at* Lucy

ON   *on* a surface: placed *on* the table, hanging *on* the wall

     on a street: the house *on* Spring Street

     on an electronic medium: *on* television, *on* the Internet

IN   *in* an enclosed space: *in* the garage, *in* the envelope

     in a geographic location: *in* San Diego, *in* Texas

     in a print medium: *in* a book, *in* a magazine

BY   *by* a landmark: *by* the fence, *by* the flagpole

uses that you must learn one at a time. For example, in English we ride *in* a car but *on* a bus, train, or subway. And when we fly *on* (not *in*) a plane, we are not sitting on top of the plane.

> **GRAMMAR CHECKERS** are of little or no help with prepositions showing time and place. The conventions of preposition use do not have the kind of mathematical precision that a computer program requires.

EXERCISE 31–4

In the following sentences, replace any prepositions that are not used correctly. If a sentence is correct, write "correct" after it. Answers to lettered sentences appear in the back of the book. Example:

>   *at*
> The play begins ~~on~~ 7:20 P.M.
>   ^

a. Whenever we eat at the Centerville Diner, we sit at a small table on the corner of the room.
b. In the 1980s, the gap between the rich and the poor in the United States became wider.
c. Usually she met with her patients on the afternoon, but in that day she stayed at home to take care of her son.
d. The clock is hanging on the wall on the dining room.
e. Our rabbi moved to the Northwest on 1994 and has been with our temple at Seattle since 1996.

1. Exhausted, Jay fell asleep on the couch in his room at the hotel.
2. I don't feel safe walking on my neighborhood at night.
3. If the train is on time it will arrive on six o'clock at the morning.
4. She licked the stamp, stuck it in the envelope, put the envelope on her pocket, and walked to the nearest mailbox.
5. The mailbox was in the intersection of Laidlaw Avenue and Williams Street.

Punctuation

32

The comma

The comma was invented to help readers. Without it, sentence parts can collide into one another unexpectedly, causing misreadings.

> **CONFUSING** If you cook Elmer will do the dishes.
>
> **CONFUSING** While we were eating a rattlesnake approached our campsite.

Add commas in the logical places (after *cook* and *eating*), and suddenly all is clear. No longer is Elmer being cooked, the rattlesnake being eaten.

Various rules have evolved to prevent such misreadings and to speed readers along through complex grammatical structures. Those rules are detailed in this section.

> **GRAMMAR CHECKERS** do not offer much advice about commas. They can tell you that a comma is usually used before *which* but not before *that* (see 32e), but they fail to flag most other missing or misused commas. For example, in an essay with ten missing commas and five misused commas, a grammar checker spotted only one missing comma (after the word *therefore*).

32a   Use a comma before a coordinating conjunction joining independent clauses.

See p. 246

When a coordinating conjunction connects two or more independent clauses—word groups that could stand alone as separate sentences—a comma must precede it. There are seven coordinating conjunctions in English: *and, but, or, nor, for, so,* and *yet.*

A comma tells readers that one independent clause has come to a close and that another is about to begin.

▶ Nearly everyone has heard of love at first sight **,** but I fell in

love at first dance.

> **EXCEPTION:** If the two independent clauses are short and there is no danger of misreading, the comma may be omitted.

The plane took off and we were on our way.

CAUTION: As a rule, do *not* use a comma to separate coordinate word groups that are not independent clauses. (See 33a.)

▶ A good money manager controls expenses **/** and invests

surplus dollars to meet future needs.

The word group following *and* is not an independent clause; it is the second half of a compound predicate.

32b Use a comma after an introductory clause or phrase.

The most common introductory word groups are clauses and phrases functioning as adverbs. Such word groups usually tell when, where, how, why, or under what conditions the main action of the sentence occurred. (See 59a–59c.)

A comma tells readers that the introductory clause or phrase has come to a close and that the main part of the sentence is about to begin.

Punctuation

▶ When Irwin was ready to eat**,** his cat jumped onto the table.

Without the comma, readers may have Irwin eating his cat. The comma signals that *his cat* is the subject of a new clause, not part of the introductory one.

▶ Near a small stream at the bottom of the canyon**,** we discov-

ered an abandoned shelter.

The comma tells readers that the introductory prepositional phrase has come to a close.

EXCEPTION: The comma may be omitted after a short adverb clause or phrase if there is no danger of misreading.

In no time we were at 2,800 feet.

Sentences also frequently begin with participial phrases describing the noun or pronoun immediately following them. The comma tells readers that they are about to learn the identity of the person or thing described; therefore, the comma is usually required even when the phrase is short. (See 59c.)

▶ Knowing that he couldn't outrun a car**,** Sy took to the fields.

▶ Excited about the move**,** Alice and Don began packing their

books.

The commas tell readers that they are about to hear the nouns described: *Sy* in the first sentence, *Alice and Don* in the second.

NOTE: Other introductory word groups include transitional expressions and absolute phrases. (See 32f.)

EXERCISE 32–1

Add or delete commas where necessary in the following sentences. If a sentence is correct, write "correct" after it. Answers to lettered sentences appear in the back of the book. Example:

> **Because it rained all Labor Day, our picnic was rather soggy.**

a. When we arrived at Salou's beach, we saw immediately that we were overdressed for the occasion.
b. The man at the next table complained loudly and the waiter stomped off in disgust.
c. If you complete the enclosed card, and return it within two weeks, you will receive a free breakfast during your stay.
d. Nursing is physically, and mentally demanding, yet the pay is low.
e. Uncle Swen's dulcimers disappeared as soon as he put them up for sale but he always kept one for himself.

1. When the runaway race car crashed the gas tank exploded.
2. He pushed the car beyond the toll gate and poured a bucket of water on the smoking hood.
3. Lighting the area like a second moon the helicopter circled the scene.
4. As the concert began we heard a tremendous explosion.
5. Many musicians of Bach's time played several instruments, but few mastered them as early or played with as much expression as Bach.

32c   Use a comma between all items in a series.

When three or more items are presented in a series, those items should be separated from one another with commas. Items in a series may be single words, phrases, or clauses.

> At Dominique's one can order fillet of rattlesnake, bison burgers, or pickled eel.

Although some writers view the comma between the last two items as optional, most experts advise using the comma because its omission can result in ambiguity or misreading.

▶ **Uncle David willed me all of his property, houses‚ and**

                                               ^

   warehouses.

   Did Uncle David will his property *and* houses *and* warehouses — or simply his property, consisting of houses and warehouses? If the former meaning is intended, a comma is necessary to prevent ambiguity.

▶ **The activities include a search for lost treasure, dubious**

   financial dealings, much discussion of ancient heresies‚ and

                                                             ^

   midnight orgies.

   Without the comma, the activities seem to include discussing orgies, not participating in them. The comma makes it clear that *midnight orgies* is a separate item in the series.

32d   Use a comma between coordinate adjectives not joined with *and.* Do not use a comma between cumulative adjectives.

When two or more adjectives each modify a noun separately, they are coordinate.

   With the help of a therapist, Mother has become a *strong, confident, independent* woman.

Adjectives are coordinate if they can be joined with *and* (strong *and* confident *and* independent) or if they can be scrambled (an *independent, strong, confident* woman).

   Adjectives that do not modify the noun separately are cumulative.

Three large gray shapes moved slowly toward us.

Beginning with the adjective closest to the noun *shapes,* these modifiers lean on one another, piggyback style, with each modifying a larger word group. *Gray* modifies *shapes, large* modifies *gray shapes,* and *three* modifies *large gray shapes.* We cannot insert the word *and* between cumulative adjectives (three *and* large *and* gray shapes). Nor can we scramble them (*gray three large* shapes).

COORDINATE ADJECTIVES

▶ Roberto is a warm, gentle, affectionate father.

The adjectives *warm, gentle,* and *affectionate* modify *father* separately. They can be connected with *and* (*warm and gentle and affectionate*), and they can be scrambled (*an affectionate, warm, gentle father*).

CUMULATIVE ADJECTIVES

▶ Ira ordered a rich/chocolate/layer cake.

Ira didn't order a cake that was rich and chocolate and layer: He ordered a *layer cake* that was *chocolate,* a *chocolate layer cake* that was *rich.* These cumulative adjectives cannot be scrambled: a *layer chocolate rich cake.*

EXERCISE 32-2

Add or delete commas where necessary in the following sentences. If a sentence is correct, write "correct" after it. Answers to lettered sentences appear in the back of the book. Example:

We gathered our essentials, took off for the great outdoors,

and ignored the fact that it was Friday the 13th.

a. She wore a black silk cape, a rhinestone collar, satin gloves and high-tops.
b. An ambulance threaded its way through police cars, fire trucks and irate citizens.
c. City Café is noted for its spicy vegetarian dishes and its friendly efficient service.
d. When air-conditioning arrived in the workplace, it had a large measurable impact on productivity.
e. My cat's pupils had constricted to small black shining dots.

1. My brother and I found a dead garter snake, picked it up and placed it on Miss Eunice's doorstep.
2. For breakfast the children ordered cornflakes, English muffins with peanut butter and cherry Cokes.
3. It was a small, unimportant part, but I was happy to have it.
4. Cyril was clad in a luminous orange rain suit and a brilliant white helmet.
5. Anne Frank and thousands like her were forced to hide in attics, cellars and secret rooms in an effort to save their lives.

32e   Use commas to set off nonrestrictive elements. Do not use commas to set off restrictive elements.

Word groups describing nouns or pronouns (adjective clauses, adjective phrases, and appositives) are restrictive or nonrestrictive. A *restrictive* element defines or limits the meaning of the word it modifies and is therefore essential to the meaning of the sentence. Because it contains essential information, a restrictive element is not set off with commas.

> **RESTRICTIVE**   For camp the children needed clothes *that were washable.*

If you remove a restrictive element from a sentence, the meaning changes significantly, becoming more general than you intended. The writer of the example sentence does not mean that the children needed clothes in general. The intended meaning is more limited: the children needed *washable* clothes.

A *nonrestrictive* element describes a noun or pronoun whose meaning has already been clearly defined or limited. Because it contains nonessential or parenthetical information, a nonrestrictive element is set off with commas.

NONRESTRICTIVE   For camp the children needed sturdy shoes, *which were expensive.*

If you remove a nonrestrictive element from a sentence, the meaning does not change dramatically. Some meaning is lost, to be sure, but the defining characteristics of the person or thing described remain the same as before. The children needed *sturdy shoes,* and these happened to be expensive.

Word groups describing proper nouns are nearly always nonrestrictive: *The Illinois River, which flows through our town, has reached flood stage.* Word groups modifying indefinite pronouns such as *everyone* and *something* are nearly always restrictive: *Joe whispered something that we could not hear.*

NOTE: Often it is difficult to tell whether a word group is restrictive or nonrestrictive without seeing it in context and considering the writer's meaning. Both of the following sentences are grammatically correct, but their meaning is slightly different.

The dessert made with fresh raspberries was delicious.

The dessert, made with fresh raspberries, was delicious.

In the example without commas, the phrase *made with fresh raspberries* tells readers which of two or more desserts the writer is referring to. In the example with commas, the phrase merely adds information about the particular dessert served with the meal.

Adjective clauses

Adjective clauses are patterned like sentences, containing subjects and verbs, but they function within sentences as modifiers of nouns or pronouns. They always follow the word they modify, usually immediately. Adjective clauses begin with a relative pronoun (*who, whom, whose, which, that*) or with a relative adverb (*where, when*).

Nonrestrictive adjective clauses are set off with commas; restrictive adjective clauses are not.

NONRESTRICTIVE CLAUSE

▶ Ed's house, which is located on thirteen acres, was completely

furnished with bats in the rafters and mice in the

kitchen.

The adjective clause *which is located on thirteen acres* does not restrict the meaning of *Ed's house,* so the information is non-essential.

RESTRICTIVE CLAUSE

▶ An office manager for a corporation/ that had government

contracts/ asked her supervisor whether she could reprimand

her co-workers for smoking.

Because the adjective clause *that had government contracts* identifies the corporation, the information is essential.

NOTE: Use *that* only with restrictive clauses. Many writers prefer to use *which* only with nonrestrictive clauses, but usage varies.

Phrases functioning as adjectives

Prepositional or verbal phrases functioning as adjectives may be restrictive or nonrestrictive. Nonrestrictive phrases are set off with commas; restrictive phrases are not.

NONRESTRICTIVE PHRASE

▶ The helicopter, with its 100,000-candlepower spotlight

illuminating the area, circled above.

The *with* phrase is nonessential because its purpose is not to specify which of two or more helicopters is being discussed.

RESTRICTIVE PHRASE

▶ One corner of the attic was filled with newspapers/ dating

from the turn of the century.

Dating from the turn of the century restricts the meaning of *newspapers,* so the comma should be omitted.

Appositives

An appositive is a noun or noun phrase that renames a nearby noun. Nonrestrictive appositives are set off with commas; restrictive appositives are not.

NONRESTRICTIVE APPOSITIVE

▶ Norman Mailer's first novel, *The Naked and the Dead,* was a

best-seller.

The term *first* restricts the meaning to one novel, so the appositive *The Naked and the Dead* is nonrestrictive.

RESTRICTIVE APPOSITIVE

▶ The song⎮ "Fire It Up⎮" was blasted out of amplifiers ten feet

tall.

Once they've read *song,* readers still don't know precisely which song the writer means. The appositive following *song* restricts its meaning.

EXERCISE 32–3

Add or delete commas where necessary in the following sentences. If a sentence is correct, write "correct" after it. Answers to lettered sentences appear in the back of the book. Example:

My youngest sister, who plays left wing on the team, now
　　　　　　　　ʌ　　　　　　　　　　　　　　　　ʌ

lives at The Sands, a beach house near Los Angeles.
　　　　　　　　　ʌ

a. B. B. King and Lucille, his customized black Gibson have electrified audiences all over the world.
b. The United States Coast Survey which was established in 1807 was the first scientific agency in this country.
c. The woman running for the council seat in the fifth district has a long history of community service.
d. Shakespeare's tragedy, *King Lear,* was given a splendid performance by the actor, Laurence Olivier.
e. Douglass's first autobiography, *Narrative of the Life of Frederick Douglass, an American Slave,* was published in 1845.

1. I had the pleasure of talking to a woman who had just returned from India where she had lived for ten years.
2. Sally's best friend Sid Phillips has been playing the guitar since the age of seven.
3. The gentleman waiting for a prescription is Mr. Rhee.
4. *Where the Wild Things Are,* the 1964 Caldecott Medal winner, is my nephew's favorite book.
5. The flame crawled up a few blades of grass to reach a low-hanging palmetto branch which quickly ignited.

32f Use commas to set off transitional and parenthetical expressions, absolute phrases, and elements expressing contrast.

Transitional expressions

Transitional expressions serve as bridges between sentences or parts of sentences. They include conjunctive adverbs such as *however, therefore,* and *moreover* and transitional phrases such as *for example, as a matter of fact,* and *in other words.* (For more complete lists, see 34b.)

When a transitional expression appears between independent clauses in a compound sentence, it is preceded by a semicolon and is usually followed by a comma. (See 34b.)

▶ Minh did not understand our language; moreover, he was
   unfamiliar with our customs.

▶ Natural foods are not always salt free; for example, celery
   contains more sodium than most people would imagine.

When a transitional expression appears at the beginning of a sentence or in the middle of an independent clause, it is usually set off with commas.

▶ As a matter of fact, American football was established
   by fans who wanted to play a more organized game of
   rugby.

▶ The prospective babysitter looked very promising; she was
   busy, however, throughout the month of January.

EXCEPTION: If a transitional expression blends smoothly with the rest of the sentence, calling for little or no pause in reading, it does not need to be set off with a comma. Expressions such as *also, at least, certainly, consequently, indeed, of course, moreover, no doubt, perhaps, then,* and *therefore* do not always call for a pause.

> Alice's bicycle is broken; *therefore* you will need to borrow Sue's.

NOTE: The conjunctive adverb *however* always calls for a pause, but it should not be confused with *however* meaning "no matter how," which does not: *However hard Bill tried, he could not match his previous record.*

Parenthetical expressions

Expressions that are distinctly parenthetical should be set off with commas. Providing supplemental information, they interrupt the flow of a sentence or appear at the end as afterthoughts.

▶ Evolution, as far as we know, doesn't work this way.

▶ The bass weighed about twelve pounds, give or take a few ounces.

Absolute phrases

An absolute phrase, which modifies the whole sentence, usually consists of a noun followed by a participle or participial phrase. (See 59e.) Absolute phrases may appear at the beginning or at the end of a sentence. Wherever they appear, they should be set off with commas.

▶ Her tennis game at last perfected, Krista won the cup.

▶ Brian was forced to rely on public transportation, his car

having been wrecked the week before.

In the first example, the absolute phrase appears at the beginning of the sentence; in the second example, it appears at the end.

CAUTION: Do not insert a comma between the noun and participle of an absolute construction.

▶ The next day/ being a school day, we turned down the

invitation.

Contrasted elements

Sharp contrasts beginning with words such as *not, never,* and *unlike* are set off with commas.

▶ Celia, unlike Robert, had no loathing for dance contests.

▶ Jane talks to me as an adult and friend, not as her little sister.

32g Use commas to set off nouns of direct address, the words *yes* and *no,* interrogative tags, and mild interjections.

▶ Forgive us, Dr. Spock, for reprimanding Jason.

▶ Yes, the loan will probably be approved.

▶ The film was faithful to the book, wasn't it?

▶ Well, cases like these are difficult to decide.

Punctuation

32h Use commas with expressions such as *he said* to set off direct quotations. (See also 37f.)

► Naturalist Arthur Cleveland Bent remarked, "In part the peregrine declined unnoticed because it is not adorable."

► "Convictions are more dangerous foes of truth than lies," wrote philosopher Friedrich Nietzsche.

32i Use commas with dates, addresses, titles, and numbers.

Dates

In dates, the year is set off from the rest of the sentence with a pair of commas.

► On December 12, 1890, orders were sent out for the arrest of Sitting Bull.

EXCEPTIONS: Commas are not needed if the date is inverted or if only the month and year are given.

The recycling plan goes into effect on 15 April 1988.

January 1996 was an extremely cold month.

Addresses

The elements of an address or place name are separated by commas. A zip code, however, is not preceded by a comma.

► John Lennon was born in Liverpool, England, in 1940.

▶ **Please send the package to Greg Tarvin at 708 Spring Street,**

Washington, Illinois 61571.

Titles

If a title follows a name, separate it from the rest of the sentence with a pair of commas.

▶ **Sandra Belinsky, M.D., has been appointed to the board.**

Numbers

In numbers more than four digits long, use commas to separate the numbers into groups of three, starting from the right. In numbers four digits long, a comma is optional.

        3,500 [*or* 3500]
      100,000
    5,000,000

EXCEPTIONS: Do not use commas in street numbers, zip codes, telephone numbers, or years.

32j Use a comma to prevent confusion.

In certain contexts, a comma is necessary to prevent confusion. If the writer has omitted a word or phrase, for example, a comma may be needed to signal the omission.

▶ **To err is human; to forgive, divine.**

If two words in a row echo each other, a comma may be needed for ease of reading.

▶ **All of the catastrophes that we had feared might happen,**
  ‸
happened.

Sometimes a comma is needed to prevent readers from grouping words in ways that do not match the writer's intention.

▶ **Patients who can, walk up and down the halls several times**
  ‸
a day.

EXERCISE 32–4: Major uses of the comma

This exercise covers the major uses of the comma listed in the chart on page 444. Add or delete commas where necessary. If a sentence is correct, write "correct" after it. Answers to lettered sentences appear in the back of the book. Example:

> **Although we invited him to the party, Gerald decided to**
>   ‸
> **spend another late night in the computer room.**

a. Cricket, which originated in England is also popular in Australia, South Africa and India.
b. At the sound of a starting pistol the horses surged forward toward the first obstacle, a sharp incline three feet high.
c. Each morning the seventy-year-old woman cleans the barn, shovels manure and spreads clean hay around the milking stalls.
d. The students of Highpoint are required to wear dull green, polyester pleated skirts.
e. Beauty is in the eye of the beholder but glamour is for anyone who can afford it.

1. After the passage of the Civil Rights Act of 1964 the Ku Klux Klan went underground for a few years but the group's racist views did not change.
2. Jan's costume was completed with bright red, snakeskin sandals.

3. Computers must be manufactured in clean climate-controlled rooms.
4. Research on Andean condors has shown that high levels of the chemical pesticide chlorinated hydrocarbon can cause the thinning of eggshells.
5. Loosening my belt I prepared myself for the richest dessert on the menu, double-chocolate cake topped with whipped cream.
6. New York City was vibrantly alive, and so was I.
7. Aunt Emilia was an impossible demanding guest.
8. The French Mirage, the fastest airplane in the Colombian air force, was an astonishing machine to fly.
9. In the showroom sat a brand-new, red convertible Porsche, a car no driver can resist.
10. Siddhartha decides to leave his worldly possessions behind and live in the forest by a beautiful river.

EXERCISE 32–5: All uses of the comma

Add or delete commas where necessary in the following sentences. If a sentence is correct, write "correct" after it. Answers to lettered sentences appear in the back of the book. Example:

> "Yes, Virginia, there is a Santa Claus," wrote the editor.

a. April 13, 1998 is the final deadline for all applications.
b. The coach having bawled us out thoroughly, we left the locker room with his last harsh words ringing in our ears.
c. Good technique does not guarantee however, that the power you develop will be sufficient for Kyok Pa competition.
d. We all piled into Sadiq's car which we affectionately referred to as the "Blue Goose."
e. As a matter of fact nationalism is a relatively modern concept.

1. Mr. Mundy was born on July 22, 1939 in Arkansas, where his family had lived for four generations.
2. Swords flashing, our heroes dashed into action.
3. President Lincoln's original intention was to save the Union, not to destroy slavery.
4. We pulled into the first apartment complex we saw, and slowly patrolled the parking lots.

Major uses of the comma

BEFORE A COORDINATING CONJUNCTION JOINING INDEPENDENT CLAUSES (32a)

No grand idea was ever born in a conference, but a lot of foolish ideas have died there.   —F. Scott Fitzgerald

AFTER AN INTRODUCTORY CLAUSE OR PHRASE (32b)

If thought corrupts language, language can also corrupt thought.   —George Orwell

BETWEEN ALL ITEMS IN A SERIES (32c)

All the things I really like to do are either immoral, illegal, or fattening.   —Alexander Woollcott

BETWEEN COORDINATE ADJECTIVES (32d)

There is a mighty big difference between good, sound reasons and reasons that sound good.   —Burton Hillis

TO SET OFF NONRESTRICTIVE ELEMENTS (32e)

Silence, which will save me from shame, will also deprive me of fame.   —Igor Stravinsky

5. Eating raw limpets, I found out, is like trying to eat art gum erasers.
6. Fortunately science is creating many alternatives to research performed on animals.
7. While the machine was printing the oversized paper jammed.
8. "The last flight" she said with a sigh "went out five minutes before I arrived at the airport."
9. The Rio Grande, the border between Texas and Mexico lay before us. It was a sluggish mud-filled meandering stream that gave off an odor akin to sewage.
10. Pittsburgh, Pennsylvania is the home of several fine colleges and universities.

33

Unnecessary commas

Many common misuses of the comma result from an incomplete understanding of the major comma rules presented in 32. In particular, writers frequently form misconceptions about rules 32a–32e, either extending the rules inappropriately or misinterpreting them. Such misconceptions can lead to the errors described in 33a–33e; rules 33f–33h list other common misuses of the comma.

33a Do not use a comma between compound elements that are not independent clauses.

Though a comma should be used before a coordinating conjunction joining independent clauses (see 32a), this rule should not be extended to other compound word groups.

▶ Jake still doesn't realize that his illness is serious/and that he will have to alter his diet to improve his chances of survival.

And links two subordinate clauses, each beginning with *that*.

▶ The director led the cast members to their positions on the stage/and gave them an inspiring last-minute pep talk.

And links the two parts of a compound predicate: *led . . . and gave.*

33b Do not use a comma after a phrase that begins an inverted sentence.

Though a comma belongs after most introductory phrases (see 32b), it does not belong after phrases that begin an inverted sentence. In an inverted sentence, the subject follows the verb, and a phrase that ordinarily would follow the verb is moved to the beginning (see 58c).

▶ At the bottom of the sound,/lies a ship laden with treasure.

33c Do not use a comma before the first or after the last item in a series.

Though commas are required between items in a series (32c), do not place them either before or after the whole series.

▶ Other causes of asthmatic attacks are,/stress, change in

temperature, humidity, and cold air.

▶ Ironically, this job that appears so glamorous, carefree, and

easy,/carries a high degree of responsibility.

33d Do not use a comma between cumulative adjectives, between an adjective and a noun, or between an adverb and an adjective.

Commas are required between coordinate adjectives (those that can be joined with *and*), but they do not belong between cumulative adjectives (those that cannot be joined with *and*). (For a full discussion, see 32d.)

▶ In the corner of the closet we found an old/maroon hatbox
from Sears.

A comma should never be used between an adjective and
the noun that follows it.

▶ It was a senseless, dangerous/mission.

Nor should a comma be used between an adverb and an
adjective that follows it.

▶ The Hurst Home is unsuitable as a mental facility for
severely/disturbed youths.

33e Do not use commas to set off restrictive or mildly
parenthetical elements.

Restrictive elements are modifiers or appositives that restrict
the meaning of the nouns they follow. Because they are essential to the meaning of the sentence, they are not set off
with commas. (For a full discussion of both restrictive and
nonrestrictive elements, see 32e.)

▶ Drivers/who think they own the road/make cycling a
dangerous sport.

The modifier *who think they own the road* restricts the meaning of *Drivers* and is therefore essential to the meaning of the
sentence. Putting commas around the *who* clause falsely suggests that all drivers think they own the road.

▶ Margaret Mead's book/*Coming of Age in Samoa*/stirred up

considerable controversy when it was published.

Since Mead wrote more than one book, the appositive contains information essential to the meaning of the sentence.

Although commas should be used with distinctly parenthetical expressions (see 32f), do not use them to set off elements that are only mildly parenthetical.

▶ Charisse believes that the Internet is/essentially/a bastion of

advertising.

33f Do not use a comma to set off a concluding adverb clause that is essential to the meaning of the sentence.

When adverb clauses introduce a sentence, they are nearly always followed by a comma (see 32b). When they conclude a sentence, however, they are not set off by commas if their content is essential to the meaning of the earlier part of the sentence. Adverb clauses beginning with *after, as soon as, because, before, if, since, unless, until,* and *when* are usually essential.

▶ Don't visit Paris at the height of the tourist season/unless

you have booked hotel reservations.

Without the *unless* clause, the meaning of the sentence would be broader than the writer intended.

When a concluding adverb clause is nonessential, it should be preceded by a comma. Clauses beginning with *although, even though, though,* and *whereas* are usually nonessential.

▶ The lecture seemed to last only a short time, although the
^
clock said it had gone on for more than an hour.

33g Do not use a comma to separate a verb from its subject or object.

A sentence should flow from subject to verb to object without unnecessary pauses. Commas may appear between these major sentence elements only when a specific rule calls for them.

▶ Zoos large enough to give the animals freedom to roam/are

becoming more popular.

▶ Francesca explained to him/that she was busy and would

see him later.

In the first sentence, the comma should not separate the subject, *Zoos*, from the verb, *are becoming*. In the second sentence, the comma should not separate the verb, *explained*, from its object, the subordinate clause *that she was busy and would see him later.*

33h Avoid other common misuses of the comma.

Do not use a comma in the following situations.

AFTER A COORDINATING CONJUNCTION (*AND, BUT, OR, NOR, FOR, SO, YET*)

▶ Occasionally soap operas are performed live, but/more often

they are taped.

AFTER *SUCH AS* OR *LIKE*

▶ Many shade-loving plants, such as/ begonias, impatiens, and coleus, can add color to a shady garden.

BEFORE *THAN*

▶ Touring Crete was more thrilling for us/ than visiting the Greek islands frequented by rich Europeans.

AFTER *ALTHOUGH*

▶ Although/ the air was balmy, the water was too cold for swimming.

BEFORE A PARENTHESIS

▶ At MCI Sylvia began at the bottom/ (with only three and a half walls and a swivel chair), but within five years she had been promoted to supervisor.

TO SET OFF AN INDIRECT (REPORTED) QUOTATION

▶ Samuel Goldwyn once said/ that a verbal contract isn't worth the paper it's written on.

WITH A QUESTION MARK OR AN EXCLAMATION POINT

▶ "Why don't you try it?/" she coaxed. "You can't do any worse than the rest of us."

EXERCISE 33-1

Delete commas where necessary in the following sentences. If a sentence is correct, write "correct" after it. Answers to lettered sentences appear in the back of the book. Example:

Loretta Lynn has paved the way for artists such as/ Reba

McEntire and Wynonna Judd.

a. We'd rather spend our money on blue-chip stocks, than speculate on pork bellies.
b. Being prepared for the worst, is one way to cope.
c. Please telephone me if you cannot send the information promptly, or if you have any questions.
d. The Marx Brothers made delightful, hilarious, movies.
e. I quickly accepted the fact that I was, literally, in third-class quarters.

1. As a child growing up in Jamaica, I often daydreamed about life in the United States.
2. He wore a thick, black, wool coat over army fatigues.
3. Often public figures, (Michael Jackson is a good example) go to great lengths to guard their private lives.
4. She loved early spring flowers such as, crocuses, daffodils, forsythia, and irises.
5. On Pam's wrist, was a tattoo of a dragon chasing a tiger.
6. Mesquite, the hardest of the softwoods, grows primarily in the Southwest.
7. Male supremacy was assumed by my father, and accepted by my mother.
8. The kitchen was covered with black soot, that had been deposited by the wood-burning stove, which stood in the middle of the room.
9. The lieutenant reported to his captain, that all of his men were present and accounted for.
10. The streets that three hours later would be bumper to bumper with commuters, were quiet and empty except for a few prowling cats.

EXERCISE 33-2

In the following paragraphs, add and delete commas as needed.

When you look at art from the tombs of ancient Egypt you are likely to ask "Why are certain human figures larger than others?" and "Why are these people always drawn in profile?" The answers to these questions can be found in the precise rigid principles followed by ancient Egyptian artists. Realism and natural perspectives were not among these principles.

Kings and other nobles, who commissioned works, required artists to make the most important person in the picture the largest; therefore nobles were often depicted as significantly larger than their spouses. In addition, artists were under pressure to make the subjects considerably more attractive, than they really were. To flatter nobles in portraits was honorable; to portray them realistically insulting.

For religious reasons, natural perspective was of little interest to Egyptian artists. The artists knew that their images were intended to accompany the dead to the other-world, and remind them of the objects and people that were important to them in life. Humans and even birds, fish, trees and other subjects were always drawn in profile because this angle was considered to offer the clearest view of all details. Human eyes, however, were always drawn as if viewed from the front. Although this perspective may seem inconsistent it was used because the eyes were such an important detail. In essence, as one historian has noted, the strategies of ancient Egyptian portrait makers were more like those of mapmakers who need to render precise details than like those of artists.

One king, Amenhopis IV, broke with tradition, and commissioned portraits that did not conform to established, artistic principles. For example, some portraits show him as an unattractive man who is bent and walking with a stick and others show him in relaxed poses. Amenhopis's pictures, needless to say, created quite a controversy. Was he on what we might today call the "cutting edge"? Yes he probably was.

LOOKING AT YOURSELF AS A WRITER
The comma and unnecessary commas

It is not necessary to learn all of the comma rules in 32 and 33; just know where to find them. If commas cause you a great deal of difficulty, however, you may want to consider some common causes and cures.

CAUSE You insert a comma whenever you take a breath.
CURE The "breath" method is too unreliable; learn to punctuate by grammatical structure instead.

CAUSE You oversimplify the rules by focusing on words. For example, because a comma goes before *and* some of the time, you conclude that it belongs before *and* all of the time.
CURE Make a conscious effort to unlearn oversimplified rules. If the word *and* gives you problems, for example, consult 32a and 33a to see whether you need the comma.

CAUSE Two of the most important comma rules (32a and 32b) refer to two different kinds of clauses — independent and subordinate — and you've never really understood clauses.
CURE You can probably grasp the rules by focusing on the examples in 32a and 32b, together with the brief definitions of clauses that are given in those sections. If not, turn to 59b and 60a for a quick review of clauses.

CAUSE You are confused about the difference between restrictive and nonrestrictive word groups (32c and 33e).
CURE You are not alone. Most writers find this distinction tricky because it requires us to think carefully about our intended meaning. When in doubt, ask two or three "test readers" to tell you how the presence or absence of commas affects your meaning.

34

The semicolon

The semicolon is used to connect major sentence elements of equal grammatical rank.

> **GRAMMAR CHECKERS** flag some, but not all, misused semicolons (34d). In addition, they can alert you to some run-on sentences (34a). However, they miss more run-on sentences than they identify, and they sometimes flag correct sentences as possible run-ons. (See also the grammar checker advice on p. 297.)

34a Use a semicolon between closely related independent clauses not joined with a coordinating conjunction.

When related independent clauses appear in one sentence, they are ordinarily linked with a comma and a coordinating conjunction (*and, but, or, nor, for, so, yet*). The coordinating conjunction signals the relation between the clauses. If the clauses are closely related and the relation is clear without a conjunction, they may be linked with a semicolon instead.

> Injustice is relatively easy to bear; what stings is justice.
> —H. L. Mencken

> Wit has truth in it; wisecracking is simply calisthenics with words. —Dorothy Parker

> When I was a boy, I was told that anybody could become president; I'm beginning to believe it. —Clarence Darrow

A semicolon must be used whenever a coordinating conjunction has been omitted between independent clauses. To use merely a comma creates a kind of run-on sentence known as a comma splice. (See 20.)

▶ Grandmother's basement had walls of Mississippi clay/; to
  ^
  me it looked like a dungeon.

CAUTION: Do not overuse the semicolon as a means of revising run-on sentences. For other revision strategies, see 20a, 20c, and 20d.

34b Use a semicolon between independent clauses linked with a transitional expression.

Transitional expressions include conjunctive adverbs and transitional phrases.

CONJUNCTIVE ADVERBS
accordingly, also, anyway, besides, certainly, consequently, conversely, finally, furthermore, hence, however, incidentally, indeed, instead, likewise, meanwhile, moreover, nevertheless, next, nonetheless, otherwise, similarly, specifically, still, subsequently, then, therefore, thus

TRANSITIONAL PHRASES
after all, as a matter of fact, as a result, at any rate, at the same time, even so, for example, for instance, in addition, in conclusion, in fact, in other words, in the first place, on the contrary, on the other hand

When a transitional expression appears between independent clauses, it is preceded by a semicolon and usually followed by a comma.

▶ I learned all the rules and regulations**;** however, I never
^

really learned to control the ball.

When a transitional expression appears in the middle or
at the end of the second independent clause, the semicolon
goes *between the clauses.*

▶ Most singers gain fame through hard work and dedication**;**
^

Evita, however, found other means.

Transitional expressions should not be confused with
the coordinating conjunctions *and, but, or, nor, for, so,* and
yet, which are preceded by a comma when they link independent clauses. (See 32a.)

34c Use a semicolon between items in a series containing internal punctuation.

▶ Classic science fiction sagas are *Star Trek,* with Mr. Spock

and his large pointed ears**;** *Battlestar Galactica,* with its
^

Cylon Raiders**;** and *Star Wars,* with Han Solo, Luke
^

Skywalker, and Darth Vader.

Without the semicolons, the reader would have to sort out the
major groupings, distinguishing between important and less
important pauses according to the logic of the sentence. By inserting semicolons at the major breaks, the writer does this
work for the reader.

34d Avoid common misuses of the semicolon.

Do not use a semicolon in the following situations.

BETWEEN A SUBORDINATE CLAUSE AND THE REST OF THE SENTENCE

▶ Unless you brush your teeth within ten or fifteen minutes after eating⫶, brushing does almost no good.

BETWEEN AN APPOSITIVE AND THE WORD IT REFERS TO

▶ Another delicious dish is the chef's special⫶, a roasted duck rubbed with spices and stuffed with wild rice.

TO INTRODUCE A LIST

▶ Some of my favorite film stars have home pages on the Web⫶: John Travolta, Susan Sarandon, Brad Pitt, and Emma Thompson.

BETWEEN INDEPENDENT CLAUSES JOINED BY *AND, BUT, OR, NOR, FOR, SO,* OR *YET*

▶ Five of the applicants had worked with spreadsheets⫶, but only one was familiar with database management.

EXCEPTIONS: If at least one of the independent clauses contains internal punctuation, you may use a semicolon even though the clauses are joined with a coordinating conjunction.

> As a vehicle [the model T] was hard-working, commonplace,
> and heroic; and it often seemed to transmit those qualities to
> the person who rode in it.   —E. B. White

Although a comma would also be correct in this sentence,
the semicolon is more effective, for it indicates the relative
weights of the pauses.

Occasionally, a semicolon may be used to emphasize a
sharp contrast or a firm distinction between clauses joined
with a coordinating conjunction.

> We hate some persons because we do not know them; and we
> will not know them because we hate them.
>   —Charles Caleb Colton

EXERCISE 34–1

Add commas or semicolons where needed in the following well-known
quotations. If a sentence is correct, write "correct" after it. Answers
to lettered sentences appear in the back of the book. Example:

> **If an animal does something, we call it instinct; if we do the**
>   ^   ^
> **same thing, we call it intelligence.**   —Will Cuppy
>   ^

a. When a woman behaves like a man why doesn't she behave like
    a nice man?   —Edith Evans
b. Do not ask me to be kind just ask me to act as though I were.
                                              —Jules Renard
c. Don't talk about yourself it will be done when you leave.
                                              —Wilson Mizner
d. The only sensible ends of literature are first the pleasurable toil
    of writing second the gratification of one's family and friends
    and lastly the solid cash.   —Nathaniel Hawthorne
e. I do not rule Russia ten thousand clerks do.   —Nicholas I

1. Everyone is a genius at least once a year a real genius has his
    [or her] original ideas closer together.   —G. C. Lichtenberg

2. When choosing between two evils I always like to try the one I've never tried before. —Mae West

3. Once the children were in the house the air became more vivid and more heated every object in the house grew more alive.

—Mary Gordon

4. We don't know what we want but we are ready to bite someone to get it. —Will Rogers

5. I've been rich and I've been poor rich is better.

—Sophie Tucker

EXERCISE 34–2

Edit the following sentences to correct errors in the use of the comma and the semicolon. If a sentence is correct, write "correct" after it. Answers to lettered sentences appear in the back of the book. Example:

Love is blind; envy has its eyes wide open.
　　　　　^

a. At the outbreak of the American Civil War, many believed that the conflict would be over in a month, others had a dreadful premonition of the future.

b. America has been called a country of pragmatists; although the American devotion to ideals is legendary.

c. The first requirement is honesty, everything else follows.

d. I am not fond of opera, I must admit; however, that I was greatly moved by *Les Misérables.*

e. The Theban plays by Sophocles consist of *Antigone,* which deals with the conscience and the state, *King Oedipus,* which explores the question of fate and circumstance, and *Oedipus at Colonus,* which presents themes of suffering and redemption.

1. The scientists were fascinated by the species *Argyroneta aquatica;* a spider that lives underwater.

2. Martin Luther King, Jr., had not intended to be a preacher, initially, he had planned to become a lawyer.

3. Severe, unremitting pain is a ravaging force; especially when the patient tries to hide it from others.

4. The Victorians avoided the subject of sex but were obsessed with death, our contemporaries are obsessed with sex but avoid thinking about death.

5. Some educators believe that African American history should be taught in separate courses, others prefer to see it integrated into survey courses.

35

The colon

The colon is used primarily to call attention to the words that follow it.

> **GRAMMAR CHECKERS** do not flag missing or misused colons. For example, they failed to catch the misused colon in this sentence: *Uncle Carlos left behind: his watch, his glasses, and his favorite pen.* Occasionally grammar checkers flag misused semicolons in contexts where a colon is required.

35a Use a colon after an independent clause to direct attention to a list, an appositive, or a quotation.

A LIST
The daily routine should include at least the following: twenty knee bends, fifty sit-ups, fifteen leg lifts, and five minutes of running in place.

AN APPOSITIVE
My roommate is guilty of two of the seven deadly sins: gluttony and sloth.

A QUOTATION
Consider the words of John F. Kennedy: "Ask not what your country can do for you; ask what you can do for your country."

For other ways of introducing quotations, see 37f.

35b Use a colon between independent clauses if the second summarizes or explains the first.

Faith is like love: It cannot be forced.

NOTE: When an independent clause follows a colon, it may begin with a lowercase or a capital letter.

35c Use a colon after the salutation in a formal letter, to indicate hours and minutes, to show proportions, between a title and subtitle, and between city and publisher in bibliographic entries.

Dear Sir or Madam:
5:30 P.M. (or p.m.)
The ratio of women to men was 2:1.
The Glory of Hera: Greek Mythology and the Greek Family
Boston: Bedford, 1997

NOTE: In biblical references, a colon is ordinarily used between chapter and verse (Luke 2:14). The Modern Language Association recommends a period instead (Luke 2.14).

35d Avoid common misuses of the colon.

A colon must be preceded by a full independent clause. Therefore, avoid using it in the following situations.

BETWEEN A VERB AND ITS OBJECT OR COMPLEMENT

▶ Some important vitamins found in vegetables are/ vitamin A, thiamine, niacin, and vitamin C.

BETWEEN A PREPOSITION AND ITS OBJECT

▶ The areas to be painted consisted of/ three gable ends, trim work, sixteen windows, and a front and back porch.

AFTER *SUCH AS, INCLUDING,* OR *FOR EXAMPLE*

▶ The trees on our campus include many fine Japanese specimens such as/ black pines, ginkgos, and weeping cherries.

EXERCISE 35–1

Edit the following sentences to correct errors in the use of the comma, the semicolon, or the colon. If a sentence is correct, write "correct" after it. Answers to lettered sentences appear in the back of the book. Example:

> Smiling confidently, the young man stated his major goal in
>
> life/: to be secretary of agriculture before he was thirty.
>   ^

a. The Greeks were right, character is fate.
b. Some examples of reptiles are: lizards, snakes, crocodiles, and turtles.
c. There are only three seasons here: winter, July, and August.
d. For example: Teddy Roosevelt once referred to the wolf as "the beast of waste and desolation."
e. Remember the words of Thomas Gray: "The paths of glory lead but to the grave."

1. The patient survived for one reason, the medics got to her in time.
2. While traveling through France, Fiona visited: the Loire Valley, Chartres, the Louvre, and the McDonald's stand at the foot of the Eiffel Tower.
3. Minds are like parachutes, they function only when open.
4. Carl Sandburg once asked three important questions, "Who paid for my freedom? What was the price? And am I somehow beholden?"
5. Robin sorts the crabs into three groups: males, females, and crabs about to molt.

36

The apostrophe

GRAMMAR CHECKERS can flag some, but not all, missing or misused apostrophes. They can catch missing apostrophes in common contractions, such as *don't*. They can also flag some problems with possessives, although they miss others. The programs usually phrase their advice cautiously, telling you that you have a "possible possessive error" in a phrase such as *a days work* or *sled dogs feet*. Therefore, you —not the grammar checker—must decide whether to add an apostrophe and, if so, whether to put it before or after the -s.

36a Use an apostrophe to indicate that a noun is possessive.

Possessive nouns usually indicate ownership, as in *Tim's hat* or *the lawyer's desk*. Frequently, however, ownership is only loosely implied: *the tree's roots, a day's work.* If you are not sure whether a noun is possessive, try turning it into an *of* phrase: *the roots of the tree, the work of a day.*

When to add -'s

1. If the noun does not end in -*s*, add -'*s*.

   Roy managed to climb out on the driver's side.

   Thank you for refunding the children's money.

2. If the noun is singular and ends in -*s*, add -'*s*.

   Lois's sister spent last year in India.

EXCEPTION: If pronunciation would be awkward with the added -'*s*, some writers use only the apostrophe. Either use is acceptable.

   Sophocles' plays are among my favorites.

When to add only an apostrophe

If the noun is plural and ends in -*s*, add only an apostrophe.

   Both diplomats' briefcases were stolen.

Joint possession

To show joint possession, use -'*s* or (-*s*') with the last noun only; to show individual possession, make all nouns possessive.

   Have you seen Joyce and Greg's new camper?

   John's and Marie's expectations of marriage couldn't have been more different.

In the first sentence, Joyce and Greg jointly own one camper. In the second sentence, John and Marie individually have different expectations.

Compound nouns

If a noun is compound, use *-'s* (or *-s'*) with the last element.

My father-in-law's sculpture won first place.

36b Use an apostrophe and *-s* to indicate that an indefinite pronoun is possessive.

Indefinite pronouns refer to no specific person or thing: *everyone, someone, no one, something.* (See 57b.)

Someone's raincoat has been left behind.

This diet will improve almost anyone's health.

36c Use an apostrophe to mark omissions in contractions and numbers.

In contractions the apostrophe takes the place of missing letters.

It's a shame that Frank can't go on the tour.

It's stands for *it is, can't* for *cannot.*
 The apostrophe is also used to mark the omission of the first two digits of a year (*the class of '95*) or years (*the '60s generation*).

We'll never forget the blizzard of '96.

Punctuation

36d Use an apostrophe and *-s* to pluralize numbers mentioned as numbers, letters mentioned as letters, words mentioned as words, and abbreviations.

> Margarita skated nearly perfect figure 8's.

> The bleachers in our section were marked with large red *J*'s.

> We've heard enough *maybe*'s.

> You must ask to see their I.D.'s.

Notice that the *-s* is not italicized when used with an italicized number, letter, or word.

EXCEPTION: An *-s* alone is often added to the years in a decade: *the 1980s.*

MLA NOTE: The Modern Language Association recommends no apostrophe in plurals of numbers and abbreviations: *figure 8s, VCRs.*

36e Avoid common misuses of the apostrophe.

Do not use an apostrophe in the following situations.

WITH NOUNS THAT ARE NOT POSSESSIVE

> *outpatients*
> ▶ Some ~~outpatient's~~ are given special parking permits.
>   ^

IN THE POSSESSIVE PRONOUNS *ITS, WHOSE, HIS, HERS, OURS, YOURS,* AND *THEIRS*

> *its*
> ▶ Each area has ~~it's~~ own conference room.
>   ^

It's means "it is." The possessive pronoun *its* contains no apostrophe despite the fact that it is possessive.

▶ This course was taught by a professional florist <del>who's</del>
                                                       whose

technique was oriental.

Who's means "who is." The possessive pronoun is *whose.*

EXERCISE 36–1

Edit the following sentences to correct errors in the use of the apostrophe. If a sentence is correct, write "correct" after it. Answers to lettered sentences appear in the back of the book. Example:

                                           Jack's.
Marietta lived above the only bar in town, Smiling <del>Jacks.</del>

a. In a democracy, anyones vote counts as much as mine.
b. He received two A's, three B's, and a C.
c. The puppy's favorite activity was chasing it's tail.
d. After we bought J. J. the latest style pants and shirts, he decided that last years faded, ragged jeans were perfect for all occasions.
e. The deed must be transferred to the purchasers name.

1. The snow does'nt rise any higher than the horse's fetlocks. [*More than one horse*]
2. For a bus driver, complaints, fare disputes, and robberies are all part of a days work.
3. Sue worked overtime to increase her families earnings.
4. We cleaned four years accumulation of trash out of the attic; its amazing how much junk can pile up.
5. Ms. Jacobs is unwilling to listen to students complaints about computer failures and damaged disks.
6. Kevins girlfriend often calls after midnight.
7. Three teenage son's can devour about as much food as four full-grown field hands. The only difference is that they dont do half as much work.
8. We handle contracts with NASA and other government agency's.
9. Luck is an important element in a rock musicians career.
10. My sister-in-law's quilts are being shown at the Fendrick Gallery.

37

Quotation marks

> **GRAMMAR CHECKERS** are good at telling you to put commas and periods inside quotation marks; they are also fairly good at flagging "unbalanced quotes," an opening quotation mark that is not balanced with a closing quotation mark. The programs can't tell you, however, when you should or shouldn't use quotation marks.

37a   Use quotation marks to enclose direct quotations.

Direct quotations of a person's words, whether spoken or written, must be in quotation marks.

> "A foolish consistency is the hobgoblin of little minds," wrote Ralph Waldo Emerson.

CAUTION: Do not use quotation marks around indirect quotations. An indirect quotation reports someone's ideas without using that person's exact words.

> Ralph Waldo Emerson believed that consistency for its own sake is the mark of a small mind.

NOTE: In dialogue, begin a new paragraph to mark a change in speaker.

> "Mom, his name is Willie, not William. A thousand times I've told you, it's *Willie*."
> "Willie is a derivative of William, Lester. Surely his birth certificate doesn't have Willie on it, and I like calling people by their proper names."

"Yes, it does, ma'am. My mother named me Willie K. Mason."
—Gloria Naylor

If a single speaker utters more than one paragraph, introduce each paragraph with quotation marks, but do not use closing quotation marks until the end of the speech.

37b Set off long quotations of prose or poetry by indenting.

When a quotation of prose runs to more than four typed lines in your paper, set it off by indenting one inch (or ten spaces) from the left margin. Quotation marks are not required because the indented format tells readers that the quotation is taken word for word from a source. Long quotations are ordinarily introduced by a sentence ending with a colon.

After making an exhaustive study of the historical record, James Horan evaluates Billy the Kid like this:

> The portrait that emerges of [the Kid] from the thousands of pages of affidavits, reports, trial transcripts, his letters, and his testimony is neither the mythical Robin Hood nor the stereotyped adenoidal moron and pathological killer. Rather Billy appears as a disturbed, lonely young man, honest, loyal to his friends, dedicated to his beliefs,

```
and betrayed by our institutions and
the corrupt, ambitious, and compro-
mising politicians of his time. (158)
```

The number in parentheses is a citation handled according to the Modern Language Association style. (See 53a.)

NOTE: When you quote two or more paragraphs from the source, indent the first line of each paragraph an additional one-half inch (or five spaces).

When you quote more than three lines of a poem, set the quoted lines off from the text by indenting one inch (or ten spaces) from the left margin. Use no quotation marks unless they appear in the poem itself. (To quote two or three lines of poetry, see 39e.)

```
Although many anthologizers "modernize" her
punctuation, Emily Dickinson relied heavily on
dashes, using them, perhaps, as a musical device.
Here, for example, is the original version of the
opening stanza from "The Snake":
        A narrow Fellow in the Grass
        Occasionally rides--
        You may have met Him--did you not
        His notice sudden is--
```

NOTE: The American Psychological Association has slightly different guidelines for setting off long quotations. (See 56c.)

37c Use single quotation marks to enclose a quotation within a quotation.

According to Paul Eliott, Eskimo hunters "chant an ancient magic song to the seal they are after: 'Beast of the sea! Come and place yourself before me in the early morning!'"

37d Use quotation marks around the titles of short works: newspaper and magazine articles, poems, short stories, songs, episodes of television and radio programs, and chapters or subdivisions of books.

> Katherine Mansfield's "The Garden Party" provoked a lively discussion in our short-story class last night.

NOTE: Titles of books, plays, Web sites, television and radio programs, and films and names of magazines and newspapers are put in italics or underlined. (See 42a.)

37e Quotation marks may be used to set off words used as words.

Although words used as words are ordinarily underlined or italicized (see 42d), quotation marks are also acceptable. Just be sure to follow consistent practice throughout a paper.

> The words "accept" and "except" are frequently confused.

> The words *accept* and *except* are frequently confused.

37f Use punctuation with quotation marks according to convention.

This section describes the conventions used by American publishers in placing various marks of punctuation inside or outside quotation marks. It also explains how to punctuate when introducing quoted material.

Periods and commas

Always place periods and commas inside quotation marks.

> "This is a stick-up," said the well-dressed young couple. "We want all your money."

This rule applies to single quotation marks as well as double quotation marks. (See 37c.) It also applies to all uses of quotation marks: for quoted material, for titles of works, and for words used as words.

EXCEPTION: In the Modern Language Association's style of parenthetical in-text citations (see 53a), the period follows the citation in parentheses.

> James M. McPherson acknowledges that the Whigs "were not averse to extending the blessings of American liberty, even to Mexicans and Indians" (48).

Colons and semicolons

Put colons and semicolons outside quotation marks.

> Harold wrote, "I regret that I am unable to attend the fundraiser for AIDS research"; his letter, however, came with a substantial contribution.

Question marks and exclamation points

Put question marks and exclamation points inside quotation marks unless they apply to the whole sentence.

> Contrary to tradition, bedtime at my house is marked by "Mommy, can I tell you a story now?"

> Have you heard the old proverb "Do not climb the hill until you reach it"?

In the first sentence, the question mark applies only to the quoted question. In the second sentence, the question mark applies to the whole sentence.

NOTE: Modern Language Association parenthetical citations create a special problem. According to MLA, the question mark or exclamation point should appear before the quotation mark, and a period should follow the parenthetical citation: *Rosie Thomas asks, "Is nothing in life ever straight and clear, the way children see it?" (77).* But because the question mark and period look rather odd so close together, perhaps it is best to restructure such a sentence: *"Is nothing in life ever straight and clear, the way children see it?" asks Rosie Thomas (77).*

Introducing quoted material

After a word group introducing a quotation, choose a colon, a comma, or no punctuation at all, whichever is appropriate in context.

If a quotation is formally introduced, a colon is appropriate. A formal introduction is a full independent clause, not just an expression such as *he said* or *she remarked.*

> Morrow views personal ads in the classifieds as an art form: "The personal ad is like a haiku of self-celebration, a brief solo played on one's own horn."

If a quotation is introduced with an expression such as *he said* or *she remarked*—or if it is followed by such an expression—a comma is needed.

> Robert Frost said, "You can be a little ungrammatical if you come from the right part of the country."

> "You can be a little ungrammatical if you come from the right part of the country," Robert Frost said.

When a quotation is blended into the writer's own sentence, either a comma or no punctuation is appropriate, depending on the way in which the quotation fits into the sentence structure.

> The future champion could, as he put it, "float like a butterfly and sting like a bee."

Charles Hudson noted that the prisoners escaped "by squeezing through a tiny window eighteen feet above the floor of their cell."

If a quotation appears at the beginning of a sentence, set it off with a comma unless the quotation ends with a question mark or an exclamation point.

"We shot them like dogs," boasted Davy Crockett, who was among Jackson's troops.

"What is it?" I asked, bracing myself.

If a quoted sentence is interrupted by explanatory words, use commas to set off the explanatory words.

"A great many people think they are thinking," wrote William James, "when they are merely rearranging their prejudices."

If two successive quoted sentences from the same source are interrupted by explanatory words, use a comma before the explanatory words and a period after them.

"I was a flop as a daily reporter," admitted E. B. White. "Every piece had to be a masterpiece—and before you knew it, Tuesday was Wednesday."

37g Avoid common misuses of quotation marks.

Do not use quotation marks to draw attention to familiar slang, to disown trite expressions, or to justify an attempt at humor.

▶ Between Thanksgiving and Super Bowl Sunday, many

American wives become ⁄football widows.⁄

Do not use quotation marks around indirect quotations. (See also 37a.)

▶ After leaving the scene of the domestic quarrel, the officer

said that /he was due for a coffee break. \

Do not use quotation marks around the title of your own essay.

EXERCISE 37–1

Add or delete quotation marks as needed and make any other necessary changes in punctuation in the following sentences. If a sentence is correct, write "correct" after it. Answers to lettered sentences appear in the back of the book. Example:

> Bill Cosby once said, **"**I don't know the key to success, but
>   ^
> the key to failure is trying to please everyone.**"**
>   ^

a. My commanding officer said, "If we wanted you to have children, we would have issued them to you."
b. As Emerson wrote in 1849, "I hate quotations. Tell me what you know.
c. Andrew Marvell's most famous poem, To His Coy Mistress, is a tightly structured argument.
d. "Ladies and gentlemen," said the emcee, "I am happy to present our guest speaker.
e. Historians Segal and Stineback note that the English settlers considered these epidemics "the hand of God making room for His followers in the "New World"."

1. "Order in the court! Order in the court!" shouts the judge, banging her wooden spoon on the kitchen table.
2. "Kick the tires and light the fires" exclaimed the pilot, giving me my cue to start the engines.

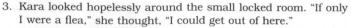

3. Kara looked hopelessly around the small locked room. "If only I were a flea," she thought, "I could get out of here."

4. After winning the lottery, Juanita said that "she would give half the money to charity."

5. At recess we stayed inside to play a card game we called "Truth or Dare".

6. Gloria Steinem once twisted an old proverb like this, "A woman without a man is like a fish without a bicycle."

7. These newly rich young men often buy expensive cars, designer shoes, and "classy" European suits.

8. As David Anable has written: "The time is approaching when we will be able to select the news we want to read from a pocket computer."

9. "Even when freshly washed and relieved of all obvious confections," says Fran Lebowitz, "children tend to be sticky."

10. Have you heard the Cowboy Junkies' rendition of Hank Williams's "I'm So Lonesome I Could Cry?"

38

End punctuation

 GRAMMAR CHECKERS occasionally flag sentences beginning with words like *Why* or *Are* and suggest that a question mark may be needed. On the whole, however, grammar checkers are of little help with end punctuation. Most notably, they neglect to tell you when your sentence is missing end punctuation.

38a The period

Use a period to end all sentences except direct questions or genuine exclamations. Also use periods in abbreviations according to convention.

To end sentences

Everyone knows that a period should be used to end most sentences. The only problems that arise concern the choice between a period and a question mark or between a period and an exclamation point.

If a sentence reports a question instead of asking it directly, it should end with a period, not a question mark.

▶ Celia asked whether the picnic would be canceled~~?~~.
                                                  ^

If a sentence is not a genuine exclamation, it should end with a period, not an exclamation point.

▶ After years of working her way through school, Pat finally

graduated with high honors~~!~~.
                            ^

In abbreviations

A period is conventionally used in abbreviations such as these:

Mr.	B.A.	B.C.	i.e.	A.M. (or a.m.)
Mrs.	M.A.	B.C.E.	e.g.	P.M. (or p.m.)
Ms.	Ph.D.	A.D.	etc.	
Dr.	R.N.	C.E.		

A period is not used with U.S. Postal Service abbreviations for states: MD, TX, CA.

Ordinarily a period is not used in abbreviations of organization names:

NATO	UNESCO	UCLA	PUSH	IBM
TVA	IRS	AFL-CIO	NBA	FTC
USA (or U.S.A.)	NAACP	SEC	FCC	NIH

Usage varies, however. When in doubt, consult a dictionary, a style manual, or a publication by the agency in question. Even the yellow pages can help.

NOTE: If a sentence ends with a period marking an abbreviation, do not add a second period.

38b The question mark

Obviously a direct question should be followed by a question mark.

> What is the horsepower of a 747 engine?

If a polite request is written in the form of a question, it too is usually followed by a question mark, although usage varies.

> Would you please send me your catalog of lilies?

CAUTION: Do not use a question mark after an indirect question, one that is reported rather than asked directly. Use a period instead.

▶ He asked me who was teaching the mythology course~~?~~.
                                                        ^

NOTE: Questions in a series may be followed by question marks even when they are not complete sentences.

> We wondered where Calamity had hidden this time. Under the sink? Behind the furnace? On top of the bookcase?

38c The exclamation point

Use an exclamation point after a word group or sentence that expresses exceptional feeling or deserves special emphasis.

> When Gloria entered the room, I switched on the lights and we all yelled, "Surprise!"

CAUTION: Do not overuse the exclamation point.

▶ In the fisherman's memory the fish lives on, increasing in

length and weight with each passing year, until at last it is

big enough to shade a fishing boat̸!.

This sentence doesn't need to be pumped up with an exclamation point. It is emphatic enough without it.

▶ Whenever I see Steffi lunging forward to put away an

overhead smash, it might as well be me̸!. She does it just the

way that I would!

The first exclamation point should be deleted so that the second one will have more force.

EXERCISE 38-1

Add appropriate end punctuation in the following paragraph.

Although I am generally rational, I am superstitious I
never walk under ladders or put shoes on the table If I spill
the salt, I go into frenzied calisthenics picking up the grains
and tossing them over my left shoulder As a result of these
curious activities, I've always wondered whether knowing the
roots of superstitions would quell my irrational responses
Superstition has it, for example, that one should never place
a hat on the bed This superstition arises from a time when
head lice were quite common and placing a guest's hat on the
bed stood a good chance of spreading lice through the host's
bed Doesn't this make good sense And doesn't it stand to reason that if I know that my guests don't have lice I shouldn't
care where their hats go Of course it does It is fair to ask,
then, whether I have changed my ways and place hats on
beds Are you kidding I wouldn't put a hat on a bed if my life
depended on it

39

Other punctuation marks: the dash, parentheses, brackets, the ellipsis mark, the slash

GRAMMAR CHECKERS rarely flag problems with the punctuation marks in this section: the dash, parentheses, brackets, the ellipsis mark, and the slash. (For a general discussion of what grammar checkers can and cannot do, see pp. 63–64.)

39a   The dash

When typing, use two hyphens to form a dash (--). Do not put spaces before or after the dash. (If your word processing program has what is known as an "em-dash," you may use it instead, with no space before or after it.) Dashes are used for the following purposes.

To set off parenthetical material that deserves emphasis

Everything that went wrong—from the peeping Tom at her window last night to my head-on collision today—was blamed on our move.

To set off appositives that contain commas

An appositive is a noun or noun phrase that renames a nearby noun. Ordinarily most appositives are set off with commas (32e), but when the appositive contains commas, a pair of dashes helps the readers see the relative importance of all the pauses.

In my hometown the basic needs of people—food, clothing, and shelter—are less costly than in Los Angeles.

To prepare for a list, a restatement, an amplification, or a dramatic shift in tone or thought

Along the wall are the bulk liquids—sesame seed oil, honey, safflower oil, and that half-liquid "peanuts only" peanut butter.

Consider the amount of sugar in the average person's diet—104 pounds per year, 90 percent more than that consumed by our ancestors.

Everywhere we looked there were little kids—a box of Cracker Jacks in one hand and mommy or daddy's sleeve in the other.

Kiere took a few steps back, came running full speed, kicked a mighty kick—and missed the ball.

In the first two examples, the writer could also use a colon. (See 35a.) The colon is more formal than the dash and not quite as dramatic.

CAUTION: Unless there is a specific reason for using the dash, avoid it. Unnecessary dashes create a choppy effect.

▶ Insisting that students use computers as instructional

tools⟋for information retrieval⟋makes good sense. Herding

them⟋sheeplike⟋into computer technology does not.

39b Parentheses

Use parentheses to enclose supplemental material, minor digressions, and afterthoughts.

After taking her temperature, pulse, and blood pressure (routine vital signs), the nurse made Becky as comfortable as possible.

> The weights James was first able to move (not lift, mind you) were measured in ounces.

Use parentheses to enclose letters or numbers labeling items in a series.

> Regulations stipulated that only the following equipment could be used on the survival mission: (1) a knife, (2) thirty feet of parachute line, (3) a book of matches, (4) two ponchos, (5) an *E* tool, and (6) a signal flare.

CAUTION: Do not overuse parentheses. Rough drafts are likely to contain more afterthoughts than necessary. As writers head into a sentence, they often think of additional details, occasionally working them in as best they can with parentheses. Usually such sentences should be revised so that the additional details no longer seem to be afterthoughts.

> ▶ Researchers have said that ~~ten million (estimates run as~~ ^*from ten to fifty million*^
>
> ~~high as fifty million)~~ Americans have hypoglycemia.

39c   Brackets

Use brackets to enclose any words or phrases that you have inserted into an otherwise word-for-word quotation.

> *Audubon* reports that "if there are not enough young to balance deaths, the end of the species [California condor] is inevitable."

The sentence quoted from the *Audubon* article did not contain the words *California condor* (since the context made clear what species was meant), so the writer needed to add the name in brackets.

The Latin word *sic* in brackets indicates that an error in a quoted sentence appears in the original source.

> According to the review, k. d. lang's performance was brilliant, "exceding [*sic*] the expectations of even her most loyal fans."

Do not overuse *sic,* however, since calling attention to others' mistakes can appear snobbish. The preceding quotation, for example, might have been paraphrased instead: *According to the review, even k. d. lang's most loyal fans were surprised by the brilliance of her performance.*

39d The ellipsis mark

The ellipsis mark consists of three spaced periods. Use an ellipsis mark to indicate that you have deleted words from an otherwise word-for-word quotation.

> Reuben reports that "when the amount of cholesterol circulating in the blood rises over . . . 300 milligrams per 100, the chances of a heart attack increase dramatically."

MLA NOTE: MLA now recommends putting brackets around ellipsis dots, like this: [. . .]. These brackets make clear that the ellipsis dots do not appear in the original work you are quoting (see pp. 576–77). You may wish to check with your instructor before following this new MLA guideline. If you are using a citation style other than MLA (such as APA), do not follow this guideline.

If you delete a full sentence or more in the middle of a quoted passage, use a period before the three ellipsis dots.

> "Most of our efforts," writes Dave Erikson, "are directed toward saving the bald eagle's wintering habitat along the Mississippi River. . . . It's important that the wintering birds have a place to roost, where they can get out of the cold wind."

CAUTION: Do not use the ellipsis mark at the beginning of a quotation; do not use it at the end of a quotation unless you

Punctuation

have cut some words from the final sentence quoted. (See also pp. 576–77.)

In quoted poetry, use a full line of ellipsis dots to indicate that you have dropped a line or more from the poem.

> Had we but world enough, and time,
> This coyness, lady, were no crime.
> ....
> But at my back I always hear
> Time's wingèd chariot hurrying near;   —Andrew Marvell

The ellipsis mark may also be used to mark a hesitation or interruption in speech or to suggest unfinished thoughts.

> Before falling into a coma, the victim whispered, "It was a man with a tattoo on his . . ."

39e The slash

Use the slash to separate two or three lines of poetry that have been run in to your text. Add a space both before and after the slash.

> In the opening lines of "Jordan," George Herbert pokes gentle fun at popular poems of his time: "Who says that fictions only and false hair / Become a verse? Is there in truth no beauty?"

More than three lines of poetry should be handled as an indented quotation. (See 37b.)

The slash may occasionally be used to separate paired terms such as *pass/fail* and *producer/director.* Do not use a space before or after the slash.

> Roger, the producer/director, announced a casting change.

Be sparing, however, in this use of the slash. In particular, avoid the use of *and/or, he/she,* and *his/her.*

EXERCISE 39–1

Edit the following sentences to correct errors in punctuation, focusing especially on appropriate use of the dash, parentheses, brackets, ellipsis mark, and slash. If a sentence is correct, write "correct" after it. Answers to lettered sentences appear in the back of the book. Example:

> Social insects/——bees, for example/——are able to
>
> communicate quite complicated messages to one another.

a. I was born in Iowa (Davenport, to be specific).

b. Pat helped Jeff put the tail on his kite—which was made of scraps from old dresses—and off they went to the park.

c. *Infoworld* reports that "customers without any particular aptitude for computers can easily learn to use it [the Bay Area Teleguide] through simple, three-step instructions."

d. Every person there—from the youngest toddler to the oldest great-grandparent, was expected to sit through the three-hour sermon in respectful silence.

e. The class stood, faced the flag, placed hands over hearts, and raced through "I pledge allegiance—liberty and justice for all" in less than sixty seconds.

1. Of the three basic schools of detective fiction, the tea-and-crumpet, the hard-boiled detective, and the police procedural, I find the quaint, civilized quality of the tea and crumpet school the most appealing.

2. The professional pool player needs to contend not only with abstract theories of math and physics but also with concrete details like the nap of the felt (usually running lengthwise) and the resiliency of the rails.

3. There are three points of etiquette in poker: 1. always allow someone to cut the cards, 2. don't forget to ante up, and 3. never stack your chips.

4. The child sang her way through the alphabet—*A, B, C . . . Z*—and then waited for our applause.

5. The old Valentine verse we used to chant says it all: "Sugar is sweet, / And so are you."

PART VIII

Mechanics

40

Abbreviations

>
>
> **GRAMMAR CHECKERS** can flag a few inappropriate abbreviations, such as *Xmas* and *e.g.*, but do not assume that a program will catch all problems with abbreviations.

40a   Use standard abbreviations for titles immediately before and after proper names.

TITLES BEFORE PROPER NAMES	TITLES AFTER PROPER NAMES
Mr. Rafael Zabala	William Albert, Sr.
Ms. Nancy Linehan	Thomas Hines, Jr.
Mrs. Edward Horn	Anita Lor, Ph.D.
Dr. Margaret Simmons	Robert Simkowski, M.D.
the Rev. John Stone	Margaret Chin, LL.D.
Prof. James Russo	Polly Stein, D.D.S.

Do not abbreviate a title if it is not used with a proper name.

>   *professor*
> ▶   My history ~~prof.~~ was an expert on America's use of the
>   ^
> atomic bomb in World War II.

Avoid redundant titles such as *Dr. Amy Day, M.D.* Choose one title or the other: *Dr. Amy Day* or *Amy Day, M.D.*

40b Use abbreviations only when you are sure your readers will understand them.

Familiar abbreviations, often written without periods, are acceptable:

CIA	FBI	AFL-CIO	NAACP
NBA	UPI	NEA	CD-ROM
YMCA	CBS	USA (or U.S.A.)	ESL

While in Washington the schoolchildren toured the FBI.

The YMCA has opened a new gym close to my office.

NOTE: When using an unfamiliar abbreviation (such as CBE for Council of Biology Editors) throughout a paper, write the full name followed by the abbreviation in parentheses at the first mention of the name. Then use the abbreviation throughout the rest of the paper.

40c Use B.C., A.D., A.M., P.M., No., and $ only with specific dates, times, numbers, and amounts.

The abbreviation B.C. ("before Christ") follows a date, and A.D. ("*anno Domini*") precedes a date. Acceptable alternatives are B.C.E. ("before the common era") and C.E. ("common era").

40 B.C. (or B.C.E.)	4:00 A.M. (or a.m.)	No. 12 (or no. 12)
A.D. 44 (or C.E.)	6:00 P.M. (or p.m.)	$150

Avoid using A.M., P.M., No., or $ when not accompanied by a specific figure.

▶ We set off for the lake early in the ~~A.M.~~
                                          morning.
                                          ^

40d Be sparing in your use of Latin abbreviations.

Latin abbreviations are acceptable in footnotes and bibliographies and in informal writing for comments in parentheses.

> cf. (Latin *confer,* "compare")
> e.g. (Latin *exempli gratia,* "for example")
> et al. (Latin *et alii,* "and others")
> etc. (Latin *et cetera,* "and so forth")
> i.e. (Latin *id est,* "that is")
> N.B. (Latin *nota bene,* "note well")

> Harold Simms et al., *The Race for Space*

> Alfred Hitchcock directed many classic thrillers (e.g., *Psycho, Rear Window,* and *Vertigo*).

In formal writing use the appropriate English phrases.

> ▶ Many obsolete laws remain on the books, ~~e.g.,~~ *for example,* a law in
>
> Vermont forbidding an unmarried man and woman to sit
>
> closer than six inches apart on a park bench.

40e Avoid inappropriate abbreviations.

In formal writing, abbreviations for the following are not commonly accepted: personal names, units of measurement, days of the week, holidays, months, courses of study, divisions of written works, states, and countries (except in addresses and except Washington, D.C.). Do not abbreviate *Company* and *Incorporated* unless their abbreviated forms are part of an official name.

> **PERSONAL NAME**   Charles (not Chas.)
>
> **UNITS OF MEASUREMENT**   pound (not lb.)

DAYS OF THE WEEK   Monday (not Mon.)

HOLIDAYS   Christmas (not Xmas)

MONTHS   January, February, March (not Jan., Feb., Mar.)

COURSES OF STUDY   political science (not poli. sci.)

DIVISIONS OF WRITTEN WORKS   chapter, page (not ch., p.)

STATES AND COUNTRIES   Massachusetts (not MA or Mass.)

PARTS OF A BUSINESS NAME   Adams Lighting Company (not Adams Lighting Co.); Kim and Brothers, Inc. (not Kim and Bros., Inc.)

▶   Eliza promised to buy me one ~~lb.~~ *pound* of Godiva chocolate for my birthday, which was last ~~Fri.~~ *Friday.*

EXERCISE 40-1

Edit the following sentences to correct errors in abbreviations. If a sentence is correct, write "correct" after it. Answers to lettered sentences appear in the back of the book. Example:

> This year ~~Xmas~~ *Christmas* will fall on a ~~Tues.~~ *Tuesday.*

a. Audrey Hepburn was a powerful spokesperson for UNICEF for many years.
b. A no. of govt. officials have been reviewing the records of some small brokerage firms in the area.
c. Mahatma Gandhi has inspired many modern leaders, including Martin Luther King, Jr.
d. The first discovery of America was definitely not in 1492 A.D.
e. Denzil spent all night studying for his psych. exam.

1. My favorite prof., Dr. Barker, is on sabbatical this semester.
2. When she arrived in Poughkeepsie to work at IBM, Pauline was overwhelmed by the sophistication and variety of product prototypes.

3. Some historians think that the New Testament was completed by A.D. 100.
4. Mark's birthday was Fri., May 13, this year.
5. Many girls fall prey to a cult worship of great entertainers — e.g., in my mother's generation, girls worshiped the Beatles.

41

Numbers

> **GRAMMAR CHECKERS** can tell you to spell out certain numbers, such as *thirty-three* and numbers that begin a sentence, but they won't help you understand when it is acceptable to use figures.

41a Spell out numbers of one or two words or those that begin a sentence. Use figures for numbers that require more than two words to spell out.

▶ Now, some ~~8~~ *eight* years later, Muffin is still with us.

▶ I counted ~~one hundred seventy-six~~ *176* CD's on the shelf.

If a sentence begins with a number, spell out the number or rewrite the sentence.

▶ ~~150~~ *One hundred fifty* children in our program need expensive dental treatment.

Rewriting the sentence will also correct the error and may be less awkward if the number is long: *In our program 150 children need expensive dental treatment.*

EXCEPTIONS: In technical and some business writing, figures are preferred even when spellings would be brief, but usage varies.

When several numbers appear in the same passage, many writers choose consistency rather than strict adherence to the rule.

When one number immediately follows another, spell out one and use figures for the other: three 100-meter events, 125 four-poster beds.

41b　Generally, figures are acceptable for dates, addresses, percentages, fractions, decimals, scores, statistics and other numerical results, exact amounts of money, divisions of books and plays, pages, identification numbers, and the time.

DATES　July 4, 1776, 56 B.C., A.D. 30

ADDRESSES　77 Latches Lane, 519 West 42nd Street

PERCENTAGES　55 percent (or 55%)

FRACTIONS, DECIMALS　½, 0.047

SCORES　7 to 3, 21–18

STATISTICS　average age 37, average weight 180

SURVEYS　4 out of 5

EXACT AMOUNTS OF MONEY　$105.37, $106,000

DIVISIONS OF BOOKS　volume 3, chapter 4, page 189

DIVISIONS OF PLAYS　act 3, scene 3 (or act III, scene iii)

IDENTIFICATION NUMBERS　serial number 10988675

TIME OF DAY　4:00 P.M., 1:30 A.M.

> $255,000
> ► Several doctors put up ~~two hundred fifty-five thousand dollars~~
>   ^
> for the construction of a golf course.

NOTE: When not using A.M. or P.M., write out the time in words (*two o'clock in the afternoon, twelve noon, seven in the morning*).

EXERCISE 41–1

Edit the following sentences to correct errors in the use of numbers. If a sentence is correct, write "correct" after it. Answers to lettered sentences appear in the back of the book. Example:

> $3.06
> By the end of the evening Ashanti had only ~~three dollars and~~
>   ^
> ~~six cents~~ left.

a. We have ordered 4 azaleas, 3 rhododendrons, and 2 mountain laurels for the back area of the garden.

b. Venezuelan independence from Spain was declared on July 5, 1811.

c. The score was tied at 5–5 when the momentum shifted and carried the Standards to a decisive 12–5 win.

d. We ordered three four-door sedans for company executives.

e. The Vietnam Veterans Memorial in Washington, D.C., had fifty-eight thousand one hundred thirty-two names inscribed on it when it was dedicated in 1982.

1. One of my favorite scenes in Shakespeare is the property division scene in act 1 of *King Lear.*

2. The botany lecture will begin at precisely 3:30 P.M.

3. 12 percent of all American marriages occur in June.

4. In nineteen hundred and forty-one, the United States entered World War II.

5. On a normal day, I spend at least 4 to 5 hours surfing the Internet.

42

Italics (underlining)

Italics, a slanting typeface used in printed material, can be produced by some word processing programs. In handwritten or typed papers, this typeface is indicated by <u>underlining</u>. Some instructors prefer underlining even if their students can produce italics.

NOTE: Current e-mail systems do not allow for italics or underlining. Many people indicate words that should be italicized by preceding and ending them with underscore marks or asterisks. Punctuation should follow the coding.

    I am planning to write my senior thesis on _Anna
    Karenina_.

In less formal e-mail messages, normally italicized words aren't marked at all.

    I finally finished reading Anna Karenina--what a
    masterpiece!

GRAMMAR CHECKERS do not flag problems with italics or underlining. (For a general discussion of what grammar checkers can and cannot do, see pp. 63–64.)

42a Underline or italicize the titles of works according to convention.

Titles of the following works should be underlined or italicized.

TITLES OF BOOKS   *The Great Gatsby, A Distant Mirror*

MAGAZINES   *Time, Scientific American*

NEWSPAPERS   the *St. Louis Post-Dispatch*

PAMPHLETS   *Common Sense, Facts about Marijuana*

LONG POEMS   *The Waste Land, Paradise Lost*

PLAYS   *King Lear, A Raisin in the Sun*

FILMS   *Casablanca, Independence Day*

TELEVISION PROGRAMS   *Friends, 60 Minutes*

RADIO PROGRAMS   *All Things Considered*

MUSICAL COMPOSITIONS   Gershwin's *Porgy and Bess*

CHOREOGRAPHIC WORKS   Twyla Tharp's *Brief Fling*

WORKS OF VISUAL ART   Rodin's *The Thinker*

COMIC STRIPS   *Dilbert*

SOFTWARE   *WordPerfect*

WEB SITES   *Barron's Online, ESPNET SportsZone*

The titles of other works, such as short stories, essays, episodes of radio and television programs, songs, and short poems, are enclosed in quotation marks. (See 37d.)

NOTE: Do not use underlining or italics when referring to the Bible, titles of books in the Bible (Genesis, not *Genesis*), or titles of legal documents (the Constitution, not the *Constitution*). Do not underline the title of your own paper.

42b Underline or italicize the names of spacecraft, aircraft, ships, and trains.

Challenger, Spirit of St. Louis, Queen Elizabeth II, Silver Streak

▶ The success of the Soviets' <u>Sputnik</u> galvanized the U.S.

space program.

42c Underline or italicize foreign words used in an English sentence.

▶ Although Joe's method seemed to be successful, I decided to

establish my own <u>modus operandi</u>.

EXCEPTION: Do not underline or italicize foreign words that have become a standard part of the English language — "laissez-faire," "fait accompli," "habeas corpus," and "per diem," for example.

42d Underline or italicize words mentioned as words, letters mentioned as letters, and numbers mentioned as numbers.

▶ Tim assured us that the howling probably came from

his bloodhound, Hill Billy, but his <u>probably</u> stuck in

our minds.

▶ Sarah called her father by his given name, Johnny, but she

was unable to pronounce <u>J</u>.

▶ A big <u>3</u> was painted on the door.

NOTE: Quotation marks may be used instead of underlining or italics to set off words mentioned as words. (See 37e.)

42e Avoid excessive underlining or italics for emphasis.

Underlining or italicizing to emphasize words or ideas is distracting and should be used sparingly.

▶ In-line skating is a sport that has become an <u>addiction</u>.

EXERCISE 42–1

Edit the following sentences to correct errors in the use of italics. If a sentence is correct, write "correct" after it. Answers to lettered sentences appear in the back of the book. Example:

<u>Leaves of Grass</u> by Walt Whitman was quite controversial

when it was published a century ago.

a. Howard Hughes commissioned the Spruce Goose, a beautifully built but thoroughly impractical wooden aircraft.
b. The old man *screamed* his anger, *shouting* to all of us, "I will not leave my money to you worthless layabouts!"
c. Even though it is almost always hot in Mexico in the summer, you can usually find a cool spot on one of the park benches in the town's zócalo.
d. Cinema audiences once gasped at hearing the word *damn* in *Gone with the Wind.*
e. "The City and the Pillar" was an early novel by Gore Vidal.

1. Bernard watched as Eileen stood transfixed in front of Vermeer's Head of a Young Girl.
2. The monastery walls were painted with scenes described in the book of Genesis.
3. My per diem allowance was $200.
4. In her first calligraphy lesson, Suzanne learned how to make a Romanesque B.
5. Redford and Newman in the movie "The Sting" were amateurs compared with the seventeen-year-old con artist who lives at our house.

43

Spelling

You learned to spell from repeated experience with words in both reading and writing, but especially writing. Words have a look, a sound, and even a feel to them as the hand moves across the page. As you proofread, you can probably tell if a word doesn't look quite right. In such cases, the solution is obvious: Look up the word in the dictionary.

> **SPELL CHECKERS AND GRAMMAR CHECKERS** are useful alternatives to a dictionary, but only to a point. A spell checker will not tell you how to spell words not listed in its dictionary; nor will it help you catch words commonly confused, such as *accept* and *except,* or some typographical errors, such as *own* for *won.* You will still need to proofread, and for some words you may need to turn to the dictionary.
>
> Grammar checkers can flag commonly confused words such as *accept* and *except* or *principal* and *principle,* but they often do this when you have used the correct word. You will still need to think about the meaning you intend.

43a Become familiar with your dictionary.

A good desk dictionary—such as *The American Heritage Dictionary of the English Language, The Random House College Dictionary,* or *Merriam-Webster's Collegiate Dictionary* or *New World Dictionary of the American Language*—is an indispensable writer's aid.

A sample dictionary entry, taken from *The American Heritage Dictionary,* appears on page 500. Labels show where various kinds of information about a word can be found in that dictionary.

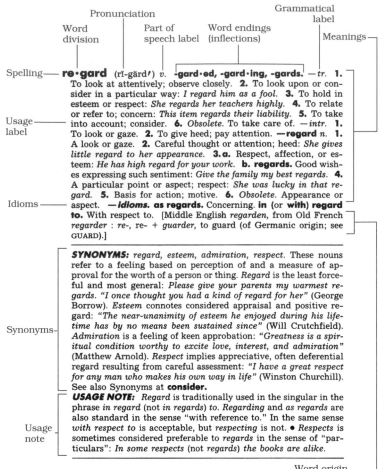

Word division | Pronunciation | Part of speech label | Word endings (inflections) | Grammatical label | Meanings

Spelling — **re·gard** (rĭ-gärd′) *v.* **-gard·ed, -gard·ing, -gards.** —*tr.* **1.** To look at attentively; observe closely. **2.** To look upon or consider in a particular way: *I regard him as a fool.* **3.** To hold in esteem or respect: *She regards her teachers highly.* **4.** To relate or refer to; concern: *This item regards their liability.* **5.** To take into account; consider. **6.** *Obsolete.* To take care of. —*intr.* **1.** To look or gaze. **2.** To give heed; pay attention. —**regard** *n.* **1.** A look or gaze. **2.** Careful thought or attention; heed: *She gives little regard to her appearance.* **3.a.** Respect, affection, or esteem: *He has high regard for your work.* **b. regards.** Good wishes expressing such sentiment: *Give the family my best regards.* **4.** A particular point or aspect; respect: *She was lucky in that regard.* **5.** Basis for action; motive. **6.** *Obsolete.* Appearance or aspect. —**idioms. as regards.** Concerning. **in** (or **with**) **regard to.** With respect to. [Middle English *regarden,* from Old French *regarder* : *re-,* re- + *guarder,* to guard (of Germanic origin; see GUARD).]

Usage label

Idioms

SYNONYMS: *regard, esteem, admiration, respect.* These nouns refer to a feeling based on perception of and a measure of approval for the worth of a person or thing. *Regard* is the least forceful and most general: *Please give your parents my warmest regards.* "*I once thought you had a kind of regard for her*" (George Borrow). *Esteem* connotes considered appraisal and positive regard: "*The near-unanimity of esteem he enjoyed during his lifetime has by no means been sustained since*" (Will Crutchfield). *Admiration* is a feeling of keen approbation: "*Greatness is a spiritual condition worthy to excite love, interest, and admiration*" (Matthew Arnold). *Respect* implies appreciative, often deferential regard resulting from careful assessment: "*I have a great respect for any man who makes his own way in life*" (Winston Churchill). See also Synonyms at **consider.**

Synonyms

USAGE NOTE: *Regard* is traditionally used in the singular in the phrase *in regard* (not *in regards*) *to. Regarding* and *as regards* are also standard in the sense "with reference to." In the same sense *with respect to* is acceptable, but *respecting* is not. • *Respects* is sometimes considered preferable to *regards* in the sense of "particulars": *In some respects* (not *regards*) *the books are alike.*

Usage note

Word origin (etymology)

Spelling, word division, pronunciation

The main entry (*re•gard* in the sample entry) shows the correct spelling of the word. When there are two correct spellings of a word (as in *collectible, collectable*, for example), both are given, with the preferred spelling usually appearing first.

The main entry also shows how the word is divided into syllables. The dot between *re* and *gard* separates the word's two syllables and indicates where the word should be divided if it can't fit at the end of a line of type (see 44f). When a word is compound, the main entry shows how to write it: as one word (*crossroad*), as a hyphenated word (*cross-stitch*), or as two words (*cross section*).

The word's pronunciation is given just after the main entry. The accents indicate which syllables are stressed; the other marks are explained in the dictionary's pronunciation key. In some dictionaries this key appears at the bottom of every page or every other page.

Word endings and grammatical labels

When a word takes endings to indicate grammatical functions (called *inflections*), the endings are listed in boldface, as with *-garded, -garding,* and *-gards* in the sample entry.

Labels for the parts of speech and for other grammatical terms are abbreviated. The most commonly used abbreviations are these:

n.	noun	adj.	adjective
pl.	plural	adv.	adverb
sing.	singular	pron.	pronoun
v.	verb	prep.	preposition
tr.	transitive verb	conj.	conjunction
intr.	intransitive verb	interj.	interjection

Meanings, word origin, synonyms, and antonyms

Each meaning for the word is given a number. Occasionally a word's use is illustrated in a quoted sentence.

Sometimes a word can be used as more than one part of speech (*regard*, for instance, can be used as either a verb or a noun). In such a case, all the meanings for one part of speech are given before all the meanings for another, as in the sample entry. The entry also gives idiomatic uses of the word.

The origin of the word, called its *etymology*, appears in brackets after all the meanings (in some dictionaries it appears before the meanings).

Synonyms, words similar in meaning to the main entry, are frequently listed. In the sample entry, the dictionary draws distinctions in meaning among the various synonyms. Antonyms, which do not appear in the sample entry, are words having a meaning opposite from that of the main entry.

Usage

Usage labels indicate when, where, or under what conditions a particular meaning for a word is appropriately used. Common labels are *informal* (or *colloquial*), *slang, nonstandard, dialect, obsolete, archaic, poetic,* and *British.* In the sample entry, two meanings of *regard* are labeled *obsolete* because they are no longer in use.

Dictionaries sometimes include usage notes as well. In the sample entry, the dictionary offers advice on several uses of *regard* not specifically covered by the meanings. Such advice is based on the opinions of many experts and on actual usage in current magazines, newspapers, and books.

43b Discriminate between words that sound alike but have different meanings.

Words that sound alike or nearly alike but have different meanings and spellings are called homophones. The following sets of words are so commonly confused that a good proofreader will double-check their every use.

affect (verb: "to exert an influence")
effect (verb: "to accomplish"; noun: "result")

its (possessive pronoun: "of or belonging to it")
it's (contraction for "it is")

loose (adjective: "free, not securely attached")
lose (verb: "to fail to keep, to be deprived of")

principal (adjective: "most important"; noun: "head of a school")
principle (noun: "a general or fundamental truth")

their (possessive pronoun: "belonging to them")
they're (contraction for "they are")
there (adverb: "that place or position")

who's (contraction for "who is")
whose (possessive form of "who")

your (possessive form of "you")
you're (contraction of "you are")

To check for correct use of these and other commonly confused words, consult the Glossary of Usage, which begins on page 773.

43c Become familiar with the major spelling rules.

1. Use *i* before *e* except after *c* or when sounded like the letter *a*, as in *neighbor* and *weigh*.

i* BEFORE *e	relieve, believe, sieve, frieze
e* BEFORE *i	receive, deceive, sleigh, freight, eight
EXCEPTIONS	seize, either, weird, height, foreign, leisure

2. Generally, drop a final silent *-e* when adding a suffix that begins with a vowel. Keep the final *-e* if the suffix begins with a consonant.

desire, desiring; remove, removable

achieve, achievement; care, careful

Words such as *argument, truly,* and *changeable* are exceptions.

3. When adding *-s* or *-d* to words ending in *-y,* ordinarily change the *-y* to *-ie* when the *-y* is preceded by a consonant but not when it is preceded by a vowel.

comedy, comedies; dry, dried

monkey, monkeys; play, played

With proper names ending in *-y,* however, do not change the *-y* to *-i* even if it is preceded by a consonant: *Dougherty, the Doughertys.*

4. If a final consonant is preceded by a single vowel *and* the consonant ends a one-syllable word or a stressed syllable, double the consonant when adding a suffix beginning with a vowel.

bet, betting; commit, committed; occur, occurrence

5. Add *-s* to form the plural of most nouns; add *-es* to singular nouns ending in *-s, -sh, -ch,* and *-x.*

table, tables; paper, papers

church, churches; dish, dishes

Ordinarily add *-s* to nouns ending in *-o* when the *-o* is preceded by a vowel. Add *-es* when it is preceded by a consonant.

radio, radios; video, videos

hero, heroes; tomato, tomatoes

To form the plural of a hyphenated compound word, add the -s to the chief word even if it does not appear at the end.

mother-in-law, mothers-in-law

NOTE: English words derived from other languages such as Latin or French sometimes form the plural as they would in their original language.

medium, media; criterion, criteria; beau, beaux

ESL

Spelling may vary slightly among English-speaking countries. This can prove particularly confusing for ESL students, who may have learned British or Canadian English. Following is a list of some common words spelled differently in American and British English. Consult a dictionary for others.

AMERICAN	BRITISH
canceled, traveled	cancelled, travelled
color, humor	colour, humour
judgment	judgement
check	cheque
realize, apologize	realise, apologise
defense	defence
anemia, anesthetic	anaemia, anaesthetic
theater, center	theatre, centre
fetus	foetus
mold, smolder	mould, smoulder
civilization	civilisation
connection, inflection	connexion, inflexion
licorice	liquorice

43d Be alert to commonly misspelled words.

absence	conceivable	humorous	privilege
academic	conferred	incidentally	proceed
accidentally	conqueror	incredible	professor
accommodate	conscience	indispensable	pronunciation
achievement	conscientious	inevitable	quiet
acknowledge	conscious	intelligence	quite
acquaintance	criticism	irrelevant	quizzes
acquire	criticize	irresistible	receive
address	decision	knowledge	referred
all right	definitely	license	restaurant
amateur	descendant	lightning	rhythm
analyze	dictionary	loneliness	roommate
answer	disastrous	maintenance	sandwich
apparently	eighth	maneuver	schedule
appearance	eligible	marriage	seize
arctic	embarrass	mathematics	separate
argument	emphasize	mischievous	sergeant
arithmetic	entirely	necessary	siege
arrangement	environment	noticeable	similar
ascend	especially	occasion	sincerely
athlete	exaggerated	occurred	sophomore
athletics	exercise	occurrence	strictly
attendance	exhaust	pamphlet	subtly
basically	existence	parallel	succeed
beginning	extraordinary	particularly	surprise
believe	extremely	pastime	thorough
benefited	familiar	permissible	tragedy
bureau	fascinate	perseverance	transferred
business	February	phenomenon	tries
calendar	foreign	physically	truly
candidate	forty	picnicking	unnecessarily
cemetery	fourth	playwright	usually
changeable	friend	practically	vacuum
column	government	precede	vengeance
commitment	grammar	preference	villain
committed	guard	preferred	weird
committee	harass	prejudice	whether
competitive	height	prevalent	writing

LOOKING AT YOURSELF AS A WRITER
Spelling

If spelling is a problem for you, consider possible sources of your difficulties. Here are some causes and cures.

CAUSE You have trouble with a few commonly misspelled words, and because these words occur so often, your spelling problem seems worse than it is.

CURE Ask someone to dictate words from the list of commonly misspelled words on page 506, and write the words as they are read to you. Once you have identified your "spelling demons," practice writing the words correctly.

CAUSE You tend to confuse words that sound alike.

CURE Keep a list of the commonly confused words that give you trouble. When they occur in a draft, consult the Glossary of Usage at the back of this book.

CAUSE Your handwriting is so poor that the words don't flow smoothly onto the paper. (Spelling is to some extent kinesthetic—a matter of how a word "feels" as you form it.)

CURE Try typing your drafts. The words may flow more smoothly as you type, reducing your misspellings. Another advantage of typing—if you use a computer—is that you'll have access to a spell checker.

CAUSE You have a learning disability. Maybe you have trouble distinguishing between sounds, or perhaps your eyes scramble or reverse letters.

CURE If possible, consult an expert on learning disabilities. With the expert's help, you can diagnose the cause of your problem and devise ways to overcome it—or work around it. Almost certainly the expert will advise you to write on a computer with a spell checker.

EXERCISE 43-1

The following memo has been run through a spell checker. Proofread it carefully, editing the spelling and typographical errors that remain.

November 1, 1996

To: Patricia Wise

cc: Richard Chang

Form: Constance Mayhew

Subject: Express Tours annual report

Thank you for agreeing to draft the annual report for Express Tours. Before you begin you're work, let me outline the initial steps.

First, its essential for you to include brief profiles of top management. Early next week, I'll provide profiles for all manages accept Samuel Heath, who's biographical information is being revised. You should edit these profiles carefully, than format them according to the enclosed instructions. We may ask you to include other employee's profiles at some point.

Second, you should arrange to get complete financial information for fiscal year 1996 from our comptroller, Richard Chang. (Helen Boyes, to, can provide the necessary figures.) When you get this information, precede according tot he plans we discuss in yesterday's meeting. By the way, you will notice from the figures that the sale of our Charterhouse division did not significantly effect net profits.

Third, you should submit first draft of the report by December 15. I assume that you won a laser printer, but if you don't, you can submit a disk and we'll print out a draft here. Of coarse, you should proofread you writing.

I am quiet pleased that you can take on this project. If I or anyone else at Express Tours can answers questions, don't hesitate to call.

44

The hyphen

> **GRAMMAR CHECKERS** can flag some, but not all, missing or misused hyphens. For example, the programs can tell you that a hyphen is needed in fractions and compound numbers, such as *two-thirds* and *sixty-four*. They can also tell you how to spell certain compound words, such as *breakup* (not *break-up*).

44a   Consult the dictionary to determine how to treat a compound word.

The dictionary will tell you whether to treat a compound word as a hyphenated compound (*water-repellent*), one word (*waterproof*), or two words (*water table*). If the compound word is not in the dictionary, treat it as two words.

▶ The prosecutor chose not to cross—examine any witnesses.

▶ Grandma kept a small note book in her apron pocket.

▶ Alice walked through the looking/glass into a backward world.

44b   Use a hyphen to connect two or more words functioning together as an adjective before a noun.

▶ Mrs. Douglas gave Toshiko a seashell and some newspaper— wrapped fish to take home to her mother.

▶ Priscilla Hood is not yet a well—known candidate.
                                        ^

Newspaper-wrapped and *well-known* are adjectives used before the nouns *fish* and *candidate.*

Generally, do not use a hyphen when such compounds follow the noun.

▶ After our television campaign, Priscilla Hood will be well⁄

known.

Do not use a hyphen to connect *-ly* adverbs to the words they modify.

▶ A slowly⁄moving truck tied up traffic.

NOTE: In a series, hyphens are suspended.

Do you prefer first-, second-, or third-class tickets?

44c Hyphenate the written form of fractions and of compound numbers from twenty-one to ninety-nine.

▶ One—fourth of my income goes to pay off the national debt.
    ^

44d Use a hyphen with the prefixes *all-, ex-* (meaning "former"), and *self-* and with the suffix *-elect.*

▶ The charity is funneling more money into self—help projects.
                                              ^

▶ Anne King is our club's president —elect.
                                    ^

44e A hyphen is used in some words to avoid ambiguity or to separate awkward double or triple letters.

Without the hyphen there would be no way to distinguish between words such as *re-creation* and *recreation.*

> Bicycling in the country is my favorite recreation.
>
> The film was praised for its astonishing re-creation of nineteenth-century London.

Hyphens are sometimes used to separate awkward double or triple letters in compound words (*anti-intellectual, cross-stitch*). Always check a dictionary for the standard form of the word.

44f If a word must be divided at the end of a line, divide it correctly.

1. Divide words between syllables.

> *recog-*
> ▶ When I returned from overseas, I didn't ~~reco-~~
> *nize*
> ~~gnize~~ one face on the magazine covers.

2. Never divide one-syllable words.

> ▶ He didn't have the courage or the ~~stren—~~
> *strength*
> ~~gth~~ to open the door.

3. Never divide a word so that a single letter stands alone at the end of a line or fewer than three letters begin a line.

▶ She'll bring her brother with her when she comes ~~a-~~
again.
~~gain.~~
˄

▶ As audience to *The Mousetrap*, Hamlet is a ~~watch-~~
watcher
~~er~~-watching watchers.
˄

4. When dividing a compound word at the end of a line, either make the break between the words that form the compound or put the whole word on the next line.

▶ My niece is determined to become a long-~~dis-~~
distance
~~tance~~ runner when she grows up.
˄

5. To divide long e-mail and Internet addresses, do not use a hyphen. Break the address after a slash, like this:

Libweb can be reached at <http://
sunsite.berkeley.edu.Libweb>.

EXERCISE 44–1

Edit the following sentences to correct errors in hyphenation. If a sentence is correct, write "correct" after it. Answers to lettered sentences appear in the back of the book. Example:

Zola's first readers were scandalized by his slice~~–~~of~~–~~life
˄ ˄

novels.

a. Gold is the seventy-ninth element in the periodic table.
b. The swiftly-moving tugboat pulled alongside the barge and directed it away from the oil spill in the harbor.
c. The Moche were a pre-Columbian people who established a sophisticated culture in ancient Peru.

d. Your dog is well-known in our neighborhood.

e. Road-blocks were set up along all the major highways leading out of the city.

1. We knew we were driving too fast when our tires skidded on the rain slick surface.

2. The Black Death reduced the population of some medieval villages by two thirds.

3. The flight attendant asked us to fasten our seat belts before lift-off.

4. A well known actress who wishes to remain anonymous has contributed $10,000 toward our scholarship fund.

5. Joan had been brought up to be independent and self-reliant.

45

Capital letters

In addition to the rules in this section, you can use a good dictionary to tell you when to use capital letters.

> GRAMMAR CHECKERS remind you that sentences should begin with capital letters and that some words, such as *Cherokee*, are proper nouns. Many words, however, should be capitalized only in certain contexts, and you must determine when to do so. The program, for example, will not know that *north pole* should be capitalized.

45a Capitalize proper nouns and words derived from them; do not capitalize common nouns.

Proper nouns are the names of specific persons, places, and things. All other nouns are common nouns. The following types of words are usually capitalized: names for the deity, religions, religious followers, sacred books; words of family relationship used as names; particular places; nationalities and their languages, races, tribes; educational institutions, departments, degrees, particular courses; government departments, organizations, political parties; historical movements, periods, events, documents; specific electronic sources; and trade names.

PROPER NOUNS	**COMMON NOUNS**
God (used as a name)	a god
Book of Jeremiah	a book
Uncle Pedro	my uncle
Father (used as a name)	my father
Lake Superior	a picturesque lake
the Capital Center	a center for advanced studies
the South	a southern state
Japan, a Japanese garden	an ornamental garden
University of Wisconsin	a good university
Geology 101	geology
Environmental Protection Agency	a federal agency
Phi Kappa Psi	a fraternity
a Democrat	an independent
the Enlightenment	the eighteenth century
the Declaration of Independence	a treaty
the World Wide Web, the Web	a home page
the Internet, the Net	a computer network
Kleenex	a tissue

Months, holidays, and days of the week are treated as proper nouns; the seasons and numbers of the days of the month are not.

Our academic year begins on a Tuesday in early September, right after Labor Day.

My mother's birthday is in early summer, on the second of June.

EXCEPTION: Capitalize Fourth of July (or July Fourth) when referring to the holiday.

Names of school subjects are capitalized only if they are names of languages. Names of particular courses are capitalized.

> This semester Austin is taking math, geography, geology, French, and English.

> Professor Anderson offers Modern American Fiction 501 to graduate students.

CAUTION: Do not capitalize common nouns to make them seem important: *Our company is currently hiring computer programmers* (not *Company, Computer Programmers*).

45b Capitalize titles of persons when used as part of a proper name but usually not when used alone.

> Professor Margaret Barnes; Dr. Harold Stevens; John Scott Williams, Jr.; Anne Tilton, LL.D.

> District Attorney Marshall was reprimanded for badgering the witness.

> The district attorney was elected for a two-year term.

Usage varies when the title of an important public figure is used alone: *The president* [or *President*] *vetoed the bill.*

45c Capitalize the first, last, and all major words in titles and subtitles of works such as books, articles, songs, and online documents.

In both titles and subtitles, major words such as nouns, pronouns, verbs, adjectives, and adverbs should be capitalized. Minor words such as articles, prepositions, and coordinating conjunctions are not capitalized unless they are the first or last word of a title or subtitle. Capitalize the second part of a hyphenated term in a title if it is a major word but not if it is a minor word.

To see why some of the following titles are italicized and some are put in quotation marks, see 42a and 37d.

> *The Impossible Theater: A Manifesto*
> *The F-Plan Diet*
> "Fire and Ice"
> "I Want to Hold Your Hand"
> *The Canadian Green Page*

Capitalize chapter titles and the titles of other major divisions of a work following the same guidelines used for titles of complete works.

> "Work and Play" in Santayana's *The Nature of Beauty*

45d Capitalize the first word of a sentence.

Obviously the first word of a sentence should be capitalized.

> When lightning struck the house, the chimney collapsed.

When a sentence appears within parentheses, capitalize its first word unless the parentheses appear within another sentence.

> Early detection of breast cancer significantly increases survival rates. (See table 2.)

> Early detection of breast cancer significantly increases survival rates (see table 2).

45e Capitalize the first word of a quoted sentence but not a quoted phrase.

> In *Time* magazine Robert Hughes writes, "There are only about sixty Watteau paintings on whose authenticity all experts agree."

> Russell Baker has written that in our country sports are "the opiate of the masses."

If a quoted sentence is interrupted by explanatory words, do not capitalize the first word after the interruption. (See 37f.)

> "If you wanted to go out," he said sharply, "you should have told me."

When quoting poetry, copy the poet's capitalization exactly. Many poets capitalize the first word of every line of poetry; a few contemporary poets dismiss capitalization altogether.

> When I consider everything that grows
> Holds in perfection but a little moment   —Shakespeare

> It was the week   that
> i felt the city's narrow breezes rush about
> me   —Don L. Lee

45f Do not capitalize the first word after a colon unless it begins an independent clause, in which case capitalization is optional.

> Most of the bar's patrons can be divided into two groups: the occasional after-work socializers and the nothing-to-go-home-to regulars.

> This we are forced to conclude: The [*or* the] federal government is needed to protect the rights of minorities.

45g Capitalize abbreviations for departments and agencies of government, other organizations, and corporations; capitalize the call letters of radio and television stations.

EPA, FBI, OPEC, IBM, WCRB, KNBC-TV

EXERCISE 45–1

Edit the following sentences to correct errors in capitalization. If a sentence is correct, write "correct" after it. Answers to lettered sentences appear in the back of the book. Example:

> On our trip to the West we visited the ~~g~~rand ~~c~~anyon and the
> ~~g~~reat ~~s~~alt ~~d~~esert.

(with editing marks: *G C* above grand canyon; *G S D* above great salt desert)

a. District attorney Bax was disgusted when the jurors turned in a verdict of not guilty after only one hour of deliberation.
b. My mother has begun to research the history of her cherokee ancestors in Georgia.
c. W. C. Fields's epitaph reads, "On the whole, I'd rather be in Philadelphia."
d. Refugees from central America are finding it more and more difficult to cross the rio Grande into the United States.
e. I obtained profiles of both candidates from a useful web site called vote smart web.

1. Whenever my brother took us to the movies, he gave us three choices: A brainless beach party flick, a foreign fluff film, or a blood-and-lust adventure movie.
2. The grunion is an unremarkable fish except for one curious habit: It comes ashore to spawn.
3. In our family, aunt Sandra was notorious for her biting tongue.
4. Historians have described Robert E. Lee as the aristocratic south personified.
5. Because Eileen enjoys working with handicapped children, she is pursuing a degree in Special Education.

PART IX

Researched Writing

College research assignments are an opportunity for you to contribute to an intellectual inquiry or debate. Most college assignments ask you to pose a question worth exploring, to read widely in search of possible answers, to interpret what you read, to draw reasoned conclusions, and to support those conclusions with valid and well-documented evidence. Such assignments may at first seem overwhelming, but if you pose a question that intrigues you and approach it like a detective, with genuine curiosity, you will soon learn how rewarding doing research can be.

Admittedly, the process takes time: time for researching and time for drafting, revising, and documenting the paper in the style recommended by your instructor (see 53 and 56). Before beginning a research project, you should set a realistic schedule of deadlines. For example, one student constructed the following schedule for a paper assigned on October 1 and due October 31.

SCHEDULE	**FINISHED BY**
1. Take the college's library tour and get familiar with computer search tools.	October 2
2. Choose a topic and plan a search strategy.	3
3. Compile a bibliography.	5
4. Read and take notes.	10
5. Decide on a tentative thesis and outline.	11
6. Draft the paper.	16
7. Visit the writing center to get help with ideas for revision.	17
8. Do further research if necessary.	20
9. Revise the paper.	25
10. Prepare a list of works cited.	26
11. Type and proofread the final draft.	28

Notice that the student built some extra time into her schedule to allow for unexpected delays. Although the due date for the paper was October 31, her schedule called for completing the paper by October 28.

46

Conducting research

Throughout Part IX, you will encounter many examples related to the two sample research papers in section 54. One, by John Garcia, debates a political issue concerning the mountain lion population in California. The other, by Karen Shaw, addresses a scholarly controversy concerning the extent to which the great apes, such as chimpanzees and gorillas, have acquired language skills. Before you begin reading the chapters in Part IX, you may want to take a look at these sample student papers.

If you have access to the Internet, you may also want to visit a useful Web site that accompanies *The Bedford Handbook: Research and Documentation in the Electronic Age* (http://www.bedfordbooks.com/rd). The site lists print sources and provides links to Internet sources for various academic disciplines. In addition, it includes guidelines for documenting both print and Internet sources in four disciplines: English and the humanities, history, the social sciences, and the biological sciences.

46a Pose possible questions worth exploring.

Working within the guidelines of your assignment, pose a few questions that seem worth researching. Here, for example, are some preliminary questions jotted down by students who were asked to write about a significant political or scholarly issue.

—Will a government-regulated rating system for television shows really curb children's exposure to violent programming?

—Which geological formations are the safest repositories for nuclear waste?

—Do genetic tests for hereditary diseases place people at a greater risk of job or insurance discrimination?

—What was Marcus Garvey's contribution to the fight for racial equality?

—How can governments and zoos help preserve China's endangered panda?

—Why was amateur archaeologist Heinrich Schliemann such a controversial figure in his own time?

If you have trouble coming up with a list of questions, you can browse through certain library references for ideas. For example, the *Opposing Viewpoints Series* compiles recent articles on controversial social issues, and *CQ Researcher* contains digests of recent articles and editorials on contemporary events. You can also discover interesting contemporary issues by skimming current magazines or by browsing the Internet. Scholarly controversies encountered in college courses are yet another potential source of ideas; ask your professors for suggestions.

Asking appropriate questions

As you formulate possible questions, make sure that they are appropriate lines of inquiry for a research paper. Choose questions that are narrow (not too broad), challenging (not too bland), and grounded (not too speculative).

CHOOSING A NARROW QUESTION   If your initial question is too broad, given the length of the paper you plan to write, look for ways to restrict your focus (see also p. 7). Here, for example, is how some students narrowed their initial questions.

TOO BROAD

—What are the hazards of fad diets?

—Is the military seriously addressing the problem of sexual harassment?

—What causes homelessness?

NARROWER

—What are the hazards of liquid diets?

—To what extent has the navy addressed the problem of sexual harassment since the Tailhook scandal?

—How has deinstitutionalization of the mentally ill contributed to the problem of homelessness?

CHOOSING A CHALLENGING QUESTION   Your research paper will be more interesting to both you and your audience if you base it on an intellectually challenging line of inquiry. Avoid bland questions that fail to provoke thought or engage readers in a debate.

TOO BLAND

—What is obsessive-compulsive disorder?

—Where is wind energy being used?

—How do lie detectors work?

CHALLENGING

—What treatments for obsessive-compulsive disorder show the most promise?

—Does investing in wind energy make economic sense?

—How reliable are lie detectors?

You may well need to address a bland question in the course of answering a more challenging one. For example, if you were writing about promising treatments for obsessive-compulsive disorder, you would no doubt answer the question "What is obsessive-compulsive disorder?" at some point in your paper. It would be a mistake, however, to use the bland question as the focus for the whole paper.

CHOOSING A GROUNDED QUESTION   Finally, you will want to make sure that your research question is grounded, not too speculative. Although speculative questions—such as those that address philosophical, ethical, or religious issues—are worth asking and may receive some attention in a research paper, they are inappropriate central questions. The central argument of a research paper should be grounded in facts; it should not be based entirely on beliefs.

TOO SPECULATIVE
—Is capital punishment moral?
—Do medical scientists have the right to experiment on animals?
—What is the difference between a just and an unjust law?

GROUNDED
—Does capital punishment deter crime?
—How have technical breakthroughs made medical experiments on animals increasingly unnecessary?
—Should we adjust our laws so that penalties for possession of powdered cocaine and crack cocaine are comparable?

Doing some preliminary research

Once you have listed some possible questions, choose the question that intrigues you most and do some preliminary research to see where your line of inquiry might lead. If it seems to be leading to a dead end—maybe because you can't find a variety of sources on the subject or because the information is too technical for you to understand—turn to another question on your list, which may prove more promising.

After doing some preliminary research, John Garcia and Karen Shaw refined their research questions as follows.

Should California voters repeal the California Wildlife Protection Act, which prevents the state fish and game commission from thinning the mountain lion population?

To what extent have the great apes—gorillas, chimpanzees, and orangutans—demonstrated language abilities akin to those of humans?

46b Map out a search strategy.

Because research is a process of discovery, it is not always orderly. Nevertheless, you will save yourself time if you impose some order on the process from the start.

A search strategy is a systematic plan for tracking down sources. To create a search strategy appropriate for the research question that you have posed, you will need to ask yourself two questions:

—What kinds of resources should I draw on?

—In what order should I conduct my search?

Appropriate resources

Academic research papers should be based to some extent on library sources, such as books and periodical articles, which meet at least minimal editorial standards. Few instructors are willing to accept papers based solely on Internet sources or on literature put out by organizations, since the reliability of such sources varies widely.

The currency of your research question dictates what kinds of resources will be appropriate. For a historical subject, you should turn to reference works, books, scholarly articles in academic journals, and primary sources such as speeches; unless your subject has been popularized or is in the news for some reason, you can ignore current magazines and newspapers.

For an up-to-date subject, however, books are less useful than recent articles in magazines and newspapers because by the time a book is published, it is already dated. In researching a 1996 debate about mountain lions in California, for example, John Garcia drew primarily on recent articles in magazines such as *National Geographic, Field and Stream,* and *Audubon,* supplementing them with newspaper articles and current information accessed on the Internet. He consulted only one book, *Cougar: The American Lion,* which he used for background information.

Order of search

Once you have decided what kinds of resources are appropriate for your research question, consider which sources to consult first, second, and so on. Often a good search strategy moves from sources that give you an overview of your subject to those that supply you with more specialized information. In other words, before making final decisions about the direction of your research, try to gain an understanding not only of your specific topic but of the intellectual or social context within which it lies. Some general reading will familiarize you with the ways in which scholars or debaters are framing issues related to your topic.

To research the topic of apes and language, Karen Shaw turned to general magazine and newspaper articles for an overview of her subject. Her librarian recommended that she check a general electronic database, *InfoTrac,* for relevant articles. Working at a computer terminal, Shaw tried the keywords *animal communication* and *primates* singly and in combination to call up abstracts (brief summaries of articles). The abstracts helped Shaw decide which articles would give her an overview of her subject.

After Shaw had located and read a few magazine and newspaper articles, she became intrigued by fairly recent research with bonobos (pygmy chimpanzees) at Yerkes Primate

Center in Atlanta. At this point, she searched for articles about bonobos in two specialized indexes, *PsycLIT* and *Sociofile.* That search yielded several more articles in magazines, newspapers, and scholarly journals.

With a narrowed topic in mind, Shaw decided to check the Internet. Using the Lycos search engine, she typed in the keyword *primate* and found Primate Info Net, a Web page offering a variety of resources on primates as well as a list of links to primate research centers across the country, including Yerkes.

Shaw didn't overlook books entirely. Many of her sources had referred to books by two key researchers, Herbert Terrace and Francine Patterson, who had published books describing the controversies surrounding early ape language studies. Shaw located these books quite easily through the library's computer catalog. Instead of trying to read the books cover to cover, Shaw used the table of contents and the index of each book to lead her to relevant chapters and pages.

By organizing her search strategy carefully, Shaw saved herself time, because most of her reading was relevant to her final approach to the topic.

46c Track down relevant library sources.

If you are an experienced Internet user, you may be tempted to skip library research altogether. In most cases, avoid this temptation. Although the Internet is a rich source of information, its chaotic organization is no match for the carefully crafted retrieval systems of a good library. And, as you are no doubt aware, anyone can post something on the Net, so judging the reliability of an Internet source can be tricky. Libraries offer more quality control. Most of a library's holdings—reference works, books, periodicals, and even pamphlets and audiovisual materials—meet at least minimal standards of reliability.

Becoming familiar with your library

If you have not already done so, explore your library to find out what it offers. Most libraries provide maps and handouts that describe their services; many conduct orientation programs or offer tours or workshops.

As you explore your library, seek out answers to at least the following questions.

— Where is the reference section?

— Does the library's computer catalog lead you to materials other than books? How are locations of different kinds of materials identified?

— Where are the periodical indexes? Do the indexes available in computerized format provide full texts of articles that you can print out?

— When full texts of articles aren't available electronically, in what form do they appear: in print, on microfiche, on microfilm?

— What computer services, such as access to databases through the campus network or the Internet, does the library offer?

— Can you access your library's catalog through your home computer?

As you get to know your library, don't forget the library staff. Librarians can save you time by helping you define what you're looking for and then telling you where to find it. Feel free to tell them about your information needs, not just to ask where to find the encyclopedias.

Reference works

Often you will want to begin by reading background information in an encyclopedia or a biographical reference. Later you may need to turn to other reference works such as atlases, almanacs, or dictionaries.

ENCYCLOPEDIAS Articles in encyclopedias introduce a topic, give you a sense of how broad or narrow it is, and often end with a bibliography of books for further reading. Here are four general encyclopedias frequently used on the college level:

Academic American Encyclopedia

Collier's Encyclopedia

Encyclopedia Americana

The New Encyclopædia Britannica

Although general encyclopedias are a good place to begin your research, do not rely too heavily on them in your finished paper. No doubt you will find more specific information later during your search.

For topics that fall within an academic discipline, consider turning to a specialized encyclopedia, such as one of the many included in the chart on pages 530–31.

BIOGRAPHICAL REFERENCES If your subject is a person, a good place to begin is with a biographical reference. *Biography and Genealogy Master Index* tells you which biographical reference books contain information on the person you are researching. If your library does not have it, try *Biography Index* or go directly to one of these general biographical references:

Contemporary Authors

Current Biography

McGraw-Hill Encyclopedia of World Biography

Webster's New Biographical Dictionary

Many specialized biographical references are available. Some are included in the chart of specialized reference works on pages 530–31.

Specialized reference works

ANTHROPOLOGY *Annual Review of Anthropology, Atlas of World Cultures, Cambridge Encyclopedia of Human Evolution, Dictionary of Anthropology, Encyclopedia of Anthropology, Encyclopedia of Cultural Anthropology, Encyclopedia of World Cultures*

ART, ARCHITECTURE, AND MUSIC *Contemporary Artists, Dictionary of Art, Encyclopedia of Popular Culture, Encyclopedia of World Art, Macmillan Encyclopedia of Architects, New Grove Dictionary of Music and Musicians, New Oxford History of Music, Oxford Companion to Art*

BIOLOGY AND EARTH SCIENCES *Bibliography and Index of Geology, Encyclopedia of Bioethics, Encyclopedia of Earth Sciences, Encyclopedia of Human Biology, Encyclopedia of the Environment, Fieldbook of Natural History, Grzimek's Animal Life Encyclopedia, Oxford Companion to Animal Behavior*

BUSINESS, ECONOMICS, AND FINANCE *Encyclopedia of Banking and Finance, Encyclopedia of Management, McGraw-Hill Dictionary of Modern Economics, New Palgrave Dictionary of Economics*

CHEMISTRY, PHYSICS, AND ASTRONOMY *Astronomy and Astrophysics Encyclopedia, Chemical Information Sources, CRC Handbook of Chemistry and Physics, Encyclopedia of Physics, Kirk-Othmer Encyclopedia of Chemical Technology, McGraw-Hill Encyclopedia of Science and Technology*

COMMUNICATIONS, THEATER, AND FILM *American Voices: Significant Speeches from American History, Film Encyclopedia, International Encyclopedia of Communications, International Television Almanac, McGraw-Hill Encyclopedia of World Drama, Oxford Companion to the Theater*

Specialized reference works (continued)

ETHNIC STUDIES *Asian and Asian American Studies, Encyclopedia of African American Civil Rights, Handbook of Hispanic Culture in the United States, Handbook of North American Indians, Harvard Encyclopedia of American Ethnic Groups, Multicultural Encyclopedia*

HISTORY *Cambridge Ancient History, Cambridge History of Africa, Dictionary of Asian American History, Dictionary of the Middle Ages, Encyclopedia of African-American Culture and History, Encyclopedia of American Social History, Encyclopedia of Asian History, Encyclopedia of the Renaissance, Encyclopedia of the United States in the Twentieth Century, Harvard Guide to American History, New Cambridge Modern History, Times Atlas of World History, Timetables of History*

LITERATURE AND LINGUISTICS *American Writers, Contemporary Literary Criticism, Dictionary of Literary Biography, Encyclopedia of World Literature in the Twentieth Century, International Encyclopedia of Linguistics, MLA International Bibliography, Oxford Companion to Classical Literature, Oxford Companion to English Literature, Oxford English Dictionary*

MATHEMATICS *CRC Handbook of Mathematical Sciences, Encyclopedic Dictionary of Mathematics, International Dictionary of Applied Mathematics*

PHILOSOPHY AND RELIGION *Anchor Bible Dictionary, Dictionary of the History of Ideas, Encyclopedia of Philosophy, Encyclopedia of Religion*

PSYCHOLOGY, SOCIOLOGY, AND EDUCATION *Encyclopedia of Education, Encyclopedia of Human Behavior, Encyclopedia of Psychology, Encyclopedia of Sociology, Mental Measurements Yearbook*

WOMEN'S STUDIES *Notable American Women, Women's Studies Encyclopedia*

ATLASES An atlas is a bound collection of maps. For current topics, make sure that you are working with an up-to-date atlas. For historical topics, consult an atlas that covers the period you are interested in. Here is a brief list of commonly used atlases; more specialized atlases are included in the chart of specialized reference works on pages 530–31.

Historical Atlas

National Geographic Atlas of the World

New York Times Atlas of the World

Rand McNally Cosmopolitan World Atlas

ALMANACS AND YEARBOOKS Almanacs and yearbooks are annual publications that record information about a year, often in the form of lists, charts, and tables. The information covers a range of subjects such as politics, world events, sports, economics, and even the weather. Here is a brief list of these useful references.

Americana Annual

Britannica Book of the Year

Statistical Abstract of the United States

World Almanac and Book of Facts

UNABRIDGED DICTIONARIES An unabridged dictionary such as one of the following is more comprehensive than an ordinary college or desk dictionary.

The Oxford English Dictionary

The Random House Dictionary of the English Language

Webster's Third New International Dictionary

Many specialized dictionaries are available. Some are included in the chart of specialized reference works on pages 530–31.

Books

Most libraries now use computer catalogs that allow you to search for books and often other materials — such as government documents, pamphlets, and audiovisuals — at a computer terminal. Computer catalogs vary widely from library to library. If you experience difficulty understanding how your library's system works, ask a reference librarian for help.

THE COMPUTER CATALOG   You can search a computer catalog by subject, by author, or by title. Subject searches are by far the most useful, especially at the beginning of a research project.

Searching the catalog by subject involves the use of keywords or subject headings, which prompt the computer to retrieve information about relevant books and other source materials. Don't become discouraged if the first keyword you type results in no finds (or "hits") — or if it yields far too many. Both problems are common and are easily remedied.

When a keyword results in no hits, try other keywords until you find some that match the subject headings used by the library catalog. You might also broaden your search using one of the techniques listed in the chart on page 536. If experimenting doesn't work, ask a librarian or consult *The Library of Congress Subject Headings*, large volumes usually placed near the catalog.

If a keyword results in too many hits, you will need to narrow your search. For example, when Karen Shaw, whose topic was apes and language, entered the term *primates* into the computer, she was faced with 174 hits, an unmanageable number. She narrowed her search by entering *primates and language* and retrieved just the eight records displayed below, a few of which looked promising. The use of *and* and other strategies for restricting a search are illustrated in the chart on page 536.

Once you have narrowed your search to a list of relevant sources, you can command the computer to display or print the complete record for each source, which includes its bibliographic information and a call number. On page 535 is the

COMPUTER CATALOG SUBJECT SEARCH: SCREEN 1

```
PRIMATES + LANGUAGE    8 ITEMS    NU Libraries
 1                                          NU  see record     1994
    Ape man [videorecording]                MV7-4971/74

 2 Bradshaw John L 1                         NU  SNELL  STACKS  1993
    The evolution of lateral asymmetries,    QP 385.5.B695 1993
    language,
 3                                          NU  SNELL  STACKS  1993
    Species, species concepts, and          QL 737.P9S69 1993
    primate evolution
 4                                          NU  SNELL  STACKS  1993
    The Undaunted Psychologist :            BF 76.5.U45 1993
    adventures in rese
 5                                          NU  SNELL  STACKS  1992
    Neurodevelopment, aging, and cognition  RC 523.N42 1992

 6                                          NU  SNELL  STACKS  1990
    "Language" and intelligence in monkeys  QL 737.P9L26 1990
    and apes
 7                                          NU  SNELL         1983
    Language in primates : perspectives     QL 737.P96L35 1983
    and implica
 8                                          NU  SNELL  STACKS  1979
    Neurobiology of social communication    QP 399.N48
    in primates

ALL ITEMS HAVE BEEN DISPLAYED.
Enter <Line number(s)> To Display Full Records (Number + B for Brief)
<P>revious For Previous Page OR <Q>uit For New Search
```

COMPUTER CATALOG SUBJECT SEARCH: SCREEN 2

```
- - - - - - - - - - - - - - - - - - - - - - - - - - - - - - - - - - - - - NU Libraries- - - - -
TITLE(s):       "Language" and intelligence in monkeys and apes:
                comparative developmental perspectives / edited by
                Sue Taylor Parker and Kathleen Rita Gibson.

                Cambridge ; New York : Cambridge University Press,
                1990.

                9009
                xviii, 590 p. : ill. ; 25 cm.
                Includes bibliographical references and index.

OTHER ENTRIES: Primates Psychology.
                Animal intelligence.
                Cognition in animals.
                Animal communication.
                Genetic psychology.
                Psychology, Comparative.
                Parker, Sue Taylor.
                Gibson, Kathleen Rita.

LOCN:    SNELL  STACKS  STATUS: Not checked out --
CALL #:  QL 737.P9L26 1990
```

complete record for title number 6 from the list generated by Shaw's search. The call number, which appears on the last line, is the book's address on the library shelf.

CARD AND MICROFORM CATALOGS   Some libraries may not include their entire collection in the computer catalog. Old titles and rare books, for example, may be in an older card catalog or microform catalog. When in doubt, consult the reference librarian.

OTHER INDEXES TO BOOKS   *Books in Print* and *Paperbound Books in Print* list books by author, title, and subject; *Cumulative Book Index* lists books by author and subject.

Researched writing

Conducting keyword searches

Ways to narrow a keyword search

1. To focus on a more specific topic, use the word *and* as a connector: *primates and sign language.*
2. To exclude unwanted subjects, use the word *not* as a connector: *primates and language not zoos.*
3. To restrict the time period of your search, specify a date or range of dates: *primates and language >=1975.*

Ways to broaden a keyword search

1. To include other topics in your search, use the word *or* as a connector: *primate or ape.*
2. To search for different words with the same root, truncate the search term (usually with an asterisk): *primates and psycholog*.*

NOTE: Computer programs vary in their default settings and in their use of terminology. If you are unfamiliar with a program, call up the help menu or ask your reference librarian for assistance.

These indexes are available electronically as well as in print form.

You may also want to consult bibliographies, lists of publications on specific topics. You can look for bibliographies in your library's computer catalog by using the relevant keyword and the word *bibliography.*

Periodicals

Periodicals are publications issued at regular intervals, such as magazines, newspapers, and scholarly or technical journals. To track down useful articles, consult a periodical index. Some periodical indexes are in print form; others are stored as electronic databases that can be accessed and read at a computer terminal.

You search for articles in an electronic database just as you look for books in the library's computer catalog—by author, title, or subject keywords. Bibliographic records appear on the screen, often accompanied by an abstract; sometimes the full text of an article can be printed.

When doing keyword searches of electronic periodical indexes, remember that you can use the same strategies to narrow or broaden a search as you do with books (see p. 536). For example, when John Garcia entered the term *cougar* into the *Readers' Guide Abstracts* database, he retrieved forty-seven records. By adding the term *hunting,* he reduced the number of hits to just four records, one of which is displayed below.

PERIODICAL INDEX SUBJECT SEARCH

```
1 RGA
   AUTHOR: Robinson, Jerome B.
   TITLE: Cat in the ballot box (California voters to decide on resumption
       of cougar hunting)
   SOURCE: Field & Stream (ISSN:8755-8580) v 100 p 30+ March'96
   CONTAINS: illustration(s)

SUBJECTS COVERED:
Puma attacks
Puma hunting
Game laws/California
ABSTRACT: For more than two decades, the California Department of Fish
and Game has been prohibited by law from taking measures to limit a
mountain lion population that has clearly overgrown its natural range and
is expanding into urban areas. Mountain lions usually eat deer, but in
locations where deer populations have become sparse, they have been
forced to find new food sources. Consequently, lions are killing
livestock, cats, dogs, and even people. Now, California voters are being
asked to decide if the "hands off" mountain lion policy should continue.
If voters pass a proposed referendum, the Fish and Game Department could
reintroduce limited sport hunting as a means of controlling mountain lion
populations.
```

Most libraries provide a list of the periodicals they own. This list tells you how each periodical has been preserved: on microfilm, on microfiche, in bound volumes, or in unbound files. It also tells you which publication years the library owns. In some libraries, all of this information appears on the screen of the computer index.

If your library does not have an index you need in either print or electronic form, your reference librarian may be able to conduct an online database search. Libraries often charge a fee for such searches, so they are usually a last resort.

GENERAL PERIODICAL INDEXES Some general periodical indexes list articles from general-interest magazines such as *U.S. News and World Report, Popular Mechanics, Science,* and *Fortune.* Others list articles from major newspapers such as the *New York Times,* the *Washington Post,* and the *Christian Science Monitor.*

Most college libraries subscribe to at least one of the following computer services, which index general periodicals.

General Periodicals Index (InfoTrac)

National Newspaper Index

Newsbank

NEXIS/LEXIS

Periodical Abstracts Ondisc

Readers' Guide to Periodical Literature

If you are looking for periodical articles that appeared before the mid-1980s, you will need to turn to print indexes, such as the following.

New York Times Index (1851–present)

Poole's Index to Periodical Literature, 1802–1881

Readers' Guide to Periodical Literature (1900–present)

SPECIALIZED PERIODICAL INDEXES To locate articles in technical and scholarly journals such as *Computer World* and *Art in America,* you can consult a specialized index. Many specialized indexes, formerly only in print form, are now available as electronic databases. For indexes covering a variety of disciplines, see the chart on page 540.

Other library sources

A library's holdings are not limited to reference works, books, and periodicals. Your library may have pamphlets, usually located in a large file cabinet known as the *vertical file,* or rare and unpublished manuscripts in a special collection. Holdings might also include government documents, records, tapes, and CD's; films, filmstrips, and videos; drawings, paintings, engravings, and slides.

If your research topic is especially complex or unusual, you may need greater resources than your library offers. In such cases, talk to a librarian about interlibrary loan, a process in which one library borrows materials from another. This procedure can take a week or more, so be sure to allow yourself plenty of time.

46d Consider using Internet sources to supplement (not to replace) library research.

Although the Internet can be a rich source of information, some of which can't be found anywhere else, it lacks quality control. And there is no Internet librarian to help you sort through its massive collection in search of reliable sources. For these reasons, most instructors will want you to use Internet sources only to supplement — not to replace — traditional library sources (see 46c).

Traditional libraries contain countless research-quality sources that have been carefully selected, classified, and indexed; some of these sources are poorly represented (or difficult to find) on the Internet. Also, because anyone can

Specialized periodical indexes

NOTE: Year in which index was first available electronically is indicated in parentheses.

ARTS AND HUMANITIES   *Art Index* (1983), *Humanities Index* (1984), *Music Index* (1981), *Philosopher's Index* (1940)

BUSINESS AND ECONOMICS   *Business and Economics* (1993), *Business Periodicals Index* (1982)

COMMUNICATIONS, THEATER, AND FILM   *Communication Abstracts, Drama Criticism Index, Film Literature Index*

ETHNIC AND WOMEN'S STUDIES   *Chicano Database on CD-ROM* (1965), *Ethnic Newswatch* (1991), *Index to Periodicals by and about Blacks, Women's Resources International* (1972)

HEALTH AND MEDICINE   *Cumulative Index to Nursing and Allied Health* (1983), *Index Medicus* (1985), *Medline* (1966)

HISTORY   *America: History and Life* (1982), *Historical Abstracts* (1982)

LITERATURE   *MLA International Bibliography* (1981)

RELIGION   *Religion Index* (1949)

SCIENCE AND TECHNOLOGY   *Applied Science and Technology Index* (1983), *Biological Abstracts* (1975), *Biological and Agricultural Index* (1983), *Chemical Abstracts* (1969), *Environmental Abstracts* (1971), *General Science Index* (1984), *MathSci* (1940), *Physics Abstracts* (1989)

SOCIAL SCIENCES   *Congressional Masterfile* (1970), *Criminal Justice Abstracts* (1968), *Education Index* (1983), *ERIC (Educational Resources Information Center)* (1966), *PAIS (Public Affairs Information Service)* (1972), *PsycINFO (Psychological Abstracts)* (1967), *PsycLIT* (1974), *Social Sciences Index* (1983), *Sociofile* (1974), *Sociological Abstracts* (1963)

publish on the Internet, you should be especially careful to evaluate the reliability and potential bias of sources that exist solely online (see 47a and 47c).

NOTE: Traditional libraries and the Internet are not mutually exclusive resources. While online, you can (and should) visit Web sites maintained by public and university libraries to browse their holdings, access some sources, and link to on-line reference materials. The Libraries of Purdue University have created an excellent Web site: http://thorplus.lib .purduc.cdu/indcx.html.

The World Wide Web

The World Wide Web (or Web) is a collection of documents, or "pages," that can be called up on a computer by using a browser such as Netscape or Microsoft Explorer. Documents on the Web are often linked to other documents, and researchers can pursue the connections at the click of a mouse. Web search engines and directories make it possible to find everything from electronic books and journals to government documents, reports from special-interest organizations, and electronic discussion groups.

SEARCH ENGINES Search engines such as Lycos (http:// www.lycos.com) are programs that allow you to locate Web sites by typing in keywords. Because the programs match only the words you type in, not their synonyms, you may need to try more than one search term. Don't be surprised when keywords lead you to irrelevant sites, because it is words—not concepts—that the programs search for. For a sample search screen, see page 542.

DIRECTORIES Directories, also known as indexes, can be more useful than search engines because their compilers evaluate sites before adding them to the list. Be aware, however, that directories are only as good as their compilers.

Some are updated frequently; others contain many sites that no longer exist or have moved. Some examples of well-maintained directories are WWW Virtual Library (http://www.w3.org/pub/DataSources/bySubject/Overview.html) and Argus Clearinghouse (http://www.clearinghouse.net). For a sample directory screen, see page 543.

Newsgroups and listservs

Newsgroups are a means of communicating with a group of people interested in a particular topic. Rather than traveling through electronic mail, newsgroup messages are public

SAMPLE SEARCH SCREEN

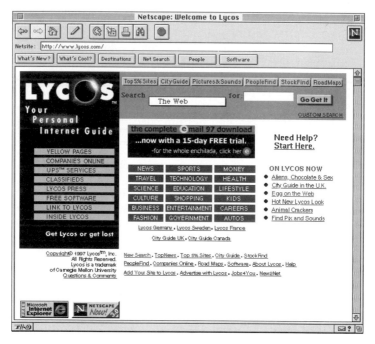

SAMPLE DIRECTORY SCREEN

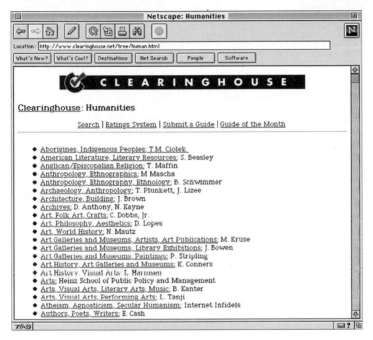

Within the browser window:

Netscape: Humanities

Location: http://www.clearinghouse.net/tree/human.html

What's New? | What's Cool? | Destinations | Net Search | People | Software

CLEARINGHOUSE

Clearinghouse: Humanities

Search | Ratings System | Submit a Guide | Guide of the Month

- Aborigines, Indigenous Peoples; T.M. Ciolek
- American Literature, Literary Resources; S. Beasley
- Anglican/Episcopalian Religion; T. Maffin
- Anthropology, Ethnographics; M Mascha
- Anthropology, Ethnography, Ethnology; B. Schwimmer
- Archaeology, Anthropology; T. Plunkett, J. Lizee
- Architecture, Building; J. Brown
- Archives; D. Anthony, N. Kayne
- Art, Folk Art, Crafts; C. Dobbs, Jr.
- Art, Philosophy, Aesthetics; D. Lopes
- Art, World History; N. Mautz
- Art Galleries and Museums, Artists, Art Publications; M. Kruse
- Art Galleries and Museums, Library Exhibitions; J. Bowen
- Art Galleries and Museums, Paintings; P. Stripling
- Art History, Art Galleries and Museums; K. Conners
- Art History, Visual Arts; L. Harrison
- Arts; Heinz School of Public Policy and Management
- Arts, Visual Arts, Literary Arts, Music; B. Kanter
- Arts, Visual Arts, Performing Arts; L. Tanji
- Atheism, Agnosticism, Secular Humanism; Internet Infidels
- Authors, Poets, Writers; E. Cash

postings that can be read by anyone; you can think of them as messages pinned to an enormous set of bulletin boards. Newsgroups are classified with abbreviations such as *alt*, *rec*, *soc*, and *sci* (standing for *alternative*, *recreational*, *society*, and *science*).

A similar but less public forum is an e-mail discussion list or "listserv." You can subscribe to a list that suits your interests and receive all the mail that members send to the list. As with newsgroups, you can also post questions to the list. Answers to your questions can at times prove quite helpful to your research, giving you a sense of public opinion about your topic, for example, or providing new leads to useful sources.

If you're looking for a newsgroup or listserv related to your topic, a good place to start is Tile.Net (http://www.tile.net), a searchable site that lists hundreds of newsgroups and listservs.

MUD's, MOO's, and IRC's

Through MUD's (multi-user dimensions), MOO's (multi-user dimensions object-oriented), and IRC's (Internet relay chats), the Internet allows for real-time communication. People can send, receive, and respond to messages while they are simultaneously connected. Often participants will communicate in a space that includes several "rooms" where different topics are under discussion.

46e   Consider doing field research.

For a sociology class, you might want to study campus trends in classroom participation: Which students are most, and least, involved in class discussions and why? At work, you might want to learn how food industry executives are responding to reports that their companies have cut portions of some products while increasing prices. Projects like these may be enhanced by, and sometimes centered on, your own field research.

Interviewing

Interviews can often shed some new light on a topic. Look for an expert who has firsthand knowledge of the subject or seek out someone whose personal experience provides an enlightening perspective to your topic. For example, for her paper on apes and language, Karen Shaw interviewed a professor on her campus who had spent seven months working with a gorilla who used sign language.

When asking for an interview, be clear about who you are, what the purpose of the interview is, whether you plan to tape it, and approximately how long it will take. If you succeed in getting an appointment, plan for the interview by writing down a series of questions. Try to avoid questions with yes or no answers or those that encourage vague rambling; instead, phrase your questions to elicit facts, anecdotes, and opinions that will add a meaningful dimension to your paper.

Accuracy is important. If you cannot tape the interview, take careful notes, and if you don't understand a point, ask for clarification. When quoting your source in your paper, you should of course be as accurate and fair as possible.

Surveying opinion

For some topics, you may find it useful to survey opinions through written questionnaires or telephone or e-mail polls. Many people are reluctant to fill out long questionnaires or answer detailed questions over the phone, so if you want a good response rate, you will need to limit your questions and frame them carefully.

When possible, ask for yes/no or multiple-choice answers, which don't take too much effort to respond to and are easy to tabulate. If necessary, ask a few open-ended questions to elicit more individual responses, some of which may be worth quoting.

Contacting organizations

Many organizations, both public and private, will mail you literature in response to a phone call, e-mail, or letter. Although this literature can provide up-to-date information, use it judiciously. Groups tend to promote their own interests; you can't always count on them to offer a balanced view.

A useful reference, *The Encyclopedia of Associations* (available both electronically and in print), lists groups by their concerns, such as environment or family planning, and provides addresses and phone numbers. Many organizations are now publishing home pages on the World Wide Web; these pages can lead you to publications sponsored by organizations and, through links, to other publications as well.

Observing and conducting experiments

For some topics you may want to supplement others' research—or break new ground—with your own observations and experiments. Most academic disciplines have specific guidelines for designing field observations and experiments, collecting and analyzing data, and reporting results. If you are unsure of the appropriate method in your discipline, consult a style manual (see 56g) or ask your instructor for advice.

47

Selecting and reading sources

By spending just an hour or two in front of your library's computer terminals, you can often locate dozens of potential sources for your topic—far more than you will have time to read. Your challenge will be to home in on a reasonable number of sources that are worth your time and attention.

47a   Read selectively.

As you search your library's catalog and periodical indexes, be alert for clues that indicate whether a book or article is worth tracking down. The language used in a title often suggests the audience at which a work is aimed. Subject headings or descriptors can give you information about the content of a book or article. In addition, many of the electronic indexes for magazines, newspapers, and scholarly journals contain abstracts—brief summaries of articles—that can help you choose which ones to take a look at. Here are some questions to guide you as you make your choices.

DECIDING WHETHER TO TRACK DOWN A SOURCE

—How relevant to your research question is the work? Does the title seem pertinent? Does the abstract address your research question?

—How recent is the source? For current topics, some books or articles may be too dated.

—How long is the source? A very short article may be too general to be helpful.

—Is the source readily available?

Once you have tracked down a source, preview it quickly to see how much of your attention, if any, it is worth. Techniques for previewing a book, an article, and a Web site are a bit different.

PREVIEWING A BOOK

—Scan the front and back covers for any information about the book's scope and its author's credentials.

—Glance through the table of contents, keeping your research question in mind.

—Skim the preface in search of a statement of the author's purposes.

—Using the index, look up a few words related to your research question.

—If a chapter seems useful, read its opening and closing paragraphs and skim any headings.

—Consider the author's style, level, and tone. Does the style invite further reading? Is the text written at a level you understand and find useful? Does the author seem to present ideas in an unbiased way?

PREVIEWING AN ARTICLE

—Consider the publication in which the article is printed. Is the publisher reputable? Who is the target audience of the publication? Might the publication be biased toward the target audience?

—For a magazine or journal article, look for an abstract or a statement of purpose at the beginning; also look for a summary at the end.

—For a newspaper article, focus on the headline and the opening sentences, known as the *lead*.

—Skim any headings and take a look at any charts, graphs, diagrams, or illustrations that might indicate the article's focus and scope.

PREVIEWING A WEB SITE

—Browse the home page. Do its contents and links seem relevant to your research question?

—Consider the reputation, credibility, and motive of the site's author. Is the site reputable enough to consider for further evaluation?

—Check to see if there is a note about when the site was last updated. For a current topic, some sites may be outdated.

—If the site looks promising, add it to the bookmarks or favorites list on your browser for easy access later.

NOTE: For advice on evaluating sources as you read them, see 47c.

47b Maintain a working bibliography.

Keep a record of any sources that you decide to consult. You will need this record, called a *working bibliography,* when you compile the list of works cited that will appear at the end of your paper. (See pp. 626, 639 for examples.) The working bibliography will contain more sources than you'll actually use and put in your list of works cited.

Traditionally, researchers recorded bibliographic information about sources on $3'' \times 5''$ cards that they sorted alphabetically before typing their list of works cited. (For an example, see p. 550.) Today, however, many researchers save time by printing out bibliographic information from the library's computer catalog and periodical indexes. (For an example, see p. 535.) Although this printed bibliographic information will not appear in the exact form required for entries in the list of works cited, it will usually contain all the information you need to create the list. That information is as follows.

FOR BOOKS

Call number

All authors; any editors or translators

Title and subtitle

Edition (if not the first)

Publishing information: city, publishing company, and date

FOR PERIODICAL ARTICLES

All authors of the article

Title and subtitle of the article

Title of the magazine, journal, or newspaper

Date and page numbers

Volume and issue numbers, if relevant

FOR INTERNET SOURCES

All authors (or sponsors)

Title and subtitle of the material you want to use (if available) and title of the longer work (if applicable)

Date of publication (or latest revision) if available

Date you visited the site

Publishing information for any print version of the material: city, publisher, date, page numbers, and volume and issue numbers

URL (address of site) or other information needed to access the site

CAUTION: Punctuation, spelling, sometimes even capitalization must be exact to access Internet sites. To ensure accuracy, you may wish to cut and paste the address from your browser into a computer file.

NOTE: For the exact bibliographic format to be used in the final paper, see 53c.

TRADITIONAL BIBLIOGRAPHY CARD

QL 737.C23 H355 1992

Hansen, Kevin. _Cougar: The American Lion._
    Flagstaff: Northland, 1992.

47c   Read with a critical eye.

When you read critically, you are not necessarily judging an author's work harshly; you are simply examining its assumptions, assessing its evidence, and weighing its conclusions. (See also 6.)

Distinguishing between primary and secondary sources

As you begin assessing the evidence in a text, consider whether you are reading a primary or a secondary source. Primary sources are original documents such as speeches, diaries, novels, legislative bills, laboratory studies, field research reports, or eyewitness accounts. Secondary sources are commentaries on primary sources.

A primary source for Karen Shaw, whose research paper appears beginning on page 627, was an article by Patricia Marks Greenfield and E. Sue Savage-Rumbaugh reporting experiments with the pygmy chimpanzee Kanzi. Shaw also consulted Flora Davis's book *Eloquent Animals*, a secondary source that reports on the studies of several researchers.

Although a primary source is not necessarily more reliable than a secondary source, it has the advantage of being a firsthand account. Naturally, you can better evaluate what a secondary source says if you have first read any primary sources it discusses.

Being alert for signs of bias

Both in print and online, some publishers and authors are more objective than others. If you were exploring the conspiracy theories surrounding the Kennedy assassination, for example, you wouldn't look to a supermarket tabloid such as the *National Enquirer* for answers. You would rely instead on newspapers and magazines with a national reputation for fair and objective reporting. Even publications that are considered reputable, however, can be editorially biased. For example, *USA Today, National Review,* and *Ms.* are all credible sources, but they are also likely to interpret certain events quite differently from one another. If you are uncertain of a particular publication's special interests, check *Magazines for Libraries* and *Book Review Digest.*

Like publishers, some authors are more objective than others. No authors are altogether objective, of course, since they are human beings with their own life experiences, values, and beliefs. But if you have reason to believe that an author is particularly biased, you will want to assess his or her arguments with special care. Here are some questions worth asking.

—Do the author and publisher have reputations for accurate and balanced reporting?

—Does the author or publisher have political leanings or religious views that could affect objectivity?

—Is the author or publisher associated with a special-interest group, such as Greenpeace or the National Rifle Association, that might see only one side of an issue?

—How fairly does the author treat opposing views?

—Does the author's language show signs of bias? (See 7g.)

For guidelines on evaluating Web sites, see page 553.

Assessing the author's argument

In nearly all subjects worth writing about, there is some element of argument, so don't be surprised to encounter experts who disagree. When you find areas of disagreement, you will want to read your sources' arguments with special care, testing them with your own critical intelligence. Questions such as the following can help you weigh the strengths and weaknesses of each author's argument.

Evaluating a Web site

It is a fairly quick and easy job to track down numerous potentially useful sources on the World Wide Web. Evaluating those sources, however, requires additional time. After previewing a Web site (see p. 548) and considering the advice given in 47c for all sources, take the following additional steps when working with Web sources.

AUTHORITY

Can you determine the author of the site? Is the author of the site knowledgeable and credible? Does the site offer links to the author's home page, résumé, or e-mail address?

OBJECTIVITY

Who, if anyone, sponsors the site? Note that a site's domain name always specifies the type of group hosting the site: commercial (.com), educational (.edu), organizational (.org), governmental (.gov), military (.mil), or network (.net).

AUDIENCE AND PURPOSE

Who is the intended audience of the site? Why is the information available: to argue a position? to sell a product? to inform readers?

DOCUMENTATION

On the Internet, traditional methods of documentation are often replaced with links to original sources. Whenever possible, check out a linked source to confirm its authority.

QUALITY OF PRESENTATION

Consider the design and navigation of the site. Is it well laid out and easy to use? Do its links work, and are they up-to-date and relevant? Is the material well written and relatively free of errors?

—What is the author's central claim or thesis?

—How does the author support this claim—with relevant and sufficient evidence or with just a few anecdotes or emotional examples?

—Are statistics accurate? Have they been used fairly? (It is possible to "lie" with statistics by using them selectively or by omitting mathematical details.)

—Are any of the author's assumptions questionable?

—Does the author consider opposing arguments and refute them persuasively? (See pp. 166–67.)

Remaining objective

When reading, you will need to be aware of your own beliefs and biases as well as those presented in the materials you are researching. Be careful not to dismiss an article simply because it doesn't mesh with your central claim or thesis. By the same token, make certain that you are critical enough of sources that do coincide with your thesis.

Be prepared to encounter logical, well-written material on both sides of an issue, and be ready to rethink your own position if you find enough persuasive evidence to the contrary.

48

Managing information; avoiding plagiarism

Once you have settled on a reasonable number of sources worth reading, you will need to choose a systematic method for managing the information gleaned from those sources.

With a systematic method, you will save yourself time. In addition, a systematic method will help you remember later, when you are drafting your paper, just which words and phrases belong to your sources and which are your own.

This is a crucial matter, for if any exact language from your sources finds its way into your final draft without quotation marks and proper documentation, you will be guilty of plagiarism, a serious academic offense. (See 48b and 50b.)

48a As you read, manage information systematically.

Not too long ago, most researchers used note cards to keep track of information. Today, however, photocopy machines and computers are changing the ways researchers work.

Using traditional note cards

If you decide to use note cards, purchase a large stack of $3'' \times 5''$ or $4'' \times 6''$ cards. Write one note on each card so you can shuffle and reshuffle the cards in different orders later as you experiment with the organization of your paper.

In the upper right corner of the card, put the last name of the author of the source, along with a short title if you are using more than one source by the author. In the upper left corner, put a subject label. If you have read enough to form a preliminary outline, use the subdivisions from your outline as subject headings on your cards.

For sample note cards, along with important advice about avoiding plagiarism while taking notes, see 48b.

Working with photocopies and printouts

Most libraries provide photocopy machines so that you can copy pages from reference books and magazine articles and other sources that can't be removed from the library. In addition, many computer indexes now allow you to print full texts of articles.

Working with photocopies and other "hard copy" has several advantages. It saves you time spent in the library. It allows you to highlight key passages, perhaps even color-coding the highlighted passages to reflect divisions in your outline. And you can annotate the text with notes in the margins and get a head start on the process of taking notes.

Finally, working with hard copy reduces the chances of unintentional plagiarism (see 48b), since you will be able to compare your use of a source in your paper with the actual source, not just with your notes.

NOTE: When researching on the Internet, you will probably find it easier to print out pages of text to work from rather than to take notes from a computer screen. In addition, it is useful to keep a hard copy of sources found on the Internet because a source may not be accessible at a future date. Be sure that your printed materials include the site's URL, the date of access, and the full title of the site so you can include them in your list of works cited. (See p. 557 for an example of a printout.)

Using computer files

Computer files are a useful alternative to traditional note cards, especially if you prefer to type rather than to handwrite your notes. Once you have a sense of the natural subdivisions of your topic, you can create a file for each one.

For his paper on the mountain lion, John Garcia created files with these labels: endangered, resurgence, attacks on humans, California propositions, and wildlife management. Working mainly with photocopied articles, Garcia typed notes into each of these files.

CAUTION: Although you can download information from the Internet into your computer files and patch parts of it into your own work, be extremely careful. Some researchers have plagiarized their sources unintentionally because they lost track of which words came from a source and which were their own. To prevent unintentional plagiarism, put quotation marks around any text that you have patched into your own work, and make sure to introduce the quoted text with a signal phrase naming the author.

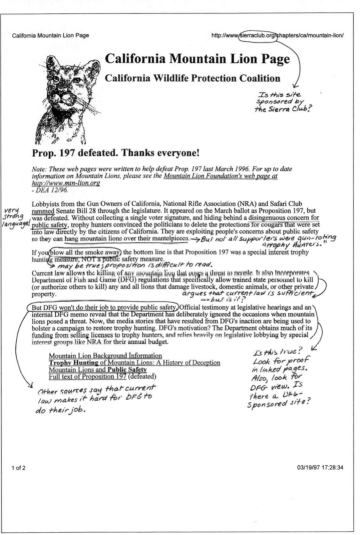

48b   As you take notes, avoid unintentional plagiarism.

You will discover that it is amazingly easy to borrow too much language from a source as you take notes. Do not allow this to happen. You are guilty of the academic offense known as *plagiarism* if you half-copy the author's sentences—either by mixing the author's phrases with your own without using quotation marks or by plugging your synonyms into the author's sentence structure. (For examples of this kind of plagiarism, see 50b.)

To prevent unintentional borrowing, resist the temptation to look at the source as you take notes—except when you are quoting. Keep the source close by so you can check for accuracy, but don't try to put ideas in your own words with the source's sentences in front of you. You should also follow this advice while drafting your paper. (See the chart on p. 583.)

There are four kinds of note taking: summarizing, paraphrasing, quoting, and writing personal comments. When you summarize, paraphrase, or quote, be sure to include exact page references, since you will need the page numbers later if you use the information in your paper.

Summarizing without plagiarizing

Summarizing is the best kind of preliminary note taking because it is the fastest. A summary condenses information, perhaps reducing a chapter to a short paragraph or a paragraph to a single sentence. A summary should be written in your own words; if you use phrases from the source, put them in quotation marks.

Here is a passage from an original source read by Karen Shaw in researching her essay on apes and language. Following the passage is Shaw's note card summarizing the source.

ORIGINAL SOURCE

Public and scientific interest in the question of apes' ability to use language first soared some 15 years ago when Washoe, a chimpanzee raised like a human child by R. Allen Gardner and Beatrice Gardner of the University of Nevada, learned to make hand signs for many words and even seemed to be making short sentences.

Since then researchers have taught many chimpanzees and a few gorillas and orangutans to "talk" using the sign language of deaf humans, plastic chips or, like Kanzi, keyboard symbols. Washoe, Sarah, a chimpanzee trained by David Premack of the University of Pennsylvania, and Koko, a gorilla trained by the psychologist Francine Patterson, became media stars.

—Eckholm, "Pygmy Chimp Readily
Learns Language Skill," p. B7

SUMMARY

Types of languages   *Eckholm, "Pygmy"*

The ape experiments began in the 1970s with Washoe, who learned sign language. In later experiments some apes learned to communicate using plastic chips or symbols on a keyboard (B7).

Paraphrasing without plagiarizing

Like a summary, a paraphrase is written in your own words; but whereas a summary reports significant information in fewer words than the source, a paraphrase retells the information in roughly the same number of words. If you retain occasional choice phrases from the source, use quotation marks so you'll know later which phrases are your own.

As you read the note card on this page, which paraphrases the first paragraph of Shaw's original source (see p. 559), notice that the language is significantly different from that in the original. Working with this note card, Shaw was in no danger of unintentional plagiarism.

Using quotation marks to avoid plagiarizing

A quotation consists of the exact words from a source. In your notes, put all quoted material in quotation marks; do not trust yourself to remember later which words, phrases,

PARAPHRASE

> *Washoe*   *Eckholm, "Pygmy"*
>
> *A chimpanzee named Washoe, trained in the 1970s by U. of Nevada professors R. Allen and Beatrice Gardner, learned words in the sign language of the deaf and may even have created short sentences (B7).*

QUOTATION

> *Washoe*   *Eckholm, "Pygmy"*
>
> *Washoe, trained by R. Allen and Beatrice Gardner, "learned to make hand signs for many words and even seemed to be making short sentences" (B7).*

and passages you have quoted and which are your own. When you quote, be sure to copy the words of your source exactly, including punctuation and capitalization.

Quotations should be reserved for special purposes: to use a writer's especially vivid or expressive wording, to allow an expert to explain a complex matter clearly, or to let critics of an opinion object in their own words. If you find yourself quoting a great deal in your notes, you are probably wasting time, because your final essay should not contain excessive quotations. (See 51.)

At the top of this page is an example of a note card with a quotation from Shaw's original source (p. 559).

Jotting down personal comments

At unexpected moments in your reading, you will experience the lucky accidents typical of the creative process: flashes of insight, connections with other reading, sharp questions, a

PERSONAL COMMENT

> *Types of training*
>
> *Washoe (and I think Koko) were raised almost like children, not in a laboratory setting. Does the setting affect the apes' performance? What about scientific objectivity?*

more restricted topic, ways to set up the arguments of two opposing positions, a vivid scenario. Write these inspirations down before you forget them. An example of such a personal note appears above.

49

Planning and drafting the paper

A look through your notes will probably suggest many ways to focus and organize your material. Before you begin writing, you should decide on a tentative thesis and construct a preliminary outline or you will flounder among the possibilities. Remain flexible, however, because you may need to revise your approach later. Writing about a subject is a way of learning about it; as you write, your understanding of your subject will almost certainly deepen.

49a   Form a tentative thesis.

Once you have read a variety of sources and considered all sides of your issue, you are ready to form a tentative thesis: a one-sentence (or occasionally a two-sentence) statement of your central idea. (See also 2a and 49d.) The thesis expresses not just your opinion, but your informed, reasoned judgment. Your paper will provide evidence to support that judgment.

In a research paper, your thesis will answer the central research question that you posed earlier (see 46a). Here, for example, are John Garcia's and Karen Shaw's research questions and their tentative thesis statements.

RESEARCH QUESTION

Should California voters repeal the California Wildlife Protection Act, which prevents the state fish and game commission from thinning the mountain lion population?

TENTATIVE THESIS

California voters should repeal the California Wildlife Protection Act because wildlife management would reduce the number of lion attacks on humans and in the long run would also protect the lions.

RESEARCH QUESTION

To what extent have the great apes--gorillas, chimpanzees, and orangutans--demonstrated language abilities akin to those of humans?

TENTATIVE THESIS

The great apes resemble humans in language abilities more than researchers once believed,

and evidence is mounting that bonobos (pygmy chimpanzees) can understand and perhaps even create
sentences.

49b Sketch a rough outline.

Before committing yourself to a detailed outline, experiment
with alternatives. Shuffle and reshuffle your note cards or
rearrange your computer notes to get a feel for the possibilities. Then create a simple list-style outline beneath your
thesis. For his outline, John Garcia used phrases similar to
the titles of the computer files into which he had typed his
notes.

> Thesis: California voters should repeal the Cali-
> fornia Wildlife Protection Act because
> wildlife management would reduce the num-
> ber of lion attacks on humans and in the
> long run would also protect the lions.
> --The once-endangered mountain lion
> --Resurgence of the mountain lion
> --Human attacks on the rise
> --The 1996 California referendum
> --Wildlife management: a reasonable
> solution

Karen Shaw sorted her notes into three batches: early
ape language studies, recent studies, and the philosophical
implications of the ape language research. Then she drafted
the following brief sentence outline.

> Thesis: The great apes resemble humans in language
> abilities more than researchers once be-
> lieved, and evidence is mounting that bono-

bos (pygmy chimpanzees) can understand and
perhaps even create sentences.

  I. Early ape language studies showed that apes
could acquire significant language skills but
failed to prove that they could create sentences.

  II. Recent research demonstrates that bonobos can
understand and perhaps even create sentences.

  III. Evidence suggests that linguistic abilities
in humans and apes are part of a continuum.

As she drafted each of the three parts of her paper, Shaw
sorted her information into smaller batches, which became
the basis for her final outline (see pp. 628–29).

49c Draft the paper in your own voice.

With a tentative thesis, a preliminary outline, and plenty of
notes, you are ready to write a first draft. Keep it rough and
keep it moving. Don't let your wish for perfect sentences stall
you at this stage. First write down your ideas and their supporting details; polish your sentences later. Writing rapidly
usually produces a more natural, individual voice and helps
you avoid echoing the language of your sources.

A chatty, breezy voice is usually not welcome in academic papers, but neither is a stuffy, pretentious style or a
timid, unsure one.

TOO CHATTY   The cougar is a lean, mean killing machine.

BETTER   The cougar is so strong, fast, and agile that it
can bring down prey five or six times its size.

TOO STUFFY   It has been determined that mountain lion on-
slaughts on humans are ascending exponen-
tially.

BETTER	Statistics show that mountain lion attacks on humans are increasing at a dramatic rate.
TOO TIMID	Although I am no expert, it seems to me that California laws should treat the mountain lion just like any other species that is not endangered.
BETTER	California laws should treat the mountain lion just like any other species that is not endangered.

Many researchers find that writing only from their outlines (rather than directly from their notes) allows them to write in their own voices without mimicking the style of their sources. In writing their first draft, they refer to their notes only for direct quotations and specific statistics. Other writers prefer to work more closely with their notes, consulting them frequently as they write. Whichever method you use, make sure that your sentences are written in your own words, not half-copied from your sources. (See 50b.)

49d   Include your thesis in the introduction.

One or two paragraphs are usually enough introduction for research papers in undergraduate courses. Most readers don't want a great deal of background; they want you to get to the point right away.

Readers are accustomed to seeing the thesis statement—the paper's main point—at the end of the first or second paragraph. The advantage of putting it in the first paragraph is that readers can immediately grasp your purpose. The advantage of delaying the thesis until the second paragraph is that you can provide a fuller context for your point. If your thesis appears in the third or fourth paragraph, however, you are providing too much context—at the risk of burying your main idea in a place where readers may miss it.

As you draft your introduction, you may change your preliminary thesis, either because you have refined (or even changed) your main point or because new wording fits more smoothly into the context you have provided for it. For example, John Garcia decided that although he was in favor of wildlife management, he opposed sport hunting. His revised thesis reflects this refined view.

TENTATIVE THESIS

California voters should repeal the California Wildlife Protection Act because wildlife management would reduce the number of lion attacks on humans and in the long run would also protect the lions.

FINAL THESIS

If California politicians decide to reconsider the mountain lion issue, a future proposition should retain the ban on sport hunting but allow the fish and game commission to control the population. Wildlife management would reduce the number of lion attacks on humans and in the long run would also protect the lions.

Karen Shaw didn't change the view expressed in her tentative thesis, but her revised thesis expresses her view more fully and ties it to sentences that appear earlier in her introduction.

TENTATIVE THESIS

The great apes resemble humans in language abilities more than researchers once believed, and evidence is mounting that bonobos (pygmy chimpanzees) can understand and perhaps even create sentences.

FINAL THESIS

These and hundreds of similar scenes played out over the last thirty years demonstrate that the great apes (gorillas, orangutans, chimpanzees, and pygmy chimpanzees) resemble humans in language abilities far more than researchers once believed. And evidence is mounting, despite opposition from some linguists and psychologists, that bonobos (pygmy chimpanzees) can understand and perhaps even create sentences.

In addition to stating your thesis and establishing a context for it, an introduction should hook readers. Sometimes you can connect your topic to something recently in the news or bring readers up to date about changing ideas. Other strategies are to pose a puzzling problem or to open with a startling statistic. John Garcia's paper begins like this: "On April 23, 1994, as Barbara Schoener was jogging in the Sierra foothills of California, she was pounced on from behind by a mountain lion." Karen Shaw's paper opens with scenes describing gorillas and chimpanzees engaged in language lessons. (For the full introductions to Garcia's and Shaw's papers, see pp. 616 and 630.)

49e Provide organizational cues.

Even if you are working with a good outline, your paper will appear disorganized unless you provide organizational cues: topic sentences, transitions between major sections of the paper, and perhaps headings.

John Garcia uses headings to help readers follow his organization (see pp. 616–26). Although Karen Shaw does not use headings, her paper is easy to follow because she begins each paragraph with a clear topic sentence and she links larger chunks of text with transitional sentences. Some of the annotations in the margins of Shaw's paper (pp. 627–40) call attention to such organizational cues.

For more about topic sentences, transitions, and headings, see 4a, 4e, and 5a.

50

Citing sources; avoiding plagiarism

50a Use a consistent system for citing sources. (See 53 for important details.)

In a research paper, you will be drawing on the work of other writers, and you must document their contributions by citing your sources. You must include a citation when you quote from a source, when you summarize or paraphrase a source, and when you borrow facts and ideas from a source that are not common knowledge. (See also 50b.)

The various academic disciplines use their own editorial styles for citing sources. Most English professors prefer the Modern Language Association's system of in-text citations, the system used in examples throughout sections 50 and 51. Here, briefly, is how an MLA in-text citation usually works:

1. The source is introduced by a signal phrase that names its author.
2. The material being cited is followed by a page number in parentheses.
3. At the end of the paper, a list of works cited (arranged alphabetically according to the authors' last names) gives complete publishing information about the source.

SAMPLE IN-TEXT CITATION

According to science writer Eugene Linden, some psychologists have adopted the oddly unscientific attitude that "the idea of the language capacity of apes is so preposterous that it should not be investigated at all" (11).

Researched writing

SAMPLE ENTRY IN THE LIST OF WORKS CITED

Linden, Eugene. <u>Silent Partners: The Legacy of the Ape
Language Experiments</u>. New York: Times, 1986.

Handling an MLA citation is not always this simple. For a detailed discussion of possible variations, see 53c. Section 53 is easy to find because its pages are marked with a vertical band in teal.

If your instructor has asked you to use the American Psychological Association (APA) style of in-text citation or the *Chicago Manual of Style* system of footnotes and endnotes, consult 56, where you will also find a list of style manuals used in various disciplines.

50b Avoid plagiarism.

Your research paper is a collaboration between you and your sources. To be fair and ethical, you must acknowledge your debt to the writers of these sources. If you don't, you are guilty of plagiarism, a serious academic offense. Universities have been known to withdraw graduate degrees from students who have plagiarized. Professional writers sue for (and often get) thousands of dollars when they discover that someone has plagiarized their work.

Three different acts are considered plagiarism: (1) failing to cite quotations and borrowed ideas, (2) failing to enclose borrowed language in quotation marks, and (3) failing to put summaries and paraphrases in your own words.

Citing quotations and borrowed ideas

You must of course document all direct quotations. You must also cite any ideas borrowed from a source: paraphrases of sentences, summaries of paragraphs or chapters, statistics and little-known facts, and tables, graphs, or diagrams.

The only exception is common knowledge — information that your readers could find in any number of general sources because it is commonly known. For example, the current population of the United States is common knowledge in such fields as sociology and economics; Freud's theory of the unconscious is common knowledge in the field of psychology.

As a rule, when you have seen certain information repeatedly in your reading, you don't need to cite it. However, when information has appeared in only one or two sources or when it is controversial, you should cite it. If a topic is new to you and you are not sure what is considered common knowledge or what is a matter of controversy, ask someone with expertise. When in doubt, cite the source.

Enclosing borrowed language in quotation marks

To indicate that you are using a source's exact phrases or sentences, you must enclose them in quotation marks unless they have been set off from the text by indenting. (See p. 578.) To omit the quotation marks is to claim — falsely — that the language is your own. Such an omission is plagiarism even if you have cited the source.

ORIGINAL SOURCE

No animal has done more to renew interest in animal intelligence than a beguiling, bilingual bonobo named Kanzi, who has the grammatical abilities of a 2½-year-old child and a taste for movies about cavemen.

—Eugene Linden, "Animals," p. 57

PLAGIARISM

According to Eugene Linden, no animal has done more to renew interest in animal intelligence than a beguiling, bilingual bonobo named Kanzi, who has

the grammatical abilities of a 2 1/2-year-old child
and a taste for movies about cavemen (57).

BORROWED LANGUAGE IN QUOTATION MARKS

According to Eugene Linden, "No animal has done
more to renew interest in animal intelligence than
a beguiling, bilingual bonobo named Kanzi, who has
the grammatical abilities of a 2 1/2-year-old child
and a taste for movies about cavemen" (57).

Putting summaries and paraphrases in your own words

When you summarize or paraphrase, it is not enough to
name the source; you must restate the source's meaning
using your own language. (See also 48b.) You are guilty of
plagiarism if you half-copy the author's sentences—either
by mixing the author's well-chosen phrases without using
quotation marks or by plugging your own synonyms into the
author's sentence structure. The following paraphrases are
plagiarized—even though the source is cited—because their
language is too close to that of the original source.

ORIGINAL SOURCE

If the existence of a signing ape was unsettling for linguists, it
was also startling news for animal behaviorists.

—Davis, *Eloquent Animals*, p. 26

UNACCEPTABLE BORROWING OF PHRASES

The existence of a signing ape unsettled linguists
and startled animal behaviorists (Davis 26).

UNACCEPTABLE BORROWING OF STRUCTURE

If the presence of a sign-language-using chimp was
disturbing for scientists studying language, it
was also surprising to scientists studying animal
behavior (Davis 26).

To avoid plagiarizing an author's language, resist the temptation to look at the source while you are summarizing or paraphrasing. Close the book, write from memory, and then open the book to check for accuracy. This technique prevents you from being captivated by the words on the page.

ACCEPTABLE PARAPHRASES

When they learned of an ape's ability to use sign language, both linguists and animal behaviorists were taken by surprise (Davis 26).

According to Flora Davis, both linguists and animal behaviorists were unprepared for the news that a chimp could communicate with its trainers through sign language (26).

51

Integrating information from sources

With practice, you will learn to integrate information from sources — quotations, summaries, paraphrases, and facts — smoothly into your own text.

51a Use signal phrases to introduce quotations; limit your use of quotations.

Using signal phrases

Readers need to move from your own words to the words of a source without feeling a jolt. Avoid dropping quotations into the text without warning. Instead, provide clear signal phrases, usually including the author's name, to prepare readers for a quotation.

DROPPED QUOTATION

```
Perhaps even more significant is the pattern that
Kanzi developed on his own in combining various
lexigrams. "When he gave an order combining two
symbols for action--such as 'chase' and 'hide'--
it was important for him that the first action--
'chase'--be done first" (Gibbons 1561).
```

QUOTATION WITH SIGNAL PHRASE

```
Perhaps even more significant is the pattern that
Kanzi developed on his own in combining various
lexigrams. According to Ann Gibbons, "When he gave
an order combining two symbols for action--such as
'chase' and 'hide'--it was important for him that
the first action--'chase'--be done first" (1561).
```

To avoid monotony, try to vary both the language and the placement of your signal phrases. The following models suggest a range of possibilities.

In the words of researcher Herbert Terrace, " . . . "

As Flora Davis has noted, " . . . "

The Gardners, Washoe's trainers, point out that " . . . "

" . . . ," claims linguist Noam Chomsky.

Psychologist H. S. Terrace offers an odd argument for this view: " . . . "

Terrace answers these objections with the following analysis: " . . . "

When your signal phrase includes a verb, choose one that is appropriate in the context. Is your source arguing a point, making an observation, reporting a fact, drawing a conclusion, refuting an argument, or stating a belief? By choosing an appropriate verb, such as one on the following list, you can make your source's stance clear.

acknowledges	comments	endorses	reasons
adds	compares	grants	refutes
admits	confirms	illustrates	rejects
agrees	contends	implies	reports
argues	declares	insists	responds
asserts	denies	notes	suggests
believes	disputes	observes	thinks
claims	emphasizes	points out	writes

Limiting your use of quotations

It is tempting to insert many long quotations in your paper and to use your own words only for connecting passages. This is an especially strong temptation if you feel that the authors of your sources are better writers than you are. But do not quote excessively. It is almost impossible to integrate numerous long quotations smoothly into your own text. In addition, heavy reliance on the words of others gives readers the impression that you cannot think for yourself.

Except for the following legitimate uses of quotations, use your own words to summarize and paraphrase your sources and to explain your own ideas.

WHEN TO USE QUOTATIONS

—When language is especially vivid or expressive

—When exact wording is needed for technical accuracy

—When it is important to let the debaters of an issue explain their positions in their own words

—When the words of an important authority lend weight to an argument

—When language of a source is the topic of your discussion (as in an analysis or interpretation)

It is not always necessary to quote full sentences from a source. To reduce your reliance on the words of others, you can often integrate a phrase from a source into your own sentence structure.

```
Bruce Bower reports that Kanzi practices "simple
grammatical ordering rules," such as putting
actions before objects (140).

Perhaps the best summation of the current state of
ape language studies comes from biologist Robert
Seyfarth, who writes that the line separating
humans from other animals "remains hastily drawn,
somewhere between the word and the sentence" (18).
```

Using the ellipsis mark and brackets

Two useful marks of punctuation, the ellipsis mark and brackets, allow you to keep quoted material to a minimum and to integrate it smoothly into your text.

THE ELLIPSIS MARK   To condense a quoted passage, you can use the ellipsis mark (three periods, with spaces between) to indicate that you have omitted words. What remains must be grammatically complete.

MLA now recommends putting brackets around ellipsis dots. These brackets make clear that the ellipsis dots do not appear in the original work you are quoting. You may wish to check with your instructor before following this new MLA guideline. If you are using a citation style other than MLA (such as APA), do not use brackets around ellipsis dots.

> In a recent <u>New York Times</u> article, Erik Eckholm
> reports that "a 4-year-old pygmy chimpanzee
> [. . .] has demonstrated what scientists say are
> the most humanlike linguistic skills ever
> documented in another animal" (A1).

The writer has omitted the words *at a research center near Atlanta,* which appeared in the original.

On the rare occasions when you want to omit one or more full sentences, use a period before the three ellipsis dots.

> According to Wade, the horse Clever Hans "could
> apparently count by tapping out numbers with his
> hoof. [. . .] Clever Hans owes his celebrity to
> his master's innocence. Von Osten sincerely
> believed he had taught Hans to solve arithmetical
> problems" (1349).

Ordinarily, do not use an ellipsis mark at the beginning or at the end of a quotation. Your readers will understand that the quoted material is taken from a longer passage, so such marks are not necessary. The only exception occurs when words at the end of the final quoted sentence have been dropped. In such cases, put bracketed ellipsis dots before the closing quotation mark and parenthetical reference: [. . .]" (103).

Obviously you should not use an ellipsis mark to distort the meaning of your source.

BRACKETS   Brackets (square parentheses) allow you to insert words of your own into quoted material. You can insert words in brackets to explain a confusing reference or to keep a sentence grammatical in your context.

> Robert Seyfarth reports that "Premack [a scientist
> at the University of Pennsylvania] taught a seven-

```
year-old chimpanzee, Sarah, that the word for
'apple' was a small, plastic triangle" (13).
```

Setting off long quotations

When you quote more than four typed lines of prose or more than three lines of poetry, set off the quotation by indenting it one inch (or ten spaces) from the left margin. Use the normal right margin and do not single-space.

Long quotations should be introduced by an informative sentence, usually followed by a colon. Quotation marks are unnecessary because the indented format tells readers that the words are taken directly from the source.

```
Desmond describes how Washoe tried signing to the
other apes when the Gardners returned her to an
ape colony in Oklahoma:
          One particularly memorable day, a snake
          spread terror through the castaways on
          the ape island, and all but one fled in
          panic. This male sat absorbed, staring
          intently at the serpent. Then Washoe was
          seen running over signing to him "come,
          hurry up." (42)
```

Notice that at the end of an indented quotation the parenthetical citation goes outside the final period.

Quoting a source quoted in another source

Occasionally you may want to quote a source that was quoted in a book or article you consulted. You can do this by putting the abbreviation "qtd. in" within the parenthetical citation, as in the example below. Make sure, however, that you integrate the quotation into your text with your own signal phrase. Do not borrow the signal phrase used by the author of the book or article you consulted.

SOURCE YOU CONSULTED

Terrace has his backers. According to linguist, semanticist, and anthropologist Thomas A. Sebeok of the University of Indiana, ape-language researchers fall into "three categories: self-delusional and self-deceptive, fraudulent, and Herb Terrace . . . we agree wholeheartedly."   — Joel Greenberg, "Ape Talk: More Than 'Pigeon' English?," p. 229

YOUR OWN SIGNAL PHRASE

One of the harshest critics of the ape language studies, Thomas A. Sebeok, sarcastically dismisses all researchers except Herbert Terrace by placing the researchers into three categories: "self-delusional and self-deceptive, fraudulent, and Herb Terrace . . . we agree wholeheartedly" (qtd. in Greenberg 229).

To borrow Joel Greenberg's signal phrase—*According to linguist, semanticist and anthropologist Thomas A. Sebeok of the University of Indiana*—without placing it in quotation marks would be plagiarism. (See 50b.) If you placed Greenberg's signal phrase in quotation marks to avoid plagiarism, however, you would find it extremely difficult to integrate the quoted signal phrase *and* the quotation *and* the name of the author smoothly into your own text. The solution is to use your own signal phrase, as in the example just given.

51b   Use signal phrases to introduce most summaries and paraphrases.

Introduce most summaries and paraphrases with a signal phrase that names the author and places the material in context. Readers will then understand that everything between the signal phrase and the parenthetical citation summarizes or paraphrases the cited source.

Without the signal phrase (underlined) in the following example, readers might think that only the last sentence is being cited, when in fact the whole paragraph is based on the source.

> Recent studies at the Yerkes Primate Center in Atlanta are breaking new ground. <u>Researchers Patricia Greenfield and Sue Savage-Rumbaugh report that</u> the pygmy chimp Kanzi seems to understand simple grammatical rules about lexigram order. For instance, Kanzi learned that in two-word utterances action precedes object, an ordering also used by human children at the two-word stage. What is impressive, say Greenfield and Savage-Rumbaugh, is that in addition to being semantically related, most of Kanzi's lexigram combinations are original (556).

There are times, however, when a signal phrase naming the author is not necessary. Most readers will understand, for example, that the citation at the end of the following passage applies to the entire anecdote, not just the last sentence.

> One afternoon, Koko the gorilla, who was often bored with language lessons, stubbornly and repeatedly signaled "red" in American Sign Language when asked the color of a white towel. She did this even though she had correctly identified the color white many times before. At last the gorilla plucked a bit of red lint from the towel and showed it to her trainer (Patterson and Linden 80-81).

Notice that when there is no signal phrase naming the author, the authors' names must be included in the parentheses along with the page number.

51c   With statistics and other facts, a signal phrase may not be needed.

When you are citing a statistic or other specific fact, a signal phrase is often not necessary. In most cases, readers will understand that the citation refers to the statistic or fact (not the whole paragraph).

> By 1991 Kanzi, a ten-year-old pygmy chimp, had
> learned to communicate about two hundred symbols
> on the computerized board that he carries with him
> (Lewin 51).

There is nothing wrong, however, with using a signal phrase to introduce a statistic or other fact.

> Roger Lewin reports that by 1991 the ten-year-old
> pygmy chimp Kanzi had learned to communicate about
> two hundred symbols on the computerized board that
> he carries with him (51).

52

Revising your draft

When you are revising any paper, it is a good idea to concentrate first on global elements — focus, organization, content, and audience appeal — and then turn to matters of style and correctness. (See 3b.) With a research paper, this strategy is especially important because reviewing your use of quotations and other source material requires considerable attention to detail.

On pages 582–83 is a two-part chart for reviewing the draft of a research paper: one part on global revision, the other on proper handling of sources.

Reviewing a research paper: Global revisions

FOCUS

—Is the thesis stated clearly enough? Is it placed where readers will notice it?

—Does each paragraph support the thesis?

ORGANIZATION

—Can readers follow the organization? Would headings help?

—Do topic sentences signal new ideas? Do transitions help readers move from one major group of paragraphs to another?

—Are ideas presented in a logical order?

CONTENT

—Is the supporting material persuasive? Are the arguments strong enough to stand up to arguments of those who disagree with the thesis?

—Are the parts proportioned sensibly? Do the major ideas receive enough attention?

—Is the draft concise—free of irrelevant, unimportant, or repetitious material?

STYLE

—Is the voice appropriate—not too chatty, too stuffy, or too timid?

—Are the sentences clear, emphatic, and varied?

Reviewing a research paper: Use of sources

USE OF QUOTATIONS

—Is quoted material enclosed within quotation marks (unless it has been set off from the text)? (See 50b.)

—Is quoted language word-for-word accurate? If not, do brackets or ellipsis marks indicate the changes or omissions? (See pp. 576–77.)

—Does a clear signal phrase (usually naming the author) prepare readers for each quotation? (See 51a.)

—Does a parenthetical citation follow each quotation? (See 53a.)

USE OF SUMMARIES AND PARAPHRASES

—Are summaries and paraphrases free of plagiarized wording—not copied or half-copied from the source? (See 50b.)

—Are summaries and paraphrases documented with parenthetical citations? (See 53a.)

—Do readers know where the material being cited begins? In other words, does a signal phrase mark the beginning of the cited material unless the context makes clear exactly what is being cited? (See 51b.)

USE OF STATISTICS AND OTHER FACTS

Are statistics and facts (other than common knowledge) documented with parenthetical citations? (See 53a.)

—If there is no signal phrase, will readers understand exactly which facts are being cited? (See 51b.)

53

MLA documentation

The various academic disciplines use their own editorial styles for citing sources and for listing the works that have been cited. The style described in this section is that of the Modern Language Association (MLA), contained in the *MLA*

Handbook for Writers of Research Papers (5th ed., 1999), which recommends that citations be given in the text of the paper rather than in footnotes or endnotes.

If your instructor prefers the American Psychological Association (APA) style of in-text citation or the footnote or endnote system of the *Chicago Manual of Style*, consult 56, where you will also find a list of style manuals used in various disciplines.

53a MLA in-text citations

The MLA's in-text citations are made with a combination of signal phrases and parenthetical references. A signal phrase indicates that something taken from a source (such as a quotation, summary, or paraphrase) is about to be used; usually the signal phrase includes the author's name. The parenthetical reference includes at least a page number.

Citations in parentheses should be as concise as possible but complete enough so that readers can find the source in the list of works cited at the end of the paper, where works are listed alphabetically by authors' last names. The following models illustrate the form for the MLA style of citation.

1. AUTHOR NAMED IN A SIGNAL PHRASE Ordinarily, you should introduce the material being cited with a signal phrase that includes the author's name. In addition to preparing readers for the source, the signal phrase allows you to keep the parenthetical citation brief.

> In his study Turback claims that "regulated sport
> hunting has never driven any wild species into
> extinction" (74).

The signal phrase—"Turback claims"—provides the name of the author; the parenthetical citation gives the page number where the quoted words may be found. By looking up the author's last name in the list of works cited, readers will find complete information about the work's title, publisher, and place and date of publication.

Notice that the period follows the parenthetical citation. For the MLA technique for handling quotations that end in a question mark or an exclamation point, see pages 472–73.

2. AUTHOR NOT NAMED IN A SIGNAL PHRASE If the signal phrase does not include the author's name (or if there is no signal phrase), the author's last name must appear in parentheses along with the page number.

> Though the number of lion attacks on humans is low, the rate of increase of attacks since the 1960s is cause for serious concern (Rychnovsky 43).

Use no punctuation between the name and the page number.

3. TWO OR MORE WORKS BY THE SAME AUTHOR If your list of works cited includes two or more works by the same author, include the title of the work either in the signal phrase or in abbreviated form in the parenthetical reference.

> In Eloquent Animals, Flora Davis reports that a chimp at the Yerkes Primate Research Center "has combined words into sentences that she was never taught" (67).

> Flora Davis reports that a chimp at the Yerkes Primate Research Center "has combined words into sentences that she was never taught" (Eloquent 67).

The title of a book should be underlined, as in the examples, or italicized. The title of an article from a periodical should be put in quotation marks.

In the rare case when both the author and a short title must be given in parentheses, the citation should appear as follows:

```
Although the baby chimpanzee lived only for a few
hours, Washoe signed to it before it died (Davis,
Eloquent 42).
```

4. TWO OR THREE AUTHORS If your source has two or three authors, name them in the signal phrase or include them in the parenthetical reference.

```
Patterson and Linden agree that the gorilla Koko
acquired language more slowly than a normal speak-
ing child (89).
```

5. FOUR OR MORE AUTHORS If your source has four or more authors, include only the first author's name followed by "et al." (Latin for "and others") in the signal phrase or in the parenthetical reference.

```
The study was extended for two years, and only
after results were duplicated on both coasts did
the authors publish their results (Doe et al. 137).
```

6. CORPORATE AUTHOR When the author is a corporation or organization, either name the corporate author in the signal phrase or include a shortened version in the parentheses.

```
The Internal Revenue Service warns businesses that
deductions for "lavish and extravagant entertain-
ment" are not allowed (43).
```

7. UNKNOWN AUTHOR If the author is not given, either use the complete title in a signal phrase or use a short form of the title in the parentheses.

> In California, fish and game officials estimate
> that since 1972 lion numbers have increased from
> 2,400 to at least 6,000 ("Lion" A21).

8. AUTHORS WITH THE SAME LAST NAME If your list of works cited includes works by two or more authors with the same last name, include the first name of the author you are citing in the signal phrase or parenthetical reference.

> Both Lucy and Koko have been reported to lie
> (Adrian Desmond 102).

> Adrian Desmond has reported that Lucy was clever
> enough to see through the lies of her trainers (102).

9. A MULTIVOLUME WORK If your paper cites more than one volume of a multivolume work, indicate in the parentheses the volume you are referring to, followed by a colon.

> Terman's studies of gifted children reveal a pattern
> of accelerated language acquisition (2: 279).

If your paper cites only one volume of a multivolume work, you will include the volume number in the list of works cited at the end of the paper and will not need to include it in the parentheses.

10. A NOVEL, A PLAY, OR A POEM In citing literary sources, include information that will enable readers to find the passage in various editions of the work. For a novel, put the page number first and then, if possible, indicate the part or chapter in which the passage can be found.

Fitzgerald's narrator captures Gatsby in a moment
of isolation: "A sudden emptiness seemed to flow
now from the windows and the great doors, endowing
with complete isolation the figure of the host"
(56; ch. 3).

For a verse play, list the act, scene, and line numbers, separated by periods. Use arabic numerals unless your instructor prefers roman numerals.

In his famous advice to the players, Shakespeare's
Hamlet defines the purpose of theater, "whose
end, both at the first and now, was and
is, to hold, as 'twere, the mirror up to nature"
(3.2.21-23).

For a poem, cite the part (if there are a number of parts) and the line numbers, separated by periods.

When Homer's Odysseus came to the hall of Circe,
he found his men "mild / in her soft spell, fed on
her drug of evil" (10.209-11).

11. THE BIBLE   Include the title, the book of the Bible, and the chapter and verse numbers either in the signal phrase or in the parentheses.

Consider the words of Solomon: "If your enemy be
hungry, give him food to eat, and if he be
thirsty, give him to drink" (New American Bible,
Prov. 25.21).

12. A WORK IN AN ANTHOLOGY   Put the name of the author of the work (not the editor of the anthology) in the signal phrase or in the parentheses.

> At the end of Kate Chopin's "The Story of an
> Hour," Mrs. Mallard drops dead upon learning that
> her husband is alive. In the final irony of the
> story, doctors report that she has died of a "joy
> that kills" (25).

13. INDIRECT SOURCE   When a writer's or speaker's quoted words appear in a source written by someone else, begin the citation with the abbreviation "qtd. in."

> "When lion sightings become common," says
> Fjelline, "trouble often follows" (qtd. in
> Robinson 30).

14. AN ENTIRE WORK   To cite an entire work, use the author's name in a signal phrase or a parenthetical reference.

> Robinson succinctly describes the status of the
> mountain lion controversy in California.

15. TWO OR MORE WORKS   To cite more than one source to document a particular point, separate the citations with a semicolon.

> The dangers of mountain lions to humans have been
> well documented (Rychnovsky 40; Seidensticker 114;
> Williams 30).

Multiple citations can be distracting to readers, however, so the technique should not be overused. If you want to alert readers to several sources that discuss a particular topic, consider using an information note instead (discussed on p. 591).

16. A WORK WITHOUT PAGE NUMBERS   You may omit the page number if a work has no page numbers or if a work is organized alphabetically (as with encyclopedias). Some electronic sources use paragraph numbers instead of page numbers. For such sources, use the abbreviation "par." or "pars." in the parentheses: (Smith, par. 4).

53b   MLA information notes

Researchers who use the MLA system of parenthetical documentation may also use information notes for one of two purposes:

1. to provide additional material that might interrupt the flow of the paper yet is important enough to include;
2. to refer readers to any sources not discussed in the paper.

Information notes may be either footnotes or endnotes. Footnotes appear at the foot of the page; endnotes appear on a separate page at the end of the paper, just before the list of works cited. For either style, the notes are numbered consecutively throughout the paper. The text of the paper contains a raised arabic numeral that corresponds to the number of the note.

TEXT

California is not alone in its concern about mountain lion attacks.[1]

NOTE

[1] For a discussion of lion attacks in other western states, see Turback 34.

Directory to MLA works cited entries

NOTE: For sample papers documented with the MLA system, see pages 616–26, 627–40, and 667–74.

53c MLA list of works cited

A list of works cited, which appears at the end of your research paper, gives publication information for each of the sources you have cited in the paper. Start on a new page and title your list "Works Cited." Then, working from your bibliography cards or computer printouts (see 47b), list in alphabetical order all the sources that you have cited in the paper.

Unless your instructor asks for them, do not include sources not actually cited in the paper, even if you read them.

Alphabetize the list by the last names of the authors (or editors); if a work has no author or editor, alphabetize by the first word of the title other than *A, An,* or *The.*

Do not indent the first line of each works cited entry, but indent any additional lines one-half inch (or five spaces). This technique highlights the names by which the list has been alphabetized (see, for example, the list of works cited at the end of the student papers on pp. 626 and 639).

The following models illustrate the form that the Modern Language Association (MLA) recommends for works cited entries.

Books

1. BASIC FORMAT FOR A BOOK   For most books, arrange the information into three units, each followed by a period and one space: (1) the author's name, last name first; (2) the title and subtitle, underlined or italicized; and (3) the place of publication, the publisher, and the date.

```
Miller, William Lee. Arguing about Slavery: The
    Great Battle in the United States Congress.
    New York: Knopf, 1996.
```

The information is taken from the title page of the book and from the reverse side of the title page (the copyright page), not from the outside cover. The complete name of the publisher (in this case Alfred A. Knopf, Inc.) need not be given. You may use a short form as long as it is easily identifiable; omit terms such as *Press, Inc.,* and *Co.* except when naming university presses (Harvard UP, for example). The date to use in your works cited entry is the most recent copyright date.

2. TWO OR THREE AUTHORS   Name the authors in the order in which they are presented on the title page; reverse the name of only the first author.

> Elders, Joycelyn, and David Chanoff. <u>Joycelyn
> Elders: From Sharecropper's Daughter to
> Surgeon General of the United States of
> America</u>. New York: Morrow, 1996.

The names of three authors are separated by commas.

> Rosenfeld, Louis, Joseph Janes, and Martha Vander
> Holk. <u>The Internet Compendium: Subject Guides
> to Humanities Resources</u>. New York: Neal,
> 1995.

3. FOUR OR MORE AUTHORS   Cite only the first author, name reversed, followed by "et al." (Latin for "and others").

> Busbey, Arthur B., III, et al. <u>The Nature Company
> Guide to Rocks and Fossils</u>. New York: Time
> Life, 1996.

4. EDITORS   An entry for an editor is similar to that for an author except that the name is followed by a comma and the abbreviation "ed." for "editor." If there is more than one editor, use the abbreviation "eds." for "editors."

> Kitchen, Judith, and Mary Paumier Jones, eds.
> <u>In Short: A Collection of Brief Creative
> Nonfiction</u>. New York: Norton, 1996.

5. AUTHOR WITH AN EDITOR   Begin with the author and title, followed by the name of the editor. In this case the abbreviation "Ed." means "Edited by," so it is the same for one or multiple editors.

> Wells, Ida B. <u>The Memphis Diary</u>. Ed. Miriam
> DeCosta-Willis. Boston: Beacon, 1995.

6. TRANSLATION   List the entry under the name of the author, not the translator. After the title, write "Trans." (for "Translated by") and the name of the translator.

> Mahfouz, Naguib. <u>Arabian Nights and Days</u>. Trans.
> Denys Johnson-Davies. New York: Doubleday,
> 1995.

7. CORPORATE AUTHOR   List the entry under the name of the corporate author, even if it is also the name of the publisher.

> Bank of Boston. <u>Bank by Remote Control</u>. Boston:
> Bank of Boston, 1997.

8. UNKNOWN AUTHOR   Begin with the title. Alphabetize the entry by the first word of the title other than *A*, *An*, or *The*.

> <u>Oxford Essential World Atlas</u>. New York: Oxford UP,
> 1996.

9. TWO OR MORE WORKS BY THE SAME AUTHOR   If your list of works cited includes two or more works by the same author, use the author's name only for the first entry. For subsequent entries use three hyphens followed by a period. The three hyphens must stand for exactly the same name or names as in the preceding entry. List the titles in alphabetical order.

> Atwood, Margaret. <u>Alias Grace: A Novel</u>. New York:
> Doubleday, 1996.
>
> ---. <u>The Robber Bride</u>. New York: Doubleday, 1993.

10. EDITION OTHER THAN THE FIRST   If you are citing an edition other than the first, include the number of the edition after the title: 2nd ed., 3rd ed., and so on.

> Boyce, David George. The Irish Question and
> British Politics, 1868-1996. 2nd ed. New
> York: St. Martin's, 1996.

11. MULTIVOLUME WORK   Include the total number of volumes before the city and publisher, using the abbreviation "vols."

> Conway, Jill Ker, ed. Written by Herself. 2 vols.
> New York: Random, 1996.

If your paper cites only one of the volumes, write the volume number before the city and publisher and write the total number of volumes in the work after the date.

> Conway, Jill Ker, ed. Written by Herself. Vol 2.
> New York: Random, 1996. 2 vols.

12. ENCYCLOPEDIA OR DICTIONARY   Articles in well known dictionaries and encyclopedias are handled in abbreviated form. Simply list the author of the article (if there is one), the title of the article, the title of the reference work, the edition number, if any, and the date of the edition.

> "Botswana." Encyclopedia Americana. 1996.

Volume and page numbers are not necessary because the entries are arranged alphabetically and therefore are easy to locate.

If a reference work is not well known, provide full publication information as well.

13. THE BIBLE   Give the version of the Bible (underlined), the editor's name (if any), and publication information.

> New American Bible. New York: Catholic Book
> Publishing, 1970.

14. WORK IN AN ANTHOLOGY   Present the information in this order, with each item followed by a period: author of the selection; title of the selection; title of the anthology; editor of the anthology, preceded by "Ed."; city, publisher, and date; page numbers on which the selection appears.

> Malouf, David. "The Kyogle Line." The Oxford
>   Book of Travel Stories. Ed. Patricia Craig.
>   Oxford: Oxford UP, 1996. 390-96.

If an anthology gives the original publication information for a selection and if your instructor prefers that you use it, cite that information first. Follow with "Rpt. in" (for "Reprinted in"), the title, editor, and publication information for the anthology, and the page numbers in the anthology on which the selection appears.

> Rodriguez, Richard. "Late Victorians." Harper's
>   Oct. 1990: 57-66. Rpt. in The Best American
>   Essays 1991. Ed. Joyce Carol Oates. New York:
>   Ticknor, 1991. 119-34.

15. TWO OR MORE WORKS FROM THE SAME ANTHOLOGY   If you wish, you may cross-reference two or more works from the same anthology. Provide a separate entry for the anthology with complete publication information.

> Craig, Patricia, ed. The Oxford Book of Travel
>   Stories. Oxford: Oxford UP, 1996.

Then list each selection separately, giving the author and title of the selection followed by a cross-reference to the anthology. The cross-reference should include the last name of the editor of the anthology and the page numbers in the anthology on which the selection appears.

> Desai, Anita. "Scholar and Gypsy." Craig 251-73.
>
> Malouf, David. "The Kyogle Line." Craig 390-96.

16. FOREWORD, INTRODUCTION, PREFACE, OR AFTERWORD   If in your paper you quote from one of these elements, begin with the name of the writer of that element. Then identify the element being cited, neither underlined nor in quotation marks, followed by the title of the complete book, the book's author, and the book's editor, if any. After the publication information, give the page numbers on which the foreword, introduction, preface, or afterword appears.

> Murray, Charles. Foreword. Unfinished Business:
> A Civil Rights Strategy for America's Third
> Century. By Clint Bolick. San Francisco:
> Pacific Research Inst. for Public Policy,
> 1990. ix-xiii.

17. BOOK WITH A TITLE WITHIN ITS TITLE   If the book title contains a title normally underlined (or italicized), neither underline (or italicize) the internal title nor place it in quotation marks.

> Abbott, Keith. Downstream from Trout Fishing in
> America: A Memoir of Richard Brautigan. Santa
> Barbara: Capra, 1989.

If the title within the title is normally enclosed within quotation marks, retain the quotation marks and underline (or italicize) the entire title.

> Faulkner, Dewey R. Twentieth Century Interpreta-
> tions of "The Pardoner's Tale." Englewood
> Cliffs: Spectrum-Prentice, 1973.

18. BOOK IN A SERIES   Before the publication information, cite the series name as it appears on the title page followed by the series number, if any.

> Marshall, Judith. Literacy, Power, and Democracy
> in Mozambique: The Governance of Learning

```
from Colonization to the Present. Conflict
and Social Change Ser. Boulder: Westview, 1993.
```

19. REPUBLISHED BOOK   After the title of the book, cite the original publication date followed by the current publication information. If the republished book contains new material, such as an introduction or afterword, include that information after the original date.

```
McClintock, Walter. Old Indian Trails. 1926.
    Foreword William Least Heat Moon. Boston:
    Houghton, 1992.
```

20. PUBLISHER'S IMPRINT   If a book was published by an imprint of a publishing company, cite the name of the imprint followed by a hyphen and the publisher's name. The name of the imprint usually precedes the publisher's name on the title page.

```
Mura, David. Where the Body Meets Memory: An
    Odyssey of Race, Sexuality, and Identity.
    New York: Anchor-Doubleday, 1996.
```

Articles in periodicals

21. ARTICLE IN A MONTHLY MAGAZINE   In addition to the author, the title of the article, and the title of the magazine, list the month and year and the page numbers on which the article appears. Abbreviate the names of months except May, June, and July.

```
Kaplan, Robert D. "History Moving North." Atlantic
    Monthly Feb. 1997: 21+.
```

This example uses "21+" because the article did not appear on consecutive pages. For articles appearing on consecutive pages, provide the range of pages (21–28).

22. ARTICLE IN A WEEKLY MAGAZINE   Handle articles in weekly (or biweekly) magazines as you do those for monthly magazines, but give the exact date of the issue, not just the month and year.

> Pierpont, Claudia Roth. "A Society of One: Zora
>
>   Neale Hurston, American Contrarian." New
>
>   Yorker 17 Feb. 1997: 80-86.

23. ARTICLE IN A JOURNAL PAGINATED BY VOLUME   Many professional journals continue page numbers throughout the year instead of beginning each issue with page 1; at the end of the year, all of the issues are collected in a volume. Interested readers need only the volume number, the year, and the page numbers to find an article.

> Barzun, Jacques. "Is Music Unspeakable?" American
>
>   Scholar 65 (1996): 193-202.

24. ARTICLE IN A JOURNAL PAGINATED BY ISSUE   If each issue of the journal begins with page 1, you need to indicate the number of the issue. Simply place a period after the volume number and follow it with the issue number.

> Baker, Peter. "Literary Theory and the Role of the
>
>   University." College Literature 22.2 (1995):
>
>   1-15.

25. ARTICLE IN A DAILY NEWSPAPER   Begin with the author, if there is one, followed by the title of the article. Next give the name of the newspaper, the date, and the page number (including the section letter).

> Knox, Richard A. "Please Don't Dial and Drive,
>
>   Study Suggests." Boston Globe 13 Feb. 1997:
>
>   A1+.

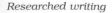

If the section is marked with a number rather than a letter, handle the entry as follows:

```
Wilford, John Noble. "In a Golden Age of
        Discovery, Faraway Worlds Beckon." New York
        Times 9 Feb. 1997, late ed., sec. 1: 1+.
```

If an edition of the newspaper is specified on the masthead, name the edition after the date and before the page reference: eastern ed., late ed., natl. ed., and so on.

26. **UNSIGNED ARTICLE IN A NEWSPAPER OR MAGAZINE**   Use the same form you would use for an article in a newspaper or a weekly or monthly magazine, but begin with the title of the article.

```
"Mammograms Get Backing." Oregonian 5 Feb. 1997: A9.
```

27. **EDITORIAL IN A NEWSPAPER**   Cite an editorial as you would an unsigned article, adding the word "Editorial" after the title.

```
"Little Loans, Big Results." Editorial. Denver
        Post 4 Feb. 1997: 8B.
```

28. **LETTER TO THE EDITOR**   Cite the writer's name, followed by the word "Letter" and the publication information for the newspaper or magazine in which the letter appears.

```
Sanford, Jane. Letter. Bangor Daily News 6 Feb.
        1997: A8.
```

29. **BOOK OR FILM REVIEW**   Cite first the reviewer's name and the title of the review, if any, followed by the words "Rev. of" and the title and author or director of the work reviewed. Add the publication information for the publication in which the review appears.

```
Greenya, John. "Home Is Where the Hurt Is." Rev.
        of Somebody Else's Children: The Courts, the
```

Kids, and the Struggle to Save America's
Troubled Children, by John Hubner and Jill
Wolfson. Washington Post Book World 12 Jan.
1997: 4.

Taubin, Amy. "Year of the Lady." Rev. of The
Portrait of a Lady, dir. Jane Campion.
Village Voice 7 Jan. 1997: 64.

Electronic sources

The documentation style for electronic sources presented in
this section is consistent with MLA's most recent guidelines,
which can be found at <http://www.mla.org> or in the *MLA
Handbook for Writers of Research Papers*, 5th ed., (1999).

30. **ONLINE SCHOLARLY PROJECT OR REFERENCE DATABASE**
For an online source accessed from within a larger scholarly
project or reference database, begin with the author (if any)
and title of the source, followed by any editors or translators.
Use quotation marks for titles of short works such as poems
and articles; underline or italicize book and periodical titles.
Include publication information for any print version of the
source before giving the title of the online project or database
(underlined or italicized), followed by the author or editor of
the project or database, the date of electronic publication (or
latest update), page or paragraph numbers (if any), the name
of any institution or organization sponsoring or associated
with the site, the date of access, and the electronic address,
or URL, of the source (in angle brackets).

Dickinson, Emily. "Hope." Poems by Emily
Dickinson. 3rd ser. Boston, 1896. Project
Bartleby Archive. Ed. Steven van Leeuwen.
Dec. 1995. Columbia U. 2 Feb. 1998
<http://www.columbia.edu/acis/bartleby/
dickinson1.html#3>.

To refer to an entire scholarly project, begin with the title of the project.

> The Einstein Papers Project. Ed. Robert Schulmann.
>
>   9 Nov. 1997. Boston U. 29 Jan. 1998 <http://
>
>   albert.bu.edu>.

31. PERSONAL OR PROFESSIONAL WEB SITE   For a citation to a personal or professional Web site, begin with the creator of the site (if available) and continue with the title of the site (or a description such as "Home page" if no title is available), the date of publication or of the latest update, the name of any organization associated with the site, the date of access, and the URL.

> Blue Note Records. Home page. 19 Mar. 1998. Blue
>
>   Note Records. 24 Mar. 1998 <http://
>
>   www.bluenote.com/>

32. ONLINE BOOK   For citations to books available online, include all available information required for printed books (see pp. 593–600), followed by the date of access and the URL.

> Brontë, Charlotte. Jane Eyre. 1846. 16 Mar. 1998
>
>   <gopher://gopher.vt.edu:10010/02/50/1>.

If the online book is part of a scholarly project or reference database, follow any information about the printed book with information about the project or database (see p. 603).

> Darwin, Charles. The Voyage of the Beagle. An
>
>   Online Library of Literature. Ed. Peter
>
>   Galbavy. 15 Jan. 1998. 11 Feb. 1998
>
>   <http://www.literature.org/Works/
>
>   Charles-Darwin/voyage/>.

33. ARTICLE IN AN ONLINE PERIODICAL   When citing online articles, follow the guidelines for printed articles (see pp. 600–03), giving whatever information is available in the online source. At the end of the citation, include the date of access and the URL.

> Coontz, Stephanie. "Family Myths, Family
>   Realities." Salon 12 Dec. 1997. 3 Feb. 1998
>   <http://www.salonmagazine.com/mwt/feature/
>   1997/12/23coontz.html>.

34. WORK FROM AN ONLINE SUBSCRIPTION SERVICE   To cite a work from a personal subscription service such as America Online, give the information about the source followed by the name of the service, the date of access, and the keyword used to retrieve the source.

> Sleek, Scott. "Blame Your Peers, Not Your Parents,
>   Author Says." APA Monitor 29:1 (1998).
>   America Online. 1 Mar. 1999. Keyword: The
>   Nurture Assumption.

For a source found in an online service accessed at a library, give the information about the source followed by the name of the service, the library, the date of access, and the URL of the service, if known.

> Miller, Christian. "Cougars Reported in Tarzana,
>   Woodland Hills." Los Angeles Times 25 Nov.
>   1997: Metro 1. Electric Lib. O'Neill Lib.,
>   Boston Coll., Chestnut Hill, MA. 12 Mar. 1998
>   <http://www.elibrary.com>.

35. ONLINE POSTING   Begin with the author's name, followed by the title or subject line (in quotation marks), the words "Online posting," the posting date, the list or group name, any identifying number of the posting, the date of access, and the URL or the e-mail address of the list.

```
Crosby, Connie. "Literary Criticism."
        Online posting. 2 Feb. 1996. Café Utne.
        17 Mar. 1998 <http://www.utne.com/motet/
        bin/show?-u4Lsul+it-la+Literature+12>.
```

36. E-MAIL   For correspondence received via electronic mail, include the author, the subject line in quotation marks, and the word "E-mail" followed by the recipient and the date of the message.

```
Schubert, Josephine. "Re: Culture shock." E-mail
        to the author. 14 Mar. 1998.
```

37. SYNCHRONOUS COMMUNICATION   To cite a synchronous communication posted in a MUD or a MOO, include the speaker's name (if relevant), a description and date of the event, the title of the forum, the date of access, and the URL. If an archival version of the communication is unavailable, include the telnet address.

```
Kelley, Heather. Jill's Borderland Tour of DU. 14
        Dec. 1995. Borderlands MOOspace. 16 Mar.
        1998 <http://www.cyberstation.net/~idd/
        v2/bordj24.htm>.
```

38. OTHER ONLINE SOURCES   For other materials accessed online, cite them as you would otherwise, including identifying labels where necessary. End the citation with the access date and the URL.

```
"No More Kings." Animation. America Rock.
        Schoolhouse Rock. ABC. 1975. 16 Mar. 1998
        <http://genxtvland.simplenet.com/
        SchoolHouseRock/song.hts?hi+kings>.
```

39. CD-ROM ISSUED IN A SINGLE EDITION   Treat a single-edition CD-ROM as you would a book, but give the medium ("CD-ROM") before the publication information.

> Sheehy, Donald, ed. <u>Robert Frost: Poems, Life,</u>
>   <u>Legacy</u>. CD-ROM. New York: Holt, 1997.

40. CD-ROM ISSUED PERIODICALLY   Cite material from a periodically issued CD-ROM as you would a printed source, followed by the title of the database (underlined or italicized), the medium ("CD-ROM"), the name of the company producing the CD-ROM, and the date of electronic publication.

> Wattenberg, Ruth. "Helping Students in the Middle."
>   <u>American Educator</u> 19.4 (1996): 2-18. <u>ERIC</u>.
>   CD-ROM. SilverPlatter. Sept. 1996.

Other sources

41. GOVERNMENT PUBLICATION   Treat the name of the government agency as the author, giving the name of the government followed by the name of the agency.

> United States. Patent and Trademark Office. <u>Setting</u>
>   <u>the Course for the Future: A Patent and</u>
>   <u>Trademark Office Review</u>. Washington: GPO, 1996.

42. PAMPHLET   Cite a pamphlet as you would a book.

> United States. Dept. of the Interior. Natl. Park
>   Service. <u>National Design Competition for an</u>
>   <u>Indian Memorial: Little Bighorn</u>
>   <u>Battlefield National Monument</u>. Washington:
>   GPO, 1996.

43. PUBLISHED DISSERTATION   Cite a published dissertation as you would a book, underlining (or italicizing) the title and giving the place of publication, the publisher, and the year of publication. After the title, add the word "Diss.," the name of the institution, and the year the dissertation was written.

> Damberg, Cheryl L. <u>Healthcare Reform: Distributional</u>
>   <u>Consequences of an Employer Mandate for</u>
>   <u>Workers in Small Firms</u>. Diss. Rand Graduate
>   School, 1995. Santa Monica: Rand, 1996.

44. UNPUBLISHED DISSERTATION   Begin with the author's name, followed by the dissertation title in quotation marks, the word "Diss.," the name of the institution, and the year the dissertation was written.

> Healey, Catherine. "Joseph Conrad's Impressionism."
>   Diss. U of Massachusetts, 1997.

45. ABSTRACT OF A DISSERTATION   Cite as you would an unpublished dissertation. After the dissertation date, give the abbreviation *DA* or *DAI* (for *Dissertation Abstracts* or *Dissertation Abstracts International*), followed by the volume number, the date of publication, and the page number.

> Chun, Maria Bow Jun. "A Study of Multicultural
>   Activities in Hawaii's Public Schools." Diss.
>   U of Hawaii, 1996. <u>DAI</u> 57 (1997): 2813A.

46. PUBLISHED PROCEEDINGS OF A CONFERENCE   Cite published conference proceedings as you would a book, adding information about the conference after the title.

> <u>Chattel, Servant, or Citizen: Women's Status in</u>
>   <u>Church, State, and Society</u>. Proc. of Irish

Conf. of Historians. Belfast, 1993. Belfast:

Inst. of Irish Studies, 1995.

47. WORK OF ART   Cite the artist's name, followed by the title of the artwork, usually underlined, and the institution and city in which the artwork can be found.

Constable, John. <u>Dedham Vale</u>. Victoria and Albert

Museum, London.

48. MUSICAL COMPOSITION   Cite the composer's name, followed by the title of the work. Underline the title of an opera, a ballet, or a composition identified by name, but do not underline or use quotation marks around a composition identified by number or form.

Copland, Aaron. <u>Appalachian Spring</u>.

Shostakovich, Dmitri. Quartet no. 1 in C, op. 49.

49. PERSONAL LETTER   To cite a letter you have received, begin with the writer's name and add the phrase "Letter to the author," followed by the date.

Cipriani, Karen. Letter to the author, 25 Apr. 1997.

50. LECTURE OR PUBLIC ADDRESS   Cite the speaker's name, followed by the title of the lecture (if any) in quotation marks, the organization sponsoring the lecture, the location, and the date.

Offenheiser, Ray. "Nongovernmental Organizations and

Peacekeeping." MIT, Cambridge. 12 Feb. 1997.

51. PERSONAL INTERVIEW   To cite an interview that you conducted, begin with the name of the person interviewed. Then write "Personal interview," followed by the date of the interview.

Meeker, Dolores. Personal interview. 21 Apr. 1997.

52. PUBLISHED INTERVIEW   Name the person interviewed, followed by the title of the interview, if there is one, in quotation marks and the publication in which the interview was printed. If the interview does not have a title, include the word "Interview" after the interviewee's name.

Renoir, Jean. "Renoir at Home: Interview with Jean
    Renoir." Film Quarterly 50.1 (1996): 2-8.

53. RADIO OR TELEVISION INTERVIEW   Name the person interviewed, followed by the word "Interview." Then give the title of the program, underlined (or italicized), and identifying information about the broadcast.

Gates, Henry Louis, Jr. Interview. Charlie Rose.
    PBS. WNET, New York. 13 Feb. 1997.

54. FILM OR VIDEOTAPE   Begin with the title. For a film, cite the director and the lead actors or narrator ("Perf." or "Narr."), followed by the distributor and year. For a videotape, add the word "Videocassette" before the distributor.

The English Patient. Dir. Anthony Minghella. Perf.
    Ralph Fiennes, Juliette Binoche, Willem Dafoe,
    and Kristin Scott Thomas. Miramax, 1996.

Sense and Sensibility. Dir. Ang Lee. Perf. Emma
    Thompson, Hugh Grant, and Alan Rickman.
    Videocassette. TriStar Home Video, 1996.

55. RADIO OR TELEVISION PROGRAM   List the relevant information in this order: the title of the program, underlined or italicized; the writer ("By"), director ("Dir."), narrator ("Narr."), producer ("Prod."), or main actors ("Perf."), if relevant; the series, neither underlined nor in quotation marks; the network; the local station that broadcast the program and the city; and the date of broadcast. For a television episode or radio segment, place the title, in quotation marks, before the program title.

    The Connection. Host Christopher Lydon. Natl.
        Public Radio. WBUR, Boston. 23 Jan.
        1997.

    In Darkest Hollywood: Cinema and Apartheid. PBS.
        WNET, New York. 13 Feb. 1997.

56. LIVE PERFORMANCE OF A PLAY   Begin with the title of the play, followed by the author ("By"). Then include specific information about the live performance: the director ("Dir."), the major actors ("Perf."), the theater company, the theater and its location, and the date of the performance.

    Six Characters in Search of an Author. By Luigi
        Pirandello. Dir. Robert Brustein. Perf.
        Jeremy Geidt, David Ackroyd, Monica Koskey,
        and Marianne Owen. American Repertory Theatre,
        Cambridge. 14 Jan. 1997.

57. SOUND RECORDING   Begin with the composer (or author, if the recording is spoken), followed by the title of the piece. Next list pertinent artists (such as performers, readers, or musicians) and the orchestra and conductor. End with the manufacturer and the date. If the recording is not on a CD, indicate the medium (such as "Audiocassette") before the manufacturer's name, followed by a period. Do not underline or italicize the name of the medium or enclose it in quotation marks.

```
Bizet, Georges. Carmen. Perf. Jennifer Larmore,
     Thomas Moser, Angela Gheorghiu, and Samuel
     Ramey. Bavarian State Orch. and Chorus. Cond.
     Giuseppe Sinopoli. Warner, 1996.
```

58. CARTOON Begin with the cartoonist's name, the title of the cartoon (if it has one) in quotation marks, the word "Cartoon," and the publication information for the publication in which the cartoon appears.

```
Klossner, John. "Hubman." Cartoon. Editorial Humor
     5-18 Feb. 1997: 7.
```

59. MAP OR CHART Cite a map or chart as you would a book with an unknown author. Underline the title of the map or chart and add the word "Map" or "Chart" following the title.

```
Winery Guide to Northern and Central California.
     Map. Modesto: Compass Maps, 1996.
```

54

MLA format; two sample research papers

54a MLA format

In most English and humanities classes, you will be asked to use the MLA (Modern Language Association) manuscript format. The following guidelines are consistent with advice in the *MLA Handbook for Writers of Research Papers,* 5th ed. (New York: MLA, 1999). For two sample MLA research papers, see 54b.

MATERIALS   Use good-quality 8½" × 11" white paper. If the paper emerges from the printer in a continuous sheet, separate the pages, remove the feeder strips from the sides of the paper, and assemble the pages in order. Secure the pages with a paper clip. Unless your instructor suggests otherwise, do not staple the pages together or use any sort of binder.

TITLE AND IDENTIFICATION   Essays written for English and humanities classes do not require a title page unless your instructor requests one. If you are not using a title page, begin the first page against the left margin about one inch from the top of the page. Type your name, the instructor's name, the course name and number, and the date on separate lines; double-space between lines. Double-space again and center the title of the paper in the width of the page. Capitalize the first and last words of the title and all other words except articles, prepositions, and coordinating conjunctions (see 45c). Double-space after the title and begin typing the text of the paper. (See p. 616.)

If you use a title page, follow the model on page 627.

MARGINS, SPACING, AND INDENTATION   Leave margins of at least one inch but no more than an inch and a half on all sides of the page.

Double-space lines and indent the first line of each paragraph one half inch (or five spaces) from the left margin.

For a quotation longer than four typed lines of prose or three lines of verse, indent each line one inch (or ten spaces) from the left margin. Double-space between the body of the paper and the quotation, and double-space between the lines of the quotation. Quotation marks are not needed when a quotation is set off from the text by indenting. See page 632 for an example; see also 37b.

PAGINATION   Put your last name followed by the page number in the upper right corner of each page, one-half inch below the top edge. (If you have a separate title page, the title page is uncounted and unnumbered.) Use arabic numerals (1, 2, 3, and so on). Do not put a period after the number and do not enclose the number in parentheses.

PUNCTUATION AND TYPING   In typing the paper, leave one space after words, commas, semicolons, and colons and between dots in ellipsis marks. MLA allows either one or two spaces after periods, question marks, and exclamation points. To form a dash, type two hyphens with no space between them; do not put a space on either side of the dash.

HEADINGS   MLA neither encourages nor discourages use of headings and currently provides no guidelines for their use. If you would like to use headings in a long essay or research paper, check first with your instructor. Although headings are not used as frequently in English and the humanities as in other disciplines, the trend seems to be changing. (See pp. 112–14 for examples of types of headings and pp. 616–26 for a paper that uses headings.)

VISUALS   MLA classifies visuals as tables and figures (figures include graphs, charts, maps, photographs, and drawings). Label each table with an arabic numeral (Table 1, Table 2, and so on) and provide a clear caption that identifies the subject; the label and caption should appear on separate lines above the table. For each figure, a label and a caption are usually placed below the figure, and they need not appear on separate lines. The word "Figure" may be abbreviated to "Fig."

Visuals should be placed in the text, as close as possible to the sentences that relate to them, unless your instructor prefers them in an appendix. See page 619 for a visual included in the text of a paper.

NOTE: See 53a for guidelines on using MLA in-text citations and 53c for preparing an MLA list of works cited.

54b Two research papers (with MLA documentation)

On the following pages are two research papers written by students in composition classes. The first, by John Garcia, takes a position on a political issue: How should California's fish and game commission be allowed to control the state's growing mountain lion population? The second, by Karen Shaw, addresses a scholarly controversy: To what extent have apes demonstrated language abilities akin to those of young children? Shaw's paper includes a title page and a formal outline, required by her professor. Both papers are documented with the MLA style of in-text citations and list of works cited.

John Garcia

Professor Hacker

English 101

21 April 1997

Title centered and
double-spaced.

The Mountain Lion:

Once Endangered, Now a Danger

On April 23, 1994, as Barbara Schoener was
jogging in the Sierra foothills of California,
she was pounced on from behind by a mountain lion.
After an apparent struggle with her attacker,

Summary: citation
with author's name
and page number
in parentheses.

Schoener was killed by bites to her neck and head
(Rychnovsky 39). In 1990, four years before this
attack, California voters had approved Proposition
117, which enacted into law the California Wildlife Protection Act. The act outlawed sport hunting
of the lions; it also took away the right of the
California Fish and Game department to thin the
mountain lion population.

In 1996, because of Schoener's death and
other highly publicized attacks, California
politicians presented voters with Proposition 197,
which contained provisions repealing much of the
1990 law. The proposition was rejected by a large
margin, probably because the debate turned into a
struggle between hunting and antihunting factions.
If California politicians decide to reconsider the
mountain lion issue, a future proposition should
retain the ban on sport hunting but allow the

Garcia 2

Department of Fish and Game to control the population. Wildlife management would reduce the number
of lion attacks on humans and in the long run
would also protect the lions.

Thesis asserts
writer's main point.

The once-endangered mountain lion

To early Native Americans, mountain lions--
also known as cougars, pumas, and panthers--were
objects of reverence. The European colonists, however, did not share the Native American view.
They conducted what Ted Williams calls an "all-
out war on the species" (29). The lions were eliminated from the eastern United States except for
a small population that remains in the Florida
Everglades.

Headings help
readers follow the
organization.

Quotation: author
named in signal
phrase; page number
in parentheses.

The lions lingered on in the west, but in
smaller and smaller numbers. At least 66,665 lions
were killed between 1907 and 1978 in Canada and
the United States (Hansen 58). As late as 1969,
the country's leading authority on the big cat,
Maurice Hornocker, estimated the United States
population as fewer than 6,500 and probably dropping (Williams 30).

Statistics
documented with
citations.

Hornocker
introduced as an
expert.

Resurgence of the mountain lion

In western states today, the mountain lion is
no longer in danger of extinction. In fact, over
the past thirty years, the population has rebounded
dramatically. In California, fish and game officials

estimate that since 1972 lion numbers have increased
from 2,400 to at least 6,000 ("Lion" A21).

Short title given in parentheses because the work has no author.

Similar increases are occurring outside of
California. For instance, for nearly fifty years
mountain lions had virtually disappeared from Yellowstone National Park, but today lion sightings
are increasingly common. In 1992, Hornocker estimated that at least eighteen adults were living in
the park (59). In the United States as a whole,
some biologists estimate that there are as many as
50,000 mountain lions, a dramatic increase over

A clear transition prepares readers for the next section.

the 1969 estimate of 6,500 (Williams 30). For the
millions of Americans interested in the preservation of animal species, this is good news, but unfortunately the increase has led to a number of
violent encounters between human and lion.

Increasing attacks on humans

There is no doubt that more and more humans
are being attacked. A glance at figure 1, a graph
of statistics compiled by mountain lion researcher
Paul Beier, confirms just how dramatically the at-

The writer explains what the graph shows.

tacks have increased since the beginning of the
century.

Ray Rychnovsky reports that thirteen people
have been killed and another fifty-seven have been
mauled by lions since 1890 (41). "What's most
startling," writes Rychnovsky, "is that nearly

For variety, the signal phrase is placed between parts of the quotation.

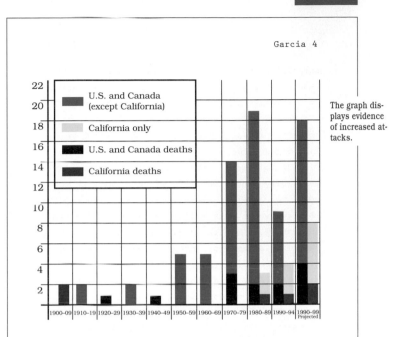

The graph displays evidence of increased attacks.

Fig. 1. Cougar attacks--a history, by Paul Beier, Northern Arizona University; rpt. in Rychnovsky (42)

Ellipsis dots in brackets indicate words omitted from original source (see p. 576).

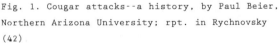

three-quarters of the attacks [. . .] have taken place in the last twenty-five years" (41).

Quotation introduced with a signal phrase.

Particularly frightening are the attacks on children. Kevin Hansen points out that children have been "more vulnerable than adults, making up 64 percent of the victims" (69). This is not

surprising, since children, being small and active,
resemble the lion's natural prey. Lion authority
John Seidensticker reports that when he worked for
the National Zoo in Washington, DC, he regularly
observed cats stalking children who passed by the
lion cages (120).

Summary
introduced with
a signal phrase.

    In California, the state where the lion is
most fully protected, 1994 was a particularly bad
year. Los Angeles Times writer Tony Perry reports
that two women were killed by lions in 1994 and
that the year brought a dramatic increase in mountain lion sightings, "many in suburban and urban
areas where the animal had previously not been
spotted" (B4). With two killings in one year and
an increasing number of sightings, it is not surprising that California politicians responded with
Proposition 197, aimed at repealing the ban on
hunting the lions.

The 1996 California referendum

    The debate over Proposition 197 was inflamed
by campaigns of misinformation on both sides of
the issue. The pro faction included the National
Rifle Association (NRA), the Safari Club, and Gun
Owners of California. On the other side were
animal rights groups such as the Sierra Club,
the Fund for Animals, and the Mountain Lion
Foundation.

Clear topic
sentences, like
this one, used
throughout the
paper.

Garcia 6

The proposition itself, introduced by Repub-
lican Tim Leslie, is laced with legalese and
deceptive phrasing. For example, in a provision
aimed at amending section 4801 of the Fish and
Game Code, the word hunters does not appear,
though the legalistic term designee clearly includes hunters:

> The department may remove or take, or
> authorize its designee, including, but
> not limited to, an appropriate govern-
> mental agency with public safety
> responsibility, an appropriate govern-
> mental agency with wildlife management
> responsibility, or an owner of land,
> to remove or take, one or more mountain
> lions that are perceived to be an imminent
> threat to public health or safety or
> livestock anywhere in the state except
> within the state park system. ("Propo-
> sition 197" sec. 5)

The proposition's euphemistic language, such as
remove or take, was echoed by the hunting
factions, who spoke much about "controlling,"
"managing," or "thinning" the lion population,
avoiding such words as kill or shoot.

Supporters of Proposition 197 were not above
exaggerating the dangers posed by mountain lions,
preferring lurid accounts of maulings and killings

Quotation set off
from text is clearly
introduced.

Quotation longer
than four lines is
indented 1″ (or ten
spaces); quotation
marks are omitted;
no period is used
after citation.

Short title given in
parentheses
because the work
has no author.

to solid statistics. For example, writing on the Internet in an attempt to sway voters, Terrence M. Eagan, Wayne Long, and Steven Arroyo appeal to human fears of being eaten: "Two small children woke up one morning without a mother because a lion ate her." To underscore the point, they describe a grisly discovery: "A lion preying upon neighborhood pets was found with parts of five different puppies in its stomach."

No parenthetical citation necessary for unpaginated Internet source when author is named in signal phrase.

Whereas the pro-hunting groups spoke in euphemistic language and exaggerated the dangers posed by lions, the pro-lion groups invoked inflammatory language and ignored the dangers. A Web page written by a coalition of wildlife preservationists is typical. Calling Proposition 197 "a special interest trophy hunting measure," the coalition claims that the Gun Owners of California, the NRA, and the Safari Club "rammed" the proposition onto the ballot while "hiding behind a disingenuous concern for public safety." After asserting that the mountain lion poses a minimal threat to humans, the coalition accuses the Department of Fish and Game of "creating a climate of fear" so that the public will choose to reinstate lion hunting (California Wildlife Protection Coalition). While it is true that human encounters with mountain lions are rare, some pro-lion publications come close to ridiculing Califor-

Transition helps readers move from one topic to another.

Internet source with no page number.

Garcia 8

nians who fear that lion attacks on humans and pets will continue to accelerate unless something is done.

Population control: A reasonable solution

Without population control, the number of attacks on Californians will almost certainly continue to rise, and the lions may become even bolder. As lion authority John Seidensticker remarks, "The boldness displayed by mountain lions just doesn't square with the shy, retiring behavior familiar to those of us who have studied these animals" (177). He surmises that the lions have become emboldened because they no longer have to contend with wolves and grizzly bears, which dominated them in the past. The only conceivable predator to reinstill that fear is the human.

Sadly, the only sure way to reduce lion attacks on humans is to thin the population. One basic approach to thinning is sport hunting, which is still legal, though restricted in various ways, in every western state except California. A second approach involves state-directed wildlife management, usually the hiring of professional hunters to shoot or trap the lions.

Sport hunting is a poor option--and not just because it is unpopular with Californians. First, it is difficult to control sport hunting. For in-

Credentials of author mentioned in signal phrase.

stance, a number of western states have restrictions on killing a female lion with kittens, but
sport hunters are rarely knowledgeable enough to
tell whether a lion has kittens. Second, because
some sport hunters are poor shots, they wound but
don't kill the lions, causing needless suffering.
Finally, certain hunting practices are anything
but sport. There is a growing business in professionally led cougar hunts, as a number of ads on
the World Wide Web attest. One practice is to tree
a lion with radio-equipped dogs and then place a
phone call to the client to come and shoot the
lion. In some cases, the lion may be treed for two
or more days before the client arrives to bag his
trophy. Such practices are so offensive that even
the California Park Rangers Association opposed
Proposition 197. As a spokesperson explained, "We
support managing the lions. But they shouldn't be
stuck on the wall in a den" (qtd. in Perry B4).

We should entrust the thinning of the lion
population to wildlife specialists guided by science, not to hunters seeking adventure or to
safari clubs looking for profits. Unlike hunters,
scientific wildlife managers have the long-term
interests of the mountain lion at heart. An uncontrolled population leads to an ecolog_cal
imbalance, with more and more lions competing for
territory and a diminishing food supply. The

Citation of
indirect source:
words quoted
in another
source.

Garcia 10

highly territorial lions will fight to the death
to defend their hunting grounds; and because the
mother lion ultimately ejects her offspring from
her own territory, young lions face an uncertain
future. Stephani Cruickshank, a spokesperson for
California Lion Awareness (CLAW), explains, "The
overrun of lions is biologically unsound and
unfair to the lions, especially those forced to
survive in marginal or clearly unnatural urban
settings" (qtd. in Robinson 35).

No citation
needed for "com-
mon knowledge"
available in
many sources.

In conclusion, wildlife management would
benefit both Californians and the California
lions. Although some have argued that California
needs fewer people, not fewer lions, humans do have
an obligation to protect themselves and their children, and the fears of people in lion country are
real. As for the lions, they need to thrive in a
natural habitat with an adequate food supply. "We
simply cannot let nature take its course," writes
Torry Mansfield of the Department of Fish and Game
(qtd. in Perry B4). In fact, not to take action in
California is as illogical as reintroducing the
lions to Central Park and Boston Common, places
they once also roamed.

The writer con-
cludes with his
own stand on the
controversy.

The paper ends
with the writer's
own words.

Works Cited

California Wildlife Protection Coalition. <u>California
Mountain Lion Page</u>. 27 Mar. 1996. Sierra Club.
9 Mar. 1997 <http://www.sierraclub.org/
chapters/ca/mountain-lion/>.

Eagan, Terrence M., Wayne Long, and Steven Arroyo.
"Rebuttal to Argument against Proposition 197."
<u>1996 California Primary Election Server</u>. 1996.
California Secretary of State. 9 Mar. 1997
<http://primary96.ss.ca.gov/e/ballot/
197again2.html>.

Hansen, Kevin. <u>Cougar: The American Lion</u>. Flagstaff:
Northland, 1992.

Hornocker, Maurice G. "Learning to Live with Lions."
<u>National Geographic</u> July 1992: 37-65.

"Lion Attacks Prompt State to Respond." <u>New York
Times</u> 18 Oct. 1995, late ed.: A21.

Perry, Tony. "Big Cat Fight." <u>Los Angeles Times</u> 8
Mar. 1996, home ed.: B1+.

"Proposition 197: Text of Proposed Law." <u>1996 California Primary Election Server</u>. 1996. California Secretary of State. 9 Mar. 1997 <http://
Primary96.ss.ca.gov/e/ballot/197txt.html>.

Robinson, Jerome B. "Cat in the Ballot Box." <u>Field
and Stream</u> Mar. 1996: 30-35.

Rychnovsky, Ray. "Clawing into Controversy." <u>Outdoor
Life</u> Jan. 1995: 38-42.

Seidensticker, John. "Mountain Lions Don't Stalk
People: True or False?" <u>Audubon</u> Feb. 1992: 113-22.

Williams, Ted. "The Lion's Silent Return." <u>Audubon</u>
Nov. 1994: 28-35.

Annotations (left margin):

Heading centered 1″ from top of page.

List is alphabetized by authors' last names.

First line of each entry is at left margin; subsequent lines are indented 1/2″ (or five spaces).

Double-spacing used throughout.

Between the Word and the Sentence:
Apes and Language

Title centered about one-third down the page.

Karen Shaw

Writer's name centered near middle of page.

English 101, Section 30
Dr. Robert Barshay
20 March 1997

Course name and section number, professor's name, and date are centered near bottom of page.

Outline pages num-
bered with small
roman numerals.

Outline begins
with thesis and
uses standard
format.

Outline

Thesis: The great apes resemble humans in language
abilities more than researchers once believed, and evidence is mounting that
bonobos (pygmy chimpanzees) can understand
and perhaps even create sentences.

I. Early ape language studies showed that apes
could acquire significant language skills,
but researchers failed to prove that apes
could create sentences.

A. Apes acquired impressive vocabularies in
sign language and in artificial languages.

B. Despite charges that they were responding
to cues, apes were using language spontaneously.

1. They performed well in experiments
that eliminated the possibility of
cuing.

2. They learned signs and symbols from
each other and initiated conversations
on their own.

Sentences are
parallel and simple.

C. Apes were using language creatively.

1. They invented creative names.

2. They may even have lied and joked.

D. There was once little evidence that apes
could order symbols grammatically to form
sentences.

Writer's name and
page number are
typed 1/2″ from top
of each page.

    1. The apes' sequences of signs were
often confusing and repetitious.

    2. Evidence of meaningful sequences was
inconclusive.

II. Recent research with Kanzi demonstrates that
bonobos can understand and perhaps even
create grammatical patterns.

    A. Kanzi can understand grammatically
complex spoken English.

    B. Kanzi has picked up simple grammatical
patterns from his caretakers.

    C. Kanzi appears to have developed his own
patterns.

III. Evidence suggests that linguistic abilities
in humans and apes are part of a continuum.

    A. The skeptics tend to apply a double stan-
dard: one for very young human children,
another for apes.

    B. In our human ancestors, the ability to
communicate in language must have preceded language itself.

Between the Word and the Sentence:

Apes and Language

One afternoon, Koko the gorilla, who was often bored with language lessons, repeatedly signaled "red" in American Sign Language when asked the color of a white towel. She did this even though she had identified the color white many times before. At last the gorilla plucked a bit of red lint from the towel and showed it to her trainer (Patterson and Linden 80-81). At Yerkes Primate Research Center, chimpanzees Sherman and Austin, who had been taught symbols for foods and tools, were put in separate rooms. To obtain food in different containers, one chimp had to ask the other for a tool, such as a wrench, by projecting symbols onto a screen. After some experimentation, the chimpanzees succeeded 97 percent of the time (Marx 1333).

These and hundreds of similar scenes played out over the last thirty years demonstrate that the great apes (gorillas, orangutans, and chimpanzees) resemble humans in language abilities far more than researchers once thought. And evidence is mounting, despite opposition from some linguists and psychologists, that bonobos (pygmy chimpanzees) can understand and perhaps even create sentences.

Although apes lack the vocal ability to

Title centered and double-spaced.

Citation with author's name and page number in parentheses.

Thesis states writer's conclusions about the ape language experiments.

Shaw 2

produce human sounds, they have acquired vocabularies
in American Sign Language (Ameslan) and in artificial languages ranging from one hundred to two
hundred signs or symbols. The apes' acquisition of
these vocabularies is not in dispute, but some researchers have questioned whether the apes are
truly learning the signs and symbols. These critics suggest that the apes may be merely imitating
their trainers or responding to cues. Psychologist
H. S. Terrace, the chief trainer of a chimp named
Nim, is one of the most formidable of the skeptics
because he was once a believer. Ultimately Terrace
concluded that in many cases "the teacher's signs
had prompted Nim's signs" (75). Terrace argued
that cuing had also played a large role in Beatrix
T. Gardner's training of the chimpanzee Washoe.

> Author named
> in signal phrase;
> page number in
> parentheses at
> end of quotation.

    While it is possible that in these early
studies many of the apes' signs were in response
to cues, Terrace and other critics failed to prove
that all of them were. Even as early as 1979, psychologists R. Allen and Beatrix T. Gardner were
performing double-blind experiments that prevented
any possibility of cuing (Sebeok and Umiker-Sebeok
81-82). When Terrace criticized these experiments
in 1979, he failed to mention the double-blind
technique.

> The writer
> interprets the
> evidence; she
> doesn't just
> report it.

    Perhaps the most convincing evidence that the

Researched writing

apes have not been simply responding to cues is that they have used signs or symbols spontaneously among themselves. Francine Patterson's gorillas Koko and Michael sign to one another, with Michael occasionally using signs that he could have learned only from Koko. "Even more intriguing," write Patterson and Linden, "is his variation of the tickle sign depending on whom he is conversing with" (176).

> For variety, the signal phrase is placed between parts of the quotation.

The most dramatic instances of spontaneous signing have involved Washoe. In 1976, she had a baby, and although the baby chimp lived only a few hours, Washoe signed to it before it died (Davis 42). Later, another baby chimpanzee placed in Washoe's care mastered more than fifty signs in Ameslan without help from humans (Toner 24). When the Gardners returned Washoe to an ape colony in Oklahoma, she desperately signaled to humans from whom she was separated by a moat, and from the start she signaled to other apes. Adrian Desmond vividly describes Washoe's efforts to converse:

> The writer supports her point with examples from a variety of sources.

> Frustrated by lack of conversationalists, she [Washoe] even tried talking to dogs. . . . One particularly memorable day, a snake spread terror through . . . the ape island, and all but one fled in panic. Then Washoe was seen running over signing to him "come, hurry up." (42)

> Brackets indicate words not in original source.

> Ellipsis dots indicate words deleted from original source.

> Quotation longer than four lines is indented 1″ (or ten spaces); quotation marks are omitted; no period is used after citation.

In addition to learning signs and using them spontaneously, apes have used language creatively. Koko has signed "finger bracelet" to describe a ring and "bottle match" for a cigarette lighter (Patterson and Linden 146). The Gardners' Lucy is reported to have called an onion "cry fruit" and a radish "cry hurt food" (Desmond 40). And the bonobo Kanzi has punched symbols for "campfire" and "TV" to ask to see Quest for Fire, a film about early primates discovering fire (Eckholm, "Kanzi" C3).

Apes who invent creative names are not simply learning by rote. They are adapting language for their own purposes. And those purposes, it turns out, may even include lying and joking. In a recent personal interview, Professor Esther Robbins, who worked with Francine Patterson's gorilla Michael for seven months, pointed out how difficult it is to verify such uses of language quantitatively. What counts as language is "a very gray area," she says. "But you know that animal, and there is very definitely communication, even lying and joking."

Although the great apes have demonstrated significant language skills, one central question remains: Can they be taught to use that uniquely human language tool we call grammar, to learn the difference, for instance, between "ape bite human" and "human bite ape"? In other words, can an ape create a sentence?

Citation includes short title because two works by Eckholm appear in list of works cited.

Use of personal interview as source.

A clear transition prepares readers for next major point.

Apes have used multisign sequences, but in the early studies there was little convincing evidence that the combinations displayed a grasp of grammar. Many of the sequences seemed confusing and repetitious, such as Nim's longest sequence: "give orange me give eat orange me eat orange give me eat orange give me you" (Terrace et al. 895).

Citation of a work with four or more authors.

More recently, however, E. Sue Savage-Rumbaugh's studies on the bonobo Kanzi are making even the skeptics take notice. Young Kanzi had played in the lab while his mother was being tutored in a language of symbols, and when he was two and a half, his mother was sent away for breeding. "To the scientists' amazement," writes Erik Eckholm, "he had been learning symbols out of the corner of his eye. He hit the symbol for apple, then proved he knew what he was saying by picking an apple from an assortment of foods" ("Kanzi" C1).

Short title needed because two works by Eckholm appear in list of works cited.

Impressed by Kanzi's ability to pick up language without explicit training, Savage-Rumbaugh decided to replace rote learning with "a more naturalistic approach": Kanzi would learn language much the way human children do (Lewin 50). Kanzi's linguistic development has taken place not in a laboratory but in a fifty-five-acre forest, which he roams in the company of his caretakers. During games of tag and hide-and-seek and other childhood

Shaw 6

activities, Kanzi communicates with his caregivers on a computerized keyboard equipped with a voice synthesizer. A word is spoken each time Kanzi touches a symbol on the board.

Evidence of Kanzi's linguistic progress was published in 1991, when Kanzi was ten. The results show that he can understand grammatically complex spoken English and that he may have developed a primitive grammar. In their studies of Kanzi and his half sister Mulika, Savage-Rumbaugh and members of her team have taken great care to avoid cuing. Lewin reports that spoken instructions to Kanzi were "delivered by someone out of his sight" and that the other team members "could not hear the instructions and so could not cue Kanzi, even unconsciously" (51). When Kanzi correctly re- sponded to sentences like "Can you put the raisins in the bowl?" his caretakers made the instructions more difficult. For example, in response to the question "Can you go to the colony room and get the telephone?" Kanzi brought back the telephone even though there were other objects in the room.

Most surprising is Kanzi's apparent grasp of grammar. The first grammatical rule that Kanzi began to display was to put action before object (as in "hide peanut" and "grab Kanzi"), a pattern probably picked up from his caregivers. In 1985,

Citation appears after quotation mark and before period.

Clear topic sen- tences, like this one, used through- out paper.

Eckholm reported that Kanzi's "two and three word statements are often made without prompting, systematically add useful information and represent his own creative responses to novel situations" ("Pygmy" B7). In the first month of study, Kanzi showed no understanding of grammatical ordering, but gradually he began to pick it up. Patricia Marks Greenfield and E. Sue Savage-Rumbaugh point out that this developmental trend "was also found for human children at the two-word stage" (559).

At times Kanzi deviated from the grammar of his keepers and began to develop his own patterns, an ability that may be more impressive than picking up rules from keepers. Without prompting, Kanzi began to combine gestures and symbols, usually pointing to the symbol first. For example, Ann Gibbons reports that when Kanzi wanted to visit the lab's dog, "he would point to the symbol for dog, then make a gesture for 'go'" (1561). Perhaps even more significant is the pattern that Kanzi developed on his own in combining various symbols. According to Gibbons, "When he gave an order combining two symbols for action--such as 'chase' and 'hide'--it was important to him that the first action--'chase'--be done first" (1561). Kanzi's consistency in combining symbols suggests that he has at least a rudimentary grasp of grammar.

Citation of a work with two authors.

Shaw 8

If Kanzi and other bonobos continue to develop grammatical patterns, the implications for the study of human evolution could be profound. Anthropologist Richard Leakey and coauthor Roger Lewin pose the issue like this:

> Is spoken language merely an extension and enhancement of cognitive capacities to be found among our ape relatives? Or is spoken language a unique human characteristic completely separate from any cognitive abilities in apes? (240)

Leakey and Lewin believe that there is a continuity in linguistic ability between apes and humans. Linguist Noam Chomsky disagrees. He describes the entire ape language field as gripped by "sentimental confusion" and dismisses the studies on Kanzi with a flippant analogy: "To maintain that Kanzi has language ability is like saying a man can fly because he can jump in the air" (qtd. in Booth A3). This is certainly strong language from a man who, in the words of Ann Gibbons, has not even "seen the new data--and doesn't care to" (1562). And philosopher Stuart Shanker notes that Savage-Rumbaugh continues to address the concerns of critics such as Chomsky. "But," he adds, "the linguists keep moving the goal post" (qtd. in Johnson C10).

Skeptics such as Chomsky seem to be applying

Smooth transition links second and third parts of paper (parts II and III of outline).

Quotation set off from text is clearly introduced.

In quotations set off from text, final punctuation mark goes before parentheses.

Citation of indirect source (words quoted in another source).

The writer addresses opposing arguments.

a double standard when they compare apes' linguistic abilities to those of young human children. As Savage-Rumbaugh puts it, "When children make up novel words it is called lexical innovation, but when chimpanzees do the same thing it is called ambiguous" (qtd. in Lewin 51). In a recent experiment comparing Kanzi and a 2-1/2-year-old child, Savage-Rumbaugh's research team discovered that both Kanzi and the child responded appropriately to about 70 percent of more than six hundred "novel sentences of request" (Rumbaugh 722).

Certainly no one expects any chimpanzee to perform linguistically far beyond the level of a very young human child. After all, a chimpanzee's brain is only one-third the size of our own. But the brains of the ancestors of <u>Homo sapiens</u> at some point were of similar size. Surely it makes more sense that an animal with whom we share 99 percent of our genetic makeup would at least have the inklings in its brain of the ability to communicate in language. And even in our human ancestors, the ability to communicate in language must have preceded language itself. Maybe I am "sentimental," to use Chomsky's word, but when I read about Kanzi's achievements, it is difficult not to believe that there is some commonality of abilities.

The writer ends with her own stand on the controversy.

Shaw 10

Works Cited

Booth, William. "Monkeying with Language: Is
     Chimp Using Words or Merely Aping Handlers?"
     Washington Post 29 Oct. 1990: A3.

Davis, Flora. Eloquent Animals: A Study in Animal
     Communication. New York: Coward, 1978.

Desmond, Adrian. The Ape's Reflexion. New York:
     Wade-Dial, 1979.

Eckholm, Erik. "Kanzi the Chimp: A Life in
     Science." New York Times 25 June 1985, local
     ed.: C1+.

---. "Pygmy Chimp Readily Learns Language Skill."
     New York Times 24 June 1985, local ed.: A1+.

Gibbons, Ann. "Déjà Vu All Over Again: Chimp-
     Language Wars." Science 251 (1991): 1561-62.

Greenfield, Patricia Marks, and E. Sue Savage-
     Rumbaugh. "Grammatical Combination in
     Pan paniscus: Processes of Learning and
     Invention in the Evolution and Development of
     Language." "Language" and Intelligence in
     Monkeys and Apes: Comparative Developmental
     Perspectives. Ed. Sue Taylor Parker and
     Kathleen Rita Gibson. Cambridge: Cambridge
     UP, 1990. 540-78.

Johnson, George. "Chimp Talk Debate: Is It Really
     Language?" New York Times 6 June 1995, local
     ed.: C1+.

List of works cited begins on separate page.

Heading, centered, 1″ from top of page.

List alphabetized by authors' last names.

First line of entry is at left margin, subsequent lines indent ¹/₂″ (or five spaces).

Shaw 11

Leakey, Richard, and Roger Lewin. <u>Origins</u>
<u>Reconsidered: In Search of What Makes Us</u>
<u>Human</u>. New York: Doubleday, 1992.

Lewin, Roger. "Look Who's Talking Now." <u>New</u>
<u>Scientist</u> 29 Apr. 1991: 49-52.

Marx, Jean L. "Ape-Language Controversy Flares
Up." <u>Science</u> 207 (1980): 1330-33.

Patterson, Francine, and Eugene Linden. <u>The</u>
<u>Education of Koko</u>. New York: Holt, 1981.

Robbins, Esther. Personal interview. 17 Mar. 1997.

Rumbaugh, Duane. "Primate Language and Cognition:
Common Ground." <u>Social Research</u> 62 (1995):
711-30.

Sebeok, Thomas A., and Jean Umiker-Sebeok.
"Performing Animals: Secrets of the Trade."
<u>Psychology Today</u> Nov. 1979: 78-91.

Terrace, H. S. "How Nim Chimpsky Changed My Mind."
<u>Psychology Today</u> Nov. 1979: 65-76.

Terrace, H. S., et al. "Can an Ape Create a
Sentence?" <u>Science</u> 206 (1979): 891-902.

Toner, Mike. "Loulis, the Talking Chimp." <u>National</u>
<u>Wildlife</u> Feb.-Mar. 1986: 24.

PART X

Literature and Other Disciplines

55

Writing about literature

Most of us know how to read and respond to literature—novels, stories, poems, and plays—in an informal way. "I like it," we say. "What was it about?" we ask. "What made it so powerful?" we might want to know. The purpose of the literary paper is to take our informal judgments about a work and, through reflection and analysis, transform them into reasoned, compelling interpretations.

All good writing about literature attempts to answer a question, spoken or unspoken, about the text: "Why doesn't Hamlet kill his uncle sooner?" "How does street language function in Gwendolyn Brooks's 'We Real Cool'?" "What might the moth symbolize in Virginia Woolf's 'The Death of the Moth'?" "How does Dickens portray lawyers in *Great Expectations?*" "In what ways does James Joyce's 'The Dead' confront traditions of love and romance?" The goal of a literature paper should be to answer such questions with a meaningful interpretation, presented forcefully and persuasively.

55a Get involved in the work; be an active reader.

Read the work closely and carefully. Think of the work as speaking to you: What is it telling you? Asking you? Trying to make you feel?

If the work provides an introduction and footnotes, read them attentively. They may be a source of important information. Use the dictionary to look up words unfamiliar to you or words with subtle nuances that may affect the work's meaning.

Rereading is a central part of the process. You should read short works several times, first to get an overall impression and then again to focus on meaningful details. With longer works, such as novels or plays, read the most important chapters or scenes more than once while keeping in mind the work as a whole.

As you read and reread, interact with the work by posing questions and looking for answers. The chart on pages 646–47 suggests some questions about literature that may help you become a more active reader.

Annotating the work

Annotating the work is a way to focus your reading. The first time through, you may want to pencil a check mark next to passages you find especially significant. On a more careful rereading, pay particular attention to these passages and jot down your ideas and reactions in a notebook or (if the book is your own) in the margins of the page.

Here is one student's annotation of a poem by Shakespeare.

> *Rhyming pattern of sonnet*
>
> Shall I compare thee to a summer's day? — *Who? (Must be a loved one.)*
> Thou art more lovely and more temperate: — *Pleasant-natured (like pleasant weather)?*
> Rough winds do shake the darling buds of May,
> And summer's lease hath all too short a date. —
> Sometime too hot the eye of heaven shines, —
> And often is his gold complexion dimmed; — *Summer is fleeting and not always perfect. (But lover is perfect?)*
> And every (fair) from (fair) sometimes declines, — *Fair = beauty, or more than beauty?*
> By chance, or nature's changing course, untrimmed.
> But thy eternal summer shall not fade,
> Nor lose possession of that fair thou ow'st
> Nor shall death brag thou wand'rest in his shade, — *Death would be proud to claim the lover but can't?*
> When in eternal lines to time thou grow'st. — *What are "eternal lines to time"? Ask in class?*
> So long as men can breathe or eyes can see,
> So long lives this, and this gives life to thee. — *Final couplet seems to signal a shift in thought.*
>
> *This = the poem? (Art, like the writer's love, is eternal.)*

Taking notes

Note taking is also an important part of rereading a work of literature. In your notes you can try out ideas and develop your perspective on the work. Here are some notes one student took on a story by Edgar Allan Poe:

> "The Fall of the House of Usher"
>
> House of Usher has two meanings—the building and the family
>
> seeing the building has an emotional impact on the narrator: "with the first glimpse of the building, a sense of insufferable gloom pervaded my spirit"
>
> narrator uses descriptive language that evokes his feelings— "dull," "dark," "soundless," "dreary," "melancholy," "insufferable gloom"
>
> produces feeling of depression in reader too
>
> Who is this narrator? What is his relationship to the Ushers?

Such notes are the raw material out of which you will build an interpretation.

55b   Form an interpretation.

After rereading and jotting notes, you are ready to start forming an interpretation. At this stage, try to focus on a central issue. Look through your notes and annotations for recurring questions and insights about a single aspect of the work.

Focusing on a central issue

In forming an interpretation, it is important to focus on a central issue. In other words, avoid trying to do everything at once. You may think, for example, that *Huckleberry Finn* is a great book because it contains brilliant descriptions of scenery, has a lot of humorous moments, but also tells a serious story of one boy's development. This is an interesting, complex response to the work, but your job in writing an essay will be to close in on one issue that you can develop into a sustained, in-depth interpretation. For example, you might focus on ways in which the runaway slave Jim uses humor to preserve his dignity. Or you might focus on ironic discrepancies between what Huck says and what his heart tells him. Or you could choose just one or two minor characters, such as the Duke and the Dauphin, and show how they represent flaws in the society at large.

Asking questions that lead to an interpretation

Think of your interpretation as answering a question about the work. Some years ago, most interpretations answered questions about literary techniques, such as the writer's handling of plot, setting, and character (see p. 646). Today the concept of literary interpretation frequently includes questions about social context as well: what a work reveals about the time and culture in which it was written (see p. 647). Frequently you will find yourself writing about both technique and social context. For example, Margaret Peel, a student who wrote about Langston Hughes's poem "Ballad of the Landlord" (see pp. 663–67), addressed the following question, which touches on both language and race:

> How does the poem's language — through its four voices — dramatize the experience of a black man in a society dominated by whites?

In the introduction of your paper, you will usually announce your interpretation in a one- or two-sentence thesis. The thesis answers the central question that you posed. Here, for example, is Margaret Peel's two-sentence thesis:

> Langston Hughes's "Ballad of the Landlord" is narrated through four voices, each with its own perspective on the poem's action. These opposing voices — of a tenant, a landlord, the police, and the press — dramatize a black man's experience in a society dominated by whites.

Questions to ask about literature

QUESTIONS ABOUT TECHNIQUE

Plot. What central conflicts drive the plot? Are they internal (within a character) or external (between characters or between a character and a force)? How are conflicts resolved? Why are events revealed in a particular order?

Setting. Does the setting (time and place) create an atmosphere, give an insight into a character, suggest symbolic meanings, or hint at the theme of the work?

Character. What seems to motivate the central characters? Do any characters change significantly? If so, what—if anything—have they learned from their experiences? Do sharp contrasts between characters highlight important themes?

Point of view. Does the point of view—the perspective from which the story is narrated or the poem is spoken—affect our understanding of events? Does the narration reveal the character of the speaker, or does the speaker merely observe others? Is the narrator perhaps innocent, naive, or deceitful?

Theme. Does the work have an overall theme (a central insight about people or a truth about life)? If so, how do details in the work serve to illuminate this theme?

Language. Does language—such as formal or informal, standard or dialect, prosaic or poetic, cool or passionate—reveal the character of speakers? How do metaphors, similes, and sensory images contribute to the work? How do recurring images enrich the work and hint at its meaning? To what extent do sentence rhythms and sounds underscore the writer's meaning?

Questions to ask about literature (continued)

QUESTIONS ABOUT SOCIAL CONTEXT

Historical context. What does the work reveal about the time and place in which it was written? Does the work appear to promote or undermine a philosophy that was popular in its time, such as social Darwinism in the late nineteenth century?

Class. How does membership in a social class affect the characters' choices and their successes or failures? How does class affect the way characters view—or are viewed by—others? What do economic struggles reveal about power relationships in the society being depicted?

Race and culture. Are any characters portrayed as being caught between cultures: between the culture of home and work or school, for example, or between a traditional and an emerging culture? Are any characters engaged in a conflict with society because of their race or ethnic background? To what extent does the work celebrate a specific culture and its traditions?

Gender. Are any characters' choices restricted because of gender? What are the power relationships between the sexes, and do these change during the course of the work? Do any characters resist the gender roles society has assigned to them? Do other characters choose to conform to those roles?

Archetypes. Does a character, image, or plot fit a pattern—or archetype—that has been repeated in stories throughout history and across cultures? (For example, nearly every culture has stories about heroes, quests, redemption, and revenge.) How does an archetypal character, image, or plot line correspond to or differ from others like it?

55c Draft a thesis and sketch an outline.

Drafting a thesis

A thesis, which nearly always appears in the introduction, announces an essay's main point (see also 2a). In a literature paper, your thesis will answer the central question that you have asked about the work. In drafting your thesis, aim for a strong, assertive summary of your interpretation. Here, for example, are two successful theses taken from student essays, together with the central question each student had posed.

QUESTION
What does Stephen Crane's short story "The Open Boat" reveal about the relation between humans and nature?

THESIS
In Stephen Crane's gripping tale "The Open Boat," four men lost at sea discover not only that nature is indifferent to their fate but that their own particular talents make little difference as they struggle for survival.

QUESTION
In the Greek tragedy *Electra,* by Euripides, how do Electra and her mother, Clytemnestra, respond to the limitations society has placed on women?

THESIS
The experience of powerlessness has taught Electra and her mother two very different lessons: Electra has learned the value of traditional, conservative sex roles for women, but Clytemnestra has learned just the opposite.

As in other writing, the thesis of a literature paper cannot be too factual, too broad, or too vague (see 2a). For an essay on Mark Twain's *Huckleberry Finn,* for example, the following would all make poor thesis sentences.

TOO FACTUAL
As a runaway slave, Jim is in danger from the law.

TOO BROAD
In *Huckleberry Finn,* Mark Twain criticizes mid-nineteenth-century American society.

TOO VAGUE
Huckleberry Finn is Twain's most exciting work.

Here is a thesis about the novel that avoids these pitfalls.

ACCEPTABLE THESIS
Because Huckleberry Finn is a naive narrator, his comments on conventional religion are ironic at every turn, allowing Twain to poke fun at empty piety.

In a literature paper, your thesis should usually appear in your introductory paragraph. If your thesis is complex, it may take up the entire opening paragraph, as in Margaret Peel's paper on a Langston Hughes poem (p. 663). Often, however, you will want to present a context for the thesis and lead up to it, as in the following paragraph, which ends with the thesis (italicized).

In *Electra,* Euripides depicts two women who have had too little control over their lives. Electra, ignored by her mother, Clytemnestra, has been married off to a farmer and treated more or less like a slave. Clytemnestra has fared even worse. Her husband, Agamemnon, has slashed the throat of their daughter Iphigenia as a sacrifice to the gods. *The experience of powerlessness has taught Electra and her mother two very different lessons: Electra has learned the value of traditional, conservative sex roles for women, but Clytemnestra has learned just the opposite.*

Sketching an outline

Your thesis may strongly suggest a method of organization, in which case you will have little difficulty jotting down your essay's key points. Consider, for example, the following informal outline, based on a thesis that leads naturally to a three-part organization.

Thesis: George Bernard Shaw's *Major Barbara* depicts the ways in which three "religions" address the problem of poverty. The Established Church ignores poverty, the Salvation Army tries rather ineffectually to alleviate it, and a form of utopianism based on guns and money promises to eliminate it—but at a terrible cost.

—The Established Church (Lady Britomart)

—The Salvation Army (Major Barbara)

—Utopianism based on guns and money (Undershaft)

If your thesis does not by itself suggest a method of organization, turn to your notes and begin putting them into categories that relate to the thesis. For example, one student who was writing about Euripides' play *Medea* constructed the following formal outline from her notes.

Thesis: Although Medea professes great love for her children, Euripides gives us reason to suspect her sincerity: Medea does not hesitate to use the children as weapons in her bloody battle with Jason, and from the outset she displays little real concern for their fate.

I. From the very beginning of the play, Medea is a less than ideal mother.
   A. Her first words about the children are hostile.
   B. Her first actions suggest indifference.

II. In three scenes Medea appears to be a loving mother, but in each of these scenes we have reason to doubt her sincerity.

III. Throughout the play, as Medea plots her revenge, her overriding concern is not her children but her reputation.
   A. Fearing ridicule, she is proud of her reputation as one who can "help her friends and hurt her enemies."
   B. Her obsession with reputation may stem from the Greek view of reputation as a means of immortality.

IV. After she kills her children, Medea reveals her real concern.
   A. She shows no remorse.
   B. She revels in Jason's agony over their death.

Whether to use a formal or an informal outline is to some extent a matter of personal preference. For most purposes, you will probably find that an informal outline is sufficient, perhaps even preferable. (See 1d.)

55d Support your interpretation with evidence from the work; avoid simple plot summary.

Your thesis and tentative outline will point you toward details in the work relevant to your interpretation. As you begin filling out the body of your paper, make good use of those details.

Supporting your interpretation

As a rule, the topic sentence of each paragraph in the body of your paper should focus on some aspect of your overall interpretation. (See 4a.) The rest of the paragraph should present details and perhaps quotations from the work that back up your interpretation. In the following paragraph, which develops part of the outline sketched on page 650, the topic sentence comes first. It sums up the religious views represented by Lady Britomart, a character in George Bernard Shaw's play *Major Barbara*.

> Lady Britomart, a member of the Established Church of England, reveals her superficial attitude toward religion in a scene that takes place in her fashionable London townhouse. Religion, according to Lady Britomart, is a morbid topic of conversation. She admonishes her daughter Barbara: "Really, Barbara, you go on as if religion were a pleasant subject. Do have some sense of propriety" (1.686–87). Religion is an unpleasant subject to Lady Britomart because, unlike Barbara, she finds no joy or humor within her religion. It is not simply that she is a humorless person, for she frequently displays a sharp wit. But in Lady Britomart's upper-class world, religion has its proper place—a serious place bound by convention

and cut off from the real world. When Undershaft suggests, for example, that religion can be a pleasant and profoundly important subject, Lady Britomart replies, "Well if you are determined to have it [religion], then I insist on having it in a proper and respectable way. Charles: ring for prayers" (1.690–93).

Notice that the writer has quoted dialogue from the play to lend both flavor and substance to her interpretation. Notice too that the writer is indeed *interpreting* the work: She is not merely summarizing the plot.

Avoiding simple plot summary

In a literature paper, it is tempting to rely heavily on plot summary and avoid interpretation. You can resist this temptation by paying special attention to your topic sentences. The following rough-draft topic sentence, for instance, led to a plot summary rather than an interpretation.

> As they drift down the river on a raft, Huck and the runaway slave Jim have many philosophical discussions.

The student's revised topic sentence, which announces an interpretation, is much better:

> The theme of dawning moral awareness is reinforced by the many philosophical discussions between Huck and Jim, the runaway slave, as they drift down the river on a raft.

Usually a little effort is all that is needed to make the difference between a plot summary that goes nowhere and a focused, forceful interpretation. As with all forms of writing, revision is key.

LOOKING AT YOURSELF AS A WRITER
Avoiding simple plot summary

When you write about a literary work that has a plot (such as a short story, a play, or a film), your instructor expects more than just a plot summary. If you—like many students—find it difficult to avoid veering off into plot summary, consider some common causes and cures.

CAUSE You assume that your audience may not have read the work and either needs to hear the plot or wants to hear it. Or you enjoyed the story and want to share it with readers.

CURE Unless you have been told otherwise, in academic writing you should assume that your readers have read the work. Your job is to share with them not the work itself but your own interpretation of it.

CAUSE Time words such as *when* and *after,* which are natural and useful transitions in literature papers, tempt you to veer off into plot summary.

CURE Continue to use these important transitions, but catch yourself if two or three sentences in a row move away from interpretation. Sometimes you can open a sentence with a subordinate clause beginning with a time word and put the interpretation in the main clause, like this: "When Sister says that the entire family has turned against her, she seems to be right, even though many of this narrator's other perceptions are not to be trusted."

CAUSE Plot summaries appeal to you because you find a chronological organization of your paper easier to manage than other kinds of organization.

CURE Although time order is indeed one of the easiest methods of organization, be aware that the easiest strategy is not always the best one.

Avoiding simple plot summary (continued)

CAUSE   Because you can't think of an interpretation, you
         turn to a plot summary.

CURE   Admittedly, interpretations are not always easy to
         come up with, but a variety of strategies may help.
         First, read the work more than once and pose ques-
         tions that might lead to an interpretation (see the
         chart on pp. 646–47 for examples). Second, take a
         look at sample papers, such as the two at the end of
         this chapter or any that appear in your literary an-
         thology. Third, discuss the work with classmates or
         friends. Finally, consider making an appointment
         with your instructor or visiting your college's writing
         center.

55e   Integrate quotations from the work.

Quotations from a literary work can lend vivid support to
your argument, but keep most quotations fairly short. Excessive use of long quotations bores readers and interrupts
the flow of your interpretation.

Integrating quotations smoothly into your own text can
present a challenge. Because of the complexities of literature, do not be surprised to find yourself puzzling over the
most graceful way to tuck in a short phrase or the clearest
way to introduce a more extended passage from the work.

NOTE: The parenthetical citations at the ends of examples in
this section tell readers where the quoted words can be
found. They indicate the lines of a poem; the act, scene, and
lines of a play; or the page number of a quotation from a
short story or novel. For guidelines on using citations, see
53a.

Introducing quotations

When writing about nonfiction essays and books, you have probably learned to introduce a quotation with a signal phrase naming the author: *According to Jane Doe, Jane Doe points out that, Jane Doe presents a compelling argument,* and so on.

When introducing quotations from a literary work, however, make sure that you don't confuse the author with the narrator of a story, the speaker of a poem, or a character in a play. Instead of naming the author, you can refer to the narrator or speaker—or to the work itself.

> **INAPPROPRIATE**
> Poet Andrew Marvell describes his fear of death like this: "But at my back I always hear / Time's wingèd chariot hurrying near" (21–22).

> **APPROPRIATE**
> Addressing his beloved in an attempt to win her sexual favors, the speaker of the poem argues that death gives them no time to waste: "But at my back I always hear / Time's wingèd chariot hurrying near" (21–22).

> **APPROPRIATE**
> The poem "To His Coy Mistress" says as much about fleeting time and death as it does about sexual passion. Its most powerful lines may well be "But at my back I always hear / Time's wingèd chariot hurrying near" (21–22).

In the last example, you could of course mention the author as well: *Marvell's poem "To His Coy Mistress" says as much . . .* Although the author is mentioned, he is not being confused with the speaker of the poem.

If you are quoting the words of a character in a story or a play, you should name the character who is speaking and provide a context for the spoken words. In the following examples, the quoted dialogue is from Tennessee Williams's play *The Glass Menagerie* and Shirley Jackson's short story "The Lottery."

> Laura's life is so completely ruled by Amanda that when urged to make a wish on the moon, she asks, "What shall I wish for, Mother?" (1.5.140).

> When a neighbor suggests that the lottery should be abandoned, Old Man Warner responds, "There's *always* been a lottery" (284).

Avoiding shifts in tense

Because it is conventional to write about literature in the present tense (see p. 226) and because literary works often use other tenses, you will need to exercise some care when weaving quotations into your own text. A first-draft attempt may result in an awkward shift, as it did for one student who was writing about Nadine Gordimer's short story "Friday's Footprint."

TENSE SHIFT
When Rita sees Johnny's relaxed attitude, "she blushed, like a wave of illness" (159).

To avoid the distracting shift from present to past tense, the writer decided to include the reference to Rita's blushing in her own text and reduce the length of the quotation.

REVISED
When Rita sees Johnny's relaxed attitude, she blushes "like a wave of illness" (159).

The writer could have changed the quotation to present tense, using brackets to indicate the change, like this: *When Rita sees Johnny's relaxed attitude, "she blushe[s] like a wave of illness" (159).* However, using brackets around just one letter of a word can seem pedantic, so the earlier revision is preferable. (For advice on using brackets around a word or more, see 39c.)

Using quotations within quotations

In writing about literature, you may sometimes want to use a quotation with another quotation embedded in it—when you are quoting dialogue in a novel, for example. In such cases, set off the main quotation with double quotation marks, as you usually would, and set off the embedded quotation with single quotation marks. (See also 37c.) The following example from a student paper quotes lines from Amy Tan's novel *The Hundred Secret Senses*.

> Early in the novel the narrator's half-sister Kwan sees—or thinks she sees—ghosts: "'Libby-ah' she'll say to me. 'Guess who I see yesterday, you guess.' And I don't have to guess she's talking about someone dead" (3).

Formatting quotations

Guidelines for formatting quotations from short stories (or novels), poems, and plays are slightly different

SHORT STORIES OR NOVELS If a quotation from a short story or a novel takes up four or fewer typed lines, put it in quotation marks and run it into the text of your essay. Include a page number in parentheses after the quotation.

> The narrator of Eudora Welty's "Why I Live at the PO," known to us only as "Sister," makes many catty remarks about her enemies. For example, she calls Mr. Whitaker "this photographer with the pop-eyes" (46).

If a quotation from a short story or a novel is five typed lines or longer, set it off from the text by indenting one inch (or ten spaces) from the left margin; when you set a quotation off from the text, you should not use quotation marks around it. (See also 37b.) Put the page number in parentheses after the final mark of punctuation.

Sister's tale begins with "I," and she makes every event
revolve around herself, even her sister's marriage:

> I was getting along fine with Mama, Papa-Daddy, and
> Uncle Rondo until my sister Stella-Rondo just sepa-
> rated from her husband and came back home again.
> Mr. Whitaker! Of course I went with Mr. Whitaker
> first, when he first appeared here in China Grove,
> taking "Pose Yourself" photos, and Stella-Rondo
> broke us up. (46)

POEMS   Enclose quotations of three or fewer lines of poetry in quotation marks within your text, and indicate line
breaks with a slash. (See also 39e.) Include line numbers in
parentheses at the end of the quotation.

> The opening lines of Frost's "Fire and Ice" strike a conversa-
> tional tone: "Some say the world will end in fire, / Some say
> in ice" (1–2).

When you quote four or more lines of poetry, set the quotation off from the text by indenting one inch (or ten spaces)
and omit the quotation marks. Put the line numbers in parentheses after the final mark of punctuation.

> The opening stanza of Louise Bogan's "Women" startles read-
> ers by presenting a negative stereotype of women:
>
>> Women have no wilderness in them,
>> They are provident instead,
>> Content in the tight hot cell of their hearts
>> To eat dusty bread. (1–4)

PLAYS   If a quotation from a play takes up four or fewer
typed lines and is spoken by only one character, put quotation marks around it and run it into the text of your essay.
Whenever possible, include the act number, scene number,
and line numbers in parentheses at the end of the quotation.
Separate the numbers with periods, and use arabic numerals unless your instructor prefers roman numerals.

Mirabell—one of Congreve's manipulative yet charming characters—adores even the faults of his beloved Mrs. Millamant, faults "so natural, or so artful, that they become her" (1.175–76).

If a dramatic quotation by a single character is five lines or longer, set it off in the same way you would set off a long prose quotation. Include the act number, scene number, and line numbers after the final mark of punctuation.

When quoting dialogue between two or more characters in a play, no matter how many lines you use, set the quotation off from the text. Type the character's name in all capital letters at a one-inch (ten-space) indent from the left margin. Indent subsequent lines under the character's name an additional quarter inch (or three spaces).

Throughout the play, Mrs. Millamant and Mirabell try to outdo each other in witty exchanges, as when they debate Mirabell's opinion that beauty is bestowed by the lover instead of being possessed by the beloved:

> MRS. MILLAMANT. One no more owes one's beauty to a lover than one's wit to an echo. They can but reflect what we look and say; vain empty things if we are silent or unseen, and want a being.
> MIRABELL. Yet to those two vain empty things you owe two of the greatest pleasures of your life.
> MRS. MILLAMANT. How so?
> MIRABELL. To your lover you owe the pleasure of hearing yourselves praised; and to an echo the pleasure of hearing yourselves talk. (2.455–64)

55f Observe the conventions of literary papers.

When you are writing a literature paper, it is important to observe certain conventions so that your readers' attention will be focused directly on your interpretation, not on the details of your presentation.

Referring to authors and titles

The first time you make reference to authors, refer to them by their first and last names: *Virginia Woolf was one of England's most important novelists.* In subsequent references, use their last names only: *Woolf's early work was largely overlooked.* As a rule, do not use titles such as Mr. or Ms. or Dr.

Titles of short stories, essays, and most poems are put in quotation marks: "The Dead" by James Joyce; "The Death of the Moth" by Virginia Woolf; "High Windows" by Philip Larkin. (See 37d.) Titles of novels, nonfiction books, plays, and epics or other long poems are underlined or italicized: *Heart of Darkness* by Joseph Conrad; *I Know Why the Caged Bird Sings* by Maya Angelou; *Macbeth* by William Shakespeare; *Howl* by Allen Ginsberg. (See 42a.)

Referring to characters and events

Refer to each character by the name most often used for him or her in the work. If, for instance, a character's name is Lambert Strether and he is always referred to as "Strether," do not call him "Lambert" or "Mr. Strether." Similarly, write "Lady Macbeth," not "Mrs. Macbeth."

When describing fictional events in a work of literature, use the present tense: "Octavia *demands* blind obedience from James and from all of her children. When James and Ty *catch* two redbirds in their trap, they *want* to play with them; Octavia, however, *has* other plans for the birds." (See also 13b and 28a.)

Referring to parts of works

Be as accurate as possible when referring to subdivisions of a literary work. Avoid using phrases like *the part where.* Instead give specific references by using the appropriate descriptive terms: *the final stanza, the scene in which Hamlet confronts his mother, the passage that refers to Jane Austen,* and so on.

55g If you use secondary sources, document them appropriately and avoid plagiarism.

Many literature papers do not rely on secondary sources — works other than the literary text under discussion. (For an example of an essay without secondary sources, see pp. 663–66.)

Other literature papers use some ideas from sources such as articles or books of literary criticism, biographies of the author, the author's own essays and autobiography, and histories of the era in which the work was written. (For an example of a paper that uses secondary sources, see pp. 667–74.) Even if you use secondary sources, your main goal should always be to develop your own understanding and interpretation of the literary work.

Whenever you use secondary sources, you must document them and you must avoid plagiarism. Plagiarism is unacknowledged borrowing — whether intentional or unintentional — of a source's words or ideas. (See 50b.)

Documenting secondary sources

Most literature papers are documented with the system recommended by the Modern Language Association (MLA). This system of documentation is discussed in detail in 53, which is easy to find because its pages have a vertical band in teal.

An MLA in-text citation usually combines a signal phrase with a page number in parentheses.

SAMPLE MLA IN-TEXT CITATION

Arguing that fate has little to do with the tragedy that befalls Oedipus, Bernard Knox writes that "the catastrophe of Oedipus is that he discovers his own identity; and for his discovery he is first and last responsible" (6).

The signal phrase names the author of the secondary source; the number in parentheses is the page on which the quoted words appear.

The in-text citation is used in combination with a list of works cited at the end of the paper. Anyone interested in knowing additional information about the secondary source can consult the list of works cited. Here, for example, is the Works Cited entry for the work referred to in the sample in-text citation.

SAMPLE ENTRY IN THE LIST OF WORKS CITED

Knox, Bernard. <u>Oedipus at Thebes: Sophocles' Tragic
Hero and His Time</u>. New York: Norton, 1971.

As you document secondary sources with in-text citations, consult 53a; as you construct your list of works cited, consult 53c.

Avoiding plagiarism

The rules about plagiarism are the same for literary papers as for other research writing. It is wrong to use other writers' ideas or language without giving credit to your source. If an interpretation was suggested to you by another critic's work or if an obscure point was clarified by someone else's research, it is your responsibility to cite the source. If you have borrowed any phrases or sentences from your source, you must put them in quotation marks and credit the author.

For important tips on avoiding plagiarism, see 50 and the chart on page 583.

Following are two sample essays. The first, by Margaret Peel, has no secondary sources. (Langston Hughes's "Ballad of the Landlord," the poem on which the essay is based, appears on pp. 666–67.) The second essay, by Angelo Ventresca, is an example of a paper that uses secondary sources.

SAMPLE ESSAY (WITHOUT SECONDARY SOURCES)

Opposing Voices in "Ballad of the Landlord"

Langston Hughes's "Ballad of the Landlord" is narrated through four voices, each with its own perspective on the poem's action. These opposing voices--of a tenant, a landlord, the police, and the press--dramatize a black man's experience in a society dominated by whites.

The main voice in the poem is that of the tenant, who, as the last line tells us, is black. The tenant is characterized by his informal, non-standard speech. He uses slang ("Ten Bucks"), contracted words ('member, more'n), and nonstandard grammar ("These steps is broken down"). This colloquial English suggests the tenant's separation from the world of convention, represented by the formal voices of the police and the press, which appear later in the poem.

Although the tenant uses nonstandard English, his argument is organized and logical. He begins with a reasonable complaint and a gentle reminder that the complaint is already a week old: "My roof has sprung a leak. / Don't you 'member I told you about it / Way last week?" (2-4). In the second stanza, he appeals diplomatically to the landlord's self-interest: "These steps is broken down. / When you come up yourself / It's a wonder you don't fall down" (6-8). In the third stanza, when the landlord has responded to his complaints with a demand for rent money, the tenant becomes more forceful, but his voice is still reasonable: "Ten

Bucks you say is due? / Well, that's Ten Bucks
more'n I'll pay you / Till you fix this house up
new" (10-12).

   The fourth stanza marks a shift in the tone
of the argument. At this point the tenant responds
more emotionally, in reaction to the landlord's
threats to evict him. By the fifth stanza, the
tenant has unleashed his anger: "Um-huh! You talking high and mighty" (17). Hughes uses an exclamation point for the first time; the tenant is raising his voice at last. As the argument gets more
heated, the tenant finally resorts to the language of violence: "You ain't gonna be able to say
a word / If I land my fist on you" (19-20).

   These are the last words the tenant speaks in
the poem. Perhaps Hughes wants to show how black
people who threaten violence are silenced. When a
new voice is introduced--the landlord's--the poem
shifts to italics:

   Police! Police!
   Come and get this man!
   He's trying to ruin the government
   And overturn the land! (21-24)

This response is clearly an overreaction to a
small threat. Instead of dealing with the tenant
directly, the landlord shouts for the police. His
hysterical voice--marked by repetitions and punctuated with exclamation points--reveals his dis-
proportionate fear and outrage. And his conclusions are equally excessive: This black man, he
claims, is out to "ruin the government" and "over-

turn the land." Although the landlord's overreaction is humorous, it is sinister as well, because
the landlord knows that, no matter how excessive
his claims are, he has the police and the law on
his side.

In line 25, the regular meter and rhyme of
the poem break down, perhaps showing how an arrest
disrupts everyday life. The "voice" in lines 25-29
has two parts: the clanging sound of the police
("Copper's whistle! / Patrol bell!") and, in sharp
contrast, the unemotional, factual tone of a police
report ("Arrest. / Precinct Station. / Iron cell.").

The last voice in the poem is the voice of
the press, represented in newspaper headlines:
"MAN THREATENS LANDLORD / TENANT HELD NO BAIL /
JUDGE GIVES NEGRO 90 DAYS IN COUNTY JAIL" (31-33).
Meter and rhyme return here, as if to show that
once the tenant is arrested, life can go on as
usual. The language of the press, like that of the
police, is cold and distant, and it gives the tenant less and less status. In line 31, he is a
"man"; in line 32, he has been demoted to a "tenant"; and in line 33, he has become a "Negro," or
just another statistic.

By using four opposing voices in "Ballad of
the Landlord," Hughes effectively dramatizes different views of minority assertiveness. To the
tenant, assertiveness is informal and natural, as
his language shows; to the landlord, it is a dangerous threat, as his hysterical response suggests.
The police response is, like the language that de-

scribes it, short and sharp. Finally, the press's view of events, represented by the headlines, is distant and unsympathetic.

By the end of the poem, we understand the predicament of the black man. Exploited by the landlord, politically oppressed by those who think he's out "to ruin the government," physically restrained by the police and the judicial system, and denied his individuality by the press, he is saved only by his own sense of humor. The very title of the poem suggests his--and Hughes's--sense of humor. The tenant is singing a ballad to his oppressors, but this ballad is no love song. It portrays the oppressors, through their own voices, in an unflattering light: the landlord as cowardly and ridiculous, the police and press as dull and soulless. The tenant may lack political power, but he speaks with vitality, and no one can say he lacks dignity or the spirit to survive.

Ballad of the Landlord

Landlord, landlord,
My roof has sprung a leak.
Don't you 'member I told you about it
Way last week?

Landlord, landlord,
These steps is broken down.
When you come up yourself
It's a wonder you don't fall down.

Ten Bucks you say I owe you?
Ten Bucks you say is due?
Well, that's Ten Bucks more'n I'll pay you
Till you fix this house up new.

What? You gonna get eviction orders?
You gonna cut off my heat?
You gonna take my furniture and
Throw it in the street?

Um-huh! You talking high and mighty.
Talk on — till you get through.
You ain't gonna be able to say a word
If I land my fist on you.

Police! Police!
Come and get this man!
He's trying to ruin the government
And overturn the land!

Copper's whistle!
Patrol bell!
Arrest.

Precinct Station.
Iron cell.
Headlines in press:

MAN THREATENS LANDLORD

TENANT HELD NO BAIL

JUDGE GIVES NEGRO 90 DAYS IN COUNTY JAIL

— Langston Hughes

SAMPLE ESSAY (WITH SECONDARY SOURCES)

Dual Narrative Perspective in

Alice Munro's "Walker Brothers Cowboy"

In "Walker Brothers Cowboy," Canadian short-
story writer Alice Munro uses what Brandon Conron
calls "a bifocal point of view" (111). The dominant perspective--a "you-are-there" present-tense
narration written in the first person from the
point of view of a child--is shaded by an adult
awareness that points toward the larger signifi-

cance of events. By manipulating point of view at crucial points in the story, Munro reveals events not only through the authentic, naive eyes of a child but also through the lens of an adult's concerns. Those concerns--passing time and mortality, along with sexual longing and lost love--give the story a sense of poignancy that childish observations alone could never achieve.

In the story, set in the 1930s, Ben Jordan, the kindly father of the young female narrator, takes her and her brother with him on his afternoon rounds as a Walker Brothers man, a traveling salesman who deals in medicines, flavorings, and even rat poison. We understand that Ben's job, at least in the eyes of his wife, is a considerable step down from his failed business of raising foxes. To Mrs. Jordan, bitter that fate has flung her family "onto a street of poor persons," her husband is "a pedlar knocking at backwoods kitchens" (Munro 4). Ben Jordan, in contrast, takes his new job with as much good humor as possible and even makes up funny songs about it to entertain his family. As a Walker Brothers man, he sings that he has "all liniments and oils, / For everything from corns to boils" (Munro 4).

The dominant point of view of the story, that of a child, reveals a sharp contrast between the magical and expansive world of Ben Jordan and the straitlaced, tightly circumscribed world of his wife. There is no doubt about which world this child prefers. In the opening line of the story,

her father asks her after supper, "Want to go down
and see if the Lake's still there?" (Munro 1).
They head out of town, for Lake Huron, encountering friendly neighbors and panhandling tramps
(just frightening enough to be intriguing), with
whom her father shares a cigarette. At the lake-
shore, with a touch of poetry, her father dwells
on the greatness of the Great Lakes, explaining
how they came to be:

> Then came the ice, creeping down from
> the north, pushing deep into the low
> places. . . . And then the ice went
> back, shrank back towards the North Pole
> where it came from, and left its fingers
> of ice in the deep places it had gouged,
> and ice turned to lakes and there they
> were today. They were new as time went.
> (Munro 3)

The child narrator describes walks with her
mother quite differently. They walk to the grocery
store, not the lake, and they are both dressed up,
the mother in "a good dress, navy blue with little
flowers, sheer, worn over a navy-blue slip," the
daughter in "wretched curls and flaunting hair
bow, scrubbed knees and white socks" (Munro 5).
"We have not walked past two houses," says the
child narrator, "before I feel we have become
objects of universal ridicule. Even the dirty
words chalked on the sidewalk are laughing at us"
(Munro 5).

Although the dominant perspective is that of

a child, Munro shifts at times to the perspective
of an adult looking back. For example, after the
child narrator learns from her father that the
Great Lakes are not new, as time goes, an adult
narrator takes over, describing how she is unsettled by her father's mortality and by her own
eventual aging and death:

> The tiny share we have of time appalls
> me, though my father seems to regard it
> with tranquility. He was not alive when
> this century started. I will be barely
> alive--old, old--when it ends. I do not
> like to think of it. (Munro 3)

In another scene, the child narrator takes us
along on a car trip with her brother and father,
bumping along on unpaved roads and noticing strange
farmhouses with upstairs doors that open onto nothing but air. But at a key moment, as the child
narrator glimpses one of the desolate farmhouses on
the route, her adult counterpart surfaces, again
dwelling on the passage of time:

> The nineteen-thirties. How much this
> kind of farmhouse, this kind of after-
> noon, seem to me to belong to that one
> decade in time, just as my father's hat
> does, his bright flared tie, our car
> with its wide running board (an Essex,
> and long past its prime). (Munro 8)

As the critic E. D. Blodgett has pointed out, the
narrator "acquires a changed level of understanding . . . after the event" (17).

The emotional height of "Walker Brothers Cowboy" occurs in a scene in which passing time and
lost love blend as the dominant themes. Ben Jordan
drives his children off his route and to the house
inhabited by Nora Cronin and her blind, aging
mother. At this point in the story, there is little
need for an adult narrator--because the child narrator's naive descriptions of events reveal details,
especially concerning sexuality, that are beyond or
just at the edge of her understanding. As critic
Ildikó de Papp Carrington writes, Munro manipulates
point of view to emphasize "the child's peripheral
position, her innocent eye's incomprehension of the
most powerful facts of life" (72).

We are never told that Nora is a former girlfriend of Ben's, but this becomes apparent through
the actions of Nora and Ben, as perceived by the
child narrator. When Nora and Ben joke at the start
of their reunion, Nora's laugh is "abrupt and somewhat angry" (Munro 11). When Nora announces to her
mother that Ben is married and the father of two
children, she does so "cheerfully and aggressively"
(Munro 12). It becomes clear to us--if not to the
narrator herself--that Nora had once hoped to be
Ben's wife.

The child narrator describes Nora with a mixture of flattering and unflattering details that
would sound catty if told by an adult. The "lavish"
dress Nora has changed into, the narrator says,
exposes her "heavy" arms, and "every bit of her
skin you can see is covered with dark little

freckles like measles" (Munro 12). As Ben and Nora
banter about the flowers in her dress, the narrator notices that Nora sends "a smell of cologne
far and wide when she moves and [displays] a
change of voice to go with the dress, something
more sociable and youthful" (Munro 13). The child's
perceptions stop just short of an outright acknowl-
edgment that Nora is trying to make herself sexu-
ally attractive to Ben.

When Nora takes a bottle out of the top of a
pump organ and pours some of its contents into
glasses for herself and Ben, the narrator knows
that the bottle holds whisky, something that Mrs.
Jordan says her husband never drinks. "But I see
he does," notes the child. "He drinks whisky and
he talks of people whose names I have never heard
before" (Munro 15).

Eventually, Nora puts a record on the gramo-
phone and encourages the narrator to dance with
her, wrapping the girl in "her strange gaiety, her
smell of whisky, cologne, and sweat" (Munro 16).
When Nora turns to Ben and asks him to dance, we
reach the climax of the story. He declines, po-
litely, on grounds of being a bad dancer. As Nora
stands there, rejected, the narrator becomes aware
of Nora's sexuality, describing "her breasts,
which a moment ago embarrassed me with their warmth
and bulk, rising and falling under her loose flow-
ered dress, her face shining with the exercise
and delight" (Munro 17). Nora's disappointment,
though controlled, is clear from her words: "I

can drink alone but I can't dance alone"
(Munro 17).

Throughout the scene in the front room, the
narrator, though sensitive to the events around
her, leaves the interpretation of what is happen-
ing between Nora and Ben largely to readers. As
Carrington writes, "The reader sees the complicated reasons for Nora's painfully confused arou-
sal, but the young narrator . . . is too young to
grasp Nora's feelings of betrayal, physical
loneliness, and loss" (73).

On the ride home the narrator realizes that
some things must not be mentioned to her mother,
but she understands these things to be just the
whisky and perhaps the dancing. She is too young
to understand the sexual tension and frustration
that she has witnessed.

At the very end of the story, the narrator
assumes her adult perspective one last time, describing her father's life as a complicated whole
that she will never understand:

> I feel my father's life flowing back
> from our car in the last of the after-
> noon, darkening and turning strange,
> like a landscape that has an enchantment
> on it, making it kindly, ordinary, and
> familiar while you are looking at it,
> but changing it, once your back is
> turned, into something you will never
> know, with all kinds of weathers, and
> distances you cannot imagine. (Munro 18)

As Blodgett writes, the narrator "becomes gradually aware that the past is a psychological domain that makes of those who appear so intimately ours something other and mysterious" (20).

In "Walker Brothers Cowboy," the adult sensibility that surfaces through the child's narration nudges readers to an understanding of what Conron calls the "complexity of personal relationships" (123). Although the people in this and other Munro stories may seem ordinary, their personal lives, as Munro has said herself, are "dull, simple, amazing, and unfathomable--deep caves paved with kitchen linoleum" (qtd. in Turbide 48).

[NEW PAGE]

Works Cited

Blodgett, E. D. Alice Munro. Twayne's World Authors Ser. 800. Ed. Robert Lecker. Boston: Twayne, 1988.

Carrington, Ildikó de Papp. Controlling the Uncontrollable: The Fiction of Alice Munro. De Kalb: Northern Illinois UP, 1989.

Conron, Brandon. "Munro's Wonderland." Canadian Literature 78 (1978): 109-23.

Munro, Alice. "Walker Brothers Cowboy." Dance of the Happy Shades. London: Penguin, 1983. 1-18.

Turbide, Diane. "The Incomparable Storyteller." Maclean's 17 Oct. 1994: 46-49.

56

Documenting sources across the curriculum

To document sources, students in most English classes use the Modern Language Association (MLA) style of in-text citation described in 53. When you are writing in other classes across the curriculum, you may be asked to use another style of documentation.

This section describes two frequently used styles: the American Psychological Association (APA) style of in-text citation, used in the social sciences, and the *Chicago Manual of Style* system of footnotes or endnotes, used in history and some humanities courses. For a list of style manuals in a variety of disciplines, see 56g. Always use the style of documentation recommended by your instructor.

A useful list of sources (both print and online) and documentation models for many disciplines can be found on a Web site that accompanies this text: *Research and Documentation in the Electronic Age*. The address is http://www.bedfordbooks.com/rd/index.html.

APA STYLE (SOCIAL SCIENCES)

In most social sciences classes, such as psychology, sociology, anthropology, and business, you will be asked to use the APA style of in-text citations and references. The guidelines in 56a–56c are based on APA's November 19, 1999, update posted on its Web site, <http://www.apa.org/journals/webref.html>. You may wish to check this Web site for future updates. For an electronic source, cite the same information that you would for a print source, and then include a retrieval statement.

Directory to APA in-text citations (56a)

NOTE: For a directory of APA references, see page 680.

NOTE: For a sample APA paper, see pages 690–99.

56a   APA in-text citations

The APA recommends an author/date style of in-text citations. These citations refer readers to a list of references at the end of the paper.

APA in-text citations provide at least the author's last name and the date of publication. For direct quotations, a page number is given as well.

1. BASIC FORMAT FOR A QUOTATION   Ordinarily, introduce the quotation with a signal phrase that includes the author's last name followed by the date of publication in parentheses. Put the page number (preceded by "p.") in parentheses at the end of the quotation.

```
According to Hart (1996), some primatologists
"wondered if apes had learned Language, with a
capital L" (p. 109).
```

When the author's name does not appear in the signal phrase, place the author's name, the date, and the page number in parentheses at the end of the quotation. Use commas between items in the parentheses: (Hart, 1996, p. 109).

2. BASIC FORMAT FOR A SUMMARY OR A PARAPHRASE   For a summary or a paraphrase, include the author's last name and the date either in a signal phrase or in parentheses at the end.

```
According to Hart (1996), researchers took
Terrace's conclusions seriously, and funding for
language experiments soon declined.
```

```
Researchers took Terrace's conclusions seriously,
and funding for language experiments soon declined
(Hart, 1996).
```

NOTE: A page number is not required, but provide one if it would help your readers find a specific page in a long work.

3. A WORK WITH TWO AUTHORS   Name both authors in the signal phrase or parentheses each time you cite the work. In the parentheses, use "&" between the authors' names; in the signal phrase, use "and."

```
Patterson and Linden (1981) agreed that the
gorilla Koko acquired language more slowly than a
normal speaking child.
```

```
Koko acquired language more slowly than a normal
speaking child (Patterson & Linden, 1981).
```

4. A WORK WITH THREE TO FIVE AUTHORS   Identify all authors in the signal phrase or the parentheses the first time you cite the source.

```
Researchers found a marked improvement in the com-
puter skills of students who took part in the pro-
```

Literature and other disciplines

```
gram (Levy, Bertrand, Muller, Vining, & Majors,
1997).
```

In subsequent citations, use the first author's name followed by "et al." in either the signal phrase or the parentheses.

```
Though school board members were skeptical at
first, the program has now won the board's full
support (Levy et al., 1997).
```

5. A WORK WITH SIX OR MORE AUTHORS   Use only the first author's name followed by "et al." in all citations.

```
Better measurements of sophistication in computer
use could be obtained through more thorough
testing (Blili et al., 1996).
```

6. UNKNOWN AUTHOR   If the author is not given, use the first word or two of the title in the signal phrase or the parenthetical citation.

```
Massachusetts state and municipal governments have
initiated several programs to improve public
safety, including community policing and after-
school activities ("Innovations," 1997).
```

If "Anonymous" is specified as the author, treat it as if it were a real name: (Anonymous, 1996). In the bibliographic references, also use the name Anonymous as author.

7. CORPORATE AUTHOR   If the author is a government agency or other corporate organization with a long and cumbersome name, spell out the name the first time you use it in a citation followed by an abbreviation in brackets. In later citations, simply use the abbreviation.

FIRST CITATION   (National Institute of Mental
                       Health [NIMH], 1997)

LATER CITATIONS   (NIMH, 1997)

8. TWO OR MORE WORKS IN THE SAME PARENTHESES When your parenthetical citation names two or more works, put them in the same order that they appear in the bibliography, separated by semicolons.

```
Recently, researchers have investigated the degree
to which gender affects the distribution of wel-
fare (Gilbert, 1995; Leira, 1994).
```

9. AUTHORS WITH THE SAME LAST NAME To avoid confusion, use initials with the last names if your bibliography lists two or more authors with the same last name.

```
Research by D. L. Johnson (1996) revealed that . . .
```

10. PERSONAL COMMUNICATION Conversations, memos, letters, e-mail, and similar unpublished person-to-person communications should be cited by initials, last name, and precise date.

```
F. Moore (personal communication, January 4, 1997)
has said that funding for the program will con-
tinue for at least another year.
```

It is not necessary to include personal communications in the bibliographic references at the end of your paper.

11. WEB SITE Cite a Web site by giving the Web address in parentheses: (http://pgweb.pg.cc.md.us). If you are referring to the entire site, you do not need a bibliographic entry; if you are referring to a specific document from the site, give the author and date of publication, and provide a bibliographic entry in the list of references (see p. 686)

56b APA references (bibliographic list)

In APA style, the alphabetical list of works cited is called "References." This section presents specific models to follow while preparing each entry in your list, along with the following general advice.

Directory to APA references (bibliographic list) (56b)

BOOKS

1. Basic format for a book
2. Two or more authors
3. Corporate author
4. Unknown author
5. Editors
6. Translation
7. Edition other than the first
8. Article in an edited book
9. Multivolume work
10. Two or more works by the same author

ARTICLES IN PERIODICALS

11. Article in a journal paginated by volume
12. Article in a journal paginated by issue
13. Article in a magazine
14. Article in a newspaper
15. Letter to the editor
16. Review
17. Two or more works by the same author in the same year

ELECTRONIC SOURCES

18. Material from an online database
19. Material from a CD-ROM database
20. Material from a database accessed via the Web
21. Document from a Web site
22. Electronic discussion list message
23. E-mail

OTHER SOURCES

24. Dissertation abstract
25. Government document
26. Conference proceedings
27. Computer program
28. Videotape

NOTE: For a sample APA paper, see pages 690–99.

TITLE AND PLACEMENT OF LIST The list of references begins on a new page at the end of your paper. Center the title "References" (without quotation marks) in the width of the page. See page 698 for an example.

INDENTING Unless your instructor suggests otherwise, do not indent the first line of an entry but indent any additional lines one-half inch (or five spaces). This technique, known as a "hanging indent," is used for final copy: student papers and actual journal articles. (For manuscripts submitted to journals, APA requires paragraph-style indents, which the publishers then convert to hanging indents.)

ALPHABETIZING THE LIST Alphabetize your list by the last name of the author (or editor); if there is no author or editor, alphabetize by the first word of the title other than *A, An,* or *The.*

AUTHORS' NAMES Invert *all* authors' names, and use initials instead of first names. With two or more authors, use an ampersand (&) rather than the word "and." Separate the names with commas. Use all authors' names; do not use "et al."

DATE Place the date of publication in parentheses immediately after the last author's name.

TITLES OF BOOKS Underline titles and subtitles of books; capitalize only the first word of the title and subtitle (as well as all proper nouns).

TITLES OF ARTICLES Do not place titles of periodical articles in quotation marks, and capitalize only the first word of the title and subtitle (and all proper nouns).

TITLES OF PERIODICALS Capitalize titles of periodicals as you would capitalize them ordinarily (see 45c). Underline the volume number of periodicals.

PAGE NUMBERS   Use the abbreviation "p." (or "pp." for plural) before page numbers of newspaper articles and works in anthologies, but do not use it before page numbers of articles appearing in magazines and scholarly journals.

PUBLISHERS' NAMES   You may use a short form of a publisher's name as long as it is easily recognizable.

Books

1. BASIC FORMAT FOR A BOOK

> Anderson, N. H. (1996). A functional theory of
>   cognition. Mahwah, NJ: Erlbaum.

2. TWO OR MORE AUTHORS

> Van Manen, M., & Levering, B. (1996). Childhood
>   secrets: Intimacy, privacy, and the self
>   reconsidered. New York: Teachers College
>   Press.

> Winncott, D. W., Shepherd, R., Johns, J., & Robin-
>   son, H. T. (1996). Thinking about children.
>   Reading, MA: Addison-Wesley.

3. CORPORATE AUTHOR   When the author is an organization, the publisher is often the same organization. In such a case, give the publisher's name as "Author."

> Bank of Boston. (1997). Banking by remote control.
>   Boston: Author.

4. UNKNOWN AUTHOR

> Oxford essential world atlas. (1996). New York:
>   Oxford University Press.

5. EDITORS

Gelman, R., & Fong, T. K. (Eds.). (1996).
Perceptual and cognitive development. San
Diego: Academic Press.

6. TRANSLATION

Eco, U. (1995). The search for the perfect language
(J. Fentress, Trans.). Cambridge, MA:
Blackwell. (Original work published 1994)

7. EDITION OTHER THAN THE FIRST

Markel, M. (1996). Technical communication:
Situations and strategies (4th ed.). New
York: St. Martin's Press.

8. ARTICLE IN AN EDITED BOOK

Moore, B. R. (1996). The evolution of imitative
learning. In C. M. and B. G. Galef, Jr.
(Eds.), Social learning in animals: The roots
of culture (pp. 291-318). San Diego: Academic
Press.

9. MULTIVOLUME WORK

Wiener, P. (Ed.). (1973). Dictionary of the history
of ideas (Vols. 1-4). New York: Scribner's.

10. TWO OR MORE WORKS BY THE SAME AUTHOR   Use the author's name for all entries. Arrange the entries by date, the earliest first.

Jones, J. M. (1988). Why should black undergraduate
students major in psychology? In P. J. Woods
(Ed.), Is psychology for them? A guide to un-

dergraduate advising (pp. 178-181).
Washington, DC: American Psychological
Association.

Jones, J. M. (1996). Racism and white racial identity: Merging realities. In B. P. Bowser
and R. G. Hunt (Eds.), Impacts of racism on
white Americans (pp. 1-23). Thousand Oaks,
CA: Sage.

Articles in periodicals

11. ARTICLE IN A JOURNAL PAGINATED BY VOLUME

Pope, K. S. (1996). Memory, abuse, and science:
Questioning claims about the False Memory
Syndrome epidemic. American Psychologist, 51,
957-974.

12. ARTICLE IN JOURNAL PAGINATED BY ISSUE

Scruton, R. (1996). The eclipse of listening. The
New Criterion, 15(3), 5-13.

13. ARTICLE IN A MAGAZINE

Steinberg, D. (1997, January). Digital underground.
Wired, 5(1), 104-110.

14. ARTICLE IN A NEWSPAPER

Chandler, D. L. (1997, February 10). Cosmos: Ever
closer, ever clearer. The Boston Globe, pp.
C1, C10.

15. LETTER TO THE EDITOR

Westberg, L. (1997). South Bronx, New York [Letter
to the editor]. Orion, 16(1), 4.

16. REVIEW

> Ehrenhalt, A. (1997, February 10). [Review of
>   the book <u>Virtuous reality</u>]. <u>The Weekly</u>
>   <u>Standard,</u> pp. 31-34.

17. TWO OR MORE WORKS BY THE SAME AUTHOR IN THE SAME YEAR
Cite the works according to the usual style, and arrange them alphabetically by title. Add lowercase letters beginning with "a," "b," and so on, within the parentheses immediately following the year.

> Benjamin, L. S. (1996a). <u>Interpersonal diagnosis</u>
>   <u>and treatment of personality disorders.</u> New
>   York: Guilford Press.
> Benjamin, L. S. (1996b). An interpersonal theory
>   of personality disorders. In J. F. Clarkin
>   and M. F. Lenzenweger (Eds.), <u>Major theories</u>
>   <u>of personality disorder</u> (pp. 141-220). New
>   York: Guilford Press.

Electronic sources

18. MATERIAL FROM AN ONLINE DATABASE

> Fletcher, M. (1990, January). Ohio law sets
>   managed care standards. <u>Business Insurance,</u>
>   32(1), 27. Retrieved June 17, 1999 from
>   DIALOG@SITE online database (Business &
>   Industry, 02035266)

19. MATERIAL FROM A CD-ROM ABSTRACT

> Cummings, A. (1995). Test review made easy
>   [Abstract]. <u>Learning, 23</u>(5), 68. Retrieved from
>   ERIC database (ERIC Reproduction Service,
>   CD-ROM, Fall 1998 release, No. ED 316 784)

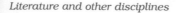

20. MATERIAL FROM A DATABASE ACCESSED VIA THE WEB

> Caruba, A. (1998, January 1). The plague of
> boredom. The World & I, 13. Retrieved
> June 17, 1999 from Electric Library
> database (Magazines) on the World
> Wide Web: http://www.elibrary.com

21. DOCUMENT FROM A WEB SITE

> Coram, J. (1999, June 4). Commencement
> grads show richness, diversity.
> Community College Times. Retrieved
> June 17, 1999 from the World Wide Web:
> http://www.aacc.nche.edu/headline/
> 060499head2.htm

22. ELECTRONIC DISCUSSION LIST MESSAGE

> Wydra, D. B. (1997, March 21). Citing sources.
> Retrieved March 27, 1997 from the listserv:
> ACW-L@listserv.ttu.edu

23. E-MAIL   E-mail messages are personal communications
and are not included in the list of references.

Other sources

24. DISSERTATION ABSTRACT

> Hu, X. (1996). Consumption and social inequality
> in urban Guangdong, China (Doctoral
> dissertation, University of Hawaii, 1996).
> Dissertation Abstracts International, 57,
> 3280A.

25. GOVERNMENT DOCUMENT

> U.S. Bureau of the Census. (1996). Statistical abstract of the United States (116th ed.). Washington, DC: U.S. Government Printing Office.

26. CONFERENCE PROCEEDINGS

> Schnase, J. L., & Cunnius, E. L. (Eds.). (1995). Proceedings of CSCL '95: The First International Conference on Computer Support for Collaborative Learning. Mahwah, NJ: Erlbaum.

27. COMPUTER PROGRAM

> TriplePlayPlus! [Computer software]. (1996). Syracuse, NY: Syracuse Language Systems.

28. VIDEOTAPE

> Harvard Graduate School of Education (Producer). (1996). Intelligence, understanding, and the mind: An illustrated presentation [Videotape]. Los Angeles: Into the Classroom Media.

56c APA manuscript format; sample research paper

This section presents guidelines for formatting a manuscript according to APA style. Also see the sample research paper formatted in APA style on pages 690–99.

MATERIALS AND TYPEFACE Use good-quality 8½" × 11" white paper. For a paper typed on a computer, make sure that the print quality meets your instructor's standards. Avoid a typeface that is unusual or hard to rea

TITLE PAGE   Begin a college paper with a title page. Type the page number, flush right (against the right margin), about one-half inch from the top of the page. Before the page number type a short title, consisting of the first two or three words of your title.

The APA manual does not provide guidelines for the placement of certain information necessary for college papers, but most instructors will want you to supply a title page similar to the one on page 690.

MARGINS, SPACING, AND INDENTATION   Use margins of at least one inch on all sides of the page. If you are working on a computer, do not justify the right margin.

Double-space throughout the paper, and indent the first line of each paragraph one-half inch (or five spaces).

For quotations longer than forty words, indent each line one-half inch (or five spaces) from the left margin. Double-space between the body of the paper and the quotation, and double-space between lines in the quotation. Quotation marks are not needed when a quotation is indented. (See 37b.)

PAGE NUMBERS AND SHORT TITLE   In the upper right-hand corner of each page, about one-half inch from the top of the page, type the page number, preceded by the short title that you typed on the title page. Number all pages, including the title page.

PUNCTUATION AND TYPING   Although the APA guidelines call for one space after all punctuation, many college professors allow (or even prefer) two spaces at the end of a sentence. Use one space after all other punctuation.

To form a dash, type two hyphens with no space between them. Do not put a space on either side of the dash.

ABSTRACT   If your instructor requires one, include an abstract right after the title page. Center the word "Abstract" about one inch from the top of the page; double-space the text of the abstract as you do the body of your paper.

An abstract is a 75-to-100-word paragraph that provides

readers with a quick overview of your essay. It should express your thesis (or central idea) and your key points; it should also briefly suggest any implications or applications of the research you discuss in the paper.

HEADINGS Although headings are not necessary, their use is encouraged in the social sciences. For most undergraduate papers, use no more than one or two levels of headings. Major headings should be centered, with the first letter of important words capitalized; minor words—articles, short prepositions, and coordinating conjunctions—are not capitalized unless they are the first word. Subheadings should be typed flush left (against the left margin) and underlined; the rules on capitalization are the same as for major headings. See pages 690–99 for an APA paper with headings.

VISUALS The APA classifies visuals as tables and figures (graphs, charts, drawings, and photographs). Keep visuals as simple as possible. Label each clearly—Table 1, Figure 3, and so on—and include a caption that concisely describes its subject. In the text of your paper, discuss the most significant features of each visual. Ask your instructor for guidelines on placement of visuals in the paper.

SAMPLE STUDENT PAPER: APA STYLE

On the following pages is a research paper written by Karen Shaw, a student in a psychology class. Shaw's assignment was to write a "review of the literature" documented with APA-style citations and references. Shaw received permission from her instructor to review the literature written by psychologists studying the linguistic abilities of apes, a topic she had previously investigated in an English class (see pp. 627–40). Shaw's two papers are quite different both in approach and in their styles of documentation.

In preparing her final manuscript, Shaw followed the APA guidelines in 56a–56c of this book. She did not include an abstract because her instructor did not require one.

Short title and page
number for student
papers.

Full title, writer's
name, name and
section number of
the course, instruc-
tor's name, and
date, all centered
and double-spaced.

Apes and Language:

A Review of the Literature

Karen Shaw

Psychology 110, Section 2

Professor Verdi

March 4, 1997

Apes and Language:

A Review of the Literature

Over the past thirty years, researchers have demonstrated that the great apes (chimpanzees, gorillas, and orangutans) resemble humans in language abilities more than had been thought possible. Just how far that resemblance extends, however, has been a matter of some controversy. Researchers agree that the apes have acquired fairly large vocabularies in American Sign Language and in artificial languages, but they have drawn quite different conclusions in addressing the following questions:

1. How spontaneously have apes used language?
2. How creatively have apes used language?
3. Can apes create sentences?
4. What are the implications of the ape language studies?

This review of the literature on apes and language focuses on these four questions.

How Spontaneously Have Apes Used Language?

In an influential article, Terrace, Petitto, Sanders, and Bever (1979) argued that the apes in language experiments were not using language spontaneously but were merely imitating their trainers, responding to conscious or unconscious cues. Terrace and his colleagues at Columbia University had trained a chimpanzee, Nim, in American Sign Lan-

Full title, centered.

The writer sets up her organization in the introduction.

Headings, centered, help readers follow the organization.

A signal phrase names all four authors and gives date in parentheses.

guage, so their skepticism about the apes' abilities received much attention. In fact, funding for ape language research was sharply reduced following publication of their 1979 article "Can an Ape Create a Sentence?"

In retrospect, the conclusions of Terrace et al. seem to have been premature. Although some of the early ape language studies had not been rigorously controlled to eliminate cuing, even as early as 1979 R. A. Gardner and B. T. Gardner were conducting double-blind experiments that prevented any possibility of cuing (Sebeok & Umiker-Sebeok, 1979). Since 1979, researchers have diligently guarded against cuing. For example, Lewin (1991) reported that instructions for bonobo (pygmy chimpanzee) Kanzi were "delivered by someone out of his sight," with other team members wearing earphones so that they "could not hear the instructions and so could not cue Kanzi, even unconsciously" (p. 51). More recently, Shanker has questioned the emphasis placed on cuing, pointing out that since human communication relies on the ability to understand cues and gestures in a social setting, it is not surprising that apes might rely on similar signals (Johnson, 1995).

There is considerable evidence that apes have signed to one another spontaneously, without train-

Because the authors of the work are not named in the signal phrase, their names appear in parentheses, along with the date.

For a quotation, a page number preceded by "p." appears in parentheses.

Apes and Language   4

ers present. Like many of the apes studied, gorillas
Koko and Michael have been observed signing to one
another (Patterson & Linden, 1981). At Central Washington University the baby chimpanzee Loulis, placed
in the care of an older, signing chimpanzee, mastered more than fifty signs in American Sign Language without help from humans. "We only used seven
signs in his presence," said psychologist Roger
Fouts. "All of his signs were learned from the
other chimps in the laboratory" (Toner, 1986,
p. 24).

     The extent to which chimpanzees spontaneously
use language may depend on their training. Terrace
trained Nim using the behaviorist technique of
operant conditioning, so it is not surprising that
many of Nim's signs were cued. Many other
researchers have used a conversational approach
that parallels the process by which human children
acquire language. In an experimental study,
O'Sullivan and Yeager (1989) contrasted the two
techniques, using Terrace's Nim as their subject.
They found that Nim's use of language was significantly more spontaneous under conversational
conditions.

     How Creatively Have Apes Used Language?
     There is considerable evidence that apes have
invented creative names. One of the earliest and

An ampersand links the names of two authors in parentheses.

The word and links the names of two authors in the signal phrase.

most controversial examples involved the Gardners'
chimpanzee Washoe. Washoe, who knew signs for
"water" and "bird," once signed "water bird" when
in the presence of a swan. Terrace et al. (1979)
suggested that there was "no basis for concluding
that Washoe was characterizing the swan as a 'bird
that inhabits water.'" Washoe may simply have been
"identifying correctly a body of water and a bird,
in that order" (p. 895).

When this article was first cited, all four authors were named. In subsequent citations of a work with three to five authors, "et al." is used after the first author's name.

Other examples are not so easily explained
away. The bonobo Kanzi has requested particular
films by combining symbols in a creative way. For
instance, to ask for Quest for Fire, a film about
early primates discovering fire, Kanzi began to
use symbols for "campfire" and "TV" (Eckholm,
1985). And the gorilla Koko has a long list of
creative names to her credit: "elephant baby" to
describe a Pinocchio doll, "finger bracelet" to
describe a ring, "bottle match" to describe a cigarette lighter, and so on (Patterson & Linden,
1981, p. 146). If Terrace's analysis of the "water
bird" example is applied to the examples just mentioned, it does not hold. Surely Koko did not
first see an elephant and then a baby before signing "elephant baby"--or a bottle and a match
before signing "bottle match."

The writer interprets the evidence; she doesn't just report it.

Can Apes Create Sentences?

The early ape language studies offered little proof that apes could combine symbols into grammatically ordered sentences. Apes strung together various signs, but the sequences were often random and repetitious. Nim's series of sixteen signs is a case in point: "give orange me give eat orange me eat orange give me eat orange give me you" (Terrace et al., 1979, p. 895). The Gardners were impressed by Washoe's multisign sequences, seeing in them the beginnings of some grasp of grammar, but their findings have been disputed. In one frequently cited film sequence, Washoe's teacher placed a baby doll in a cup. Washoe signed "baby in baby in my drink," a series of signs that seemed to make grammatical sense. Terrace et al. (1979) noted, however, that Washoe had previously been drilled in similar patterns and that the teacher had pointed to the objects.

Recent studies with bonobos at the Yerkes Primate Research Center in Atlanta have broken new ground. Kanzi, a bonobo trained by Savage-Rumbaugh, seems to understand simple grammatical rules about lexigram order. For instance, Kanzi learned that in two-word utterances action precedes object, an ordering also used by human children at the two-word stage. In a major article reporting on their re-

The writer draws attention to an important article.

search, Greenfield and Savage-Rumbaugh (1990) wrote
that Kanzi rarely "repeated himself or formed combinations that were semantically unrelated" (p. 556).

   More important, Kanzi began on his own to
create certain patterns that may not exist in
English but can be found among deaf children and
in other human languages. For example, Kanzi used
his own rules when combining action symbols. Lexigrams that involved an invitation to play, such
as "chase," would appear first; lexigrams that indicated what was to be done during play ("hide")
would appear second. Kanzi also created his own
rules when combining gestures and lexigrams. He
would use the lexigram first and then gesture, a
practice often followed by young deaf children
(Greenfield & Savage-Rumbaugh, 1990, p. 560).

The writer gives a page number for this summary because the article is long.

   In a recent study, Kanzi's abilities have
been shown to be similar to those of a 2-1/2-year-
old human, Alia. According to Rumbaugh (1995),
"Kanzi's comprehension of over 600 novel sentences
of request was very comparable to Alia's; both
complied with the requests without assistance on
approximately 70% of the sentences" (p. 722).

For quotations, a page number is required.

                What Are the Implications of the
                   Ape Language Studies?
   Kanzi's linguistic abilities are so impressive that they may help us understand how

humans came to acquire language. Pointing out that
99% of our genetic material is held in common with
the chimpanzees, Greenfield and Savage-Rumbaugh
(1990) have suggested that something of the
"evolutionary root of human language" can be found
in the "linguistic abilities of the great apes"
(p. 540). Noting that apes' brains are similar to
those of our human ancestors, Leakey and Lewin
(1992) argued that in ape brains "the cognitive
foundations on which human language could be built
are already present" (p. 244).

The suggestion that there is a continuity in
the linguistic abilities of apes and humans has created much controversy. Linguist Noam Chomsky has
strongly asserted that language is a unique human
characteristic (Booth, 1990). Terrace has continued
to be skeptical of the claims made for the apes, as
have Petitto and Bever, coauthors of the 1979 article that caused such skepticism earlier (Gibbons,
1991). However, according to Lewin (1991), "Many
psychologists are extremely impressed with Kanzi and
the implications of the observations" (p. 52).

> The writer presents a balanced view of the philosophical controversy.

Although the ape language studies continue to
generate controversy, researchers have shown over
the past thirty years that the gap between the
linguistic abilities of apes and humans is far
less dramatic than was once believed.

> The tone of the conclusion is objective.

List of references
begins on a new
page. Heading is
centered.

References

Booth, W. (1990, October 29). Monkeying with
    language: Is chimp using words or merely
    aping handlers? The Washington Post, p. A3.

Eckholm, E. (1985, June 25). Kanzi the chimp: A
    life in science. The New York Times, pp.
    C1, C3.

Gibbons, A. (1991). Déjà vu all over again:
    Chimp-language wars. Science, 251,
    1561-1562.

Greenfield, P. M., & Savage-Rumbaugh, E. S.
    (1990). Grammatical combination in Pan
    paniscus: Processes of learning and invention
    in the evolution and development of language.
    In S. T. Parker & K. R. Gibson (Eds.), "Lan-
    guage" and intelligence in monkeys and
    apes: Comparative developmental perspectives
    (pp. 540-578). Cambridge: Cambridge
    University Press.

Johnson, G. (1995, June 6). Chimp talk debate:
    Is it really language? The New York Times,
    pp. C1, C10.

Leakey, R., & Lewin, R. (1992). Origins
    reconsidered: In search of what makes us
    human. New York: Doubleday.

Lewin, R. (1991, April 29). Look who's talking
    now. New Scientist, 130, 49-52.

List is alphabetized
by authors' last
names.

In student papers
the first line of an
entry is at left mar-
gin; subsequent
lines indent ½″ (or
five spaces). (See
p. 681.)

Double-spacing
used throughout.

O'Sullivan, C., & Yeager, C. P. (1989). Communicative
    context and linguistic competence: The effect of
    social setting on a chimpanzee's conversational
    skill. In R. A. Gardner, B. T. Gardner, & T. E.
    Van Cantfort (Eds.), Teaching sign language to
    chimpanzees (pp. 269-279). Albany: SUNY Press.

Patterson, F., & Linden, E. (1981). The education of
    Koko. New York: Holt, Rinehart & Winston.

Rumbaugh, D. (1995). Primate language and cognition:
    Common ground. Social Research, 62, 711-730.

Sebeok, T. A., & Umiker-Sebeok, J. (1979, November).
    Performing animals: Secrets of the trade.
    Psychology Today, 13, 78-91.

Terrace, H. S., Petitto, L. A., Sanders, R. J., &
    Bever, T. G. (1979). Can an ape create a
    sentence? Science, 206, 891-902.

Toner, M. (1986, February-March). Loulis, the talking
    chimp. National Wildlife, 24, 24.

CHICAGO STYLE
(HISTORY AND HUMANITIES)

Professors in history and the humanities often require foot-notes or endnotes based on *The Chicago Manual of Style*, 14th ed. (Chicago: U of Chicago P, 1993). When you use *Chicago*-style notes, you will usually be asked to include a bibliography at the end of your paper. (See 56e.)

Although *The Chicago Manual of Style* does not include guidelines for documenting online sources, the University of Chicago Press recommends following the system developed by Andrew Harnack and Eugene Kleppinger in *Online! A Reference Guide to Using Internet Sources* (New York: St. Martin's, 1997). The examples of online sources given in this section are based on Harnack and Kleppinger's guidelines.

56d *Chicago*-style footnotes or endnotes

Notes provide complete publication information either at the bottom of the page (footnotes) or at the end of the paper (end-notes). A raised arabic numeral in the text indicates that a quotation, summary, or paraphrase has been borrowed from a source; to find the publication information for that source, readers consult the footnote or endnote with the corre-sponding number.

Individual notes are single-spaced, and the first line is indented one-half inch (or five spaces); double-spacing sep-arates entries. Notes are numbered consecutively through-out the paper.

TEXT

Governor John Andrew was not allowed to recruit black soldiers out of state. "Ostensibly," writes Peter Burchard, "no recruiting was done outside

```
Massachusetts, but it was an open secret that
Andrew's agents were working far and wide."¹
```

The first time you cite a source, the note should include publication information for that work as well as the page number on which the specific quotation, paraphrase, or summary may be found.

NOTE

```
    1. Peter Burchard, One Gallant Rush: Robert
Gould Shaw and His Brave Black Regiment (New York:
St. Martin's Press, 1965), 85.
```

For subsequent references to a source you have already cited, you may simply give the author's last name, followed by a comma and the page or pages cited.

```
    2. Burchard, 31.
```

If you cite more than one work by the same author, include a short form of the title in subsequent citations. A short form of the title of a book is underlined or italicized; a short form of the title of an article is put in quotation marks.

```
    2. Burchard, One Gallant Rush, 31.

    4. Burchard, "Civil War," 10.
```

NOTE: *Chicago* style no longer requires the use of "ibid." to refer to the work cited in the previous note. The Latin abbreviations "op. cit." and "loc. cit." are no longer used.

The following examples for first references to a source are consistent with the guidelines set forth in *The Chicago Manual of Style*, 14th edition.

Books

1. BASIC FORMAT FOR A BOOK

1. James M. McPherson, Battle Cry of Freedom: The Civil War Era (New York: Oxford University Press, 1988), 87.

2. TWO OR THREE AUTHORS

2. Rudolph O. de la Garza, Z. Anthony Kruszewski, and Tomás A. Arciniega, Chicanos and Native Americans: The Territorial Minorities (Englewood Cliffs, N.J.: Prentice-Hall, 1973), 8.

3. FOUR OR MORE AUTHORS

3. Martin J. Medhurst et al., Cold War Rhetoric: Strategy, Metaphor, and Ideology (New York: Greenwood, 1990), 88.

4. UNKNOWN AUTHOR

4. The Men's League Handbook on Women's Suffrage (London, 1912), 23.

5. AUTHOR'S NAME IN TITLE

5. Long Walk to Freedom: The Autobiography of Nelson Mandela (Boston: Little, Brown, 1995), 435.

6. EDITED WORK WITHOUT AN AUTHOR

6. Marshall Sklare, ed., Understanding American Jewry (New Brunswick, N.J.: Transaction Books, 1982), 49.

7. EDITED WORK WITH AN AUTHOR

7. William L. Riordan, Plunkitt of Tammany Hall, ed. Terrence J. McDonald (Boston: Bedford Books, 1994), 33.

8. TRANSLATED WORK

8. Shintaro Ishihara, The Japan That Can't Say No, trans. Frank Baldwin (New York: Simon and Schuster, 1989), 65-83.

9. EDITION OTHER THAN THE FIRST

9. C. H. Lawrence, Medieval Monasticism: Forms of Religious Life in Western Europe in the Middle Ages, 2d ed. (London: Longman, 1989), 163-64.

10. UNTITLED VOLUME IN A MULTIVOLUME WORK

10. New Cambridge Modern History (Cambridge: Cambridge University Press, 1957), 1:52-53.

11. TITLED VOLUME IN A MULTIVOLUME WORK

11. William Wood and Ralph Henry Gabriel, In Defense of Liberty, vol. 7 of The Pageant of America (New York: United States Publishers, 1928), 135-42.

or

11. William Wood and Ralph Henry Gabriel, The Pageant of America, vol. 7, In Defense of Liberty (New York: United States Publishers, 1928), 135-42.

12. WORK IN AN ANTHOLOGY

12. Michelle T. Clinton, "For Strong Women," in Home Girls: A Black Feminist Anthology, ed. Barbara Smith (New York: Kitchen Table, 1983), 325-27.

13. LETTER IN A PUBLISHED COLLECTION

13. James Thurber to Harold Ross, 27 December 1948, Selected Letters of James Thurber, ed. Helen Thurber and Edward Weeks (Boston: Little, Brown, 1981), 65-66.

14. WORK IN A SERIES

14. Robert M. Laughlin, Of Cabbages and Kings: Tales from Zinacantán, Smithsonian Contributions to Anthropology, vol. 23 (Washington, D.C.: Smithsonian Institution Press, 1977), 14.

15. ENCYCLOPEDIA OR DICTIONARY

15. Encyclopaedia Britannica, 15th ed., s.v. "evolution."

NOTE: The abbreviation "s.v." is for the Latin *sub verbo* ("under the word").

16. BIBLICAL REFERENCE

16. Matt. 20.4-9 Revised Standard Version.

Articles in periodicals

17. ARTICLE IN A JOURNAL PAGINATED BY VOLUME

17. Laura E. Hein, "In Search of Peace and Democracy: Postwar Japanese Economic Debate in Political Context," Journal of Asian Studies 53 (1994): 752.

18. ARTICLE IN A JOURNAL PAGINATED BY ISSUE

18. Robert Darnton, "The Pursuit of Happiness," Wilson Quarterly 19, no. 4 (1995): 42.

19. ARTICLE IN A MAGAZINE

19. Andrew Weil, "The New Politics of Coca," <u>New Yorker</u>, 15 May 1995, 70.

20. ARTICLE IN A NEWSPAPER

20. Lena H. Sun, "Chinese Feel the Strain of a New Society," <u>Washington Post</u>, 13 June 1993, sec. A.

21. UNSIGNED ARTICLE

21. "Radiation in Russia," <u>U.S. News and World Report</u>, 9 August 1993, 41.

22. BOOK REVIEW

22. Dauril Alden, review of <u>Vanguard of Empire: Ships of Exploration in the Age of Columbus</u>, by Roger C. Smith, <u>Journal of World History</u> 6 (1995): 137.

Electronic sources

23. WORLD WIDE WEB SITE

23. Jerome J. McGann, "Dante Gabriel Rossetti: A Brief Biography," <u>The Complete Writings and Pictures of Dante Gabriel Rossetti: A Hypermedia Research Archive</u>, 19 March 1997, <http://jefferson.village.virginia.edu/rossetti/dgrbio.html> (23 March 1997).

24. E-MAIL MESSAGE

24. Constance McCready, <ctm9417@unh.edu> "Civil War Battles," 14 January 1997, personal e-mail (17 January 1997).

25. **LISTSERV MESSAGE**

     25. Nancy Stegall, <stegall@primenet.com>
"Web Publishing and Censorship," 2 February 1997,
<acw-1@ttacs6.ttu.edu> via <http://www.ttu.edu
/lists/acw-1> (18 March 1997).

26. **NEWSGROUP MESSAGE**

     26. Richard J. Kennedy, <rkennedy@orednet
.org> "Re: Shakespeare's Daughters," 18 March
1997, <humanities.lit.authors.shakespeare>
(23 March 1997).

27. **SYNCHRONOUS COMMUNICATION**

     27. Diversity University MOO, Group Discussion, 16 March 1997, telnet moo.du.org (16 March
1997).

28. **TELNET SITE**

     28. Case Western Reserve University, "Historical Timeline," Cleveland Freenet, n.d., telnet
freenet-in-c.cwru.edu login as visitor, press 11,
press 2, press 5 (17 March 1997).

29. **FTP OR GOPHER SITE**

     29. Michael Trietel, "The Great Hunger of
1044: The Progress of a Medieval Famine," 1 May
1992, <ftp://ftp2.cc.ukans.edu/pub/history
/Europe/Medieval/articles/famine.art>
(14 February 1997).

30. **ELECTRONIC DATABASE**

     30. Paul D. Hightower, "Censorship," in Contemporary Education (Terre Haute: Indiana State

University, School of Education, winter 1995), 66,
Dialog, ERIC, ED 509251.

31. COMPUTER SOFTWARE

31. Lotus 1-2-3 Rel. 4, Lotus Development
Corporation, Cambridge, Mass.

Other sources

32. GOVERNMENT DOCUMENT

32. U.S. Department of State, <u>Foreign
Relations of the United States: Diplomatic
Papers, 1943</u> (Washington, D.C.: GPO, 1965),
562.

33. UNPUBLISHED DISSERTATION

33. Cheryl D. Hoover, "East Germany's Revolution" (Ph.D. diss., Ohio State University, 1994),
450-51.

34. PERSONAL COMMUNICATION

34. Sara Lehman, letter to author, 13
August 1996.

35. Hector LaForge, telephone interview
by author, 4 April 1996.

36. Martha Carlin, e-mail to author, 18
June 1996.

35. INTERVIEW

37. Jesse Jackson, interview by Marshall
Frady, <u>Frontline</u>, Public Broadcasting System, 30
April 1996.

36. FILM OR VIDEOTAPE

38. <u>North by Northwest</u>, prod. and dir.
Alfred Hitchcock, 2 hr. 17 min., MGM/UA, 1959,
videocassette.

37. SOUND RECORDING

39. Gustav Holst, <u>The Planets</u>, Royal Philharmonic, André Previn, Telarc compact disc
80133.

38. SOURCE QUOTED IN ANOTHER SOURCE

40. George Harmon Knoles, <u>The Jazz Age Revis-</u>
<u>ited: British Criticism of American Civilization</u>
<u>during the 1920s</u> (Stanford: Stanford University
Press, 1955), 31, quoted in C. Vann Woodward, <u>The</u>
<u>Old World's New World</u> (Oxford: Oxford University
Press, 1991), 46.

56e   *Chicago*-style bibliography

A bibliography, which appears at the end of your paper, lists
every work you have cited in your notes; in addition, it may
include works that you consulted but did not cite. For advice on constructing the list, see pages 718–19. A sample
bibliography appears on page 723.

The following models are based on guidelines set forth
in *The Chicago Manual of Style*, 14th edition.

Books

1. BASIC FORMAT FOR A BOOK

McPherson, James M. <u>Battle Cry of Freedom: The</u>
<u>Civil War Era</u>. New York: Oxford University
Press, 1988.

Directory to Chicago-style bibliography (56e)

BOOKS

1. Basic format for a book
2. Two or three authors
3. Four or more authors
4. Unknown author
5. Author's name in title
6. Edited work without an author
7. Edited work with an author
8. Translated work
9. Edition other than the first
10. Untitled volume in a multivolume work
11. Titled volume in a multivolume work
12. Work in an anthology
13. Letter in a published collection
14. Work in a series
15. Encyclopedia or dictionary
16. Biblical reference

ARTICLES IN PERIODICALS

17. Article in a journal paginated by volume
18. Article in a journal paginated by issue
19. Article in a magazine
20. Article in a newspaper
21. Unsigned article
22. Book review

ELECTRONIC SOURCES

23. World Wide Web site
24. E-mail message
25. Listserv message
26. Newsgroup message
27. Synchronous communication
28. Telnet site
29. FTP or gopher site
30. Electronic database
31. Computer software

OTHER SOURCES

32. Government document
33. Unpublished dissertation
34. Personal communication
35. Interview
36. Film or videotape
37. Sound recording
38. Source quoted in another source

2. TWO OR THREE AUTHORS

Garza, Rudolph O. de la, Z. Anthony Kruszewski, and Tomás A. Arciniega. Chicanos and Native Americans: The Territorial Minorities. Englewood Cliffs, N.J.: Prentice-Hall, 1973.

3. FOUR OR MORE AUTHORS

Medhurst, Martin J., et al. Cold War Rhetoric: Strategy, Metaphor, and Ideology. New York: Greenwood, 1990.

4. UNKNOWN AUTHOR

The Men's League Handbook on Women's Suffrage. London, 1912.

5. AUTHOR'S NAME IN TITLE

Mandela, Nelson. Long Walk to Freedom: The Autobiography of Nelson Mandela. Boston: Little, Brown, 1995.

6. EDITED WORK WITHOUT AN AUTHOR

Sklare, Marshall, ed. Understanding American Jewry. New Brunswick, N.J.: Transaction Books, 1982.

7. EDITED WORK WITH AN AUTHOR

Riordan, William L. Plunkitt of Tammany Hall. Edited by Terrence J. McDonald. Boston: Bedford Books, 1994.

8. TRANSLATED WORK

Ishihara, Shintaro. <u>The Japan That Can't Say No</u>.
Translated by Frank Baldwin. New York: Simon
and Schuster, 1989.

9. EDITION OTHER THAN THE FIRST

Lawrence, C. H. <u>Medieval Monasticism: Forms of
Religious Life in Western Europe in the
Middle Ages</u>. 2d ed. London: Longman, 1989.

10. UNTITLED VOLUME IN A MULTIVOLUME WORK

<u>New Cambridge Modern History</u>. Vol. 1. Cambridge:
Cambridge University Press, 1957.

11. TITLED VOLUME IN A MULTIVOLUME WORK

Wood, William, and Ralph Henry Gabriel. <u>In
Defense of Liberty</u>. Vol. 7 of <u>The Pageant of
America</u>. New York: United States Publishers,
1928.

or

Wood, William, and Ralph Henry Gabriel. <u>The
Pageant of America</u>. Vol. 7, <u>In Defense of
Liberty</u>. New York: United States Publishers,
1928.

12. WORK IN AN ANTHOLOGY

Clinton, Michelle T. "For Strong Women." In <u>Home
Girls: A Black Feminist Anthology</u>, edited by
Barbara Smith. New York: Kitchen Table, 1983.

13. **LETTER IN A PUBLISHED COLLECTION**

Thurber, James. Letter to Harold Ross, 27 December
    1948. In Selected Letters of James Thurber,
    edited by Helen Thurber and Edward Weeks,
    65-66. Boston: Little, Brown, 1981.

14. **WORK IN A SERIES**

Laughlin, Robert M. Of Cabbages and Kings: Tales
    from Zinacantán. Smithsonian Contributions to
    Anthropology, vol. 23. Washington, D.C.:
    Smithsonian Institution Press, 1977.

15. **ENCYCLOPEDIA OR DICTIONARY**   Encyclopedias and dictionaries are usually not included in the bibliography.

16. **BIBLICAL REFERENCE**   The Bible is usually not included in the bibliography.

Articles in periodicals

17. **ARTICLE IN A JOURNAL PAGINATED BY VOLUME**

Hein, Laura E. "In Search of Peace and Democracy:
    Postwar Japanese Economic Debate in Political
    Context." Journal of Asian Studies 53 (1994):
    752-78.

18. **ARTICLE IN A JOURNAL PAGINATED BY ISSUE**

Darnton, Robert. "The Pursuit of Happiness."
    Wilson Quarterly 19, no. 4 (1995): 42-52.

19. **ARTICLE IN A MAGAZINE**

Weil, Andrew. "The New Politics of Coca." New
    Yorker, 15 May 1995, 70.

20. ARTICLE IN A NEWSPAPER

Sun, Lena H. "Chinese Feel the Strain of a New
     Society." Washington Post, 13 June 1993,
     sec. A.

21. UNSIGNED ARTICLE

"Radiation in Russia." U.S. News and World Report,
     9 August 1993, 40-42.

22. BOOK REVIEW

Alden, Dauril. Review of Vanguard of Empire: Ships
     of Exploration in the Age of Columbus, by
     Roger C. Smith. Journal of World History 6
     (1995): 137-39.

Electronic sources

23. WORLD WIDE WEB SITE

McGann, Jerome J. "Dante Gabriel Rossetti: A
     Brief Biography." The Complete Writings
     and Pictures of Dante Gabriel Rossetti:
     A Hypermedia Research Archive. 19
     March 1997. <http://jefferson.village
     .virginia.edu/rossetti/dgrbio.html> (23
     March 1997).

24. E-MAIL MESSAGE

McCready, Constance. <ctm9417@unh.edu> "Civil War
     Battles." 14 January 1997. Personal e-mail
     (17 January 1997).

25. LISTSERV MESSAGE

Stegall, Nancy. <stegall@primenet.com> "Web
     Publishing and Censorship." 2 February 1997.
     <acw-1@ttacs6.ttu.edu> via <http://www.ttu.edu
     /lists/acw-1> (18 March 1997).

26. NEWSGROUP MESSAGE

Kennedy, Richard J. <rkennedy@orednet.org> "Re:
     Shakespeare's Daughters." 18 March 1997.
     <humanities.lit.authors.shakespeare>
     (23 March 1997).

27. SYNCHRONOUS COMMUNICATION

Diversity University MOO. Group Discussion. 16
     March 1997. Telnet moo.du.org (16 March
     1997).

28. TELNET SITE

Case Western Reserve University. "Historical Time-
     line." Cleveland Freenet. n.d. Telnet freenet-
     in-c.cwru.edu login as visitor, press 11,
     press 2, press 5 (17 March 1997).

29. FTP OR GOPHER SITE

Trietel, Michael. "The Great Hunger of 1044: The
     Progress of a Medieval Famine." 1 May 1992.
     <ftp://ftp2.cc.ukans.edu/pub/history/Europe
     /Medieval/articles/famine.art> (14 February
     1997).

30. ELECTRONIC DATABASE

Hightower, Paul D. "Censorship." In Contemporary
   Education. Terre Haute: Indiana State Univer-
   sity, School of Education, winter 1995. 66,
   Dialog, ERIC, ED 509251.

31. COMPUTER SOFTWARE

Lotus 1-2-3 Rel. 4. Lotus Development Corporation,
   Cambridge, Mass.

Other sources

32. GOVERNMENT DOCUMENT

U.S. Department of State. Foreign Relations of the
   United States: Diplomatic Papers, 1943. Washington, D.C.: GPO, 1965.

33. UNPUBLISHED DISSERTATION

Hoover, Cheryl D. "East Germany's Revolution."
   Ph.D. diss., Ohio State University, 1994.

34. PERSONAL COMMUNICATION

Personal communications are not included in the bibliography.

35. INTERVIEW

Jackson, Jesse. Interview by Marshall Frady.
   Frontline. Public Broadcasting System, 30
   April 1996.

36. FILM OR VIDEOTAPE

North by Northwest. Produced and directed by
   Alfred Hitchcock. 2 hr. 17 min. MGM/UA, 1959.
   Videocassette.

37. SOUND RECORDING

Holst, Gustav. The Planets. Royal Philharmonic. André Previn. Telarc compact disc
   80133.

38. SOURCE QUOTED IN ANOTHER SOURCE

Knoles, George Harmon. The Jazz Age Revisited:
   British Criticism of American Civilization
   during the 1920s, 31. Stanford: Stanford
   University Press, 1955. Quoted in C. Vann
   Woodward, The Old World's New World (Oxford:
   Oxford University Press, 1991), 46.

56f *Chicago*-style manuscript format; sample pages

The following guidelines on manuscript formatting are based
on *The Chicago Manual of Style,* 14th edition.

   TITLE AND IDENTIFICATION   On the title page, include the
full title of your paper and your name. Your instructor may
also want you to include the course title, the instructor's
name, and the date. Do not type a number on the title page
but count it in the manuscript; that is, the first page of text
will usually be numbered page 2. In the unusual case that
your paper includes extensive preliminary material such as
a table of contents, list of illustrations, or preface, you may
be required to number that material separately. See page
720 for a sample title page.

MARGINS AND SPACING   Leave margins of at least one inch at the top, bottom, and sides of the page. Double-space the entire manuscript, including block quotations, but single-space individual entries in notes and the bibliography.

PAGINATION   Using arabic numerals, number all pages except the title page in the upper right corner. Depending on your instructor's preference, you may also use a short title or your last name before page numbers to help identify pages in case they come loose from your manuscript.

Preparing the endnotes page

On page 722 are sample endnotes for a paper in *Chicago* style. (You may choose to or be required to use footnotes instead.) Endnote pages should be numbered consecutively with the rest of the manuscript, and the title "Notes" should be centered on the first page about one inch from the top of the page. Indent only the first line of each entry one-half inch (or five spaces) and begin the note with the arabic numeral corresponding to the number in the text. Follow the number with a period and one space. Do not indent any other lines of the entry. Single-space individual notes but double-space between notes.

AUTHORS   Authors' names are not inverted in notes. With two or more authors, use "and," not an ampersand (&). In notes for works with four or more authors, use the first author's name followed by "et al."

PAGE NUMBERS   Page numbers are not preceded by the abbreviation "p." or "pp."

Preparing the bibliography page

Typically, the notes in *Chicago*-style papers are followed by a bibliography, an alphabetically arranged list of all of the works cited or consulted. Page 723 shows a sample bibliography in *Chicago* style.

Type the title "Bibliography," centered, about one inch from the top of the page. Number bibliography pages consecutively with the rest of the paper. Begin each entry at the left margin, and indent any additional lines one-half inch (or five spaces). Single-space individual entries but double-space between entries.

ALPHABETIZING THE LIST Alphabetize the bibliography by the last names of the authors (or editors); when a work has no author or editor, alphabetize by the first word of the title other than *A, An,* and *The.*

If your list includes two or more works by the same author, use three dashes (or three hyphens) instead of the author's name in all entries after the first. You may arrange the entries alphabetically by title or chronologically; be consistent throughout the bibliography.

AUTHORS Invert the name of the first author or editor. With two or more authors, use "and," not an ampersand (&). For works with four or more authors, use the first author's name, inverted, followed by "et al."

NOTE: The sample notes and bibliography pages show you how to type bibliographic information for *Chicago*-style papers. For more information about the exact format of notes, see 56d; for bibliography entries, see 56e.

SAMPLE *CHICAGO* TITLE PAGE

Page number not
typed on title page.

                      The Forgotten Pioneers:
            African Americans on the Western Frontier

Title page includes   Robert Diaz
full title, writer's
name, course title,
name of instructor,
and date.

                          History 120
                       Professor Marshall
                        3 March 1997

SAMPLE CHICAGO PAGE

Diaz 2

Most Americans know something of Billy the
Kid, Sitting Bull, and General Custer; their lives
have been featured as subjects of high school
lectures as well as books, films, and TV dramas.
But how many people have heard of Clara Brown, an
African American who helped bring groups of her
people west by wagon train, or of Bill Pickett, a
black cowboy who was one of the most famous rodeo
riders in the United States?[1] How many know of the
"Buffalo soldiers," black cavalrymen who rode and
fought on the western plains?[2] Until recently, the
role of African Americans in the settlement of the
West has been largely ignored in schools and in the
media. A growing body of historical research, however, has pointed out the significance of African
Americans to the westward development of the
United States.

From the American Revolution to the turn of
the twentieth century, thousands of African Americans headed west looking for opportunity and a new
start in a new land, hoping to escape slavery and
racist conditions in the East. They often discovered, however, that discriminatory attitudes
had preceded them. As William Lorenz Katz writes,
the white pioneers who headed west "carried the
virus of racism with them, as much a part of their
psyche as their heralded courage and their fears."[3]

Page number in
upper right corner;
first page after title
page is page 2;
writer's last name
precedes page num-
ber (optional).

Raised arabic num-
ber (placed outside
punctuation) indi-
cates citation.

Thesis announces
central claim of
paper.

SAMPLE *CHICAGO* ENDNOTES

Notes page is numbered consecutively.

Heading "Notes" is centered 1″ from top of page.

First line of each note indented ½″ (or five spaces).

Note number is not raised and is followed by period.

Author names are not inverted.

Entries singlespaced; doublespacing between entries.

Last names refer to an earlier note by the same author.

Notes

1. Ruth Pelz, <u>Black Heroes of the Wild West</u> (Seattle: Open Hand Publishing, 1990), 15-36.

2. William H. Leckie, <u>The Buffalo Soldiers</u> (Norman: University of Oklahoma Press, 1967), 5.

3. William Lorenz Katz, <u>The Black West: A Pictorial History</u>, 3d ed. (Seattle: Open Hand Publishing, 1987), 307.

4. Katz, <u>Black West</u>, 307.

5. William Lorenz Katz, <u>The Westward Movement and Abolitionism</u> (Austin: Steck-Vaughn Publishers, Raintree, 1992), 32.

6. Scott Minerbrook, "The Forgotten Pioneers," <u>U.S. News and World Report</u>, 8 August 1994, 53.

7. Katz, <u>Black West</u>, 49.

8. Ginia Bellafante, "Wild West 101," <u>Time</u>, 22 February 1993, 75.

9. John Mack Faragher, "The Frontier Trail: Rethinking Turner and Reimagining the American West," <u>American Historical Review</u> 98 (1993): 106-7.

10. Faragher, 110.

11. Bellafante, 75.

12. Kenneth W. Porter, <u>The Negro on the American Frontier</u> (New York: Arno Press, 1971), 42-45.

13. Porter, 60.

14. Faragher, 107.

SAMPLE *CHICAGO* BIBLIOGRAPHY

Diaz 16

Bibliography

Bellafante, Ginia. "Wild West 101." Time, 22
    February 1993, 75.

Crouch, Barry A. The Freedmen's Bureau and Black
    Texans. Austin: University of Texas Press,
    1992.

Dolan, Edward F. Famous Builders of California.
    New York: Dodd, Mead, 1924.

Faragher, John Mack. "The Frontier Trail: Rethink-
    ing Turner and Reimagining the American
    West." American Historical Review 98 (1993):
    106-17.

Katz, William Loren. The Black West: A Pictorial
    History. 3d ed. Seattle: Open Hand Publishing,
    1987.

---. The Westward Movement and Abolitionism.
    Austin: Steck-Vaughn Publishers, Raintree,
    1992.

Leckie, William H. The Buffalo Soldiers. Norman:
    University of Oklahoma Press, 1967.

Minerbrook, Scott. "The Forgotten Pioneers." U.S.
    News and World Report, 8 August 1994, 53-55.

Pelz, Ruth. Black Heroes of the Wild West. Seattle:
    Open Hand Publishing, 1990.

Porter, Kenneth W. The Negro on the American
    Frontier. New York: Arno Press, 1971.

Wheeler, B. Gordon. Black California: The History
    of African Americans in the Golden State. New
    York: Hippocrene Books, 1993.

Bibliography page
is numbered
consecutively.

Heading "Bibliogra-
phy" is centered 1˝
from top of page.

Entries are alpha-
betized by authors'
last names.

Three hyphens
indicate work by
same author as in
previous entry.

First line of entry
begins at left mar-
gin; additional lines
indent ⅛˝ (or five
spaces).

Entries single-
spaced; double-
spacing between
entries.

OTHER STYLES

56g A list of style manuals for various disciplines

The Bedford Handbook describes three commonly used systems of documentation: MLA, used in English and the humanities (see 53); APA, used in psychology and the social sciences (see 56a–56c); and *Chicago,* used primarily in history (see 56d–56f). Following is a list of style manuals used in a variety of disciplines.

BIOLOGY
Council of Biology Editors. *Scientific Style and Format: The CBE Manual for Authors, Editors, and Publishers.* 6th ed. New York: Cambridge UP, 1994.

CHEMISTRY
Dodd, Janet S., ed. *The ACS Style Guide: A Manual for Authors and Editors.* Washington: Amer. Chemical Soc., 1986.

ENGLISH AND THE HUMANITIES (SEE 53.)
Gibaldi, Joseph. *MLA Handbook for Writers of Research Papers.* 5th ed. New York: MLA, 1999.

GEOLOGY
Bates, Robert L., Rex Buchanan, and Marla Adkins-Heljeson, eds. *Geowriting: A Guide to Writing, Editing, and Printing in Earth Science.* 5th ed. Alexandria: Amer. Geological Inst., 1992.

GOVERNMENT DOCUMENTS
Garner, Diane L. *The Complete Guide to Citing Government Information Resources: A Manual for Writers and Librarians.* Rev. ed. Bethesda: Congressional Information Service, 1993.

United States Government Printing Office. *Manual of Style.* Washington: GPO, 1988.

HISTORY (SEE 56d–56f.)

The Chicago Manual of Style. 14th ed. Chicago: U of Chicago P, 1993.

JOURNALISM

Goldstein, Norm, ed. *Associated Press Stylebook and Libel Manual.* 31st ed. New York: Associated Press, 1996.

LAW

Columbia Law Review. *A Uniform System of Citation.* 16th ed. Cambridge: Harvard Law Rev. Assn., 1996.

LINGUISTICS

Linguistic Society of America. "LSA Style Sheet." Published annually in the December issue of the *LSA Bulletin.*

MATHEMATICS

American Mathematical Society. *The AMS Author Handbook: General Instructions for Preparing Manuscripts.* Providence: AMS, 1994.

MEDICINE

Iverson, Cheryl, et al. *American Medical Association Manual of Style.* 8th ed. Baltimore: Williams and Wilkins, 1989.

MUSIC

Holoman, D. Kern, ed. *Writing about Music: A Style Sheet from the Editors of 19th-Century Music.* Berkeley: U of California P, 1988.

PHYSICS

American Institute of Physics. *Style Manual: Instructions to Authors and Volume Editors for the Preparation of AIP Book Manuscripts.* 5th ed. New York: AIP, 1995.

POLITICAL SCIENCE

American Political Science Association. *Style Manual for Political Science.* Rev. ed. Washington: Amer. Political Science Assn., 1993.

PSYCHOLOGY AND THE SOCIAL SCIENCES (SEE 56a–56c.)

American Psychological Association. *Publication Manual of the American Psychological Association.* 4th ed. Washington: APA, 1994.

SCIENCE AND TECHNICAL WRITING

American National Standard for the Preparation of Scientific Papers for Written or Oral Presentation. New York: Amer. Natl. Standards Inst., 1979.

Rubens, Philip, ed. *Science and Technical Writing: A Manual of Style.* New York: Holt, 1992.

SOCIAL WORK

National Association of Social Workers. *Writing for NASW.* 2nd ed. Silver Springs: Natl. Assn. of Social Workers, 1994.

Grammar Basics

57

Parts of speech

Traditional grammar recognizes eight parts of speech: noun, pronoun, verb, adjective, adverb, preposition, conjunction, and interjection. Many words can function as more than one part of speech. For example, depending on its use in a sentence, the word *paint* can be a noun (*The paint is wet*) or a verb (*Please paint the ceiling next*).

A quick-reference chart of the parts of speech appears on pages 742–44.

57a Nouns

As most schoolchildren can attest, a noun is the name of a person, place, or thing.

> The *cat* in *gloves* catches no *mice*.

In addition to the traditional definition of a noun, grammarians describe a noun as follows:

—the kind of word that is often marked with an article (a *spoon*, an *apple*, the *newspaper*)

—the kind of word that can usually be made plural (one *cat*, two *cats*) or possessive (the *cat's* paw)

—the kind of word that when derived from another word typically takes one of these endings: play*er*, just*ice*, happi*ness*, divis*ion*, guid*ance*, refer*ence*, pave*ment*, child*hood*, king*dom*, agen*cy*, tour*ist*, sincer*ity*, censor*ship*

—the kind of word that can fill one of these positions in a sentence: subject, direct object, indirect object, subject complement, object complement, object of the preposition (See 58a and 58b.)

Nouns, in other words, may be identified as much by their form and function as by their meaning.

Nouns sometimes function as adjectives modifying other nouns. Because of their dual function, nouns used in this manner may be called *noun/adjectives.*

You can't make a *silk* purse out of a *sow's* ear.

Nouns are classified for a variety of purposes. When capitalization is the issue, we speak of *proper* versus *common nouns* (see 45a). If the problem is one of word choice, we may speak of *concrete* versus *abstract nouns* (see 18b). The distinction between *count nouns* and *noncount nouns* is useful primarily for nonnative speakers of English (see 30a and 30b). The term *collective noun* refers to a set of nouns that may cause problems with subject-verb or pronoun-antecedent agreement (see 21f and 22b).

EXERCISE 57–1

Underline the nouns (and noun/adjectives) in the following sentences. Answers to lettered sentences appear in the back of the book. Example:

Idle <u>hands</u> **are the** <u>devil's</u> <u>workshop</u>**.**

a. The sun will set without your assistance. —Hebrew proverb
b. Pride is at the bottom of all great mistakes. —John Ruskin
c. The trouble with being in the rat race is that even if you win, you're still a rat. —Lily Tomlin
d. The ultimate censorship is the flick of the dial.

—Tom Smothers
e. Figures won't lie, but liars will figure. —Anonymous

1. Truthfulness so often goes with ruthlessness.   —Dodie Smith
2. Luck is a matter of preparation meeting opportunity.
                                                —Oprah Winfrey
3. Problems are only opportunities in work clothes.
                                                —Henry Kaiser
4. A woman must have money and a room of her own.
                                                —Virginia Woolf
5. The devil often cites Scripture for his purpose.
                                                —Shakespeare

57b Pronouns

There are thousands of nouns, and new ones come into the language every year. This is not true of pronouns, which number about one hundred and are extremely resistant to change. Most of the pronouns in English are listed in this section.

A pronoun is a word used in place of a noun. Usually the pronoun substitutes for a specific noun, known as its *antecedent*.

When the *wheel* squeaks, *it* is greased.

Although most pronouns function as substitutes for nouns, some can function as adjectives modifying nouns.

This hanging will surely be a lesson to me.

Because they have the form of a pronoun and the function of an adjective, such pronouns may be called *pronoun/adjectives*.

Pronouns are classified as personal, possessive, intensive and reflexive, relative, interrogative, demonstrative, indefinite, and reciprocal.

PERSONAL PRONOUNS Personal pronouns refer to specific persons or things. They always function as noun equivalents.

Singular: I, me, you, she, her, he, him, it

Plural: we, us, you, they, them

POSSESSIVE PRONOUNS Possessive pronouns indicate ownership.

Singular: my, mine, your, yours, her, hers, his, its

Plural: our, ours, your, yours, their, theirs

Some of these possessive pronouns function as adjectives modifying nouns: *my, your, his, her, its, our, their.*

INTENSIVE AND REFLEXIVE PRONOUNS Intensive pronouns emphasize a noun or another pronoun (The senator *herself* met us at the door). Reflexive pronouns, which have the same form as intensive pronouns, name a receiver of an action identical with the doer of the action (Paula cut *herself*).

Singular: myself, yourself, himself, herself, itself

Plural: ourselves, yourselves, themselves

RELATIVE PRONOUNS Relative pronouns introduce subordinate clauses functioning as adjectives (The man *who robbed us* was never caught). In addition to introducing the clause, the relative pronoun, in this case *who*, points back to a noun or pronoun that the clause modifies (*man*). (See 59b.)

who, whom, whose, which, that

Some grammarians also treat *whichever, whoever, whomever, what,* and *whatever* as relative pronouns. These words introduce noun clauses; they do not point back to a noun or pronoun. (See 59b.)

INTERROGATIVE PRONOUNS   Interrogative pronouns introduce questions (*Who* is expected to win the election?).

who, whom, whose, which, what

DEMONSTRATIVE PRONOUNS   Demonstrative pronouns identify or point to nouns. Frequently they function as adjectives (*This* chair is my favorite), but they may also function as noun equivalents (*This* is my favorite chair).

this, that, these, those

INDEFINITE PRONOUNS   Indefinite pronouns refer to nonspecific persons or things. Most are always singular (*everyone, each*); some are always plural (*both, many*); a few may be singular or plural (see 21e). Most indefinite pronouns function as noun equivalents (*Something* is burning), but some can also function as adjectives (*All* campers must check in at the lodge).

all	anything	everyone	nobody	several
another	both	everything	none	some
any	each	few	no one	somebody
anybody	either	many	nothing	someone
anyone	everybody	neither	one	something

RECIPROCAL PRONOUNS   Reciprocal pronouns refer to individual parts of a plural antecedent (By turns, we helped *each other* through college).

each other, one another

NOTE: Pronouns cause a variety of problems for writers. See pronoun-antecedent agreement (22), pronoun reference (23), distinguishing between pronouns such as *I* and *me* (24), and distinguishing between *who* and *whom* (25).

EXERCISE 57-2

Underline the pronouns (and pronoun/adjectives) in the following sentences. Answers to lettered sentences appear in the back of the book. Example:

Beware of persons <u>who</u> are praised by <u>everyone</u>.

a. He has every attribute of a dog except loyalty.

—Thomas Gore

b. A fall does not hurt those who fly low.   —Chinese proverb

c. I have written some poetry that I myself don't understand.

—Carl Sandburg

d. I am firm. You are obstinate. He is a pig-headed fool.

—Katherine Whitehorn

e. She never lets ideas interrupt the easy flow of her conversation.

— Jean Webster

1. Doctors can bury their mistakes, but architects can only advise their clients to plant vines.   —Frank Lloyd Wright

2. Nothing is interesting if you are not interested.

—Helen MacInness

3. We will never have friends if we expect to find them without fault.   —Thomas Fuller

4. The gods help those who help themselves.   —Aesop

5. You never find yourself until you face the truth.

—Pearl Bailey

57c Verbs

The verb of a sentence usually expresses action (*jump, think*) or being (*is, become*). It is composed of a main verb possibly preceded by one or more helping verbs:

       MV
The best fish *swim* near the bottom.

       HV   **MV**
A marriage *is* not *built* in a day.

Grammar basics

HV   HV   MV
Even God *has been defended* with nonsense.

Notice that words can intervene between the helping and the main verb (*is* not *built*).

Helping verbs

There are twenty-three helping verbs in English: forms of *have, do,* and *be,* which may also function as main verbs; and nine modals, which function only as helping verbs. The forms of *have, do,* and *be* change form to indicate tense; the nine modals do not.

> **FORMS OF *HAVE, DO,* AND *BE***
> have, has, had
>
> do, does, did
>
> be, am, is, are, was, were, being, been
>
> **MODALS**
> can, could, may, might, must, shall, should, will, would

The phrase *ought to* is often classified as a modal as well.

Main verbs

The main verb of a sentence is always the kind of word that would change form if put into these test sentences:

BASE FORM	Usually I (*walk, ride*).
PAST TENSE	Yesterday I (*walked, rode*).
PAST PARTICIPLE	I have (*walked, ridden*) many times before.
PRESENT PARTICIPLE	I am (*walking, riding*) right now.
-S FORM	Usually he/she/it (*walks, rides*).

If a word doesn't change form when slipped into these test sentences, you can be certain that it is not a main verb. For example, the noun *revolution,* though it may seem to suggest an action, can never function as a main verb. Just try to make it behave like one (*Today I revolution . . . Yesterday I revolutioned . . .*) and you'll see why.

When both the past-tense and the past-participle forms of a verb end in *-ed,* the verb is regular (*walked, walked*). Otherwise, the verb is irregular (*rode, ridden*). (See 27a.)

The verb *be* is highly irregular, having eight forms instead of the usual five: the base form *be;* the present-tense forms *am, is,* and *are;* the past-tense forms *was* and *were;* the present participle *being;* and the past participle *been.*

Helping verbs combine with the various forms of main verbs to create tenses. For a survey of tenses, see 28a.

NOTE: Some verbs are followed by words that look like prepositions but are so closely associated with the verb that they are a part of its meaning. These words are known as *particles.* Common verb-particle combinations include *bring up, call off, drop off, give in, look up, run into,* and *take off.*

> A lot of parents *pack up* their troubles and *send* them *off* to camp. —Raymond Duncan

NOTE: Verbs cause many problems for writers. See subject-verb agreement (21), standard English verb forms (27), verb tense, mood, and voice (28), and ESL problems with verbs (29).

EXERCISE 57–3

Underline the verbs in the following sentences, including helping verbs and particles. If a verb is part of a contraction (such as *is* in *isn't* or *would* in *I'd*), underline only the letters that represent the verb. Answers to lettered sentences appear in the back of the book. Example:

A full cup <u>must</u> <u>be</u> <u>carried</u> steadily.

a. Great persons have not commonly been great scholars.
—Oliver Wendell Holmes, Sr.
b. There are no atheists on turbulent airplanes.   —Erica Jong
c. One arrow does not bring down two birds.   —Turkish proverb
d. If love is the answer, could you please rephrase the question?
—Lily Tomlin
e. Throw a lucky man into the sea, and he will emerge with a fish in his mouth.   —Arab proverb

1. Do not needlessly endanger your lives until I give you the signal.
—Dwight D. Eisenhower
2. Wrong must not win by technicalities.   —Aeschylus
3. Love your neighbor, but don't pull down the hedge.
—Swiss proverb
4. I'd rather have roses on my table than diamonds around my neck.   —Emma Goldman
5. He is a fine friend. He stabs you in the front.
—Leonard Louis Levinson

57d Adjectives

An adjective is a word used to modify, or describe, a noun or pronoun. An adjective usually answers one of these questions: Which one? What kind of? How many?

the *lame* elephant [Which elephant?]

valuable old stamps [What kind of stamps?]

sixteen candles [How many candles?]

Grammarians also define adjectives according to their form and their typical position in a sentence, as follows:

—the kind of word that usually comes before a noun in a noun phrase (a *frisky* puppy, an *amiable young* man)

—the kind of word that can follow a linking verb and describe the subject (The ship was *unsinkable;* Talk is *cheap*) (see 58b)

—the kind of word that when derived from another part of speech typically takes one of these endings: wonder*ful,* courte*ous,* luck*y,* fool*ish,* pleasur*able,* colon*ial,* help*less,* defens*ible,* urg*ent,* disgust*ing,* friend*ly,* spectacul*ar,* secret*ive*

The definite article *the* and the indefinite articles *a* and *an* are also classified as adjectives.

Some possessive, demonstrative, and indefinite pronouns can function as adjectives: *their, its, this* (see 57b).

NOTE: Writers sometimes misuse adjectives (see 26b). Speakers of English as a second language often encounter problems with the articles *a, an,* and *the* and occasionally have trouble placing adjectives correctly (see 30 and 31d).

57e Adverbs

An adverb is a word used to modify, or qualify, a verb (or verbal), an adjective, or another adverb. It usually answers one of these questions: When? Where? How? Why? Under what conditions? To what degree?

Pull *gently* at a weak rope. [Pull how?]

Read the best books *first.* [Read when?]

Adverbs that modify a verb are also defined according to their form and their typical position in a sentence, as follows:

—the kind of word that can appear nearly anywhere in a sentence and is often movable (he *sometimes* jogged after work; *sometimes* he jogged after work)

—the kind of word that when derived from an adjective typically takes an *-ly* ending (nice, nice*ly;* profound, profound*ly*)

Adverbs modifying adjectives or other adverbs usually intensify or limit the intensity of the word they modify.

Be *extremely* good, and you will be *very* lonesome.

Adverbs modifying adjectives and other adverbs are not movable. We can't say "Be good *extremely*" or "*Extremely* be good."

The negators *not* and *never* are classified as adverbs. A word such as *cannot* contains the helping verb *can* and the adverb *not*. A contraction such as *can't* contains the helping verb *can* and a contracted form of the adverb *not*.

Adverbs can modify prepositions (Helen left *just* before midnight), prepositional phrases (The budget is *barely* on target), subordinate clauses (We will try to attend, *especially* if you will be there), or whole sentences (*Certainly* Joe did not intend to insult you).

NOTE: Writers sometimes misuse adverbs (see 26a). Speakers of English as a second language may have trouble placing adverbs correctly (see 31d).

EXERCISE 57–4

Underline the adjectives and circle the adverbs in the following sentences. If a word is a pronoun in form but an adjective in function, treat it as an adjective. Also treat the articles *a, an,* and *the* as adjectives. Answers to lettered sentences are in the back of the book. Example:

A wild goose (never) laid a tame egg.

a. General notions are generally wrong.

—Lady Mary Wortley Montagu

b. The American public is wonderfully tolerant.   —Anonymous
c. Gardening is not a rational act.   —Margaret Atwood
d. A clean glove often hides a dirty hand.   —English proverb
e. Sleep faster. We need the pillows.   —Yiddish proverb

1. Success is a public affair; failure is a private funeral.
     —Rosalind Russell
2. Their civil discussions were not interesting, and their interesting discussions were not civil.   —Lisa Alther
3. Money will buy a pretty good dog, but it will not buy the wag of its tail.   —Josh Billings
4. A little sincerity is a dangerous thing, and a great deal of it is absolutely fatal.   —Oscar Wilde
5. Feelings are untidy.   —Esther Hautzig

57f Prepositions

A preposition is a word placed before a noun or pronoun to form a phrase modifying another word in the sentence. The prepositional phrase nearly always functions as an adjective or as an adverb. (See 59a.)

> The road *to hell* is usually paved *with good intentions.*

To hell functions as an adjective, modifying the noun *road; with good intentions* functions as an adverb, modifying the verb *is paved.*
     There are a limited number of prepositions in English. The most common ones are included in the following list.

about	around	besides	despite	inside
above	as	between	down	into
across	at	beyond	during	like
after	before	but	except	near
against	behind	by	for	next
along	below	concerning	from	of
among	beside	considering	in	off

on	past	than	under	upon
onto	plus	through	underneath	with
opposite	regarding	throughout	unlike	within
out	respecting	till	until	without
outside	round	to	unto	
over	since	toward	up	

Some prepositions are more than one word long. *Along with, as well as, in addition to,* and *next to* are common examples.

NOTE: Except for certain idiomatic uses (see 18d), prepositions cause few problems for native speakers of English. For second-language speakers, however, prepositions can cause considerable difficulty (see 29d and 31f).

57g Conjunctions

Conjunctions join words, phrases, or clauses, and they indicate the relation between the elements joined.

COORDINATING CONJUNCTIONS A coordinating conjunction is used to connect grammatically equal elements. The coordinating conjunctions are *and, but, or, nor, for, so,* and *yet.*

> Poverty is the parent of revolution *and* crime.

> Admire a little ship, *but* put your cargo in a big one.

In the first sentence, *and* connects two nouns; in the second, *but* connects two independent clauses.

CORRELATIVE CONJUNCTIONS Correlative conjunctions come in pairs: *either . . . or; neither . . . nor; not only . . . but also; whether . . . or; both . . . and.* Like coordinating conjunctions, they connect grammatically equal elements.

Either Jack Sprat *or* his wife could eat no fat.

SUBORDINATING CONJUNCTIONS   A subordinating conjunction introduces a subordinate clause and indicates its relation to the rest of the sentence. (See 59b.) The most common subordinating conjunctions are *after, although, as, as if, because, before, even though, how, if, in order that, once, rather than, since, so that, than, that, though, unless, until, when, where, whether, while,* and *why.*

If you want service, serve yourself.

CONJUNCTIVE ADVERBS   A conjunctive adverb may be used with a semicolon to connect independent clauses; it usually serves as a transition between the clauses. The most common conjunctive adverbs are *consequently, finally, furthermore, however, moreover, nevertheless, similarly, then, therefore,* and *thus.* (See the chart on p. 744 for a more complete list.)

When we want to murder a tiger, we call it sport; *however,* when the tiger wants to murder us, we call it ferocity.

NOTE: The ability to distinguish between conjunctive adverbs and coordinating conjunctions will help you avoid run on sentences and make punctuation decisions (see 20, 32a, and 32b). The ability to recognize subordinating conjunctions will help you avoid sentence fragments (see 19).

57h Interjections

An interjection is a word used to express surprise or emotion (*Oh! Hey! Wow!*).

Grammar basics

Parts of speech

A **NOUN** names a person, place, thing, or idea.

> N   N   N
> *Repetition* does not transform a *lie* into *truth.*

A **PRONOUN** substitutes for a noun.

>   PN PN   PN
> When the gods wish to punish *us, they* heed *our* prayers.

Personal pronouns: I, me, you, he, him, she, her, it, we, us, they, them

Possessive pronouns: my, mine, your, yours, her, hers, his, its, our, ours, their, theirs

Intensive and reflexive pronouns: myself, yourself, himself, herself, itself, ourselves, yourselves, themselves

Relative pronouns: that, which, who, whom, whose

Interrogative pronouns: who, whom, whose, which, what

Demonstrative pronouns: this, that, these, those

Indefinite pronouns: all, another, any, anybody, anyone, anything, both, each, either, everybody, everyone, everything, few, many, neither, nobody, none, no one, nothing, one, several, some, somebody, someone, something

Reciprocal pronouns: each other, one another

A **HELPING VERB** comes before a main verb.

Modals: can, could, may, might, must, shall, should, will, would (*also* ought to)

Forms of be: be, am, is, are, was, were, being, been

Parts of speech (continued)

Forms of have: have, has, had

Forms of do: do, does, did

(The forms of *be, have,* and *do* may also function as main verbs.)

A **MAIN VERB** asserts action, being, or state of being.

       MV   HV   MV
Charity *begins* at home but *should* not *end* there.

A main verb will always change form when put into these positions in sentences:

Usually I _____ .	(*walk, ride*)
Yesterday I _____ .	(*walked, rode*)
I have _____ many times before.	(*walked, ridden*)
I am _____ right now.	(*walking, riding*)
Usually he _____ .	(*walks, rides*)

There are eight forms of the highly irregular verb *be: be, am, is, are, was, were, being, been.*

An **ADJECTIVE** modifies a noun or pronoun, usually answering one of these questions: Which one? What kind of? How many? The articles *a, an,* and *the* are also adjectives.

   ADJ   ADJ
Useless laws weaken *necessary* ones.

An **ADVERB** modifies a verb, adjective, or adverb, usually answering one of these questions: When? Where? Why? How? Under what conditions? To what degree?

        ADV   ADV
People think *too historically.*

Parts of speech (continued)

A **PREPOSITION** indicates the relationship between the noun or pronoun that follows it and another word in the sentence.

>   P   P
> A journey *of* a thousand miles begins *with* a single step.

Common prepositions: about, above, across, after, against, along, among, around, as, at, before, behind, below, beside, besides, between, beyond, but, by, concerning, considering, despite, down, during, except, for, from, in, inside, into, like, near, next, of, off, on, onto, opposite, out, outside, over, past, plus, regarding, respecting, round, since, than, through, throughout, till, to, toward, under, underneath, unlike, until, unto, up, upon, with, within, without

A **CONJUNCTION** connects words or word groups.

Coordinating conjunctions: and, but, or, nor, for, so, yet

Subordinating conjunctions: after, although, as, as if, because, before, even though, how, if, in order that, once, rather than, since, so that, than, that, though, unless, until, when, where, whether, while, why

Correlative conjunctions: either . . . or, neither . . . nor, not only . . . but also, both . . . and, whether . . . or

Conjunctive adverbs: accordingly, also, anyway, besides, certainly, consequently, conversely, finally, furthermore, hence, however, incidentally, indeed, instead, likewise, meanwhile, moreover, nevertheless, next, nonetheless, otherwise, similarly, specifically, still, subsequently, then, therefore, thus

An **INTERJECTION** expresses surprise or emotion. (*Oh! Wow! Hey! Hooray!*)

58

Sentence patterns

Most English sentences flow from subject to verb to any objects or complements. The vast majority of sentences conform to one of these five patterns:

subject / verb / subject complement

subject / verb / direct object

subject / verb / indirect object / direct object

subject / verb / direct object / object complement

subject / verb

Adverbial modifiers (single words, phrases, or clauses) may be added to any of these patterns, and they may appear nearly anywhere—at the beginning, the middle, or the end.

Predicate is the grammatical term given to the verb plus its objects, complements, and adverbial modifiers.

For a quick-reference chart of sentence patterns, see page 752.

58a Subjects

The subject of a sentence names who or what the sentence is about. The *complete subject* is usually composed of a *simple subject*, always a noun or pronoun, plus any words or word groups modifying the simple subject. To find the complete subject, ask Who? or What?, insert the verb, and finish the question. The answer is the complete subject.

┌── COMPLETE SUBJECT ──┐
The purity of a revolution usually lasts about two weeks.

Who or what lasts about two weeks? *The purity of a revolution.*

┌─────────── COMPLETE SUBJECT ───────────┐
Historical books that contain no lies are extremely tedious.

Who or what are extremely tedious? *Historical books that contain no lies.*

COMPLETE SUBJECT
┌──────────┐
In every country the sun rises in the morning.

Who or what rises in the morning? *The sun.* Notice that *In every country the sun* is not a sensible answer to the question. *In every country* is a prepositional phrase modifying the verb *rises.* Since sentences frequently open with such modifiers, it is not safe to assume that the subject must always appear first in a sentence.

To find the simple subject, strip away all modifiers in the complete subject. This includes single-word modifiers such as *the* and *historical,* phrases such as *of a revolution,* and subordinate clauses such as *that contain no lies.*

┌─SS─┐
The purity of a revolution usually lasts about two weeks.

┌─SS─┐
Historical books that contain no lies are extremely tedious.

┌SS┐
In every country *the sun* rises in the morning.

A sentence may have a compound subject containing two or more simple subjects joined with a coordinating conjunction such as *and, but,* or *or.*

┌──SS──┐   ┌──SS──┐
Much industry and little conscience make us rich.

In imperative sentences, which give advice or issue commands, the verb's subject is understood but not actually present in the sentence. The subject of an imperative sentence is understood to be *you*, as in the following example.

[*You*] Hitch your wagon to a star.

Although the subject ordinarily comes before the verb, occasionally it does not. When a sentence begins with *There is* or *There are* (or *There was* or *There were*), the subject follows the verb. The word *There* is an expletive in such constructions, an empty word serving merely to get the sentence started.

┌─── ss ───┐
There is *no substitute for victory.*

Occasionally a writer will invert a sentence for effect.

┌─ ss ─┐
Happy is *the nation that has no history.*

Happy is an adjective, so it cannot be the subject. Turn this sentence around and its structure becomes obvious: *The nation that has no history is happy.*

In questions, the subject frequently appears in an unusual position, sandwiched between parts of the verb.

┌ ss ┐
Do *married men* make the best husbands?

Turn the question into a statement, and the words will appear in their usual order: *Married men do make the best husbands.* (*Do make* is the verb.)

NOTE: The ability to recognize the subject of a sentence will help you edit for a variety of problems such as sentence fragments (19), subject-verb agreement (21), and choice of pronouns such as *I* and *me* (24). If English is not your native language, see also 31a and 31b.

Grammar basics

EXERCISE 58–1

In the following sentences, underline the complete subject and write *ss* above the simple subject(s). If the subject is an understood *you*, insert it in parentheses. Answers to lettered sentences appear in the back of the book. Example:

> <u>Fools and their money</u> are soon parted.

a. Sticks and stones may break my bones, and words can sting like anything. —Anonymous
b. To some lawyers, all facts are created equal.
> —Felix Frankfurter
c. Speak softly and carry a big stick. —Theodore Roosevelt
d. There is nothing permanent except change. —Heraclitus
e. The only difference between a rut and a grave is their dimensions. —Ellen Glasgow

1. The secret of being a bore is to tell everything. —Voltaire
2. Don't be humble. You're not that great. —Golda Meir
3. In the eyes of its mother, every beetle is a gazelle.
> —Moorish proverb
4. The price of hating other human beings is loving oneself less.
> —Eldridge Cleaver
5. There are no signposts in the sea. —Vita Sackville-West

58b Verbs, objects, and complements

Section 57c explains how to find the verb of a sentence, which consists of a main verb possibly preceded by one or more helping verbs. A sentence's verb is classified as linking, transitive, or intransitive, depending on the kinds of objects or complements the verb can (or cannot) take.

Linking verbs and subject complements

Linking verbs link the subject to a subject complement, a word or word group that completes the meaning of the subject by renaming or describing it. If the subject complement renames the subject, it is a noun or noun equivalent (sometimes called a *predicate noun*).

```
┌──────────── s ──────────────┐ ┌─ v ─┐ ┌─ sc ─┐
The handwriting on the wall may be a forgery.
```

If the subject complement describes the subject, it is an adjective or adjective equivalent (sometimes called a *predicate adjective*).

```
s  v   sc
Love is blind.
```

Whenever they appear as main verbs (rather than helping verbs), the forms of *be*—*be, am, is, are, was, were, being, been*—usually function as linking verbs. In the preceding examples, for instance, the main verbs are *be* and *is*.

Verbs such as *appear, become, feel, grow, look, make, seem, smell, sound,* and *taste* are sometimes linking, depending on the sense of the sentence.

```
         ┌── s ──┐ ┌── v ──┐ ┌─ sc ─┐
At the touch of love, everyone becomes a poet.
```

```
      ┌── s ──┐          ┌─ v ─┐┌ sc ┐
At first sight, original art often looks ugly.
```

When you suspect that a verb such as *becomes* or *looks* is linking, check to see if the word or words following it rename or describe the subject. In the sample sentences, *a poet* renames *everyone,* and *ugly* describes *art.*

Transitive verbs and direct objects

A transitive verb takes a direct object, a word or word group that names a receiver of the action.

```
┌──────── s ────────┐ ┌─ v ─┐ ┌────────── DO ──────────┐
The little snake studies the ways of the big serpent.
```

In such sentences, the subject and verb alone will seem incomplete. Once we have read *The little snake studies,* for example, we want to know the rest: *The little snake studies what?* The answer to the question What? (or Whom?) is the complete direct object: *the ways of the big serpent.* The simple direct object is always a noun or pronoun, in this case *ways.* To find it, simply strip away all modifiers.

Transitive verbs usually appear in the active voice, with the subject doing the action and a direct object receiving the action. Active-voice sentences can be transformed into the passive voice, with the subject receiving the action instead. (See 58c.)

Transitive verbs, indirect objects, and direct objects

The direct object of a transitive verb is sometimes preceded by an indirect object, a noun or pronoun telling to whom or for whom the action of the sentence is done.

> **S   V   IO ┌─DO─┐   S┌──V──┐ IO ┌── DO──┐**
> You show me a hero, and I will write you a tragedy.

The simple indirect object is always a noun or pronoun. To test for an indirect object, insert the word *to* or *for* before the word or word group in question. If the sentence makes sense, the word or word group is an indirect object.

> You show [to] me a hero, and I will write [for] you a tragedy.

An indirect object may be turned into a prepositional phrase using *to* or *for: You show a hero to me, and I will write a tragedy for you.*

Only certain transitive verbs take indirect objects. Common examples are *give, ask, bring, find, get, hand, lend, offer, pay, pour, promise, read, send, show, teach, tell, throw,* and *write.*

Transitive verbs, direct objects, and object complements

The direct object of a transitive verb is sometimes followed by an object complement, a word or word group that completes the direct object's meaning by renaming or describing it.

```
 ┌─S─┐      ┌─V─┐┌─ DO ─┐┌──────────── OC ────────────┐
 People now call a spade an agricultural implement.
```

```
 ┌─S─┐┌─ V ─┐┌────── DO──────┐┌─OC─┐
 Love makes all hard hearts gentle.
```

When the object complement renames the direct object, it is a noun or pronoun (such as *implement*). When it describes the direct object, it is an adjective (such as *gentle*).

Intransitive verbs

Intransitive verbs take no objects or complements. Their pattern is always subject/verb.

```
    S      V
 Money talks.
```

```
 ┌──────S──────┐      ┌─V─┐
 Revolutions never go backward.
```

Nothing receives the actions of talking and going in these sentences, so the verbs are intransitive. Notice that such verbs may or may not be followed by adverbial modifiers. In the second sentence, *backward* is an adverb modifying *go*.

NOTE: The dictionary will tell you whether a verb is transitive or intransitive. Some verbs have both transitive and intransitive functions.

TRANSITIVE   Sandra flew her Cessna over the canyon.

INTRANSITIVE   A bald eagle flew overhead.

Sentence patterns

Subject / linking verb / subject complement

```
┌──s──┐ v ┌────sc────┐
```
Advertising is legalized lying. [*Legalized lying* renames *Advertising*.]

```
┌───s───┐ v ┌─sc─┐
```
Great intellects are skeptical. [*Skeptical* describes *Great intellects*.]

Subject / transitive verb / direct object

```
┌──s──┐┌───v───┐┌DO┐
```
A stumble may prevent a fall.

Subject / transitive verb / indirect object / direct object

```
s   v   IO ┌───DO───┐
```
Fate gives us our relatives.

Subject / transitive verb / direct object / object complement

```
┌──s──┐┌─v─┐ DO   OC
```
Our fears do make us traitors. [*Traitors* renames *us*.]

```
┌─s─┐ v ┌─DO─┐ OC
```
The pot calls the kettle black. [*Black* describes *the kettle*.]

Subject / intransitive verb

```
s   v
```
Time flies.

In the first example, *flew* has a direct object that receives the action: *her Cessna*. In the second example, the verb is followed by an adverb (*overhead*), not by a direct object.

EXERCISE 58-2

Label the subject complements, direct objects, indirect objects, and object complements in the following sentences. If an object or complement consists of more than one word, bracket and label all of it. Answers to lettered sentences appear in the back of the book. Example:

$$\text{DO} \quad \overbrace{\text{OC}}$$
All work and no play make Jack a dull boy.

a. The best mind-altering drug is truth.   —Lily Tomlin
b. No one tests the depth of a river with both feet.
                                                —West African proverb
c. All looks yellow to a jaundiced eye.   —Alexander Pope
d. Luck never made a man [or a woman] wise.
                                                —Seneca the Younger
e. You show me a capitalist and I will show you a bloodsucker.
                                                —Malcolm X

1. Accomplishments have no color.   —Leontyne Price
2. Victory has a hundred fathers, but defeat is an orphan.
                                                —Count Galeazzo Ciano
3. Acting is a form of confession.   —Tallulah Bankhead
4. I never promised you a rose garden.   —Hannah Green
5. Some folk want their luck buttered.   —Anonymous

58c Pattern variations

Although most sentences follow one of the five patterns in the chart on the facing page, variations of these patterns commonly occur in questions, commands, sentences with delayed subjects, and passive transformations.

Questions and commands

Questions are sometimes patterned in normal word order, with the subject preceding the verb.

$$\text{s} \quad \overbrace{\text{v}}$$
Who will take the first step?

Grammar basics

Just as frequently, however, the pattern of a question is inverted, with the subject appearing between the helping and main verbs or after the verb.

> **HV   S   MV**
> Will you take the first step?
>
> **V ┌───S───┐**
> Why is the first step so difficult?

In commands, the subject of the sentence is an understood *you.*

> [You] Keep your mouth shut and your eyes open.

Sentences with delayed subjects

Writers sometimes choose to delay the subject of a sentence to achieve a special effect such as suspense or humor.

> **V ┌───S───┐**
> Behind the phony tinsel of Hollywood lies the real tinsel.

The subject of the sentence is also delayed in sentences opening with the expletive *There* or *It.* When used as expletives, the words *There* and *It* have no strict grammatical function; they serve merely to get the sentence started.

> **V ┌───────S───────┐**
> There are many paths to the top of the mountain.
>
> **V   ┌───────S───────┐**
> It is not good to wake a sleeping lion.

The subject in the second example is an infinitive phrase. (See 59c.)

Passive transformations

Transitive verbs, those that can take direct objects, usually appear in the active voice. In the active voice, the subject does the action and a direct object receives the action.

ACTIVE The early bird sometimes catches the early worm.

Sentences in the active voice may be transformed into the passive voice, with the subject receiving the action instead.

┌────── S ──────┐ HV   MV
PASSIVE The early worm is sometimes caught by the early bird.

What was once the direct object (*the early worm*) has become the subject in the passive-voice transformation, and the original subject appears in a prepositional phrase beginning with *by*. The *by* phrase is frequently omitted in passive-voice constructions.

PASSIVE The early worm is sometimes caught.

Verbs in the passive voice can be identified by their form alone. The main verb is always a past participle, such as *caught* (see 57c), preceded by a form of *be* (*be, am, is, are, was, were, being, been*): *is caught.* Sometimes adverbs intervene (*is sometimes caught*).

NOTE: Writers sometimes use the passive voice when the active voice would be more appropriate (see 14a). For a review of the uses of the active and the passive voice, see 28c.

59

Subordinate word groups

Subordinate word groups include prepositional phrases, subordinate clauses, verbal phrases, appositives, and absolutes. Not all of these word groups are subordinate in quite the same way. Some are subordinate because they are modifiers; others function as noun equivalents, not as modifiers.

59a Prepositional phrases

A prepositional phrase begins with a preposition such as *at*, *by*, *for*, *from*, *in*, *of*, *on*, *to*, or *with* (see 57f) and usually ends with a noun or noun equivalent: *on the table*, *for him*, *with great fanfare*. The noun or noun equivalent is known as the *object of the preposition*.

Prepositional phrases function either as adjectives modifying a noun or pronoun or as adverbs modifying a verb, an adjective, or another adverb. When functioning as an adjective, a prepositional phrase nearly always appears immediately following the noun or pronoun it modifies.

Variety is the spice *of life.*

Adjective phrases usually answer one or both of the questions Which one? and What kind of? If we ask Which spice? or What kind of spice? we get a sensible answer: *the spice of life.*

Adverbial prepositional phrases that modify the verb can appear nearly anywhere in a sentence.

Do not judge a tree *by its bark.*

Tyranny will *in time* lead to revolution.

To the ant, a few drops of rain are a flood.

Adverbial word groups usually answer one of these questions: When? Where? How? Why? Under what conditions? To what degree?

Do not judge a tree *how? By its bark.*

Tyranny will lead to revolution *when? In time.*

A few drops of rain are a flood *under what conditions? To the ant.*

If a prepositional phrase is movable, you can be certain that it is adverbial; adjectival prepositional phrases are wedded to the words they modify. At least some of the time, adverbial modifiers can be moved to other positions in the sentence.

> *By their fruits* you shall know them.

> You shall know them *by their fruits*.

In questions and subordinate clauses, a preposition may appear after its object.

> *What* are you afraid *of?*

> We avoided the clerk *whom* John had warned us *about*.

NOTE: The ability to recognize the object of a preposition will help you distinguish between pronouns such as *I* and *me* (see 24b).

EXERCISE 59-1

Underline the prepositional phrases in the following sentences. Be prepared to explain the function of each phrase. Answers to lettered sentences appear in the back of the book. Example:

> You can stroke people <u>with words</u>. *(Adverb phrase modifying can stroke)*

a. A résumé is a balance sheet without any liabilities.
>   —Robert Half

b. Any mother could perform the job of several air traffic controllers with ease.   —Lisa Alther

c. She wears her morals like a loose garment.
>   —Langston Hughes

d. You can tell the ideals of a nation by its advertising.
>   —Norman Douglas

e. In France, cooking is a serious art form and a national sport.
>   — Julia Child

1. We know that the road to freedom has always been stalked by death. —Angela Davis
2. The quarrels of friends are the opportunities of foes. —Aesop
3. Some people feel with their heads and think with their hearts. —G. C. Lichtenberg
4. By a small sample, we may know the whole piece. —Cervantes
5. You and I come by road or rail, but economists travel on infrastructure. —Margaret Thatcher

59b Subordinate clauses

Subordinate clauses are patterned like sentences, having subjects and verbs and sometimes objects or complements. But they function within sentences as adjectives, adverbs, or nouns. They cannot stand alone as complete sentences.

A subordinate clause usually begins with a subordinating conjunction or a relative pronoun.

SUBORDINATING CONJUNCTIONS

after	before	rather than	though	where
although	even though	since	unless	whether
as	how	so that	until	while
as if	if	than	when	why
because	in order that	that		

RELATIVE PRONOUNS

that	who	whom	whose	which

The chart on page 762 classifies these words according to the kinds of clauses (adjective, adverb, or noun) they introduce.

Adjective clauses

Like other word groups functioning as adjectives, adjective clauses modify nouns or pronouns. An adjective clause nearly always appears immediately following the noun or pronoun it modifies.

The arrow *that has left the bow* never returns.

Relatives are persons *who live too near and visit too often.*

To test whether a subordinate clause functions as an adjective, ask the adjective questions: Which one? What kind of? The answer should make sense. Which arrow? *The arrow that has left the bow.* What kind of persons? *Persons who live too near and visit too often.*

Most adjective clauses begin with a relative pronoun (*who, whom, whose, which,* or *that*), which marks them as grammatically subordinate. In addition to introducing the clause, the relative pronoun points back to the noun that the clause modifies.

The fur *that warms a monarch* once warmed a bear.

Relative pronouns are sometimes "understood."

The things [*that*] *we know best* are the things [*that*] *we haven't been taught.*

Occasionally an adjective clause is introduced by a relative adverb, usually *when, where,* or *why.*

Home is the place *where you slip in the tub and break your neck.*

The parts of an adjective clause are often arranged as in sentences (subject/verb/object or complement).

          S   **V** **DO**
We often forgive the people *who bore us.*

Frequently, however, the object or complement appears first, violating the normal order of subject/verb/object.

DO   S   V

We rarely forgive those *whom we bore.*

To determine the subject of a clause, ask Who? or What? and insert the verb. Don't be surprised if the answer is an echo, as in the first adjective clause above: Who bore us? *Who.* To find any objects or complements, read the subject and the verb and then ask Who? Whom? or What? Again, be prepared for a possible echo, as in the second adjective clause: We bore whom? *Whom.*

NOTE: For punctuation of adjective clauses, see 32e and 33e. If English is not your native language, see 31c for a common problem with adjective clauses.

Adverb clauses

Adverb clauses usually modify verbs, in which case they may appear nearly anywhere in a sentence—at the beginning, at the end, or in the middle. Like other adverbial word groups, they tell when, where, why, under what conditions, or to what degree an action occurred or a situation existed.

When the well is dry, we know the worth of water.

Venice would be a fine city *if it were only drained.*

When do we know the worth of water? *When the well is dry.* Under what conditions would Venice be a fine city? *If it were only drained.*

Unlike adjective clauses, adverb clauses are frequently movable. In the preceding example sentences, for instance, the adverb clauses can be moved without affecting the meaning of the sentences.

We know the worth of water *when the well is dry.*

If it were only drained, Venice would be a fine city.

When an adverb clause modifies an adjective or an adverb, it is not movable; it must appear next to the word it modifies. In the following examples the *because* clause modifies the adjective *angry,* and the *than* clause modifies the adverb *faster.*

> Angry *because the mayor had not kept his promises,* we worked for his defeat.

> Joan can run faster *than I can bicycle.*

Adverb clauses always begin with a subordinating conjunction (see the chart on p. 744 for a list). Subordinating conjunctions introduce clauses and express their relation to the rest of the sentence.

Adverb clauses are sometimes elliptical, with some of their words being "understood."

> *When* [*it is*] *painted,* the room will look larger.

Noun clauses

Because they do not function as modifiers, noun clauses are not subordinate in the same sense as are adjective and adverb clauses. They are called subordinate only because they cannot stand alone: They must function within a sentence, always as nouns.

A noun clause functions just like a single-word noun, usually as a subject, subject complement, direct object, or object of a preposition.

> ┌────── S ──────┐
> *Whoever gossips to you* will gossip of you.

> ┌──────── DO ────────┐
> We never forget *that we buried the hatchet.*

A noun clause begins with a word that marks it as subordinate (see p. 762 for a list). The subordinating word may

Words that introduce subordinate clauses

WORDS INTRODUCING ADVERB CLAUSES

Subordinating conjunctions: after, although, as, as if, because, before, even though, if, in order that, rather than, since, so that, than, that, though, unless, until, when, where, whether, while

WORDS INTRODUCING ADJECTIVE CLAUSES

Relative pronouns: that, which, who, whom, whose

Relative adverbs: when, where, why

WORDS INTRODUCING NOUN CLAUSES

Relative pronouns: that, which, who, whom, whose

Other pronouns: whoever, whomever, what, whatever, whichever

Subordinating conjunctions: how, if, when, whenever, where, wherever, whether, why

or may not play a significant role in the clause. In the preceding example sentences, *whoever* is the subject of its clause, but *that* does not perform a function in its clause.

As with adjective clauses, the parts of a noun clause may appear out of their normal order (subject/verb/object).

> **DO   S   V**
> Talent is *what you possess.*

The parts of a noun clause may also appear in their normal order.

> **S   V   DO**
> Genius is *what possesses you.*

EXERCISE 59–2

Underline the subordinate clauses in the following sentences. Be prepared to explain the function of each clause. Answers to lettered sentences appear in the back of the book. Example:

> **Dig a well <u>before you are thirsty</u>.** *(Adverb clause modifying <u>Dig</u>)*

a. It is hard to fight an enemy who has outposts in your head.
                                                    —Sally Kempton
b. A rattlesnake that doesn't bite teaches you nothing.
                                                    — Jessamyn West
c. When I am an old woman, I shall wear purple.   — Jenny Joseph
d. Dreams say what they mean, but they don't say it in daytime language.   —Gail Godwin
e. A fraud is not perfect unless it is practiced on clever persons.
                                                    —Arab proverb

1. What history teaches us is that we have never learned anything from it.   —Georg Wilhelm Hegel
2. When the insects take over the world, we hope that they will remember our picnics with gratitude.   —Anonymous
3. A woman who will tell her age will tell anything.
                                                    —Rita Mae Brown
4. Science commits suicide when it adopts a creed.
                                                    — T. H. Huxley
5. He gave her a look that you could have poured on a waffle.
                                                    —Ring Lardner

59c   Verbal phrases

A verbal is a verb form that does not function as the verb of a clause. Verbals include infinitives (the word *to* plus the base form of the verb), present participles (the *-ing* form of the verb), and past participles (the verb form usually ending in *-d, -ed, -n, -en,* or *-t*). (See 27a and 57c.)

INFINITIVE	PRESENT PARTICIPLE	PAST PARTICIPLE
to dream	dreaming	dreamed
to choose	choosing	chosen
to build	building	built
to grow	growing	grown

Instead of functioning as the verb of a clause, a verbal or a verbal phrase functions as an adjective, a noun, or an adverb.

ADJECTIVE   *Stolen* grapes are especially sweet.

NOUN   Continual *dripping* wears away a stone.

ADVERB   Were we born *to suffer?*

Verbals can take objects, complements, and modifiers to form verbal phrases; the phrases usually lack subjects.

Living well is the best revenge.

Governments exist *to protect the rights of minorities.*

The verbal *Living* is modified by the adverb *well;* the verbal *to protect* is followed by a direct object, *the rights of minorities.*

Like single-word verbals, verbal phrases function as adjectives, nouns, or adverbs. In the sentences just given, for example, *living well* functions as a noun used as the subject of the sentence, and *to protect the rights of minorities* functions as an adverb, answering the question Why?

Verbal phrases are ordinarily classified as participles, gerunds, and infinitives. This classification is based partly on form (whether the verbal is a present participle, a past participle, or an infinitive) and partly on function (whether the whole phrase functions as an adjective, a noun, or an adverb).

NOTE: For advice on editing dangling verbal phrases, see 12e.

Participial phrases

Participial phrases always function as adjectives. Their verbals are either present participles, always ending in *-ing*, or past participles, frequently ending in *-d, -ed, -n, -en,* or *-t* (see 27a).

Participial phrases frequently appear immediately following the noun or pronoun they modify.

Congress shall make no law *abridging the freedom of speech or of the press.*

Truth *kept in the dark* will never save the world.

Unlike other adjectival word groups, however, which must always follow the noun or pronoun they modify, participial phrases are often movable. They can precede the word they modify.

Being weak, foxes are distinguished by superior tact.

They may also appear at some distance from the word they modify.

History is something that never happened, *written by someone who wasn't there.*

Gerund phrases

Gerund phrases are built around present participles (verb forms ending in *-ing*), and they always function as nouns: usually as subjects, subject complements, direct objects, or objects of a preposition.

Justifying a fault doubles it.

```
        ┌─────── SC ───────┐
```
The secret of education is *respecting the pupil.*

```
        ┌─────── DO ───────┐
```
Kleptomaniacs can't help *helping themselves.*

```
        ┌─── OBJ OF PREP ───┐
```
The hen is an egg's way of *producing another egg.*

Infinitive phrases

Infinitive phrases, usually constructed around *to* plus the base form of the verb (*to call, to drink*), can function as nouns, as adjectives, or as adverbs.

When functioning as a noun, an infinitive phrase may appear in almost any noun slot in a sentence, usually as a subject, subject complement, or direct object.

```
┌─────── S ───────┐
```
To side with truth is noble.

```
        ┌─────────── DO ───────────┐
```
Never try *to leap a chasm in two jumps.*

Infinitive phrases functioning as adjectives usually appear immediately following the noun or pronoun they modify.

We do not have the right *to abandon the poor.*

The infinitive phrase modifies the noun *right.* Which right? *The right to abandon the poor.*

Adverbial infinitive phrases usually qualify the meaning of the verb, telling when, where, how, why, under what conditions, or to what degree an action occurred.

He cut off his nose *to spite his face.*

Why did he cut off his nose? *To spite his face.*

NOTE: In some constructions, the infinitive is unmarked; in other words, the *to* does not appear: *No one can make you [to] feel inferior without your consent.* (See 29c.)

EXERCISE 59-3

Underline the verbal phrases in the following sentences. Be prepared to explain the function of each phrase. Answers to lettered sentences appear in the back of the book. Example:

> **Do you want <u>to be a writer</u>? Then write.** *(Infinitive phrase used as direct object of Do want)*

a. The best substitute for experience is being sixteen.
> —Raymond Duncan

b. The trouble with being punctual is that nobody is there to appreciate it. —Franklin P. Jones

c. Poetry is the impish attempt to paint the color of the wind.
> — Maxwell Bodenheim

d. Being a philosopher, I have a problem for every solution.
> —Robert Zend

e. For years I wanted to be older, and now I am.
> —Margaret Atwood

1. The thing generally raised on city land is taxes.
> —C. D. Warner

2. Do not use a hatchet to remove a fly from your friend's forehead.
> —Chinese proverb

3. He has the gall of a shoplifter returning an item for a refund.
> —W. I. E. Gates

4. Tact is the ability to describe others as they see themselves.
> —Mary Pettibone Poole

5. He could never see a belt without hitting below it.
> —Harriet Braiker

59d Appositive phrases

Though strictly speaking they are not subordinate word groups, appositive phrases function somewhat as adjectives do, to describe nouns or pronouns. Instead of modifying nouns or pronouns, however, appositive phrases rename them. In form they are nouns or noun equivalents.

Appositives are said to be "in apposition" to the nouns or pronouns they rename.

Politicians, *acrobats at heart,* can sit on a fence and yet keep both ears to the ground.

Acrobats at heart is in apposition to the noun *politicians.*

59e Absolute phrases

An absolute phrase modifies a whole clause or sentence, not just one word, and it may appear nearly anywhere in the sentence. It consists of a noun or noun equivalent usually followed by a participial phrase.

His words dipped in honey, the senator mesmerized the crowd.

The senator mesmerized the crowd, *his words dipped in honey.*

60

Sentence types

Sentences are classified in two ways: according to their structure (simple, compound, complex, and compound-complex) and according to their purpose (declarative, imperative, interrogative, and exclamatory).

60a Sentence structures

Depending on the number and types of clauses they contain, sentences are classified as simple, compound, complex, or compound-complex.

Clauses come in two varieties: independent and subordinate. An independent clause is a full sentence pattern that does not function within another sentence pattern: It contains a subject and verb plus any objects, complements, and modifiers of that verb, and it either stands alone or could stand alone. A subordinate clause is a full sentence pattern that functions within a sentence as an adjective, an adverb, or a noun but that cannot stand alone as a complete sentence. (See 59b.)

Simple sentences

A simple sentence is one independent clause with no subordinate clauses.

> ┌────── **INDEPENDENT CLAUSE** ──────┐
> Without music, life would be a mistake.

This sentence contains a subject (*life*), a verb (*would be*), a complement (*a mistake*), and an adverbial modifier (*Without music*).

A simple sentence may contain compound elements—a compound subject, verb, or object, for example—but it does not contain more than one full sentence pattern. The following sentence is simple because its two verbs (*enters* and *spreads*) share a subject (*Evil*).

> ┌────── **INDEPENDENT CLAUSE** ──────┐
> Evil enters like a needle and spreads like an oak.

Compound sentences

A compound sentence is composed of two or more independent clauses with no subordinate clauses. The independent clauses are usually joined with a comma and a coordinating conjunction (*and, but, or, nor, for, so, yet*) or with a semicolon. (See 8.)

```
  ┌──INDEPENDENT CLAUSE──┐      ┌──────INDEPENDENT CLAUSE──────┐
```
One arrow is easily broken, but you can't break a bundle of ten.

```
  ┌──────────INDEPENDENT CLAUSE──────────┐ ┌──INDEPENDENT──┐
```
We are born brave, trusting, and greedy; most of us have

```
  ┌─CLAUSE─────────┐
```
remained greedy.

Complex sentences

A complex sentence is composed of one independent clause with one or more subordinate clauses. (See 59b.)

	SUBORDINATE ┌───CLAUSE───┐
ADJECTIVE	They that sow in tears shall reap in joy.

	SUBORDINATE ┌───CLAUSE───┐
ADVERB	If you scatter thorns, don't go barefoot.

	┌──────SUBORDINATE CLAUSE──────┐
NOUN	What the scientists have in their briefcases is terrifying.

Compound-complex sentences

A compound-complex sentence contains at least two independent clauses and at least one subordinate clause. The following sentence contains two full sentence patterns that can stand alone.

```
  ┌INDEPENDENT CLAUSE┐    ┌──INDEPENDENT CLAUSE──┐
```
Tell me what you eat, and I will tell you what you are.

And each independent clause contains a subordinate clause, making the sentence both compound and complex.

```
  ┌──────IND CL──────┐      ┌──────IND CL──────┐
  │  ┌───SUB CL───┐   │      │  ┌───SUB CL───┐   │
```
Tell me what you eat, and I will tell you what you are.

60b Sentence purposes

Writers use declarative sentences to make statements, imperative sentences to issue requests or commands, interrogative sentences to ask questions, and exclamatory sentences to make exclamations.

DECLARATIVE	The echo always has the last word.
IMPERATIVE	Love your neighbor.
INTERROGATIVE	Are second thoughts always wisest?
EXCLAMATORY	I want to wash the flag, not burn it!

EXERCISE 60-1

Identify the following sentences as simple, compound, complex, or compound-complex. Be prepared to identify the subordinate clauses and classify them according to their function: adjective, adverb, or noun. (See 59b.) Answers to lettered sentences appear in the back of the book. Example:

The frog in the well knows nothing of the ocean. *(Simple)*

a. People who sleep like a baby usually don't have one.
   —Leo Burke
b. My folks didn't come over on the *Mayflower*, they were there to meet the boat. —Will Rogers
c. The impersonal hand of the government can never replace the helping hand of a neighbor. — Hubert Humphrey
d. If you don't go to other people's funerals, they won't go to yours.
   —Clarence Day
e. Tell us your phobias, and we will tell you what you are afraid of.
   —Robert Benchley

1. The tragedy of life is that people don't change.
   —Agatha Christie
2. Those who write clearly have readers; those who write obscurely have commentators. —Albert Camus

3. The children are always the chief victims of social chaos.

—Agnes Meyer

4. Morality cannot be legislated, but behavior can be regulated.

— Martin Luther King, Jr.

5. When an elephant is in trouble, even a frog will kick him.

—Hindu proverb

Glossary of Usage

This glossary includes words commonly confused (such as *accept* and *except*), words commonly misused (such as *hopefully*), and words that are nonstandard (such as *hisself*). It also lists colloquialisms and jargon. Colloquialisms are expressions that may be appropriate in informal speech but are inappropriate in formal writing. Jargon is needlessly technical or pretentious language that is inappropriate in most contexts. If an item is not listed here, consult the index. For irregular verbs (such as *sing, sang, sung*), see 27a. For idiomatic use of prepositions, see 18d.

a, an   Use *an* before a vowel sound, *a* before a consonant sound: *an apple, a peach*. Problems sometimes arise with words beginning with *h*. If the *h* is silent, the word begins with a vowel sound, so use *an: an hour, an heir, an honest senator, an honorable deed*. If the *h* is pronounced, the word begins with a consonant sound, so use *a: a hospital, a hymn, a historian, a hotel*. When an abbreviation or acronym begins with a vowel sound, use *an: an EKG, an MRI, an AIDS* patient.

accept, except   *Accept* is a verb meaning "to receive." *Except* is usually a preposition meaning "excluding." *I will accept all the packages except that one. Except* is also a verb meaning "to exclude." *Please except that item from the list.*

adapt, adopt   *Adapt* means "to adjust or become accustomed"; it is usually followed by *to. Adopt* means "to take as one's own." *Our family adopted a Vietnamese orphan, who quickly adapted to his new surroundings.*

adverse, averse *Adverse* means "unfavorable." *Averse* means "opposed" or "reluctant"; it is usually followed by *to*. *I am averse to your proposal because it could have an adverse impact on the economy.*

advice, advise *Advice* is a noun, *advise* a verb. *We advise you to follow John's advice.*

affect, effect *Affect* is usually a verb meaning "to influence." *Effect* is usually a noun meaning "result." *The drug did not affect the disease, and it had adverse side effects. Effect* can also be a verb meaning "to bring about." *Only the president can effect such a change.*

aggravate *Aggravate* means "to make worse or more troublesome." *Overgrazing aggravated the soil erosion.* In formal writing, avoid the colloquial use of *aggravate* meaning "to annoy or irritate." *Her babbling annoyed* (not *aggravated*) *me.*

agree to, agree with *Agree to* means "to give consent." *Agree with* means "to be in accord" or "to come to an understanding." *He agrees with me about the need for change, but he won't agree to my plan.*

ain't *Ain't* is nonstandard. Use *am not, are not* (*aren't*), or *is not* (*isn't*). *I am not* (not *ain't*) *going home for spring break.*

all ready, already *All ready* means "completely prepared." *Already* means "previously." *Susan was all ready for the concert, but her friends had already left.*

all right *All right* is written as two words. *Alright* is nonstandard.

all together, altogether *All together* means "everyone gathered." *Altogether* means "entirely." *We were not altogether certain that we could bring the family all together for the reunion.*

allude To *allude* to something is to make an indirect reference to it. Do not use *allude* to mean "to refer directly." *In his lecture the professor referred* (not *alluded*) *to several pre-Socratic philosophers.*

allusion, illusion An *allusion* is an indirect reference. An *illusion* is a misconception or false impression. *Did you catch my allusion to Shakespeare? Mirrors give the room an illusion of depth.*

a lot *A lot* is two words. Do not write *alot*. *We have had a lot of rain this spring.* See also *lots, lots of.*

among, between See *between, among.*

amongst In American English, *among* is preferred.

amoral, immoral *Amoral* means "neither moral nor immoral"; it also means "not caring about moral judgments." *Immoral* means "morally wrong." *Until recently, most business courses were taught from an amoral perspective. Murder is immoral.*

amount, number   Use *amount* with quantities that cannot be counted; use *number* with those that can. *This recipe calls for a large amount of sugar. We have a large number of toads in our garden.*

an   See *a, an.*

and etc.   *Et cetera* (*etc.*) means "and so forth"; therefore, *and etc.* is redundant. See also *etc.*

and/or   Avoid the awkward construction *and/or* except in technical or legal documents.

angry at, angry with   To write that one is *angry at* another person is nonstandard. Use *angry with* instead.

ante-, anti-   The prefix *ante-* means "earlier" or "in front of"; the prefix *anti-* means "against" or "opposed to." *William Lloyd Garrison was one of the leaders of the antislavery movement during the antebellum period. Anti-* should be used with a hyphen when it is followed by a capital letter or a word beginning with *i.*

anxious   *Anxious* means "worried" or "apprehensive." In formal writing, avoid using *anxious* to mean "eager." *We are eager* (not *anxious*) *to see your new house.*

anybody, anyone   *Anybody* and *anyone* are singular. (See 21e and 22a.)

anymore   Reserve the adverb *anymore* for negative contexts, where it means "any longer." *Moviegoers are rarely shocked anymore by profanity.* Do not use *anymore* in positive contexts. Use *now* or *nowadays* instead. *Interest rates are so low nowadays* (not *anymore*) *that more people can afford to buy homes.*

anyone   See *anybody, anyone.*

anyone, any one   *Anyone,* an indefinite pronoun, means "any person at all." *Any one,* the pronoun *one* preceded by the adjective *any,* refers to a particular person or thing in a group. *Anyone from Chicago may choose any one of the games on display.*

anyplace   *Anyplace* is informal for *anywhere.* Avoid *anyplace* in formal writing.

anyways, anywheres   *Anyways* and *anywheres* are nonstandard. Use *anyway* and *anywhere.*

as   *As* is sometimes used to mean "because." But do not use it if there is any chance of ambiguity. *We canceled the picnic because* (not *as*) *it began raining. As* here could mean "because" or "when."

as, like   See *like, as.*

as to   *As to* is jargon for *about. He inquired about* (not *as to*) *the job.*

averse   See *adverse, averse.*

awful   The adjective *awful* means "awe-inspiring." Colloquially it is used to mean "terrible" or "bad." The adverb *awfully* is sometimes used in conversation as an intensifier meaning "very." In formal writing, avoid these colloquial uses. *I was very* (not *awfully*) *upset last night. Susan had a terrible* (not *an awful*) *time calming her nerves.*

awhile, a while   *Awhile* is an adverb; it can modify a verb, but it cannot be the object of a preposition such as *for.* The two-word form *a while* is a noun preceded by an article and therefore can be the object of a preposition. *Stay awhile. Stay for a while.*

back up, backup   *Back up* is a verb phrase. *Back up the car carefully. Be sure to back up your hard drive.* A *backup* is a duplicate of electronically stored data. *Keep your backup in a safe place. Backup* can also be used as an adjective. *I regularly create backup disks.*

bad, badly   *Bad* is an adjective, *badly* an adverb. (See 26a and 26b.) *They felt bad about being early and ruining the surprise. Her arm hurt badly after she slid headfirst into second base.*

being as, being that   *Being as* and *being that* are nonstandard expressions. Write *because* or *since* instead. *Because* (not *Being as*) *I slept late, I had to skip breakfast.*

beside, besides   *Beside* is a preposition meaning "at the side of" or "next to." *Annie Oakley slept with her gun beside her bed. Besides* is a preposition meaning "except" or "in addition to." *No one besides Terrie can have that ice cream. Besides* is also an adverb meaning "in addition." *I'm not hungry; besides, I don't like ice cream.*

between, among   Ordinarily, use *among* with three or more entities, *between* with two. *The prize was divided among several contestants. You have a choice between carrots and beans.*

bring, take   Use *bring* when an object is being transported toward you, *take* when it is being moved away. *Please bring me a glass of water. Please take these flowers to Mr. Scott.*

burst, bursted; bust, busted   *Burst* is an irregular verb meaning "to come open or fly apart suddenly or violently." Its principal parts are *burst, burst, burst.* The past-tense form *bursted* is nonstandard. *Bust* and *busted* are slang for *burst* and, along with *bursted*, should not be used in formal writing.

can, may   The distinction between *can* and *may* is fading, but many careful writers still observe it in formal writing. *Can* is traditionally reserved for ability, *may* for permission. *Can you ski down the advanced slope without falling? May I help you?*

capital, capitol *Capital* refers to a city, *capitol* to a building where lawmakers meet. *Capital* also refers to wealth or resources. *The capitol has undergone extensive renovations. The residents of the state capital protested the development plans.*

censor, censure *Censor* means "to remove or suppress material considered objectionable." *Censure* means "to criticize severely." *The library's new policy of censoring controversial books has been censured by the media.*

cite, site *Cite* means "to quote as an authority or example." *Site* is usually a noun meaning "a particular place." *He cited the zoning law in his argument against the proposed site of the gas station.* Locations on the Internet are usually referred to as *sites. The library's Web site improves every week.*

climactic, climatic *Climactic* is derived from *climax,* the point of greatest intensity in a series or progression of events. *Climatic* is derived from *climate* and refers to meteorological conditions. *The climactic period in the dinosaurs' reign was reached just before severe climatic conditions brought on an ice age.*

coarse, course *Coarse* means "crude" or "rough in texture." *The coarse weave of the wall hanging gave it a three-dimensional quality. Course* usually refers to a path, a playing field, or a unit of study; the expression *of course* means "certainly." *I plan to take a course in car repair this summer. Of course, you are welcome to join me.*

compare to, compare with *Compare to* means "to represent as similar." *She compared him to a wild stallion. Compare with* means "to examine the ways in which two things are similar." *The study compared the language ability of apes with that of dolphins.*

complement, compliment *Complement* is a verb meaning "to go with or complete" or a noun meaning "something that completes." *Compliment* as a verb means "to flatter"; as a noun it means "flattering remark." *Her skill at rushing the net complements his skill at volleying. Mother's flower arrangements receive many compliments.*

conscience, conscious *Conscience* is a noun meaning "moral principles." *Conscious* is an adjective meaning "aware or alert." *Let your conscience be your guide. Were you conscious of his love for you?*

continual, continuous *Continual* means "repeated regularly and frequently." *She grew weary of the continual telephone calls. Continuous* means "extended or prolonged without interruption." *The broken siren made a continuous wail.*

could care less   *Could care less* is a nonstandard expression. Write *couldn't care less* instead. *He couldn't* (not *could*) *care less about his psychology final.*

could of   *Could of* is nonstandard for *could have. We could have* (not *could of*) *had steak for dinner if we had been hungry.*

council, counsel   A *council* is a deliberative body, and a *councilor* is a member of such a body. *Counsel* usually means "advice" and can also mean "lawyer"; *counselor* is one who gives advice or guidance. *The councilors met to draft the council's position paper. The pastor offered wise counsel to the troubled teenager.*

criteria   *Criteria* is the plural of *criterion,* which means "a standard or rule or test on which a judgment or decision can be based." *The only criterion for the scholarship is ability.*

data   *Data* is a plural noun technically meaning "facts or propositions." But *data* is increasingly being accepted as a singular noun. *The new data suggest* (or *suggests*) *that our theory is correct.* (The singular *datum* is rarely used.)

different from, different than   Ordinarily, write *different from. Your sense of style is different from Jim's.* However, *different than* is acceptable to avoid an awkward construction. *Please let me know if your plans are different than* (to avoid *from what*) *they were six weeks ago.*

differ from, differ with   *Differ from* means "to be unlike"; *differ with* means "to disagree." *She differed with me about the wording of the agreement. My approach to the problem differed from hers.*

disinterested, uninterested   *Disinterested* means "impartial, objective"; *uninterested* means "not interested." *We sought the advice of a disinterested counselor to help us solve our problem. He was uninterested in anyone's opinion but his own.*

don't   *Don't* is the contraction for *do not. I don't want any. Don't* should not be used as the contraction for *does not,* which is *doesn't. He doesn't* (not *don't*) *want any.* (See 27c.)

double negative   Standard English allows two negatives only if a positive meaning is intended. *The runners were not unhappy with their performance.* Double negatives used to emphasize negation are nonstandard. *Jack doesn't have to answer to anybody* (not *nobody*).

due to   *Due to* is an adjective phrase and should not be used as a preposition meaning "because of." *The trip was canceled because of* (not *due to*) *lack of interest. Due to* is acceptable as a subject complement and usually follows a form of the verb *be. His success was due to hard work.*

each *Each* is singular. (See 21e and 22a.)

effect See *affect, effect.*

e.g. In formal writing, replace the Latin abbreviation *e.g.* with its English equivalent: *for example* or *for instance.*

either *Either* is singular. (See 21e and 22a.) (For *either . . . or* constructions, see 21d and 22d.)

elicit, illicit *Elicit* is a verb meaning "to bring out" or "to evoke." *Illicit* is an adjective meaning "unlawful." *The reporter was unable to elicit any information from the police about illicit drug traffic.*

emigrate from, immigrate to *Emigrate* means "to leave one country or region to settle in another." *In 1900, my grandfather emigrated from Russia to escape the religious pogroms. Immigrate* means "to enter another country and reside there." *Many Mexicans immigrate to the United States to find work.*

eminent, imminent *Eminent* means "outstanding" or "distinguished." *We met an eminent professor of Greek history. Imminent* means "about to happen." *The announcement is imminent.*

enthused Many people object to the use of *enthused* as an adjective. Use *enthusiastic* instead. *The children were enthusiastic* (not *enthused*) *about going to the circus.*

-ess Many people find the *-ess* suffix demeaning. Write *poet,* not *poetess; Jew,* not *Jewess; author,* not *authoress.*

etc. Avoid ending a list with *etc.* It is more emphatic to end with an example, and in most contexts readers will understand that the list is not exhaustive. When you don't wish to end with an example, *and so on* is more graceful than *etc.* See also *and etc.*

eventually, ultimately Often used interchangeably, *eventually* is the better choice to mean "at an unspecified time in the future" and *ultimately* is better to mean "the furthest possible extent or greatest extreme." *He knew that eventually he would complete his degree. The existentialist considered suicide the ultimately rational act.*

everybody, everyone *Everybody* and *everyone* are singular. (See 21e and 22a.)

everyone, every one *Everyone* is an indefinite pronoun. *Every one,* the pronoun *one* preceded by the adjective *every,* means "each individual or thing in a particular group." *Every one* is usually followed by *of. Everyone wanted to go. Every one of the missing books was found.*

except See *accept, except.*

expect   Avoid the colloquial use of *expect* meaning "to believe, think, or suppose." *I think* (not *expect*) *it will rain tonight.*

explicit, implicit   *Explicit* means "expressed directly" or "clearly defined"; *implicit* means "implied, unstated." *I gave him explicit instructions not to go swimming. My mother's silence indicated her implicit approval.*

farther, further   *Farther* usually describes distances. *Further* usually suggests quantity or degree. *Chicago is farther from Miami than I thought. You extended the curfew further than you should have.*

female, male   The terms *female* and *male* are jargon when used to refer to specific people. *Two women* (not *females*) *and one man* (not *male*) *applied for the position.*

fewer, less   *Fewer* refers to items that can be counted; *less* refers to general amounts. *Fewer people are living in the city. Please put less sugar in my tea.*

finalize   *Finalize* is jargon meaning "to make final or complete." Use ordinary English instead. *The architect prepared final drawings* (not *finalized the drawings*).

firstly   *Firstly* sounds pretentious, and it leads to the ungainly series *firstly, secondly, thirdly, fourthly,* and so on. Write *first, second, third* instead.

further   See *farther, further.*

get   *Get* has many colloquial uses. In writing, avoid using *get* to mean the following: "to evoke an emotional response" (*That music always gets to me*); "to annoy" (*After a while his sulking got to me*); "to take revenge on" (*I got back at him by leaving the room*); "to become" (*He got sick*); "to start or begin" (*Let's get going*). Avoid using *have got to* in place of *must. I must* (not *have got to*) *finish this paper tonight.*

good, well   *Good* is an adjective, *well* an adverb. (See 26.) *He hasn't felt good about his game since he sprained his wrist last season. She performed well on the uneven parallel bars.*

hanged, hung   *Hanged* is the past-tense and past-participle form of the verb *hang* meaning "to execute." *The prisoner was hanged at dawn. Hung* is the past-tense and past-participle form of the verb *hang* meaning "to fasten or suspend." *The stockings were hung by the chimney with care.*

hardly   Avoid expressions such as *can't hardly* and *not hardly,* which are considered double negatives. *I can* (not *can't*) *hardly describe my elation at getting the job.*

has got, have got   *Got* is unnecessary and awkward in such constructions. It should be dropped. *We have* (not *have got*) *three days to prepare for the opening.*

he   At one time *he* was commonly used to mean "he or she." Today such usage is inappropriate. (See 17f and 22a.)

he/she, his/her   In formal writing, use *he or she* or *his or her.* For alternatives to these wordy constructions, see 17f and 22a.

hisself   *Hisself* is nonstandard. Use *himself.*

hopefully   *Hopefully* means "in a hopeful manner." *We looked hopefully to the future.* Do not use *hopefully* in constructions such as the following: *Hopefully, your daughter will recover soon.* Indicate who is doing the hoping: *I hope that your daughter will recover soon.*

hung   See *hanged, hung.*

i.e.   In formal writing, replace the Latin abbreviation *i.e.* with its English equivalent: *that is.*

if, whether   Use *if* to express a condition and *whether* to express alternatives. *If you go on a trip, whether it be to Nebraska or New Jersey, remember to bring traveler's checks.*

illusion   See *allusion, illusion.*

immigrate, emigrate   See *emigrate from, immigrate to.*

imminent   See *eminent, imminent.*

immoral   See *amoral, immoral.*

implement   *Implement* is a pretentious way of saying "do," "carry out," or "accomplish." Use ordinary language instead. *We carried out* (not *implemented*) *the director's orders with some reluctance.*

imply, infer   *Imply* means "to suggest or state indirectly"; *infer* means "to draw a conclusion." *John implied that he knew all about computers, but the interviewer inferred that John was inexperienced.*

in, into   *In* indicates location or condition; *into* indicates movement or a change in condition. *They found the lost letters in a box after moving into the house.*

individual   *Individual* is a pretentious substitute for *person.* *We invited several persons* (not *individuals*) *from the audience to participate in the experiment.*

ingenious, ingenuous   *Ingenious* means "clever." *Sarah's solution to the problem was ingenious. Ingenuous* means "naive" or "frank." *For a successful manager, Ed is surprisingly ingenuous.*

in regards to   *In regards to* confuses two different phrases: *in regard to* and *as regards.* Use one or the other. *In regard to* (or *As regards*) *the contract, ignore the first clause.*

irregardless   *Irregardless* is nonstandard. Use *regardless*.

is when, is where   These mixed constructions are often incorrectly used in definitions. *A run-off election is a second election held to break a tie* (not *is when a second election breaks a tie*). (See 11c.)

it is   *It is* is nonstandard when used to mean "there is." *There is* (not *It is*) *a fly in my soup*.

its, it's   *Its* is a possessive pronoun; *it's* is a contraction for *it is*. (See 36c and 36e.) *The dog licked its wound whenever its owner walked into the room. It's a perfect day to walk the twenty-mile trail.*

kind(s)   *Kind* is singular and should be treated as such. Don't write *These kind of chairs are rare*. Write instead *This kind of chair is rare*. *Kinds* is plural and should be used only when you mean more than one kind. *These kinds of chairs are rare*.

kind of, sort of   Avoid using *kind of* or *sort of* to mean "somewhat." *The movie was somewhat* (not *kind of*) *boring*. Do not put *a* after either phrase. *That kind of* (not *kind of a*) *salesclerk annoys me*.

lead, led   *Lead* is a noun referring to a metal. *Led* is the past tense of the verb *lead*. *He led me to the treasure*.

learn, teach   *Learn* means "to gain knowledge"; *teach* means "to impart knowledge." *I must teach* (not *learn*) *my sister to read*.

leave, let   *Leave* means "to exit." Avoid using it with the nonstandard meaning "to permit." *Let* (not *leave*) *me help you with the dishes*.

less   See *fewer, less*.

let, leave   See *leave, let*.

liable   *Liable* means "obligated" or "responsible." Do not use it to mean "likely." *You're likely* (not *liable*) *to trip if you don't tie your shoelaces*.

lie, lay   *Lie* is an intransitive verb meaning "to recline or rest on a surface." Its principal parts are *lie, lay, lain. Lay* is a transitive verb meaning "to put or place." Its principal parts are *lay, laid, laid*. (See 27b.)

like, as   *Like* is a preposition, not a subordinating conjunction. It can be followed only by a noun or a noun phrase. *As* is a subordinating conjunction that introduces a subordinate clause. In casual speech you may say *She looks like she hasn't slept* or *You don't know her like I do*. But in formal writing, use *as. She looks as if she hasn't slept. You don't know her as I do*. (See prepositions and subordinating conjunctions, 57f and 57g.)

loose, lose   *Loose* is an adjective meaning "not securely fastened." *Lose* is a verb meaning "to misplace" or "to not win." *Did you lose your only loose pair of work pants?*

lots, lots of   *Lots* and *lots of* are colloquial substitutes for *many, much,* or *a lot.* Avoid using them in formal writing.

male, female   See *female, male.*

mankind   Avoid *mankind* whenever possible. It offends many readers because it excludes women. Use *humanity, humans, the human race,* or *humankind* instead.

may   See *can, may.*

maybe, may be   *Maybe* is an adverb meaning "possibly." *May be* is a verb phrase. *Maybe the sun will shine tomorrow. Tomorrow may be a brighter day.*

may of, might of   *May of* and *might of* are nonstandard for *may have* and *might have. We may have* (not *may of*) *had too many cookies.*

media, medium   *Media* is the plural of *medium. Of all the media that cover the Olympics, television is the medium that best captures the spectacle of the events.*

most   *Most* is colloquial when used to mean "almost" and should be avoided. *Almost* (not *Most*) *everyone went to the parade.*

must of   See *may of.*

myself   *Myself* is a reflexive or intensive pronoun. Reflexive: *I cut myself.* Intensive: *I will drive you myself.* Do not use *myself* in place of *I* or *me. He gave the flowers to Melinda and me* (not *myself*). (See also 24.)

neither   *Neither* is singular. (See 21e and 22a.) For *neither . . . nor* constructions, see 21d and 22d.

none   *None* is usually singular. (See 21e.)

nowheres   *Nowheres* is nonstandard for *nowhere.*

number   See *amount, number.*

of   Use the verb *have,* not the preposition *of,* after the verbs *could, should, would, may, might,* and *must. They must have* (not *of*) *left early.*

off of   *Off* is sufficient. Omit *of. The ball rolled off* (not *off of*) *the table.*

OK, O.K., okay   All three spellings are acceptable, but in formal speech and writing avoid these colloquial expressions for consent or approval.

parameters   *Parameter* is a mathematical term that has become jargon for "fixed limit," "boundary," or "guideline." Use ordinary English instead. *The task force was asked to work within certain guidelines* (not *parameters*).

passed, past   *Passed* is the past tense of the verb *pass*. *Mother passed me another slice of cake. Past* usually means "belonging to a former time" or "beyond a time or place." *Our past president spoke until past midnight. The hotel is just past the next intersection.*

percent, per cent, percentage   *Percent* (also spelled *per cent*) is always used with a specific number. *Percentage* is used with a descriptive term such as *large* or *small*, not with a specific number. *The candidate won 80 percent of the primary vote. Only a small percentage of registered voters turned out for the election.*

phenomena   *Phenomena* is the plural of *phenomenon*, which means "an observable occurrence or fact." *Strange phenomena occur at all hours of the night in that house, but last night's phenomenon was the strangest of all.*

plus   *Plus* should not be used to join independent clauses. *This raincoat is dirty; moreover* (not *plus*), *it has a hole in it.*

precede, proceed   *Precede* means "to come before." *Proceed* means "to go forward." *As we proceeded up the mountain path, we noticed fresh tracks in the mud, evidence that a group of hikers had preceded us.*

principal, principle   *Principal* is a noun meaning "the head of a school or organization" or "a sum of money." It is also an adjective meaning "most important." *Principle* is a noun meaning "a basic truth or law." *The principal expelled her for three principal reasons. We believe in the principle of equal justice for all.*

proceed, precede   See *precede, proceed.*

quote, quotation   *Quote* is a verb; *quotation* is a noun. Avoid using *quote* as a shortened form of *quotation*. *Her quotations* (not *quotes*) *from Shakespeare intrigued us.*

raise, rise   *Raise* is a transitive verb meaning "to move or cause to move upward." It takes a direct object. *I raised the shades. Rise* is an intransitive verb meaning "to go up." It does not take a direct object. *Heat rises.*

real, really   *Real* is an adjective; *really* is an adverb. *Real* is sometimes used informally as an adverb, but avoid this use in formal writing. *She was really* (not *real*) *angry.* (See 26a.)

reason is because   Use *that* instead of *because*. *The reason I'm late is that* (not *because*) *my car broke down.* (See 11c.)

reason why   The expression *reason why* is redundant. *The reason (not The reason why) Jones lost the election is clear.*

relation, relationship   *Relation* describes a connection between things. *Relationship* describes a connection between people. *There is a relation between poverty and infant mortality. Our business relationship has cooled over the years.*

respectfully, respectively   *Respectfully* means "showing or marked by respect." *Respectively* means "each in the order given." *He respectfully submitted his opinion to the judge. John, Tom, and Larry were a butcher, a baker, and a lawyer, respectively.*

sensual, sensuous   *Sensual* means "gratifying the physical senses," especially those associated with sexual pleasure. *Sensuous* means "pleasing to the senses," especially those involved in the experience of art, music, and nature. *The sensuous music and balmy air led the dancers to more sensual movements.*

set, sit   *Set* is a transitive verb meaning "to put" or "to place." Its principal parts are *set, set, set. Sit* is an intransitive verb meaning "to be seated." Its principal parts are *sit, sat, sat. She set the dough in a warm corner of the kitchen. The cat sat in the warmest part of the room.*

shall, will   *Shall* was once used as the helping verb with *I* or *we: I shall, we shall, you will, he/she/it will, they will.* Today, however, *will* is generally accepted even when the subject is *I* or *we.* The word *shall* occurs primarily in polite questions (*Shall I find you a pillow?*) and in legalistic sentences suggesting duty or obligation (*The applicant shall file form 1080 by December 31*).

should of   *Should of* is nonstandard for *should have. They should have* (not *should of*) *been home an hour ago.*

since   Do not use *since* to mean "because" if there is any chance of ambiguity. *Since we won the game, we have been celebrating with a pitcher of beer. Since* here could mean "because" or "from the time that."

sit   See *set, sit.*

site, cite   See *cite, site.*

somebody, someone   *Somebody* and *someone* are singular. (See 21e and 22a.)

something   *Something* is singular. (See 21e.)

sometime, some time, sometimes   *Sometime* is an adverb meaning "at an indefinite or unstated time." *Some time* is the adjective *some* modifying the noun *time* and is spelled as two words to mean "a period of time." *Sometimes* is an adverb meaning "at times, now and then." *I'll see you sometime soon. I haven't lived there for some time. Sometimes I run into him at the library.*

suppose to   Write *supposed to.*

sure and   *Sure and* is nonstandard for *sure to. We were all taught to be sure to* (not *and*) *look both ways before crossing a street.*

take   See *bring, take.*

than, then   *Than* is a conjunction used in comparisons; *then* is an adverb denoting time. *That pizza is more than I can eat. Tom laughed, and then we recognized him.*

that   See *who, which, that.*

that, which   Many writers reserve *that* for restrictive clauses, *which* for nonrestrictive clauses. (See 32e.)

theirselves   *Theirselves* is nonstandard for *themselves. The two people were able to push the Volkswagen out of the way themselves* (not *theirselves*).

them   The use of *them* in place of *those* is nonstandard. *Please send those* (not *them*) *flowers to the patient in room 220.*

there, their, they're   *There* is an adverb specifying place; it is also an expletive. Adverb: *Sylvia is lying there unconscious.* Expletive: *There are two plums left. Their* is a possessive pronoun. *Fred and Jane finally washed their car. They're* is a contraction of *they are. They're later than usual today.*

they   The use of *they* to indicate possession is nonstandard. Use *their* instead. *Cindy and Sam decided to sell their* (not *they*) *1975 Corvette.*

this kind   See *kind(s).*

to, too, two   *To* is a preposition; *too* is an adverb; *two* is a number. *Too many of your shots slice to the left, but the last two were right on the mark.*

toward, towards   *Toward* and *towards* are generally interchangeable, although *toward* is preferred in American English.

try and   *Try and* is nonstandard for *try to. The teacher asked us all to try to* (not *and*) *write an original haiku.*

ultimately, eventually   See *eventually, ultimately.*

unique   Avoid expressions such as *most unique, more straight, less perfect, very round.* Something either is unique or it isn't. It is illogical to suggest degrees of uniqueness. (See 26c.)

usage   The noun *usage* should not be substituted for *use* when the meaning intended is "employment of." *The use* (not *usage*) *of computers dramatically increased the company's profits.*

use to   Write *used to*.

utilize   *Utilize* means "to make use of." It often sounds pretentious; in most cases, *use* is sufficient. *I used* (not *utilized*) *the best workers to get the job done fast.*

wait for, wait on   *Wait for* means "to be in readiness for" or "await." *Wait on* means "to serve." *We're only waiting for* (not *waiting on*) *Ruth to take us to the game.*

ways   *Ways* is colloquial when used to mean "distance." *The city is a long way* (not *ways*) *from here.*

weather, whether   The noun *weather* refers to the state of the atmosphere. *Whether* is a conjunction referring to a choice between alternatives. *We wondered whether the weather would clear up in time for our picnic.*

well, good   See *good, well*.

where   Do not use *where* in place of *that*. *I heard that* (not *where*) *the crime rate is increasing.*

which   See *that, which* and *who, which, that*.

while   Avoid using *while* to mean "although" or "whereas" if there is any chance of ambiguity. *Although* (not *While*) *Gloria lost money in the slot machine, Tom won it at roulette.* Here *While* could mean either "although" or "at the same time that."

who, which, that   Do not use *which* to refer to persons. Use *who* instead. *That*, though generally used to refer to things, may be used to refer to a group or class of people. *Fans wondered how an old man who* (not *that* or *which*) *walked with a limp could play football. The team that scores the most points in this game will win the tournament.*

who, whom   *Who* is used for subjects and subject complements; *whom* is used for objects. (See 25.)

who's, whose   *Who's* is a contraction of *who is; whose* is a possessive pronoun. *Who's ready for more popcorn? Whose coat is this?* (See 36c and 36e.)

will   See *shall, will*.

would of   *Would of* is nonstandard for *would have*. *She would have* (not *would of*) *had a chance to play if she had arrived on time.*

you   In formal writing, avoid *you* in an indefinite sense meaning "anyone." (See 23d.) *Any spectator* (not *You*) *could tell by the way John caught the ball that his throw would be too late.*

your, you're   *Your* is a possessive pronoun; *you're* is a contraction of *you are. Is that your new motorcycle? You're on the list of finalists.* (See 36c and 36e.)

Answers to Tutorials and Lettered Exercises

TUTORIAL 1, page xxii

1. A verb has to agree with its subject. (21)
2. Each pronoun should agree with its antecedent. (22)
3. You should avoid sentence fragments. (19)
4. Don't write a run-on sentence, you must connect the clauses with a comma and a coordinating conjunction or with a semicolon. (20)
5. Discriminate carefully between adjectives and adverbs. (26)
6. Proofread to see if you left any words out. (10)
7. Check for -ed verb endings that have been dropped. (27d)
8. In most contexts, avoid passive-voice verbs. (14a or 28c)
9. In choosing proper pronoun case, follow the example of us teachers, who are the experts. (24 and 25)
10. Don't use double negatives. (26d)
11. Watch out for dangling modifiers. (12e)
12. It's important to use apostrophes correctly. (36)
13. A writer must be careful not to shift his or her [*not* their] point of view. *Or* Writers must be careful not to shift their point of view. (13a)
14. If your sentence begins with a long introductory word group, use a comma to separate the word group from the rest of the sentence. (32b)
15. Avoid clichés. (18e)

TUTORIAL 2, page xxiii

1. The index entry "*anybody*" mentions that the word is singular, so you might not need to look further to realize that the plural *their* is incorrect. The second page reference leads you to section 22, which suggests non-sexist strategies for revision, such as *Students taking the school bus to the volleyball game must bring in a permission slip signed by their parents* or *Anybody taking the school bus to the volleyball game must bring in a permission slip signed by his or her parents.* is correct.

2. The index entry "*lay, lie*" (or "*laying* versus *lying*") takes you to section 27b and to the Glossary of Usage, where you will learn that *lying* (meaning "reclining or resting on a surface") is correct.

3. Look up "*only*" and you will be directed to section 12a, which explains that limiting modifiers such as *only* should be placed before the words they modify. The sentence should read *We looked at only two houses before buying the house of our dreams.*

4. Looking up "*you*, inappropriate use of" leads you to page 56, section 23d, and the Glossary of Usage, which all explain that *you* should not be used to mean "anyone in general." You can revise the sentence by using *a person* or *one* instead of *you*, or you can restructure the sentence completely: *In Saudi Arabia, accepting a gift is considered ill-mannered.*

5. The index entries "*I* versus *me*" and "*me* versus *I*" take you to section 24, which explains why *me* is correct.

TUTORIAL 3, page xxiii

1. Section 32c tells you that although usage varies, most experts advise using a comma between all items in a series—to prevent possible misreadings or ambiguities. To find this section, Ray Farley would probably use the menu system.

2. Maria Sanchez and Mike Lee would consult section 30, on articles. This section is easy to locate on either the brief or the detailed menu.

3. Section 24 explains why *Jane and me* is correct. To find section 24, John Pell could use the menu system to locate section 24, "Pronoun case" (*I* or *me*, etc.). Or he could look up "*I* versus *me*" in the index. Pell could also look up "*myself*" in the index or he could consult the Glossary of Usage, where a cross-reference would direct him to section 24.

4. Selena Young's employees could turn to sections 21 and 27c for help. Young could use the menu system to find these sections if she knew to look under "Subject-verb agreement" or "Standard English verb forms." If she wasn't sure about the grammatical terminology, she could look up "*-s*, as verb ending" or "Verbs, *-s* form of" in the index.

5. Section 26b explains why *I felt bad about her death* is correct. To find section 26b, Joe Thompson could use the menu system if he knew that *bad* versus *badly* is a choice between an adjective and an adverb. Otherwise he could look up "*bad, badly*" in the index or the Glossary of Usage.

TUTORIAL 4, page xxiv

1. The *number* of horses a Comanche warrior had in his possession indicated the wealth of his family.
2. Correct
3. That is the most *unusual* floral arrangement I have ever seen.
4. Changing attitudes *toward* alcohol have *affected* the beer industry.
5. Jenny *should have* known better than to attempt that dive.
6. Everyone in our office is *enthusiastic* about this project.
7. George and Pat are selling *their* house because now that *their* children are grown, *they're* planning to move to Arizona.
8. Correct
9. It is *human* nature to think wisely and act foolishly.
10. Dr. Newman and *I* have agreed to arrange the retirement party.

TUTORIAL 5, page xxv

Codoga, Helen. E-mail to the author. 10 Apr. 1997.

Cooper, Mary H. "Native Americans' Future: Do U.S. Policies Block Opportunities for Progress?" CQ Researcher 6 (1996): 603-19.

Dao, James. "Gambling Proponents See Indian Casinos as Alternative." New York Times 30 Jan. 1997: B2. New York Times on America Online. Online. America Online. 5 Apr. 1997.

Johansen, Bruce E. Life and Death in Mohawk Country. Golden, CO: North American, 1993.

Ridgebear, Sam. "Guilty Hands: Traditionalism and the Indian Gaming Industry." Many Voices: American Indian Students Journal 1.1 (1995): n. pag. Online. Internet. 2 Apr. 1997. Available http://thecity.sfsu.edu/users/BANN/journal /guiltyhands.html.

Schine, Eric. "First Gambling, Then a Bank: California Has Reservations." Business Week 9 Sept. 1996: 47.

EXERCISE 7–1, page 175

a. hasty generalization; b. false analogy; c. emotional appeal; d. faulty cause-and-effect reasoning; e. *either . . . or* fallacy

EXERCISE 8–2, page 190

Possible revisions:

a. A user-friendly instruction manual is enclosed with your computer.
b. Part of my earnings went toward the purchase of a ten-speed bicycle, which I hoped would serve as my primary form of transportation.
c. There are five fishing piers on the island, each with a bait and tackle shop.
d. Student volunteers from Baltimore City Community College help the younger children with reading and math, their weakest subjects.
e. Because the home study course seemed to have everything I was looking for, I thought my troubles were over, but in reality they were just beginning.

EXERCISE 8–3, page 193

Possible revisions:

a. During a routine morning at the clinic, an infant in cardiac arrest arrived by ambulance.
b. My 1969 Camaro, an original SS396, is no longer street legal.
c. This highly specialized medical training, called a "residency," usually takes four years to complete.
d. Although outsiders have forced changes on them, native Hawaiians try to preserve their ancestors' sacred customs.
e. Ash Lawn, located only two miles from Monticello, is the restored home of our fifth president, James Monroe.

EXERCISE 9–1, page 199

Possible revisions:

a. The system has capabilities such as communicating with other computers, processing records, and performing mathematical functions.
b. The personnel officer told me that I would answer the phone, welcome visitors, distribute mail, and do some typing.
c. The African elephants are endangered primarily because poachers kill them and because they have less and less space to live in.
d. How ideal it seems to raise a family here in Winnebago instead of in the air-polluted suburbs.
e. In combat the soldiers were brave but sometimes foolish—because of poor training, lack of confidence, and inexperience.

EXERCISE 10–1, page 206

Possible revisions:

a. Dip the paintbrush into the paint remover and spread a thick coat on a small section of the door.

b. Christopher had an attention span longer than that of the other students.
c. SETI (the Search for Extraterrestrial Intelligence) has excited and will continue to excite interest among space buffs.
d. Samantha got along better with the chimpanzees than with Albert. [*or . . .* than Albert did.]
e. We were glad to see that Yellowstone National Park was recovering from the devastating forest fire.

EXERCISE 11–1, page 212

Possible revisions:

a. The name of the song is "Words Unspoken."
b. A trial conducted in England, which included both pre- and post-menopausal women, showed slightly different results.
c. It is through the misery of others that old Harvey has become rich.
d. A cloverleaf allows traffic on limited-access freeways to change direction.
e. Bowman established the format that future football card companies would emulate for years to come.

EXERCISE 12–1, page 217

Possible revisions:

a. At our warehouse sale, only cash, MasterCard, or Visa will be accepted.
b. Not all thin people are anorexic or bulimic.
c. Celia received a flyer from a Japanese nun about a workshop on making a kimono.
d. Jurors are encouraged to sift through the evidence carefully and thoroughly.
e. Each state would set into motion a program of recycling all reusable products.

EXERCISE 12–2, page 221

Possible revisions:

a. Reaching the heart, the surgeon performed a bypass on the severely blocked arteries.
b. To enter college early, students need more than good grades.
c. While we dined at night, the lights along the Baja coastline created a romantic atmosphere perfect for our first anniversary.
d. While my sister was still a beginner at tennis, the coaches recruited her to train for the Olympics.
e. After Marcus Garvey returned to Jamaica, his Back to Africa movement slowly died.

EXERCISE 13–1, page 230

Possible revisions:

a. My hopes rose and fell as Joseph's heart started and stopped. The doctors inserted a large tube into his chest, and blood flowed from the incision onto the floor.

b. After the count of three, Mikah and I placed the injured woman on the scoop stretcher. Then I took her vital signs.
c. Ministers often have a hard time because they have to please so many different people.
d. We drove for eight hours until we reached the South Dakota Badlands. We could hardly believe the eeriness of the landscape at dusk.
e. The question is whether ferrets bred in captivity have the instinct to prey on prairie dogs or whether this is a learned skill.

EXERCISE 14–1, page 236

Possible revisions:

a. The Prussians defeated the Saxons in 1745.
b. Ahmed, the producer, manages the entire operation.
c. Emphatic and active; no change.
d. Players fought on both sides of the rink.
e. Emphatic and active; no change.

EXERCISE 16–1, page 254

Possible revisions:

a. The drawing room in the west wing is said to be haunted.
b. Ten terry cloth towels stuffed under the door did nothing to stop the flow.
c. Bloom's race for the governorship is futile.
d. Mr. Barker still hasn't paid last month's rent.
e. In the heart of Beijing lies the Forbidden City, an imperial palace built during the Ming dynasty.

EXERCISE 17–1, page 260

Possible revisions:

a. Ignore those who try to dissuade you from reaching your goals.
b. This conference will help me serve my clients better.
c. Have you ever been accused of beating a dead horse?
d. When Sal was laid off from his high-paying factory job, he learned what it was like to be poor.
e. Passengers should try to complete the customs declaration form before leaving the plane.

EXERCISE 17–3, page 269

Possible revisions:

a. Dr. Geralyn Farmer is the chief surgeon at University Hospital. Dr. Paul Green is her assistant.
b. A young graduate who is careful about investments can accumulate a significant sum in a relatively short period.
c. An elementary school teacher should understand the concept of nurturing if he or she intends to be a success.
d. The vice president for community affairs asked Elizabeth and Joseph to serve as cochairs of the Red Cross blood drive.

e. If we do not stop polluting our environment, we will perish.

EXERCISE 18–3, page 275

Possible revisions:

a. We regret this delay; thank you for your patience.
b. Those who believe that books written for children are all sweetness and light are suffering from an illusion.
c. Liu Kwan began his career as a lawyer, but now he is a real estate mogul.
d. When Robert Frost died at age eighty-eight, he left a legacy of poems that will make him immortal.
e. In general, the Internet has had a positive effect on our society.

EXERCISE 18–4, page 277

Possible revisions:

a. Queen Anne was so angry with Sarah Churchill that she dismissed her once faithful servant.
b. Correct
c. Dad told us to be sure to visit the ghost towns of Nevada.
d. For the frightened refugees, the dangerous trek across the mountains was preferable to life in a war zone.
e. The baby fell off the couch and landed on the soft cushion of the dog's bed.

EXERCISE 18–5, page 280

Possible revisions:

a. John stormed into the room like a hurricane.
b. The president thought that the scientists were using science as a means to further their political goals.
c. The Cubs easily beat the Mets, who were in trouble early in the game today at Wrigley Field.
d. We ironed out the wrinkles in our relationship.
e. Sasha told us that he wasn't willing to take a chance.

EXERCISE 19–1, page 291

Possible revisions:

a. As I stood in front of the microwave, I recalled my grandmother bending over her old black stove and remembered what she taught me: that any food can have soul if you love the people you are cooking for.
b. The resort was full of attractions: three swimming pools, four restaurants, five bars, and every game imaginable, including a life-sized chess set.
c. Correct
d. We need to stop believing myths about drinking—that strong black coffee will sober you up, for example, or that a cold shower will straighten you out.

e. On Sundays, James scrupulously read the newspaper's employment listings, scrutinizing every position that held even the remotest possibility.

EXERCISE 20–1, page 302

Possible revisions:

a. The city had one public swimming pool that stayed packed with children all summer long.
b. The building is being renovated, so at times we have no heat, water, or electricity.
c. Why shouldn't a divorced wife receive half of her husband's pension and retirement benefits? She was her husband's partner for many years.
d. Suddenly there was a loud silence; the shelling had stopped.
e. The experience taught Juanita a lesson: She could not always rely on her parents to bail her out of trouble.

EXERCISE 20–2, page 303

Possible revisions:

a. Although Ted never drove the vintage cars that he had inherited, he could not bring himself to sell them.
b. Correct
c. In the Middle Ages, when the streets of London were dangerous places, it was safer to travel by boat along the Thames.
d. Researchers studying the fertility of Texas land tortoises X-rayed all the female tortoises to see how many eggs they had.
e. We had planned to spend the last few days of our vacation at the beach; the hurricane, however, brought us home in a hurry.

EXERCISE 21–1, page 320

a. Subject: history and life; verb: have. b. Subject: shelters; verb: offer. c. Subject: each; verb: was. d. Subject: chances; verb: are. e. Subject: signs or traces; verb: were.

EXERCISE 21–2, page 321

a. High concentrations of carbon monoxide result in headaches, dizziness, unconsciousness, and even death.
b. Correct
c. Correct
d. Crystal chandeliers, polished floors, and a new oil painting have transformed Sandra's apartment.
e. Correct

EXERCISE 22–1, page 327

Possible revisions:

a. I can be standing in front of a Xerox machine, with parts scattered around my feet, and someone will ask me for permission to make a copy.

b. Correct
c. The instructor has asked students to bring their own tools to carpentry class.
d. An eighteenth-century architect was also a classical scholar who was often at the forefront of archaeological research.
e. Anyone caught smoking on the premises will be severely reprimanded.

EXERCISE 23–1, page 335

Possible revisions:

a. The detective removed the bloodstained shawl from the body and then photographed the body.
b. In Professor Jamal's class, students are lucky to earn a C.
c. We have a staff of experienced technicians who will service your copier within two hours of a service call.
d. The Comanche braves lived violent lives; they gained respect for their skill as warriors.
e. All students can secure parking permits from the campus police office, which is open from 8 A.M. until 8 P.M.

EXERCISE 24–1, page 343

a. My Ethiopian neighbor was puzzled by the dedication of us joggers.
b. Correct
c. Sue's husband is ten years older than she.
d. Everyone laughed whenever Sandra described how her brother and she had seen the Loch Ness monster and fed it sandwiches.
e. We appreciate your bringing this problem to our attention.

EXERCISE 25–1, page 350

a. In his first production of *Hamlet*, whom did Laurence Olivier replace?
b. Correct
c. Correct
d. The bank doors were locked, and whoever was inside remained there until the police officers arrived.
e. One of the women whom Martinez hired became the most successful lawyer in the agency.

EXERCISE 26–1, page 358

Possible revisions:

a. When Tina began breathing normally, we could relax.
b. All of us on the team felt bad about our performance.
c. This incident could have been handled more professionally if lines of communication had been kept open.
d. Correct
e. Fiona has developed the most unusual Web site I've ever seen.

EXERCISE 27–1, page 365

a. Noticing that my roommate was shivering and looking pale, I rang for the nurse.
b. When I get the urge to exercise, I lie down until it passes.
c. Grandmother had driven our new jeep to the sunrise church service on Savage Mountain, so we were left with the station wagon.
d. Last June my cousin Lucia swam the length of the lake in forty minutes.
e. Correct

EXERCISE 27–2, page 375

a. The cops were after my hot rod Lincoln. We were passing cars like they were standing still.
b. The museum visitors were not supposed to touch the exhibits.
c. Our church has all the latest technology, even a closed-circuit television.
d. We often don't know whether he is angry or just joking.
e. Correct

EXERCISE 28–1, page 385

a. Correct
b. Watson and Crick discovered the mechanism that controls inheritance in all life: the workings of the DNA molecule.
c. In 1941 Hitler decided to kill the Jews. But Himmler and his SS were there three years ahead of him; they had had mass murder in mind since 1938.
d. Correct
e. In the feminist rewriting of "Sleeping Beauty," the girl is not awakened by a prince.

EXERCISE 28–2, page 388

Possible revisions:

a. Fra Angelico painted each cell in the monastery.
b. Scientists use carbon dating to determine the approximate age of an object.
c. As the patient undressed, we saw scars on his back, stomach, and thighs. We suspected child abuse.
d. We noted right away that the taxi driver had been exposed to Americans because he knew all the latest slang.
e. Researchers have discovered diseases more often than cures.

EXERCISE 29–1, page 395

a. We will make this a better country.
b. There is nothing in the world that TV has not touched on.
c. Did the landlord tell you that he's going to raise the rent?
d. A hard wind was blowing while we were climbing the mountain.
e. The child's innocent world has been taken away from him.

EXERCISE 29–2, page 397

Possible revisions:

a. He would have won the election if he had gone to the inner city to campaign.
b. If Martin Luther King, Jr., were alive today, he would be appalled by the violence in our inner cities.
c. Whenever there is a fire in our neighborhood, everybody comes out to watch.
d. We will lose our largest client unless we update our computer system.
e. If I lived in southern California, I wouldn't need to buy a winter coat.

EXERCISE 29–3, page 401

Possible answers:

a. I enjoy riding my motorcycle.
b. Will you help Samantha study for the test?
c. The team hopes to work hard and win the championship.
d. Ricardo and his brothers miss surfing during the winter.
e. The babysitter let Roger stay up until midnight.

EXERCISE 31–1, page 416

a. There are some cartons of ice cream in the freezer.
b. There are several emergency telephone numbers listed next to the phones at the hotel.
c. The prime minister is the most popular leader in my country.
d. Juana wants to travel to many countries that she has read about.
e. The king, who had served since the age of sixteen, was an old man when he died.

EXERCISE 31–2, page 420

a. an attractive young Vietnamese woman
b. a dedicated Catholic priest
c. her old blue wool sweater
d. Joe's delicious Scandinavian bread
e. many beautiful antique bird cages

EXERCISE 31–3, page 422

a. Listening to everyone's complaints all day was irritating.
b. During the long lecture, many students appeared tired.
c. Correct
d. The violence in recent movies is often disgusting.
e. Correct

EXERCISE 31–4, page 424

a. Whenever we eat at the Centerville Diner, we sit at a small table in the corner of the room.

b. Correct
c. Usually she met with her patients in the afternoon, but on that day she stayed at home to take care of her son.
d. The clock is hanging on the wall in the dining room.
e. Our rabbi moved to the Northwest in 1994 and has been with our temple in Seattle since 1996.

EXERCISE 32–1, page 429

a. Correct
b. The man at the next table complained loudly, and the waiter stomped off in disgust.
c. If you complete the enclosed card and return it within two weeks, you will receive a free breakfast during your stay.
d. Nursing is physically and mentally demanding, yet the pay is low.
e. Uncle Swen's dulcimers disappeared as soon as he put them up for sale, but he always kept one for himself.

EXERCISE 32–2, page 431

a. She wore a black silk cape, a rhinestone collar, satin gloves, and high-tops.
b. An ambulance threaded its way through police cars, fire trucks, and irate citizens.
c. City Café is noted for its spicy vegetarian dishes and its friendly, efficient service.
d. When air-conditioning arrived in the workplace, it had a large, measurable impact on productivity.
e. Correct

EXERCISE 32–3, page 436

a. B. B. King and Lucille, his customized black Gibson, have electrified audiences all over the world.
b. The United States Coast Survey, which was established in 1807, was the first scientific agency in this country.
c. Correct
d. Shakespeare's tragedy King Lear was given a splendid performance by the actor Laurence Olivier.
e. Correct

EXERCISE 32–4, page 442

a. Cricket, which originated in England, is also popular in Australia, South Africa, and India.
b. At the sound of a starting pistol, the horses surged forward toward the first obstacle, a sharp incline three feet high.
c. Each morning the seventy-year-old woman cleans the barn, shovels manure, and spreads clean hay around the milking stalls.
d. The students of Highpoint are required to wear dull green polyester pleated skirts.

e. Beauty is in the eye of the beholder, but glamour is for anyone who can afford it.

EXERCISE 32–5, page 443

a. April 13, 1998, is the final deadline for all applications.
b. The coach having bawled us out thoroughly, we left the locker room with his last, harsh words ringing in our ears.
c. Good technique does not guarantee, however, that the power you develop will be sufficient for Kyok Pa competition.
d. We all piled into Sadiq's car, which we affectionately referred to as the "Blue Goose."
e. As a matter of fact, nationalism is a relatively modern concept.

EXERCISE 33–1, page 451

a. We'd rather spend our money on blue-chip stocks than speculate on pork-bellies.
b. Being prepared for the worst is one way to cope.
c. Please telephone me if you cannot send the information promptly or if you have any questions.
d. The Marx Brothers made delightful, hilarious movies.
e. I quickly accepted the fact that I was literally in third-class quarters.

EXERCISE 34–1, page 458

a. When a woman behaves like a man, why doesn't she behave like a nice man?
b. Do not ask me to be kind; just ask me to act as though I were.
c. Don't talk about yourself; it will be done when you leave.
d. The only sensible ends of literature are first, the pleasurable toil of writing; second, the gratification of one's family and friends; and lastly, the solid cash.
e. I do not rule Russia; ten thousand clerks do.

EXERCISE 34–2, page 459

a. At the outbreak of the American Civil War, many believed that the conflict would be over in a month; others had a dreadful premonition of the future.
b. America has been called a country of pragmatists, although the American devotion to ideals is legendary.
c. The first requirement is honesty; everything else follows.
d. I am not fond of opera; I must admit, however, that I was greatly moved by *Les Misérables*.
e. The Theban plays by Sophocles consist of *Antigone*, which deals with the conscience and the state; *King Oedipus*, which explores the question of fate and circumstance; and *Oedipus at Colonus*, which presents themes of suffering and redemption.

EXERCISE 35–1, page 462

a. The Greeks were right: Character is fate.
b. Some examples of reptiles are lizards, snakes, crocodiles, and turtles.
c. Correct
d. For example, Teddy Roosevelt once referred to the wolf as "the beast of waste and desolation."
e. Correct

EXERCISE 36–1, page 467

a. In a democracy, anyone's vote counts as much as mine.
b. Correct
c. The puppy's favorite activity was chasing its tail.
d. After we bought J. J. the latest style pants and shirts, he decided that last year's faded, ragged jeans were perfect for all occasions.
e. The deed must be transferred to the purchaser's name.

EXERCISE 37–1, page 475

a. Correct
b. As Emerson wrote in 1849, "I hate quotations. Tell me what you know."
c. Andrew Marvell's most famous poem, "To His Coy Mistress," is a tightly structured argument.
d. "Ladies and gentlemen," said the emcee, "I am happy to present our guest speaker."
e. Historians Segal and Stineback note that the English settlers considered these epidemics "the hand of God making room for His followers in the 'New World.'"

EXERCISE 39–1, page 485

a. I was born in Davenport, Iowa.
b. Pat helped Jeff put the tail on his kite, which was made of scraps from old dresses, and off they went to the park.
c. Correct
d. Every person there—from the youngest toddler to the oldest great-grand-parent—was expected to sit through the three-hour sermon in respect-ful silence.
e. The class stood, faced the flag, placed hands over hearts, and raced through "I pledge allegiance . . . liberty and justice for all" in less than sixty seconds.

EXERCISE 40–1, page 491

a. Correct
b. A number of government officials have been reviewing the records of some small brokerage firms in the area.
c. Correct
d. The first discovery of America was definitely not in A.D. 1492.
e. Denzil spent all night studying for his psychology exam.

EXERCISE 41–1, page 494

a. We have ordered four azaleas, three rhododendrons, and two mountain laurels for the back area of the garden.
b. Correct
c. Correct
d. We ordered three 4-door sedans for the company executives.
e. The Vietnam Veterans Memorial in Washington, D.C., had 58,132 names inscribed on it when it was dedicated in 1982.

EXERCISE 42–1, page 498

a. Howard Hughes commissioned the *Spruce Goose,* a beautifully built but thoroughly impractical wooden aircraft.
b. The old man screamed his anger, shouting to all of us, "I will not leave my money to you worthless layabouts!"
c. Even though it is almost always hot in Mexico in the summer, you can usually find a cool spot on one of the park benches in the town's *zócalo.*
d. Correct
e. *The City and the Pillar* was an early novel by Gore Vidal.

EXERCISE 44–1, page 512

a. Correct
b. The swiftly moving tugboat pulled up alongside the barge and directed it away from the oil spill in the harbor.
c. Correct
d. Your dog is well known in our neighborhood.
e. Roadblocks were set up along all the major highways leading out of the city.

EXERCISE 45–1, page 518

a. District Attorney Bax was disgusted when the jurors turned in a verdict of not guilty after only one hour of deliberation.
b. My mother has begun to research the history of her Cherokee ancestors in Georgia.
c. Correct
d. Refugees from Central America are finding it more and more difficult to cross the Rio Grande into the United States.
e. I obtained profiles of both candidates from a useful Web site called Vote Smart Web.

EXERCISE 57–1, page 729

a. sun, assistance; b. Pride, bottom, mistakes; c. trouble, rat (noun/adjective), race, rat; d. censorship, flick, dial; e. Figures, liars

EXERCISE 57–2, page 733

a. He, every (pronoun/adjective); b. those, who; c. I, some (pronoun/adjective), that, I, myself; d. I, You, He; e. She, her (pronoun/adjective)

EXERCISE 57–3, page 735

a. have been; b. are; c. does bring down; d. is, could rephrase; e. Throw, will emerge

EXERCISE 57–4, page 738

a. Adjectives: General, wrong; adverb: generally; b. Adjectives: The (article), American, tolerant; adverb: wonderfully; c. Adjectives: a (article), rational; adverb: not; d. Adjectives: A (article), clean, a (article), dirty; adverb: often; e. Adjective: the (article); adverb: faster

EXERCISE 58–1, page 748

a. Complete subjects: Sticks and stones, words; simple subjects: Sticks, stones, words; b. Complete subject: all facts; simple subject: facts; c. Complete subject: (You); d. Complete subject: nothing except change; simple subject: nothing; e. Complete subject: The only difference between a rut and a grave; simple subject: difference

EXERCISE 58–2, page 753

a. Subject complement: truth; b. Direct object: the depth of a river; c. Subject complement: yellow; d. Direct object: a man [or a woman]; object complement: wise; e. Indirect objects: me, you; direct objects: a capitalist, a bloodsucker

EXERCISE 59–1, page 757

a. without any liabilities (adjective phrase modifying *sheet*); b. of several air traffic controllers (adjective phrase modifying *job*), with ease (adverb phrase modifying *could perform*); c. like a loose garment (adverb phrase modifying *wears*); d. of a nation (adjective phrase modifying *ideals*), by its advertising (adverb phrase modifying *can tell*); e. In France (adverb phrase modifying *is*)

EXERCISE 59–2, page 763

a. who has outposts in your head (adjective clause modifying *enemy*); b. that doesn't bite (adjective clause modifying *rattlesnake*); c. When I am an old woman (adverb clause modifying *shall wear*); d. what they mean (noun clause used as direct object of *say*); e. unless it is practiced on clever persons (adverb clause modifying *is*)

EXERCISE 59–3, page 767

a. being sixteen (gerund phrase used as subject complement); b. being punctual (gerund phrase used as object of the preposition *with*), to appreciate it (infinitive phrase modifying *is*); c. to paint the color of the wind (infinitive phrase modifying *attempt*); d. Being a philosopher (participial phrase modifying *I*); e. to be older (infinitive phrase used as direct object of *wanted*)

EXERCISE 60–1, page 771

a. Complex; who sleep like a baby (adjective clause); b. compound; c. simple; d. complex; If you don't go to other people's funerals (adverb clause); e. compound-complex; what you are afraid of (noun clause)

(continued from p. iv)

Paul Beier, "Cougar Attacks on Humans in the United States and Canada." *Wildlife Society Bulletin, Winter 1991.* Copyright © 1991 by The Wildlife Society. Reprinted with permission of The Wildlife Society.

William Bennett, "Drug Policy and the Intellectuals," from *Drug Prohibition and the Conscience of Nations,* edited by Arnold S. Trebach and Kevin B. Zeese. Washington, DC: Drug Policy Foundation Press, 1990, pp. 14–20. Reprinted with permission of the Drug Policy Foundation.

Eugene Boe, from "Pioneers to Eternity: Norwegians on the Prairie," from *The Immigrant Experience,* edited by Thomas C. Wheeler. Copyright © 1971 by Thomas C. Wheeler. Reprinted by permission of Doubleday, a division of Bantam Doubleday Dell Publishing Group, Inc.

Louise Bogan, first stanza of "Women," from *The Blue Estuaries.* Copyright © 1968 by Louise Bogan. Reprinted by permission of Farrar, Straus & Giroux, Inc.

Jane Brody, from *Jane Brody's Nutrition Book.* Copyright © 1981 by Jane E. Brody. Reprinted by permission of W. W. Norton & Company, Inc. and Wendy Weil Agency, Inc.

California Mountain Lion Page from the Sierra Club Web site (http://www .sierraclub.org/chapters/ca/mountain-lion). © 1996 by the Sierra Club.

Roger Caras, from "What's a Koala?" Copyright © 1983 by Roger Caras. First appeared in *Geo* magazine, May 1983. Reprinted by permission of Curtis Brown, Ltd.

Bruce Catton, from "Grant and Lee: A Study in Contrasts," from *The American Story,* edited by Earl Schenck Miers. Copyright © 1956 U.S. Capitol Historical Society, all rights reserved.

Earl Conrad, from *Harriet Tubman.* © 1943, 1969 by Earl Conrad. Reprinted by permission of Paul S. Eriksson, Publisher.

James Underwood Crockett, Oliver E. Allen, and the Editors of Time-Life Books, from *The Time-Life Encyclopedia of Gardening: Wildflower Gardening.* © 1977 Time-Life Books, Inc.

Emily Dickinson, from "The Snake." Reprinted by permission of the publishers and the Trustees of Amherst College from *The Poems of Emily Dickinson,* Thomas H. Johnson, Ed. Cambridge, Mass.: The Belknap Press of Harvard University Press. Copyright 1951, 1955, 1979, 1983 by the President and Fellows of Harvard College.

Annie Dillard, from *Teaching a Stone to Talk.* Copyright © 1982 by Annie Dillard. Reprinted by permission of HarperCollins Publishers and Blanche C. Gregory, Inc.

Excerpt from *The Dorling Kindersley Encyclopedia of Fishing.* Copyright © 1994 Dorling Kindersley. Reprinted with permission.

Erik Eckholm, from "Pygmy Chimp Readily Learns Language Skill," *The New York Times.* Copyright © 1985 by The New York Times Company. Reprinted by permission.

Robert Frost, lines from "Fire and Ice," from *The Poetry of Robert Frost,* edited by Edward Connery Lathem, copyright 1923, Copyright © 1969 by Henry Holt and Company, copyright © 1951 by Robert Frost. Reprinted by per mission of Henry Holt & Company, Inc.

Stephen Jay Gould, from "Were Dinosaurs Dumb?" from *The Panda's Thumb: More Reflections on Natural History.* Copyright © 1978 by Stephen Jay Gould. Reprinted by permission of W. W. Norton & Company, Inc.

Dan Gutman, from *The Way Baseball Works.* Reprinted with permission of Simon & Schuster. Copyright © 1996 by Byron Preiss/Richard Ballantine, Inc.

Andrew Harnack and Eugene Kleppinger, guidelines from Chapter 7 of *Online! A Reference Guide to Using Internet Sources.* Copyright © 1997. Reprinted with permission of St. Martin's Press.

Hilary Hauser, from "Exploring a Sunken Realm in Australia," *Natural Geographic*, January 1984. Reprinted by permission of the National Geographic Society.

Langston Hughes, "Ballad of the Landlord." From *Collected Poems* by Langston Hughes. Copyright © 1994 by the Estate of Langston Hughes. Reprinted by permission of Alfred A. Knopf, Inc. and Harold Ober Associates, Inc.

Xia Li and Nancy Crane, "Electronic Sources: APA Style of Citation" (http://www.uvm.edu/~ncrane/estyles/apa.html), from *Electronic Styles: A Handbook for Citing Electronic Information* by Xia Li and Nancy Crane. Reprinted with permission of Information Today, Inc., Medford, NJ (http://www.infotoday.com).

The Lycos "Catalog of the Internet" and Netscape browser frame. Copyright © 1994–1997 Carnegie Mellon University. All rights reserved. Lycos is a trademark of Carnegie Mellon University. Used by permission. Copyright © 1996 Netscape Communications Corp. All Rights Reserved. This electronic file or page may not be reprinted or copied without the express written permission of Netscape.

Margaret Mead, from "New Superstitions for Old," *A Way of Seeing*. Reprinted by permission of William Morrow & Company, Inc.

Alice Munro, from "Walker Brothers Cowboy," from *Dance of the Happy Shades*. Copyright © 1983. Reprinted with permission of Penguin Books and McGraw-Hill Book Company.

Portland Community College home page and Netscape browser frame. Copyright © 1997 by Portland Community College. Reprinted with permission of Russell Banks, Division of Publications, Portland Community College. Copyright © 1996 Netscape Communications Corp. All Rights Reserved. This electronic file or page may not be reprinted or copied without the express written permission of Netscape.

Chet Raymo, from "Curious Stuff, Water and Ice." *The Boston Globe*, January 27, 1986.

Paul Reps, from "The Moon Cannot Be Stolen," from *Zen Flesh, Zen Bones*. Reprinted by permission of Charles E. Tuttle Co., Inc., of Rutland, Vermont, and Tokyo, Japan. First printing 1957.

Richard Rodriguez, from "Aria: A Memoir of a Bilingual Childhood." Copyright © 1980 by Richard Rodriguez. Reprinted by permission of Georges Borchardt, Inc., for the author. First published in *The American Scholar*.

Lewis Thomas, from "On Societies as Organisms." Copyright © 1971 by the Massachusetts Medical Society, from *The Lives of a Cell* by Lewis Thomas. Reprinted by permission of Viking Penguin, a division of Penguin Books USA Inc.

James Thurber, from "University Days." © 1933, 1961 by James Thurber. From *My Life and Hard Times*, published by Harper & Row.

Olivia Vlahos, from *Human Beginnings*. Published by Viking Penguin, Inc. Reprinted by permission of the author.

Alice Walker, from "In Search of Our Mothers' Gardens," from *In Search of Our Mothers' Gardens*. Copyright © 1967 by Alice Walker. Reprinted by permission of Harcourt Brace & Company and David Higham Associates Ltd.

Janice R. Walker, specifications from style sheet endorsed by the Alliance for Computers and Writing (http://www.cas.usf.edu/english/walker/mla.html). Copyright © 1996 J. Walker. Reprinted by permission of the author.

Webster's New World Dictionary, synonyms for *fertile, fecund, fruitful*, and *prolific*. Reprinted with the permission of Simon & Schuster from *Webster's New World Dictionary*, Third Edition, edited by Victoria Neufeldt and David B. Guralnik. Copyright © 1996 by Simon & Schuster.

Eudora Welty, excerpt from "Why I Live at the P.O." Copyright © 1941 and renewed 1969 by Eudora Welty. Reprinted with permission of Harcourt Brace & Company and Russell & Volkening.

Index

T

Special Help for ESL Students

A complete section on major ESL problems:

ESL notes in other sections:

A List of Charts

A List of Charts

abbr	faulty abbreviation **40**
ad	misuse of adverb or adjective **26**
add	add needed word **10**
agr	faulty agreement **21, 22**
appr	inappropriate language **17**
art	article **30**
awk	awkward
cap	capital letter **45**
case	error in case **24, 25**
cliché	cliché **18e**
coh	coherence **4e**
coord	faulty coordination **8b**
cs	comma splice **20**
dev	inadequate development **4b**
dm	dangling modifier **12e**
-ed	error in *-ed* ending **27d**
emph	emphasis **14**
ESL	English as a second language **29–31**
exact	inexact language **18**
frag	sentence fragment **19**
fs	fused sentence **20**
gl/us	see Glossary of Usage
hyph	error in use of hyphen **44**
idiom	idioms **18d**
inc	incomplete construction **10**
irreg	error in irregular verb **27a**
ital	italics (underlining) **42**
jarg	jargon **17a**
lc	lowercase letter **45**
mix	mixed construction **11**
mm	misplaced modifier **12a–d**
mood	error in mood **28b**
nonst	nonstandard usage **17d, 27**
num	error in use of numbers **41**
om	omitted word **10, 30, 31a**

p	error in punctuation
⌃	comma **32**
no ,	no comma **33**
;	semicolon **34**
:	colon **35**
⌄	apostrophe **36**
" "	quotation marks **37**
. ? !	period, question mark, exclamation point **38**
— ( ) [ ] ... /	dash, parentheses, brackets, ellipsis mark, slash **39**
¶	new paragraph **4f**
pass	ineffective passive **14a, 28c**
pn agr	pronoun agreement **22**
proof	proofreading problem **3d**
ref	error in pronoun reference **2**
run-on	run-on sentence **20**
-s	error in *-s* ending **21, 27c**
sexist	sexist language **17f, 22a**
shift	distracting shift **13**
sl	slang **17d**
sp	misspelled word **43**
sub	faulty subordination **8c–d**
sv agr	subject-verb agreement **21, 27c**
t	error in verb tense **28a**
trans	transition needed **4e**
usage	see Glossary of Usage
v	voice **14a, 28c**
var	lack of variety in sentence structure **8, 15**
vb	verb error **27, 28**
w	wordy **16**
//	faulty parallelism **9**
∧	insert
✗	obvious error
#	insert space
⌒	close up space

absolute phrase **59e**
active voice **28c, 58c**
adjective **57d**
adjective clause **59b**
adverb **57e**
adverb clause **59b**
agreement **21, 22**
antecedent **22, 23, 57b**
appositive phrase **59d**
article **30**
case **24, 25**
clause **59b, 60**
comparative **26c**
complement **58b**
complete subject **58a**
complex sentence **60a**
compound-complex sentence **60a**
compound sentence **60a**
compound subject **58a**
conjunction **57g**
conjunctive adverb **57g**
coordinating conjunction **57g**
correlative conjunction **57g**
demonstrative pronoun **57b**
dependent clause (*See* subordinate clause.)
determiner **30**
direct object **58b**
expletive **58a, 58c**
future tense **28a**
gerund **59c**
gerund phrase **59c**
helping verb **57c**

indefinite pronoun **57b**
independent clause **60a**
indirect object **58b**
infinitive **59c**
infinitive phrase **59c**
intensive pronoun **57b**
interjection **57h**
interrogative pronoun **57b**
intransitive verb **58b**
inverted sentence pattern **58a**
irregular verb **27a**
linking verb **58b**
main clause (*See* independent clause.)
main verb **57c**
modal **29a, 57c**
mood **28b**
noun **57a**
noun/adjective **57a**
noun clause **59b**
object complement **58b**
object of the preposition **59a**
particle **29d**
participial phrase **59c**
participle, present and past **27a, 57c**
parts of speech **57**
passive voice **28c, 58c**
past tense **28a**
perfect tense **28a**
personal pronoun **57b**
possessive pronoun **57b**
predicate **58**

predicate adjective (*See* subject complement.)
predicate noun (*See* subject complement.)
preposition **57f**
prepositional phrase **57f, 59a**
present tense **28a**
progressive tenses **28a**
pronoun **57b**
pronoun/adjective **57b**
reciprocal pronoun **57b**
reflexive pronoun **57b**
regular verb **27a, 57c**
relative adverb **59b**
relative pronoun **57b, 59b**
-s form of verbs **21, 27c**
sentence patterns **58**
sentence types **60**
simple sentence **60a**
simple subject **58a**
subject **58a**
subject complement **58b**
subordinate clause **59b**
subordinating conjunction **57g, 59b**
subordinate word group **59**
superlative **26c**
tense **28a**
transitive verb **58b**
understood subject **58a**
verb **57c, 58b**
verbal phrase **59c**

Detailed Menu